The Fiery Test of Critique

The Fiery Test of Critique

A Reading of Kant's Dialectic

IAN PROOPS

Great Clarendon Street, Oxford, OX2 6DP,
United Kingdom

Oxford University Press is a department of the University of Oxford.
It furthers the University's objective of excellence in research, scholarship,
and education by publishing worldwide. Oxford is a registered trade mark of
Oxford University Press in the UK and in certain other countries

© Ian Proops 2021

The moral rights of the author have been asserted

First Edition published in 2021

Impression: 1

All rights reserved. No part of this publication may be reproduced, stored in
a retrieval system, or transmitted, in any form or by any means, without the
prior permission in writing of Oxford University Press, or as expressly permitted
by law, by licence or under terms agreed with the appropriate reprographics
rights organization. Enquiries concerning reproduction outside the scope of the
above should be sent to the Rights Department, Oxford University Press, at the
address above

You must not circulate this work in any other form
and you must impose this same condition on any acquirer

Published in the United States of America by Oxford University Press
198 Madison Avenue, New York, NY 10016, United States of America

British Library Cataloguing in Publication Data
Data available

Library of Congress Control Number: 2020943336

ISBN 978–0–19–965604–2

DOI: 10.1093/oso/9780199656042.001.0001

Printed and bound by
CPI Group (UK) Ltd, Croydon, CR0 4YY

Links to third party websites are provided by Oxford in good faith and
for information only. Oxford disclaims any responsibility for the materials
contained in any third party website referenced in this work.

To my father, Jim,

—and to the memories of my mother, Pat, and my sister, Helen

Contents

List of Figures	xiii
Introduction	1
0.1 The fiery test of critique	8
0.2 Method and experiment	14
0.3 The sceptical method	15
0.4 Pyrrhonian postponement	22
0.5 Kantian charity	24
0.6 Denying knowledge	25
0.7 Speculation	27
0.8 The pre-eminence of the Antinomies	29
0.9 Four masters of method	30
0.10 Approach	31
0.11 Rigour	32
0.12 Typographical conventions	33
0.13 Jargon and dating the reflections	33
0.14 Acknowledgements	34

PART I: RATIONAL PSYCHOLOGY

1. Transcendental Illusion	39
1.1 Introduction	39
1.2 Illusions: logical, empirical, and transcendental	40
1.3 The sources of transcendental illusion	42
1.4 The simplified account	52
1.5 The necessity of transcendental illusion	53
1.6 Some recalcitrant texts	55
2. Empirical and Rational Psychology	59
2.1 Introduction	59
2.2 Wolff	60
2.3 Gottsched	67
2.4 Baumgarten	69
2.5 Meier	71
2.6 Rational psychology in the *Metaphysics L1*	72
2.7 *Pure* rational psychology	78
2.8 Pure rational psychology as the science of self-consciousness	79
2.9 The critique of pure rational psychology	85
2.10 Two ways of proceeding in pure rational psychology	87

3. The First Paralogism: Preliminaries	90
3.1 Introduction	90
3.2 Substance	92
3.3 Transcendental illusion in the first paralogism	93
3.4 Kant's notion of a paralogism	97
3.5 Transcendental paralogism	102
4. The *B*-edition First Paralogism	104
4.1 Introduction	104
4.2 The paralogism	104
4.3 Objections and replies	111
4.4 Ameriks's interpretation	125
5. The *A*-edition First Paralogism	127
5.1 Introduction	127
5.2 A closer look at transcendental illusion	130
5.3 Wuerth's interpretation	134
5.4 A problem with Kant's characterization of a paralogism	137
5.5 Two ways of viewing a paralogism	138
6. The Second Paralogism	140
6.1 Introduction	140
6.2 The Achilles	141
6.3 The *A*-edition second paralogism as a paralogism$_k$	148
6.4 Kant's criticism evaluated	149
6.5 A Cartesian application of the major premise	151
6.6 The I as 'simple in concept'	154
6.7 The *B*-edition second Paralogism	156
6.8 The possibility of monism	158
7. The Third Paralogism	161
7.1 Introduction	161
7.2 The major premise	164
7.3 The minor premise	166
7.4 The practical use of the concept of a person	170
7.5 The *B*-edition third paralogism	173
7.6 Immortality	175
7.7 Mendelssohn's argument	177
7.8 Fordyce's argument	178
7.9 Fordyce's argument evaluated	188
8. The Fourth Paralogism	190
8.1 Introduction	190
8.2 The paralogism	191
8.3 External-world scepticism rejected	193
8.4 Anti-materialism	196
8.5 Monism	197

8.6 The *B*-edition fourth paralogism 198
8.7 Transcendental illusion again 199
8.8 Architectonic and method 200
8.9 Descartes 203

PART II: RATIONAL COSMOLOGY

9. The Mathematical Antinomies Presented 209
    9.1 Introduction 209
    9.2 The phenomenon of antinomy 212
    9.3 The form of an antinomy 217
    9.4 The thesis of the first antinomy: time 221
    9.5 Infinity 223
    9.6 The antithesis of the first antinomy: time 227
    9.7 The thesis of the first antinomy: space 231
    9.8 The antithesis of the first antinomy: space 234
    9.9 The second antinomy: preliminaries 236
    9.10 The thesis of the second antinomy 237
    9.11 The antithesis of the second antinomy 240

10. The Mathematical Antinomies Resolved 245
    10.1 Introduction 245
    10.2 The first line of resolution 246
    10.3 The second line of resolution 249
    10.4 Proofs by *reductio* 254
    10.5 Regresses *ad infinitum* and *ad indefinitum* 255
    10.6 The cosmological syllogism 257
    10.7 The sceptical representation 261
    10.8 The Lambert analogy 263
    10.9 The indifferentists 265
    10.10 The indirect argument for Transcendental Idealism 270
    10.11 The road not taken: nonsense 273
    10.12 Zeno 275

11. The Third Antinomy Presented 277
    11.1 Introduction 277
    11.2 The thesis and antithesis 277
    11.3 Terminology 281
    11.4 Causes in Kant 284
    11.5 Kant's determinism 287
    11.6 The antinomies: lessons learned 289
    11.7 The thesis argument 289
    11.8 The antithesis argument 293

x CONTENTS

12. The Third Antinomy Resolved 299
    12.1 Introduction 299
    12.2 Empirical and intelligible character 301
    12.3 What kind of freedom? 303
    12.4 Another indirect argument for Transcendental Idealism 304
    12.5 Moral responsibility, moral growth, and rational blame 305
    12.6 The moral argument for freedom 309
    12.7 Is Kant a compatibilist? 313
    12.8 Against Leibnizian compatibilism 314
    12.9 Kant's alleged libertarianism 317
13. The Fourth Antinomy 325
    13.1 Introduction 325
    13.2 The thesis argument 326
    13.3 The antithesis argument 327
    13.4 The resolution 329
    13.5 De Mairan and the moon 331

PART III: RATIONAL THEOLOGY

14. The Ontological Argument 337
    14.1 Introduction 337
    14.2 Kant's presentation of the ontological argument 339
    14.3 What is a 'real predicate'? 346
    14.4 Wolff and Baumgarten on existence 348
    14.5 The 'inconsistency' objection 351
    14.6 *Existence, being,* and *actuality* 353
    14.7 *Actuality* is not a real predicate 354
    14.8 The 'hundred thalers' argument 356
    14.9 Evaluation of the argument 359
    14.10 The disputational form of Kant's criticism 362
15. The Cosmological Argument 364
    15.1 Introduction 364
    15.2 Kant's presentation of the cosmological argument 367
    15.3 The role of contingency 371
    15.4 The remaining phases of the argument 373
    15.5 Contingency and the *PSR* 383
    15.6 Kant's third main criticism: the *nervus probandi* and its converse 384
16. The First *Critique* on the Physico-Theological Argument 390
    16.1 Introduction 390
    16.2 The ordinary physico-theology 391
    16.3 Kant's revised physico–theology 396
    16.4 The pre-critical revised physico-theology: concluding remarks 403

  16.5 The revised physico-theology in the first *Critique*   404
  16.6 The first *Critique* on the physico-theological argument   406
  16.7 Kant's criticisms of the dogmatic physico-theological argument   410
  16.8 Do we observe end-directedness?   415
  16.9 The doctrinal belief in an Author of Nature   418
  16.10 The non-dogmatic argument: criticisms and prospects   419

17. The Regulative Use of the Ideas   422
  17.1 Introduction   422
  17.2 The Idea of the soul as a regulative principle   426
  17.3 The Idea of God as a regulative principle   427
  17.4 Laws expressing the purposes of nature   430
  17.5 Lazy reason and perverted reason   432
  17.6 The Idea of systematic unity   432
  17.7 The first *Critique* on the courses of the heavenly bodies   440
  17.8 The transcendental principles   445
  17.9 The co-applicability of the logical principles   448
  17.10 The *focus imaginarius*   448

18. Closing Reflections   453
  18.1 Further conclusions   454
  18.2 Denying knowledge (again)   457
  18.3 Transcendental Realism as a logical impossibility   459
  18.4 The loss of innocence   460
  18.5 Exhaustiveness   461

Appendix: Abbreviations   463

Bibliography   467
Index   475

List of Figures

2.1 Division of empirical and rational psychology	73
8.1 Circle of topics	202
9.1 The form of an antinomy	218
17.1 Diagram from Newton's *Opticks* (1704)	449

Introduction

At the opening of the second edition of the first *Critique* Kant is pondering the future of metaphysics. Will this enterprise, he wonders, ever be put on the secure path of a science? Is such a path even possible, and if not, why has nature nonetheless implanted in us a restless striving to find it?[1] On the basis of an intermittently conjectural survey of the development of the established sciences he arrives at the upbeat conclusion that—yes—such a path is indeed possible. But he warns that getting metaphysics onto it will not be easy. It will require—or so his quasi-survey leads him to believe—nothing short of an intellectual *revolution*: a transformation in our mode of thinking that consists, like its Copernican archetype, in a radical reversal of perspective. Whereas for Copernicus the reversal had involved a shift in the inquirer's cosmic frame of reference, for Kant it involves a reversal in our expectations about the direction of epistemic fit: instead of taking our cognition to conform to objects, we are to 'experiment' with the supposition that objects, being partly constituted by the contribution of our cognitive faculties, conform to our cognition (B *xvi*).[2] It is clear that Kant regards this experiment, which he takes to disclose the truth of Transcendental Idealism, as an unqualified success (B *xviii*).

Thanks to the patient efforts of generations of scholars, the theory Kant develops in aiming to enact philosophy's Copernican revolution—his so-called 'metaphysics of experience'—has by now been examined in minute detail. Less closely studied, however, have been the intellectual pressures that precipitate the crisis to which that revolution is a response. In particular, much remains to be said about Kant's examination in the Transcendental Dialectic of the pathologies—or, more precisely, illusions, delusions, and (antinomial) paradoxes—that he supposes to lie within and behind, dogmatic speculative metaphysics.[3] A number of

---

[1] See B *vii*, B *ix–xi* and, especially, B *xv*. Quotations from Kant's writings are drawn from the Prussian Academy edition, the first *Critique* being cited by the A/B pagination. Immanuel Kant, *Gesammelte Schriften* (Berlin: Königlich-Preussischen Akademie der Wissenschaften zu Berlin [now de Gruyter], 1900–). English translations are my own, though often indebted to some selection of the translations listed in the Bibliography.

[2] Kant's decision to present his Transcendental Idealism as a hypothesis to be experimentally tested reinforces his analogy; for he sees Copernicus as having formulated one of the most celebrated hypotheses of all (24: 223).

[3] I take it that an antinomy is a 'paradox' in the 'modern' sense identified by Roy Sorensen, namely: 'a small set of propositions that are individually plausible but jointly inconsistent'. See Roy Sorensen, *A Brief History of the Paradox: Philosophy and the Labyrinths of the Mind* (Oxford: Oxford University Press, 2003) at 120. In an antinomy, the small set in question is a *pair* of propositions. If '*A*' is a name of

2 THE FIERY TEST OF CRITIQUE

specific questions arise: First, what, if anything, unifies the various instances of the 'worm-eaten dogmatism' to which Kant is, much of the time, reacting? Do they stem from a single source, and, if so, what is its nature? Second, assuming there is a single source, is it peculiar to dogmatic speculative metaphysics or does it underlie a broader range of problematic approaches? Third, and relatedly, exactly which outlooks, besides dogmatism, is Kant meaning to oppose in the Transcendental Dialectic? Fourth, is any particular part of speculative dogmatic metaphysics especially revelatory of the source of its predicament? Fifth, does Kant regard any part of speculative metaphysics as worth saving? And, if so, how does this salutary part of the enterprise differ from the parts to be discarded?

To answer these and related questions, I have found it necessary to attempt a study of the Transcendental Dialectic as a whole. The 'Dialectic', as this part of the work is colloquially known, accounts for some two fifths of Kant's masterwork. In it we are offered—among *many* other things—a searching examination of the dogmatic speculative metaphysics of certain of the critical Kant's modern predecessors—among them, most notably: Descartes, Leibniz, Wolff, Mendelssohn, and (less explicitly) Kant's earlier 'pre-critical' self.[4] The metaphysics of these philosophers qualifies as *dogmatic*, in Kant's view, because it hastens to its attempted proofs without undertaking a preparatory examination of the mind's capacities and powers.[5] It is *speculative* because it rests on 'theoretical' grounds, such as the Principle of Sufficient Reason, rather than 'practical' grounds, such as the fact that we stand under moral obligations.[6]

In Kant's view, the ultimate goal of dogmatic speculative metaphysics is to prove certain 'cardinal propositions' of pure reason—including, pre-eminently, the existence of God, on the one hand, and the natural immortality of the human

---

the relevant antinomy, then the pair would be: 'The thesis and antithesis of A are contradictories' and 'The thesis and antithesis of A are each supported by sound arguments.' The antinomial paradox would be resolved if one could show either or both of these propositions to be false. As we will see, Kant in fact supposes that he can show both to be false.

[4] More accurately, in the Dialectic we are offered a treatment of some but not all of the dogmatic views of these philosophers. Leibniz's commitment to the identity of indiscernibles, for example, receives its critique in the appendix on 'The amphiboly of concepts of reflection', which immediately precedes the Transcendental Dialectic. In this earlier section Kant's critique is directed not towards the faculty of reason and its purported products—as it tends to be in the Dialectic—but rather towards certain conclusions drawn from 'mere acts of reflection' (A 278/B 335). Kant has in mind certain errors that occur in the performance of 'transcendental reflection': the practice of assigning representations to their appropriate cognitive faculties (compare 9: 73).

[5] B *xxxv*; 8: 226; 9: 83–4. Kant insists that there is nothing *in itself* problematic about seeking strict proofs from principles known a priori—the so-called 'dogmatic procedure' of reason (B *xxxv*). But he believes that we must use this procedure only within its proper domains.

[6] As we will see, however, the word 'speculative' is not always pejorative for Kant (compare A *xxi*). In particular, when it modifies 'reason', it can mean merely 'theoretical' as opposed to 'practical' (compare B *xliii*).

soul, on the other.[7] The objects—whether actual or merely putative—with which this metaphysics deals fall into two overlapping groups. On the one hand, there are the three 'supersensible objects' connected with Kant's doctrine of practical faith, namely, God, immortality, and freedom.[8] On the other, there are the objects studied by the three branches of Wolffian 'special' metaphysics. These are the intentional—or, as Kant puts it, 'imagined'—objects of the 'Transcendental Ideas' of: the world (conceived of as an absolute totality of objects of sense); the soul (conceived of as a simple substance); and God (conceived of as the supreme intelligence).[9] As we will see, Kant takes a different epistemic attitude towards the existence of each of these objects: he rejects the first as non-existent, is agnostic about the existence of the second, and believes in the third—though on this last point he is not, I fear, entirely consistent.[10] In all three cases, however, he insists that we can have no theoretically-grounded *knowledge* [*Wissen*] of these objects, and he disdains, as a hallmark of dogmatism, the ambition to acquire it.[11]

This ambition—along with its characteristic attitudes and alleged products—constitutes the main target of Kant's critique of speculative metaphysics in the Dialectic, and, perhaps unsurprisingly, my first and most basic goal will be to scrutinize the details of that critique.[12] But I have, in addition, a number of less predictable goals, which I would like to spend a moment outlining.

---

[7] See R 5637 (18: 273) and A 741–2/B 669–70. This choice of 'cardinal propositions' is entirely appropriate because Descartes in his *Dedicatory Letter to the Sorbonne* describes God and the soul as two topics concerning which demonstrative proofs can and should be provided with the aid of philosophy rather than theology (*AT* VII, 1; *CSM* II, 3). Kant occasionally characterizes the freedom of the will and the ideality of space and time as cardinal propositions of metaphysics, though when he does so he is expressing his own view of the appropriate target propositions of metaphysics rather than that of his opponents (see A 799–800/B 828, R 6349, and R 6353).

[8] At 5: 469 Kant calls these supersensible objects 'res fidei' ('matters of faith') (see also 20: 350, R 6317, and 20: 295). Immortality, being a 'future life <vita futura>' that follows necessarily from the nature of the soul (28: 763), is a phase of temporal existence (compare 20: 298). Accordingly, Kant's reason for deeming it 'supersensible' cannot be that it is atemporal. The reason is rather that it is not a possible object of experience (4: 477; 29: 945). This is so for two reasons. First, the day will never come when I am able empirically to verify my unending existence; second, for Kant, immortality requires the post-mortem *necessary* endurance of the soul—a feature that cannot, he insists, be read off of the deliverances of the senses. Incidentally, the fact that immortality is a phase of temporal existence suggests that Kant does not conceive of the supersensible objects that are matters of faith as *in general* things in themselves; for things in themselves are in every case atemporal—though he certainly conceives of some of them in this way.

[9] Kant refers to freedom as a transcendental Idea at A 533/B 561 and A 558/B 586, but he does not treat it as the primary object of any branch of Wolffian metaphysics.

[10] To be clear, Kant is agnostic about the existence of the soul *when it is conceived of as a substance*; he is *not* agnostic about its existence when it is conceived of, more neutrally, as whatever it is in a human being that thinks—the so-called 'thinking I'. Second, the inconsistency with respect to Kant's belief in God arises because he is apt to characterize the objects of the transcendental Ideas—which he also terms 'concepts of reason'—as mere 'heuristic fictions' (A 771/B 799).

[11] In the case of God, Kant even seems to think that such knowledge is not even to be *desired*. Were we to possess it, he thinks, we would be incapable of genuinely morally motivated action; for we would envisage reward and punishment so distinctly that morality would be transformed into self-interest. See, for example, 28: 1292 and compare R 4996; 18: 55.

[12] This is not to deny that there is some overlap between the goals of the Dialectic and other parts of the first *Critique*. Indeed, Kant supposes that the Dialectic confirms a result already proved in the

4 THE FIERY TEST OF CRITIQUE

My second main goal—the first of the less obvious ones—is to emphasize a point originally noted some six decades ago by Lewis White Beck, namely, that although he unequivocally rejects the dogmatic project of attempting to gain theoretically grounded knowledge of the supersensible, Kant nonetheless endorses certain theoretically grounded *arguments* concerning these matters, arguments that he sees as producing something less than knowledge.[13] These arguments, which occur in the first *Critique*, draw on three elements: (a) empirical premises, (b) the principle of analogy, and (c) one or other principle of reason governing inquiry (a principle of the form 'proceed in your empirical inquiries on the assumption that *p*'). They seek to produce, not knowledge but rather certain firmly held (hence stable), in part *theoretically grounded* beliefs that are, in spite of their stability, not wholly unshakable (A 827–8/B 855–6). These beliefs are instances of a phenomenon Kant terms 'doctrinal belief' [*doctrinalen Glauben*], a phenomenon that includes, at minimum, beliefs in a human afterlife (B 425–6) and in 'a god' (A 826–7/B 854–5)—understood not as a perfect being, but merely as a 'wise and great originator of the world' (B *xxxiii*).

Kant illustrates the notion of doctrinal belief with his own belief that other planets are inhabited—a belief, he tells us, on which, if there were a realistic chance of settling the question empirically (so that there would be a point to making a bet), he'd stake 'many of life's advantages', including all he owns (A 825/B 853). Since he takes betting behaviour to be the touchstone of the strength of a belief (A 825–6/B 852–3; 24: 853), the example suggests that Kant conceives of doctrinal beliefs as somewhat akin to high-credence partial belief states.[14] The upshot is that he must be adjudged a believer in 'a god'—a very great and wise originator or 'Author of Nature'—and in an afterlife. And we must suppose him to hold these views on *theoretical* rather than merely practical (that is, moral) grounds.

Beck made his observation that Kant endorses a theoretically based argument for a doctrinal belief in the afterlife in an easy-to-miss footnote in a book on Kant's second *Critique*. So, it is perhaps not all that surprising that the topic of doctrinal belief has, until recently, been largely neglected by scholars of the first.[15]

Transcendental Analytic: namely, that 'all of our inferences that seek to take us beyond the realm of possible experience are deceptive and baseless' (A 642/B 671). He supposes that one thing the Dialectic adds to this already established result (beyond its confirmation) is an illustration of the fact that we have a *'natural propensity* to overstep this realm's boundary' (ibid., emphasis added).

[13] See Lewis White Beck, *A Commentary on Kant's Critique of Practical Reason* (Chicago: University of Chicago Press, 1960) at 266, n18.

[14] More precisely, he takes betting *and oath taking* to be the touchstones of the sufficiency of holding-to-be true when that holding-to-be true constitutes belief (9: 73). We will later see a reason to think that the affinity between doctrinal beliefs and what we call beliefs today is actually not as close as one might at first suppose.

[15] Owing to the insightful work of Andrew Chignell, Kant's attachment to the notion of doctrinal belief is now becoming more widely known. But even Chignell's otherwise excellent discussion of the phenomenon of doctrinal belief (or as he prefers to call it 'Theoretical Belief') fails to register Beck's

Nonetheless, his observation is of the first importance for our understanding of Kant's critical project. It suggests that Kant sees two branches of traditional speculative metaphysics in particular, namely rational theology and rational psychology—the latter being the branch of rational metaphysics to which he assigns the argument for a doctrinal belief in an afterlife (28: 441–2, 28: 591–2)—as *in part* legitimate enterprises.[16]

If this is right, then Kant's bugbear in the Dialectic is not speculative or theoretical metaphysics per se but rather something more specific. What exactly? A prime candidate, I would suggest, is *dogmatism*—understood as an unrealistically inflated estimation of how much one can *know* on theoretical grounds alone (along with the project of trying to fulfil this expectation).[17] In Kant's view, dogmatism can take the form either of dogmatic speculative metaphysics or of a somewhat paradoxically labelled 'dogmatic *scepticism*'—the pragmatically self-defeating attempt to establish with certainty that nothing is certain, an aspiration that Kant associates, somewhat frowningly, with Academic scepticism.[18]

The scepticism of Pyrrho, by contrast, he treats as worthy of respect. The Pyrrhonian 'critical' or 'problematic' sceptic, he supposes, doubts only in order to eventually gain certainty (24: 214). Kant plainly has great sympathy for Pyrrho, though, equally plainly, *his* Pyrrho is not to be confused with the founder of traditional Pyrrhonism. Indeed, Kant regards as a complete non-starter the position usually termed 'Pyrrhonism'—namely, the philosophy that advocates the balancing of claims, followed by the suspension of judgment, with the aim of attaining *tranquillity*. He rejects this approach mainly because he supposes that on certain questions there simply is no permitted ignorance—hence no prospect

---

point that Kant argues for a doctrinal belief in the afterlife. See Andrew Chignell, 'Belief in Kant', *Philosophical Review*, 116 (3) (2007), 323–60.

[16] Kant takes 'metaphysics'—when the term is used for something distinct from a natural predisposition (B 22)—to have at least three meanings (A 843/B 869). In its widest sense, the term connotes the philosophy of pure reason. This divides into critique (or propaedeutic), on the one hand, and the system of pure reason on the other, the latter qualifying as 'metaphysics' in a second, narrower sense. The system of pure reason in turn divides into the speculative use of pure reason (or 'metaphysics of nature'), on the one hand, and the practical use of reason (or 'metaphysics of morals'), on the other. Kant supposes that the term 'metaphysics' is usually used for the metaphysics of nature. Since doctrinal beliefs are products of the speculative or theoretical use of pure reason, it is plausible to suppose that they—or the arguments justifying them at least—count as belonging—somewhat paradoxically given their content—to the metaphysics of nature.

[17] Kant also treats dogmatism as involving certain attitudes and stances. At A 485–6/B 514, for example, he associates it with an attitude of 'erudition', and at A 757/B 785 with one of 'boastfulness'—an attitude he regards as capable of being punctured, if at all, then only by an antinomy. In the *Jäsche Logic* he equates the attitude of dogmatism with a 'blind trust in the faculty of reason to expand itself *a priori* through mere concepts, without critique, merely on account of its seeming success' (9: 84).

[18] See 24: 214 and 24: 745–6; compare 24: 216 and R 4164 (17: 440). The dogmatic sceptic engages in dogmatic doubt, which Kant also calls 'the doubt of decision', a notion that contrasts with the critical sceptic's 'doubt of postponement' (24: 205). When one engages in the doubt of decision one decides that one must remain uncertain. When one engages in the doubt of postponement, by contrast, one resolves to keep on searching.

of tranquillity [*Ruhestand*] arising therefrom (see *Prolegomena* 4: 274).[19] He is no less staunchly opposed to a certain, harder-to-label brand of scepticism that he finds in Hume—a brand he sometimes, but not always, treats as a species of dogmatic scepticism—as well as to a certain rather elusive 'indifferentism' about which I'll later have more to say. Since the philosophical landscape of Kant's time is densely populated and, to date, only sketchily surveyed, a third major aim of the book is to gain a clearer view of the full range of positions against which Kant is opposing his critical philosophy.[20]

One of the more catchy slogans of the first *Critique* is Kant's confession that he found it necessary to 'deny'—or perhaps 'annul' [*aufheben*]—'knowledge [*Wissen*] in order to make room for faith [*Glaube*]' (B xxx).[21] Tantalizingly, he leaves this signature claim somewhat under-elaborated. Why exactly—one wants to know—should having knowledge of certain matters—or at least the ambition to acquire it—threaten, in the absence of the critical philosophy, to leave no room for faith? A fourth goal of the book is to shed some light on this matter.

The *Critique of Pure Reason*, we are (rightly) told, is Pure Reason's critique of itself.[22] But what exactly is Kantian 'critique'? A fifth goal is to address this question. I will argue that for Kant critique has both a subjective and an objective side. Subjectively—as is well known—it is an investigation of the limits of the

---

[19] In another sense, he allows that a *true* tranquillity may indeed be obtained so long as it arises not from our settling for ignorance on the antinomial questions but rather from the litigation made possible by critique (A 751–2/B 779–80). This means that we are to pursue a *verdict* on the antinomial questions not a *victory*—and the verdict is to consist not in a ruling in favour of one side of the antinomial dispute and against the other but rather in a judgment about the source of the controversy, a judgment made possible by critique (ibid.). The sceptic's tranquillity, Kant supposes, provides an inappropriately short path to philosophical tranquillity (A 757/B 785): the implication would seem to be that Kant's own approach provides the more appropriate longer path.

[20] Kant is apt to liken his task in metaphysics to that of a maritime explorer in search of a navigable channel through treacherous waters. The frequency with which he employs this specifically maritime image is sometimes obscured by a tendency among his translators to render the term '*Weg*' as 'road' rather than 'route' even in contexts where the dominant image is plainly one of aquatic endeavour (see, for example, the standard translations of Kant's use of '*Weg*' at 11: 76). The nautical image comes to the fore when Kant describes himself as wishing to steer a course for pure reason between the looming 'cliffs' [*Klippen*] of fanaticism, on the one hand, and scepticism, on the other (B 128). This wish seems to be an aspect of his more general desire to steer a course between the twin perils of dogmatism, on the one hand, and scepticism, on the other (compare: R 5645; 18: 287). (For the distinction between 'fanaticism' [*Schwärmerei*] and 'enthusiasm' [*Enthusiasmus*], see 2: 251n.)

[21] I take it that 'annulling' knowledge is a matter of annulling the *claim* to know. I render '*Glaube*' in *this* context as 'faith' rather than 'belief' because the beliefs that Kant takes to be jeopardized by pursuing speculative metaphysics dogmatically—beliefs in God, freedom, and immortality—are ones that he terms 'doctrines of faith [*Glaubenslehren*]' (20: 298–9). The term '*Glaubenslehre*' plausibly relates to faith rather than belief in general, because it occurs in such phrases as: '*Kongregation für die Glaubenslehre*' ('Congregation for the doctrine of the faith'). This is one reason to disfavour a uniform translation of '*Glaube*' as 'belief'. Another is that Kant uses the term '*fides*' for the state one is in when one attains a practical *Glaube*—namely, 'rational faith [*Vernunftglaube*]' (24: 734).

[22] Echoing Pope's famous dictum that the proper study of mankind is man, Kant claims that pure reason 'is in fact occupied with nothing but itself. Nor can it have any other vocation' (A 680/B 708). The *way* in which it is so occupied, of course, is through critique.

mind's ability to acquire a priori knowledge, and, more generally, an investigation of the mind's active powers—a critique of 'the entire faculty of pure reason' (20: 321), which proceeds by means of an examination of the sources of cognition (A 758/B 786). But objectively—as is less well known—it is a kind of *test* of (what Kant sees as) the main disciplines of traditional metaphysics.[23] Viewed in this second way, critique is a kind of winnowing exercise in which one separates the wheat of good speculative metaphysics from the chaff of bad, though, as we will see, Kant employs a less familiar metaphor to make the same point.

The goal of achieving a clearer view of Kant's conception of critique dovetails with a sixth and final goal of the book, namely, to deepen our understanding of Kant's methodological self-conception. I argue that, although an assortment of influences shape Kant's methodology, his most profound sympathies lie with Pyrrho's method—or, more precisely, with a component of Kant's own rather idiosyncratic conception of Pyrrho's method—the idea, namely, that inquiry should be prolonged and a final judgment postponed, but *not* indefinitely. Although in Kant's view the best philosophical inquiry takes its time, it both aims at, and eventually attains, certainty. This certainty, however, does not concern quite the same subject matter as had been originally in question. Kant's favoured method, which he calls 'the sceptical method', and which he distinguishes sharply from scepticism, is one he associates most closely with the method of the antinomies when they are viewed, not merely as snares into which human reason is prone to fall but as instructive and salutary instruments which can yield insights into the human predicament and so generate self-knowledge of an especially profound kind.

These are the main goals of the book. My plan is to work through the Dialectic, guided by the order of its chapters. But there are two prefatory discussions. One concerns the nature of transcendental illusion and the role it plays in Kant's diagnosis of the human impulse towards metaphysical overreach (Chapter 1), the other, the notions of empirical and rational psychology as they are developed in the period from Wolff to Kant (Chapter 2).

In what remains of the introduction I begin digging into some of the themes just mentioned, starting with Kant's conception of *critique* and, more specifically, with the light shone on the objective side of critique by his metaphor of a 'fiery test' (A 406/B 433).

---

[23] The subjective side of critique is in fact rather involved. For further details, see 29: 782. And for a discussion of the meaning of the term 'critique' prior to Kant, see Giorgio Tonelli, '"Critique" and Related Terms Prior to Kant: A Historical Survey', *Kant-Studien*, 69 (2) (1978), 119–48. I should stress that I do not mean to put any great weight on the labels 'subjective' and 'objective' in this context: it may perhaps be better to speak of the 'faculty-directed' and 'discipline-directed' sides of critique. These do not come to the same thing because, as we will see, the doctrines belonging to a given discipline need not uniformly result from the exercise of a single faculty.

0.1 The fiery test of critique

Kant divides the Dialectic into three main sections, each of which contains the critique of a separate sub-discipline of Wolffian 'special' metaphysics (A 334–5/B 391–2). To a first approximation at least, 'rational psychology' is dealt with in the Paralogisms chapter, 'rational cosmology' in the Antinomies chapter, and 'rational theology' in the 'Ideal of pure reason'—though these chapters include much else besides these critiques and Kant's targets are not confined to the views of the Wolffians. It is no simple matter to say what these putatively 'rational' sciences amount to in the forms in which Kant receives them. For example, the 'rational psychology' he discusses in the first *Critique* is not simply the purportedly a priori doctrine of the soul articulated by the four paralogisms of pure reason. For, as we will see in Chapter 7, Kant conceives of rational psychology as including a certain empirically based argument for the soul's survival after death, which argument he deems legitimate so long as it is understood to produce a doctrinal belief rather than knowledge (28: 441–2; compare 28: 591–2).

Officially speaking, critique is the systematic investigation of the mind's capacity for acquiring metaphysical knowledge—and so also a systematic investigation of the limits of that knowledge (4: 365, 4: 378–9). It is a task in which the responsible philosopher must engage before constructing a system of metaphysical science (B *xxxv*; 4: 371). But, unofficially, it is also a kind of test of the worth of various branches and sub-branches of speculative metaphysics—a test whose results turn out to be interestingly variegated. This point is not obvious, but it emerges from a close reading of a metaphor Kant deploys in the Antinomies chapter in the course of reflecting on the results of his recently concluded investigations in the Paralogisms. 'Pneumatism', he says,

> cannot deny that inner defect through which its entire plausibility [*Schein*] dissolves into mere haze [*Dunst*] when put to the fiery test of critique [*Feuerprobe der Kritik*]. (A 406/B 433, Guyer–Wood translation—I will shortly amend this translation)

Kant is telling us that the putative science of pneumatism comes to naught when subjected to a certain test, namely: the '*Feuerprobe*' of critique. 'Pneumatism', as we will see, turns out—on Kant's lips at least—to refer to the dogmatic, non-empirical part of rational psychology, namely, the (in ambition) a priori doctrine of the nature of thinking beings in general—the doctrine of so-called 'spirits'.[24]

---

[24] Spirits, more precisely, are for Kant thinking beings that are conceived of as capable of possessing *consciousness* without possessing a body (20: 309). Sometimes, he also uses 'pneumatism' [*pneumatismus*] for the doctrine that the mind is not matter (A 379). But in the present context, where he is reflecting on the results of the Paralogisms, this term refers to the purported science that aims to establish, among other things, that the soul is a spirit. Used in this way, 'pneumatism' is equivalent to

But what exactly is a '*Feuerprobe*'? Some of Kant's most accomplished translators have suggested that it is an ordeal by fire; and I have heard the same suggestion made by native German speakers.[25] In the present context, however, such an interpretation would be jarringly inapt; for it would portray Kant as modelling his supposedly enlightened programme of 'critique' on a paradigm of religious superstition: the so-called *iudicium dei* (*judgment of God*) of medieval European Christianity. This is an ordeal in which a person who stands accused of a crime for which there are no earthly witnesses is tried (in a religious ceremony) in the eyes of God (the unique divine witness and judge). In an ordeal specifically 'by fire' the accused, having volunteered for the ordeal, might be required to carry a red-hot iron bar for a certain distance. Afterwards, their hand would be bandaged and after a specified interval (of a few days) examined by a priest. If the wound were found to have healed (festered), the judgment of God would be taken to be that the accused was innocent (guilty).[26]

An ordeal of this kind is hardly a fitting metaphor for critique, which, being an instrument of properly enlightened intellectual progress, is supposed to enjoy certain qualities of openness, autonomy, and independence of religious authority.[27] The unwanted connotations of benightedness and superstition may, of course, be merely accidental—many a metaphor, after all, carries some unwanted baggage in its train. However, even with that point given due weight, this interpretation still leaves the reader wondering why Kant—usually sure-footed in his handling of figuration—should have fastened upon an image so starkly at odds with the spirit of enlightened critique. Nor, on this interpretation, would the *Feuerprobe* passage really make sense: Kant would have to be understood to be claiming that something undergoes an ordeal by fire with the result that it vanishes in a puff of smoke.

Fortunately, a more satisfactory account of Kant's '*Feuerprobe*' metaphor is available. And it is one that suggests important lessons about the nature of his critical undertaking. According to this alternative account, the 'fiery test' is not a religious ordeal but rather a *metallurgical assay*—a 'fire assay' or 'cupellation test' to be precise. In such a procedure, a coin or a sample of metal-containing ore is

---

'pneumatology' [*pneumotologie*], the discipline that Kant variously characterizes as a 'metaphysical-dogmatic psychology', a 'doctrine of spirits [*Geisterlehre*]' (28: 679), and a 'science of thinking beings in general' (28: 222, compare 28: 555).

[25] Kemp Smith suggests 'the fiery ordeal of critical investigation', Pluhar 'the critique's ordeal by fire' (A 406/B 433).

[26] For details—and a surprising assessment of the efficacy of the practice—see Peter T. Leeson, 'Ordeals', *Journal of Law and Economics*, 55 (2012), 691–714.

[27] That said, one might think of Kant as likening a particular *part* of critique to another kind of ordeal, namely a trial by combat, for he explicitly figures the parties in the antinomies as combatants. However, this is not the part of critique on which Kant is focusing here.

tested for its precious metal content.[28] The test involves placing the sample in a porous crucible—technically a 'cupel'—where it is burned in a furnace in the presence of a lead catalyst. When this happens the sample's base metals—iron, zinc, and so forth—form oxides (as we'd now call them) that are either driven off in fumes or drawn into the pores of the crucible by capillary action. At the end of the procedure, if one is lucky, one finds a nugget of silver or gold sitting at the bottom of the crucible.[29]

Would Kant have been familiar with this use of the term '*Feuerprobe*'? There is reason to think he would. For one thing, he lectured on minerology in the early 1770s and owned several works on the subject. In one of these works, J. J. Lange's *Einleitung zur Mineralogica Metallica*, there is an unmistakable use of '*Feuerprobe*' for a fire assay.[30] Secondly, the related image of using a furnace to recover the gold of truth from the rust and dross of falsehood, thereby purifying our putative knowledge in the process, occurs in another work Kant owned, namely, Abraham Tucker's *The Light of Nature Pursued*.[31] Thirdly, Kant's familiarity with fire assays is actually on display in his 1796 essay 'On a recently prominent tone of superiority in philosophy'. There, criticizing certain unnamed 'philosophers of feeling', he says:

> It cannot be demanded that the betterment of a human being... should be certified by an assay-master [*Münzwarden*] of his or her morality, trying it in an assay-cupel [*Probierkapelle*]; for, to be sure, the weight [*Schrot*] of good actions can indeed be feather light, but as to how much sterling metal [*Mark Fein*] they contain at heart, who can bear a **publicly valid** testimony to this?
>
> (8: 402)

Here Kant is alluding to the customary distinction between the weight of a metal [*das Schrot*] in a coin and its inner value [*das Korn*]—the latter being the coin's precious-metal content (technically its 'fine weight') as opposed its base-metal 'vehicle'.[32] He is saying that one cannot follow the philosophers of feeling in demanding certification of the moral worth of an action by a figurative

---

[28] One of Kant's nineteenth-century translators, J. M. D. Meiklejohn, appears to have been alert to this interpretation; for he renders '*Feuerprobe*' as 'crucible'. J. M. D. Meiklejohn, *Critique of Pure Reason: Translated from the German of Immanuel Kant* (London: Henry G. Bohm, 1855) at 255.

[29] The procedure is discussed at length in a classic work on mining by Georgius Agricola, *De re metallica* (Basel: Froben, 1556).

[30] J. J. Lange, *Einleitung zur Mineralogica Metallica* (Halle: J. J. Curt, 1770) at 184. For Kant's ownership of this work, see Arthur Warda, *Immanuel Kants Bücher* (Bibliographien und Studien; Berlin: Martin Breslauer, 1922) at 29.

[31] Abraham Tucker, *The Light of Nature Pursued*, 7 vols (1; London: R. Faulder and T. Payne, 1768–78) at *xxxv* and *xlvi*. Kant owned a German translation of the first volume of 1771 by J. C. P. Erxleben (Tucker published under the pseudonym, 'Edward Search').

[32] See J. C. Adelung, *Grammatisch-kritisches Wörterbuch der hochdeutschen Mundart* (Leipzig, 1811), 1661–2.

assay-master—presumably conscience or moral feeling—who applies a cupellation test or fire assay to determine the action's inner worth. One cannot do so simply because there is no applicable test of the inner worth of actions. Similar imagery occurs again in a reflection on anthropology where Kant speaks of subjecting certain products of the mind to 'the cupel assay of reason' [*'der Capellenprobe der Vernunft'*] (15: 407–8). In this instance the envisaged valuable product [*Korn*] is explicitly identified as fine metal [*fein Metall*]. And finally, Kant obliquely invokes the image of a fire assay in a separate part of the first *Critique* when he speaks of an 'assay balance [*Problierwaage*] of critique' (A 767/B 795). Balances of this kind were used specifically for weighing the inputs and outputs of metallurgical fire assays: they were a standard part of the equipment of '*Probierkunst*'.

In the light of these facts, two linguistic points about the '*Feuerprobe*' passage assume a heightened significance. The first is that the word '*Schein*', which Guyer and Wood render as 'plausibility', could in eighteenth-century German mean not just 'illusion' (its more usual translation), but also 'shine'—as in '*Mondschein*' (moonshine).[33] This makes it possible that the '*falsche Schein*' mentioned in the '*Feuerprobe*' passage may be the false *glister* or *glint* of the sample to be tested (think of fool's gold). The second point is that the phrase '*sich in Dunst auflösen*', which Guyer and Wood render 'to dissolve into a haze', has the idiomatic meaning of 'to go up in smoke'. Together, these points suggest the following amended translation:

> Pneumatism... cannot deny that hereditary flaw [*Erbfehler*] on account of which all its promising glister goes up in mere smoke in the fire assay of critique.
> (A 406/B 433)[34]

Only a single question remains: Why should an ore sample be thought to contain an 'hereditary flaw'? This is not obvious, but the answer may be that Kant is here interweaving his metallurgical metaphor with a certain genealogical metaphor that happens also to involve metals. This genealogical metaphor alludes to the so-called 'myth of the metals' in Plato's *Republic*—a myth that is to be taught to the citizens of the republic as part of a 'noble falsehood'. The citizens are to be told that they are 'earthborn brothers', who must defend their motherland. The rulers among them are to be told that the god who made them mixed some gold into them, the auxiliaries that their metal is silver, and the craftsmen and farmers that their metal is bronze or iron. Significantly for our purposes, each member of the

---

[33] See the relevant entry in Adelung, *Grammatisch-kritisches Wörterbuch der hochdeutschen Mundart*.

[34] The broader context runs: '[*In der transcendentale Paralogismus*] *der Vorteil ist gänzlich auf der Seite des Pneumatismus, obgleich dieser den Erbfehler nicht verleugnen kann, bei allem ihm günstigen Schein in der Feuerprobe der Kritik sich in lauter Dunst aufzulösen*' (A 406/B 433).

republic is to be told 'for the most part, you will produce children like yourself'.[35] It follows that a low-born citizen will typically possess the 'hereditary flaw' of containing a base metal. Kant, I suggest, is figuring pneumatism as one of the lowly, base-metal containing citizens of Plato's republic. His metaphor is not merely nested but also double-layered: pneumatism is figured as a person (because treated as a potential denier of things), but also as a metal-containing sample. By alluding to Plato's metaphor, Kant is dexterously combining his personification of pneumatism with, on the one hand, the metaphor of a fire assay and, on the other, his own genealogical metaphor—a leitmotif of the first *Critique*.[36]

I conclude that in the '*Feuerprobe*' passage Kant is figuring pneumatism as a sample to be tested for its precious-metal content. When he says that pneumatism yields nothing but smoke when subjected to the fire assay of critique, he is telling us that this particular sample of metaphysics contains nothing but base metals. I take this metallurgical re-interpretation of Kant's guiding metaphor to matter because it indicates the need for a corresponding re-orientation of our conception of Kantian critique.[37] If we conceive of the objective side of critique on the model of a theologico-juridical ordeal, we will consider it an all-or-nothing affair: a branch of traditional 'rational metaphysics' will either come through the trial unscathed or it will not. If, on the other hand, we conceive of it on the model of a fire assay, we will conceive of it as a test whose results may be interestingly various and subject to degree, and accordingly, the possibility will open up that the object of the test might receive, so to speak, partial credit. In applying the test, moreover, we will seek to learn whether the branch contains something of value, and if so, how much of this precious metal there is, and of what kind. And most importantly of all, we might come to learn that a certain branch of metaphysics, while containing much dross, also contains some precious nuggets. Since a fire assay is usually conducted in the hope of finding something of value in the sample to be tested (whether it be gold, silver, or, in the case of a coin, a certain fine weight), the metaphor might even suggest a positive, hopeful role for critique: the critical philosopher might, in part at least, be seeking to recover something good from the samples of metaphysics to be tested. At any rate, whether Kant is alluding to a prospecting assay or to a numismatic cupellation test, the main conclusion is the same: unlike a medieval ordeal, the test is not pass–fail.

---

[35] *Republic*, book III, 415a–c. Plato, *Republic*, trans. G. M. A. Grube (Indianapolis: Hackett, 1992) at 91–2.

[36] For details of Kant's genealogical metaphor see Dieter Henrich, 'Kant's Notion of a Deduction and the Methodological Background to the First *Critique*', in Eckart Förster (ed.), *Kant's Transcendental Deductions: The Three 'Critiques' and the 'Opus Postumum'* (Stanford: Stanford University Press, 1989), 29–46, and Ian Proops, 'Kant's Legal Metaphor and the Nature of a Deduction', *Journal of the History of Philosophy*, 41 (2) (2003), 209–29.

[37] Only a partial re-orientation because Kant deploys a range of metaphors to illuminate this conception of critique, including, most famously, the notion of a public tribunal.

What hidden nuggets might Kant have supposed traditional speculative rational metaphysics to contain? I want to suggest that he thinks that there is both gold and silver to be found—though he doesn't use these images himself. The gold, I will argue, is a cogent proof of Transcendental Idealism—a proof that, unlike those given in the Aesthetic, proceeds indirectly (that is, by *reductio ad absurdum*), and so, in Kant's view, promises to establish its result with greater evidence [*Evidenz*] than the previously given direct proofs (A 790/B 818).[38] The silver, I will argue, includes at least the doctrinal beliefs in a 'god' (understood as a wise and great being) and in an afterlife. These are high-credence, stable, partial beliefs that Kant takes to admit of (partly empirically based) non-demonstrative proofs. For Kant, these 'doctrinal beliefs' are to be justified on what he seems to consider 'theoretical' grounds related to their role in advancing natural scientific inquiry. They are not to be confused with the beliefs in God and an afterlife that are justified on moral grounds. The theoretical justification for the doctrinal belief in the afterlife, as we will see in more detail in Chapter 7, takes the form of an argument by analogy, which inhabits the empirically grounded, non-dogmatic part of rational psychology (B 425–6, A 827/B 855). The theoretical justification for the doctrinal belief in a wise and great originator, as we will see in Chapter 16, is a version of the design argument and is given in the part of rational theology known as 'physicotheology' (A 826–7/B 854–5).

Since the argument for an afterlife 'from the analogy of nature with other beings in general' is supposed to proceed in part from dubitable, empirical premises, and purports to yield a highly stable belief rather than knowledge, it does not count as dogmatic. And since Kant nonetheless includes it within rational psychology (28: 441–2, 28: 591–2), that purported science—and so traditional rational metaphysics as a whole—must, by his lights, have a *non*-dogmatic part. The same point may explain why it is 'pneumatism' rather than 'rational psychology' that is said to go up in mere smoke in the fire assay of critique. If I am right, it would not do for Kant to describe rational psychology in this way in the '*Feuerprobe*' passage precisely because, in his view, this branch of speculative metaphysics leaves a valuable residue, namely, what I am calling 'the silver' of a doctrinal belief in an afterlife.[39] Exactly how this doctrinal belief is argued for is a story that will require much telling. The point for now is just that certain parts of traditional speculative metaphysics do, in Kant's view, reveal themselves to have some inner worth when

---

[38] As we will see in the conclusion, 'evidence' is a technical notion for Kant: a claim has greater evidence the more closely the kind of certainty it enjoys approximates 'intuitive certainty'—the kind of certainty produced by demonstrations, which, in Kant's view, are found exclusively in mathematics—as opposed to acroamatic or discursive proofs, which are found in philosophy. We will also see that Kant holds that indirect proofs are, in another respect, inferior to direct ones: unlike the latter, the former afford no insight into the grounds of a claim.

[39] At one point in the A edition, Kant says 'the whole of rational psychology falls, as a science surpassing all powers of human cognition' (A 382). I take it that here he is using 'rational psychology' to mean specifically *dogmatic* rational psychology.

subjected to the fire assay of critique. For Kant, then, traditional speculative metaphysics is not *mere* dogmatism, and the objective side of critique is not merely the exercise of showing that rational metaphysics is so much smoke and dross.

One of the main—and hopefully distinctive—aims of this book is to throw into sharper relief these points about Kant's conception of what I'm calling the objective side of critique, and especially about its positive, hopeful, and investigatory aspect. But this does not mean that I wish to downplay the obvious importance of either Kant's diagnostic project, which, insofar as it provides an explanation of our predicament is also positive in aim, or indeed his many and varied specific criticisms of arguments within *dogmatic* speculative metaphysics. Quite the reverse, the study of these topics will be the main business of this book. However, when I turn to these more familiar topics the novelty in my discussion will be of a more familiar kind: it will consist not in lessons learned from any radical re-interpretation of a guiding metaphor but rather, first, in the details of my analyses of Kant's critical arguments and diagnostic explanations, and, second, in the emphasis I place on certain broad themes, the first of which is the importance Kant attaches to the experimental method as a model for critical philosophy.

0.2 Method and experiment

The theme of critique as experiment comes to the fore when Kant discusses his indirect argument for Transcendental Idealism. In the *Prolegomena*, for example, he portrays the antinomies—which severally rehearse this argument—as providing a 'crucial experiment [*entscheidender Versuch*], which must disclose to us a fault [*Unrichtigkeit*] that lies hidden in the presuppositions of reason' (4: 340–1). That fault, as we will see in Chapters 10, 12, and 13, is the tacit, and indeed generally *unnoticed*, background assumption of Transcendental Realism. In the *B* preface to the first *Critique* Kant assigns to the antinomies this same role, but now only implicitly; and he treats them now as providing an experimental cross check [*Gegenprobe*] on—that's to say, a confirmation of—his proposal that objects should be assumed to conform to our cognition (B *xx–xxi*). The experiment runs as follows: If we assume that the objects of sense are things in themselves, we run into a contradiction; if, however, we assume that they are mere appearances, the contradiction disappears (B *xx*).

Kant develops this idea through the metaphor of chemical analysis. The antinomies and their resolution, he implies, confirm an experimental analysis already performed in the Transcendental Aesthetic—one whose distinct products are *appearances*, on the one hand, and *things in themselves*, on the other. The antinomies and their resolution show that these elements cannot be recombined except in the way envisaged by Transcendental Idealism—namely, under the condition that Transcendental Idealism is true (compare B *xxi*, note 'a'). More specifically, the objects of sense ('appearances' in a theory-neutral sense) are shown to be combinable with things in themselves not as *being identical with them* (as Transcendental Realism holds), but rather only as *being the appearances of them* (as Transcendental Idealism holds)—and now the term 'appearances' has the loaded Kantian sense of things whose make-up is partly constituted by the contribution of certain human faculties.[40] Insofar as it involves conducting this analysis, the method of the critical inquirer imitates that of the investigator of nature (note to B *xviii*) and, in particular, it imitates the method of the (proto)-chemist who, having isolated certain (relatively) elementary substances, confirms their distinctness by showing that they cannot be recombined except under certain special conditions (see B *xxi*, note 'a').[41] The antinomies, then, provide a confirmatory test of the results of the Transcendental Aesthetic, one that yields 'a discovery about the true character (or constitution [*Beschaffenheit*]) of things as objects of the senses' (A 507/B 535; compare 20: 291). What we discover is that the objects of the senses are not things in themselves but rather 'appearances' in Kant's technical sense. That is to say, we discover that they are objects whose make-up is constituted partly by the operation of our faculty of sensible intuition and partly—when the objects of sense are thought of collectively as 'experience'— by the operation of the understanding through concepts (B *xvii*). Kant, at any rate, is guided by the ambition to model philosophical method on the investigative procedures of natural science, including those of chemistry and metallurgy—but also, most famously, astronomy (B *xvi–xvii*).

0.3 The sceptical method

A second important theme of this book is Kant's embrace of 'the sceptical method' (A 424/B 451–2). In his logic lectures Kant is reported by his student note-takers to have drawn a distinction between two species of doubt. (In the interests of tedium-avoidance, I'll hereafter dispense with the practice of indicating that Kant is merely reported to have said the things attributed to him in the transcripts of his lectures. I will write as if he had actually said those things, but I will always intend

---

[40] Accordingly, one way to express Transcendental Idealism—or at least one central plank in this doctrine—is as the claim that appearances in the neutral sense are appearances in the loaded sense. Of course, a fuller statement of Transcendental Idealism would include the claim that space and time are nothing but the forms of our sensible intuition.

[41] An example of this procedure in the phlogiston chemistry of Kant's time would be the separation of phlogiston from a metal through burning (calcination). The two components obtained—phlogiston and the calcinated metal—would be capable of recombination only when heated in the presence of charcoal.

to be understood as having made the more cautious claim that he is merely reported as having said them.)[42] The first species of doubt is the doubt of the Academic sceptics—philosophers who maintain dogmatically that nothing is certain, thereby earning for themselves the paradoxical-sounding title of 'dogmatic sceptics'.[43] Since the generalization, 'Nothing is certain', subsumes itself, Kant regards their position as self-refuting.[44] The second species of doubt is that of Kant's Pyrrho and his (by Kant's lights) *authentic* followers. The Pyrrhonian 'sect', Kant says, 'did not really doubt all truths' but instead 'lengthened investigation and postponed decision'.[45] This remark seems to be inspired by Sextus Empiricus's characterization of the (Pyrrhonian) sceptics as philosophers who 'keep on searching'.[46] In other respects, however, Kant's understanding of Pyrrhonism is idiosyncratic. In particular, he supposes that the true Pyrrhonist does not respond to the balancing of the grounds, by permanently suspending belief, with the goal of attaining tranquillity (*ataraxia*). Instead, Kant's Pyrrhonist, having balanced the grounds for opposed claims, continues to inquire, with the goal of attaining *certainty*. Kant's 'Pyrrhonist', then, is not a Pyrrhonist on the popular understanding of that figure today; indeed, he is not even, in the ordinary sense, a sceptic.

Kant seems to appreciate this last point because, although he sometimes calls his authentic Pyrrhonian doubters 'sceptics', he takes them to be more accurately described as '*zetetici*' (investigators) or 'seekers' (24: 213). They seek, inquire, and investigate, postponing a decision until a thorough investigation has been completed (24: 209–10). This idea about the value of thorough investigation, lengthened inquiry, and deferred decision must have sent its tentacles deep into Kant's imagination, for it is one to which he frequently recurs. The theme emerges when he presents dogmatism as characterized by *hastiness* of judgment (A 309/B 366), and again when he equates the method of 'keeping on searching' with the 'sceptical method' of which he so heartily approves. In the early 1770s, for example, he remarks:

---

[42] *Blomberg Logic*, 24: 208–9; *Vienna Logic*, 24: 885–6.
[43] *Dohna-Wundlacken Logic*, 24: 745.
[44] See 24: 216 and 24: 745. In claiming that dogmatic scepticism is self-refuting Kant would seem to be tacitly assuming that assertion is governed by the norm that we should not assert something unless we take it to be known with certainty. This is not a norm he follows consistently in his own writings, however.
[45] *Blomberg Logic*, 24: 213. The reason why this lengthening of investigation counts as 'doubt' is that it standardly involves a balancing of claims or equilibrium: a state in which one has no more reason to believe a claim than its opposite. Kant conceives of this as a state of subjective doubt (*Zweifel, dubitatio*) and contrasts it with a state that involves the possession of an unbalanced objective ground, however small, for holding a claim to be false (*Bezweifelung, dubium*) (*Dohna-Wundlacken Logic*, 24: 743).
[46] Sextus Empiricus, *Outlines of Pyrrhonism*, trans. R. G. Bury (Loeb Classical Library; Cambridge, MA: Harvard University Press, 1933) at 3.

Sceptical method is a true investigating of truth by means of postponement, in that one does not accept or reject anything at once, but instead first lets there be dispute about it. (*Blomberg Logic*, 24: 210)

And some two decades later he makes the same equation:

The sceptical method is that of postponing one's approval, where one is equally open to opposing grounds. (*Dohna-Wundlacken Logic*, 1792, 24: 744)

The sceptical method, however, is not to be confused with scepticism. The former, although unhurried in its progress, nonetheless pursues certainty; the latter, however, decisively declares itself for ignorance (compare A 424/B 451). In Kant's phrase, it treats ignorance as a 'dwelling place for constant residence' (A 761/B 789). Sceptical method, moreover, is dynamic—one forges ahead in one's inquiries; scepticism, on the other hand, is static—it brings one to a 'standstill [*Stillestand*] of reason' (20: 328).[47]

This distinction between scepticism and sceptical method corresponds to another Kant draws between two kinds of epistemic stance one might adopt after balancing the grounds for opposed claims in the manner of Pyrrho. On the one hand, there is the 'sceptical' or 'renunciatory' suspension of judgment—a permanent refusal to deliver a verdict on the question under dispute, which Kant rejects because it leaves the disputed matter 'forever in darkness' (24: 640).[48] On the other, there is the Kant-approved 'critical' or 'investigative' suspension of judgment—a temporary stance that leads eventually to certainty, and which Kant associates—approvingly—with Pyrrho's 'non liquet' ('It is not evident').[49] It is this second kind of suspension that Kant has in mind when he says in the *Blomberg Logic* '**Suspensio** should only help [one] not to accept something until one has sufficient grounds [for doing so], but not on this account to reject every hope whatsoever of being able to attain full certainty concerning a thing or a cognition' (24: 161). The Kant-approved form of suspension, Kant maintains, is practised by

---

[47] That Kant himself endorses a form of Pyrrhonism aimed ultimately at certainty shows that he does not espouse a mitigated scepticism of the kind advocated by Philo of Larissa or Cicero. He does not, that is to say, believe that one side of an antinomial dispute is to be defended as, though not certain, nonetheless more probable or more warranted than its opposite. As we will see, the certainty at which he thinks the authentic Pyrrhonian should aim in fact turns out to attach not to the thesis or antithesis of an antinomy, but rather to the negation of a certain presupposition shared by the two disputants. And the doctrinal beliefs Kant regards as justified on—or officially produced and stabilized by— theoretical grounds in rational psychology and rational theology, though indeed possessed of non-demonstrative warrant, do not, in his view, belong to antinomially opposed pairs. Indeed, in these disciplines he sees dogmatic error as arising exclusively from a merely 'one-sided' illusion since the psychological and theological Ideas contain no antinomy at all (compare A 406/B 433 and A 673/B 701). I am grateful to an anonymous referee for getting me to think about where Kant stands with respect to mitigated scepticism.
[48] Compare 24: 545–6. [49] See 24: 214; 24: 885; and 9: 74.

18   THE FIERY TEST OF CRITIQUE

the 'honest' sceptic—he cites Bayle as a modern example—who 'postpones his final judgment for a good while before he dares to settle something fully' (24: 210–11). This use of 'sceptic' for an adherent of Kant-approved Pyrrhonism is, however, rare in Kant: more often he reserves the term for one or other school of thought of which he does not approve.

'Pyrrho', he says, in the *Vienna Logic*,

> maintained that philosophy lies in the equilibrium of our judgment and in the skill of being able to uncover all false illusion without otherwise being able to discover anything decisive.   (24: 803, delivered *c.*1780s)

Kant's 'otherwise' suggests the view that by following Pyrrho's method we *can* discover something decisive: namely, the existence of some kind of false illusion. And in this respect his take on Pyrrho's method accords with his own remarks about the sceptical method in the first *Critique*. 'The sceptical method', he says, 'aims at *certainty*, seeking to discover the point of misunderstanding in disputes that are honestly intended and conducted with intelligence by both sides' (A 424/B 451–2, emphasis added). As we will see in Chapter 18, the certainty to which Kant is alluding here is that which he sees as attaching to the conclusion of his indirect argument for Transcendental Idealism in the Antinomies chapter.

Kant places great value on the postponement of decision through the lengthening of inquiry. The lengthening can be extreme, involving, it seems, the *exhaustive* examination of one's starting assumptions. For Kant equates criticism itself with the maxim 'never to assume anything to be true except after [a] complete **examination of principles**' (R 5645 (18: 293)). He values the enactment of disputes, partly because this activity has the power to bring to light an otherwise unnoticed illusion and partly because it serves to sharpen our intellectual faculties. Indeed, even dogmatism, he suggests, can be of value when it enacts disputes that are grist for the Kant-approved Pyrrhonian's critico-sceptical mill.[50] 'The contradictions and conflict of systems', he says,

> are the only thing that have in modern times prevented human reason from falling into complete dereliction in matters of metaphysics. Although [these systems] are all dogmatic to the highest degree, they still represent perfectly the position of sceptics for one who surveys this game as a whole. For this reason we can thank a Crusius as well as a Wolff for the fact that through the new paths that they trod they at least prevented the understanding from allowing its rights to

---

[50] Kant appears to take the same view of Leibniz's philosophy, for he conceives of the Wolffian philosophy as its 'daughter' (8: 187).

become superannuated in stupid idleness and still preserved the germ of a secure knowledge.[51]

This passage combines its main point with a subsidiary aside. The main point is that Crusius and Wolff can at least claim to have provided a temporary bulwark against the threat of indifferentism (compare A x). They are serious thinkers, who made an honest stab at advancing the project of dogmatic metaphysics. And their dogmatism at least had the merit of keeping the human understanding *limber*.[52] As we will see in Chapter 10, what Kant means by 'indifferentism' is a kind of pseudo-intellectual posturing that privileges ridicule and disingenuous rhetoric over open and honest critique. Its practitioners are guilty of a kind of hypocrisy; for even while proudly scorning metaphysics they quietly arrive at dogmatic metaphysical positions. In Kant's eyes, the indifferentist movement—if one can call it that—is no more than a distasteful fad, and its proponents unworthy of serious intellectual engagement. Nonetheless it is—or so he ruefully judges—the dominant outlook of his age (A x, A xi note).

The passage's subsidiary aside makes the point that when a serious-minded metaphysical dispute is viewed externally, each disputant can be regarded as playing their part in the construction of an antinomy, and thus as doing internally a portion of the work of a (Kant-approved) Pyrrhonian sceptic who, looking upon the dispute from without, notes the equilibrium of grounds and continues to inquire into the source of the apparent contradiction. Interestingly, in another reflection from the same period Kant suggests that the critical philosopher must occupy both perspectives—internal and external—at the same time. They must, that is, simultaneously rehearse the two sides of a dispute and impartially observe it. 'Two metaphysicians <metaphysici>', he says,

> one of whom proves the thesis, the other the antithesis, occupy in the eyes of a third observer the position of a sceptical examination. *One must do both oneself.*
> (R 5015 (18: 60), 1776–78, emphasis added)

In these last two passages Kant is giving his approval to the work of the sceptical observer. So, the 'scepticism' in question must be that of the Kant-approved Pyrrhonist. But since that is so, Kant would seem to regard the construction of antinomies as part of the method of the authentic Pyrrhonian sceptic.

That having been said, Andrew Chignell and Colin McLear are right to observe (against Michael Forster) that Kant does not make an absolutely explicit

---

[51] R 4936, 1776–78, 18: 33–4.
[52] Significantly, Kant sometimes portrays Wolff as an especially adept practitioner of dogmatic speculative metaphysics, on one occasion going so far as to describe him as a 'virtuoso of reason' [*Vernunftkünstler*] (R 4866, 1776–78, 18: 14).

connection between the antinomies and what he takes to be Pyrrho's method of *critical* suspension.[53] There is, as they say, no smoking gun. I would claim, however, that while there may indeed be no single text that states the connection, a tolerably plausible case can be made for its existence by linking together a series of texts from the first *Critique* and the logic lectures—texts which Forster does not himself cite. Thus, one observes that while in the first *Critique* Kant identifies the method of occasioning antinomies with the sceptical method (A 423/B 451; and compare R 5639 (18: 276)), in the *Blomberg Logic* he identifies the sceptical method with the lengthening of investigation (24: 210), and lengthened investigation with the method of the (by his lights) authentic Pyrrhonist (24: 213). If these links hold firm, Kant must be identifying the method of occasioning antinomies with his favoured form of Pyrrhonism—and so with the method of critical suspension. But, since some of the links are forged only in student notes, these texts can provide only relatively weak evidence. The same conclusion, however, is at least strongly hinted at by the more authoritative 'two-metaphysicians' remark already quoted from R 5015. It is also confirmed—albeit in another remark from these same Blomberg lectures—by Kant's characterization of 'the Pyrrhonic doubter'. 'The Pyrrhonic, that is, sceptical doubter', he says, 'holds that to each and every one of our judgments, or at least most, another judgment may always be opposed which maintains exactly the opposite of what is contained in the former judgment' (24: 209). If—as seems likely—by 'opposing one judgment to another' Kant means furnishing competing, balanced grounds for the opposed claims, this remark implicitly equates the method of constructing antinomies with the method of Kant's Pyrrhonist.

In Kant's view, while Pyrrho taught the investigative or critical kind of suspension, his followers corrupted his teachings by recommending the renunciatory kind. These followers, Kant supposes, sometimes accompany their recommendation of the permanent suspension of belief with the judgment that nothing is certain. When this happens, inauthentic Pyrrhonism turns into self-undermining Academic scepticism (24: 210). He further supposes that the Academic sceptics were well aware that their view undermined itself and that they accordingly adopted the strategy—by Kant's lights an unconvincing ruse—of likening their scepticism to a self-expelling emetic. 'Scepticism', he says,

---

[53] Andrew Chignell and Colin McLear, 'Three Skeptics and the *Critique*: Critical Notice of Michael Forster's *Kant and Skepticism*', *Philosophical Books*, 51 (4) (2010), 228–44 at 230–1. These authors are, I think, right to claim that Forster fails to make a persuasive case for such a connection. I also agree with them that *contra* Forster, far from rejecting Pyrrhonism Kant sees the critical philosophy as an embodiment of Pyrrhonism *as he understands it* (Chignell and McLear, 'Three Skeptics', 234). What he does reject is Pyrrhonism understood as recommending the balancing of claims followed by the *permanent* suspension of belief—a practice he regards as a perversion of Pyrrho's doctrine. See Michael N. Forster, *Kant and Skepticism* (Princeton: Princeton University Press, 2008).

was in the beginning actually very rational, but its followers spoiled it and earned it a bad reputation. These latter were so subtle that they even went so far as to say that everything is uncertain, even that it is uncertain that everything is uncertain. That [they said] was actually a kind of purgative of human reason, which was such that after it cleansed our understanding completely of all impurities, i.e., of all false delusion, prejudices, [and] incorrect judgments, it disposed of itself in turn. (24: 210)

Here Kant seems to be relying on the characterization of scepticism offered by Diogenes Laertius in the chapter on Pyrrho in his *Lives of Eminent Philosophers*.[54]

A trace of this image survives into the first *Critique*, where Kant describes the sober critique made possible by the sceptical method as a *true* purgative (or 'cathartic'). By means of the sceptical method, he says,

> one can with little expense spare oneself a great dogmatic jumble, and put in its place a sober critique, which, as a true cathartic [*Kathartikon*], will happily purge us of delusion along with its attendant, namely, the attitude of erudition.
> (A 485–6/B 514)

By speaking of a 'true cathartic' Kant is implicitly contrasting his own method with what he sees as the false cathartic (or purgative) of Academic scepticism—as practised, for example, by Arcesilaus (24: 886). The sceptical method, Kant seems to be implying, is the right kind of purgative because it eliminates the rubbish *without* eliminating itself. It does not eliminate itself, one supposes, because, being a method rather than a doctrine, the sceptical method is not the kind of thing that could be eliminated.

Though he favours the sceptical method, Kant does not regard it as the only legitimate method of critique. Rather, it is the *best* such method: 'In the critique of metaphysics', he says,

> one can make use of two kinds of method. The first is to examine [the proofs] in detail and to search for [the metaphysicians'] paralogisms <paralogismos> or petitiones principii. The second is to oppose one proof to another, indeed a proof equally convincing as the opposite. This latter method is the best.
> (R 4454 (17: 557))

---

[54] L. Diogenes, *Lives of Eminent Philosophers* (Loeb Classical Library; Cambridge, MA: Harvard University Press) at 489–91. We know that Kant was familiar with this work first because he alludes to it at B xi, and, secondly, because at A 167/B 208 he refers to Epicurus's use of the Greek word that we transliterate as 'prolepsis'. Diogenes discusses this usage in his chapter on Epicurus in book 10, paragraph 33 of his work.

22   THE FIERY TEST OF CRITIQUE

As one might expect, the method of attempting to identify paralogisms—that is, (roughly) incorrect inferences—is the method practised in the Paralogisms chapter, that of opposing one proof to another the method of the Antinomies.⁵⁵ In Chapter 16 we will see that Kant takes the traditional physico-theological proof to involve a *petitio principii*. And in Chapter 9 we will see why he favours the method of opposing one proof to another.

0.4 Pyrrhonian postponement

Kant's Pyrrhonism leads him to reject a certain established method of inquiry. 'I am not of the same opinion', he declares in a reflection,

> as an excellent man who recommends that when one has once convinced oneself of something one should afterward not doubt it any more.... One must rather weigh the propositions in all sorts of applications and even borrow a particular proof from these, one must try out the opposite, and postpone decision until the truth is illuminated from all sides.⁵⁶

In the *Jäsche Logic* he goes so far as to suggest that we should remain open to the opposite view even after we have achieved knowledge of the matter in question. 'With knowledge [*Wissen*]', he says, 'one still listens to opposed grounds' (9: 72). This open-mindedness comes to an end, he suggests, only in the case of practically grounded faith [*Glaube*]. He continues: '[one still listens to opposed grounds with knowledge] but not with faith [*Glaube*], because here one does not depend on objective grounds but on the moral interest of the subject' (ibid.). Kant's Pyrrhonism, then, is a methodological stance adopted only in regard to *theoretically* grounded inquiry: morally grounded faith, perhaps surprisingly, is in a certain sense more robust than theoretically grounded knowledge.⁵⁷

In the reflection just quoted, Kant leaves the 'excellent man' unnamed, but Descartes is a likely suspect. For in the 'Synopsis' to his *Mediations*, Descartes says: 'The eventual result of this doubt is to make it impossible for us to have any further doubts about what we subsequently discover to be true.'⁵⁸ And in his *Principles of Philosophy*—a work Kant also owned—Descartes includes the following recommendation on his list of 'rules to be observed in order to philosophize correctly':

---

⁵⁵ The qualification 'roughly' is needed because, as we will see in Chapter 3, Kant's notion of a paralogism turns out to be wider than that of a formally invalid argument.
⁵⁶ R 5036, 1776–78, 18: 69.
⁵⁷ Notice that this is another reason to avoid translating '*Glaube*', when it refers to morally grounded faith, as 'belief'.
⁵⁸ *AT* VII, 12; *CSM* II, 9.

We must give our attention in an orderly way to the notions that we have within us, and we must judge to be true all and only those [notions] whose truth we clearly and distinctly cognize [*cognoscemus*] when we attend to them in this way.[59]

The 'all' part of this rule implies that we ought not to continue to doubt any proposition whose truth has been clearly and distinctly cognized. Instead, we must take care to conclusively judge all such propositions true. Against such a view, Kant insists that

> reason must not count so boldly on the premises that ground it as if it were unnecessary for it frequently to look back and consider whether there might not be errors in the progress of its inferences to be discovered that were overlooked in its principles and that make it necessary either to determine them further or else to alter them entirely. (A 735–6/B 763–4)

By Kant's lights, then, Descartes is insufficiently alive to the possibility that his first principles might be either mistaken or else too weak to adequately ground the conclusions he draws from them. In this respect Descartes is, in Kant's eyes, quintessentially anti-Pyrrhonian. In another respect, however, Descartes shares an affinity with *Kant's* Pyrrho, for in the *Meditations* he doubts not in order to permanently suspend belief, but only in order to eventually attain certainty. Kant, it seems, focuses on the contrast at the expense of the comparison.

This is one aspect of Kant's take on the Pyrrhonian idea that we should 'continue to inquire'. Another, arguably, is that we should be constantly on the lookout for ways to re-prove results already proven. This explains why he should offer—in the form of his four, or strictly five, antinomies—a cluster of arguments that provide, through the need for their several resolutions—a cluster of distinct indirect proofs of Transcendental Idealism. It also explains why he should provide these indirect arguments even after having already provided his direct proof of this view in the Aesthetic, and why he should offer several indirect arguments while also maintaining that each individual antinomy-resolution establishes Transcendental Idealism with *apodictic* certainty. And, finally, it explains why he should offer two distinct styles of resolution of the mathematical antinomies (see Chapter 10).

These considerations suggest that we may express Kant's favoured 'sceptical method' in the form of a recipe. First, construct antinomies for yourself, by

---

[59] *Principles of Philosophy*, Part I, §75 (*AT* VIII, 38; *CSM* I, 221). Kant owned the edition of 1650. Contrast Kant's remark in a reflection: 'I do not approve of the rule that when in the use of pure reason one has proven something, one should subsequently no longer cast doubt upon it, as if it were a firm principle' (R 5019, 1776–78, 18: 62–3).

devising the most compelling arguments you can for pairs of opposed propositions in dogmatic speculative metaphysics. Next, note that the arguments just constructed are equally convincing, and temporarily suspend belief. But don't stop there! Instead, continue to investigate, both by re-examining the proofs, and by seeking the source of the apparent disagreement in a false presupposition shared by the two sides of the dispute. In particular, try to uncover an illusion that might make that false presupposition appear to be true. Only when this illusion has been found, 'make a determination'—that is, assign truth values to the thesis and antithesis. Next, appeal to the discovered illusion to explain why this assignment of truth values did not seem possible initially. Repeat this procedure as many times as seems appropriate in the context of a range of different antinomies. Finally, remain permanently alert to the possibility of having somewhere made a mistake in following this very recipe.

0.5 Kantian charity

Related to the theme of postponing judgment is the idea of charitably *cultivating* one's opponent's position before subjecting it to critique. Kant supposes that criticism can proceed effectively only if the positions to be critiqued are first afforded the freedom to develop themselves properly (compare A 507/B 535), and even nourished with fresh arguments. 'The germ of the contestations [of the dogmatic metaphysicians]', he says,

> which lies in the nature of human reason, must be extirpated; but how can we extirpate it if we do not give it freedom, indeed even nourishment, to send out shoots, so that we can discover it and afterwards uproot it? Thus, think up for yourself the objections which have not yet occurred to any opponent, and even lend him the weapons or concede him the most favourable position he could desire. (A 777/B 805-6).

The charitable development of dogmatic views is essential to the practice of critique because it provides something to clutch onto—shoots—when the time comes to uproot the weed. These shoots also help us to locate the germ of dogmatic metaphysics, to locate, that is to say, the fundamental error on which it rests—an error that, in the Antinomies at least, Kant identifies with Transcendental Realism.[60] In Chapter 15 we will see that an especially transparent

---

[60] As will become clearer when we consider the Antinomies, Kant views the Transcendental Realist's very conception of the sensible world (as an absolute totality of things in themselves) as a dogmatic conception (see A 521/B 549, note).

instance of this kind of charitable development of a dogmatic position occurs in Kant's criticism of the cosmological argument.

Kant's appreciation of the value of charity is on display in a reflection apparently composed shortly before the appearance of the first *Critique*. 'In judging the writings of others', he says:

> one must adopt the method of participation in the general matters of human reason. In the attempt to discover in them that which pertains to the whole, it is worthwhile to extend a helping hand to the author, or rather to the common good, and to treat errors as incidentals. (R 4992, 1776–78, 18: 53)

In keeping with these generous sentiments Kant disavows the critique of particular 'books or systems' (A *xii*; compare 8: 218 note *). His target is an idealized dogmatic speculative metaphysics, one freed from the incidental errors of this or that particular author. As we will see in Chapter 2, one example of this aspect of Kant's charity is his selection of a properly purified—and accordingly charitably *improved*—version of dogmatic rational psychology as the target of his criticisms.

0.6 Denying knowledge

Even prior to his critical turn, Kant saw metaphysics, when properly practised, as a shield of religion and morality. 'Metaphysics', he says in a pre-critical reflection, 'is not the mother of religion but its bulwark'.[61] More expansively:

> It is religion that derives the greatest profit from [metaphysics]: everything in religion that is moral is secured by metaphysics, protected from fanaticism and unbelief, and freed from dependence on scholastic subtleties.
> (R 4284 (17: 495), 1770s)

By 'religion', of course, Kant means his *own* non-sectarian, creed-transcending 'moral religion'—a religion in which moral progress displaces the observance of religious rites, and whose cardinal propositions, insofar as it has them at all, are the existence of God (conceived of as a being who proportions happiness to worthiness-to-be-happy), and the existence of an afterlife. Kant takes one especially sturdy shield of religion and morality to be his own doctrine of Transcendental Idealism. He sees this doctrine as a bulwark against 'fanaticism and unbelief' for two reasons. First, he regards this view as an antidote to

---

[61] See R 4865, 1776–78, 18: 14. And for similar statements during the critical period (with 'foundation' substituted for 'mother') compare A 849/B 877 and R 5675 (18: 325).

Spinozism, a view traditionally associated with atheism and by Kant with 'fanaticism' [*Schwärmerei*].[62] Second, he regards Transcendental Idealism as making possible the resolution of the antinomies—apparent contradictions which, if left unresolved, would in Kant's view lead to either scepticism or dogmatism.[63] Scepticism—by which in this context Kant means ignorance-asserting dogmatic scepticism—is, for Kant, an 'evil' because it 'rob[s] human reason of all hope in the most important questions of reason' (R 4645, 18: 294). He is thinking, in particular, of the questions of the existence of a Highest Being and an afterlife—matters about which he believes we can attain morally grounded faith. Dogmatism, for its part, is damaging to religion and morality partly because it can lead to fanaticism and partly because, resting on dubious scholastic proofs and demanding that one close one's mind to the opposing view, it fails to provide religion with the justification it seeks.

Kant believes that metaphysics, when properly conducted, can free religion from its dependence on scholastic *subtleties*. It is to be conducted not by means of the ambitious and obscurely hair-splitting proofs of the dogmatists but rather by certain proofs, less ambitious and more accessible, that can hope to appeal to 'common human reason'. These proofs include, on the one hand, the various 'moral proofs', and, on the other, certain theoretically (as opposed to morally) based, and in part empirical, arguments for the rationality of the aforementioned 'doctrinal beliefs'. By limiting one's ambitions to providing these more accessible proofs, Kant thinks, one makes room for faith partly because one avoids the self-defeatingly fussy, obscure, and unconvincing dogmatic proofs. A paradigm of one of these hair-splitting dogmatic proofs is Mendelssohn's 'proof' of the immortality of the soul (B 413–15). Kant would, I think, see this proof as self-defeating: it perversely impedes one's faith in an afterlife because, failing through its subtlety to appeal to 'common human reason' (4: 383), it rightly arouses our suspicion (B 424).[64] Kant, by contrast, holds that:

---

[62] See 28: 1052–3; and compare R 6050, 18: 436 and 5: 101–2. And for the distinction between 'fanaticism' [*Schwärmerei*] and 'enthusiasm' [*Enthusiasmus*], see 2: 251n. It is interesting to note in this connection that in the *Prolegomena* Kant describes school metaphysics as 'the *final* hiding place of fanaticism' (4: 383, emphasis added). This suggests that as Transcendental Realism leads to fanaticism, so fanaticism, for Kant, leads to school metaphysics—presumably of a Spinozist stripe. This point brings out that Kant is prepared to apply the term 'school metaphysics' to views beyond medieval Aristotelianism and German school metaphysics.

[63] A 407/B 434; compare 20: 327.

[64] Such sentiments, as Kant would have known, were commonplace. David Fordyce, for example, maintains that because the metaphysical proofs of the soul's immortality depend on 'intricate reasonings' they are 'not obvious to ordinary understandings, and are seldom so convincing...as not to leave some doubts behind them' (David Fordyce, *The Elements of Moral Philosophy* (Indianapolis: Liberty Fund, 2003) at 152). David Hume suggests, more strongly still, that when 'the religious philosophers' indulge their 'rash curiosity' by seeing how far they can 'establish religion upon the principles of reason', they are more likely to 'excite' than 'satisfy' the doubts that arise from a diligent inquiry (see David Hume, *Enquiries Concerning Human Understanding and Concerning the Principles of Morals* (Oxford: Clarendon Press, 1975) at 135). More strongly yet—and more pithily—Anthony Collins is reputed to have quipped: 'No one doubted [God's] existence until [Samuel] Clarke tried to prove it'

The proofs that are usable for the world [of human beings] here [that is, with respect to the question of an afterlife] preserve their undiminished worth, and rather gain in clarity and unaffected conviction through the removal of those dogmatic pretensions, since [these usable proofs] place reason in its proper domain, namely, the order of ends [*Zwecke*] that is yet at the same time an order of nature. (B 425)

In Chapters 7 and 16 we will see that the non-dogmatic, yet still (in part) theoretically grounded, arguments that Kant regards as capable of producing the justified doctrinal beliefs in a wise and great Author of Nature and in an afterlife, do indeed proceed from certain assumptions about the existence of *ends* or *purposes* in nature (compare B *xxxiii*). They are, accordingly, good candidates— together, of course, with the more familiar moral proofs—for the accessible faith-producing (and faith-justifying/stabilizing) arguments that Kant expects to come into their own when we abandon the ambition to attain metaphysical knowledge by dogmatic speculative means.[65]

0.7 Speculation

The three main targets of Kant's critical philosophy are: first, the dogmatic speculative metaphysics of (among others): Plato, Epicurus, Descartes, Leibniz, Crusius, Wolff, Mendelssohn, and Baumgarten—as well, of course, as that of Kant himself in certain of his pre-critical writings; second, various forms of dogmatic *scepticism*, including both the scepticism of Kant's Hume (A 764/B 792; 4: 262; 24: 217) and that of the Academic sceptics;[66] and third, the stance of the 'indifferentists',

---

(quoted in Roy Porter, *Enlightenment: Britain and the Creation of the Modern World* (London: Penguin, 2000) at 104).

[65] Kant tends to present the relevant arguments as generating *very firmly held* or *almost unshakeable* doctrinal beliefs rather than *justified* ones. But there are signs that the concept of justification does gain a foothold in application to doctrinal beliefs. Kant says, for example, that by expanding the order of ends 'beyond the bounds of experience and life', as one does when conducting an argument supporting the doctrinal belief in an afterlife, reason is *'justified* in going beyond the order of nature' (B 425, emphasis added). For this reason, I will portray Kant as regarding doctrinal beliefs as justified, while also acknowledging that his emphasis lies on their firmness and (near) unshakeability.

[66] Kant describes Hume as 'perhaps the most brilliant of the sceptics' (A 764/B 792). He supposes that Hume begins by following the salutary practice of the true Pyrrhonian sceptic, but in the end lapses into dogmatic scepticism because he finally 'complains about the uncertainty of all our cognition whatsoever' (24: 217). After a promising start, then, Hume, in Kant's view, ends up revealing himself to have merely *affected* to employ the Pyrrhonian sceptical method (24: 211). This may explain why, in the context of a discussion of Hume's scepticism, Kant says that Hume's path 'began on the trail of truth' (A 764/B 792) and that he *'capitulated* entirely to scepticism' (B 128, emphasis added). But there is also another aspect of Kant's criticism of Hume that has to be taken into account. Kant sees Hume as having undertaken an incomplete and non-systematic criticism of the alleged principles of dogmatic meta- physics, thus engaging in a piecemeal 'censure' of reason, which reveals only its 'limits' (that is, some of

as represented—or so I will argue—principally by the French *philosophes*, on the one hand, and the German popular philosophers, on the other.[67] In the first *Critique* Kant focuses mainly on the dogmatic speculative metaphysicians and the sceptics, depicting his own critical philosophy as steering a middle course between these undesirable extremes.[68] But, even while opposing dogmatism, Kant regards 'speculative reason' as capable of accomplishing much that is of value, including—as we'll see in Chapters 10 and 12—the provision of a theoretically grounded indirect argument for Transcendental Idealism. That argument, in turn, makes room for a practically grounded extension of our cognition because, by establishing that nature does not exclude freedom, it makes room for a practically grounded argument for the existence of a genuinely spontaneous human causal faculty.[69]

This point about what speculative reason can achieve confirms that, as used by Kant, 'speculative' is not always a pejorative word (compare B *xliii*). The same point is confirmed by three further textual facts: first, he portrays the table of categories as a blueprint for a 'planned speculative science' (B 110), second, he describes pure mathematics as a pure science of reason with 'merely speculative' content (A 480/B 508), and third, he presents his slumber-piercing recollection of David Hume as having caused him not to *abandon* his speculative inquires, but rather to give them a completely different direction (4: 260). What is objectionable for Kant is not speculative reason per se, but rather its *misuse*—something that occurs when speculative reason is developed in the absence of a prior critique of the mind's capacities—when, that is to say, it becomes dogmatic.

'A theoretical cognition', Kant says, 'is **speculative** if it concerns such an object, or such concepts, as one cannot reach in any experience' (A 634/B 662). On the face of it, this claim specifies only a sufficient condition: any cognition—and, in particular, any judgment—that concerns the supersensible is speculative. But for Kant speculative cognition is not confined to the supersensible. He is clear, for example, that cognition of certain objects existing within possible experience also counts as speculative.[70] When making such claims he seems to be thinking of the cognition of certain not-directly-perceivable features of possibly experienced objects—cognition afforded by our knowledge of the principles of the possibility of experience.

---

reason's contingent limitations, rather than a systematic critique, which reveals its principled 'boundaries' (A 767/B 795)). This lack of a systematic critique, Kant believes, led Hume to overlook the legitimate metaphysics of experience that Kant endorses, and so to indulge in a disastrous baby-out-with-the-bathwater, sceptical over-reaction—an over-reaction that, at its most extreme, became self-undermining (A 767–8/B 795–6).

[67] In Chapter 10, I go further into the question: 'Who are the indifferentists?'
[68] *Prolegomena* §58 (4: 360); also 24: 745.
[69] The Third Antinomy contains no clear suggestion that the faculty for which Kant wishes to make room through the antinomy's resolution is specifically *human* free will. In §12.3, however, I offer evidence that this is in fact the case.
[70] See A 395 and A 471/B 499; and compare A 702/B 730.

Intriguingly, Kant occasionally claims that even certain arguments whose conclusions possess only empirical (as opposed to apodictic) certainty—for example, arguments by analogy—belong to speculation. Thus, speaking initially of his doctrine of practical faith, he says:

> The only precariousness to be found in [my morally-based belief in God and an afterlife] is the fact that this rational belief is based on the presupposition of moral attitudes. If we abandon this presupposition and assume someone who is entirely indifferent with regard to moral laws, then the question posed by reason becomes merely a problem for speculation; *and it can indeed then be supported by strong grounds taken from analogy*, but not by grounds to which the most obstinate scepticism would have to yield. (A 829/B 857, emphasis added)

As we will see in Chapter 7, a certain argument for the afterlife, which Kant treats as producing a doctrinal belief, fits the profile of one of these 'strong grounds taken from analogy', as, arguably, does the physico-theological argument when it is construed in a duly modest Kantian fashion (see Chapter 16). In Kant's view, then, speculative metaphysics contains a non-dogmatic part in which one constructs, on the basis of *theoretical* premises, arguments aimed at producing justified beliefs rather than knowledge. Speculative reason thus has both legitimate and illegitimate 'uses' for Kant, where only the latter—which he calls 'pure' or 'transcendental' uses—are bad or 'dialectical' in themselves.[71]

0.8 The pre-eminence of the Antinomies

In the *Prolegomena* Kant urges 'the critical reader' to be concerned chiefly with the phenomenon of antinomy (4: 341n). This recommendation reflects his view that the construction of antinomies is the best critical method, but it also reflects his conception of the arguments of the antinomies as unique among our transcendental illusion-induced inferences in *compelling* reason's critical self-examination (ibid.). The phenomenon of antinomy, he says in the second *Critique*, is 'the most beneficial error into which human reason could ever have fallen, inasmuch as *it finally drives us to search for the key to escape from this labyrinth*' (5: 107, emphasis added).

The 'key' in question—or so I will argue—is Transcendental Idealism. The antinomies, Kant thinks, can be resolved if *but only if* Transcendental Idealism is true. And since they must be resolved if reason is to be coherent, their resolution provides an indirect or 'apagogic' argument for the Transcendental Idealism

---

[71] See A 777/B 806 and compare A 329/B 386 as well as 5: 104 and 5: 146.

already argued for by direct or 'ostensive' means in the Aesthetic.[72] Insofar as they play this role, the antinomies distinguish themselves from the arguments of the Paralogisms and the Ideal, which play no such role because the merely 'one-sided' illusion that prompts them, forcing no crisis, creates no special pressure to reject Transcendental Realism.[73]

Kant believes that if the antinomies are left unresolved, there will be no end to 'the cosmological dispute that reason has with itself' (A 497/B 525). And since that dispute plays out within the human rational faculty, in the absence of this resolution our theoretical allegiances will, he further supposes, be doomed to persist in a fruitless oscillation between the thesis and antithesis of each antinomy (A 475/B 503). As Kant recognizes, the pendulum swing is *in practice* stabilized, but only by means of prejudice and other non-evidentiary factors.[74] One can appreciate why he should have found such a situation intolerable. For this oscillation—whether left unchecked or merely artificially stabilized—risks creating the suspicion that reason is permanently in conflict with itself. Once established, this suspicion has the potential to erode our very trust in 'reason's government' (A 669/B 697), hence in pure *practical* reason, hence in morality, and so, finally, in the morally based arguments for God, freedom, and an afterlife.

For the same reasons, the resolution of the *dynamical* antinomies is no less urgent. But in their case the urgency has another source too. For, left unresolved, one of these antinomies threatens to make Kant's own metaphysics of experience seem dogmatic. The antithesis of the third antinomy, after all, is tantamount to a statement of Kant's causal principle, a principle that he takes to be known a priori as a condition of the possibility of experience. Without a resolution of this antinomy, therefore, Kant will seem, through his positive metaphysics of experience, to have taken sides in an antinomial dispute and so to have himself lapsed into dogmatism (broadly construed).

0.9 Four masters of method

Kant characterizes the first *Critique* as a treatise on method (B *xxii*). It is, he implies, the propaedeutic to an envisaged—if unrealized—system of the science of metaphysics (B *xliii*).[75] His favoured philosophical method shows the influence of a quartet of luminous figures in the Western tradition: Copernicus, Francis Bacon, Pyrrho, and Socrates. From Copernicus, as we have seen, Kant takes the idea that genuine intellectual progress in any (would-be) scientific field requires a

---

[72] For a discussion of these labels see 24: 233.
[73] See A 406/B 433, 4: 340, and 5: 107. Also see Chapter 3 for further discussion of this point.
[74] A 465–75/B 493–503.
[75] Kant at one point conceived of this envisaged systematic work as a metaphysics textbook, or brief handbook, to be used in academic lectures (10: 346).

revolutionary shift in perspective. In metaphysics, as we have noted, this idea yields the thought that objects should conform to our cognition rather than the reverse (B *xvi*). Arguably, a trace of the perspective-shift idea is also present in Kant's related thought that the mind can gain a priori knowledge only insofar as it recovers—or, in the case of mathematics, *develops*—a certain a priori element that it has itself put into things (B *xviii*). From Bacon, whose programme for reforming the sciences Kant honours in the *B* edition's epigraph, he takes certain empirical models and metaphors that guide his somewhat analogous programme for reforming metaphysics—though Copernicus, obviously, is also a model for this.[76] From Pyrrho Kant takes the idea that philosophy should be 'zetetic' or investigatory—that it should proceed by asking questions—and, most importantly of all, that it should lengthen inquiry, postponing judgment until the question has been examined from all sides. From Socrates, whom Kant thinks of as something of a Pyrrhonian *avant la lettre*,[77] he takes the idea that true knowledge is *self-knowledge*—knowledge of one's own ignorance (compare A *xi*).[78] Kant regards Socrates as possessing 'a laudable ignorance', which consists, somewhat paradoxically, in 'a knowledge of non-knowledge'.[79] His procedure is thus a model for the critical Kant's own approach of seeking a 'modest but thorough self-knowledge'—a 'knowledge of non-knowledge' that for Kant has the status of a *science* (A 758/B 786).[80] And significantly, Kant conceives of this science of the boundaries of human reason as producing a kind of enlightenment (in the pre-Kantian sense of 'intellectual illumination'). In the darkness in which we find ourselves, he says, 'the critique of reason lights a torch, although it illuminates not the regions unknown to us beyond the sensible world, but the dark space of our own understanding'.[81]

0.10 Approach

Approaches to Kant's theoretical philosophy run the gamut from the purely historiographical and contextualist at one extreme, to the analytical, reconstructive, and even boldly idea-raiding at the other. Kant scholarship is a broad church, and which approach one favours is (and, I think, ought to be) largely a matter of aptitude and taste. The present work occupies a position towards the middle of this spectrum. I provide historical context for the conceptions Kant employs, but

---

[76] See B *xx–xxi*, B *xvi–xvii*, A 770/B 798, and R 5645 (18: 287–8).
[77] *Logic Herder*, 24: 4; *Blomberg Logic*, 24: 292.
[78] *Blomberg Logic*, 24: 212, compare 24: 72. Kant also recommends the use of Socratic method, understood now as the method of exposing one's opponent's ignorance, for use against those who raise objections to morality and religion (B *xxxi*).
[79] *Jäsche Logic*, 44–5.   [80] A 736/B 764; compare A *xi* and A 680/B 708.
[81] R 5112, 1776–78, 18: 93.

also attempt to reconstruct his arguments with a degree of rigour. On occasion, I relate Kant's views to problems of contemporary interest; but I avoid lengthy discussions of those problems for their own sake. Equally, although I delve into the intellectual background when it seems relevant, I avoid lengthy discussions of Kant's immediate predecessors as philosophers of interest in their own right (as several of them were). The one possible exception to this last rule might be the chapter on empirical and rational psychology (Chapter 2), where I go into the Wolffian background in some detail.[82]

I have aimed to offer a more-or-less complete treatment of the Dialectic. This has required me to confine my attention to the most immediately relevant secondary literature, lest the book, already lengthy, should become unmanageable. Those readers who lack a taste for lengthy books should be assured that almost every chapter may be read as a more-or-less self-standing discussion (The two exceptions to this rule are Chapters 4 and 5, which presuppose some knowledge of Chapter 3.) Readers who choose this approach are advised to consult the appendix for explanations of abbreviative jargon introduced in earlier chapters.

0.11 Rigour

I tend to formulate both Kant's own arguments and those he presents on his opponents' behalf in the form of (in intention) rigorous proofs. I consider this approach to be in keeping with the spirit of Kant's critical philosophy, first, because he regards his own critical method as 'scholastic' rather than 'popular' in style (A *xviii*, B *xxxvi*, B *liii*);[83] second, because he sometimes claims that the reasoning he presents informally could, in principle, be treated with scholastic

---

[82] This background has recently been opened up by the painstaking scholarship of Corey Dyck. See his *Kant and Rational Psychology* (Oxford: Oxford University Press, 2014). His is an approach which I find congenial and to which I am indebted. In taking seriously the influence on Kant of Wolff and the Wolffians, Dyck and I both us depart from Jonathan Bennett (*Kant's Dialetic* (Cambridge: Cambridge University Press, 1974)), who confesses:

> I am unable to explore Wolff's yard-long shelf of philosophy, in which Leibniz's views are developed inaccurately and in infinite detail. I shall mainly ignore Wolff and write as though Kant's only Leibnizian source was Leibniz. I think no harm will come of this.
>
> (*Kant's Dialectic*, at 6)

But compare:

> I am unable to explore the Amazon's higher reaches, in which mermaids feud with river monsters. I shall mainly ignore the Amazon and write as though South America's only long river is the Orinoco. Etc.

[83] This, of course, is a non-pejorative use of 'scholastic'—a use tantamount to 'scientific [*scientifische*]' (see 9: 148). As a sign of Kant's willingness to use the scholastic method of presentation we may note that he sometimes conforms his critical arguments to the rules for conducting a 'learned dispute' or '*controversia*' that are set out in §499 of Meier's *Auszug*. In Chapter 14, I will argue that attending to the details of these rules, and to the disputational context they govern, sheds crucial light on a key move Kant makes in his most famous criticism of the ontological argument.

rigour (A 352); and third, because he tells us that the deceptions involved in flawed arguments are discovered most easily if those arguments are presented 'in a manner complying with school standards' (A 608/B 636).[84] This approach will also be of value insofar as it will help us to learn, through our examination of the proofs involved in the antinomies, a great deal about what Kant takes the commitments of Transcendental Realism to be. The formal system in which I give these reconstructed proofs is an amended version of the natural deduction system of Warren Goldfarb's excellent introductory text, *Deductive Logic*.[85]

0.12 Typographical conventions

Words and phrases that Kant borrows from foreign or dead languages I set in roman type and encase in angle brackets after supplying the English translation (if there is one) in the main text. When there is no natural English translation, I set the phrase in italics (for example, '*focus imaginarius*'). When the word or phrase is the same in (current) English and Latin—for example, the late Latin word 'hypothesis'—I set it in roman type and leave it unenclosed. Those phrases that appear in the Academy edition in separated type (*Sperrdruck*) I set in bold type, those that appear in heavy type (*Fettdruck*) in bolded italics. Finally, when referring to the individual arguments constituting the paralogisms or antinomies, I use lower case (thus: 'paralogisms', 'antinomies'), but when referring to the corresponding chapters (or relevant passages within those chapters) I set the initial letter in upper case (thus: 'Paralogisms', 'Antinomies').

0.13 Jargon and dating the reflections

I employ certain space-saving sub-scripted abbreviations, including: 'substance$_1$', 'substance$_2$', 'paralogism$_k$', and 'minor premise$_y$'. These abbreviations are explained when they are first introduced and a second time in the appendix. When citing Kant's reflections (indicated by 'R'), I supply Erich Adickes's suggested dates, except when they are so tentative as to be almost useless. However, because much of Adickes's dating is conjectural, when I say such things as 'in a reflection of 1776' this should be understood to mean 'in a reflection that Adickes dates, somewhat conjecturally, to 1776'.

---

[84] The scholastic mode of presentation, we should note, concerns not just the rigour of proofs, but also the order in which the book's topics are presented. Kant tells us that, but for his wish to respect 'school's rights', he would have begun the first *Critique* with the Antinomy of Pure Reason—a part of the work that he believed would have whetted the reader's appetite for getting to the bottom of this controversy (10: 269–70).

[85] Warren Goldfarb, *Deductive Logic* (Indianapolis: Hackett, 2003). For details of how I depart from Goldfarb see note 34 in Chapter 9.

0.14 Acknowledgements

I would like to thank the following people for comments, criticisms, and discussion: Lucy Allais, Ralf Bader, Gordon Belot, Omri Boehm, Daniel Bonevac, Ray Buchanan, John Carriero, Emily Carson, Andrew Chignell, Randolph Clarke, Brian Cutter, Michael Della Rocca, Sinan Dogramaci, Katherine Dunlop, Matt Evans, Krasi Filcheva, Karen Gorodeisky, Sean Greenberg, Alex Grzankowski, Daniel Guevara, Derek Haderlie, Arata Hamawaki, Jim Hankinson, Jeremy Heis, Ivan Heyman, Kathleen Higgins, Thomas Hofweber, Des Hogan, Ed Holland, Jim Joyce, Cory Juhl, Tom Kelly, Boris Kment, Rob Koons, James Kreines, Martin Lin, Jon Litland, Dustin Locke, Paul Lodge, Louis Loeb, Béatrice Longuenesse, Bennett McNulty, Liz Mallett, Mike Martin, Al Martinich, Christia Mercer, Michelle Montague, Adrian Moore, Alex Mourelatos, Alan Nelson, Charles Parsons, Laurie Paul, Christopher Peacocke, Michael Pendelbury, Bryan Pickel, Annika Pierson, Michael Potter, Jim Proops, Joan Proops, Peter Railton, Tobias Rosefeldt, Jacob Ross, Mark Sainsbury, Sahotra Sarkar, Karl Schafer, Tamar Schapiro, Anat Schechtman, Tad Schmaltz, David Schroeren, Lisa Shabel, Jon Shaheen, Sanford Shieh, Joel Smith, Nicole Smith, Roy Sorensen, David Sosa, Galen Strawson, Peter Sullivan, Zoltán Szabó, Jamie Tappenden, Michael Tye, Deb Olin Unferth, Eric Watkins, Timothy Williamson, Kenneth Winkler, and Susan Wolf.

I owe special thanks to no fewer than six philosophers: Ralf Bader, Brian Cutter, Katherine Dunlop, Derek Haderlie, Roy Sorensen, and David Sosa. Ralf, a Harrington Fellow at UT during the 2015–16 academic year, read several draft chapters and provided perceptive—and often devastating—critical comments. It was exhilarating to learn so much from him over tea and coffee during our weekly, five-hour-long Kantathons. Brian served as my research assistant and provided insightful feedback on early drafts along with eagerly sought tutorials on sundry topics in metaphysics. Katherine gave numerous invaluable comments on, and criticisms of, draft chapters in the context of co-teaching seminars with me on Kant and Leibniz at UT Austin. Her erudite comments and objections led to many a face-saving improvement. Derek read late drafts of several chapters and provided thoughtful comments and criticisms on each—as well as much-needed encouragement. Roy read the whole work just as it was nearing completion. His generous, probing questions helped me to see numerous connections to issues of contemporary interest—they also helped me correct a number of embarrassing blunders. I should also like to thank David Sosa in his capacity as Chair of the UT philosophy department for his unwavering support during the project and for creating an unusually favourable environment for conducting research—both for me personally and for my colleagues at UT.

Five chapters of the book were drafted during my time as a Fellow at the National Humanities Center, Research Triangle Park, North Carolina. I am grateful to the Center and its staff for the extraordinarily supportive intellectual environment it created during the nine happy months I spent there. I am grateful also to GlaxoSmithKlein for generously funding my Fellowship and to the University of Texas at Austin for providing generous supplementary funding. I owe thanks to Karen Carroll, the copyeditor of the Center, for her editorial assistance with Chapters 14 and 15.

Embryonic drafts of many chapters in this book were given as talks at various universities and professional meetings. I am grateful to audiences at the following venues for probing questions and helpful suggestions: The Pacific meetings of the APA in 2011 and 2017; The National Humanities Center; The Autonomous University of Barcelona, North Carolina State University, Notre Dame University, Princeton University, The University of Cambridge, The University of California at Irvine, The University of Manchester, The University of Michigan, Ann Arbor, The University of North Carolina, Chapel Hill, The University of Oxford, The University of Stockholm, The University of Texas at Austin, and Yale University. I am also grateful to my session chair at the 2011 Pacific meetings of the APA, Des Hogan, for thoughtful comments on some of the material that made it into Chapter 14.

Some material in Chapters 3–5, though now substantially revised and expanded, was originally published in my article 'Kant's First Paralogism', *The Philosophical Review*, vol. 119, no. 4, 449–95. Copyright, 2010, Cornell University. All rights reserved. Chapter 14 is a substantive revision of my article 'Kant on the Ontological Argument,' *Noûs*, vol. 49.1, 2015, 1–27 (first published electronically in 2013). And Chapter 15 is a revised version of my article 'Kant on the Cosmological Argument', *Philosophers' Imprint*, vol. 14, no. 12, May 2014, 1–21. I am grateful to these journals for permission to use this material.

I am grateful for the helpful comments of two anonymous referees for Oxford University Press and to Peter Momtchiloff for his encouragement, wise guidance, and seemingly inexhaustible patience. Finally, I owe a tremendous debt of gratitude to Stephanie Hollub-Fletcher, Michelle Botello, Sally Jackman, Ben Fest, and Fatima Bayo for their administrative assistance.

PART I
RATIONAL PSYCHOLOGY

1
Transcendental Illusion

1.1 Introduction

According to Kant, human beings, by virtue of their very rationality, are subject to a peculiar kind of systematic illusion, which he terms 'transcendental illusion'. Illusion of this kind is not erroneous belief or false judgment but rather a non-perceptual *seeming* that produces in rational human subjects an inclination to make false judgments and to form false beliefs. More specifically, it produces in these subjects a temptation to embrace a wide range of dogmatic metaphysical positions. The project of 'transcendental dialectic' is the *critique* of this 'dialectical' illusion (A 63/B 88). It aims to alert us to the existence of transcendental illusion, to explain its workings, and, most ambitiously of all, to persuade us that this species of illusion lies behind all serious and sincere theoretically grounded dogmatic metaphysics—the kind of metaphysics that makes claims to know a priori and on theoretical grounds (and with apodictic certainty) a range of claims about the supersensible.

In calling his critique of dialectical illusion transcendental 'dialectic' Kant is intentionally bestowing a new meaning an old word. In the hands of the ancients, he tells us, dialectic was 'a technique of illusion or a sophistical art' (R 5063, 18: 76-7). It was the art—in Kant's view a wholly disreputable one—of *creating* illusion.[1] Kant's own 'transcendental' dialectic, by contrast, is the art of *exposing* transcendental illusion by means of critique. One does so with the intention not of deceiving others but rather of preventing transcendental illusion from deceiving oneself (A 297/B 354).

---

[1] *Vienna Logic*, 24: 794; *Jäsche Logic*, 9: 17. Kant nods to this older usage when he figures speculative reason as a tricky dialectical illusionist (A 606/B 634). One suspects, therefore, that a further reason why he calls the part of the *Critique* that lays out the arguments of dogmatic speculative metaphysics 'The Transcendental Dialectic' is that he is likening these arguments to the work of such an illusionist. Thus, while transcendental illusion is natural, Kant is prepared to grant that certain of the arguments it encourages might involve contrivance. At the opening of the Transcendental Dialectic Kant characterizes dialectic in yet a third way, namely, as the 'logic of illusion' [*Logik des Scheins*] (A 293/B 349). Here he is nodding—with some subtle wordplay ('*Schein*' versus '*Wahrscheinlichkeit*')—to an alternative tradition according to which dialectic is the logic of probability (*logica probabilium*). Kant, however, alludes to this tradition only to distance himself from it. For details see Giorgio Tonelli, 'Die historische Ursprung der Kantischen Termini "Analytik" und "Dialektik"', *Archiv für Begriffsgeschichte*, 7 (1962), 120-39 at 135-6.

The Fiery Test of Critique: A Reading of Kant's Dialectic. Ian Proops, Oxford University Press (2021). © Ian Proops.
DOI: 10.1093/oso/9780199656042.003.0002

1.2 Illusions: logical, empirical, and transcendental

Kant characterizes illusion in general as the enticement [*Verleitung*] to erroneous judgment (A 293/B 350). It comes in logical, empirical, and transcendental flavours. *Logical* illusion is the enticement to logically fallacious inference. It is operative when, owing to inattention to the logical rule, one adjudges an argument that is in fact invalid to be valid (A 297/B 353). This variety of illusion counts as 'artificial', in Kant's view, because there is nothing in our make-up dictating that we must ever experience it. Because logical illusion arises *merely* from inadvertence (A 298/B 354), it 'entirely disappears' as soon as we attend to the correct logical rule—presumably with the knowledge that it *is* correct (A 297/B 353).[2] Insofar as it possesses a certain fleetingness and fragility, logical illusion contrasts sharply with transcendental illusion, which enjoys a certain robustness befitting its character as 'natural' and 'unavoidable' (A 297–8/B 353–4).

Empirical illusion comprises instances of naturally occurring perceptual illusion—and paradigmatically, naturally occurring optical illusions (A 295/B 351-2). A subject in the grip of an empirical illusion—that is, a subject who is perceptually appeared to in a certain deceptive way but who is not hallucinating—is tempted to make a false judgment about an actually perceived object. And when the subject succumbs to this temptation their faculty of judgment is 'misled through the influence of the imagination' (ibid.). Kant mentions as examples of this kind of illusion the appearance that the sea is higher in the middle than at the shores, as well as the so-called 'moon illusion', in which the moon appears larger on the horizon than at its zenith (A 297/B 354).

Officially, the source of transcendental illusion is the *understanding* (A 581/B 609), but unofficially it is *reason*. Kant, after all, characterizes the dialectical inferences of pure reason as having sprung from 'the nature of reason' (see, for example, A 339/B 397) and he asserts that the illusion involved in the paralogisms has its *ground* in the nature of human reason (A 341/B 399). The discrepancy between the official and unofficial accounts can be explained by the fact that he sometimes treats the understanding as a sub-faculty of the faculty of reason (in the broad sense). For example, in the dynamical antinomies, when he portrays reason as seeming to be in conflict with itself, he treats the antithesis as satisfying the needs of the understanding, the thesis those of reason (now in the narrow sense) (see A 531/B 559).

Kant sees transcendental illusion as sharing three important affinities with empirical illusion. First, as we have already mentioned, it is *natural* and, since

---

[2] Kant understands 'applied logic' as the discipline that deals with (among other things) attention, including, one presumes, attention to the logical rule (A 54/B 79). In applied logic, one learns (among other things) how to dispel logical illusion.

incapable of being dispelled, also *permanent* (A 298/B 354).[3] Just as anyone equipped with properly functioning visual faculties will, Kant supposes, be subject to the moon illusion, so anyone equipped with a properly functioning faculty of reason will be subject to transcendental illusion.[4]

The second feature that Kant takes transcendental illusion to share with empirical illusion is its status as 'not irresoluble' [*nicht unauflöslich*] (A 341/B 399). He means that although it can never be dispelled, transcendental illusion remains in principle ultimately innocuous insofar as its usual consequences are *correctible* (A 644/B 672).[5] Thus, just as one need not be 'taken in' by an optical illusion—in the sense of actually forming a judgment or belief on its basis—so a subject experiencing transcendental illusion need not be led to adopt any dogmatic belief on its basis. We can, as Kant says, 'forestall the error' (A 339/B 397; compare A 644-5/B 672-3), even if 'we can never fully rid ourselves of the illusion' (A 339/B 397).[6]

It would be hard to exaggerate the importance Kant attaches to the distinction between avoidable error and inevitable illusion. As Michelle Grier has observed, if one fails to draw it, Kant will seem to be making the patently false claim that the unsound arguments of the Transcendental Dialectic are themselves inevitable.[7] With the distinction drawn, however, it becomes clear that rather than vainly cautioning us against inevitable error, Kant is merely alerting us to the existence and workings of transcendental illusion in the hope of fortifying us against its

---

[3] That Kant regards transcendental illusion as permanent is clear from his remark that transcendental dialectic (that is, the critique of illusion) 'can never bring it about that transcendental illusion should [not merely cease to deceive us] but also disappear (as logical illusion does [when detected]) and cease to be an illusion' (A 297-8/B 354).

[4] Kant seems to imply that the optical illusions he describes affect all (properly functioning) human beings. But whether that is in fact so is a question for empirical psychology.

[5] I avoid saying that the illusion *itself* is 'correctible' because this might suggest a view Kant did *not* hold, namely, that transcendental illusion is capable of being neutralized by a compensating counter-illusion. As Roy Sorensen has remarked (in conversation), it is puzzling that Kant held out no hope of someone's eventually designing such a counter-illusion (as British road engineers seeking 'traffic calming' nudges have designed roadway striping to create the illusion of speed). Why was he pessimistic about finding such a permanent fix to the problem of transcendental illusion? Wouldn't that have been better than simply recommending *Critique* as an endlessly needed—and difficult to apply—expedient? This is a good question. Kant was not, after all, ignorant of the idea of a compensating counter-illusion. He knew, for example, about John Dollond's 'achromatic doublet'—a pairing of a concave flint glass lens with a convex crown glass lens to correct for chromatic aberration in telescopes (29: 915). Of course, he would also presumably have known about corrective spectacles, and very possibly also—given his lively interest in architecture—about the illusion-compensation theory of column entasis espoused by Vitruvius (see *The Ten Books on Architecture*, III, iii, 13). Incidentally, for similar reasons, I avoid describing the illusion as 'resistible'—as indeed does Kant, who in fact explicitly calls it 'irresistible' (A 642/B 670).

[6] Accordingly, when at A 642/B 676 Kant says that the illusion's deception is something that one can 'barely' [*kaum*] prevent through the most acute critique, he does not mean that one *cannot* prevent it but merely that one can *only just* prevent it.

[7] See Michelle Grier, 'Illusion and Fallacy in Kant's First Paralogism', *Kant-Studien*, 83 (1993), 257-82 at 263-4 and also her book *Kant's Doctrine of Transcendental Illusion* (Cambridge: Cambridge University Press, 2001) at 116 and 28-30.

customary effects. In particular, by attending to the existence of transcendental illusion, we will, he hopes, be better able to resist the appearance of soundness attaching to certain arguments within speculative dogmatic metaphysics that are in fact not known to be sound. His idea is that, being able to resist forming the judgments that constitute the conclusions of these arguments, we will be better equipped to cast a sceptical eye over the arguments themselves.

The third feature that transcendental illusion shares with empirical illusion relates to an aspect of its independence from belief and judgment, namely, its *persistence* in the face of countervailing beliefs. Transcendental illusion does not 'cease even though it is uncovered and its nullity [*Nichtigkeit*] clearly seen into by transcendental criticism' (A 297/B 353). In other words, it survives detection and even—Kant is perhaps saying—*explanation*. In today's jargon we would say that, like the Müller-Lyer illusion, transcendental illusion 'resists cognitive penetration'.[8] This means that a subject who, being wise to the illusion, forms a belief contrary to the erroneous one it standardly tempts a person to form will still experience the illusion and still feel tempted to form the false belief.

The persistence of transcendental illusion has implications for the practice of critique. Owing to it, Kant thinks, human reason will be perpetually propelled into 'momentary aberrations that always need to be removed' (A 298/B 355). And in consequence the work of transcendental criticism will never be finished.

1.3 The sources of transcendental illusion

Although he believes that transcendental illusion has a number of 'sources' (A 581/B 609) or 'causes' (A703/B 731), Kant singles out one cause as pre-eminent. This, he tells us, is the fact that

> in our reason (considered subjectively as a human faculty of cognition) there lie fundamental rules and maxims for its use, which [while subjective in character] have entirely the look of objective principles, and through them it comes about that the subjective necessity of a certain connection of our concepts for the benefit of the understanding is taken for an objective necessity, the determination of things themselves. (A 297/B 353)

Kant characterizes one of these subjective rules or maxims as a 'demand of reason'. 'Multiplicity [*Mannigfaltigkeit*] of rules and unity of principles', he says, 'is a demand of reason, [something demanded] in order to bring the understanding into thoroughgoing accordance with itself' (A 305/B 362). This demand is a

---

[8] See A 581/B 609; and compare A 703/B 731 and 7: 149–50.

methodological principle; in Kant's language it is a 'subjective' principle (or law) or, again, a 'logical prescription [*Vorschrift*]' (A 309/B 365). Kant is telling us that the use of our reason in theory construction is governed by the norm that we should strive to bring our knowledge into a system in which the richest variety of rules is unified by the smallest—or, better, most explanatorily deep—set of principles, something, he goes on to make clear, that involves, among other things, minimizing the theory's conceptual inventory (I take it that 'principles' therefore are fundamental components of a theory—basic concepts as well as basic propositions).[9] This last point is not spelled out in the text, but it is suggested by Kant's referring to the demand in question as a 'subjective law of housekeeping [*Haushaltung*]' aimed at economizing on the 'supplies of the understanding' (A 306/B 362). Kant, I take it, is deploying this image of domestic frugality to suggest that one aspect of theoretical unity is the minimization of the number of concepts that the theory treats as undefined—the minimization, in Quinean terms, of the theory's 'ideology'. The demand in question, Kant is suggesting, is *inter alia* the demand to minimize ideology through conceptual reductions in which one concept is characterized in terms of others. That this is part of what Kant has in mind is suggested by his speaking of effecting the reduction in the number of concepts by *comparing* one with another (ibid.); for the language of comparison is the language he employs when speaking of reduction in other contexts. (See, for example, A 649/B 677, where he envisages the reduction of one power to another.) Kant's image of efficient housekeeping, I take it, is intended to work by suggesting that just as a housekeeper stands under a *ceteris paribus* prudential obligation to use up the household's provisions (so that food doesn't spoil), so the empirical scientist stands under a *ceteris paribus* prudential obligation not to leave concepts unreduced (so that theories don't conceptually bloat). If this is right, then Kant's implied image of an over-stocked pantry or storehouse is playing a role in connection with ideology exactly parallel to the role played by Quine's image of an over-populated slum in connection with ontology.[10]

All of this suggests that we may formulate the aforementioned demand of reason as a norm on theory construction that tells us to seek that theory among those fitting the data which maximizes the combination of explanatory power and ideological parsimony. Kant doesn't consider whether the principle in question could always identify a uniquely preferred empirically adequate theory, but since trade-offs between explanatory power and parsimony are plausibly possible, this question is one he might have considered.

---

[9] The qualification about explanatory depth is needed because a theory with a single, highly disjunctive or gerrymandered axiom would not count as highly unified in the sense Kant clearly intends.

[10] The image of concepts as residing in 'the storehouse of the mind' would have been familiar to Kant from Descartes's fifth *Meditation*.

Kant's model for the procedure by which one arrives at reason's methodological principles or rules is 'reason's formal and logical procedure in syllogisms' (A 306/B 363). This is the procedure in which one constructs polysyllogisms, by seeking ever higher logical grounds or logical conditions for a given conclusion.[11] In the *Logik Hechsel* Kant illustrates this procedure with the following example: 'Everything that thinks is simple, the soul thinks, hence it is simple. Everything that is simple is indivisible. The soul is simple, hence it is indivisible.'[12] Here the first syllogism purports to establish the minor premise of the second (namely, 'The soul is simple'). To supply the first syllogism when presented with the second is just to take the first step in a procedure which involves linking together ever higher syllogisms into a polysyllogistic chain, advancing to ever more general principles (considered as premises) as one does so.

Although this particular illustrative example fails to do justice to the idea of ideological parsimony, it is adequate for Kant's purposes—namely, to illustrate how a merely methodological principle (a 'logical maxim') might, through a misunderstanding, be taken for a substantive principle generating dogmatic metaphysics (a 'principle of pure reason') (A 306-7/B 363-4).[13] Kant likes the example partly because it makes vivid the point that sometimes we seek unification at a level of abstraction higher than that of the subject matter of our science. His thought is that just as we do not need to intuit particular features of objects in order to apply the norm of seeking to unify our judgments about them by searching for ever more general logical conditions in constructing polysyllogisms, so we do not need to note any particular necessary features of objects—such as that every occurrence has a cause—in order to apply the general norm on theory construction in theorizing about them (see A 306/B 363). The example of constructing polysyllogisms thus serves to illustrate the idea, which Kant is clearly anxious to underscore, that the theoretical unity we are urged to seek by his general norm on theory construction differs in *kind* from the object-level unity— expressed, for example, by the causal principle—of possible experience (A 307/B 363). One imagines that he feels the need to stress this point as forcefully as he does because he thinks that, owing to transcendental illusion, we are especially prone to overlook the distinction that it makes salient.

---

[11] See, A 307-8/B 363-5 and note Kant's talk at A 500/B 528 of 'the logical demand to assume complete premises for a given conclusion'. For an illuminating treatment of Kant's account of conditions in connection with polysyllogisms, see Tobias Rosefeldt, 'Subjects of Kant's First Paralogism', in A. Stephenson and A. Gomes (eds), *Kant and the Philosophy of Mind: Perception, Reason, and the Self* (Oxford: Oxford University Press, 2017), 221–44.

[12] Tillmann Pinder, *Immanuel Kant Logik-Vorlesung Unveröffentlichte Nachschriften, Logik Hechsel; Warschauer Logik* (2; Hamburg: Meiner, 1998) at 484.

[13] That one use of 'logical' as qualifying 'principle' or 'maxim' in the first *Critique* has the meaning of 'methodological' (or 'subjective') is apparent in many places, but perhaps most clearly of all at the end of the first full paragraph of A 648/B 676. This same passage makes clear that 'logical' in this sense is opposed to 'transcendental' and 'objective'.

Kant's illustrative example is designed also to bring out how *repeated* application of his envisaged general norm on theory construction can, through its capacity to generate an ascending polysyllogistic chain, lead to the construction of a *regress* of ever more general conditions (A 307/B 364). And it further helps to bring out that there is nothing *in itself* problematic about applying the methodological norm in question. Trouble arises, Kant thinks, only because we are inclined to mistake reason's injunction to proceed in our theorizing by seeking ever higher logical conditions—whether premises or principles—for a *doctrine* of reason, namely, the thesis that we inhabit a world characterized by a series of world-states or objects of sense ordered by the *real* conditioning relation and either containing an unconditioned condition as its first member or, being infinite, containing an infinite series of conditions that is itself unconditioned. Either way, Kant thinks, when we yield to this inclination we lapse into error.[14]

Since the example of polysyllogism construction fails to illustrate the part of the general norm that urges us to advance theoretical unification by reducing one concept to another (or others), it is only a partial illustration of the procedure recommended by the norm on theory construction Kant is envisaging at A 305/B 361-2. This is not a serious problem, however, for two reasons. First, as Kant himself stresses, the example of polysyllogism construction by itself already suffices to illustrate the two points just mentioned—for *these* purposes, there is no need to advert to the second part of the general norm. Second, another discussion in the first *Critique* provides the material for an especially clear-cut illustration of how misinterpreting the norm of maximal ideological parsimony might lead us into dogmatism. This example involves the *ontological* parsimony of powers rather than an ideological parsimony, but it is readily adaptable to our purposes. It concerns, in particular, the generation of the rational psychologist's belief that all the powers of the soul—imagination, memory, wit, and so forth—are reducible to a single fundamental power (A 649/B 677).[15] Kant's idea is that by

---

[14] Kant, it should be noted, has no *general* objection to an infinite series' bearing the real conditioning relation to something. He allows, for example, that a given moment of time is (really) conditioned by the infinite series of times preceding it. He says: 'The entire elapsed time, *as condition of the given instant*, is thought necessarily as given' (A 412/B 439, emphasis added). He is able to allow that a given instant of time is borne the relation of real conditioning by an infinite series of times because time is an infinite *totum analyticum*. What he does reject (as leading to antinomies) is the assumption that real conditioning relation should be borne to something by an infinite *totum syntheticum* (for example, by the series of world-states prior to a given world state). We discuss the notions of *totum analyticum* and *totum syntheticum* in Chapter 9. Note, incidentally, that Kant does not say—and, I think, does not hold—that an instant is conditioned by any allegedly 'immediately previous' time. His view would seem to be that no time is immediately preceded by another (see B 413-14, for Kant's apparent rejection of the view that there could be two distinct times with no time between them).

[15] This isn't, however, quite how every rational psychologist would *express* the view Kant has in mind. Baumgarten, for example, regards the faculties that are derivable from the soul's basic power not as powers properly speaking, but rather merely as modes of the power of representation. See Baumgarten, *Metaphysics* §744; and Gary Hatfield, 'Baumgarten, Wolff, Descartes, and the Origins of Psychology', in Courtney D. Fugate and John Hymers (eds), *Baumgarten and Kant on Metaphysics* (Oxford: Oxford University Press, 2018), 61-77 at 66.

confusing the demand for ontological parsimony in our theories with imagined knowledge of unification in the phenomena themselves we are led to suppose, without justification, that there is a single power of which all the others are determinations or sub-kinds (sub-powers). As Kant would have been aware, Wolff believed that the soul did indeed possess only a single power, namely, its power of representing the world from the point of view of its associated body (see Chapter 2). In Wolff, therefore, Kant has a flesh-and-blood example of a philosopher to whom the present diagnosis might apply.

Although this example involves an ontological rather than conceptual reduction, it may be adapted to a yield an illustration of a case in which a legitimate push for *conceptual* reduction leads to a parallel mistake. One might, for example, try to *define* memory as, say, the power to veridically *represent* something as past, thereby seeking to diminish the number of concepts needed to describe the phenomena. Such a conceptual reduction might be a reasonable thing to attempt, but in Kant's view such a project will tend to encourage the unfounded belief that the relevant powers themselves admit of a corresponding ontological reduction.

Noting the centrality of Kant's idea that we are inclined to confuse a methodological, prescriptive principle with a constitutive one, Michelle Grier has recommended that we interpret Kant as taking transcendental illusion to be 'manifested' by the conflation of two principles. The idea is that we conflate a 'logical prescription' governing theory construction (A 309/B 365), namely, *P* (Grier's 'P1'):

P: Find for the conditioned cognitions of the understanding the unconditioned whereby its [that is, the understanding's] unity is completed   (cf. A 307/B 364)

with a descriptive claim about the world, namely, *D* (Grier's 'P2'):

D: If the conditioned is given, the whole series of conditions subordinated to one another, a series which is therefore itself unconditioned, is likewise given
(cf. A 307–8/B 364 & B 436).[16]

I agree with Grier that this conflation—mistaking *P* for *D*—is certainly included among the mistakes encouraged by transcendental illusion, but I think that

---

[16] See Grier, 'Illusion and Fallacy'. And also Grier, *Kant's Doctrine* at 268–79. My labels '*P*' (for 'prescription') and '*D*' (for 'description') are intended as arguably more suggestive replacements for Grier's 'P1' and 'P2'. Although I agree with much of what she says, I disagree with Grier on three points of detail. First, I would not endorse her characterization of *D* as something we must assume as a condition of 'using' *P* (Grier, *Kant's Doctrine*, 126). Being a prescription, *P* is not something that can be used, but only something that can be complied with or contravened. Instead, I think the correct thing to say about the relationship between *P* and *D* is that the illusion that *D* is true is one that is, in Kant's view, inevitably generated in rational human minds in virtue of their being subject to the demand of reason expressed by the prescription *P*. Second, as we will see in Chapter 5, it is in fact not quite *D* itself but a closely related claim that expresses the content of the illusion. Third, I differ from Grier on the form of the first paralogism (see Chapter 4).

transcendental illusion in fact admits of a more general characterization. Most generally characterized, it is the illusion that something that is in fact (in a broad sense) merely subjective—methodological demands on theory construction included—is an objective feature of the world.[17] Nonetheless, the mistake of taking P for D is certainly one central *instance* of the error that can arise when we succumb to this illusion—and, arguably, it is the most important such instance.

Prescription, P, enjoins us to seek the most unified theory that is empirically adequate. Descriptive claim, D, on the other hand, declares that for every phenomenon (in the theory-neutral sense of that term) there exists a series constituted by its unconditioned condition. In Kant's view, when through a 'misunderstanding' we are deceived by transcendental illusion, the 'need of reason' expressed by P is 'taken for a transcendental principle of reason' that 'over hastily postulates...an unlimited completeness in the series of conditions' (cf. A 309/B 366).[18] In other words, we mistake the prescription, P for the putative statement of fact, D. In Kant's jargon, we mistake a 'regulative' for a 'constitutive' principle.[19]

Although Kant characterizes the 'misunderstanding' (A 309/B 365) that leads to certain fallacious 'inferences of reason' in terms of our having 'taken' the need of reason expressed by the prescription, P, for the truth of the principle, D (A 309/B 366),[20] the path from the former to the latter may, I think, be usefully be characterized in more fine-grained terms. It seems that our first mistake must be to misconstrue a prescription concerning *cognitions* (that is, in this context, rules and maxims governing theory construction) as a prescription concerning the worldly objects themselves. That is to say, we hear P as saying:

P*: Find for the object of any given cognition, that object's unconditioned series of conditions.

It seems plausible that, being a command of *reason*, the legitimate prescription, P, will be viewed as *authoritative*. Moreover, P is plausibly experienced as *reasonable* because reason's authority strikes those subject to it as reasonably exercised. But since the prescription, P, strikes us as reasonable and authoritative, the same will be true of our misconstrual of it, namely, P*. We will accordingly find it natural to

---

[17] This broad characterization of transcendental illusion is bound up with yet another understanding of dialectic, not now as the critique of illusion, but rather as 'the doctrine of the subjective laws of the understanding insofar as they are taken for objective' (R 1579; 16: 23).

[18] Kant gives this explanation in the form of a lengthy question in the course of announcing the topic to be investigated. We might paraphrase the question as: 'Has the need of reason expressed by P been taken for the transcendental principle expressed by D?' It is clear from his subsequent discussion that, as far as traditional dogmatic metaphysics goes, Kant's answer is yes.

[19] See A 619–20/B 647–8; A 647/B 675; A 686/B 713; A 690/B 718; and *Prolegomena*, §56, 4: 350.

[20] Kant also implies that *instances* of P are apt to be taken for instances of D, for he says that the various specific fundamental maxims and rules contributed by human reason and governing its use 'look entirely like objective principles' (A 297/B 313).

suppose that what the apparently authoritative prescription P^* enjoins us to seek is in fact actually there to be found. In this way, the appearance of the standing authority of P (and so also of P^*) will generate in us the permanent inclination to regard D as true.

Or so, at least, runs a plausible interpretation of Kant's first-pass view. However, I will argue in Chapter 5 that his considered view is that it is not D itself that states the content of this sub-illusion, but rather the related proposition, D^*, which omits the reference to a series: 'If a conditioned object is given, an absolutely unconditioned object is likewise given.' Because the reasons for this qualification are complicated, however, it will be convenient, for the time being, to continue our preliminary exposition with reference to D.

In portraying the immediate illusion lurking behind much of dogmatic speculative metaphysics as the illusion that D is true, Kant may seem to be lumping his predecessors together in an unduly high-handed way. Is it really true that much of dogmatic speculative metaphysics flows from a single principle? Such qualms may, however, be alleviated somewhat by the observation of Predrag Cicovacki that D can be regarded as one formulation of the Principle of Sufficient Reason (hereafter '*PSR*')—a principle which does indeed have a claim to be a substantive principle which generates many of the claims of dogmatic speculative metaphysics.[21] This idea might also explain why Kant refers to D as 'this supreme principle of pure reason' (A 308/B 365).

In Kant's view, we are inclined to regard D not just as true but as *necessarily* true. This circumstance, he maintains, is owed to our readiness to mistake the 'subjective necessity' of 'a certain connection of our concepts' for an 'objective necessity, the determination of things in themselves' (A 297/B 353). Kant doesn't say what this 'subjective necessity' is supposed to consist in; but it is plausibly the necessity involved in the following conditional injunction: 'If you wish to proceed rationally in inquiry, you *must* seek, for the object of any cognition, the series constituting its unconditioned condition.' The necessity involved here counts as 'subjective' because the imperative is conditional upon our having a certain goal or desire.[22] Kant supposes that, owing to transcendental illusion, this subjective necessity is apt to be misconstrued as the objective necessity involved in the

---

[21] Predrag Cicovacki, 'Kant's Debt to Leibniz', in Bird Graham (ed.), *A Companion to Kant* (Oxford: Blackwell 2006), 79–92 at 87. See also James Kreines, 'Metaphysics Without Pre-Critical Monism', *The Bulletin of the Hegel Society of Great Britain*, 29 (1–2) (2008), 48–70 at 49; and Omri Boehm, *Kant's Critique of Spinoza* (Oxford: Oxford University Press, 2014) at 51. Two caveats: first, D is plausibly equivalent to the *PSR* only on the Kantian assumption—to be discussed in Chapter 15—that nothing can be a condition of itself. If something could be its own condition, then the demands of the *PSR* might be satisfied while D was false. Second, I disagree with Boehm's view that P (his 'P1') is a formulation of the *PSR* (Boehm, *Kant's Critique of Spinoza*, 51). It is rather a methodological principle urging us to pursue economically constructed theories. I had overlooked this last point in Ian Proops, 'Kant's First Paralogism', *Philosophical Review*, 119 (4) (2010), 449–95.

[22] Elsewhere, Kant indicates that he sees the prescriptive force of a certain postulate as similarly conditional on our desires. We should, he says, think of events in such a way that we can apply our

claim: 'Necessarily, for the object of any cognition, the series constituting its unconditioned condition exists.' The illusion that D holds *of necessity*, then, is itself a component of transcendental illusion.

To clarify the slide that I take Kant to be envisaging it will be helpful to break it up into three transitions between four claims:

[1] If you desire to proceed rationally in inquiry, you must seek—that is, strive to formulate—the most unified theory, where unification is understood in terms of finding ever higher logical conditions (that is, principles) for one's cognitions.
[2] If you desire to proceed rationally in inquiry, you must seek, for the object of any cognition, the series constituting its unconditioned (real) condition.
[3] You must seek, for the object of any cognition, the series constituting its unconditioned (real) condition.
[4] Necessarily, for the object of any cognition, the series constituting its unconditioned (real) condition exists.

Claim [4] is just the claim that principle D (slightly reformulated) holds with necessity.

As I read him, Kant supposes that we are apt to confuse [1] with [2] because a certain principle governing theory construction looks like a principle guiding worldly investigation. This *seeming*, I take it, is an instance of transcendental illusion because it involves seeing a subjective unity (the unity that would be enjoyed by a regressing chain of syllogisms if it could be extended to a logically unconditioned minor premise) as an objective unity (the unity that would be enjoyed by a series of worldly states if it were to have an ultimate unconditioned real condition).[23] Thus, when we are taken in by the sub-illusion that [1] says what is said by [2] we are apt to slide from acceptance of [1] to acceptance of [2]. The confusion involved in the slide from [1] to [2] is thus a confusion about the nature of the object for which the inquirer is seeking.

Beyond this, we are further inclined to misconstrue [2] as meaning [3] simply because, being rational beings, we *do* naturally desire to proceed rationally when we inquire. Since this desire is so natural and pervasive its presence is easily overlooked, and we thus fail to appreciate that the necessity in [3] is merely the conditional necessity expressed in the consequent of [2]. The sub-illusion that [2] says the same as [3] is the illusion that an intellectual—as opposed to practical—*hypothetical* imperative is an intellectual *categorical* imperative.

---

understanding to them 'if we want our understanding to be in unison with itself in accordance with principles' (R 6109, 1783–84, 18: 457).

[23] Recall that, as Kant sets things up, at each step of the polysyllogism it is the *minor* premise that is derived by a further syllogism.

Finally, we are further inclined to misconstrue [3] as saying [4] because we hear [3] as specifically an injunction of *reason*, and so regard it as rational. This in turn inclines us to believe that what we are enjoined to seek actually exists. We are thus inclined to misconstrue the injunctive modality in [3] as the alethic modality in [4]. That is to say, we are inclined to mistake the 'must' of (what we regard as) a binding intellectual categorical imperative for the 'must' of an indicative claim purporting to express a necessary fact.[24]

Each of these sub-illusions may be regarded as a matter of our being inclined to take something that is, in some respect or other, merely subjective for something objective. Each one, therefore, is plausibly viewed as an instance of the general inclination Kant identifies sometimes with transcendental illusion and sometimes with its cause. The upshot is that we are inclined to slide all the way from an acceptance of the (eminently reasonable) hypothetical imperative of inquiry [1] to an endorsement of the strong metaphysical claim [4]. But whether we do so in practice will depend on whether we have been tipped off by the critical philosophy to the instances of transcendental illusion that constitute the misleading appearance that the content of [1] is the same as that of [2], that the content of [2] is the same as that of [3], and so forth. Transcendental illusion is thus to be invoked in *explaining* the slide between judgments, but an aspect of it can also be thought of as the *product* of the slide insofar as the three sub-illusions combine to transform the veridical appearance that [1] is a maxim of rational inquiry into the illusory appearance that [4] is true.

In support of our explanation of the steps leading from [2] to [3] and from [3] to [4], we may observe that on one occasion Kant himself draws the distinction between objective and subjective necessity in precisely the terms we have suggested—although he does so in a less familiar setting. In religion lectures from the mid-1780s, speaking of his earlier attempted proof of the existence of an *ens realissimum* (or 'most real being') in his 1763 work *The Only Possible Basis for a Demonstration of the Existence of God* (hereafter 'OPB'), he says that although this proof is, contrary to his former hope, unable to establish the objective necessity of an original being, it nonetheless succeeds in establishing the subjective necessity of accepting such a being (28: 1034).[25] His point in these lectures is that although I cannot demonstrate the existence of a being that is the ground of everything possible, my reason makes it necessary for me to *accept* the existence of such a being because otherwise I would be unable to *cognize* in what in general the possibility of something consists (ibid.).[26] Kant thus comes to believe that his earlier 'proof' in *OPB*, although it hadn't attained its professed goal, had

---

[24] I am indebted to Derek Haderlie for help in formulating this last claim.
[25] *OPB* is dated 1763, but was in fact published in 1762.
[26] This passage has been raised to prominence by Andrew Chignell. See 'Belief in Kant', *Philosophical Review*, 116 (3) (2007), 323–60 at 349. I follow his translation.

nonetheless succeeded in establishing the merely subjective necessity involved in the conditional claim: 'If we want to cognize in what in general the possibility of a thing consists, then we must accept that the *ens realissimum* exists.' Because in OPB Kant had taken the 'proof' to establish the dramatically stronger claim that the *ens realissimum* exists, the clear implication of his later remarks is that he believes that we are inclined in this case to slide from a hypothetical imperative of inquiry, expressed as a conditional, to an objective claim of necessity—namely, the claim that the *ens realissimum* must exist—precisely because we *do* wish to cognize in what in general the possibility of a thing consists. Kant is appealing to this idea in his religion lectures in order to diagnose his own earlier dogmatic mistake.

I think a similar slide is involved in the transition from [2] to [4]. To be sure, in the case of our hypothetical imperative, [2], what figures in the consequent is not, as in OPB, the notion of *accepting* a proposition. It is rather that of *seeking* the unconditioned. This difference of attitude, however, does nothing to undermine the parallel between the relevant passages with respect to Kant's use of the terms 'subjective' and 'objective' in their role as qualifying the term 'necessity'.

Our description of the process leading from [1] to [4] amounts to an account of how rational human agents can be led to form certain *beliefs* within dogmatic speculative metaphysics—beliefs, namely, in instances of the general claim, [4]. But more would need to be said if Kant is to invoke transcendental illusion—as he seems to wish to do—to explain why philosophers of the calibre of a Descartes or a Leibniz should have come to believe that they have genuine *knowledge* of instances of [4].[27] Kant leaves this lacuna unfilled, but we might fill it by continuing our story in the following way.

Having arrived at a given dogmatic speculative belief—that is, a given instance of [4]—Kant's dogmatic speculative metaphysician, not supposing that his belief could have any source other than pure reason, proceeds to imagine that his grounds for it must be principles known a priori. He then tries to make explicit the reasoning he takes himself to have implicitly relied on in forming his belief. This involves constructing a proof of the relevant instance of [4]. Since he imagines this proof to be sound and to proceed by a priori reasoning from

---

[27] 'Through the explanation of illusion', Kant says, 'one grants to the one who erred a kind of fairness' (9: 56). He means, I take it, that by explaining the illusion prompting an error we render that error comprehensible as arising from something other than obtuseness. Nowhere, it seems, is the need for such an explanation more urgent than in connection with Leibniz. For Kant's estimation of Leibniz's intellect could hardly be higher. 'No philosopher', he rhapsodizes, 'has ever shown such extensive skill in philosophizing dogmatically as Leibniz' (24: 804). Charity, then, is one reason to posit transcendental illusion. Another, I think (though this is more speculative), is the need to posit a *real* ground for error. For, unlike Descartes, Kant sees error [*Irrtum*] as a reality rather than a lack [*Mangel*] or negation (see 28: 1272). It would therefore have been natural for him to seek a reality to ground this reality. Transcendental illusion would, I think, have filled this bill.

principles known a priori, he thereby comes to believe himself possessed of theoretically based *knowledge* of the metaphysical proposition in question.

1.4 The simplified account

Our story has emphasized passages in which Kant suggests that the first error we make upon succumbing to transcendental illusion is that of confusing a logical (that is to say, methodological) imperatival principle—a conditional injunction concerning theory construction—with a real or metaphysical imperatival principle—a conditional injunction concerning the discovery of worldly phenomena. However, our account would be incomplete if we did not give due weight to the existence in the *B* edition of a simpler account of how transcendental illusion operates. This rival account makes no mention of the confusion of a logical with a real principle. Instead, Kant puts the blame on a misapplication of reason's legitimate demand for the unconditioned. In the *B*-edition preface, he says:

> [W]hat necessarily impels us to go beyond the boundary of experience and of all appearances is the **unconditioned**, which reason demands in things in themselves; [within the realm of things in themselves] reason necessarily and with full right—demands this unconditioned for everything conditioned, thus demanding that the series of conditions be completed by means of that unconditioned. (B *xx*)[28]

One clear implication of this remark is that so long as the 'things' in question are things in themselves, the categorial injunction to seek the unconditioned in things (rather than in theories) is perfectly legitimate. Kant says nothing here to explain why this demand should cause us to illegitimately go beyond the boundary of experience, but the following story seems likely. If, having succumbed to transcendental illusion, we mistake the objects of sense for things in themselves, we will go beyond experience in attempting to comply with this (in itself legitimate) demand of reason. For, taking the objects of sense to be things in themselves, we will take an injunction that, in truth, applies only to the latter, to apply to the former. We will thus suppose that what it enjoins us to seek is in fact there to be found. And so we will come to believe that the spatio-temporal world series contains an unconditioned object or state of affairs (or, alternatively, a series of them) that is not an object of experience.

---

[28] And compare the following remark from a reflection: 'The proposition that if the conditioned is given, the whole series of all conditions through which the conditioned is determined is also given is, if I abstract from the objects or take it merely intellectually, correct' (R 5553 (18: 223); compare 4: 354).

This new account dispenses with steps [1] and [2] of our reconstruction, rejoining it at step [3]. It seems to have been an attempt by Kant to streamline his explanation of how transcendental illusion induces error. It does so by emphasizing that the content of transcendental illusion is equivalent to Transcendental Realism. Unfortunately, however, Kant fails to remove certain traces of his more complicated (and presumably earlier) account from the second edition. This is not all that surprising because those traces occur in the parts of the *Critique* that he did not substantially revise.

1.5 The necessity of transcendental illusion

As we have seen, Kant believes that rational human beings *inevitably* experience transcendental illusion.[29] Unsurprisingly, commentators have wondered what his argument for this inevitability thesis is supposed to be.[30] Possibly, Kant intends to be offering an argument by analogy with the perceptual case. The idea would be that just as human beings inevitably experience various perceptual illusions in virtue of possessing properly functioning perceptual faculties, so they inevitably experience transcendental illusion in virtue of having a properly functioning rational faculty. The grounds for such an inference would include the numerous similarities noted between (theoretical) reason and sense perception: each faculty, for example, operates on an input of a certain characteristic kind (in the case of perception, sensation; in the case of reason, judgment), each is apt, in virtue of its very organization, sometimes to lead the judgmental faculty astray, and so forth. The inference would consist in affirming one more similarity on the basis of these: namely, that whatever it is that inclines the judgmental faculty towards error must, like perceptual illusion, be universal in rational human subjects.

Such an argument belongs to a genre of which Kant certainly approved; for as we will see in later chapters, he recognizes arguments by analogy as legitimate so long as they are held to be capable of producing only 'empirical certainty' (9: 132–3). The interpretive proposal, then, has its merits. But it also faces a

---

[29] Kant associates transcendental illusion with specifically *human* reason. He does not seem to think that angels would be subject to it, and he plainly does not regard non-human animals as subject to it. If the first point sets him in tension with the tradition (for wasn't Lucifer tempted?), the second sets him against experience. For Kant's most general characterization of transcendental illusion—as the systematic appearance that something in fact subjective is an objective feature of the world—would seem to imply that some non-human animals are subject to it. Take, for example, my cat, Gremlin. She sometimes suffers from UTIs. When thus afflicted, she will not urinate in the same place twice. She behaves as if she is taken in by the illusion that something subjective (her pain) is an objective (and localized) feature of the world, as if there existed painful areas of the litter box (or sofa!) which, once discovered, are to be studiously avoided.

[30] For a discussion of relevant literature see Michael Rohlf, 'The Ideas of Pure Reason', in Paul Guyer (ed.), *The Cambridge Companion to Kant's Critique of Pure Reason* (Cambridge: Cambridge University Press, 2010), 190–209.

difficulty—albeit one of which Kant seems unlikely to have been aware—the difficulty, namely, that its motivating parallel is in fact undermined by the empirical data. Unfortunately for Kant, certain optical illusions turn out *not* to be universal in human beings, and so cannot be psychologically necessary. For example, subjects brought up in different environments within a single culture have been found to differ in their susceptibility to the Müller-Lyer illusion.[31] One premise of the argument by analogy therefore fails.

A second possible argument for the necessity thesis would appeal to the idea that reason has an essence. It is of the essence of reason—or so this argument would maintain—that rational beings feel motivated by an injunction of reason to ask theoretical *why*-questions and to press them as far as possible.[32] To engage in such inquiries, this line further holds, is therefore a fundamental need of human reason. From this assumption one would conclude that the production of transcendental illusion is, for this very reason, inevitable in rational human beings, for it is inevitably produced by the imperatives governing this kind of inquiry. This strategy has the advantage of making use of the idea of a 'need of reason'—a notion to which Kant himself often appeals. It has the obvious weakness, however, of being anthropologically dubious. For it is not at all clear that human rationality must always lead to scientific or metaphysical curiosity. In some individuals it might rather find expression in, for example, one or more of the following activities: chess, music appreciation, pigeon keeping, cineastry, cooking, carpentry, or floral art.

For these reasons, I'm inclined to doubt that Kant has a strong argument for the thesis that transcendental illusion is necessary—even psychologically—in rational human beings. But perhaps this matters less than it appears. After all, what should matter for Kant—or so one might have thought—is merely to draw attention to the existence of transcendental illusion and to make a plausible case that it is sufficiently pervasive and enduring as to be capable of explaining the *apparently* universal and unceasing human drive to engage in dogmatic speculative metaphysics. In defending such a claim Kant would, I think, be on firmer ground.

---

[31] A. Ahluwalia, 'An Intra-Cultural Investigation of Susceptibility to "Perspective" and "Non-Perspective" Spatial Illusions', *British Journal of Psychology*, 69 (2) (1978), 233–41. Nor is this an isolated case: a casual dip into the relevant literature reveals the existence of variable susceptibilities, whether cross-cultural or individual, to other illusions, including, for example, the Ponzo and Ebbinghaus illusions.

[32] Compare R 4117 (17: 423), where Kant suggests that in the cosmological argument a necessary being is posited in order to bring to a close the series of *why*-questions arising from inquiring about the reasons for the existence of alterable things, thereby making the existence of alterable things fully comprehensible. Kant must mean that it is the fact of the *existence* of this being rather than the being itself that is taken by proponents of the cosmological argument to be the answer to the final envisaged *why*-question. I am grateful to James Kreines for this last point.

1.6 Some recalcitrant texts

Up to now I have for expository reasons been suppressing certain texts that complicate Grier's otherwise helpful picture. Like Grier, I have emphasized the point that for Kant, although transcendental illusion unavoidably tempts us to err, it does not force our hand.[33] But although such a view seems to be well supported by the texts, Kant does not always use the term 'transcendental illusion' for illusion in contrast to error. Indeed, in a number of places he uses the terms 'illusion' [*Schein*] and 'transcendental illusion' for preventable, false *judgment* or *belief*. I end this chapter with a brief look at these recalcitrant texts.

Consider, first of all, some passages in which Kant uses the term 'transcendental illusion' for something that we are able to remove or prevent. One such passage occurs in the Antinomies. In the course of discussing his general solution to these apparent conflicts of reason, Kant says:

> If one regards the two propositions, "The world is infinite in magnitude," [and] "The world is finite in magnitude," as contradictory opposites, then one assumes that the world (the whole series of appearances) is a thing in itself.... But if I take away this presupposition, *or rather this transcendental illusion* [*transcendentalen Schein*], and deny that [the world] is a thing in itself, then the contradictory conflict of the two assertions is transformed into a merely dialectical conflict....
> (A 504–5/ B 532–3, emphasis added)

The suggestion that transcendental illusion can be removed appears again in the *Real Progress* of 1793:

> [In] the concept of the unconditioned in the totality of all mutually subordinated conditions.... there is need to remove that illusion [*Schein*] which creates an antinomy of pure reason, by confusion of appearances with things in themselves ... (*Real Progress*, 20: 311)

Each of these passages uses the term 'illusion' for something removable, and each suggests—the first more explicitly than the second—that this removable something is a belief (or presupposition) in whose rejection the resolution of the antinomies consists, namely, the belief in Transcendental Realism.[34]

One supposes that Kant may have found it natural to describe Transcendental Realism as an 'illusion' because he would have regarded the belief in this doctrine

---

[33] See: A 644–5/B 672–3; A 821/B 849; *Prolegomena*, 4: 328, and 28: 583.
[34] It is not clear that the content of transcendental illusion should in general be equated with the content of the belief in Transcendental Realism, but it is plausible that the instance of it associated with the cosmological Ideas should be.

as an especially deep, yet overlooked, feature of pre-critical philosophy. And yet, such talk is, strictly speaking, inconsistent with his official line on transcendental illusion; for Transcendental Realism consists not in an unavoidable illusion but rather in an avoidable belief. Kant's better thought would seem to be that Transcendental Realists are taken in by transcendental illusion (proper) in rational cosmology insofar as they fall prey to the illusion that the world exists as an absolute totality (the illusion, that is, that Transcendental Realism is true). This better thought is expressed in the first *Critique* when Kant says that in the antinomies 'Transcendental illusion has portrayed a reality to [the transcendental realist] where none is present' (A 501/B 29–30).

A second group of recalcitrant texts suggests that Kant sometimes uses the term 'transcendental illusion' to refer to the *product* of dialectical inferences rather than to their cause. Such a usage coheres with (what I have argued to be) Kant's view that the illusion that *D* is true is the product of certain other sub-illusions. But the usage, I think, indicates something that goes beyond this idea. At the opening of the Antinomies he says:

> We have shown in the introduction to [the Dialectic] that *every* transcendental illusion [*transcendentale Schein*] of pure reason *rests on* [*beruhe auf*] dialectical inferences. (A 405/B 432, emphases added)

And again, in the Ideal he says:

> [In the cosmological argument] speculative reason seems to have summoned up all its dialectical art so as to bring about the greatest possible transcendental illusion [*transcendentalen Schein*]. (A 606/B 634)

The context of this last remark makes clear that here Kant is referring to the untrustworthy inferences involved in the cosmological argument. He is personifying reason as an ancient dialectician, fluent in the deceptive art of creating illusion—and by 'illusion' here he seems to mean the body of conclusions of these untrustworthy inferences.

Further passages suggest that Kant occasionally uses the word 'illusion' to refer either to a judgment or to the 'taking' of one thing for another—a mental act that is itself naturally construed as a judgment. Consider, for example, the following three remarks:

> It is correctly said that the senses do not err; yet not because they always judge correctly, but because they do not judge at all. Hence truth, as much as error, *and thus also illusion* [*Schein*] *as leading to the latter, are to be found only in judgments*, i.e., only in the relation of the object to our understanding.
> (A 293/B 350, emphasis added).

> One can place all **illusion** [*Schein*] in the taking of a **subjective** condition of thinking for the cognition of an **object**. (A 396)

> [N]othing is more natural and seductive than the illusion [*Schein*] of taking the unity in the synthesis of thoughts for a perceived unity in the subject of these thoughts. (A 402)

In these passages Kant is speaking not of the illusion (in the sense of a seeming) *underlying* the formation of false dogmatic beliefs, but rather of the illusion (in the sense of an error) that results from the commission of a fallacy. This error, under its most general description, is that of *taking* something that is in fact merely subjective for something objective. As we will see, this description fits perfectly the error under discussion in the Paralogisms chapter, where Kant scrutinizes certain inferences that he describes as containing an illusion *within* themselves (A 396).

What these last-considered passages reveal, I think, is simply that Kant is engaging in equivocation. He uses the word 'illusion' sometimes for a kind of pervasive, seductive, and systematic *seeming*, and sometimes for a judgment, belief, inference, or phenomenon that is 'false' in one of the following senses: mistaken, invalid, specious. An adjectival occurrence of 'illusion' corresponding to this last usage occurs in a remark from Kant's metaphysics lectures. 'We will be able', he says,

> to secure morality and religion against the specious objections of speculative reason [*Schein Einwurfe der speculativen Vernunft*].
> (*Mrongovius Metaphysics*, 29: 781)[35]

Some of the passages just considered also suggest that Kant occasionally uses the whole phrase 'transcendental illusion' equivocally. In particular, when the 'illusion' (in the sense of 'error') has its source in 'transcendental illusion' (a seeming), Kant is prepared to term it 'transcendental illusion'.

These complications of the initial picture help to explain why it should have taken so long for Grier's point to be made. Her insight arose because she noticed a central strand of Kant's thought that tracked a certain sub-set of occurrences of the terms 'illusion' and 'transcendental illusion'. By identifying this strand and emphasizing its importance, Grier has revealed the coherence of Kant's position on transcendental illusion and opened up the Dialectic as never before.

As we noted at the beginning of this chapter, Kant characterizes 'transcendental dialectic' as the 'critique of illusion'.[36] We have now arrived a clearer view of what this critique involves, namely, at minimum, the detection of transcendental

---

[35] Kant's note-taker capitalizes '*Schein*' when it occurs as an attributive adjective. Compare: '*Schein Weisheit*' (29: 766).
[36] R 5063, 18: 76–7.

illusion—understood as a pervasive and permanent illusion of reason that systematically tempts the unwary philosopher into dogmatic error (A 297/B 354). I would venture that, beyond this, the critique of illusion also involves some account of the *workings* of this illusion: some account along the lines, perhaps, of the transitions leading from [1] to [4] in §1.2. Finally, it involves the tracing of reason's itinerary as it works through its natural dialectic. We begin our examination of that itinerary with a consideration of the claims and prospects of rational psychology.

2
Empirical and Rational Psychology

2.1 Introduction

When Kant tackles dogmatic rational psychology in the Paralogisms chapter he chooses as his target a specifically *pure* version of this self-proclaimed science—a 'pure doctrine of the soul [*reinen Seelenlehre*]' (A 348). The purity of this doctrine consists in its purporting to demonstrate on theoretical and non-empirical grounds, and by purely a priori means, certain so-called 'pure predications' of the soul or 'thinking I', including its substantiality, simplicity, and natural immortality.[1] Although the critical Kant views this putative pure 'science' of the soul as a failure, he does grant that we can be conscious of certain features pertaining to the inner nature of the soul on practical grounds. In particular, he maintains that on the basis of our consciousness of the moral law, we can be conscious that the soul possesses freedom. We will discuss this aspect of Kant's view in Chapters 11 and 12. For now, however, our focus will be on the views of Kant and of certain of his predecessors about how much, if anything, we can cognize of the nature and inner constitution of the soul on purely theoretical grounds.

Kant's dogmatic rational psychologist operates with a radically pared-down concept of the soul—namely, 'the thinking I' (A 351). Variant locutions intended to express this same concept include: 'the thinking self' (B 430) and 'the thinking subject' (A 334/B 392). But when speaking on his own behalf, Kant sometimes employs certain designations for the soul that reflect his own, specifically Transcendentally Idealist, perspective. These designations include: 'the transcendental subject of all inner appearances' (A 478/B 506, note), 'a transcendental subject of thoughts = X' (A 346/B 404), and 'the transcendental object of inner sense' (A 361).

As this list suggests, in the first *Critique* Kant conceives of 'the thinking I' as both the *subject* of thoughts and the *object* of inner sense (A 379). It counts as a *transcendental* subject of thoughts because I have no knowledge of how it is in itself. It is, as Kant says, known to me only through 'the thoughts that are its predicates'—or, more precisely, through the appearances of those thoughts in inner sense (A 346).[2] These thoughts—or their appearances—include our belief-

---

[1] See A 342/B 400 and A 343/B 401.
[2] 'The soul', Kant says in the *Metaphysics Mrongovius*, 'as a thing in itself does not at all produce its actions in a time sequence, rather they only appear to us that way' (29: 924). Since our token

states, perceptions, intentions, and volitions. By contrast, the thinking I's constitution (or 'character' [*Beschaffenheit*]) and nature [*Natur*], lie entirely beyond our theoretical-grounded ken (A 398, A 345–6/B 403–4). What we do know (on theoretical grounds) about the soul as it is in itself is only that it exists and *appears* to us as having certain thoughts (broadly understood).

During the critical period, but not before, Kant sometimes suggests that *rational* psychology can properly be so called only if it is a *pure* doctrine of the soul (see, for example, A 347/B 405–6). Sometimes, therefore, his talk of 'pure rational psychology' is pleonastic. When it is not, such talk marks a contrast either with the Kant-approved empirically grounded rational psychology he discusses in his metaphysics lectures (see 28: 441–2) or with an in-intention dogmatic rational psychology that incorporates certain empirical elements. As we will see, Kant endorses the former project in the first *Critique* while rejecting the latter.

To understand Kant's conception of pure rational psychology it will help to examine the conceptions of rational and empirical psychology espoused by his broadly Wolffian predecessors. I will argue that Kant's target in the Paralogisms chapter is a putative pure science of the soul that, although influenced by these conceptions, actually departs from them in important respects. That target turns out to incorporate elements from two sources, namely, Baumgarten's *Metaphysics*, on the one hand, and Kant's own immediately pre-critical rational psychology in his *Metaphysics L1* lectures, on the other. The second of these, I will argue, counts as a pure rational psychology if, but only if, its claims and conceptions are understood as Kant would come to understand them from the perspective of the first *Critique*. When Kant was defending this putative science in the late 1770s, however, he would have conceived of it as an *impure* rational psychology. Finally, Descartes is another possible target—and very plausibly *the* target of the fourth Paralogism, but one suspects that Kant's immediate targets are, for the most part, more recent, and to some extent idealized, practitioners of what the ever-charitable Kant would have regarded as a properly 'corrected' science of pure rational psychology.

2.2 Wolff

Let's begin by examining the conception of rational psychology developed by the self-proclaimed originator of this discipline, Christian Wolff.[3] In his *German*

---

psychological states *are* temporally ordered, they cannot be identical with the actions of our soul (that is, 'thoughts'), but only with their appearances. I am indebted to Ralf Bader for this point.

[3] That Wolff claims to have been the originator of this science is noted by Dyck, *Kant and Rational Psychology* at 4. For Wolff's claim to novelty see: Wolff (1740c, vol. 1, first published 1728 (hereafter '*PD*' for '*Preliminary Discourse*')), §112.

Metaphysics of 1719 (hereafter '*GM*'), Wolff divides psychology into two parts.[4] The first part (*GM*, chapter 3), left at this stage unnamed, treats of the soul insofar as we perceive its actions and insofar as we derive its concept—which Wolff equates with its nominal essence—from experience (§727). The second part (*GM*, chapter 5), similarly unnamed, investigates

> in what the [real] essence of the soul and of a spirit in general consists, and how that which we have perceived of them and noted is grounded in that essence, in the course of which a variety of things will be treated to which experience does not immediately lead. (*GM*, §727)[5]

The first part of Wolff's psychology consists largely of an empirical study of the human soul, but it also includes a proof of the soul's existence (*GM*, §6). The empirical study catalogues the soul's various operations; it also seeks to identify the soul's nominal essence, which it conceives of as an empirically derived concept. The second part endeavours, first, to derive the soul's real essence from this nominal essence and thereby to determine the real essence's identity, second, to test the correctness of this derivation by examining whether everything that we note of the soul in the first part of psychology—apart from its existence, which in any case we strictly prove rather than 'note'—can be derived from the already derived real essence in the second. If the answer to this last question is yes, the correctness of the derivation of the soul's real essence from its nominal essence is confirmed; if no, we must attempt to derive the real essence anew. The derivation of the empirically observed properties of the soul from its real essence thus provides a crosscheck on the correctness of the derivation of that real essence. Wolff accordingly describes experience as the 'touchstone' [*Probier-Stein*] of what we imagine ourselves to have learned about the real essence of the soul in the second part of psychology (*GM*, §727). That second part, however, does *not*, conversely, contain the touchstone of our purported experience of the soul as reported by the first part (*GM*, §727): it is not an adequacy condition on the work done in psychology's first, empirical part that it should contain introspective observations of *every* feature allegedly derivable from the soul's real essence in psychology's second part. In consequence, the second part of psychology may extend beyond the first without detriment to the reputation of either part of this science. Wolff's procedure in *GM* does not, then, involve any Rawlsian or

---

[4] Wolff (1751, orig. pub. 1719) (hereafter '*GM*').
[5] I was alerted to this passage, and to many others I quote in this chapter, by Corey Dyck's instructive discussion of rational and empirical psychology in the first three chapters of his book (*Kant and Rational Psychology*). Although I disagree with Dyck on several points, I am profoundly indebted to him for opening up this rich seam of historical inquiry. For the sake of brevity, I will not indicate every occasion on which I first learned about a noteworthy text from Dyck's discussion—readers of his book will be able to discern that for themselves. Let me simply acknowledge that those occasions are not few.

Goodmanian 'reflective equilibrium' between theory and data. Instead, in the event of a conflict between the two, the data hold sway. In the event of a discrepancy the psychologist is meant to stick with the data and conclude that the soul's real essence has been mis-derived and so mis-identified.

Wolff maintains that the nominal essence of the soul is the concept: 'that thing which is conscious of itself and of other things outside itself' (*GM*, §192).[6] The envisaged external 'things' are not the soul's mental states, but rather, on the one hand, bodies—including, for example, buildings—and, on the other, persons [*Personen*] (§197).[7] He maintains that the real essence of the soul is its power of representing the world from the point of view of its associated body (§§753, 755). In view of the way that Wolff specifies the soul's nominal essence, we can already draw one concrete conclusion about Kant's targets in the Paralogisms chapter: his target in the fourth Paralogism is not Wolff. For Wolff supposes that the soul cognizes itself as conscious of things outside of it: our self-concept is such that in knowing that we exist, we also know the existence of the external world. The paralogist, by contrast, argues by means of the fourth paralogism for the opposite conclusion: the soul cognizes itself 'not as the consciousness of several things outside it, but as [the consciousness] of **the existence of itself only** and of other things merely as its representations' (A 404).

The main philosophical work done in the second part of Wolff's psychology consists in deriving the soul's real essence from the its nominal essence. This line of reasoning is worth examining. It begins with the following sub-argument for the thesis that bodies are incapable of thinking. The alterations of a body are grounded in the magnitude, figure, and position of its parts. Consciousness cannot arise from changes in these features; therefore, bodies cannot be conscious. In consequence, since thought is a kind of consciousness, bodies cannot think (§738).

With this sub-argument completed, the reasoning continues as follows. Since the soul can think, it cannot be a body. Since anything composite is a body, the soul is not composite and so must be simple (§742). Since it is simple, it is something that exists for itself, hence a substance (§114). But every substance has a power from which its alterations flow (§744). Hence, the soul has a power from which its alterations flow (ibid.).[8] But, since the soul is simple, it cannot have a plurality of basic powers; for each such power would need to be grounded in its

---

[6] In *GM* Wolff does not yet describe this as the soul's nominal definition, but that he so regards it is made clear by what he says in his *Psychologia empirica* of 1732. Wolff, Christian (1738), *Psychologia empirica* (2nd edn.) (first published 1732), in Christian Wolff, *Gesammelte Werke*, Part 2. Lateinische Schriften, vol. 5. (Hildesheim: Olms, 1968) (hereafter '*PE*') at §20. Certain of Wolff's followers also appreciated that this was supposed to be a nominal definition. See, for example, the definition of 'Anima' (definition number 689) in Friedrich Christian Baumeister, (1767), *Philosophia Definitiva* (Wittenberg) (orig. pub. 1735) at 128.

[7] The first of these claims is also suggested by Wolff's observation that we are accustomed to calling the things that we represent as outside ourselves 'bodies' (*GM*, §217).

[8] One might be tempted to say 'a single *fundamental* power', but Wolff does not in fact speak this way.

own substance (§745). Therefore, the soul has only a single power from which each of its alterations flow (§745). This single power bears various names, including 'understanding', 'imagination', and 'will'—names bestowed on it in accordance with its sundry effects or manifestations (§§746–7). Nonetheless, it remains a single power. To illustrate this point Wolff draws an analogy with a flame, whose single power, namely, the power to impart motion, receives various names according to its various effects or manifestations. It is called 'an illuminating power', 'a burning power', and so forth (§746).

Having argued that the soul is a substance with a single power, Wolff reasons as follows: The alterations that we perceive in the soul are perceptions (§749), and these perceptions represent something outside of us, namely the human body (ibid.). The human body is part of the world (§753). Consequently, the soul has a power of representing various parts of the world according to the position of its body in the world (§753). Since this power is the single ground from which the soul's alternations flow, it is the soul's real essence (§755).

In this way, starting from an empirically acquired concept of the soul (its nominal essence), Wolff argues that the soul's real essence—that feature by virtue of which it *is* a soul—is a power of representing the world according to the position in the world of its body. It would be a dry and fruitless chore to pick over all the flaws and gaps in Wolff's reasoning. I want instead to extract from this sketch three lessons about the Wolff of *GM*'s conception of the second part of psychology.

The first lesson is that two theses that Kant will later treat as paradigm deliverances of dogmatic pure rational psychology, namely, the claims that the soul is simple and that it is a substance, are in the second part of Wolff's psychology derived from an empirically acquired concept of the soul merely en route to trying to derive the soul's real essence. Simplicity and substantiality, then, are not themselves properties that the second part of psychology aims to show to be grounded in the real essence of the soul. One wonders whether Wolff has these features in mind when he says that in the course of developing the second part of psychology one treats of various things to which experience 'does not immediately lead' (*GM*, §727).

The second lesson is that Wolff's alleged derivation of the soul's real essence draws upon certain assumptions that are not plausibly viewed, even from his own perspective, as analytic truths. One such assumption is the claim that the soul perceives its own body (§749). This assumption is clearly empirical in character. Wolff nonetheless regards it as an acceptable assumption to make in the second part of psychology, and he does so because he regards it as *indubitable* (compare *GM* §1 and §6).[9] For Wolff indubitability renders an empirical claim admissible as

---

[9] I owe this observation to Katherine Dunlop.

a premise of rational psychology because for him the principles of demonstration permissibly drawn upon in rational psychology include 'nothing except definitions, *indubitable* experiences, axioms, and propositions already demonstrated'.[10] Insofar as the second part of psychology in *GM* corresponds to a 'rational psychology', therefore, it is permitted to proceed in its proofs by drawing on indubitable empirical claims.

The third lesson is that, Wolff's programmatic remarks notwithstanding, the second part of rational psychology in *GM* actually contains very few attempts to demonstrate theses to the effect that a certain feature noted in empirical psychology is grounded in the real essence of the soul. In fact, to my knowledge, the only clear such example occurring in *GM* is the attempt to show that the faculty of sensible desire—something we observe through its various exercises—is grounded in the soul's single faculty of representing the world, hence in its real essence, by arguing that to desire something is just to represent it as good (*GM*, §878). Nor, it must be said, do the features actually catalogued in the first part of *GM*'s psychology always appear to be of a kind that *could* be shown to be grounded in the essence of the soul. In practice, the deliverances of the psychology developed in the first part of *GM* turn out to be a medley of observations on disparate topics, not all of which belong to what we'd today think of as psychology. We do find a few observations about the operations of the mind—Wolff observes, for example, that the content of the imagination is not fully within one's power (§243). And there are explications of certain faculties whose operations might plausibly be taken to be empirically observed—for example: understanding (§277), reason (§368), and memory (§249), along with explications of various cognitive and affective states, for example: attention (§268), pain (§421), and joy (§446). But cohabiting with these expected topics are others far removed from empirical psychology as we might understand that discipline today. Thus, the first part Wolff's psychology in *GM* contains explications of various phenomena belonging to what we'd today call 'moral psychology'—for example, benevolence (§471) and *schadenfreude* (§458), along with explications of epistemological phenomena—such as: knowledge [*Wissen*] (§361), experience (§325), opinion (§384), and uncertainty (§392). At still more of a stretch, the first part of psychology contains explications of notions from: logic, for example, inference (§340) and demonstration (§347); ethics, for example, good (§422); and the philosophy of language, for example, common nouns (§300) and pronouns (§306). The subject matter of the

---

[10] Emphasis added. Christian Wolff, *Psychologia Rationalis*, ed. Georg Olms (*Gesammelte Werke*, Part 2. Lateinische Schriften; Frankfurt am Main: Hildesheim, 1740a) at §3. This point already follows from Wolff's claim that those things that are treated of in rational psychology are things to be demonstrated (*demonstranda*). For demonstrations, as Wolff makes clear in his *Latin Logic*, draw upon nothing but definitions, indubitable experiences, axioms and propositions already demonstrated (§498, §562). Wolff, moreover, cites just this section of the *Latin Logic* when characterizing the resources of rational psychology in §3 of his *Rational Psychology*.

first part of Wolff's psychology thus turns out to be a large and polymorphous assortment of topics sharing little in common with one another beyond their status as items of 'broad philosophical interest'.

We have now nearly completed our discussion of psychology in *GM*, but before turning to later works, we should first say a word about Wolff's proof of the soul's existence. Two points about this proof are especially noteworthy. First, Wolff locates the proof in the first part of his psychology. Second, he conducts the argument in the first-person *plural*. It runs as follows:

Whoever is conscious of himself and other things exists.
We are conscious of ourselves and other things.
Therefore, we exist. (*GM*, §6)[11]

The argument resembles a pluralized version of the *cogito* when that exercise is construed as an inference, but it has a much stronger minor premise than the *cogito*. Because Wolff describes this premise as an indubitable experience (*GM*, §7) the proof might permissibly be located in the second part of psychology; so it is perhaps surprising to find it in the first.

The conception of psychology presented in *GM* of 1719 survives into later works, where it is elaborated and made more explicit. In *PD* of 1728 Wolff uses the term 'rational psychology' for the first time and characterizes this science in a manner reminiscent of his characterization of the second part of psychology in *GM*. 'In rational psychology', he says,

> we derive a priori from a unique concept of the human soul all the things which are observed a posteriori to pertain to the human soul and all the things which are deduced from these observations, insofar as they are proper to philosophy.
> (*PD*, §112)

One supposes that by 'all the things which are observed a posteriori to pertain to the human soul' Wolff has in mind only those things that pertain to one's soul *qua* human soul, namely, its characteristic features, capacities, and modes of experience. He is not thinking, for example, of a preference for beer over wine.[12] Nonetheless, it remains a flaw of his exposition that he fails to provide a more precise characterization of the domain of a posteriori psychology.

What Wolff means by 'a unique concept of the human soul' here would seem to be its real essence; for the idea that the second part of psychology should derive what is observed of the soul in empirical psychology from its putative real essence is a stable feature of Wolff's view, occurring both before *PD* (in *GM*) and also after

---

[11] A similar argument is presented later in *PE* at §14, see also §11.
[12] I'm grateful to Ralf Bader for getting me to think about this point.

it in the *PE* (1732). In this later work Wolff refers the reader to the section of *PD* in which the passage just quoted occurs for an explanation of why rational and empirical psychology should be distinguished from one another. He also indicates in the same work that it is in rational psychology that one aims to show *what* the soul is—to exhibit, in other words, its real essence.[13]

In his *Rational Psychology* of 1734 Wolff makes explicit the previously unspoken point that rational psychology 'reveals those things which had been impervious [*impervia*] to observation alone' (§9). He now further claims that such things as are noted in empirical psychology are *understood* [*intelliguntur*] more fully and more correctly through rational psychology (§§7–8, emphasis added). He makes clear that this envisaged improvement in the completeness and accuracy of our understanding is owed to the fact that in rational psychology one provides the reason *why* the soul has a certain feature (§8). In doing so, he further suggests, one increases the keenness of one's observations regarding the soul (§8).

In making this last claim Wolff would seem to be positing an instance of what we'd today call 'cognitive penetration'. Here's how this might work—whether things do in fact work this way is an empirical question on which I'll remain neutral. Consider some undistinguished novice student of French, Bob. Suppose Bob were to come across a French-speaking donkey. Upon first encountering this beast, he would in all likelihood fail to hear its speech as language. For, first, not expecting a donkey to be able to speak, he would not be poised to try consciously to impose a syntax on its (as it happens) articulate braying; and, second, having only a tenuous grip on the French language, neither would he automatically impose a syntax on it. But upon being told by someone whose testimony Bob trusted that the cause of the unfamiliar sounds he was hearing was indeed a French-speaking (monoglot) donkey, he'd be able, equipped as he is with his shaky French, to start to begin to hear at least some snatches of the beast's throaty racket as sentences of that language. In this way, Bob's understanding of the causal ground of the relevant sounds would sharpen and, arguably, enrich his perception of them.

Returning to reality, we may note that certain elements of Wolff's conception of psychology are taken up by the Wolffians. Especially influential is the idea that empirical and rational psychology constitute two alternative routes to knowledge of one and the same sub-set of the soul's properties. On the one hand, there is an 'empirical' route based on experience of the soul and its operations, and, on the other, a so-called 'a priori' route, which takes as its foundation, logic, the *PSR*, and the concept of the soul, along with certain *indubitable* claims of experience. The term 'a priori' in Wolff's writings, when used to qualify judgments or routes to knowledge, thus has a sense rather different from the one, usually associated with

---

[13] Wolff, *PE* at §20, 15.

Kant, of 'involving no experiential grounds'.[14] It seems rather to mean 'proceeding by means of derivations that include complex chains of reasoning and which rest on nothing but the following: definitions, non-experientially justified principles, and *indubitable* experientially justified principles'. The intended contrast would seem to be with the idea of 'proceeding by means of reasoning that includes among its grounds one or more *dubitable* experientially justified claim'.

But while Wolff's followers inherit the idea that there are multiple routes to some parts of our knowledge of the soul, they also modify his conception of rational psychology in certain ways relevant to Kant's understanding of this putative science. For this reason, it will be worth examining the development of the broadly Wolffian conception of rational psychology in the period between Wolff's *Rational Psychology* of 1734 and Kant's own musings on the subject on the eve of the critical philosophy. Let's begin with the views of one of Wolff's earliest and most faithful disciples, the Leipzig-based philosopher, Johann Christoph Gottsched (1700–1766).

2.3 Gottsched

In the fourth part of his *Erste Gründe der gesamten Weltweisheit* (*First Grounds of Philosophy taken as a whole*, first edition, 1733–4) Gottsched sets forth a '*Geisterlehre*' or 'doctrine of spirits', which he also refers to as a 'pneumatology' [*pneumatologia*].[15] Being a doctrine of thinking substances in *general*, the *Geisterlehre* treats of three classes of thinking being: human souls, the souls of non-human animals, and God (volume 1, §859). The *Geisterlehre* has three parts. The first, based entirely on experience, concerns the powers and actions of finite souls and spirits (1, §§860–1). The second treats of the essence and nature of souls and spirits. Echoing Wolff's characterization of the second part of psychology in *GM*, Gottsched describes this part of his *Geisterlehre* as 'concerned to display

---

[14] As Desmond Hogan has convincingly argued, however, this is not the only sense of 'a priori' in Kant. Sometimes it rather means 'known through the ground'. See Desmond Hogan, 'How to Know Unknowable Things in Themselves', *Noûs*, 43 (1) (2009), 49–63 at 52. See also Heinz Heimsoeth, *Transzendentale Dialektik: Ein Kommentar zu Kant's Kritik der reinen Vernunft*, 4 vols (Berlin: De Gruyter, 1966–71) at 239 note 72.

[15] Johann Christoph Gottsched, *Erste Gründe der gesamten Weltweisheit* (7th edn; Leipzig: Breitkopf, 1762). See volume 1, pages 473–596. As Dyck notes, this use of the term 'pneumatology' for the doctrine of spirits in general goes back at least to Leibniz, who conceives of pneumatology as treating of 'knowledge of God, souls, and simple substances in general' (see Dyck, *Kant and Rational Psychology* at 4, note 4). And as Dyck further notes, Crusius uses the term in a similar way (ibid.)—although he focuses on a distinctively 'metaphysical pneumatology', which he conceives of as an a priori science. 'By *metaphysical pneumatology* [*metaphysische Pneumatologie*]', he says, 'I understand the science of the necessary essence of a spirit, of its distinctions and properties, which permit of being understood a priori'. Christian August Crusius, *Entwurf der Nothwendigen Vernunft-Wahrheiten, wiefern sie den zufälligen Entgegengesetzt werden*, ed. Giorgio Tonelli, 4 vols (*Die Philosophischen Hauptwerke*, 2; Hildesheim: Georg Olms, 1745) at §424.

[*anzuzeigen*] in the nature and essence of the soul or spirit, the grounds of all those things that have been noted [in empirical psychology]' (1, §862). This part of *Geisterlehre*, Gottsched adds, must, in contrast to the first part, 'be discerned through inferences of reason [*Vernunftschlüsse*]'—that is, through valid syllogisms (ibid.).[16] The third part of the *Geisterlehre* deals with the essence and attributes of God (1, §§1099–1146).

Gottsched follows Wolff in attempting to derive the real essence of the soul from its nominal essence, though he departs from him in employing a slightly different preliminary explication of the soul, namely, as 'that in us which thinks and is conscious of itself' (1, §872). In this formulation, there is no Wolffian reference to consciousness of things outside the soul. Nonetheless, the conclusion Gottsched reaches is the Wolffian one that the real essence or nature of the soul is its unique power: the power of representation (1, §§1019–20).

One last noteworthy feature of Gottsched's presentation of his *Geisterlehre* is that it begins with the following attempt to demonstrate the soul's existence:

Everything that thinks, exists [Proved from the principle of contradiction (1, §870)] We think [Known on the basis of experience (1, §868)[17]]
Therefore, we exist. (1, §871)

This amounts to a simplified version of Wolff's own existence proof—the ungainly predicate 'is conscious of itself and other things outside itself' being replaced with the pithy, and, in this context, Cartesian, 'thinks'. Notably, however, this modification deprives Gottsched of Wolff's justification for treating the minor premise as empirical. There may perhaps be some intuitive plausibility in the claim that our knowledge that we think rests on experience, but this is less plausibly an empirical claim than the claim that we are conscious of things outside of ourselves.

As should be clear from this brief discussion, the significance of Gottsched's conception of rational psychology lies not so much in its novelty as in its nearly faithful adherence to Wolff's conception of the relationship between empirical and rational psychology. This fact matters because it makes Gottsched a possible conduit for Kant's knowledge of Wolff's rational psychology. Indeed, Gottsched seems an especially likely such conduit for three reasons. First, we know that Kant kept a copy of *Erste Gründe* in his library; second, he seems to be referring to this

---

[16] I am indebted to Dyck for raising this passage to prominence and noting its connection with Wolff's conception of rational psychology. However, my translation differs from his in removing an ambiguity: his translation leaves it unclear whether it is the features observed in empirical psychology or their grounds that are to be displayed in the essence of the soul. I take the German to be clear that it is the latter. See Dyck, *Kant and Rational Psychology* at 45.

[17] The heading of this section runs: 'Experience teaches that we think' ('*Experientia docet, nos cogitare*').

work when he speaks of 'Gottsched's compendium' in the *Hechsel Logic*; and third, as Lewis White Beck notes, *Erste Gründe* was regarded as the chief Wolffian textbook of its day.[18] To make this observation is not, of course, to deny that Kant could have learned of these conceptions directly from Wolff's writings. But these considerations do make it likely that he would have known of them by one avenue or another. This matters because, as we'll see, there is a case to be made that Kant's conception of rational psychology on the eve of the first *Critique*, as witnessed by his *Metaphysics L1* lectures, incorporates Wolff's view that rational psychology may draw on empirical premises so long as they are indubitable. Before we examine that conception, however, we should first consider the views on psychology of Wolff's disciple, Alexander Baumgarten—views to which Kant's conception of *pure* rational psychology in the first *Critique* seems to be to some degree indebted.

2.4 Baumgarten

Baumgarten draws the distinction between empirical and rational psychology in the following terms:[19]

> Psychology (1) deduces its assertions on the basis of experience that is nearest to hand, in which case it is EMPIRICAL PSYCHOLOGY, and (2) deduces its assertions on the basis of the concept of the soul through a longer series of arguments, in which case it is RATIONAL PSYCHOLOGY.
>
> (*Metaphysics*, 1739, §503)

For Baumgarten, then, the science of empirical psychology consists of the body of assertions that can be drawn from 'experience that is nearest to hand'. As one might expect, many of these assertions take the form of descriptions and categorizations of the various faculties of the mind. But, beyond this, Baumgarten's empirical psychology includes certain short *arguments*, including the following argument for the existence of the soul:

> If there is something in a being that can be conscious of something, that is a SOUL.

---

[18] Pinder, *Immanuel Kant Logik-Vorlesung Unveröffentlichte Nachschriften II, Logik Hechsel; Warschauer Logik* at 491. Kant owned the 1748–9 edition of *Erste Gründe*. See Warda, *Immanuel Kants Bücher* at 49. See also Lewis White Beck, *Early German Philosophy: Kant and His Predecessors* (Cambridge, MA: Belknap, 1969) at 260.

[19] Alexander Baumgarten, *Metaphysics: A Critical Translation with Kant's Elucidations, Selected Notes, and Related Materials*, trans. Courtney D. Fugate and John Hymers (London: Bloomsbury, 2013). From the 1760s onward Kant used the 4th edition of 1757 as the textbook for his metaphysics lectures.

Something exists in me (§55), that can be conscious of something (§57).
Therefore a soul exists in me (I, a soul, exist).   (*Metaphysics*, §504)

Insofar as it reasons about a singular subject, this argument represents a departure from the corresponding arguments of Wolff and Gottsched.[20]

In other short arguments, also officially located within empirical psychology, Baumgarten reasons that my soul *is* (rather than *has*) a power (*Metaphysics*, §505) for representing (§506) the universe (§507) according to the position of its body (§512). Baumgarten thus introduces a striking point of novelty: he *identifies* the soul with the power that Wolff had taken to be its real essence, and he does so in the *empirical* part of his psychology. Later, however, in the part of his *Metaphysics* dealing with rational psychology, he characterizes this power in more Wolffian terms, namely, as the 'nature' [*natura*] of the human soul (§758). In a further departure from Wolff and Gottsched, Baumgarten takes rational psychology to begin from the concept, not of a soul in general, but of the *human* soul in particular—a soul, as he puts it, 'in the closest interaction with the human body' (§740).

Further departing from Wolff and Gottsched, Baumgarten does not assign to rational psychology the task of showing how what was observed of the soul in empirical psychology is grounded in the soul's nature or real essence. Instead, to the extent that he pursues the latter project at all, he does so within empirical psychology, where, for example, my faculty of imagination is represented as but an aspect of my power of representing the universe according to the position of my body (§557). For Baumgarten the main task of rational psychology is rather to establish certain results about the human soul that are not established in empirical psychology. These results include assertions to the effect that the human soul is: a substance, a monad, and a spirit (§742), immaterial and incorporeal (§757), not a substantiated phenomenon (§743), finite and contingent (§743), able to originate only from nothing and perish only through annihilation (§745), indivisible (§746), unextended (§747), the sufficient ground for the inherence of some accidents (§755), possessed of personality and freedom (§756). And finally—the culmination of all these—naturally immortal (§782).[21]

Since the items on this list are all, arguably, pure predications of the soul, the list suggests that the part of Baumgarten's rational psychology that is concerned with establishing the properties of the soul is by the lights of the first *Critique* a *pure*

---

[20] This departure is noted by Corey Dyck, 'The Divorce of Reason and Experience: Kant's Paralogisms of Pure Reason in Context', *Journal of the History of Philosophy*, 47 (2) (2009), 249–75 at 258–9. Notice that Baumgarten's argument has the curious feature that in it 'I' and 'me' are not co-referential (I exist in me). We'll see that in the *Metaphysics L1* Kant also treats the first person singular personal pronoun as ambiguous.

[21] Notice that, curiously, Baumgarten seems to hold that the soul is *both* a power *and* a substance.

rational psychology. It makes no appeal to experience in its ground except to establish that the soul exists, and its predicates are arguably pure concepts.

2.5 Meier

A somewhat more Wolffian conception of rational psychology is developed by Baumgarten's student and successor at Halle, Georg Friedrich Meier (1718–77).[22] In the third part of his forbidding four-volume work, *Metaphysics* (1755–9), Meier divides psychology into its empirical and rational parts.[23] He says:

> I have completely convinced myself *through empirical psychology* taken in its entirety that my soul is a substance, which possesses a power of representation though which it represents the world according to the position of its body, partly distinctly and partly indistinctly. (*Metaphysics*, 3, §735, emphasis added)

For Meier, then, empirical psychology reveals my human soul to be a substance that *possesses* the power with which Baumgarten had identified the human soul. In this respect Meier's position (at least as it is stated here—it's not clear that Meier is consistent) approximates Wolffian orthodoxy more closely than does Baumgarten's. It is striking, though, that Meier sides with Baumgarten (and against Wolff) in assigning the discovery that my soul posssesses this power to empirical rather than rational psychology. This prompts the question: if *rational* psychology is not directed toward making this important discovery, what is it for? Meier's answer runs as follows:

> **Rational psychology** is that science [*Wissenschaft*] of the soul that is derived from the abstract concept of the soul through longer and wider-ranging proofs [than one finds in empirical psychology]. It proves of all human souls that which one has cognized of his own soul in the empirical psychology; it treats of the nature and essence of the soul; it treats of such matters as can in no way be decided by experience; it seeks to discover the grounds of the alterations of the soul, and the way in which they come to be; and it treats of the remaining finite spirits and souls outside of the human. (*Metaphysics*, 3, §474)

---

[22] Meier, the chief follower of Baumgarten, grew to be the bitter antagonist of Gottsched, the most faithful disciple of Wolff. As Beck notes, the depth of their animosity is evident in the nakedly contemptuous title of Meier's article: 'Exposition of the reasons why it appears to be impossible to carry on a useful and rational controversy with Herr Professor Gottsched' (1754). Apparently, Gottsched had committed the inexcusable *faux pas* of condemning Klopstock. See Beck, *Early German Philosophy* at 281.

[23] Georg Friedrich Meier, *Metaphysik*, 4 vols (3; Halle: Gebauer, 1765).

Empirical psychology, Meier is saying here, discloses that I possess the power of representing the world according to the position of my body. But rational psychology shows that to possess this power is characteristic of human souls in general: it constitutes their essence. Meier is suggesting that the point of demonstrating within rational psychology that the human soul possesses certain properties that it has already been shown to possess in empirical psychology is that in doing so one shows that these properties are not peculiar to one's own soul but rather pertain to human souls in general.[24] Moreover, for Meier, as for Gottsched, rational psychology goes farther insofar as it treats of *non*-human finite spirits and souls (§474), including the souls of brutes, angels, and even the devil (§734). But since this science does not treat of God's nature, Meier does not label it a 'pneumatology'. Nonetheless, it seems reasonable to think of it as a truncated pneumatology.

As we will see, Kant holds that rational psychology should aim to be a science of thinking beings in general. And since Kant's God, not possessing a discursive (that is, concept-employing) understanding, strictly speaking, does not think (8: 400 note *; 18: 631; 29: 888–9), this means that, strictly speaking, Kant shares Meier's view that rational psychology does not treat of God's nature.

We are now nearly ready to consider Kant's conception of rational psychology in the first *Critique*, but before we do so, we must examine his pre-critical conception of this discipline in his metaphysics lectures from 1777–80 (the *Metaphysics L1*). As we will see, this conception borrows from Wolff and Gottsched the broad lesson that rational psychology should be in *some* way constrained by empirical psychology, but it also departs from that tradition in radically reconceiving the nature of the constraining relation. Kant's pre-critical view also equips *rational* psychology with a new starting concept, namely, the Cartesian 'I'. The result is a distinctive conception of rational psychology—one which, to my knowledge, is endorsed in this exact form by no thinker besides the immediately pre-critical Kant.

2.6 Rational psychology in the *Metaphysics L1*

Kant opens his discussion of psychology in the *Metaphysics L1* lectures of 1777–80 with a general taxonomy of the sciences, a taxonomy in which the broadest distinction is that between *physiology* and *transcendental philosophy*—two sciences that differ with respect to the source of their objects of study (28: 221–2). The former discipline borrows the concepts of the objects it studies from experience, the latter from 'pure concepts of reason' (ibid.). Because Kant treats the

---

[24] Meier maintains that we can establish the nature of the soul on non-deductive grounds—from observations of the behaviour of others—with the same degree of rigour (*Gründlichkeit*) that attaches to inductively established empirical claims, such as the claim that every portion of air is heavy (§735).

objects of experience as identical with the objects of sense (compare R 5926; 18: 388), he defines *physiology* as 'the cognition of the objects of the senses' (28: 221). This science in turn divides into two sub-disciplines, depending on whether the objects to be cognized belong to outer or inner sense. The part of physiology that studies the objects of outer sense is physics, while that which studies the objects of inner sense is psychology (28: 222). Sometimes Kant speaks as if inner sense has only a single object, namely, the soul (28: 265).[25] Both physics and psychology, finally, further sub-divide into their empirical and rational branches according to their grounds of cognition. Empirical psychology 'is the cognition of the objects of inner sense insofar as it is obtained from experience' (28: 223), while rational psychology 'is the cognition of the objects of inner sense insofar as it is borrowed from pure reason' (28: 222–3). And what it is to cognize an object of the senses 'a priori' is to derive knowledge about that object from a consideration of its concept.

A portion of the 'division' to which Kant at this stage takes empirical and rational psychology to belong thus takes the form shown in Figure 2.1. As this division suggests, at this stage Kant conceives of rational psychology as that discipline in which one cognizes by a priori means an object of inner sense (hence of experience)—namely, the soul. However, as we have already observed, he departs from Wolff in regarding the concept of the soul from which rational psychology is to be developed not as the concept of *that which is conscious of itself*

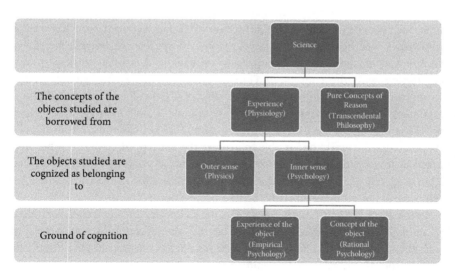

Figure 2.1 Division of empirical and rational psychology

---

[25] Compare Baumgarten, who says that 'INTERNAL SENSE... represents the state of my soul' (*Metaphysics*, §535).

and of other things outside itself but rather as the more Cartesian-sounding 'concept of I'.[26]

Kant supposes the pronoun 'I' has both a broad and a narrow sense. Taken in the broad sense, it refers to an object of both inner *and* outer sense, something which Kant refers to using the phrase '**I as human being**'; in the narrow sense, however, it refers only to an object of inner sense, which Kant refers to with the phrase '**I as intelligence**' (28: 224). It is clear that he takes the concept from which the doctrine of the soul is to be developed to be the 'I' taken in the narrow sense, for it is this expression whose referent he equates with the soul (28: 265).[27]

A complication is introduced by Kant's choice of concept from which to develop the science of rational psychology in the *Metaphysics L1*. For in these lectures he expressly describes 'the concept of [the] I' as merely 'a concept of empirical psychology' (28: 224), and he portrays our knowledge that we have a soul as empirically grounded (28: 263). But then one wonders how a rational psychology founded on this concept could aspire to be the entirely pure, a priori, general science of the soul that Kant takes it to be.

Part of the answer, I think, is that Kant takes everything that we learn about the nature as opposed to the existence of the soul in rational psychology to be cognized a priori. 'The concept of the soul', he says, 'is a concept of experience. But in rational psychology we take nothing more from experience than the mere concept of the soul, **that** we have a soul. The rest must be cognized from pure reason' (*Metaphysics L1*, 28: 263).

This last remark exhibits an interesting quirk of Kant's idiolect. If his student note-taker is to be trusted, when Kant speaks of 'taking' a concept from experience sometimes what he means is not deriving that concept from experience but rather verifying its exemplification by appeal to experience. A similar quirk occurs in connection with the concept of God in the *Metaphysics Mrongovius*. There, temporarily speaking from the point of view of a defender of the cosmological argument, Kant tells us that through the world one is able 'to arrive at [*aufkommen*] the concept of God' (29: 748). The context makes clear that he means not that through the world one is able to acquire the concept of God but rather that one is by this means able to 'cognize God's existence' (29: 748). In the first *Critique* Kant uses the phrase 'to take a proposition [from some domain]' as similarly referring to the grounds through which a proposition is cognized (A 353).

In the *Metaphysics L1*, then, Kant treats the claim that one has a soul as rational psychology's sole empirical claim. Since he now identifies the concept of the soul with the concept of the I—that is, the thinking subject—he regards the claim that I have a soul as equivalent to the claim, 'I am'. As we have seen, there's nothing un-

---

[26] See 28: 224, 28: 266, and compare the use he makes of this concept in the actual development of rational psychology at 28: 225–7.

[27] See Dyck, *Kant and Rational Psychology* at 64.

Wolffian in treating the basis of rational psychology as incorporating an empirical claim, so long as that claim is *indubitable*. And since Kant regards the claim 'I am' as known with certainty (28: 206), he is in this respect (in his own eyes) being thoroughly Wolffian. Where he does depart from Wolff is in adopting the concept 'I' as the basic concept from which rational psychology is to proceed in preference to Wolff's concept of *that which is conscious of itself and of other things outside itself*. This change would seem to be motivated, at least in part, by Kant's holding (at *this* stage) that I am *not* certain of the existence of things outside of me (28: 206). It follows that for Kant at this stage the claim that Wolff's concept of the soul is exemplified cannot be part of the basis of rational psychology.

Where the immediately pre-critical Kant departs from *Baumgarten* is, first, in treating the soul as unambiguously a substance rather than a power, and second, in taking the starting point of rational psychology to be the concept of the 'I'. To be sure, Baumgarten had employed this concept in his *empirical* psychology, but the starting point for his rational psychology had always been the concept of 'the human soul'.

A further noteworthy innovation in the *Metaphysics L1* is Kant's reconceptualization of the manner in which empirical psychology constrains rational psychology. 'Cognition', he says, 'can come **up to the boundaries** of experience, as much by a priori means as by a posteriori, but **not [go] beyond the boundaries of experience**'.[28] He means that in rational psychology we can establish by a priori means only such results about the nature or constitution of the soul as are independently confirmable by experience in empirical psychology.

Such a view marks a striking departure from Wolff; for Kant's constraint is in fact tantamount to the *converse* of Wolff's. While Wolff demands that rational psychology be able to derive from the soul's essence *all* those things that we note about the soul in empirical psychology, Kant demands that it should be able to derive from the concept of 'the I' *only* such things about the soul's nature (as opposed to its existence) as we note about that nature in empirical psychology. If Kant's constraint is not the perfect converse of Wolff's that is only because the concepts of the soul in question differ.[29]

Where, then, does the immediately pre-critical Kant take the boundaries of experience to lie? Given the constraint just stated, we know that he takes them to

---

[28] *Metaphysics L1*, 28: 264.

[29] In discerning a radical discontinuity here I depart from Dyck, who asserts a continuity (Dyck, *Kant and Rational Psychology* at 70). We differ, I think, because we disagree about Kant's conception of the relationship between empirical and rational psychology. While Dyck takes Kant in the *Metaphysics L1* to maintain that the doctrines of rational psychology are to be *founded upon* what is disclosed in empirical psychology, I take him to regard this science—insofar as it concerns the nature rather than the existence of the soul—as merely *constrained by* what is so disclosed insofar as it is subject to the constraint that it may prove on a priori grounds only what has already been independently verified on empirical grounds. In my view, Kant's rational psychology is at this stage *founded upon* only the concept, *I*, on the one hand, and the proposition 'I am', on the other. Contrast ibid., at 69.

extend at least as far as the results of rational psychology. In the *Metaphysics L1* Kant makes clear that he conceives of rational psychology as capable of establishing that the soul is a simple and single substance (28: 265)—and that, having such a nature, it will continue to exist at all future times (28: 285). But he does not regard this science as capable of establishing that the soul is a spirit (28: 278), or pre-existent (28: 268), or immortal (28: 287)—this last property requiring that the soul's future existence should be a natural necessity rather than a contingency (28: 285). The lecture transcripts are less definite about whether at this stage Kant thinks that rational psychology can establish the soul's immateriality. At the beginning of 28: 273 he is represented as answering no, but later on the same page he is represented as answering yes. A similar obscurity attaches to his position on the provability of transcendental freedom, understood as absolute spontaneity (28: 268, 28: 270). But, since he takes the substantiality, simplicity, and singleness of the soul to be provable within rational psychology, we can infer—from the fact that the constraint just mentioned is in place—that on the eve of the *Critique* he supposes us to actually introspect these features of the soul.

In spite of its non-Wolffian reconceptualization of the way in which empirical psychology constrains rational psychology, Kant's position in the *Metaphysics L1* shares an important affinity with that of his Wolffian predecessors. For the Kant of this period, as for the Wolffians, *some* class of facts about the nature of the soul—not necessarily the same class—can be known by either of two independent routes: either directly from experience or indirectly from the concept of the soul by means of derivations exploiting logic, a priori truths, and such empirical facts as are indubitable. Moreover, for the Kant of this period, as for the Wolffians, an appeal to experience is involved in our knowledge of the *existence* of the soul, though, while the majority of Wolffians take the soul's existence to be demonstrated in empirical psychology, Kant takes it to be an undemonstrated premise—the sole empirically grounded basic truth of rational psychology. On the other hand, since he sees the soul's existence as an *indubitable* truth, in adopting this position Kant does not thereby depart from Wolff's conception of rational psychology. For the most part, however, Kant's own rational psychology in the *Metaphysics L1* is conceived of as an a priori science because, although it must appeal to experience to establish the soul's existence, its detailed articulation of the inner constitution of the soul, being based solely on an analysis of the soul's concept (taken together with the principles of pure reason), remains a straightforwardly a priori matter. For these reasons, I take it that when in the *Metaphysics L1* Kant characterizes rational psychology as an a priori science whose principles are borrowed from pure reason he intends to be speaking only of the part of rational psychology that deals with the nature as opposed to the existence of the soul.[30]

---

[30] See 28: 223; 28: 262–3; 28: 269.

In choosing to delineate the boundaries of legitimate rational psychology in the way he does in the *Metaphysics L1* Kant is engaging in a kind of 'pre-critical' criticism. He warns that if one attempts to prove by a priori reasoning things not independently established through experience, one engages in false sophistry and dogmatism (28: 264–5). Such a remark is entirely 'critical' insofar as it expresses the results of a preliminary investigation of the mind's capacity to acquire a priori self-knowledge. And yet Kant's position at this stage remains in two respects stubbornly 'pre-critical'. First, he supposes that we are able to *perceive* the soul's substantiality, simplicity, and singleness. Second, he supposes that theoretically based a priori metaphysics *can* prosper within certain limits even though its principles are not yet conceived of as conditions of the possibility of experience.

In the first *Critique* Kant finally arrives at the view that we are incapable of acquiring any theoretically based a priori knowledge about the nature or intrinsic properties of the soul. At this point, he also comes to hold that neither can inner sense afford such knowledge. What inner sense can afford, he thinks, is just knowledge of my existence and my 'inner state'—understood as the particular thoughts I am having at a given time—or, strictly speaking, their appearances (A 33/B 49 and A 38/B 55). As he says in the preamble to the A Paralogisms:

> Through this I, or he, or it (the thing) that thinks, nothing more is represented than a transcendental subject of thoughts = X, which is cognized [*erkannt*] only through the thoughts that are its predicates.   (A 346/B 404)

In the *Metaphysics L1* Kant had already supposed us to have knowledge of our inner state, but at that earlier stage this knowledge had been taken to cohabit with some limited knowledge of the soul's intrinsic nature.[31] By the time of the first edition of the first *Critique*, however, the cohabitation is over.

In summary, then, there are three respects in which rational psychology, as Kant conceives of this discipline in the late 1770s, may be said to 'involve' experience. First, rational psychology—or part of it—*rests on* experience insofar as experience grounds the soul's knowledge of its own *existence* (as opposed to its nature). Second, rational psychology *makes an appeal to* experience insofar as it assigns experience a role in delimiting its own proper domain. Third, rational psychology incorporates claims with experiential content insofar as the predicates that are attributed to the soul on a priori grounds in rational psychology are supposed to be independently attributable to it on empirical grounds in empirical psychology.

---

[31] 'Consciousness', he says in the *Metaphysics L1*, is 'a knowledge [*Wissen*] of that which belongs to me' (28: 227). It is 'a representation of my representations, it is a self-perception' (ibid.). Here Kant is using 'consciousness' in the way he will later use 'inner sense' and 'empirical apperception'.

Rational psychology, then—as it is conceived in the *Metaphysics L1*—aims to attribute to the soul certain predicates that are, by Kant's lights at the time of delivering those lectures, empirical.[32] For this reason, the rational psychology presented in the *Metaphysics L1* is not, according to its self-conception, a 'pure' rational psychology in the sense of the first *Critique*. As we will see, however, from the point of view of the first *Critique* this same rational psychology *does* count as a pure rational psychology (in that same sense) because, first, the predicates attributed to the soul in rational psychology are, by the critical period, no longer supposed to be also attributable to it on empirical grounds, and, second, the claim 'I am' is no longer thought of as resting on a determinate empirical intuition.

2.7 *Pure* rational psychology

In both editions of the first *Critique* Kant chooses for his target a distinctively *pure* version of rational psychology (A 342–3/B 400–1)—a doctrine of the soul, or *Seelenlehre*, whose unique object is the thinking I. In what does the purity of this envisaged doctrine consist? Partly, I think, in the fact that the predicates of this putative science are wholly free of empirical elements. Speaking of the thought 'I think', for example, Kant says:

> We readily see that this thought, if it is to be related to an object (myself), can contain nothing but transcendental predicates; because the slightest empirical predicate would corrupt the rational purity and independence from all experience of the science. (A 343/B 401)

What it is for a predicate to count as 'transcendental' or 'non-empirical', I take it, is for it to be a pure concept of the understanding—that is, either a category or a concept derived from the categories through their combination either with the modes of pure sensibility or with one another—in short, a 'predicable' in Kant's Aristotelian jargon (A 82/B 108).[33] Already, in the *Metaphysics L1* Kant had supposed that the predicates to be demonstrated of the soul in rational psychology would be transcendental predicates (28: 265). He had not expected the theorems of rational psychology to include such claims as 'I currently have a headache', 'I fear spiders', or 'I am conscious of objects outside of me'. Nonetheless, his view remained unsatisfactory from the point of view of the critical philosophy because he had supposed that the application of certain transcendental predicates would be capable of an independent empirical verification. He had thus in effect

---

[32] They are thought of as empirical predicates insofar as they are conceived as being such that their exemplification is capable of being directly verified on the basis of experience.

[33] I take it that Kant is speaking slightly inaccurately when he says at A 478–9/B 506–7 that 'transcendental psychology' asks whether the *categories* apply to the soul.

misrepresented what he would later come to regard as pure predications of the soul as impure predications—or so his fully critical position would have held.

A second requirement Kant places on a properly pure rational psychology in the first *Critique* is that *its basis* should contain nothing empirical. He says:

> If in [the rational doctrine of the soul] the least empirical element of my thought, or any particular perception of my inner state, were still intermingled with the grounds of cognition of this science, it would no longer be a rational but an **empirical** doctrine of the soul. (A 342/B 400)

I take this to mean that any properly *pure* rational psychology would need to exclude from its foundation everything one perceived of one's particular mental goings on, including any observations one might make about the 'play' of one's thoughts (A 405/B 347). But it is clear that Kant also wishes to exclude from rational psychology's purview any putative 'natural laws of our thinking self' that we might formulate on the basis of these observations (A 405/B 347).

The requirement that rational psychology should not include any claims about mental goings on is not, I think, supposed to disqualify the rational psychology of the *Metaphysics L1* from the status a pure rational psychology by the lights of the first *Critique*. For, as we will see in the next section, the critical Kant holds that the claim 'I think' does not express an empirical claim about the soul. Moreover, since he also views this claim as equivalent to 'I am' (A 354–5), it seems safe to suppose that by the time of the first *Critique* Kant has retreated from his pre-critical view that the basis of rational psychology includes one empirical claim—namely, 'I am' (contrast 28: 263). Viewed from the perspective of Kant's critical philosophy, then, the rational psychology developed in the *Metaphysics L1* fits the profile of a pure rational psychology: its basis contains no claim that would be seen, from that later point of view, as empirical, and it attributes to the soul no predicate that would be seen, from that later point of view, as impure. Since that is so, it constitutes an appropriate target of Kant's criticisms in the Paralogisms chapter. In the light of these facts, we should not be surprised that certain of the paralogistic arguments criticized in the first *Critique* correspond to arguments that he had himself previously offered in the *Metaphysics L1* (I substantiate this point in the relevant chapters).[34]

2.8 Pure rational psychology as the science of self-consciousness

As should by now be clear, the first *Critique*'s conception of the part of rational psychology that aims at apodictic certainty, since it incorporates the requirement

---

[34] On this point I'm in full agreement with Corey Dyck. See Dyck, *Kant and Rational Psychology* at 97.

that the predicates and grounds of this putative science must be pure, differs from the conceptions of the majority of Wolffian rational psychologists.[35] And, as we have also seen, the nearest approximation to Kant's critical conception of this part of rational psychology—aside from his own view in the *Metaphysics L1*—is not Wolff's but Baumgarten's version of this science. Nonetheless, while departing from Wolff on the issue of purity, the critical Kant shares with him the idea that an apodictic rational psychology would have to be a rational science of *self-consciousness*. This idea is explicit in the critical Kant insofar as he takes rational psychology to begin from the representation of pure self-consciousness, 'I think' (B 132; A 344/B 402). It appears in Wolff's philosophy through the idea that rational psychology must proceed from the concept of *that which is conscious of itself and of other things outside itself*. Kant's affinity with Wolff on this point is confirmed in the preamble to the Paralogisms, where he raises the question of how rational psychology, as a science of specifically self-conscious beings, could aspire to be a science of thinking beings in general. He says:

> But right at the start it must seem strange that the condition under which I think in general [that is, self-consciousness or apperception], and which is therefore merely a property of my [own] subject, is at the same time to be valid for everything that thinks, and that on an empirical-seeming proposition we can presume to ground an apodictic and universal judgment, [the judgment,] namely, that everything that thinks is constituted as the claim of self-consciousness asserts of me. (A 346/B 404)

There are two components to the strangeness mentioned here, each of which generates a separate *prima facie* objection to the procedure of pure rational psychology. The first oddity is that a science purporting to contain truths about thinking beings in general should be based on anything so parochial as my own, specifically *self-conscious*, mode of thought. The second is that such a science should be grounded on the empirical-seeming judgment 'I think'—empirical seeming because the proponent of impure rational psychology regards it as expressing an empirical claim (B 421–2; cf. A 402).

Kant addresses only the first of these concerns directly. 'I cannot', he says,

> have the least representation of a thinking being through an external experience, but only through self-consciousness. Thus such objects [as other thinking beings] are nothing further than the transference [*Übertragung*] of this consciousness of

---

[35] Recall that Wolff's *rational* psychology, in addition to attempting to derive the real essence of the soul from its nominal essence, also seeks to derive the deliverances of empirical psychology from that real essence.

mine to other things, which [things] can be represented as thinking beings only in this way. (A 347)

Kant is suggesting that the reason why the science of self-conscious thinking beings amounts to a science of thinking beings in general is simply that we cannot regard a being as capable of thought unless we also regard it as self-conscious. Although, strictly speaking, Kant speaks here only of a transference of 'consciousness' rather than of 'self-consciousness', the passage is naturally read as claiming that other thinking beings are nothing beyond the transference of my peculiar kind of consciousness, *to wit self-consciousness*, to other thinking things. Since such a reading fits with Kant's taking the 'I think' to be the sole text of rational psychology, I take his position to be that I can conceive of something as a thinking being distinct from me only if I conceive of it as a *self-conscious* thinking being.

Such a position would enable the rational psychologist to extend any results they might have established about possessors of their own, specifically self-conscious, mode of thought to thinking beings in general. But it would seem to have the consequence that Kant cannot take non-human animals to be thinking beings; for he clearly regards them as lacking self-consciousness. This need not be a problem for our interpretation, however, for there is reason to think that Kant does indeed deny that non-human animals can think. In the *Metaphysics Mrongovius*, for example, he is explicit first, that all three species of thinking, namely, understanding, judgment, and reasoning, require concepts, and second, that non-human animals lack concepts. They lack them, he thinks, because they lack apperception, which is bound up with using the self-representation, 'I'—a representation whose possession is a condition of possessing concepts.[36]

Somewhat surprisingly, Kant takes his 'transference' story to be *obvious*. In the second Paralogism he says:

It is obvious that, if one wishes to represent a thinking being, one must put oneself in its place, and thus substitute one's own subject for the object one wants to consider (which is not the case in any other kind of investigation). (A 353–4)

We might fairly wonder whether this claim really is 'obvious'—there has, after all, been a lively debate between 'the simulation theory' and the 'theory-theory' in the philosophy of mind. But if we were to object to Kant's transference story, he would be entitled to respond that we thereby problematize the very idea that there could be a general science of thinking beings. For with the transference story rejected the

---

[36] See 29: 888–9 and compare 29: 878–9 and 28: 276. Kant does not, however, deny that non-human animals are capable of acting in accordance with representations. Indeed, he insists that they can do just that, and takes this point to distinguish his own position from that of Descartes. For relevant texts and for a discussion of Kant's views on animal mentality more generally see Colin McLear, 'Kant on Animal Consciousness', *Philosophers' Imprint*, 11 (15) (2011), 1–16.

worry about our overgeneralizing from a peculiarity of our own constitution will gain traction. For this reason, Kant can expect his envisaged rational-psychologist opponent to readily grant his transference story.

Before we consider how Kant addresses the second worry—the concern, namely, that the 'I think' is 'empirical seeming'—it will be convenient to examine more closely his famous claim that '**I think** is the sole text of rational psychology' (A 343/B 401). This claim invites the question: what other candidate 'texts' might one have naïvely imagined rational psychology to include, instead of, or along with, 'I think'? One candidate for an accompanying rather than displacing 'text' is the claim that the soul perceives its own body. For, as we have seen, this claim was essential to Wolff's attempted derivation of the soul's real essence from its nominal essence in *GM*. The context of Kant's 'sole text' claim, however, suggests that he has something broader in mind. The intended contrast class seems to be the whole body of claims comprising the content of run-of-the-mill empirical psychology, and especially reports of our current mental states. Thus, in the preamble to the 'sole text' remark Kant says that rational psychology would no longer be a pure science 'if the least bit of anything empirical in my thinking, *a particular perception of my inner state*, were intermingled with the grounds of cognition of this science' (A 342/B 400, emphasis added). He adds, by way of illustration, that rational psychology would be transformed into empirical psychology if 'the least object of perception (e.g., pleasure or displeasure)' were added to the general representation of self-consciousness (A 343/B 401).

The 'I think', then, is to be the sole text of (the in-intention apodictic part of) rational psychology precisely because this science—at least on Kant's conception of it—is supposed to have a wholly non-empirical basis. But what assurance do we have that the 'I think' fits this bill? How do we know that it *is* a non-empirical claim? Kant's answer to this question runs as follows:

> The reader must not object that in this proposition, which expresses the perception of the self, I have an inner experience, and that therefore the rational doctrine of the soul founded upon it is never pure and is in part grounded on an empirical principle. For this inner perception is nothing beyond the mere apperception, **I think**, which even makes possible all transcendental concepts.
> (A 342–3/B 400–1)

Here Kant is conceding that the 'I think' expresses something that might—in some sense—be described as an 'inner perception'.[37] But he is also denying that this fact undermines the claim of (apodictic) rational psychology—as he conceives of it—to be a *pure* science. Why so? How does labelling what is expressed by the 'I think'

---

[37] At times Kant seems to state this concession quite strongly. At A 848/B 876, for example, he characterizes the 'I think' as an 'empirically inner representation'.

'mere apperception' enable us to resist the conclusion that when I judge 'I think' I self-ascribe an empirical predicate? The continuation of this passage, though suggestive, cannot be said to answer this question definitively:

> Inner experience as such and its possibility, or perception as such and its relation to other perception, without any particular distinction or determination of such inner experience or perception being given empirically, cannot be regarded as empirical cognition; it must rather be regarded as cognition of the empirical as such and it belongs to the inquiry into the possibility of any experience—an inquiry that is indeed transcendental. (A 343/B 401)

Kant's idea would seem to be that the 'I think' furnishes us with nothing beyond some highly indeterminate experience, namely: the awareness of inner experience or inner perception as such. This awareness is insufficiently determinate to count as cognition proper, and for that reason fails to compromise the purity of a rational psychology founded on the 'I think'—or so Kant seems to think.

A remark that occurs only in the B edition enlarges on this idea. 'I would not say', Kant explains,

> that the I [in the proposition 'I think'] is an empirical representation, for it is rather purely intellectual because it belongs to thinking in general. Without some empirical representation to supply the material [*Stoff*] for the thought, the *actus*, 'I think', would not, indeed, take place; but the empirical is only the condition of the application, or of the employment of the pure intellectual faculty.
> (B 422, note*)

Experience, then, stands to the exercise of the pure intellectual faculty as clay stands to the exercise of the potter's skill: it constitutes the material on which the thinking agent operates in exercising that faculty. Accordingly, what the 'I think' expresses (in the first instance, at least) is just an *act* that constitutes an exercise of the pure intellectual faculty 'of thinking in general'. But because this act requires for its performance that the mind performing it should have some experience or other on which to operate, in a derivative sense it expresses 'an indeterminate empirical intuition, i.e., [a] perception' (B 422–3). The perception in question is indeterminate because what the 'I think' expresses is not any particular empirical intuition but rather the general fact that some empirical intuition is being had. The 'I think' succeeds in expressing this fact simply because the report of the performance of an action signals the obtaining of the known enabling conditions for that action. If, for example, I say 'I did some pottery yesterday', then, if you believe me, you understand that I operated on some clay, and so my statement expresses the presence to me yesterday of clay. It appears that Kant is assuming it to be as widely known that thought requires experience as that pottery requires clay. This assumption may be wrong, of course, but the important point for our purposes is just the following. Since according to Kant what is expressed by the 'I think' is not a perception of the soul or self that acts but rather the fact of experience in general, the 'I think' can be considered (as far as its relation to the self goes) to be a wholly pure representation and so an appropriate basis for a distinctively pure apodictic rational psychology.[38]

This helps somewhat, but a stubborn doubt remains. Surely, one supposes, when one acts with the consciousness of doing so, one is at some level aware of the existence of the author of one's action. And the question then arises why the self-awareness expressed by the 'I think', and performed in the act of 'determining my existence' (B 157), should not therefore amount to an inward *perception* of the acting, determining self. Kant answers this question in the *B* edition: 'The consciousness of myself in the representation I', he says, 'is not intuition at all, but a merely **intellectual** representation of the self-activity of a thinking subject' (B 278). In a note to the *B*-edition preface he goes further and speaks of an '**intellectual consciousness** of my existence' expressed by the representation '**I am**' (B xl).[39] This suggests that in the *B* edition Kant takes each of us to have an intellectual consciousness of both our self-activity and our existence.

Kant, however, fails to explain what this 'intellectual consciousness' could amount to if it is not a state of cognition—as it *cannot* be given his view that we have no intuition of the acting, determining self (B 407, compare A 402).[40] Since he seems to be positing an epistemic state that has no official place in his epistemology, Kant's position, at this point, seems precarious. It should therefore come as no surprise that, for a while at least, he strives to avoid this commitment. In the *Prolegomena*, for example, he experiments with the idea that the I is (or expresses) a mere *feeling*.[41] He says:

> If the representation of apperception, **the I**, were a concept through which anything might be thought, it could then be used as a predicate for other things, or contain such predicates in itself. But it is nothing more than a feeling of an existence [*Gefühl eines Daseins*] without the least concept, and is only a representation of that to which all thinking stands in relation (*relatione accidentis*).
>
> (*Prolegomena*, §46, note, 4: 334)

---

[38] On this point I agree with Henry Allison. See Henry Allison, *Kant's Transcendental Idealism: An Interpretation and Defense* (New Haven: Yale University Press, 2004) at 354.

[39] Relatedly, in a late reflection Kant remarks: 'The "I am" is not an experiential proposition' (R 6316, 1790–91, 18: 623).

[40] Kant grants that in inner sense I *do* intuit the *determined* self—that is, the self as it appears to itself. I can intuit the self as thinking that p, desiring that q, and so forth.

[41] In making this suggestion Kant seems to be drawing on the resources of a tradition. For helpful discussions of 'feeling-of-self' theories of inner sense and consciousness see Udo Thiel, 'Varieties of Inner Sense: Two Pre-Kantian Theories', *Archiv für Geschichte der Philosophie*, 79 (79) (1997), 58–79. Also see Patricia Kitcher, *Kant's Thinker* (Oxford: Oxford University Press, 2011) at 62–5.

In both editions of the first *Critique* Kant maintains that feeling [*Gefühl*] 'is not a power for the representation of things, *but lies outside the cognitive power altogether*' (A 801/B 829 note, emphasis added).[42] Kant's position in the *Prolegomena* would therefore seem to involve denying that what the word 'I' expresses has the status of a cognition. This is a more forthright position than the one he adopts in the B edition, where the word 'consciousness' seems to serve as a rug under which to hide an awkward tension, namely, the point that although we cannot intuit the soul as it is in itself, we can nonetheless know that it acts and exists.

2.9 The critique of pure rational psychology

In the A edition Kant suggests that associated with the unity of apperception is the illusion 'of taking the unity in the synthesis of thoughts for a perceived unity in the subject of these thoughts' (A 402). He adds that one could call this illusion 'the subreption of a hypostatized consciousness' (ibid.). As Dyck has observed, in this context Kant is attaching a Wolffian sense to the term 'subreption'. In his *Philosophia Rationalis sive Logica* ('*Latin Logic*') Wolff describes a '*vitium subreptionis in experiundo*' (a fallacy of subreption in what is to be tested or proved) as an instance in which 'we seem to experience that which we do not experience in the least'.[43]

The label 'subreption' is aptly applied to the error arising from the illusion that Kant takes to lie behind dogmatic rational psychology because he supposes that we take ourselves to experience the unity of the subject—a unity that is understood as consisting in its instantiating the category of substance—when all we in fact

---

[42] Compare A 49/B 66.

[43] Christian Wolff, *Philosophia Rationalis sive Logica*, 3 vols (3rd edn, Christian Wolff, *Gesammelte Werke*, Pt. 2. Lateinische Schriften, 1; Hildesheim: Olms, 1983b) at §668. See Dyck, *Kant and Rational Psychology* at 86, and Hanno Birken-Bertsch, *Subreption und Dialektik bei Kant: Der Begriff des Fehlers der Erschleichung in der Philosophie des 18. Jahrhunderts* (Stuttgart: Frommann-Holzboog, 2006) at 49, note 130. More generally, by a 'subreption' Kant means an instance of the fallacy known as '*vitium subreptionis*' (literally, the vice of pilfering). One commits this fallacy when one mistakes a thing of one kind for a thing of another kind. Kant's examples often involve cases in which something subjective is wrongly mistaken for something objective, for example, when a judgment of perception is mistaken for a judgment of experience (24: 767), or when a concept—'the subjective of thinking'—is mistaken for a thing—'the objective of what is thought' (*Real Progress*, 20: 349). Kant also explains the fallacy of '*vitium subreptionis*' as the fallacy from which there arises 'the mixing of concepts of experience and of reason' (*Blomberg Logic*; §255; 24: 254–5), and here by a 'concept of reason' he means a pure concept of the understanding. One commits this fallacy when, for example, one wrongly takes the concept of cause and effect to be derived from experience (ibid.). In the *Inaugural Dissertation* Kant suggests that the reverse error—that of taking a 'sensitive concept' for a pure concept of the understanding—also counts as an instance of the subreptive fallacy (2: 412). There, however, he is explicit that he means to be using the term only by analogy with its accepted meaning. Finally, a *transcendental* subreption is the error of taking a thing of one kind (and usually something subjective) for a thing of another kind (and usually something objective) where this error is grounded in transcendental illusion.

perceive, or more correctly 'judge', is a certain unity in our thoughts: the unity of apperception, which itself consists in all of our thoughts' belonging to one subject.[44] In a reflection from the late 1770s or early 1780s, Kant portrays the phenomenon of paralogism as an instance of this kind of subreption. 'The paralogism of pure reason', he says, 'is properly a transcendental subreption [*Subreption*], since our judgment about objects and the unity of consciousness in them is held to be a perception [*Wahrnehmung*] of the unity of the subject' (R 5553; 18: 223). In the B edition he goes further and portrays this mistake as nothing short of the original sin of rational psychology. 'Rational psychology', he says,

> has its origin in a mere misunderstanding. The unity of consciousness, which grounds the categories, is here taken for an intuition of the subject as an object, and the category of substance applied to it. (B 421–2)

This remark makes clear that to think of the subject as a 'unity' is, in the first instance, to think of it as exemplifying the category of substance. The misunderstanding in question consists in wrongly taking the unity of consciousness to be an intuition of an object, namely, the thinking, *determining* self (the self as it is in itself), which one then judges to be a substance. This is a mistake because the self that we can intuit as an object is only the *determinable* self (the self as it appears to itself).

But why should the mistaken belief that we are able to *perceive* the determining self as a substance amount to the founding error of pure *rational* psychology? Why isn't it just a mistake in empirical psychology? The answer, I think, is that, once made, this mistake about what we can perceive encourages another: we come to suppose that certain of the proofs given in pure rational psychology meet the constraint on legitimate pure rational psychology laid down in the *Metaphysics L1*—the constraint, namely, that this science may show the soul to possess only such features as are perceived to hold of it in empirical psychology. The problem is that since we imagine ourselves to perceive the soul to be a substance we also imagine that we can demonstrate this fact a priori in pure rational psychology.

We are nearly ready to delve a little further into Kant's conception of the method of dogmatic rational psychology, but before we do so it would be well to consider a rival reading of his discussion at B 421–2. This (possible) interpretation maintains that Kant takes dogmatic rational psychology to go wrong for the much simpler reason that it takes as part of its basis certain empirical propositions

---

[44] This unity is an instance of what Kant calls 'the unity of the multiplicity', which in this case consists in the unity of the predicates in a subject. See R 4385, 1771 (17: 528).

that purport to describe our perceptions of certain features of the self that the critical Kant takes to be expressed by pure predicates.[45] I have two doubts about this reading. First, to level such a charge seems fundamentally to mischaracterize Wolffian rational psychology. For as we have seen, in Wolff's view, rational psychology includes within its basis only such empirical propositions as are *indubitable*. And yet the simplicity and substantiality of the soul, for example, do not seem to have this status. Second, in the first *Critique* Kant presents various claims about the intrinsic nature of the soul—claims which correspond to the conclusions of the paralogistic arguments—as figuring among the alleged *fruits* of dogmatic rational psychology rather than, as the rival reading would have it, as belonging to its basis.

2.10 Two ways of proceeding in pure rational psychology

In the B edition Kant sketches two contrasting procedures [*Verfahren*] in accordance with which pure rational psychology might be developed (B 416-19). According to the 'synthetic' procedure, one begins with a concept of the soul, taken 'problematically'—that is, considered without prejudice to its implicit claim to be exemplified—and then proceeds to derive from this concept certain features that the soul would have to have if it were to exist. Only once this investigation is complete does one argue for the soul's existence (B 416-17). According to the 'analytic' procedure, by contrast, one begins with knowledge of the existence of the soul and seeks to extract from the representation 'I think' various results about what pertains to a thinking being in general (B 418-19). In the process, one is supposed to gain knowledge of the character of something already known to exist.[46]

It is clear that in the A edition Kant conceives of pure rational psychology as developed only in accordance with the synthetic procedure. The proposition 'I think', he tells us, is taken in rational psychology

> only problematically; not insofar as it may contain a perception of an existence (the Cartesian 'I think, therefore I am' <cogito, ergo sum>), but only in its mere

---

[45] Dyck sometimes seems to recommend such a reading, though, since I am not altogether clear about the precise sense in which he takes Wolffian rational psychology to 'rest on' experience, I'm not certain that he endorses it.

[46] The present distinction is *not* an application of Wolff's distinction between analytic and synthetic methods to the science of the soul. Wolff takes the analytic method to follow the order of actual and possible discovery, the synthetic to involve arranging truths in their natural hierarchy 'according as one can be more easily understood and demonstrated from another'. (See *Latin Logic*, Part 3, §885.) Both of Kant's procedures count as analytic in Wolff's sense.

possibility, in order to see which properties pertaining to its subject might flow from so simple a proposition (whether that subject be existent or not).

(A 347/B 405)[47]

To say that in rational psychology the proposition 'I think' is 'taken' only problematically is to say that one conceives of the 'I think' as merely expressing the *concept* of a self-conscious thinking being—a concept that, for all that is known to us at the outset, may or may not be exemplified. In pursuing the synthetic procedure with respect to this concept, one asks what might be obtained from this concept by analysis and logical reasoning. It is only after one has derived a number of claims about the kind of thing a self-conscious thinking being would be, if it existed, that one attempts to demonstrate its existence.

Unfortunately, Kant says nothing in the first *Critique* to indicate which philosophers he regards as having employed the synthetic procedure.[48] Concerning the analytic procedure, however, it seems possible that he'd take one of its practitioners to have been his own former self in the *Metaphysics L1*. For there he presents the rational psychologist as taking himself to perceive the existence of the soul in inner sense (28: 263). This suggestion, however, can only be tentative, for in the relevant passage Kant says nothing definite about the order in which the soul's existence and properties are cognized.

This completes our preliminary examination of dogmatic rational psychology. We have seen that the classic conception of this science is owed to Wolff, who is prepared to include empirical claims within its basis, but only so long as they are indubitable. Kant's own conception of rational psychology in the *Metaphysics L1* shares this feature with Wolff's; for he includes the claim 'I am'—viewed as both empirical and indubitable—within the basis of this science. But it also departs from Wolff's insofar it treats the concept from which rational psychology is to proceed as the concept of *the I* rather than Wolff's concept of *that which is conscious of itself and of other things outside it*. The Kant of the *Metaphysics L1* also differs from Wolff in treating rational psychology as governed by a constraint that is tantamount to the converse of Wolff's. While Wolff holds that a legitimate rational psychology must be able to demonstrate of the soul *all* those intrinsic features that are independently noted of it in empirical psychology, the Kant of the

---

[47] In Chapter 8 we will see reason to think that this is not the conception of the *B* edition; so the retention of this statement in that edition should be attributed merely to Kant's failure to make the needed revision.

[48] It is tempting to suppose that Kant might have regarded the Wolffians as employing the synthetic procedure, but the temptation is better resisted. For Kant assumes that an attempted proof of the soul's existence would have formed the final part of a *rational* psychology developed in accordance with the synthetic method. Yet, as we have seen, Wolff and his followers present their proofs of the soul's existence at the start of their *empirical* psychologies. See Wolff, *PE*, §§14–21; Baumgarten, *Metaphysics*, §504; Meier, *Metaphysics*, volume 3, §§480–1; and Ludwig Philipp Thümmig, *Institutiones Philosophiae Wolffianae in usus academicos adornate*, 2 vols (1; Frankfurt am Main and Leipzig: Renger, 1725–6) at Part 3, §§8–9.

Metaphysics L1 holds that a legitimate rational psychology can demonstrate *only* those same features. Finally, I have suggested that in the first *Critique* Kant sees dogmatic rational psychology as founded on the original sin of supposing that we intuit or perceive the soul precisely because he takes this belief to encourage the view that certain of the soul's intrinsic features will be independently demonstrable in rational psychology. I take the critical Kant to see this mistake as arising in different ways in the cases of Wolff and the pre-critical Kant. In the former case, he supposes that the belief that we intuit or perceive the soul produces the further belief that the features in question *must* be provable of the soul in rational psychology. In the latter case, he supposes that this same belief produces the belief these same features *may* be so proved. In consequence, since owing to transcendental illusion we imagine that we perceive the character of the soul, we also suppose it either obligatory (Wolff) or permissible (pre-critical Kant) to derive certain substantive conclusions about the soul a priori either from the concept that expresses the soul's real essence (Wolff) or from the concept of the thinking I (Kant). In the next six chapters we will examine Kant's criticisms in the Paralogisms chapter of various attempts to provide these (in ambition) a priori arguments.

3
The First Paralogism
Preliminaries

3.1 Introduction

The paralogisms are four arguments by means of which the dogmatic rational psychologist seeks to establish certain substantive claims about the soul. More precisely, they are four (in intention) categorical syllogisms—or, as Kant's terms them, 'inferences of reason [*Vernunftschlüsse*]'—which the rational psychologist views as sound, but which Kant views either as (a) invalid, (b) valid-but-not-known-to-be-sound, or (c) sound-but-establishing-a-conclusion-too-weak-to-be-of-interest. The claims they seek to establish are, for the most part, relevant to the question of the soul's ability to survive bodily death—a question that itself bears on, though it is not identical with, that of the soul's natural immortality.[1] These arguments conceive of the soul as the subject of thought, something that Kant calls 'the thinking I'. Collectively, they purport to demonstrate that the subject of thought is: a substance, simple (that is, not a plurality or group mind), a person, and, finally, aware of the objects of outer sense, not directly, but only by means of a 'doubtful'—by which Kant means not wholly reliable—inference.

In Kant's view, owing to a certain 'one-sided' instance of transcendental illusion, we are predisposed to accept the conclusions of these arguments even prior to their being rehearsed. The instance of transcendental illusion in question is the illusion that a certain subjective unity of our representations is an objective unity in the soul. This illusion counts as 'one-sided' because, unlike the illusion lying behind the antinomies, its products are a set of conclusions all of which tend in the same direction, namely, towards the family of dogmas characteristic of 'pneumatism'—the doctrine that the subject is an immaterial thinking substance capable of existing and being conscious without a body—in short, a 'spirit' in the traditional sense of that word (20: 309). I say that these arguments *tend towards* pneumatism because they argue for conclusions compatible with this doctrine even if they do not amount collectively to a statement of it.

---

[1] In the *Critique of Practical Reason*, Kant presents reason's efforts to grapple with the problem of immortality as generating nothing but paralogisms (5: 133).

Kant's treatment of the paralogisms is not without its growing pains. And it is not surprising that in the second edition he subjects the Paralogisms chapter to a comprehensive overhaul. Although he tries to downplay the importance of the changes he makes, portraying them as merely cosmetic changes in 'the manner of exposition' (B xxxviii), they are in truth significant and substantive. Nowhere is this more obvious than in the first Paralogism, where Kant's critical analysis changes dramatically between the two editions; nowhere is it more important than in the second Paralogism, where Kant comes to regard as flatly false his A-edition claim that one of the argument's crucial premises—the so-called *nervus probandi*—lacks grounds (for details see Chapter 6).

In the first edition he officially portrays the paralogisms as committing a fallacy of equivocation—the fallacy known as *sophisma figurae dictionis* (A 402). In practice, however, in this same edition Kant treats the first paralogism as vitiated—though not in our sense invalidated—by what we'd now regard as the informal fallacy of '*ignoratio elenchi*' ('ignorance of the refutation'). This fallacy arises when one of the participants in an academic disputation gets confused about *which* thesis is to be established and ends up arguing for a claim weaker than the one he was supposed to prove.[2] Since the disputant who makes this mistake remains ignorant of his error, he commits a fallacy of misinterpretation—and indeed, of *overestimation*—of what he has proved.[3] In the second edition, the A-edition analysis, which portrays the paralogism actually stated as sound, is replaced with one that conforms with Kant's official diagnosis of paralogisms as *sophismata figurae dictionis*. That is to say, in the second edition the paralogism is treated as involving a fallacy of equivocation on the apparent middle term of what would otherwise be a valid first-figure syllogism (in an expanded Aristotelian logic that recognizes as valid certain arguments containing singular minor premises).[4] This change is so obviously substantive that one has to wonder whether Kant is being quite honest when he portrays the changes between the two editions, which involve the paralogisms among other chapters, as concerning merely the manner of exposition (B xxxviii–xlii). My colleague, Roy Sorensen, recently asked me whether Kant ever told an outright lie: the present case affords the best evidence I know supporting an affirmative answer. To defend Kant, one would have to

---

[2] The method of disputation relevant here (and elsewhere in this book) is the so-called 'argument' method, where one attacks one's opponent by trying to demonstrate the negation of their thesis. This contrasts with the 'question' method, where one attempts to trap one's opponent by asking them questions until they give contradictory answers. This way of framing the distinction between kinds of disputation is owed to Fredericus Heine. For a discussion see, Ignacio Angelelli, 'The Techniques of Disputation in the History of Logic', *Journal of Philosophy*, 67 (20) (3) (1970), 800–15 at 801.

[3] The fallacy of '*ignoratio elenchi*' is thus aptly so-called because it is a fallacy arising from ignorance of what would suffice to refute one's opponent in a disputation.

[4] I call the middle term 'apparent' because such an argument, strictly speaking, has no middle term since it contains no univocal term common to both premises. In the logical tradition, an argument of this kind is regarded as having four terms. Kant shows his allegiance to this tradition when he says that such an argument 'walks on four feet [*geht auf vier Füßen*]' (8: 197).

insist either that he draws the line between expository and substantive changes very differently from how we do today, or that when he makes his claim about the manner of exposition he is standing back from his book and considering his claims at an extremely high level of abstraction. I'll leave the reader to decide whether they find such defences convincing.

3.2 Substance

In the *B* edition Kant maintains that transcendental illusion inevitably produces in rational minds a standing temptation to believe that the soul (understood as the subject of thoughts or thinking I) is a substance in the sense of 'something that can exist only as **subject**, not as a mere determination of other things'.[5] A substance in this sense is a necessarily non-inhering subject of inherence. It is a thing or object rather than a judgmental component—a thing that *cannot* inhere in another thing as a determination of it. And by a 'determination' in this context Kant means, not a judgmental component occurring in predicate position but rather either a property that inheres in *one* other thing as an accident of it or a configuration that inheres in a *plurality* of other things as what we might call a 'complex' composed of those things.[6] By 'complexes' I understand relatively straightforward composite objects, such as molecules, along with more recondite metaphysical entities such as fists.[7] In the *B* edition Kant adds that a substance is something that *need not* inhere in another thing as a determination because it is a 'self-**subsisting being**' (B 407; cf. B 412, B 149).

I take it that Kant intends to be speaking of substance in this sense whenever he invokes what commentators have come to call the 'unschematized' category of substance. But he also appeals to a distinct concept of substance corresponding to the 'schematized' category. This is the concept of something that 'persists' (A 144/B 183, A 182) in the sense of existing at every moment (A 182). For convenience, I will follow Jonathan Bennett's convention of calling the first of these notions 'substance$_1$', the second 'substance$_2$'.[8] Kant employs only a single term—'*Substanz*'—for both notions, but he is not prone to conflate them.

In the *B* edition Kant claims that in the 'General Note on the System of Principles' (B 288–94) and the chapter on Phenomena and Noumena,

---

[5] Compare B 407, B 288; *MFNS* 4: 503, and *On a Discovery* (8: 225).

[6] In the *Metaphysics Herder* Kant takes composition to be an accident (28: 48). It is the manner in which a *plurality* of substances exists: a way in which the members of the plurality are configured. This idea represents a broadening of Kant's official understanding of 'accident', namely, as a particular way of existing of a (single) substance (A 186/B 229).

[7] My notion of a 'complex' corresponds to James Van Cleve's notion of a 'mode'. See James Van Cleve, *Problems from Kant* (Oxford: Oxford University Press, 1999) at 105.

[8] Jonathan Bennett, *Kant's Analytic* (Cambridge: Cambridge University Press, 1966) at 182.

it was proved that the concept of a thing that can exist for itself as subject but not as mere predicate [*als bloßes Prädikat*] as yet [*noch*] carries with it no objective reality at all, i.e., that one cannot know [*Wissen*] whether it can apply [*zukommen könne*] to any object, since one has no insight into the possibility of such a way of existing, and consequently that it yields absolutely no cognition [*Erkenntnis*].

(B 412)

As the word '*noch*' indicates, Kant is telling us that we cannot *yet* have the knowledge in question. I take this to mean that we cannot have such knowledge so long as we limit ourselves to the customary pre-critical a priori resources (that is, logic, definitions, and the PSR). In Kant's view, in order to know that the concept of substance₁ has application we would rather need to provide a proof that experience is possible only if there is substance₂. And Kant, of course, takes himself to provide such a proof in the first Analogy.⁹ One supposes that the exemplification of the concept of *substance₁* would then follow because the way in which a substance₁ exists within experience is just as some part of the sum-total of substance₂.

3.3 Transcendental illusion in the first Paralogism

How are we to apply Kant's model of transcendental illusion to the appearance that the soul is a substance₁? One way to do so, I think, would be to arrive at a plausible specification of the series of conditions that reason might, in this case, be supposed to enjoin us to complete.¹⁰ In the case of the world's existence in time the relevant series was the series of temporally ordered states of the world. In the present case, a very different series would have to be involved. But what kind of entities would make it up? In the first *Critique* Kant's view on this matter is hard to discern, but in the *Prolegomena* he states it clearly:

> Pure reason demands that for each predicate of a thing we should seek its own [*zugehöriges*] subject, but that for this subject, which is in turn necessarily only a predicate, we should seek its subject again, and so forth to infinity (or as far as we

---

[9] I am grateful to Ralf Bader for alerting me to the significance in this context of the word '*noch*'. The alternative reading, according to which the awaited extra resource would be an intuition of the permanent as permanent, is contraindicated simply because the permanent cannot be perceived as permanent by something within time.

[10] If we suppose that the Rational Psychologist believes that something's possessing a single fundamental power requires its being a single substance₁, then a second way of applying Kant's diagnosis of how transcendental illusion operates—taking that diagnosis now on its broadest construal—might run through the account we gave in Chapter 1 of how the demand for ideological parsimony can, through a confusion of a prescription with a descriptive claim, generate the belief that the soul has a single fundamental power.

get). But from this it follows that we should take nothing that we can attain for an ultimate [*letztes*] subject, and that the substantial itself could never be thought by our ever-so-deeply penetrating understanding, even if the whole of nature were laid bare before it.   (§46, 4: 333)[11]

Pure reason demands that we strive to complete a series in which each apparent subject is conceived of as (really) a predicate of some further subject conditioning or grounding it.[12] Kant is clear that the regressive series of conditions in question here is supposed to stand on all fours with the various regressive series comprehended under the 'cosmological Idea' (*the world*). He makes this point in passing when, as it happens, denying that the 'theological Idea' (*God*) generates a similar series:

> [In the case of the theological idea] reason does not, *as with the psychological and the cosmological idea*, start from experience and become seduced by the ascending sequence of grounds into aspiring, if possible, to absolute completeness in their series, but instead breaks off entirely from experience and descends from bare concepts of what would constitute the absolute completeness of a thing in general... to the determination of the possibility, hence the actuality, of all other things.   (*Prolegomena*, §55, 4: 348, emphasis added)

The passage quoted from *Prolegomena* §46 makes clear which kind of regressive or 'ascending' series Kant has in mind in connection with the self: it is a series of ever more fundamental subjects of inherence.[13] However, although helpful, the

---

[11] Here one expects 'cognized' or 'known' rather than 'thought'. And there is reason to think that this is indeed what Kant means. For there are other occasions on which he uses 'thought' for 'cognized' or 'known'. In the 'Amphiboly of the Concepts of Reflection', for example, he says, 'If by merely intelligible objects we understand those things that are *thought* through pure categories, without any schema of sensibility, then things of this sort are impossible' (A 286/B 342, emphasis added). Here 'thought' cannot mean 'conceived' because Kant does not deny the conceivability of noumena (see A 256/B 311). He must rather mean 'cognized' or 'known'. He seems to have eventually become conscious of this quirk of his usage because in his marginal notes in his own copy of the first edition he suggests that the passage from A 286 be corrected to read 'cognized by us' rather than 'thought' (23: 49).

[12] This conception has a precedent in Baumgarten's view of composites as capable of being regarded both as accidents and also (by courtesy) as bearers of accidents. 'A composite substance', Baumgarten says, 'can exist only as a collection of other substances posited mutually outside of one another and composed in a certain way. Therefore, it can exist only as a determination of others. Therefore, it is an accident, and, if it seems to subsist by itself and if a power is attributed to it, then this is a substantiated phenomenon' (*Metaphysics* §233). Baumgarten believes that accidents can exist only in substances or in aggregates of them (*Metaphysics* §194). For him, composite substances, while they appear to be substances, are in truth merely accidents, which entails that they inhere in other things. They may also have powers attributed to them (presumably by courtesy), so they are (or at least seem to be) inhered in by other things. They are, therefore, excellent candidates to play the role of the non-terminal members of the series Kant sketches in the *Prolegomena*.

[13] Accidents, which Kant usually refers to simply as 'determinations', can be considered 'subjects' relative to further, less fundamental, accidents that inhere in them: they are 'comparative' rather than 'absolute' subjects.

passage is also potentially misleading. For it seems to suggest that Kant is considering a demand of reason that might be expressed by the injunction: 'For each subject, seek another in which the first inheres as a predicate.' But although Kant's words do suggest such a picture, it cannot be quite what he intends. For such an injunction, since it implies that we should never take ourselves to have arrived at an ultimate subject, would tend to generate in humans the belief that there is *no* ultimate subject, and hence that nothing—not even the self—is a substance$_1$. But such a belief is obviously not Kant's intended target in the first Paralogism.

A better story would, I think, run as follows. For each subject we encounter, we are enjoined to seek some ultimate subject in which the associated regressive series of subjects terminates. Accordingly, we must try to construe each subject we encounter as in turn a 'predicate' (that is, a property or a complex) of something else (or some other things), hoping as we do so that at some stage our attempt will fail precisely because we will have arrived at an ultimate subject. In obeying this injunction we will, of course, be acting as if we are trying to show that there are no ultimate subjects; but we will be doing so only as a means to discovering a subject that resists our efforts to construe it as a predicate of another thing. Our ultimate goal, then, will be to discover an ultimate—or 'absolute'—subject. Understanding the injunction in this way yields the satisfactory result that the dogmatic belief that we form when deceived by the relevant instance of transcendental illusion is the belief that the soul or thinking I is a substance$_1$. We do so because we confuse the injunction of reason associated with the Transcendental Idea of the soul—a regulative principle— with a constitutive claim, namely, that the soul exists as an ultimate subject—a 'substance$_1$'. The continuation of the discussion suggests that this is indeed the right picture:

> Now it does appear as if we have something substantial in the consciousness of ourselves (in the thinking subject), and indeed have it in an immediate intuition; for all the predicates of inner sense are referred to the I as subject, and this cannot again be thought as the predicate of some other subject. It therefore appears that in this case completeness in the referring of the given concepts to a subject as predicates is not a mere idea, but that the object, namely the **absolute subject** itself, is given in experience. But this expectation is disappointed [*vereitelt*].
>
> (*Prolegomena*, §46, 4: 334)

Here Kant is suggesting that in the case of at least one series generated by the relation of subsistence and inherence—namely, the series associated with the Idea of the soul—pure reason's injunction to seek an ultimate subject inclines us to form the belief that there is such a thing. In the soul we seem to have a subject that cannot be conceived of as a predicate—that is, accident—of another thing.[14] The soul, in other words, seems to be an 'absolute subject'. But this appearance, he adds, gives rise to an expectation that is 'disappointed'. For, although we *are* aware of the soul as it appears in inner sense, this awareness amounts only to knowledge that something in us is the subject of our states of considering, willing, desiring, intending, and so forth. We do not know that this subject is a substance$_1$.

Why is our expectation disappointed? Not, surely, because introspection reveals that we are *not* substances$_1$. For if introspection did reveal such a thing, it would, contrary to Kant's view, reveal something substantive (if negative), about the nature of the soul as it is in itself. And, in any case, since Kant holds that each of us is transcendentally illuded, when we peer into ourselves we will, on his own telling, all *seem* to find there an absolute subject (that is, a substance$_1$). His theory, then, predicts that we will not be disappointed in *this* way. It seems that if we are disappointed, it must be on theoretical rather than introspective grounds. But on which grounds exactly?

Here is one possible story. Suppose we were to accept Kant's point that if, *per impossibile*, we were to veridically perceive the soul as a substance$_1$ then this could only be as a consequence of having an intuition of the soul as falling under the *schematized* category of substance, and so as permanent. We might then reason as follows. Even if we could perform the (apparently psychologically impossible) feat of keeping our mind's eye introspectively focused on a single object of inner sense for an entire lifetime, this would still not suffice to verify the permanence of the object so intuited; for permanence requires lasting forever, while our experience lasts only for a lifetime. By thus reflecting on what it would take for something to appear to inner sense as a substance$_1$ we come to appreciate that such an appearance is not to be had. It is in this way that we are disappointed.

Since this suggestion relies on certain of Kant's own (critical) commitments, it is worth noting that we can also tell an alternative story, which assumes only pre-critical commitments. Recall that on Kant's conception of rational psychology in the *Metaphysics L1* there is no obstacle to our deriving a priori from the soul's concept such and so many of its features as we perceive of it in empirical psychology. That being so, if our efforts to derive the soul's substantiality$_1$ a priori from its concept are repeatedly frustrated, this will undermine our naïve assumption that we introspect this feature. A single failure will not, of course, be decisive, but the evidence for our not perceiving this feature will build with each qualitatively distinct failed attempt at a derivation. Our expectation that we perceive the

---

[14] As Heiner F. Klemme notes, Crusius had defined the notion of an 'absolute subject' in a similar way, though omitting the needed modality. 'An absolute subject', Crusius says, 'would be that which would not again subsist in another thing'. For details see Heiner F. Klemme, *Kants Philosophie des Subjekts: Systematische und Entwicklungsgeschichtliche Untersuchungen zum Verhältnis von Selbstbewußtsein und Selbsterkenntnis* (Hamburg: Felix Meiner, 1996) at 312, n88.

substantiality₁ of the soul, will thus be disappointed if, after repeated attempts, we find that we cannot prove this result on a priori grounds in rational psychology.

The theory of transcendental illusion predicts that each person, insofar as they are finite and rational, will be predisposed to believe that they are a substance₁. But Kant supposes that in practice we will yield to this inclination only when it is accompanied by the specious reasoning of the first paralogism. The next two chapters are devoted to examining this paralogism, but before we do so, it will be useful to get clearer about what exactly Kant takes a 'paralogism' to be.

3.4 Kant's notion of a paralogism

It is a simple matter to say what Kant takes the arguments grouped under the heading of 'The Paralogisms of Pure Reason' to have in common. They are, first, categorical syllogisms (A 405–6/B 432–3) that are false 'in respect of form' [*der Form nach*] (A 341/B 399), and, second, inferences in which our inferring falsely has a transcendental ground (A 341/B 399).[15] It is a less simple matter, however, to say what it is for an argument to be 'false in respect of form'. I will argue that this notion turns out to be broader than the modern notion of a 'formally invalid' argument.[16]

The term Kant uses for a syllogism is '*Vernunftschluß*', literally an 'inference of reason'. As we will see shortly, he divides *Vernunftschlüße* into those that are false in respect of form and those that are correct in form but false in respect of matter. In the *Jäsche Logic* he characterizes fallacies (*fallacia*) as those inferences that, while being false in respect of form give the illusion of not being so (§90, 9: 134–5). And, in these same lectures, he divides fallacies in this sense into 'paralogisms', on the one hand, and 'sophisms', on the other, where a fallacy counts as a paralogism insofar as one deceives oneself through it (unintentionally, of course), but as a sophism insofar as by its means one intentionally seeks to deceive another (ibid.).

This characterization, which treats *paralogism* and *sophism* as mutually exclusive concepts, is, I think, a poor guide to Kant's use of the term 'paralogism' in the first *Critique*. It seems to derive from Wolff, who in the second part of his *Latin Logic* distinguishes between two kinds of syllogism that possess a defect of form. On the one hand, there are sophisms, in which the defect is concealed and, on the other, paralogisms in which it lies open to view.[17] An argument that contains a

---

[15] As I noted in my 2010, Kant does not reserve the term 'paralogism' for arguments about the self. See Proops, 'Kant's First Paralogism', 468.

[16] An argument is formally invalid in the usual contemporary sense just in case it is schematized by no valid schema. And a schema is valid if and only if it has no interpretation that makes all of its premises true and its conclusion false.

[17] Wolff, *Philosophia Rationalis* at §635. The same distinction is offered as a classification of fallacies by J. P. Reusch in his *Systema Logicum*, orig. pub. 1734, in Christian Wolff, *Gesammelte Werke, Materialien und Dokumente*, 3 abt, volume 26 (Hildesheim: Olms, 1990), §733.

concealed fallacy, obviously, is suitable for deceiving others, while one where the fallacy is patent would be unsuited to sophistry and would likely be committed only unwittingly by a novice.

Although the present contrast is the one by means of which Kant introduces the notion of a paralogism in the *Jäsche Logic*—the transcription of his logic lectures often held to be the most authoritative—it cannot be the classification that guides his use of the term 'paralogism' in the first *Critique*. For there Kant treats *paralogism* and *sophism* as overlapping categories. 'The paralogism in the dialectical syllogisms of the rational doctrine of the soul', he says, 'is a *sophisma figurae dictionis*' ('a sophism of a figure of speech') (A 402). In the view of the critical Kant, then, some paralogisms are sophisms. Does Kant regard a paralogism as a species of sophism or the reverse? On the plausible assumption that Kant, insofar as his usage on this point departs from Wolff's, is following the usage of Wolff's *disciples*, we would have to rule in favour of the latter alternative. For all three of Feder, Baumgarten, and Meier treat a sophism as a species of paralogism.

Thus, for example, in his *Logic and Metaphysics*, Feder says:

A defective inference [*Fehlschluß*] (*Paralogismus*) in general is an inference in which the consequence (*Form, Schlußart*) is not correct. In particular it is called a fallacy [*Trugschluß*] (*Sophisma, Captio*), if one can be easily deceived by its means.[18]

And Baumgarten, for his part, says:

A syllogism that errs in form is a PARALOGISM, and a concealed paralogism is a SOPHISM (*captio, fallacia*). (*Acroasis Logica*, §385)[19]

For Feder and Baumgarten, then, a paralogism is an inference that is defective in form, while a sophism is the particular species of paralogism in which the defect of form is concealed. We will shortly see that on this point Meier concurs, but first we should pause to argue for our as yet unsubstantiated claim that Kant follows Feder and Baumgarten in treating a paralogism as an inference in which the form or mode of inference is incorrect.

This point is made clearly enough in the first *Critique*. 'The logical paralogism', Kant says:

---

[18] The phrases in parentheses are Kant's interpolations, those in square brackets, my own. Johann Georg Heinrich Feder, *Logik und Metaphysik* (5th edn.; Göttingen: J. C. Dieterich, 1778) at §50. According to Warda, Kant owned a 1778 printing of the fifth edition. See Warda, *Immanuel Kants Bücher* at 48.

[19] Alexander Baumgarten, *Acroasis Logica* (2nd edn.; Halle and Magdeburg, 1773). Kant recommends this logic text of Baumgarten under the description 'Toellner's manual', to his follower Ludwig Heinrich Jakob in a letter of 1787 (10: 494). Toellner was the volume's editor.

consists in the falsity of an inference of reason [*Vernunftschlusses*] in respect of form [*der Form nach*], whatever its content may be.[20] A transcendental paralogism, however, has a transcendental ground for inferring falsely in respect of form. (A 341/B 399)

The part of this passage dealing with logical paralogisms is echoed in the logic lectures. In the *Blomberg Logic* Kant says 'Every inference false in form is a paralogism' (24: 287), while in the *Dohna-Wundlacken Logic* he says: 'An inference of reason... if it is false in form <*forma*> [is called] a paralogism' (24: 777). It is also echoed by a marginal note that Kant added to his own copy of the A edition: 'A paralogism is an inference of reason that is false in *forma*' (E *CLV*, 23: 38).

Clearly, then, Kant takes a paralogism to be an inference that is, in some sense yet to be elucidated, 'false' in (or 'with respect to', or 'as to') form. But there is more to it than that, as a reflection from the *Duisburg Nachlaß* makes clear: 'A **paralogism** is an inference of reason that is false in respect to form, although as far as its matter (the premises) are concerned [*bei Vordersätzen*] it is correct [*richtig*]' (R 5552: 18: 218).[21] A paralogism, then, is false with respect to its form, but correct with respect to its matter, where the matter is constituted by the premises, and the form by the mode of connection of premises and conclusion. Or so at least the reflection suggests. In the *Jäsche Logic*, however, Kant sketches a rather different picture. There he identifies the form of an inference of reason not with the mode of connection of premises and conclusion, but rather with 'the conclusion insofar as it contains the **consequentia**' (§59, compare 29: 847). Which of these two incompatible understandings of the 'form' of an inference of reason is relevant to Kant's characterization of the paralogisms as 'false with respect to form'? Not, I would suggest, the latter, because such a view would commit Kant to dogmatically adjudging the conclusion of a paralogism to be false rather than of unknown truth value. It is, in my view, the former; but this point needs careful handling because, as we will see, for Kant in the first *Critique* the mode of connection of the propositions in a paralogism—the 'logical form' in our contemporary sense—may be correct (that is, truth preserving) while the argument is nonetheless by Kant's lights 'false as to form'.

The issues, then, are delicate, and this should justify us in proceeding slowly. Let us note, first, that the idea of the form as the mode of connection of premises and conclusion rather than the conclusion is present in the Wolffian tradition.

---

[20] Here I follow Kemp Smith in leaving '*übrigens*' untranslated. Guyer and Wood's 'otherwise' risks creating the misleading impression that the inference's form is an aspect of its content.
[21] Compare A 398, where Kant classifies a certain inference as a paralogism which is false in form 'alone'. In rendering the dative plural phrase '*bei Vordersätzen*' in these lectures as 'the premises' I am guided partly by Kant's speaking of '*Vordersätzen oder Prämissen*' in §59 of the *Jäsche Logic* and partly by Meier's having offered '*praemissae*' as one of the Latin equivalents for the closely related term '*Vorderurtheile*' in his *Auszug*. See Georg Friedrich Meier, *Auszug aus der Vernunftlehrer* (Halle: Gebauer, 1752) at §356.

Wolff himself says: 'with inferences one is to look in part to the correctness of the propositions, in part to their mode of connection with one another, that is, as one usually says for short, *in part to the matter, in part to the form...*' (*GM*, §390, emphasis added). The same idea occurs in Baumgarten's *Acroasis Logica*, where in his own German commentary on the Latin text he equates an inference's erring in respect of form with its erring in respect of its 'mode of inference' ('*Art und Weise zu Schliessen*').[22] It is also found in Leibniz's *Preliminary Dissertation on the Conformity of Faith with Reason* in his *Theodicy*.[23] And, indeed, it goes back at least as far as Aquinas's commentary on Aristotle's *Physics*: '[E]ach argument of both Melissus and Parmenides is sophistic', says Aquinas, 'for they err in matter, whence [Aristotle] says that they have accepted what is false, i.e., they assume false propositions, and they err in form, whence he says they are not syllogizing.'[24] Notably, however, this kind of application of the form–matter distinction to arguments is absent from the passages of Aristotle on which Aquinas is commentating.

The Thomistic understanding of how the form–matter distinction applies to arguments, at any rate, is firmly entrenched in the tradition upon which Kant is drawing. Nonetheless, one suspects that his most immediate source for it would have been the textbook he used in his logic lectures, namely, Meier's *Auszug aus der Vernunftlehre*. For in that work Meier identifies the *matter* of an argument with its premises (*Vorderurtheilen*) and the *form* with 'the following of the conclusion from the premises'.[25] And, most importantly of all for our purposes, Meier anticipates Kant in defining a paralogism—the word he uses is '*paralogismus*'—as 'an inference of reason in which the form is incorrect [*unrichtig*]'.[26]

Taken together, these points suggest that what Kant means by a 'paralogism' is an inference that is false (or incorrect) in respect of its form, but correct in matter, where being correct in matter amounts to having premises that are true. But incorrectness of form, interestingly, is not, according to the Wolffian tradition, confined to arguments that are, in today's sense, 'formally invalid'. Meier, for example, classifies as incorrect in form certain arguments that have true premises but are deficient owing to a kind of fallacy of misinterpretation of their validly

---

[22] Baumgarten, *Acroasis Logica*, §302.
[23] G. W. Leibniz, *Theodicy*, trans. E. M. Huggard (La Salle, IL: Open Court, 1985) at 89.
[24] Thomas Aquinas, *Commentary on Aristotle's Physics*, trans. R. J. Spath, R. J. Blackwell, and W. Edmund Thirkel. Rev. (South Bend, IN: Dumb Ox Books, 1999) at 10.
[25] Meier, *Auszug* at §359.
[26] Ibid., at §402. Two other works, both owned by Kant, are also likely to have been among Kant's immediate sources for this conception. The first is Reimarus's *Vernunftlehrer*—Kant owned the edition of 1756—where the 'matter' of an inference is equated with the premises (a premise being referred to as a '*Vordersatz*'). See Hermann Samuel Reimarus, *Die Vernunftlehre, als eine Unweisung zum richtigen Gebrauche der Vernunft in der Erkenntnis der Wahrheit als zwoen ganz natürlichen Regeln der Einstimmung und des Wiederspruchs hergeleitet* (Hamburg: H.S.R. P.J.H, 1756) at §208, §10, and § 11. The other candidate source is Feder's *Logic and Metaphysics*—which Kant also owned—where a paralogism is characterized as an inference which is 'not correct' [*nicht richtig*] in form or mode of inference, and where the falsity of a premise is treated as rendering an inference defective with respect to its matter (Feder, *Logik und Metaphysik* at 50).

drawn conclusion.[27] Examples of these fallacies include the '*sophisma heterozeteseos*', in which a disputant wrongly believes that they have *demonstrated* a claim stronger than the one they have in fact established, as well as the '*sophisma ignoratio elenchi*' in which a disputant wrongly believes that they have *refuted* a claim weaker than the one they have in fact refuted.[28]

That these last two kinds of inference count as 'incorrect in form' (hence as paralogisms) is not a point that leaps off the page of Meier's textbook. But it does emerge from a consideration of the division he provides for the concept of an 'inference of reason'. This runs as follows. 'Inferences of reason' [*Vernunftschluße*] divide into those that are false as to form, which Meier terms paralogisms, and those that are not. Paralogisms, in turn, divide into those in which the defect is hidden, which Meier terms both '*Betrugschlüße*' and 'sophisma[ta]', and those in which it is not.[29] Inferences in which the defect is hidden [*Betrugschlüße*], in turn, divide into no fewer than *seven* kinds, including the *sophisma figurae dictionis*, in which the middle term is 'twofold' [*zweifache*], the fallacy of confusing a qualified with an unqualified sense of a term (usually known as the sophism '*a dicto secundum quid, ad dictum simpliciter*'), as well as the *heterozeteseos* and the *ignoratio elenchi*.

Two points concerning this taxonomy are worth noting. First, Meier's notion of a *Betrugschluß* corresponds to that of a *sophism* in Baumgarten's and Feder's classifications, for it is an inference that is false as to form where the defect is concealed.[30] Second, the fact that *Betrugschlüße* constitute a species of paralogism suggests that the sophisms of *heterozeteseos* and *ignoratio elenchi* are conceived of as fallacies that constitute an argument false as to form—and this remains so even though they are in the contemporary sense merely informal fallacies. The tradition in which Meier is working classes them as false as to form simply because, although incorrect, they need not be incorrect as to matter, for they may have true premises.

With regard to this second point it is worth noting that Kant himself treats these same two—by today's lights informal—fallacies as examples of inferences that are 'false in form'. This becomes clear from the juxtaposition of two passages that occur in close proximity in the *Dohna-Wundlacken* logic of 1792:

An inference of reason which is false with respect to (matter) is called a fallacy (*Trugschluß*) and if it is false with respect to form—[a] paralogism. Sophism is an inference that is false in form [*in forma*]. (24: 777)

---

[27] Meier, *Auszug* at §402.   [28] Ibid., at §405.

[29] Ibid., §402. An example in which the defect was not hidden would be some overtly invalid syllogism, such as for example, any argument overtly of the form All F are G; Some G is H; so some F is H. In a case such as this there is no equivocation or other hidden flaw.

[30] Kant sometimes uses '*Trugschluß*' in this same way (1: 124), but as the remark we quote next shows he also uses this same term somewhat differently.

> The **sophisma heterozeteseos,** when it concerns a disputed question [*Streitfrage*], is called a *sophisma ignorationis elenchi.* E.g., the proof of the immortality of the soul [is an instance of the latter sophism] where one would prove a future life [for the soul when one was supposed to prove its immortality]. (24: 778)

Here, if his student note-taker is to be believed, Kant is treating the *sophisma ignorationis elenchi* as a species of *sophisma heterozeteseos*. But what matters for our purposes is that, since Kant classes both inferences as *sophisms*, he is treating each of them as 'false in form'. Such a classification may sound odd to us, but it makes sense in this context because, as the first of these passages shows, the contrast class is inferences that are false in matter. It makes sense that these sophisms should *not* be false in matter because there is no suggestion that they need have false premises. And Kant seems to treat 'false in respect of form' as a catch-all category into which he places any defective argument that is not false as to matter.

The point that Kant sees inferences that are false in form (that is, paralogisms) as including these two (in today's sense) *informal* fallacies is further suggested by (and explains) the fact that the *A*-edition paralogisms include at least one argument that we would today class as formally *valid*, namely, the first paralogism. In the first edition, the flaw that Kant detects in this argument—as we will see in more detail in Chapter 5—is not that it contains an equivocal middle term, but rather that it purports to have proved something relevant to the question of the soul's immortality, when in reality it has proved only a triviality (compare, A 350-1). The first paralogism in *A*, then, is a fallacy of *misinterpretation*—and indeed, of overestimation—of what has been proved. It can be viewed either as a *sophisma heterozeteseos* or as a *sophisma ignorationis elenchi*, depending on how one conceives of its role in a disputation—that is to say, depending on whether one sees it as a purported demonstration or as a purported refutation. But the important point is that it counts as formally incorrect—and so as a paralogism— only because it exemplifies one of these traditionally 'formal', but nowadays informal, fallacies. The *A*-edition first paralogism, moreover, is both a paralogism and a sophism, for its contained 'error of form'—in the Pickwickian sense currently under discussion—is one in which the defect is 'concealed' in the sense of being easily overlooked.

3.5 Transcendental paralogism

Kant classifies the four paralogisms he discusses as *transcendental* paralogisms. By this he means that they have a transcendental ground—namely, transcendental illusion—that bestows on them a certain naturalness and inevitability. 'They are', he says, sophistries not of human beings but of pure reason itself, and even the wisest of all human beings cannot get free of them; after much effort he perhaps succeeds in guarding himself against error, but he can never be wholly rid of the illusion, which ceaselessly teases and mocks him. (A 339/B 397)

Owing to the transcendental paralogisms we imagine ourselves capable of acquiring (what Kant would classify as) synthetic a priori knowledge of the intrinsic character of the subject of thought. In truth, however:

> The subject of inherence [that in which thoughts inhere] is designated only transcendentally through the I that is attached [*angehängte*][31] to thoughts, without [our] noting the least property of it, or being acquainted with it or knowing it [through propositions] at all. (A 355)

Kant means both that we cannot have acquaintance with the self it is in itself and that we cannot acquire propositional knowledge of it—by which he presumably means propositional knowledge of its intrinsic character; for, as we saw in the previous chapter, he had earlier claimed that the self is 'cognized [*erkannt*] through the thoughts that are its predicates' (A 346/B 404). Thus, while in Kant's view I can know, for example, that I am thinking that it's raining, I cannot know whether or not the subject of this thought is a substance$_1$.

In Kant's view, transcendental illusion renders us permanently predisposed to find the conclusions of the paralogisms plausible, while the arguments themselves convert this temptation into actual ungrounded judgments or doctrines. In the next five chapters we will scrutinize these arguments, beginning with the *B*-edition treatment of the first paralogism.

---

[31] Here I follow Kemp Smith in favouring the looser 'attached' to the more literal 'appended'. I do so because the 'I think' is typically prefixed, rather than appended, to thoughts.

4
The *B*-Edition First Paralogism

4.1 Introduction

Kant offers different treatments of the first paralogism in the two editions of the first *Critique*. We examine the *B*-edition treatment in the present chapter, and the more obscure *A*-edition treatment in the next.[1] I want to begin by stating two desiderata for a viable interpretation of the *B*-edition first Paralogism. First, the interpretation should portray the argument as formally invalidated by equivocation on its middle term. It is, as Kant says, drawn '*per sophisma figurae dictionis*' (B 411)—a phrase that, following Meier, he consistently explains as referring to a fallacy of equivocation on the middle term (see, for example, 9: 135). Second, the interpretation should portray the fallacy in question as sufficiently subtle that it could have been committed by thinkers of real sophistication.

4.2 The paralogism

In the *B* edition Kant sets out the first paralogism as follows:

> What cannot be thought otherwise than as subject does not exist otherwise than as subject, and is therefore substance.
>
> Now a thinking being, considered merely as such, cannot be thought otherwise than as subject.
>
> Therefore it also exists only as such a thing, i.e., as substance.   (B 410–11)

Superficially, this argument appears to be valid. It seems to be a first-figure categorical syllogism in the mood of Barbara:

All *M* are *P*—major premise
All *S* are *M*—minor premise
Therefore: All *S* are *P*—conclusion

---

[1] Kant acknowledged the obscurity of the *A*-edition discussion. See *Prolegomena*, 4: 381 and B *xxxviii–xlii*.

A more regimented version of the paralogism may be obtained by making the following substitutions in this schema:

M: entities that cannot be thought otherwise than as subject
P: entities that cannot exist otherwise than as subjects, and therefore (by definition) are substances
S: entities that are thinking beings (considered merely as such)

Here I have supplied the term 'entities', which is intended to be categorially neutral, merely in order to work the argument into the apparent form of a first-figure categorical syllogism in Barbara. This requires construing all three of the syllogism's 'terms' as plural noun-phrases. And, to achieve consistency with Kant's definitions of substance at B 149, B 288, and B 289, I have strengthened the substituend for *P* to 'entities that *cannot* exist otherwise than as subjects' in preference to Kant's actually stated phrase: 'entities that *do not* exist otherwise than as subjects...'. The need for this strengthening is confirmed by the note to B 411, in which Kant presents as a consequence of the argument's intended (but not attained) conclusion the claim that 'I *cannot* exist otherwise than as a subject' (emphasis added). I will treat Kant's failure to indicate the needed modal force as merely a slip.

The cleaned-up paralogism runs:

All entities that cannot be thought otherwise than as subjects are entities that cannot exist otherwise than as subjects, and are therefore (by definition) substances.

Entities that are thinking beings (considered merely as such) are entities that cannot be thought otherwise than as subjects.

So:

Entities that are thinking beings (considered merely as such) are entities that cannot exist otherwise than as subjects, and are therefore (by definition) substances.

From this argument one obtains a dogmatic conclusion about the thinking I merely by adding the premise that the thinking I is a thinking being considered merely as such.[2]

---

[2] As Dyck notes, Kant himself endorses an argument structurally similar to the B-edition first paralogism in the *Metaphysics L1*. See Dyck, *Kant and Rational Psychology* at 96–7. And see *Metaphysics L1*, 28: 225–6, and 266. The fact that he had himself earlier endorsed a version of the paralogistic argument helps to explain why he should have seen it as so seductive.

Kant supposes that, owing to equivocation on its middle term, the argument does not in fact have the form of a first-figure categorical syllogism (A 402). He traces the equivocation to the word 'thought':

> 'Thought' [*Das Denken*] is taken in an entirely different meaning [*Bedeutung*] in the two premises: in the major premise, as it applies to an object in general (hence as it may be given in intuition); but in the minor premise only as it subsists in relation to self-consciousness, where, therefore, no object is thought, but only the relation to oneself as subject (as the form of thinking) is represented.
>
> (note to B 411–12)

Our first task is to identify the two senses of 'thought' in question by considering the meaning of each of the premises. The major premise says, in effect, that if it is impossible to *conceive* of some entity as a property, then that entity cannot *exist* as a property.[3] Since the premises of the paralogism are, by Kant's lights, true, we must take him to be endorsing this generalized conditional.[4] He nonetheless denies that we can know the minor premise to be true when its predicate is construed as uniform in meaning with the subject of the major premise. Kant takes such a view because he supposes it to be at least arguable that the thinking self or soul can be conceived 'otherwise than as a subject'. Indeed, one version of such a view is standardly attributed to Spinoza, who holds that the human mind inheres in the intellect of the one true substance: God.[5] Spinoza may or may not be right about this, but his position is at least not known to be unintelligible—and the same may be said for the idea that the soul is merely a power of a thing.[6] But such facts are all Kant needs in order to argue that the minor premise, interpreted as it

---

[3] More fully, it would have to be taken to say, in addition, that if an entity cannot be conceived as a complex of other entities, it cannot exist as such a complex. But to streamline exposition I suppress this detail.

[4] Recall that Kant says that a paralogism can be titled a *sophisma figurae dictionis* insofar as its premises are correct (A 402; compare R 5552 (18: 218)). One might wonder how Kant takes himself to know the truth of the major premise. I address this issue in the 'Objections and Replies'.

[5] In the *Ethics* Spinoza says that 'the human mind is part of the infinite intellect of God' (*Ethics* II, Proposition 11, Corollary). See Baruch Spinoza, *Complete Works*, trans. Samuel Shirley (Indianapolis: Hackett, 2002) at 250. For Spinoza everything is either a mode or a substance. Since God is the only substance, the self must be a mode. Kant, moreover, knew of this opinion of Spinoza (see 5: 101–2 and 28: 1052–3).

[6] Kant knew that Baumgarten identified the human soul with its power of representing the universe from the position of its body (see *Metaphysics Mrongovius*, 29: 906, and compare Baumgarten, *Metaphysics* at §741). As Ameriks notes, Kant attributes a similar view to Wolff (28: 261), and he takes it to imply that the soul is an accident (ibid.). See Karl Ameriks, *Kant's Theory of Mind: An Analysis of the Paralogisms of Pure Reason* (New Edition; Oxford: Clarendon Press, 2000) at 82, n94.). However, Kant fails to support this attribution with a citation, and if Wolff ever held such a view, he was certainly not consistent in doing so. For in *GM* Wolff clearly maintains that the soul is a self-subsisting thing that *has* powers (see §§743–4). What matters for our purposes, however, is just that, although Kant does not himself subscribe to the view that the soul is a power, neither does he regard it as unintelligible (see 28: 261–2 and 29: 906).

would need to be in order to mesh with the major, is not known to be true.[7] In consequence, even if the argument were to be interpreted as valid, it would still not be known to be sound, and so would not constitute a successful proof.

I take it, then, that Kant views the word 'thought' as it occurs in the major premise as meaning 'conceived'. He supposes that when the minor premise is interpreted in such a way that it can plausibly be taken to be known to be true the term 'thought' does not have this sense. What sense, then, does it have in the minor premise? The answer is contained in the continuation of the note to B 411:

> In the first premise, one talks about things that cannot be thought of other than as subjects; in the second, however, one talks not about **things**, but about **thought** (in that one abstracts from every object), in which the I always serves as subject of consciousness; hence in the conclusion it cannot follow that I cannot exist otherwise than as subject, but rather only that, in thinking my existence, I can use myself only as the subject of the judgment, which is an identical proposition that discloses absolutely nothing about the manner of my existence.
>
> (note to B 411)

Let's focus on the conclusion about the self that Kant supposes we *are* entitled to draw from the premises of the first paralogism, namely:

[1]   In thinking my existence I can use myself only as the subject of the judgment.

Because Kant supposes that we are entitled to infer [1] from the premises of the argument, and because he takes those premises to be true, he must also take [1] to be true. Accordingly, a charitable interpretation of [1] is in order. But even a charitable interpretation must take Kant to be committing an error that is the analogue at the level of judgment of a confusion of use and mention. After all, what I 'use' as the subject of a judgment expressing my existence is not my self but only a judgmental component representing my self.[8] So Kant must mean:

---

[7] *Contra* C. Thomas Powell, Kant's point is not that one or other of the premises is known to be false. See C. Thomas Powell, *Kant's Theory of Self-Consciousness* (Oxford: Oxford University Press, 1990) at 67.

[8] A discussion of the use of more ordinary concepts in the *Metaphysical Foundations of Natural Science* sheds light on Kant's talk of 'using' the self. When explaining the notions of substance and accident, he says: 'In the categorical judgement: **The stone is hard**, the **stone** is used as subject, and **hard** as predicate, in such a way that the understanding is still free to exchange the logical function of these concepts, and to say that something hard is a stone' (4: 475, continuation of note '*'). Here when Kant says 'the **stone** is used as subject' he means that the concept *stone* is used as subject. The emphasis on 'stone' indicates that here this word refers not to an object (a stone), but only to a concept. The same typographical convention seems to be in play in Kant's use of the phrase 'the **I**' at A 349 when he says: 'in all our thinking the **I** is the subject, in which thoughts inhere only as determinations, and this **I** cannot be used as the determination of another thing'. The parallel with the phrase 'the **stone**' suggests that the emphasis on the word 'I' in the phrases 'the **I**' and 'this **I**'—indicated in the Academy edition by spaced lettering [*Sperrdruck*]—is intended to signal that Kant is referring to the judgmental component

[2]   In thinking my existence I can use the representation of my self only as the subject of the judgment.

This is an improvement on [1], but we are not yet finished with our charitable reformulations; for [2] is, strictly speaking, false. To see why, consider the judgment: 'Something instantiates the property of being identical with me'. In this judgment I think my existence without using the representation of myself as a subject, for it is used only as a component of the predicate. Nor do I use the representation of myself as a subject in the judgment: 'The property of being me is exemplified', for here my representation, 'me', is used only as a component of the subject concept. To do justice to Kant's thought, therefore, we must suppose that when he says such things as [1] he does so against the background of the assumption that any sub-sentential component of a categorical judgment occurs either as a subject or as a predicate.[9] Although this assumption is, strictly speaking, false, it does little harm to Kant's reasoning. To correct for it, we need only suppose that when he says that a judgmental component 'can be used only as [the] subject of the judgment' what he actually means is that it 'cannot be used as [the] predicate of the judgment'—where by a 'predicate' here one means not a property but a judgmental component occurring in a predicative role. What Kant must mean by [1], then, is just:

[3]   In thinking my existence I cannot use the representation of my self as [the] predicate of the judgment.

Kant describes [1] as an 'identical proposition', meaning that it is an analytic judgment.[10] Presumably, he conceives of it in this way because it contains necessity while not plausibly being construed as stating a condition of the possibility of experience. One supposes that Kant would have regarded [1] as analytic because it amounts to [3] and because it is analytic of our concept of the word 'Ich' that it has the grammatical distribution it does. Presumably, it would be thought of as 'That German word whose phonetic signal (in such-and-such a dialect) is so-and-so, whose meaning is such-and-such, and whose grammatical distribution is so-and so', where this last 'so-and-so' would contain the component 'does not occur as a predicate'. Such an account might be satisfactory for the word 'Ich', though one has to wonder whether it would carry over to the level of judgmental components.

expressed by the word 'I'—which component is presumably the concept of the soul spoken of at A 351. His point, therefore, is that the concept expressed by the word 'I' cannot be employed in a judgment in a predicative role.

[9] Kant treats the copula as expressing not a judgmental component but rather the judgment's form (see, for example, *Jäsche Logic*, §24 (9: 105)).
[10] A 7/B 10; 9: 111.

In the note to B 411 Kant suggests that the most we may infer from the premises of the paralogism is [3] in contradistinction to the (metaphysically loaded) claim that 'I cannot exist otherwise than as subject'. The focus on existence in these claims suggests that he endorses the following view:

[4]   What follows from the premises of the paralogism as far as my existence is concerned is not that I cannot exist otherwise than as subject but merely that in thinking my existence I cannot use the representation of myself as a predicate.

It is easy to see why Kant should take [3] to follow from the premises of the paralogism; for it follows from a combination of the minor premise, construed as saying

[5]   The representation of a thinking being, considered merely as such, cannot be used as the predicate of a judgment.

with the independently plausible claim that

[6]   The representation 'I' (or 'me')—or, strictly, the judgmental component expressed by these words—is the representation of a thinking being considered merely as such.

The note to B 411 therefore provides reason to interpret the minor premise as meaning [5]. And, so construed, it can be regarded as true. After all, the representation of any thinking being considered merely as such will be a singular representation, and representations of this kind—or so Kant supposes—are incapable of playing the grammatical role of predicates, though they may, of course, figure as parts of predicates.[11] In the case of a term for a universal, by contrast, that term can occupy either subject or predicate position in a judgment. For example, both 'Blue is a colour' and 'American mailboxes are blue' are grammatical. (The same goes, *mutatis mutandis*, for what really concerns us: the judgmental components these words express. Hereafter, I will suppress this qualification.)

Kant's key observation about the *B*-edition first paralogism is that this fact about the grammatical distribution of the first-person singular personal pronoun entails nothing about how the self can or cannot be conceived. *A fortiori*, it entails nothing about whether or not the self is a substance$_1$. Thus, although it is true that

---

[11] One might be inclined to doubt this on the ground that in the judgment, for example, that 'Allah is God', it looks as though 'God' occupies predicate position. However, this judgment does not in fact contain a predicate position since it is not of subject-predicate form, but rather an identity judgment with relational form.

the representation of the self cannot be used as the predicate of a judgment, this fact 'discloses absolutely nothing about the manner of my existence' (note to B 411). This point can be made more vivid by considering the case of an ordinary proper name. Suppose I were to name my right fist 'Fred'. Kant would grant that 'Fred' cannot occur as the sole occupant of the predicate position in a judgment; but this does not show that Fred is a substance$_1$. Indeed, since Fred is something whose existence depends on the configuration of other things (my fingers), it must be deemed a complex, hence a 'determination' of other things. Being a *phenomenon* that is also a substratum of other phenomena, it counts as a substance only in a 'comparative' sense, rather than as a substance proper.[12]

On this reading, the equivocation on which the paralogism trades is, as Kant suggests, located in the word 'thought'. While in the major premise to 'think' of a thing is to conceive of it; in the minor it is to assign the thing's representation a certain role in a judgment. Accordingly, in the sense appropriate to the major premise, an entity that cannot be 'thought' as a predicate is something that cannot be conceived as a property (or complex) of another thing (or things); while in the sense appropriate to the minor premise an entity that cannot be 'thought' as a predicate is something whose representation cannot play the grammatical role of a predicate. Exploiting the ambiguity of 'predicate', which in Kant's writings sometimes means a property (or complex) and sometimes a judgmental component in predicative role, we might characterize the equivocation in question as that between the notion of something that cannot be *conceived* as a predicate and the notion of something that cannot be *deployed* as a predicate. At any rate, the kernel of Kant's critical insight amounts to the observation that the fact that a thing's representation cannot be deployed as a predicate in judgments doesn't entail that that thing itself cannot be conceived as a property of another thing (or as a complex of other things). And *a fortiori*, it doesn't entail that it cannot exist in this manner. This observation, I take it, constitutes a philosophical insight of real depth.[13]

---

[12] R 5312 (18: 150). For texts suggesting Kant equates comparative substances with substantiated phenomena see Dyck, *Kant and Rational Psychology* at 95, note 55. And for a more general discussion of substantiated phenomena, see Rae Langton, *Kantian Humility: Our Ignorance of Things in Themselves* (Oxford: Clarendon Press, 1998), at ch. 3.

[13] This account of the formal fallacy in the B-edition paralogism differs markedly from Grier's, who proposes that the argument be reconstructed as the invalid inference: '$\forall x\,(Ox \rightarrow (Sx \rightarrow Ex))$, Sa; so Ea', where 'Ox' is 'x is an object of possible experience'; 'Sx' is 'x cannot be thought otherwise than as subject', and 'Ex' is 'x does not exist otherwise than as subject' (Grier, *Kant's Doctrine of Transcendental Illusion*, 163). Grier neglects to say what she takes 'a' to be, but one supposes it must be the singular term 'the self', or, perhaps, 'the thinking subject (considered merely as such)'. This reconstruction has, I think, several shortcomings. First, and most obviously, it fails to portray the paralogism as a syllogism. Second, since it portrays the second premise as a singular judgment, it would seem to fit the A-edition version better than the B-edition version. Third, the very suggestion that the first premise incorporates a restriction that is absent from the second seems to run counter to Kant's words. For he describes the first premise as talking of a being that can be thought of 'in every respect' and the second as speaking of

4.3 Objections and replies

Our account of the *B*-edition first paralogism satisfies our two desiderata: it portrays the paralogism as fallacious in virtue of equivocation on its middle term, and it portrays the fallacy as sufficiently subtle that it might have been committed by thinkers of real sophistication. It also has the virtue of locating the equivocation precisely where Kant says it is located—namely, in the word 'thought'. So, the reading has its merits; but what are its points of vulnerability?

One possible objection alleges that the interpretation would commit Kant to detecting dogmatism where it is in fact absent. If transcendental illusion encourages the error I have described, it seems that it should also encourage a similar mistake in other cases. Suppose, for example, that I name my right fist 'Fred'. Since this representation cannot occur as sole occupant of predicate position, our account seems to suggest that, owing to transcendental illusion, we should also be inclined to judge Fred to be a substance$_1$.

The reply, I take it, would run as follows. We are not tempted to make this mistake in the case of Fred simply because we perceive Fred to be a complex, and so come (perhaps tacitly) to understand that it is something whose existence consists in the configuration of other things, hence that it is a determination of those things. In the case of the self, by contrast, all one has to go on in considering whether or not it can be conceived of as a determination of another thing (or group of things) are the features that can be known to attach to it at the terminus of Cartesian doubt. But, crucially, none of those features would indicate that the self is not a substance$_1$. They include only the general property of having thoughts, feelings, and desires, along with the particular properties of believing that *p*, doubting that *q*, intending that *r*, and so forth.[14] It is because, in considering the character of the self, our resources are restricted in this way that, in this case, the fallacy is so easy to commit.

So much, then, for the first possible line of objection. A second line questions the evidence for attributing to Kant the view that the judgmental component expressed by 'I' cannot occur as a predicate. Some putative grounds for this worry are mentioned by Patricia Kitcher.[15] Although Kitcher herself wants to attribute something like this claim to Kant as part of her interpretation of the *A*-edition first Paralogism, she does so only with reservations. 'Kant,' she says, 'never says why the "I" cannot occur as a predicate. Further, he himself points out that any concept can occur in either the subject or the predicate position in a sentence.' As support

---

this being only 'relative to thinking and the unity of consciousness'. This suggests that, on the contrary, the second premise is in fact more restricted than the first.

[14] Compare: A 346/B 404.
[15] Patricia Kitcher, 'Kant's Paralogisms', *Philosophical Review*, 91 (4) (1982), 515–47 at 526.

for the second of these claims, Kitcher cites the texts: A 349, B 128–9, and A 242–3/B 300–1. Kitcher's contention, if correct, would pose a difficulty for my reading only if what she means by a 'concept' is a judgmental component in general. For the sake of argument, therefore, I shall suppose that this is so.

To meet this objection it suffices to observe that the passages cited do not in fact support the conclusion Kitcher draws from them. Consider A 349. Far from suggesting that any judgmental component can play the role of predicate, this passage actually suggests that the judgmental component expressed by 'I' cannot do so. It contains the claim that 'in all our thinking the I is the subject, in which thoughts inhere only as determinations, and *this I cannot be used as the determination of another thing*' (A 349, emphasis added). If I am right that when Kant speaks of 'using the I' he means employing the self's representation in a judgment, this would mean that the judgmental component expressed by the word 'I' cannot occur as a predicate in a judgment. At any rate, there is no suggestion at A 349 that this representation *can* function as a predicate. Nor, so far as I can tell, is there any hint of this idea at A 242–3/B 300–1. The only text cited by Kitcher that might seem to support the attribution to Kant of such a view is the passage from B 128–9. Here Kant offers a certain characterization of the categories:

> [The categories] are concepts of an object in general, by means of which its intuition is regarded as **determined** with regard to one of the **logical functions** for judgments. Thus, the function of the **categorical** judgment was that of the relationship of the subject to the predicate, e.g., "All bodies are divisible". Yet in regard to the merely logical use of the understanding it would remain undetermined which of these two concepts will be given the function of the subject and which will be given that of the predicate. For one can also say: "Something divisible is a body". Through the category of substance, however, if I bring the concept of a body under it, it is determined that its empirical intuition in experience must always be considered as subject, never as mere predicate; and likewise with all the other categories. (B 128–9)

As I read this passage, Kant is not claiming that any representation whatsoever can occur as a predicate in a judgment. He is rather claiming that, prior to the application of the category of substance, any general term might play either subject- or predicate-role in a subject-predicate judgment. As we have already noted (with our example of 'blue'), this flexibility is typical of general terms. Kant is saying that if we were to regard body as a substance, we would be thereby committed to denying that its representation has the role of a predicate. That idea, however, is far from entailing that 'I' can occur in predicate position, for 'I' is a representation that purports to stand for a particular.

A third possible objection levels a charge of incompleteness. It asserts that I have failed to do justice to the apparently rather different explanation of the paralogism's deceptiveness that occurs in the body of the text. This explanation runs as follows:

> In the major premise one talks about a being that can be thought of in general, in every respect, and hence also as it may be given in intuition. But in the minor premise one talks about this being only insofar as it considers itself as subject, only relative to thinking and the unity of consciousness, but not at the same time in relation to the intuition whereby it is given as an object for thinking. (B 411)

The objection is fair: I have not yet taken account of this remark. What then, is going on here? Let's start with the idea of a thinking being 'considered merely as such'. This, I believe, is a thinking being singled out under no aspect but that of a subject of thought. When I consider a thinking being 'merely as such' I do not think of it as, for example, the possessor of such-and-such a body. Nor do I think of it as an object of inner sense—an idea Kant expresses by saying that it is not thought of 'in relation to the intuition through which it is given as an object for thinking'. On the other hand, I do think of myself 'merely as a thinking being' when—and in Kant's view only when—I think thoughts of the form 'I think x'. A thinking being 'considered merely as such', then, is a thinking being thought of in no more determinate way than as a thinker of certain thoughts. With this matter clarified, the line of criticism Kant is running in the body of the text also becomes clear. He is saying that in the minor premise the phrase 'cannot be thought except as subject' means 'cannot be thought except as subject *when thought of merely as a thinking being*'.[16] In the major it means 'cannot be thought except as subject *simpliciter*' or, in other words, 'cannot be thought as inhering in a thing (or in some things)'. In the body of the text, then, the posited equivocation is just this equivocation on the phrase 'cannot be thought of except as subject'. If this explanation is correct, the third possible objection is thereby answered.

A fourth possible objection challenges my claim that Kant would have regarded the major premise as true.[17] The objector asks how Kant could possibly take himself to know this premise given that it purports to be a necessary truth, and yet is, at first sight, neither analytic nor synthetic a priori. This objection can, I think, be answered by arguing that Kant would have regarded the major premise as analytic.

Consider what we might call the 'core' of the major premise, namely: 'What(ever) cannot be thought otherwise than as a subject does not exist otherwise than as a subject'. I have suggested that in order to be consistent Kant ought

---

[16] If I think of myself as, for example, a mode of God's intellect, then I'm thinking of myself under a mode of presentation richer than that of a mere 'thinking thing'.

[17] I am grateful to an anonymous referee for pressing this question, and to Kenneth Winkler for discussion of some possible responses. The response I finally settled upon was, in its essentials, suggested to me by Ivan Heyman.

to replace 'does not' with 'cannot'. Applying this emendation, and replacing the phrase 'otherwise than as a subject' with the (in this context) equivalent phrase 'as a determination', we obtain: 'Whatever cannot be thought as a determination cannot exist as a determination.' To appreciate why Kant should have regarded this claim as analytic it is necessary to attend to the modalities involved. For each occurrence of 'cannot', we need to ask whether the impossibility in question is real or logical. The answer, I believe, is that the first impossibility is logical, the second real. Accordingly, the claim should be read: 'Whatever is such that there is always a contradiction in representing it as a determination of another thing cannot, as a matter of real possibility, exist as a determination of another thing.' Such a claim is analytic because it is analytic of the notion of 'real possibility' that whatever is really possible is logically possible, with the consequence that whatever is logically impossible is really impossible (compare 29: 811).

In support of this reading we may observe that when Kant speaks of what we 'can think' he sometimes clearly has in mind what can be represented as logically possible. For example, in the B-edition preface he says '[Although I cannot cognize freedom as a property of my soul], nevertheless, I can think freedom to myself, i.e., the representation of it at least contains no contradiction in itself' (B *xxviii*). This provides some support for the idea that the first kind of impossibility in the major premise is logical impossibility. More precisely, it suggests that the whole phrase 'whatever cannot be thought otherwise than as subject' means 'whatever is such that there is always a contradiction in representing it as a determination of another thing'. That the second impossibility is real impossibility is only to be expected because the notion of impossibility figuring in the definition of substance$_1$ (as that which cannot exist as a determination of another thing) is very plausibly real impossibility. The major premise, then, is plausibly analytic. And we can therefore suppose that Kant would have regarded it as true—both by his own lights and by those of the rational psychologist.

Yet a fifth objection has been raised by Julian Wuerth.[18] Taking issue with my claim that in the B edition Kant holds that for all we know the self might not be a substance$_1$, Wuerth claims that Kant 'repeatedly' rejects the claims that the soul could be a power and that it could be an accident.[19] 'Kant', he adds, 'goes on to repeatedly and specifically underscore that it is indeed inconceivable to think of the I as anything other than a subject.'[20] If this last claim is to amount to an objection to my reading, Wuerth must mean by a 'subject' something that Kant calls an 'absolute subject' and which I have called a 'substance$_1$'.[21] For the sake of considering a focused objection, I'll assume this to be so.

---

[18] Julian Wuerth, *Kant on Mind, Action, and Ethics* (New York: Oxford University Press, 2014).
[19] Proops, 'Kant's First Paralogism' at 472. Wuerth, *Kant on Mind* at 164, note 9.
[20] Wuerth, *Kant on Mind* at 164, note 9.
[21] This, recall, is a necessarily non-inhering subject of inherence.

The first thing I should like to say in reply is that, on the face of it, Wuerth's criticism clashes with Kant's claim that the I, or he, or it that thinks 'is cognized only through the thoughts that are its predicates' (A 346/B 404). For if Kant did regard my soul's being a substance₁ as a conceptual impossibility, then by his own lights I *would* be able to cognize something about the self as it is in itself, namely, that it is *not* (and cannot be) a substance₁. Such a proposition would be cognizable because it would amount to a conceptual or analytic truth. Nor could Wuerth respond by denying that the insight gained through analytic judgments qualifies as 'cognition', for Kant speaks explicitly of 'analytic cognition' at A 47/B 64–5 and A 151/B 191. If he were to try to claim that the negative knowledge that the soul (as it is in itself) is not a substance₁ is not, strictly speaking, 'cognition' on the ground that it is not knowledge of intrinsic features of the soul (as it is in itself), then I would give the following reply. The soul's predicates are similarly not intrinsic features of the soul as it is in itself, and yet they are surely things that we 'cognize'; for they are the means by which we cognize the soul. We cognize the soul as it appears because we cognize them. Now, Wuerth might, of course, have some other ground for claiming that the alleged negative knowledge in question is not cognition, but the burden lies with him to say what it is.

Wuerth's position would also seem to be in tension with the following remark:

> [In the "General Note on the System of Principles" (B 288–B 294) and the chapter on "Phenomena and Noumena" (A 235–60/B 294–B 315)] it was proved that the concept of a thing that can exist for itself as subject but not as mere predicate [*als bloßes Prädikat*] as yet [*noch*] carries with it no objective reality at all, i.e., that one cannot know [*Wissen*] whether it can apply [*zukommen könne*] to any object, since one has no insight into the possibility of such a way of existing, and consequently that it yields absolutely no cognition [*Erkenntnis*].
>
> (B 412)[22]

As I argued in the previous chapter, this passage suggests that until a proof is given that experience is possible only on the condition that the concept of substance₁ finds application within it, we cannot know that this concept has application. If Wuerth is right, however, so long as we know that the soul (conceived merely as the thinking I) exists we will be able to know that the concept of a substance₁ has application; for, on his reading, this will follow from the inconceivability of the soul's being something other than a substance₁.

If Wuerth is to defend his interpretation of Kant's *B*-edition views in the face of these passages, he will need to adduce equally authoritative countervailing texts

---

[22] Notice that 'as subject' and 'as mere predicate' are in this context the envisaged roles of a thing, not merely of a representation: they describe two mutually exclusive ways in which this thing might be conceived of as existing.

that bear on Kant's views at the time of composing the *B* edition. And yet such texts as he does adduce occur only in markedly less authoritative texts and usually hail from other periods. He appeals, for example, to passages from the *Metaphysics Herder* student lecture notes of 1762–64, as well as to remarks from the *Metaphysics L1* of 1777–80.²³ In certain other lectures upon which Wuerth relies it is unclear whether Kant is speaking in his own voice or merely rehearsing the reasoning of some imagined rational psychologist (see, for example, *Metaphysics L2*, 28: 590). I do not propose to quibble over whether all of these texts really show what Wuerth takes them to show simply because, in the present context, that question is moot. What matters, for our purposes, is Kant's position in authoritative texts at the time of writing the second edition of the first *Critique*.

That having been said, one of these less authoritative texts does seem worth discussing; for it is close in date to the *B* edition and, if reliable, would raise a sharp problem for my interpretation of the *B*-edition first Paralogism.²⁴ The passage occurs in the *Pölitz* religion lectures of 1783–84. It runs:

> Fundamentally one might just as well call **Spinozism a great fanaticism as a form of atheism**. For Spinoza, treating God as the unique substance, affirmed two predicates of Him: **extension** and **thinking**. All souls, he said, are only modifications of divine thought, all bodies only modifications of His extension. Thus Spinoza assumed that everything that exists is to be found in God. But he thereby fell into major contradictions [*große Widersprüche*]. For if only a single substance exists, then either I must myself be this substance and consequently I must be God—but this conflicts with [*widerspricht*] my dependency—or else I am an accident—but this conflicts with [*widerspricht*] the concept of my I, in which I think of myself as an ultimate subject which is not in turn the predicate of any other thing. (28: 1052–3)

In this passage Kant is declaring what he calls 'the concept of my I' to be in *conflict* with the assumption that I am an accident. This suggests that he thinks I know— either on conceptual grounds or at least on the basis of some a priori synthetic principle—that I am not an accident. The former kind of ground might be suggested by the language of 'major contradictions', but since this remark occurs in a transcript compiled from student notes, and since this language is somewhat undermined by the double occurrence of the weaker term, 'conflicts', it wouldn't do to rest too much on this point. A second relevant passage occurs later in the same transcript:²⁵

---

[23] Wuerth, *Kant on Mind* at 164.
[24] Wuerth cites this passage in discussing Kant's attitude towards Spinoza, rather than in a direct criticism of my reading (*Kant on Mind* at 91, note 4). But I adduce it on his behalf because it does, I think, raise a question that my reading needs to address.
[25] Wuerth adduces this passage as evidence against my reading (*Kant on Mind* at 164, note 9).

> The consciousness of my self testifies that I do not relate all my actions to God, as to the ultimate subject, which is not a predicate of another thing, and thus the concept of a substance arises, since I perceive in myself that I am not the predicate of any further thing. For example, when I think, I am conscious that my I, and not perhaps some other thing, thinks in me. Thus I infer that this thinking in me does not inhere in another thing external to me but in myself, and consequently also that I am a substance, i.e., that I exist for myself, without being the predicate of another thing. I myself am a thing and therefore also myself a substance. (28: 1042)

Here, although Kant does not claim it to be *inconceivable* that I am a substance (that is, in our terms, he does not claim that I am a substance$_1$), he does say that I perceive in myself that I am not a predicate of another thing and that I infer from this that I am a substance—a position that is, I freely admit, far removed from the agnosticism about the subject's substantiality$_1$ that I wish to attribute to Kant in both editions of the first *Critique*.

What are we to say about these apparently countervailing texts? The answer, I think, is that although they should indeed be taken seriously as reflecting Kant's views at the time he gave these lectures, they do not reflect his views in either edition of the first *Critique*. Instead, they merely show that he becomes temporarily dogmatic about the soul's substantiality$_1$ in the period between the two editions. What might explain this temporary lapse into dogmatism? The key to answering this question is, I think, an observation made by Ralf Bader, namely, that in the period between the two editions Kant came to regard his formulation of the *A*-edition first analogy as inadvertently committing him to the dogmatic view that the soul is permanent.[26] What Kant came to realize, Bader suggests, is that in its *A*-edition formulation the principle of the first analogy applies to the object of inner sense—the soul as it appears to itself. He thus came to see that in the first edition he was, contrary to his intentions, committed by the principle of the first analogy to the existence of a permanent object of inner sense. It was this realization, Bader argues, that prompted Kant to reformulate the principle of the first analogy in the *B* edition so that it applied only to the objects of *outer* sense.

If Bader is right, we should not be surprised to find Kant waxing dogmatic about the substantiality$_1$ of the soul in lectures from 1783–84; for it is only substances$_1$ that can be necessarily permanent. And since the motivations for this temporary dogmatism would have lapsed with the reformulation of the first analogy's principle in the *B* edition, we can also understand why his position in that edition should have reverted to the agnosticism of the *A* edition. So, Bader's

---

[26] Ralf Bader, 'The Refutation of Idealism', in James O'Shea (ed.), *Kant's Critique of Pure Reason: A Critical Guide* (Cambridge: Cambridge University Press, 2017), 205–22 at 213–15.

story predicts precisely the oscillation of views that I am attributing to Kant. But is it right?

Let's first consider Kant's formulation of the *A*-edition analogy, the so-called 'principle of persistence of substance':

> All appearances contain the permanent [*das Beharrliche*] (**substance**) as the object itself, and the changeable [*das Wandelbare*] as its mere determination, i.e., a way in which the object exists. (A 182)

Since the soul appears to itself in inner sense, this principle entails that the soul's appearance must contain something permanent. And since this principle is supposed to be known a priori, it commits Kant to maintaining that we know a priori that the appearance of the soul in inner sense contains something permanent. But since this permanent in appearance—our substance$_2$—is just what exemplifies the concept that results from the schematization of the pure category (that pure category being substance$_1$), the appearance of the soul in inner sense must also contain a substance$_1$. Moreover, this is necessarily so, for what is known a priori is necessary.

For these reasons, if he had acknowledged these commitments and sought to make his views consistent with them, Kant would, in the immediate wake of the *A* edition, have come to espouse a position every bit as dogmatic as the one he seems to espouse in the *Pölitz* religion lectures. Granted, the positions are not identical; for knowing some truth a priori on the basis of a principle of the possibility of experience is not the same thing as knowing it on the basis of a concept. But I think it would be wrong to attach too much weight to this difference here. A student note-taker, after all, coming to Kant's lectures from a Wolffian background—and with an accompanying conceptualist understanding of necessity—would have found it natural to equate the claim that Spinoza's view of the soul is in conflict with what we know a priori about the I with the idea that Spinoza's view is in *contradictory* conflict with the *concept* of the I.[27] At any rate, Bader's reflections provide us with an intellectually satisfying account of why Kant should have become dogmatic about the nature of 'the thinking I' in the period between the two editions of the first *Critique*.

Is there any evidence to corroborate this picture of a temporary lapse into a more dogmatic position between the two editions? Yes, there is. For the *Prolegomena* (1783) contains several passages suggesting that we can know the

---

[27] Since Wolff was well known to have supposed the *PSR* derivable from the law of contradiction (Christian Wolff, *Philosophia prima sive ontologia methodo scientifica pertractata qua omnis cognitionis humanae principia continentur*, ed. J. École (2nd edn, *Christian Wolff, Gesammelte Werke*; Hildesheim: Olms, 1736) at §70), neither would the student, in all likelihood, have seen a 'conflict' with the former principle as being distinct from a logical contradiction.

soul to persist in a sense stronger than that of merely persisting through this or that particular alteration. Consider, for example, the following remark:

> If... we want to infer the permanence of the soul from the concept of the soul as substance, *this can... hold good of the soul only for the purpose of possible experience*, and not as a thing in itself and beyond all possible experience.
> (*Prolegomena* §48, 4: 335, emphasis added)

What it means to say we can infer the permanence of the soul 'only for the purpose of possible experience' is, I think, that we can prove that the soul endures *throughout our this-worldly lifetimes* but not after our bodily death. In other words, we can establish only the soul's relative permanence—its permanence during life. Kant continues:

> But the subjective condition of all our possible experience is life: consequently, only the permanence of the soul during life can be inferred, for the death of a human being is the end of all experience as far as the soul as an object of experience is concerned.... Therefore the permanence of the soul can be proven only during the life of the human being (which proof will surely be granted us), but not after death (which is actually our concern)—and indeed then from the universal ground, because the concept of substance, insofar as it is to be considered as connected necessarily with the concept of permanence, can be so connected only in accordance with a principle of possible experience, and hence only for the purpose of the latter. (*Prolegomena* §48, 4: 335)

As these passages show, Kant's strategy is to concede that we can prove the endurance of the soul insofar as, and for the period during which, it is an object of inner sense. The period for which this result can, in Kant's view, be proved, however, does not extend beyond the life of the body. Such a position is consistent with Kant's conception of the principles of the analogies as principles holding only of objects of possible experience. It demands, however, that after my bodily death, even if I should survive, I will no longer be an object of inner sense.

As we will see in Chapter 7, Kant does in fact believe in an afterlife, and so he must also believe that after our bodily deaths, we will continue to exist while ceasing to appear to ourselves in inner sense. The question therefore arises: Why will we cease to appear to ourselves in inner sense when our bodies die? Kant's answer, articulated in metaphysics lectures delivered during the years 1782–85, draws on a view that was already present in the *Metaphysics L1* lectures. In those earlier lectures he says:

> But when the soul separates itself from the body, then it will not have the same sensible intuition of this world; it will not intuit the world as it appears, but rather

as it is. Accordingly, the separation of the soul from the body consists in the **alteration of sensible intuition into spiritual intuition; and that is the other world**. The other world is accordingly not another place [*Ort*], but rather only another intuition. The other world remains the same with respect to its objects; it is not different with respect to the substances, but it is **intuited spiritually**.

(*Metaphysics L1*, 28: 297–8)

The same view appears, more succinctly stated, in the *Metaphysics Mrongovius* of 1782–83:

We are now already conscious through reason of finding ourselves in an intelligible realm; after death we will intuit and cognize it and then we are in an entirely different world that, however, is altered only in form, namely, where we cognize things as they are in themselves. (*Metaphysics Mrongovius*, 29: 920)

It also occurs in the *Metaphysics Volckmann* of 1784–85:

If the soul lives after death then where is it? . . . [I]f the souls [in the afterlife] will cognize the same things [as they cognize in this life] as they are [as opposed to as they appear], then this [afterlife] is another world. . . . [T]he transition into the other world would be merely the [change in kind of] intuition, [this transition] is called coming into another world; the latter is another [world] only with respect to form, but with respect to content it is always the same world.[28]

The views reported in these lectures are, I think, just things that Kant believes at certain stages in his career, not things he takes himself to know. But the later-occurring among them do seem to be motivated by his commitment in the years between the A- and B- editions to the soul's substantiality. For if that commitment is to be limited, as Kant wants it to be, to knowledge of the soul's persistence in *this* (pre-bodily-death) world, it must be true that after bodily death the soul either does not exist at all or else exists without its sensible forms of intuition. After all, it is the temporal form of intuition that enables the soul to appear to itself in sensible intuition. Since Kant takes our belief in the afterlife to be justified, he will not endorse the first of these alternatives, and so he is left in the interval between the two editions in the somewhat awkward position of endorsing a view which, by his own lights, demands that upon bodily death we will come to lose our spatio-temporal forms of intuition. The position is not a happy one, for—among other things—a change in our form of intuition upon the death of our body would seem to have to be conceived of as an event taking place in time. And yet in acquiring

---

[28] *Metaphysics Volckmann*, 28: 445; compare 29: 857 and 29: 927.

the spiritual form of intuition we are supposed to divest ourselves of our sensible forms of intuition, including the temporal form.[29] We are left wondering, therefore, how we could exchange our sensible forms of intuition for a non-sensible form when this transition takes place in time.[30]

Fortunately, however, the difficulties faced by this dogmatic and paradoxical position need not detain us. For these commitments lapse as soon as Kant reformulates the principle of the first analogy. In the *B* edition that principle comes to say:

> In all change of appearances substance persists, and its quantum in nature is neither increased nor diminished. (B 224)

This new formulation affords Kant the necessary leeway to avoid his former commitment to the (relative) permanence of the soul. For he can interpret 'change of appearances' [*Wechsel der Erscheinungen*] as comprehending only episodes in which an object of *outer* intuition arises or perishes. In other words, he can now hold that alterations [*Veränderungen*] of the mind—transitions in which the object of inner sense takes on or loses a determination—are not changes of appearances and so are not subsumed by the reformulated principle.

But why think that the extension of the term 'changes of appearances' comes to be restricted in this way? The answer, as Bader has observed, is that Kant indicates this change in marginalia to his own copy of the *A* edition.[31] When commenting on A 182, he says: 'Here the proof must be so conducted that it applies only to substances as **phenomena** of outer sense' (R LXXX E 32, 23: 30). And, apparently commenting on the principle itself, he says: 'Here it must be shown that this proposition does not pertain to any other substances than those whose alteration is effected only through moving causes, and also consists in motion, consequently in alteration of relations' (R LXXVII, E 31, 23: 30). Those objects whose alteration is effected only through *moving* causes are, of course, bodies. In the reflection R LXXXIII, E 32, Kant concludes that for these reasons 'my [own] permanence is not proven' (23: 31). The same point is confirmed in lectures form the early 1790s, where Kant makes clear that the principle of the first analogy holds only of the objects of outer sense:

---

[29] The tempting idea that Kant might hold only that we lose our spatial form of intuition while retaining our temporal form must be rejected. For, first, it is the temporal form that allows us to appear to ourselves in inner sense, and second Kant supposes that inner sense presupposes outer sense (*Metaphysics K2*, 28: 771; B 274-9). No afterlife, accordingly, could be a world of purely temporal experience.

[30] Kant presumes that the future world will not be a spatial world spatially discontinuous from the present one because 'space makes of all things only one single world' (28: 690). Instead, he holds that it will consist in nothing more than our standing in a different epistemic relation to the very same objects (that is, substances) that exist in this world. It is this change in our epistemic situation that *constitutes* the separation of the soul from the body—or so Kant, at this stage, seems to believe.

[31] Bader, 'The Refutation of Idealism' at 214.

The soul cannot perish through division, but clearly through remission of powers .... The extinguishing of the human soul until complete evanescence can therefore be quite easily thought. There will also be no leap <saltus> here, but rather all can go according to the laws of continuity. With one degree of power the soul is there in one time; between this and the moment where it wholly disappears there are a multitude of moments where the degrees are various. This representation seems to contradict [the idea] that in all alterations in nature the substance perdures and only the accidents change. *But here the talk is merely of bodily substances, with which we are acquainted, but with the human soul we are acquainted with nothing perduring, not even the concept of the I, since consciousness occasionally disappears.* (Metaphysics K2, 28: 763–4, emphasis added)[32]

By the time of the *B* edition, then, the crisis has passed. Kant has reformulated the principle of the first analogy in such a way that it no longer entails the permanence of the soul. For these reasons I take it that Kant's position on the substantiality of the soul between the two editions of the first *Critique* is more dogmatic than in either edition. It reflects his temporary acceptance of a consequence of the principle of the first analogy as that principle is formulated in the *A* edition—a consequence he'd overlooked in the first edition and from which he came to distance himself in the second. His statements of that temporally held view, and of positions associated with it (and in some respects stronger than it), in lectures given, or texts composed, between the two editions cannot, therefore, be treated as evidence of Kant's views about substance in either edition of the first *Critique*. Accordingly, since Wuerth offers no evidence for his reading drawn from authoritative texts contemporaneous with the *B* edition, I regard his objection as ultimately lacking in force.

A sixth and final objection has been raised by Béatrice Longuenesse in her book: *I, Me, Mine: Back to Kant, and Back Again*.[33] Longuenesse takes issue with my suggestion that the concept of substance$_1$ plays a central role in the *B*-edition first paralogism. This cannot be so, she contends, because Kant would not have recognized my (and Bennett's and Van Cleve's) 'substance$_1$' as the unschematized category of substance. The unschematized category, she says, 'reduces' to a logical function; and by this she seems to mean that it is *identical* with its associated logical function. If that is what she means, I would have to disagree. Categories are concepts; and concepts, as Kant makes clear, are not identical with functions but rather 'rest on' [*beruhen auf*] them (A 68/B 93). Moreover, at B 128–9 Kant explicitly distinguishes the logical functions of judgment—which I take to be

---

[32] The passage and others cited in support of the present point were drawn to my attention by Ralf Bader.
[33] Béatrice Longuenesse, *I, Me, Mine: Back to Kant and Back Again* (Oxford: Oxford University Press, 2017) at 137–8, n44.

identical with the logical functions of the understanding in judgments—from the categories. He stresses that only the latter play the role of determining how the object is to be thought (for example, in the case of the category of substance, 'always as subject and never as predicate'). Nor is it clear how the categories *could* be identical with the functions since the latter seem to be not concepts but rather (something like) ways in which concepts are combined.

That said, there is some *prima facie* support for Longuenesse's reading. Kant, after all, does seem to identify the categories with the functions of judgment when he says: 'The **categories**, however, are indeed nothing but precisely these functions of judgment insofar as the manifold of a given intuition is determined in regard to them' (B 143). This is a powerful text for Longuenesse's reading and indeed one that formerly led me to myself endorse the same identification.[34] Nonetheless, on reflection, it is not quite as powerful as it seems. For '*X* is identical with *Y* insofar as *Y* is *F*' does not in fact entail '*X* is identical with *Y*'. Consider, for example, 'My fist is identical with my hand insofar as my hand is configured in such and such a way.' This claim does not entail 'My hand is identical with my fist'. After all, my hand will usually outlive any associated fist.

Developing her criticism further, Longuenesse claims that there is 'no sense at all in which an entity can be said to *be* substance' (ibid.). This objection, I think, contains a small inaccuracy of formulation. I'm not suggesting that it makes sense to say that any entity *is* substance$_1$—indeed, I agree that this makes no sense at all. Rather, I hold that it makes sense to classify an entity as *a* substance$_1$. In short, insofar as the word 'substance' expresses the unschematized concept, it is, for Kant, a count noun, not a mass term. Moreover, when an entity is *correctly* classified as a substance$_1$ I hold that the unschematized category of substance, namely, *substance$_1$* is exemplified by an entity. Longuenesse does not make clear what she takes the alternative to be. 'The category of substance', she says, 'does not apply to any actual or possible object: nothing is left but the concept of subject as a mere role in the logical function of categorical judgment' (138, n44). I can't fully follow this thought because I'm not clear what it would be for something to be a role *in* a logical function of judgment. But Longuenesse's words do clearly suggest that she sees that which exemplifies the unschematized category as a *role* rather than an object—a role perhaps of a judgmental component (the role of 'occurring as subject'). This, however, is not Kant's view. To be sure, he does characterize *functions* as roles played by conceptual components (B 128-9), but not *categories*. 'The categories', he says, 'are concepts of an object as such' (B 128), and this would seem to suggest that when a category is exemplified, what exemplifies it is precisely that: an object. At any rate, in the *A* edition Kant clearly treats the unschematized or 'bare' category of substance as exemplified, if at all, then by objects (things)

---

[34] Proops, 'Kant's Legal Metaphor and the Nature of a Deduction' at 222-3.

rather than roles. This is clear from the fact that he describes the significance of calling the soul a 'substance' in the following way: 'If I say through the mere category that the soul is a simple substance, then I am using [the] understanding's bare concept of substance which contains nothing more than that *a thing* is to be represented as a subject in itself and not in turn as a predicate of another subject' (A 401, emphasis added). Kant explains that the significance of calling a thing a substance (in the sense of the bare category) is that the thing is to be represented as a 'subject in itself' (ibid.). This means, I take it, that the thing in question is to be thought of as a self-subsistent entity: it is to be represented as existing in itself and not as a property of another thing. At any rate categories seem to be exemplified by things. To be sure, they *catalogue* the roles played by those things: but that is not the same as being exemplified by roles.

Kant, moreover, treats substance in this same way in the B edition. Consider, for example, a remark from B 407 where he is telling us that a certain proposition—in this context it matters not which—is too weak to report a metaphysically interesting conclusion: '[T]his proposition', he says, 'does not mean that I am, as an **object**, a **being subsisting** in myself or **substance**' (emphasis in the original). The 'or' here has the sense of the Latin '*sive*': it means 'or, in other words'. Accordingly, Kant is treating 'substance' here as applying to a self-subsistent being (an object). He does not take this term to designate a mere role or function or anything else that might (with some licence) be described as 'not an entity'.

Kant's religion lectures point to the same conclusion. 'God', he says,

> is a substance. This predicate belongs to God merely as a thing, since all things are substances. A substance is understood to be a reality existing merely for itself, without being a determination of another thing.... God ... is a thing for itself and *eo ipso* a substance. If we would dispute God's substantiality, we would have to deny him thinghood as well, and thus remove the whole concept of God.
>
> (28: 1037)

To deny God 'thinghood', I take it, would be to deny that he is an 'entity' in the technical Wolffian sense of a 'possibilium'. Kant is saying that if we were to dispute God's substantiality we would 'remove' or 'annul' the concept of God in the sense of rendering it inconsistent. In other words, he is telling us that it is part of the concept of God to be a substance in a sense of 'substance' that entails that God is not a determination of another thing—a sense compatible with Kant's thinking of God as a 'substance$_1$'. And since he also holds that God is a being outside of time (28: 1067; compare A 641–2/B 669–70), the notion of substance involved here cannot be the temporal notion of permanence (my 'substance$_2$'). Since Kant believes in God, he must take us to be able to think thoughts about Him and so also—because he regards substantiality as part of God's concept—to attach sense to the notion of God's substantiality. But God is clearly an entity or object, so Kant would again seem to be perfectly comfortable with regarding the unschematized category of substance as exemplified by an entity.

4.4 Ameriks's interpretation

The closest rival I know to my interpretation of the *B*-edition first Paralogism is Karl Ameriks's account in his 1982 and 2000.[35] According to Ameriks, the reason why there can be no sound argument of the kind the first paralogism attempts to be is that (when the equivocation in the paralogism is resolved so that the argument is formally valid) 'despite systematically misleading appearances, we don't have sufficient evidence to make any subsumption under the first premise'.[36] Although I agree with him on this point, my interpretation of the *B*-edition first Paralogism differs from Ameriks's in a number of respects.

First, I maintain that the focus of the minor premise lies not, as Ameriks would have it, on the idea that I must think of myself as subject, which, on my reading, would mean that the representation 'I' must occur as the exclusive occupant of subject position. It lies rather on the point that the representation 'I' cannot occur as the exclusive occupant of predicate position. This, I take it, is the more charitable interpretation because, as we have seen, it is simply false to say that 'I' can only occur in subject position. A second difference concerns my suggestion that, 'in relation to self-consciousness' (that is, in the epistemic situation in which I would find myself at the terminus of Cartesian doubt), my resources for thinking of myself are impoverished to such a degree that, under the influence of transcendental illusion, it will easily seem to me that when considering whether or not I can conceive of myself as a determination I have nothing to appeal to except an (in fact) inappropriate grammatical test. So far as I can tell, no such suggestion occurs in Ameriks's discussion of the first Paralogism. A third difference is that, while Ameriks concentrates on the note, I offer a reading of Kant's diagnosis of the paralogism both in the note and in the body of the text—and I try to bring out the differences between these diagnoses. A fourth and final difference relates to Ameriks's claim that the major premise is a definition (he calls it a 'valid transcendental definition').[37] By contrast, I take the major premise to be a non-definitional analytic claim that merely *incorporates* a definition in the added tag 'and therefore is substance'.[38] I take it that the main part of the major premise is the non-definitional but analytic claim: 'That which cannot be thought otherwise

---

[35] Karl Ameriks, *Kant's Theory of Mind: An Analysis of the Paralogisms of Pure Reason* (Oxford: Clarendon Press, 1982).
[36] Ibid., at 71.   [37] Ibid.
[38] Because the major premise incorporates this definition of substance, the first paralogism in *B* in fact takes the form of an abridged *polysyllogism*. Fully spelled out, it would contain two syllogisms

than as subject does not exist otherwise than as subject.' (The added tag indicates that the consequent of this generalized conditional is the definition of *substance*.) I take the analyticity of this claim to be far from obvious—the claim is not, after all, itself a definition. I also hold that appreciating why it is analytic requires a detailed consideration of Kant's views on modality. My reading thus goes beyond Ameriks's also insofar as it seeks to explain why Kant should have regarded the premises of the *B*-edition first paralogism as analytic. I should stress that in spite of these differences, I have learned a great deal from Ameriks's pioneering account, and, in particular, I agree both with his having taken seriously Kant's claim that the *B*-edition first paralogism involves equivocation on the word 'thought' and also with his criticisms of other interpretations.[39]

This concludes our examination of the *B*-edition first Paralogism. In the next chapter we turn to the more obscure discussion in the *A* edition.

---

linked together, where the first—in the tradition the 'prosyllogism'—purports to establish the minor premise of the second—the 'episyllogism' (for these terms, see Meier, *Auszug*, §407). It would run:

First syllogism (prosyllogism)
All entities that cannot be thought otherwise than as subject cannot exist otherwise than as subject. (Major premise)
All thinking beings (considered merely as such) cannot be thought otherwise than as subject. (Minor premise)
Therefore: All thinking beings (considered merely as such) cannot exist otherwise than as subject.

Second syllogism (episyllogism)
All entities that cannot exist otherwise than as subject are substances. (Major premise)
All thinking beings (considered merely as such) cannot exist otherwise than as subject. (Minor premise—established by the first syllogism)
Therefore: All thinking beings (considered merely as such) are substances.

[39] Ameriks, *Kant's Theory of Mind* (1982 edn) at 68, 71–3.

5
The *A*-edition First Paralogism

5.1 Introduction

The *A*-edition first paralogism is an argument that purports to show that the soul, understood as *the thinking I*, is, in a sense yet to be discussed, a substance. It runs as follows:

> That the representation of which is the **absolute subject** of our judgments and hence cannot be used as the determination of another thing, is *substance*.
> I, as a thinking being, am the **absolute subject** of all my possible judgments, and this representation of myself cannot be used as the predicate of any other thing.
> Therefore I, as thinking being (soul), am *substance*. (A 348)[1]

As stated, this argument bears little resemblance to a first-figure categorical syllogism in Barbara. The major premise is a definition rather than a universal claim stating a sufficient condition for being a substance; while the minor premise is a conjunction of two distinct singular judgments. Eliminating certain redundancies, we may charitably reformulate the argument as follows:

> Any entity whose representation cannot be used as a determination of another thing is a substance.
> The thinking I is an entity whose representation cannot be used as a determination of another thing.
> Therefore, the thinking I is a substance.

Here I have assumed that the word 'determination' in the major premise means the same as the word 'predicate' in the minor. On this assumption the argument is valid—indeed, manifestly so. And because we plausibly know that the representation 'I' cannot occur as the sole occupant of predicate position in a judgment, the minor premise is known to be true.[2] Obviously, the major premise is also known

---

[1] The token of 'I' at the start of the second premise does double duty. When first encountered, it *refers* to the thinking subject but later—as one reads on—it is, so-to-speak, revisited insofar as it is now enlisted to *express* the referent of the phrase 'this representation of myself'.
[2] Recall our discussion in the previous chapter (section 4.2) of what Kant means by 'using' myself in a certain grammatical role. Here Kant is speaking, more accurately, of using the 'representation' of the

to be true because it is a consequence of a definitional truth. The argument, therefore, is plausibly known to be sound.

Thus reformulated, the argument appears to have just one shortcoming: its conclusion is simply too weak to advance the rational psychologist's project. Our considerations in the previous chapter suggest that when it is deciphered it will be seen to show that the thinking I is a 'substance' only in the relatively uninteresting, grammar-driven sense of *something whose representation cannot occur as the sole occupant of predicate position in a judgment*. In Kant's terms, the argument establishes that the thinking I is a 'substance only in the idea' (A 351) or, equivalently, that 'the mere apperception, (I)' is '[a] substance in concept' (A 400). In order to indicate that this is the weakest of the conceptions of substance we have encountered so far I will dub it 'substance$_0$'.[3]

Kant's verdict on the A-edition first paralogism, then, is not that it is (in today's terms) formally invalid but rather that, although valid, and, indeed, sound, it fails to establish anything metaphysically interesting.[4] Since Kant's criticism takes this form, there is no need to posit a fallacy of equivocation to neutralize the argument's force.[5] We saw in Chapter 3 that Kant allows arguments of this kind to count as 'false in respect of form'—hence as paralogisms—simply because for him such arguments include certain sophisms—namely, the *sophisma ignoratio elenchi* and the *sophisma heterozeteseos*—in which the conclusion of a valid, and indeed sound, argument, is misinterpreted as stronger than it actually is.

For precisely this reason, Ameriks is right to say that Kant's A-edition criticisms of the first paralogism, insofar as they involve detecting invalidity, are directed at an invalid *extended* argument for the permanence of the soul.[6] Ameriks supposes

---

thinking I, but the same lessons, *mutatis mutandis*, apply. For an alternative account of the first Paralogism that is somewhat in sympathy with my own, see Rosefeldt, 'Subjects of Kant's First Paralogism'. Rosefeldt's account departs from my own insofar as he takes the all-important feature of the representation 'I' that I treat as (quasi-) grammatical or syntactic to be what he calls 'logico-semantical'.

[3] Kant's notion of substance$_0$ has no obvious precedent in the tradition. It might perhaps be thought to correspond loosely to Aristotle's notion of something that is not 'said of' a subject (*Categories*, §5); for it's possible to read Aristotle there as offering a characterization of substance that rests, partly, on grammatical considerations. But that idea is only an element of Aristotle's notion of primary substance, not the notion itself.

[4] A 350–1; A 400; compare *Prolegomena* §47.

[5] Still less is there reason to view either of its premises as false. Even so, interpretive positions of this kind have been taken over the years. Adickes and, following him, Alfons Kalter, take Kant to hold *each* of the four paralogisms to be a *valid* inference with a false minor premise. See Erich Adickes, *Immanuel Kants Kritik der reinen Vernunft* (Berlin: Meyer & Müller, 1889) at 717 note 1 and Alfons Kalter, *Kant's vierter Paralogismus: eine entwicklungsgeschichtliche Untersuchung zum Paralogismenkapitel der ersten Ausgabe der Kritik der reinen Vernunft* (Meisenheim am Glan: Anton Hain, 1975) at 121. Matthias Kossler, for his part, takes both premises to be false. See Matthias Kossler, 'Der transzendentale Schein in den Paralogismen der reinen Vernunft nach der ersten Auflage der Kritik der reinen Vernunft', Kant Studien, 90 (1) (1999), 1–22 at 13.

[6] Ameriks, *Kant's Theory of Mind* at 68. I say 'permanence' because the thesis which Kant portrays the rational psychologist as attempting to demonstrate in the first Paralogism is that the soul is a

that the rational psychologist's error consists in illicitly moving from the conclusion that I cannot be a determination of another thing (that is, that I am a substance$_1$) to the stronger conclusion that I am a substance$_2$. Such a step enacts the fallacy that Jonathan Bennett calls 'inflating' the first paralogism.[7]

But although I agree with the gist of this reading, I would claim that the conclusion that gets inflated—or, better, *misinterpreted*—is not the claim that the soul is a substance$_1$ but rather the weaker claim that it is a substance$_0$.[8] The claim that the soul is a substance$_1$, after all, is not one that Kant could regard as having been established unless he were prepared to take a dogmatic stand on a metaphysical question; for the claim that the soul is a substance$_1$ is a substantive claim involving necessity—a substance$_1$, recall, is a *necessarily* non-inhering subject of inherence. Since Kant wholly rejects dogmatism in both editions of the first *Critique* he can hardly—*contra* Ameriks—grant that the argument establishes that the thinking I is a substance$_1$.[9]

I take it, then, that Kant's criticism of the A-edition first paralogism boils down to the claim that the rational psychologist who rehearses it commits the fallacy of *ignoratio elenchi*.[10] I have only one reservation about such a reading: it entails that Kant speaks inaccurately at A 402 when he portrays *every* paralogism as a *sophisma figurae dictionis*. But this is, I think, an interpretive cost worth incurring—and one that is not as high as it might at first appear. Kant, after all, wholly re-drafted the Paralogisms in the B edition; and, accordingly, we should not be shocked if the A-edition version of this chapter turns out to contain some inaccuracies.

I take it that the main change between the A- and B-edition versions of the first Paralogism chapter—a change that enables Kant to portray the first paralogism as a formally invalid argument—is the change in the definition of substance from 'that the representation of which cannot be employed as a determination of another thing'—that is, substance$_0$ (compare, A 348)—to 'that which cannot exist otherwise than as subject'—that is, substance$_1$ (B 149, B 288, B 289).[11] This

---

substance insofar as it 'cannot arise or perish by natural alterations', a point that entails that, barring a miracle, it will always exist and has always existed. Thus, the rational psychologist takes the argument to establish something about the self's 'origin' as well as its 'future state' (compare A 400).

[7] Jonathan Bennett, *Kant's Dialectic* (Cambridge: Cambridge University Press, 1974) at 76-7.
[8] I am grateful to Kenneth Winkler for persuading me that the conclusion of the A-edition first paralogism has to be weaker than the proposition that the soul is a substance$_1$.
[9] Ameriks, *Kant's Theory of Mind* at 68.
[10] Kant is thinking of the rational psychologist as rehearsing the argument in the context of a rule-governed formal disputation. The argument commits the fallacy in question in virtue of the disputant's doing so. The argument is false as to form, hence a paralogism, because the fallacy of *ignoratio elenchi* is a species of sophism, and sophisms are, as we saw in Chapter 3, classified by the tradition on which Kant is drawing as false with respect to form.
[11] Recall that I am treating the omission of modal force in the predicate of the major premise in the B version as merely a slip.

thought is confirmed by the absence of the latter notion from the *A* edition, and by Kant's omission of the former from the parts of the *B* edition that he revised.

5.2 A closer look at transcendental illusion

It is now time to consider some apparent obstacles to applying to the Paralogisms chapter the account of transcendental illusion outlined in Chapter 1. While that account is, I think, broadly correct, it does stand in need of further elaboration and defence. Two problems need to be addressed. First, although there is much in the first *Critique* to support the interpretive hypothesis that the illusion tempting us to commit the fallacy of the first paralogism is the illusion that *D* is true, there are also numerous passages that, on the face of it, suggest a rather different story. Second, the picture from the *Prolegomena* that seemed helpful—namely, that of a regressive series of conditions whose imagined ultimate member would, if it existed, be an absolute subject—is expressly repudiated at one point in the second edition of the first *Critique*.

Let's begin with this second problem. In the course of defending the completeness of the table of cosmological ideas stated at B 443, Kant says:

> [The category of substance and its accidents] is not suited to a transcendental idea, i.e., in regard to this category reason has no ground to proceed regressively toward conditions. (A 414/B 441)[12]

Does this mean that the *Prolegomena*'s story is a temporary aberration, a view held only fleetingly during the period between the two editions of the first *Critique*? This seems doubtful because the *B* edition retains a number of remarks from the first edition in which the *Prolegomena*'s account seems to be present. These remarks all occur in the chapter of the first *Critique* dealing with the general notion of a transcendental idea, which chapter occurs before the point at which Kant stopped revising.

First, Kant describes the 'totality of conditions and the unconditioned' as the 'common title of all concepts of reason' (A 324/B 380). But since one of these 'concepts of reason' is the transcendental Idea of the soul, this Idea would seem to have as part of its content the notion of an unconditioned totality of conditions. Second, in the course of arguing that there are just as many species of deceptive

---

[12] Kant goes on to concede that we have one concept of substance that might 'still seem' to be an idea of transcendental reason, namely, the concept of what he calls the "**substantiale**". In this context, he understands this to be the concept of a subsisting object that lacks any predicates (A 414/B 441). But since this would not, if it did exist, be an appearance (that is, an object of possible experience), Kant thinks it plain that it cannot be thought of as a final member in a regressive series *of appearances*, which is what would be required in the present context.

syllogistic inference as there are transcendental Ideas, Kant says that in each species of [dialectical] syllogism 'prosyllogisms proceed to the unconditioned: one, to a subject that is no longer a predicate, another to a presupposition that presupposes nothing further... [etc.]' (A 323/B 379–80, emphasis added). Here an absolute subject is cited as an 'unconditioned', and the idea of a series of conditions is suggested by the idea of prosyllogisms 'proceeding' to the unconditioned. These remarks suggest that in both editions of the first *Critique* Kant takes seriously at least some parts of the *Prolegomena*'s picture of the soul as the unconditioned ultimate condition of a regressive series of conditions. The passage from the Antinomies chapter suggests that he takes other parts back. So which parts of the *Prolegomena*'s story are supposed to go and which to stay? A clue is provided by the prominent position accorded in both editions to the following passage:

> There will be as many pure concepts of reason as there are kinds of relation represented by the understanding by means of the categories; and so we must seek an **unconditioned**, *first*, for **the categorical** synthesis in a **subject**, *second* for the **hypothetical** synthesis of the members of a **series**, and *third* for the **disjunctive** synthesis of the parts in a **system**. (A 323/B 380)[13]

This remark constitutes the fourth paragraph of the section dealing with the transcendental Ideas. It thus occurs in a part of the first *Critique* in which Kant is laying out the grosser features of the Dialectic's architectonic. Here he is trying to forge a connection between, on the one hand, the various kinds of synthesis represented by the Ideas and, on the other, the three species of dialectical syllogism. The three species of 'unconditioned' in question are intended to match up with the transcendental Ideas of the soul, the world, and God.

Kant's words at A 323/B 380 suggest that he conceives of the transcendental Idea of the soul as the Idea of an 'unconditioned' associated specifically with categorical synthesis. But he now implies that this unconditioned is not to be thought of as the first member of a *series*. Instead, the notion of such a first member is reserved for the unconditioned as it relates to hypothetical synthesis, a form of synthesis that Kant elsewhere associates with the Antinomies (A 406/B 432–3). In view of the prominence of this remark, it seems wisest to assume that Kant's more considered thought involves rejecting the *Prolegomena*'s conception of transcendental illusion as operative in portraying the referent of the 'I' as the final member of a regressive series. In the Antinomies Kant explains the reason for this rejection as follows: '[A]ccidents (insofar as they inhere in a single substance)

---

[13] Compare a partial quotation from R 5553:
  1. The unconditioned of *inherence* (or of the aggregate). 2. That of dependence or of the *series*. 3. That of the concurrence of all *possibility* in one and of one for all. (R 5553, 18: 228)

are coordinated with one another, and do not constitute a series' (A 414/B 441). One suspects that at this point Kant is impressed by the thought that the inherence relation—as it is viewed by one who is in the grip of transcendental illusion—is transitive, with the result that the terms of any apparent series generated by this relation all ultimately inhere in the ultimate subject, and so are, fundamentally speaking, merely coordinated.

At any rate, to answer our question about the application of Kant's model of transcendental illusion to the first paralogism: what goes (or, at any rate, should go) is the idea of a series of conditions, while what stays (or should stay) is the idea of a subject that is not (and cannot be) a predicate of something else, and which is, in that sense, absolutely unconditioned. Kant is not entirely consistent on this point, but this seems like the best way to try to make him consistent.[14]

Owing to transcendental illusion, we are inclined to think of the self not just as unifying its representations but as unifying them in virtue of standing to them as their unconditioned condition. This idea perhaps makes the most sense in connection with the 'unconditioned unity of relation', which is the unconditioned in the series generated by the relational category of subsistence and inherence. For we can understand why Kant might have taken transcendental illusion to tempt us to view the self as an unbearable bearer of 'the thoughts that are its predicates' (A 346/B 404). In this case transcendental illusion tempts us to confuse the unity of consciousness with the unconditioned unity of relation, and so to suppose that the 'I' of apperception represents something that is indeed an unbearable bearer of properties, or, in our terms, a substance$_1$.

Since the thought that the self is imagined by one in the grip of transcendental illusion to be an unconditioned condition outlives the thought that it is imagined to be the unconditioned condition specifically *in a series*, it is possible to see Kant's various remarks about mistaking one kind of subjective unity for another as indeed in keeping with the spirit (if not, admittedly, the letter) of our original account of transcendental illusion.[15] This is possible because the illusion operative in the first paralogism can now be thought of as simply the illusion that there is an unconditioned condition for any mental predicate in a particular consciousness— that is, a necessarily non-inhering subject in which they all inhere. Kant supposes that this illusion inclines us to mistake the subjective unity of our thoughts—the unity of apperception—for the objective unity of the thinking subject, namely, its

---

[14] The account of transcendental illusion in the introduction to the Dialectic and in the chapter on Ideas is not entirely consistent with Kant's remarks in the Antinomies. For in the two former places he maintains that all ideas give rise to regressive series of conditions. (See especially, A 307–8/B 364 and A 336/B 393.) It seems likely that in the *B* edition Kant simply failed to correct fully the parts of the text he did not wholly redraft.

[15] I have in mind such texts as the following: '[N]othing is more natural and seductive than the illusion of taking the unity in the synthesis of thoughts for a perceived unity in the subject of these thoughts. We might call it a subreption of the hypostatized consciousness (*apperceptionis substantiae*)' (A 402). Compare: R 5553, 18: 223–4.

apparent property of being incapable of inhering in another thing. However, because principle D makes an essential reference to a series of conditions, the present account is compatible only with a modified version of our original account of the content of transcendental illusion. We must now say that the illusion to which P gives rise is the illusion not that D is true, but that another principle, D^*, is:

D^*:   If the conditioned is given, then so is its absolutely unconditioned condition.

Kant recommends the *Prolegomena*'s account of the paralogisms as an improvement on the account given in the A edition (4: 381). But it's clear from his remarks in the Antinomies that he also harbours doubts about the idea of characterizing transcendental illusion specifically as the illusion that a regressive series of conditions has an unconditioned ultimate member. Why should he have entertained these doubts? Kant doesn't say; but one possible source of his qualms is the fact that such a conception would invite the question: 'Why is there not an antinomy of the self?' This question would arise because, if the relation of inherence were to generate a regressive series of conditions, the situation would, as far as transcendental illusion goes, be structurally parallel to the case of an antinomy. We would be able to seek the unconditioned either in an ultimate member of the regress or, supposing the regress to be unending, in an infinite totality of members occurring earlier in the series than a given conditioned member. Kant in fact indicates the availability of these two options in the parenthetical remark in the passage from the *Prolegomena*. He says, 'Pure reason demands that for each predicate of a thing we should seek its own subject, but that for this subject, which is in turn necessarily only a predicate, we should seek its subject again, and so forth to infinity (*or as far as we get*)' (*Prolegomena*, §46; 4: 333, emphasis added). The existence of these two possible ways of finding the unconditioned in a series, neither one of them uniquely recommended by reason, would generate what Kant calls a 'two-sided illusion', and so an impulse toward antinomy.[16] And yet in the first *Critique* he is keen to maintain that each of the paralogisms 'effects a merely one-sided illusion regarding the idea of the subject of our thought, and for the opposite assertion there is not the least plausibility forthcoming from concepts of reason' (A 406/B 433). Kant is wedded to this view for architectonic reasons. It matters to him to maintain that there are only four antinomies, one for each 'title'

---

[16] To be clear, my position—both here and in my 'Kant's First Paralogism'—is not, *contra* Wuerth, that the first paralogism *is*, in effect, an antinomy (Wuerth, *Kant on Mind* at 163, note 9). On the contrary, I hold that it is plainly a paralogism—the result of a one-sided illusion—and, indeed, Kant is explicit that the psychological idea contains no antinomy (A 673/B 701). My point—both here and in 'Kant's First Paralogism'—is rather that Kant's account of how transcendental illusion functions in connection with the self in the *Prolegomena* would, if strictly thought through, cause one to wonder why he did not see this instance of transcendental illusion as engendering an antinomy rather than a paralogism.

of the table of categories (A 415/B 442; compare A 462/B 490), because he sees this correspondence as a sign that he has succeeded in identifying all the instances of dialectical inference associated with the hypothetical syllogism. This is part of the important idea that *Critique* should be systematic.

Kant's actual view in the Paralogisms avoids the worry about a two-sided illusion by dispensing with the picture of a regressive series; but when fully thought through, this change demands a corresponding change in the general account of transcendental illusion. Principle D^* rather than D must now be regarded as the relevant statement of the content of transcendental illusion.

5.3 Wuerth's interpretation

In the previous chapter we examined Wuerth's criticisms of my interpretation of the B-edition first Paralogism. I turn now to his own positive views. Wuerth's account runs as follows. Kant believes that although I cannot *cognize* or *know* features of the self as it is in itself, I can nonetheless have an indeterminate *consciousness* or *apperception* of the soul as falling under the pure or 'unschematized' categories of substance, simplicity, and so forth.[17] Wuerth supposes that I am able in *this* sense to 'apply' these pure categories to the soul as it is in itself. He further holds that when Kant intends to speak of our consciousness of the soul's instantiating the pure concept of substance he speaks in terms of our being conscious of our underlying 'substantiale'.[18] Insofar as Kant denies that we have insight into our own substantiality, Wuerth maintains, he merely means that we are not justified in applying to the soul the useful, empirical, and determinate concept of *persistence* (understood as permanence).[19] Importantly, on Wuerth's view, the sense in which we can 'apply' to the self the pure categories of substance, simplicity, and so forth is not that we *cognize* the self as having these properties, but merely that in being conscious of them we stand to them in what Wuerth seems to regard as a *sui generis* state of 'epistemic contact'.[20] Wuerth holds that in the B edition Kant continues to grant the applicability to the self of each of the pure, unschematized categories.[21] He thus supposes that in both editions Kant allows that we have, among other things, what Wuerth calls 'a pure, indeterminate apperception of our soul as a noumenal substance'.[22]

Wuerth's reading is original and intriguing. There are certainly some texts, particularly from Kant's religion lectures, that can seem to support it. In the end, however, I find the view—considered as an interpretation of Kant's position specifically in the first *Critique*—to be lacking in genuine textual support and, indeed, to be undermined by several of Kant's remarks in his more authoritative

---

[17] Wuerth, *Kant on Mind* at 167–8, 173. [18] Ibid., at 165; compare n11, 169.
[19] Ibid., at 160.   [20] Ibid., at 122.   [21] Ibid., at 167.   [22] Ibid., at 168.

texts. I will enumerate my objections before substantiating them. They are three in number.

First, certain authoritative texts contradict Wuerth's claim that 'consciousness' affords us a kind of unmediated insight into the soul's inner nature—an insight distinct in kind from cognition.[23] Second, although Kant does allow that we are conscious in pure apperception of the *substantiale*, this is not something that we are held to be conscious of as exemplifying the unschematized category of substance. It is rather the referent of the I thought of merely as a something that bears accidents; it is the self considered in abstraction from its accidents (29: 904). To think of the I in this way is emphatically *not* to think of it as exemplifying the unschematized concept of substance, for the latter concept includes the modal notion of being *incapable* of inhering in another thing. Third, as we saw in the previous chapter, although between the two editions Kant does take the soul (understood as the thinking subject) to be a substance$_1$, this is only a briefly held commitment—one from which Kant frees himself in the second edition.

To substantiate the first of these criticisms it suffices to consider a famous remark from the *B* Deduction. In the synthetic original unity of apperception, Kant says, 'I am conscious of myself not as I appear to myself, nor yet as I am in myself, but only **that** I am' (B 157). If Wuerth is right, Kant ought to say no such thing; for according to his interpretation Kant maintains, in both editions of the first *Critique*, that in pure apperception I am indeed conscious of myself *as I am in myself* insofar as I am conscious of my noumenal self as instantiating certain unschematized categories.[24]

Second, consider a remark from the 'Discipline of Pure Reason':

> As plausible as the supposed proof of the simple nature of our thinking substance from the unity of apperception may be, yet it unavoidably faces the difficulty that, since absolute simplicity is not a concept that can be immediately related to a perception, but rather... must be merely inferred, there can be no insight at all into how the mere consciousness that is contained or at least can be contained **in all thinking** should, even though it is on this account a simple representation, lead to the consciousness [*Bewußtsein*] and acquaintance [*Kenntnis*] with a thing **in which** alone thinking can be contained. (A 784/B 812)

I take it that when he claims here that we lack insight into how it is, or can be, that such and such is the case, Kant does not mean that such and such *is* the case, though we lack insight into *how* it could be the case. For on that reading he would be allowing that we have consciousness of *and acquaintance with* our thinking substance, while lacking insight into how we do so. But Kant explicitly denies that

---

[23] Ibid., at 173. [24] Ibid., at 126, 134, 166–7.

we have acquaintance with the thinking subject (A 355). The passage from A 784/B 812, therefore, is better read as denying that we have the alleged consciousness or acquaintance at all. But such a denial runs directly counter to Wuerth's interpretation.

What, then, *is* the purpose of this remark from A 784/B 812? Its function, I think, is just to apply the constraint on rational psychology that Kant articulates in the *Metaphysics L1* and which we discussed in Chapter 2.6, namely, that rational psychology may prove of the soul only what we can experience of it. Kant is suggesting that this constraint is infringed by the rational psychologist's claim to be able to prove the simplicity of the soul simply because we do not experience the soul's simplicity.

A third relevant passage occurs in the Appendix to the Transcendental Dialectic. There Kant says that the 'dogmatic spiritualist' explains our interest in the afterlife 'by our consciousness of the immaterial nature, and so forth, of ourselves as thinking subjects' (A 690/B 718). The context makes clear that Kant views the dogmatic spiritualist's explanation as mistaken. If Wuerth is right, however, Kant would himself qualify as a 'dogmatic spiritualist'. For on Wuerth's view, he maintains that we are conscious of the inner nature of the self, including, its simplicity—and hence presumably also its immateriality. I take it that because Kant would plainly disavow the label 'dogmatic spiritualist' he would also disavow Wuerth's interpretation of his view.

A fourth problem-passage for Wuerth's reading runs as follows:

[Although I know no a priori answer to the question: "What, in general, is the character of a thing that thinks"], it does seem to me that I can give such an answer in a particular case, viz., in the proposition that expresses self-consciousness: I think. For this I is the premier subject; i.e., substance; it is simple, etc. But then these propositions would all have to be experiential ones; yet in fact they could not contain such predicates (which are not empirical) without a universal rule stating a priori the conditions of the possibility of thinking as such. In this way, my [presumed] insight (so plausible at the start) into the nature of a thinking being, and indeed judged from mere concepts, becomes suspect, even though I have not yet uncovered the error in it.

This error can be uncovered, however, by further investigation into the origin of these attributes that I attribute to myself as a thinking being as such. (A 398–9)

At the start of this passage Kant is temporarily speaking from the point of view of the dogmatic rational psychologist. He means that this figure's *alleged* insight into the nature of the thinking being, which this figure initially takes to be afforded by the self-consciousness expressed in the 'I think', although *apparently* genuine on first appearances, can be recognized, in the end, as specious. The implication is that self-consciousness does not, after all, reveal features of the subject as it is in itself. Again, such an implication seems to run directly contrary to Wuerth's interpretation.

Wuerth would presumably read this passage as saying merely that self-consciousness can afford no insight into which *schematized* categories apply to the soul. He would take Kant to hold that self-consciousness does afford an insight into the fact that the soul instantiates the pure or unschematized concept of, for example, substance. But, if that were really Kant's position, then, contrary to what he says here, he would indeed have an answer to the question: 'What is the character of the thing that thinks?' For he would be able to say that it is a substance, simple, and so forth (in the sense of the unschematized categories). In short, on Wuerth's interpretation, Kant would be vulnerable here to the reproach of misleading his reader.

Kant's view seems rather to be that all that is represented to me through the consciousness expressed by the proposition 'I think' (that is, through pure apperception) is that I am a mere *something* in which accidents—thoughts—inhere. This 'something', I take it, is what Kant means by 'the substantiale'. 'The substantiale', he says in metaphysics lectures from 1789–91, 'is in general the concept of something [*Etwas*] in which the accidents inhere' (28: 511). Such a thing is not to be confused with something exemplifying the unschematized category of substance; for that category, as I have already emphasized, has a *modal* component: it is the concept of something that *cannot* be an accident of another thing. *Contra* Wuerth, then, the substantiale in me is not my soul thought of as subsumed under the unschematized category of substance: it is rather simply the transcendental subject, understood as a mere indeterminate (that is, categorially undetermined) something [*Etwas*] in which certain accidents—my thoughts—inhere (compare A 355).

5.4 A problem with Kant's characterization of a paralogism

Kant's explanation of the fallacy involved in the paralogisms, as it is stated in the *A* edition, is problematic; for it seems to mis-locate the alleged equivocation. Kant says that the fallacy arises because

> the major premise makes a merely transcendental use of the category, in regard to its condition, but...the minor premise and the conclusion, in respect of the soul that is subsumed under this condition make an empirical use of this same category. (A 402–3)

If one takes Kant at his word, while also supposing that the argument features equivocation on its middle term, one is forced to conclude that in the first edition Kant is portraying the paralogisms as having the following form:

Major premise: All M^T are P^T
Minor premise: The I, as thinking being, is M^E
Conclusion: Therefore the I, as thinking being, is P^E

Here I use a superscript 'T' for the transcendental use of the category, and a superscript 'E' for the empirical use.

This form fits *none* of the paralogisms in either edition; for, with the sole exception of the *A*-edition first paralogism, which, in any case, lacks an equivocal middle term, the major premise and conclusion feature an unequivocal predicate. This problem is, I think, intractable, but it does help to explain why Kant should have felt it necessary to subject the Paralogisms chapter to a thoroughgoing overhaul. In the second edition what survives of Kant's description of a paralogism at A 402–3 is just the idea that the paralogism is a *sophisma figurae dictionis* (B 411). But the business about the predicate's possessing both empirical and transcendental uses rightly disappears.

5.5 Two ways of viewing a paralogism

The faulty inferences Kant discusses in the Paralogisms chapter share the feature that if they are genuinely *sophismata figurae dictionis* then they may be interpreted in either of two incompatible ways. On the one hand, we may interpret the argument as having known premises but containing an equivocal middle term. On the other, we may interpret it so that the equivocation is remedied, but now accept that the minor premise is not known to be true.

Since these two ways of regarding a paralogism will become important in later chapters it will be useful to adopt some abbreviations. Let us call the minor premise when its middle term is so interpreted that the premise meshes with the major into a valid argument 'the minor$_v$' ('v' for a premise in a *valid* argument). And let's call the minor premise when its middle term is so interpreted that the premise is known to be true 'the minor$_k$' ('k' for a *known* premise). In line with this practice, let us also use the term 'paralogism$_v$' for a *rectified* paralogism, that is to say, an argument in which the predicate of the minor premise is construed as univocal with the subject term of the major premise, with the result that the argument is in fact valid, though its minor premise is not known to be true. Finally, let us use the term 'paralogism$_k$' for a *sophisma figurae dictionis* where the ambiguity is resolved in such a way that the argument is invalid while its premises are known to be true.

It should be obvious that a paralogism$_v$ is, *strictly speaking*, no more a paralogism than a repaid debt is a debt or a filled-in hole is a hole. In speaking (for convenience) of 'two ways of regarding a paralogism' and of a 'paralogism$_v$', therefore, I am using words informally and, strictly speaking, inaccurately.

However, since Kant himself discusses certain paralogisms$_v$ under the heading of the 'Paralogisms' chapter, I think this way of speaking is appropriate and does no great harm. Indeed, it avoids a good deal of fuss. One should never forget, however, that it is *only* an unofficial way of speaking.[25]

With this terminology in place, we can note that three styles of criticism are available to Kant in the Paralogisms chapter. He can treat one of the paralogist's arguments as a paralogism$_v$ and criticize it on the ground that its minor premise is not known to be true. Or he can treat it as a paralogism$_k$ and criticize it on the ground that it equivocates on its middle term. Finally, he can treat it as an *ignoratio elenchi*, which is to say a valid argument with known premises whose promulgator misconstrues its conclusion as stronger than it actually is. As we will see, Kant in fact makes use of all three styles of criticism in his discussion of the paralogisms.

To sum up: Kant's critique of the *A*-edition first paralogism consists, at bottom, in the observation that it operates with an incorrect conception of substance—'incorrect' because it fails to correspond to any notion that the rational psychologist might have in mind when claiming that the self is a 'substance'. Consequently, the argument suffers from the fallacy of *ignoratio elenchi*: it establishes less than was required to refute an envisaged opponent who denies the permanence of the soul. The *A*-edition first paralogism traffics in a conception of substance—namely, substance$_0$—that turns out to make an essential appeal to considerations having to do with where a judgmental component can (and cannot) occur in a judgment. Since that is so, the main flaw in the *A*-edition first paralogism is one of *irrelevance*: the paralogism establishes a conclusion that is too weak to be of interest to the rational psychologist. We learn only that the soul is a substance$_0$, and to learn that is not to learn a lot.

---

[25] On this last point I find myself disagreeing with Marcus Willaschek, who claims that what I am calling the unofficial way of speaking should be taken seriously. That is to say, he insists, *contra* my 2010, that there are two ways of diagnosing a paralogism (now using this term in a strict sense), corresponding to the two ways of disambiguating its middle term. I remain unpersuaded, however, because a paralogism is by definition false with respect to form, and this means that when the paralogism is a *sophisma figurae dictionis* (rather than merely an *ignoratio elenchi*) resolving the ambiguous middle term so that it is taken in the same sense in both premises will produce an argument that is strictly speaking *not* a paralogism. The extent of our disagreement, however, should not be exaggerated. The two large grains of truth in Willaschek's position are, first, that Kant does include within the Paralogisms chapter, along with discussion of those arguments that I am calling paralogisms$_k$, discussion of certain arguments that I am unofficially (and with reservations and due warnings) calling 'paralogisms$_v$'; and, second, that the latter do exhibit one of two ways of diagnosing what might go wrong in a *sophisma figurae dictionis* (the other diagnosis involving treating the argument as a paralogism$_k$). Unfortunately, however, having made these important observations, Willaschek proceeds to muddy the waters by inaccurately characterizing the two ways of diagnosing the arguments in question. We may, he says, read each paralogism either as 'valid but not sound' or as 'sound but invalid'. But since a sound argument is a *valid* argument all of whose premises are true, the latter characterization is contradictory; while the former fails to recognize that for the purposes of his criticism all that Kant needs to say about the alternative disambiguation is that the argument is valid but not *known to be* sound (because not known to have true premises). See Marcus Willaschek, *Kant on the Sources of Metaphysics: The Dialectic of Pure Reason* (Cambridge: Cambridge University Press, 2018) at 195, n16 and 195–6.

6
The Second Paralogism

6.1 Introduction

The *A*-edition second paralogism argues that the soul, understood as the subject of thoughts or 'thinking I', is simple, hence non-composite, or, more precisely, non-plural: it is one thing as opposed to many. The argument turns on the idea that the thinking I thinks not in the manner in which a composite would think if *per impossibile* it could do so, but in the manner of a unitary subject. Kant has a specific understanding of what would be required for something to think in the manner of a composite; but before we get into that we should consider how he presents the second paralogism in the *A* edition.

Like the first paralogism, the second takes the form of a categorical syllogism with a singular minor premise. It runs as follows:

That thing, whose action can never be regarded as the concurrence [*Concurrenz*] of many acting things, [*Dinge*] is **simple**.
Now the soul, or the thinking I, is one such [thing].
Therefore, etc. (A 351)

Here by 'simple' the paralogist means 'not a plurality of things'.[1] The major premise, accordingly, asserts that that thing whose action *can never be conceived of as* the concurrence of a plurality of things *is not* a plurality of things. We can think of this premise as derived from two others. First: 'That thing whose action *can never be conceived of as* the concurrence of a plurality of acting things is such that its action *is not* the concurrence of a plurality of acting things'. Second: 'That thing whose action *is not* the concurrence of a plurality of acting things *is not* (itself) a plurality of acting things'. The first of these assumptions shares a structural affinity with the major premise of the *B*-edition first paralogism. The second is, if not completely obvious, then at least plausible; and Kant leaves it unchallenged, devoting his critical energies to arguing that the minor premise is

---

[1] The rival reading, according to which to be simple is to be one substance$_1$, is to be rejected because it would make the *major* premise unacceptably dogmatic and hard to know. Why should a non-plural actor not rather be a predicate of another thing, as Spinoza, for example, had supposed concerning finite minds? Kant, recall, questions our knowledge of the major premise in none of the paralogisms.

not known to be true. He thus treats the *A*-edition second paralogism as (in our terms) a paralogism$_v$.[2] That is to say, he portrays the argument as flawed not because it is 'false as to form' but merely because one of its premises is not known to be true. He argues that the minor premise—that is, in our terms the minor premise$_v$—is not known to be true because its traditional supporting argument—the so-called Achilles—relies on a premise that is itself not known to be true. He refers to this premise as the argument's '*nervus probandi*' or 'nerve of what is to be proved'.

6.2 The Achilles

The Achilles endeavours to prove that nothing composite can think *qua* composite. The qualification '*qua* composite' is needed because the Achilles does not seek to rule out that a composite might think in virtue of one of its members' thinking. (That hypothesis would be ruled out by the arbitrariness of the assumption that it thinks in virtue of one particular member rather than any other.) Kant supposes that if the conclusion of the Achilles could be established, the minor premise$_v$ would follow as a corollary. He offers no defence of this last claim, but the argument for the entailment would plausibly run as follows:

We wish to show that the soul (understood merely as a thinking subject) is something whose action can never be regarded as the concurrence of many acting things (that is, we wish to establish the minor premise$_v$). We assume that nothing composite can think *qua* composite. The proof then proceeds as follows. Suppose, for *reductio*, that one of the soul's (token) actions could be the (token) action of a plurality of things acting jointly. Then the soul, whose action is to think, would be a composite that thinks in the manner of a composite. But then it would be possible for something composite to think *qua* composite. But, by our premise, nothing composite can think *qua* composite. Contradiction. QED.

If we interpret 'composite' here as meaning 'plurality', this argument is valid. Kant's (tacit) objection to it is only that its main premise—namely, that nothing composite can think *qua* composite—is not known to be true. This premise is not known to be true, he thinks, because its supporting argument, the Achilles, relies on a premise, the *nervus probandi*, that is not known to be true. Kant formulates the *nervus probandi* in two ways, the first of which runs as follows:

Nervus probandi (containment formulation):
In order for many representations to make up one thought, they must be contained in the absolute unity of the thinking subject. (A 352)

---

[2] Recall that the notions of a paralogism$_v$, the minor premise$_v$, a paralogism$_k$, etc. are explained in the appendix.

I take it that a thinking subject's 'absolute unity' consists in its being a non-plural thinker of the thoughts it thinks—in, that is to say, its not being a thinking committee or group mind.[3] The alternative natural interpretation of the phrase 'absolute unity', according to which a thing counts as an absolute unity just in case it is a single *substance₁*, is, I take it, less charitable because it would present the *nervus probandi* as being stronger—and so less plausibly known to be true.

In the second formulation of the *nervus probandi* the language of containment is replaced with the language of causality.

Nervus probandi (causal formulation):
A thought can only be the effect of the absolute unity of the thinking being. (A 353)

I take this to mean:

> Necessarily, every thought is caused to exist by the action of at least one non-plural thinking thing, which action is the total cause of that thought.

In this formulation 'every thought' is intended to have wide scope with respect to 'at least one'. The formulation allows for the possibility of causal over-determination; for it allows that a thought might be caused to exist by several things each of which functions as a distinct total cause of that thought. What the formulation rules out is the possibility that a plurality of things should, *qua* plurality, cause some thought to exist—a case in which the action of each thing in the plurality would be required for the existence of the thought, and so a case in which each thing in the plurality would be merely a *partial* cause of the thought.

Kant embeds the Achilles argument in an intricate passage, whose main parts I label for convenience.

> [**Apology**] This is the Achilles of all dialectical inferences of pure psychology. It is by no means merely a sophistical game that a dogmatist contrives in order to provide his assertions with a fleeting air of plausibility, it is rather an inference that seems to withstand even the keenest examination and the most scrupulous investigation. Here it is:
>
> [**Setup and premises**] Every **composite** substance is an aggregate of many substances, and the action of a composite, or whatever inheres in it as such a composite, is an aggregate of many actions or accidents, which is distributed among the plurality [*Menge*] of substances. Now an effect which arises from the concurrence [*Concurrenz*] of many acting substances is indeed possible, namely,

---

[3] At A 629/B 657 Kant uses 'absolute unity' in this sense when speaking of the originator's alleged property of being a non-plural (cause of the universe).

when this effect is external only (as, for instance, the motion of a body is the united motion of all its parts.). [**Thesis**] But with thoughts, as accidents belonging internally to a thinking being, it is otherwise. [**Argument**] For suppose [for *reductio* that] the composite were to think: then every part of it would contain a part of the thought, and only all of them taken together would contain the whole thought. But this is contradictory. For representations (for instance, the single words of a verse), distributed among different beings, [can] never make up a whole thought (a verse), and it is therefore impossible that a thought should inhere in a composite as such. [**Conclusion**] Hence a thought is only possible in **one** substance, which is not an aggregate of many, and hence is absolutely simple.

(A 351–2)

The 'apology' presents the second paralogism, the heart of which is contained in the Achilles argument, as the most convincing of all the dialectical inferences of reason. In the tradition, an 'Achilles' is that argument which makes the best case for a certain position.[4] But since Kant sees this particular Achilles as unsuccessful, the thought behind his application of the label would presumably be merely that the argument offers the best prospect of advancing pure rational psychology by theoretical means. Kant's respect for the argument is entirely fitting; for, as Dyck notes, it boasts a long and venerable lineage, and as Heiner Klemme and Allison note, Kant had himself been attracted to it in the 1760s and 1770s.[5]

The 'setup and premises' section makes three important points. The first point concerns the relationship between a composite substance and the accidents that inhere in it or, alternatively, the effects that it has. The action of a composite that acts *as* a composite, Kant tells us, is thought of as *distributed* among the composite's parts. Moreover, when the composite is acting *as a composite* its action is

---

[4] Dyck traces this usage to Bayle. Dyck, *Kant and Rational Psychology* at 104, note 1. We may also note that the Oxford English Dictionary records a 1579 use of the adjective 'Achillean' with the meaning 'invulnerable or invincible'.

[5] Klemme, *Kants Philosophie des Subjekts* at 316. Allison, *Kant's Transcendental Idealism* at 341. See also *Dreams of a Spirit Seer*, 2: 322 and 2: 327 note †, and *Metaphysics L1*, 28: 266–7. Kemp Smith notes that Kant may have known of the argument from Mendelssohn's *Phädon* (see Norman Kemp Smith, *A Commentary to Kant's Critique of Pure Reason* (2nd edn; Atlantic Highlands, NJ: Humanities Press International, 1992) at 458–9). But he could also have learned of it from his teacher, Martin Knutzen, who in his *Philosophical Treatise on the Immaterial Nature of the Soul* of 1744 presents a version of the argument that takes the form of a trilemma of roughly the following form: Suppose matter thinks. Then in an aggregate of monads constituting a lump of matter either one monad thinks a whole thought (so to speak on behalf of the composite), or each thinks a separate part of the thought, or again each thinks the whole thought. Knutzen proceeds to argue that whichever disjunct obtains this does not amount to a case of matter's thinking a thought. The Achilles proper is appealed to in arguing against the second disjunct. Our description, however, simplifies Knutzen's argument. For details see Martin Knutzen, *Philosophische Abhandlung von der immateriellen Natur der Seele* (Königsberg, 1744) at §7. This trilemma argument, which goes back to Plotinus, would also have been familiar to Kant from Ralph Cudworth's exposition of Plotinus's version of the argument in his work *The True Intellectual System of the Universe*. See Ralph Cudworth, *The True Intellectual System of the Universe*, 3 vols. (1845) at volume 3, 388. Kant owned J. L. Mosheim's Latin translation of 1733.

constituted by the several actions of its parts. In the text, the fact that the composite is conceived of as thinking the thought *as a composite* is indicated by the phrase 'as such', which corresponds to the Latin qualification '*qua talis*'.[6] The contrast is with a case in which a composite might be supposed to think a thought merely in virtue of one of its parts' thinking the thought.[7] Such a case, it seems reasonable to assume, is one that Kant would have regarded as ruled out for the rational psychologist by a properly consistent use of the *PSR*. For, if one supposes that a composite thinks in virtue of the thinking of a particular one of its members, there would have to be a sufficient reason why that particular member enjoyed this privilege rather than some other. And yet there would seem to be none.

The second point made in the 'setup and premises' is that both Kant and his rational psychologist opponent suppose that if thinking composites were to exist, the relationship between their actions and the actions of their parts would share the transparency of the relation between the motion of a body and the motions of its parts: the action of the whole would be the sum of the actions of the parts. This conception calls to mind a passage from Newton's *Principia* with which Kant would have been familiar.

> The motion of the whole [body] is the same as the sum of the motions of the parts; that is, the translation of the whole out of its place is the same thing as the sum of the translations of the parts out of their places.[8]

For Kant, however, the analogy conveys merely a conception of how composites would have to think if, *per impossibile*, they could do so.

The third point made in the 'setup and premises' is that Kant's rationalist conceives of a *composite* substance as an *aggregate* of many substances ('substances' here being understood neutrally as things rather than as substances$_1$). Composites are naturally thought to have *parts*, aggregates *members*; so the two notions would not usually be equated. But since Kant seems not to insist on this distinction himself, I will permit myself a similar leeway in explicating both his own views and his take on the views of his opponent.

Kant's handling of the thesis features a minor glitch. Whereas the thesis actually stated is the minor premise of the second paralogism, the thesis argued for in the 'argument' section is not this claim exactly, but rather the claim from which—on assumptions Kant shares with his opponent—it follows as a corollary, namely, that no composite can think. This shows, I think, that Kant is apt to run these two claims together. Nonetheless, they *are* distinct and it is worth registering their distinctness in our reconstruction.

---

[6] Compare 29: 1034. [7] This case is considered explicitly by Knutzen. See note 5 above.
[8] Isaac Newton, *Philosophiae Naturalis Principia Mathematica* ('*Mathematical Principles of Natural Philosophy*'), trans. Florian Cajori, 2 vols (Los Angeles: University of California Press, 1934) at volume 1, 7.

In the 'argument' section we are finally presented with the Achilles argument, which I take to run as follows:

Thesis to be proven: Nothing composite can think *qua* composite.

Argument:

We first prove the weaker claim that nothing composite *does* think in this manner.
P1.   (*Reductio* premise). Something composite thinks (*qua* composite), [1].
P2.   What it is for a composite to act (*qua* composite) is for each of its parts to produce a distinct part of its action while none of them produces the action as a whole, [2].
P3.   (*The nervus probandi*) Necessarily, every thought has at least one non-plural total efficient cause, [3].
P4.   The action of a thinking composite is to think, [4].

So,

L1. What it is for a thinking composite to think (*qua* composite) is for each of its parts to produce a distinct part of a given one of its thoughts while none of them produces the thought as a whole. (from P2 and P4), [2, 4].

So,

L2. Something composite produces a thought in the following manner: each of its parts produces a distinct part of the thought while none produces the thought as a whole ("every part of the composite would contain a part of the thought, and only all of the parts taken together would contain the whole thought") (from P1 and L1), [1, 2, 4].

But,

L3.   Contradiction (from L2 and P3. We will scrutinize this controversial step shortly), [1, 2, 3, 4].
So,
L4.   Nothing composite thinks (from L3, discharging P1), [2, 3, 4].
But,
P5.   Each of the premises P2–P4 is a necessary truth and the steps in our proof correspond to entailments, [5].

So,

C. No composite *can* think (from L4 and P5 by a basic principle of modal logic), [2, 3, 4, 5].

This is a natural reconstruction of the argument that Kant states, but the reasoning as it stands is flawed. The problem lies with the step leading to L3. For the contradiction alleged there does not in fact exist. Consider, for example, a world in which a composite's token thought was causally overdetermined, being produced *both* by the composite itself (*qua* composite) and by God. At this world, although the composite would (by L2) not be a *non-plural* total cause of the thought, the thought would still possess such a cause, namely God. And L2 and P3 would both be true. Such a situation is not ruled out by our premises. In order to rule it out we need to appeal to a further premise, namely, that no token thought has more than one total cause. With this further assumption made, the argument becomes valid. But what could justify this further premise? The answer, I think, is the *inherence* model of the relation between a thought and a thinker. After all, our supplementary premise will be justified if we think of each thought as inhering in its total cause. Or rather, it will be justified if we combine this assumption with the idea that token thoughts are tropes (particularized universals), for no trope can inhere in more than one thing. If the argument is repaired in this way, the inherence model will figure essentially.

Kant views the Achilles as a valid argument that relies on an unknown premise—namely, the *nervus probandi* (our P3). He might also have questioned our right to affirm P2, but he seems to grant this premise—either for the sake of argument or because he regards it as true. His main criticism is that P3 is not known to be true. He maintains that we can cognize its truth neither 'from concepts'—which in this context means on the basis of analytic truths including definitions, nor from 'experience'.[9]

In the course of claiming that we cannot know P3 'from concepts' Kant briefly considers one purported conceptual proof of the *nervus probandi*. The main (tacit) premise of this purported proof is the principle that the total cause must have at least as much reality as the effect—a principle that the Descartes of the *Meditations* takes to be known by the natural light.[10] Kant, who grants the analyticity of this principle for the sake of argument, envisages his rationalist opponent as applying it to the case of thoughts in the following way. One begins by assuming, first, that thoughts are absolute unities, and second, that absolute

---

[9] Dyck claims that Kant might have also objected to the argument on the ground that it takes the form of a *reductio ad absurdum* (*Kant and Rational Psychology*). As we will see in Chapter 10, however, Kant is in fact committed to rejecting only a limited class of *reductio* arguments in metaphysics—a class to which the present one does not belong.

[10] *Meditations* III, paragraph 14 (*AT* VII, 40; *CSM* II, 28).

unities have more reality than mere 'collective' unities (that is, organized or united pluralities). One then argues that the total cause of any thought must also be an absolute unity, and so not a plurality. For, by the just-mentioned tacit premise, no merely collective unity will have sufficient reality to bring a thought into existence.

Kant blocks this argument by denying its starting assumption. The unity of a thought, he claims, is not in fact absolute but merely *collective*:

> Since the thought consists of many representations, its unity is collective [*collectiv*] and can, as far as mere concepts are concerned, just as well relate to [*sich beziehen auf*] the collective unity of the substances acting on the thought [in producing it] as to the absolute unity of the subject. (A 353)

Kant's point is simply that since a thought is made up of a plurality of representations its unity is of the 'collective' kind: the unity, namely, enjoyed by pluralities—for example, herds. And since that is so, it is compatible with the Cartesian causal principle that a thought should have for its total cause a plurality of things rather than a single thing.[11]

Apparently assuming that the rational psychologist views the Cartesian causal principle as a conceptual truth, Kant seems to regard this (by his lights) flawed argument as the only remotely plausible candidate for a conceptually based demonstration of the *nervus probandi*. For he concludes: 'There can be no insight according to the rule of identity into the necessity of presupposing a simple substance for a composite thought' (A 353). He means, of course, that we cannot know the *nervus probandi* to be true on conceptual grounds, whether those grounds be those just considered or others. Nor, in Kant's opinion, can we treat the claim as a synthetic a priori truth known *merely* from concepts, for, in his view, there are no such truths: all synthetic a priori truth is, for him, grounded in the possibility of experience, and it is clear that Kant sees no way to establish such a ground for the *nervus probandi* (A 353).

Nor, finally, can we know the *nervus probandi* 'from experience'. For, first, the principle purports, through its use of the word 'must', to express a necessary connection (A 353), and yet 'experience does not allow us to cognize any necessity' (ibid.). Second, 'absolute unity' is 'far above [experience's] sphere' (ibid.). In other words, the concept of something's being *one* thing as opposed to many is not a concept whose exemplification we can verify on the basis of mere experience— anything that seems to be one thing could turn out, upon closer inspection, to be many. The *nervus probandi*, Kant concludes, cannot be known to be true.

---

[11] It is, I think, no accident that this argument, which appeals to the same principle as the Third Mediation argument for God, is on Kant's mind in this context. For, as we will see, an assumption made in the course of this same Cartesian argument provides the model for the second paralogism's major premise.

6.3 The A-edition second paralogism as a paralogism$_k$

Up to now we have followed Kant in analysing the A-edition second paralogism as a paralogism$_v$. But since the A edition claims that each of the paralogisms can be viewed as a *sophisma figurae dictionis* we need to consider how the second paralogism might be construed as a paralogism$_k$. In particular, we need to ask: which known truth are we supposed to be apt to confuse with the unknown minor premise (or, treating the diagnosis more loosely, the with *nervus probandi*)? Kant's answer runs as follows:

> [I]t is obvious that we require, in order to have any thought, the absolute unity of the subject only because otherwise we could not say *I think* (the manifold in one presentation). For although the whole of the thought could be divided and distributed among many subjects, still the subjective *I* cannot be divided and distributed, and yet we presuppose this *I* in all thought. (A 353–4)

The known truth in question is supposed to be the truth that the subjective *I*—the *I* that refers to the subject of thought as opposed to the human being—cannot be divided and distributed among a plurality of thinkers.

This suggests the following interpretation for the second paralogism when it is conceived of as an invalid argument with known premises (a paralogism$_k$ in our jargon):

> That thing whose action cannot be conceived of as the concurrence of many acting things is simple.
>
> The thinking I is something that cannot be divided and distributed among many subjects.
>
> Therefore, the thinking I is simple.

Here we have exhibited how the middle term must be disambiguated if we are to treat the argument as a paralogism$_k$. But what does it mean to say that the thinking *I* cannot be 'divided and distributed among many subjects'? What would it be to wrongly imagine that it *could* be? And *why* can't it be?

Kant answers none of these questions explicitly; so we'll have to answer them ourselves. Let's focus on the second. One thing that might constitute wrongly imagining that the *I* could be divided and distributed among several subjects would be to imagine that I might be able to think a thought in virtue of myself thinking only some proper subset of its components—the work of thinking the remaining components being delegated to other minds. One instance of this supposition would be to suppose that I might be able to think the thought that *aRb* by having my mum think '*a*' and my dad think '*R*', while I myself think only '*b*'. It is obvious that I could not think the thought that *aRb* in this manner. I take it that Kant supposes that we are apt to confuse the perfectly obvious thought that the distribution of intellectual labour just described could not amount to *my* thinking the thought that *aRb* with the unwarranted thought that this exercise could not constitute the thinking of this thought by *some* mind—and in particular by the group mind consisting of the three family members just mentioned. Neither, of course, do I know that it *does* constitute such a thing, but that is beside the point. The present question is just whether recognition of the impossibility currently under consideration gives me any reason to conclude that pluralities are incapable of thinking *qua* pluralities. And Kant is quite right to maintain that it does not.

6.4 Kant's criticism evaluated

In the A edition Kant focuses on the point that the second paralogism, construed as a paralogism$_v$, is not known to be sound because P3 is not known to be true. If his criticism is to carry conviction, he will need to persuade us that no sound argument *could* be constructed for P3—by establishing, for example, that this premise is actually false. But, as we have seen, far from establishing this result, Kant merely criticizes a single attempt to argue for P3. His criticism is therefore at the very least incomplete. In order to shore it up we would need to describe a possible situation in which a thought *is* entertained by a group mind. In an effort to do that one might adapt an example from Michael Tye.[12]

Consider a group of minds organized under the complex relation whose obtaining constitutes the minds in question the voting committee of a philosophy department. The committee could choose something, intend to do something, settle on a plan, and so forth without a single one of its members choosing that thing, intending to do that thing, or settling on that plan. For a situation could arise in which each individual member ranked an action, plan, or whatnot, second in an ordered list of preferences while the votes cast nonetheless so aggregated as to render that action, plan, or whatnot the *committee*'s first choice. That the preferences of a group can diverge in this way from the preferences of its individual members gives us a reason to think of the committee itself as a *subject* of deciding, choosing, planning, etc.—in short, a group mind distinct from its members.

Kant seems never to have considered such a model of group thinking. His own examples always involve cases in which a plurality of thinkers thinks a thought in

---

[12] See Michael Tye, 'Homunculi Heads and Silicon Chips: The Importance of History to Phenomenology', in Adam Pautz and Dan Stoljar (eds), *Blockheads! Essays on Ned Block's Philosophy of Mind and Consciousness* (Cambridge, MA: MIT Press, 2019), 545–70.

virtue of its members' pairing up with the thought's components, each one thinking its assigned component. In Kant's day, this distributive conception was the standard way to conceive of the alleged possibility of a composite thinker thinking *qua* composite, and it would be anachronistic to represent Kant as having even considered examples in the style of Tye's. Nonetheless, it seems worth asking whether Kant would have endorsed the current example as a counter-example to the *nervus probandi* had he been presented with it. One reason to think that he would *not* have done so is his commitment to the spontaneity of thought.[13] If what it takes for the thinking of a thought to be a spontaneous act is that there should be nothing involved in its production other than the mental activities of its subject, then Tye's model will be ruled out. The committee, after all, reaches its decision in virtue of the mental acts of its members. A second reason to doubt whether Kant would have accepted this as a counter-example to the *nervus probandi* is that he conceives of thoughts not broadly as acts of the mind, but more specifically as truth-evaluable combinations of concepts (that is, as judgments). It would take some further argument to make plausible that Tye's committee thinks thoughts in the latter and not merely the former sense.

This second objection is, I think, more decisive than the first. For the first suffers from a doubt about whether Kant could have been understanding the spontaneity of thought in quite the way envisaged. After all, if he had been doing so, he would have possessed precisely what he claims we cannot have, namely, an argument for the *nervus probandi*. For, *any* model of group thought that represents the thinking of a thought by a group as the joint operation of several simultaneously acting causes will depict the thinker as *depending* for their thinking on the actions of those causes. Had he been thinking of the spontaneity of thought in this way, then, Kant would have had a very quick argument against the idea that a thought could be entertained by a group of thinkers that think the thought in the distributive manner he envisages.

On the other hand, it is also possible that in the A edition Kant *was* thinking of the spontaneity of thought in this way, but had yet to appreciate that such a conception had the consequence of supporting the *nervus probandi*. One reason to think that this might be what is going on is that in the B edition he comes to present the second paralogism as *succeeding* in establishing that I am a singular— that is, non-plural—subject. At this later stage, the fallacy in the argument—as we will shortly see—is presented as consisting not in the failure of the *nervus probandi* to be known, but in an illicit inference from the conclusion that I am a non-plural subject to the conclusion that I am a substance (now in the sense of a substance₁). Might it be, then, that by the second edition Kant had finally recognized that he was indeed committed to the *nervus probandi* by his

---

[13] A 68/B 93; A 77/B 102; B 158 note. I am grateful to Ralf Bader for this suggestion.

endorsement of the spontaneity of thought? This is certainly possible. But the issue is complicated by the fact that in the second edition Kant takes on a new commitment, one which, if he had thought it through, ought to have led him to this same conclusion. What I have in mind is a commitment to viewing the copula as the unifying element in a categorical judgment, to viewing it, in other words, as expressing that special combination of representations that constitutes them parts of a judgment. With this new commitment in place, Kant is, I would argue, committed to conceiving of categorical thoughts as incapable of being thought by a plurality of thinkers thinking in the distributive way Kant envisages. For in order to think the unifying element as a unifying element a given member of the plurality will also have to think all the other elements that are unified. After all, to think of the combination of the elements by the copula it is not enough to think of copulative combination in abstraction. One must rather think of the copula under the aspect of playing its particular combining role, namely, as combining the subject and predicate into a thought. But thinking of the copula in this way involves thinking the whole thought. In consequence, the division of labour must necessarily be unequal: one member of the plurality—the one responsible for thinking the copula—will have to think the whole thought and the actions of the other members will therefore be redundant.

Since Kant nowhere rehearses this reasoning himself one might doubt whether it had occurred to him. I would argue, however, that he was likely familiar with this style of reasoning. For an argument having precisely this form—albeit with a different subject matter—occurs in Descartes's *Meditations*—a work Kant owned. It is worth examining Descartes's presentation of this argument closely. By doing so, we will see not only that there is indeed reason to think that Kant would have been familiar with this style of argument but also that an assumption very like the major premise of the second paralogism plays a role in the Cartesian argument. The major premise, accordingly, emerges as less apparently contrived for the special, ad hoc, purpose of rehearsing the second paralogism.

6.5 A Cartesian application of the major premise

In the Third Meditation Descartes attempts to argue for the existence of God by arguing that one's idea of God must have God himself as its cause. His argument makes crucial use of the principle that when the effect is an idea, its total and efficient cause must have at least as much reality 'formally' as the effect has 'objectively'.[14] In addition to this principle, Descartes's argument relies on the

---

[14] This is a simplification of the principle Descartes uses, which is tailored to chains of entities related by causation, and requires that the first member of the chain have at least as much reality

assumptions first, that the meditator possesses the idea of God (conceived of as a most perfect being), second, that this idea has the maximum degree of objective reality, and, third, that this idea is indeed *caused* to exist in the meditator's mind. It follows from the combination of these three assumptions with the just-stated causal principle that any total and efficient cause of this idea must have the highest degree of formal reality, and so be a most perfect being.[15] To amount to an argument for God the argument must be supplemented with further reasoning to show that there can be at most one such being, but that reasoning needn't detain us.

In the course of defending this argument, Descartes raises—and answers—the potential objection that our idea of God might be the causal upshot, not of the creative act of some *total* efficient cause, but rather of a plurality of *partial* causes acting together. The worry is that if each of these partial causes were to produce a separate part of the idea of God, while none of them produced the whole, then there would be no *total* cause of the idea (or at least none that could with any plausibility be identified with God), with the consequence that the causal principle, which speaks only of total causes, could not be invoked.[16] Here is Descartes simultaneously raising, and disposing of, this potential objection:

> Nor can it be supposed that several partial causes have perhaps concurred in bringing about my existence [*ad me efficiendum concurrisse*], and that from one I have received the idea of one of the perfections that I attribute to God and from another the idea of another, so that all these perfections would surely be found somewhere in the universe, but not all joined together in some one being, who would be God. For—on the contrary—the unity, simplicity, or the inseparability of all the things that are in God is one of the foremost perfections that I understand to be in him. And the idea of this unity of all his perfections certainly could not have been posited in me by any cause from which I had not also the ideas of the other perfections. For it could not have effected that I would understand these perfections as joined together and inseparable unless it simultaneously had effected that I would recognize which perfections they would be.[17]

The reply Descartes states here involves making two claims. First, the idea of God is the idea of something that *unites* the divine perfections. Second, whatever cause

---

formally as the final member (an idea) has objectively. For our purposes, however, nothing turns on these complications, and it will be convenient to suppress them.

[15] I say 'any cause' to allow for cases of causal over-determination.
[16] For all that has been argued, the plurality of partial causes might itself be the total cause, but, obviously, not being simple, such a plurality could not be identified with God.
[17] René Descartes, *Meditations on First Philosophy: Meditationes de Prima Philosophia: A Bilingual Edition*, trans. George Heffernan (Notre Dame, IN: University of Notre Dame Press, 1990) at 147.

implants the idea of this unity in me must have also implanted the idea of the perfections united. The rationale for the second of these claims runs as follows: the relevant idea of unity is not unity per se, but rather *such-and-such perfections existing as unified*. For suppose that a plurality of beings were to have severally implanted in me the ideas of each of the divine perfections save unity. And suppose that, in addition, a being distinct from these were to have implanted in me the idea of unity per se. On these assumptions, I would not receive the idea of all the divine perfections or attributes *as unified*. Instead, I would have separate ideas of each of God's various attributes—unity included. It would be as if I were trying to think of God under the description 'a being that has perfections $A, B \ldots Y, Z$ and *unity*', while the idea I would actually need is 'a being that has perfections $A, B \ldots Y, Z$ unified'.

In other words, in order to possess the idea of the perfections that are in fact the divine attributes *as unified*—hence the idea of the unity of God—I would have to possess the idea of the unifying relation *as playing its unifying role*. And that means, I would have to think of the entities that it unifies and think of them *as unified*. But since to think of the divine attributes in this way is just to have an idea of God, the member of the plurality of causes that produces the idea of unity would have to *thereby* produce an idea of God and so itself be a most real being. It would therefore be a total cause of this idea, and the other supposed partial causes in the plurality would merely operate redundantly. For Descartes, then, God is a being one of whose actions—namely, the action of implanting an idea of God in the meditator—cannot be conceived of as the concurrence or joint action of several acting substances, each of which is merely a partial cause of the implanting.

Never mind whether this argument is sound. What matters for our purposes is that Descartes is one philosopher in the broadly 'rationalist' tradition who, in a work known to Kant, first, gives an argument precisely in the style of the one I am suggesting would have motivated the Kant of the second edition to endorse the *nervus probandi*, and second, in the course of doing so invokes the very principle that functions as the major premise in the second paralogism. Moreover, he does the latter in an argument about something other than the human soul. One thing whose action cannot be thought of as the concurrence of several acting things is, in Descartes's case, a cause of our idea of God.

There is, then, nothing contrived about Kant's attributing this style of argument to the rational psychologist. Indeed, he may well be using the Cartesian argument as his *model* for the argument of the second Paralogism. For, first, the word Kant employs in the major premise for the notion of a joint action is '*Concurrenz*', and, as we have seen, Descartes uses a form of the verb '*concurrere*', namely, '*concurrisse*', to express the joint action of the causes.[18] And, second, both

---

[18] The word '*concurrisse*' is the perfect active infinitive of '*concurrere*', which means to run with others, flock, concur, or coincide. In contemporary German, the term '*die Konkurrenz*' has lost the

philosophers, in the context of invoking simplicity in an argument for a certain thing's having a cause that is *one* thing rather than many, equate simplicity with *unity* (A 352–3).

Insofar as these points make it likely that Kant had noticed this argument of Descartes, they also make it likely that he would have seen that his adoption in the second edition of the view that the copula provides for the unity of a judgment commits him to the view that we know that categorical judgments cannot be thought by composites—or at least by composites thinking in the non-emergent, distributive manner in which both Kant and his opponent suppose that composites would have to think. At any rate, since it is hard to deny that I *can* think categorical thoughts, it does seem clear that, had he been aware of this style of reasoning, he would have appreciated that he needed to find a rather different flaw in the second paralogism than that of failing to establish that the thinker of certain sub-class of my thoughts—the categorical ones—is a single or non-plural subject. We'll shortly see that in the second edition he does just this.

6.6 The I as 'simple in concept'

In the A edition Kant supposes that we know the self or I to be 'simple in concept' (A 400). This claim is exceedingly weak. It means merely that one's self-*representation* has certain features that we associate with simplicity. Kant takes these features to be two in number.

> **I am simple** signifies no more than that this representation I encompasses not the least manifoldness within itself, and that it is [an] absolute (though merely logical) unity. (A 355)

The qualification 'though merely logical' indicates that Kant is taking the notion of 'absolute unity' to be equivocal. I take it that an absolute unity in the logical sense is just a singular representation (the analogue of a singular term in natural language), while an absolute unity in the *non*-logical sense is a solitary or non-plural entity. Something that is simple in this weakest of senses then is just

---

connotation of concurrence and means 'competition'. One presumes that over time the word must have narrowed its meaning to one particular kind of 'running together', namely, the running together of athletes *in a race*. But in Kant's day this term, along with its Latin cognate, was applied to causes as meaning 'acting together'. Thus, in a reflection Kant says: 'A concurrence [*Concursus*] is contradistinguished from a solitary [*solitariae*] action' (R 4748, 17: 696). In the major premise of the second paralogism a concurrence would be the effect of a set of jointly operating causes, the actions of whose members are individually necessary and jointly sufficient for the production of the effect.

something whose representation is (a) singular and (b) contains nothing manifold. Let's call something that has this property a simple₀.

Kant claims that the simplicity of my self (as soul) is 'not actually **inferred** from the proposition "I think"' but rather 'lies already in every thought itself' (A 354–5). Perhaps appreciating just how gnomic this remark is, he seeks to illuminate it through a comparison with the *cogito*. 'The proposition **I am simple**', he says, 'must be regarded as an immediate expression of apperception, just as the putative Cartesian inference *cogito, ergo sum* is in fact tautological, since the *cogito* (*sum cogitans*) immediately asserts the actuality [*Wirklichkeit*]' (A 354–5).[19] Kant would seem to be interpreting the *cogito* argument as an abbreviated form of the argument '*sum cogitans, ergo sum*' ('I exist thinking, therefore I exist'). He supposes that contrary to Descartes (outside of the *Meditations*), the *cogito* is not to be conceived of as a knowledge-extending inference. It is not to be so conceived, he thinks, because anyone who appreciates the truth of the argument's premise already thereby appreciates the truth of its conclusion. In a somewhat similar fashion, we should not, in his view, conceive of the claim 'I am simple' as an informative claim. Rather, what I try to express when I say 'I am simple' is something I already appreciate in understanding the first-person singular personal pronoun. What I understand is that I am a single subject (or single thinker)—a single *total* cause of the whole of each of my thoughts.[20] My grasp that I am a single thinker is expressed through my choice of a grammatically singular term for this thinking existent entity. I know that I am an *I* not a *we*. This is why Kant refers to the transcendental subject = *X* as 'this I, or he, or it (the thing) that thinks' (A 346/B 404). The possibility that it is a 'we' who think—a plurality of *total* causes of one's thoughts—*can*, assuming thoughts are tropes, be ruled out. But this only means that each of my thoughts has a single thinker (that is, one and only one thinker *of the whole*). In the A edition, at least, it is not taken to rule out that this single subject of each thought should be constituted by a plurality of things—even of thinking things—that serve as partial causes of my thought. I know that each of my token thoughts is grasped as a whole by exactly *one* mind, but I don't know whether or not this one mind is a group mind—or so at least Kant maintains in the A edition.

---

[19] Kant would have been familiar with Latin formulations of the argument or inference 'I think, therefore I am' both from Descartes's *Principles of Philosophy*—a work he owned—and from his reading of the Latin translation of the *Discourse on Method*, a work which, according to his student note-taker, he refers to (slightly inaccurately) as '*Tractat[us] de methodo*' in the *Metaphysics Dohna* (28: 680), where he also sets forth the *cogito* inference in Latin.

[20] As Henry Allison notes, the point that the *cogito* argument is tautological was already made by Leibniz in a work available to Kant (Allison, *Kant's Transcendental Idealism* at 353). Leibniz says: 'To say *I think therefore I am* is not really to prove existence from thought, since *to think* is already to say *I am*' (*New Essays*, bk 4, ch. 7, §7). One supposes that what Leibniz intends to say is 'To think "I think" is already to think "I am".'

6.7 The *B*-edition second Paralogism

I have argued that the minor premise of the *A*-edition paralogism says that the soul is something whose action—thinking—cannot be regarded as the concurrence of many acting *subjects* (that is, thinkers). I have suggested that *arguably* in the *A* edition Kant ought, in view of his understanding of thought as spontaneous, to have regarded this claim as known to be true and that accordingly—by his own lights at least—his *A*-edition criticism fails. In the *B* edition Kant seems to have registered that the *A*-edition criticism—whether for this reason or some other—fails. For there he makes an altogether different criticism of the argument. He now takes the claim that a thought cannot be thought by a composite of thinkers each of whom thinks only a component of the thought to be both true and known to be true. So much is suggested by his saying 'the unity of apperception in thought permits the rationalist no explanation of the soul from what is composite' (B 417).[21] This is not a momentary aberration, for the same idea appears again in the *Real Progress* of 1793, where Kant says:

> The unity of consciousness, which must necessarily be met with in every cognition... makes it impossible that representations distributed among many subjects should constitute unity of thought.[22]

At least from the *B* edition onwards, then, Kant is prepared to affirm that no composite can think in the manner of a composite.

This striking development has weighty consequences for how Kant formulates the second paralogism. For in the *B* edition he can no longer happily portray this paralogism as an unsuccessful argument for the thesis that the soul is a non-plural thinker. It is perhaps not surprising, then, that in the *B* edition Kant treats the second paralogism as running along altogether different lines. He now treats it as designed to show that the soul is simple in the sense of being one substance$_1$ and he changes his objection accordingly. His complaint is now that the argument's conclusion, namely, that the soul is a non-plural subject, though *successfully* established, gets inflated to the claim that the soul is a single substance$_1$. The (by Kant's *B*-edition lights) sound argument to the uninflated conclusion runs as follows:

> Anything whose action can never be regarded as the concurrence of many acting things is **simple** (that is, not constituted by a plurality of other things).

---

[21] Kant makes a similar comment in the *Metaphysics K2*. He says: 'But representations cannot occur in a composite <*composito*>; for here they are divided among several subjects' (28: 762).

[22] *Real Progress*, 20: 308. There is no article before 'unity'.

The soul, or thinking I, is something whose action can never be regarded as the concurrence of many acting things.
Therefore,
The soul, or thinking I, is simple (that is, not constituted by a plurality of other things).

Kant's B-edition criticism of this argument relates not so much to its soundness as to its ambitions. He says:

> That the I of apperception, consequently in every thought, is a **single thing** [*ein Singular*] that cannot be resolved [*aufgelöset*] into a plurality of subjects, and consequently that it denotes a logically simple subject, lies already in the concept of thinking and is therefore an analytic proposition; but this does not mean that the thinking I is a simple **substance**, which would be a synthetic proposition.
> (B 407)

In this context, to resolve the 'I' of apperception into a plurality of subjects means to treat my thoughts as the non-emergent products of the joint activity of a plurality of subjects of representation. The first part of this remark, accordingly, amounts to the claim that the minor premise of the argument just stated is an analytic truth. Since Kant adds that this claim entails that the 'I' of apperception *denotes* a logically simple subject, it is clear that 'logical simplicity' is now a stronger notion than it had been in the *A* edition. Indeed, whereas in the *A* edition logical simplicity had been a property of representations, it is now treated as a property of what is denoted by a representation. The second part of the remark warns us that we cannot infer from this conclusion the stronger conclusion that the thinking I is a single substance, and I would claim that here 'single substance' means a single substance$_1$. In the *B* edition, then, Kant's criticism effectively amounts to the charge that the second paralogism is an *ignoratio elenchi*: the paralogist commits the fallacy of misconstruing (and exaggerating) what has been established. That Kant (implicitly) levels such a charge may come as a surprise, for one might have expected the criticism to rather be that the inference is a *sophisma figurae dictionis*. However, in the second edition only the first paralogism is expressly characterized as having this form (B 411). Nor, it must be said, would an analysis of the *B*-edition second paralogism as a *sophisma figurae dictionis* be at all satisfactory. For, given the explanation at B 407 just quoted, such a diagnosis would involve representing the paralogism as running as follows:

Anything whose action can never be regarded as the concurrence of many acting things (substances$_1$) is **simple** (that is, one substance$_1$).
The soul, or thinking I, is something whose action can never be regarded as the concurrence of many acting things (that is, subjects of representation).

Therefore,
The soul, or thinking I, is simple (that is, one substance$_1$).

Kant *would* take the minor premise of this argument to be known. But—and herein lies the rub—he would not take the major premise to be known. For the fact that something cannot be conceived of as a plurality of substances$_1$ does not entail that it is a single substance$_1$. It might, for example, be a single accident. Since Kant always represents the major premise of a paralogism as something we are in a position to know, this analysis won't do.

6.8 The possibility of monism

In addition to containing Kant's presentation and diagnosis of the rational psychologist's argument for the simplicity of the soul, the second Paralogism also contains an intriguing discussion of a view we might today consider a version of 'monism'. Kant invites us to conduct a thought experiment in which we are to suppose that the soul had after all been shown to be a simple substance (A 356). He asks us to consider what this would show about the real issue that concerns us (insofar as we are pursuing the traditional concerns of rational psychology), namely, whether the soul can be distinguished from all matter, and so, exempted from the decay to which matter is subject. He claims that it would show no such thing. For, even if the soul were shown to be a simple substance, it would remain epistemically possible for it to be of fundamentally the same kind as the noumenal substratum of matter. Thus, as Kant says:

> We cannot make the least use of [the proposition that everything that thinks is a simple substance] in deciding whether the soul is distinct in kind from, or akin to, matter. (A 357)[23]

We cannot do so, he explains, because it is (as we'd say today) epistemically possible that matter should be the appearance in sensible intuition of noumenal stuff that thinks. In Kant's own words:

> Something lies at the basis of outer appearances and affects our sense in such a way that this sense acquires the representations of space, matter, shape, etc. And this something considered as noumenon (or better, as transcendental object), might yet at the same time also be the subject of thoughts—although, because of the way in which our outer sense is affected by this something, we acquire no

---

[23] At this point Kant merely poses the question whether we can make such a use of this proposition, but he goes on to answer his own question in the negative (compare A 359).

intuition of [this something's] representations, of [its] will, etc., but acquire merely intuitions of space and its determinations. (A 358)

If the noumenal substratum of matter were thinking stuff, it would be of the same kind as our own noumenal stuff. And we know this conditional to be true because we know at least that our noumenal stuff thinks—or more precisely that it has properties of which our thoughts are the appearances. Kant even supposes it epistemically possible that the substratum of matter might be something *simple* which, through the way in which it affects our sensibility, produces in us the intuition of what is extended and composite (A 359).

We might describe the (epistemic) possibility that matter might be underlain by noumenal thinking stuff as the possibility of 'monism', but Kant himself lacks any term for this 'hypothesis' (A 360).[24] For him, the value of a hypothesis—at least in the sense of this term intended here—is that it enables one to defend against dogmatism by describing an epistemic possibility that is incompatible with some particular dogmatic claim (A 776-82/B 804-10). So his purpose in raising the epistemic possibility of monism may be just to show that, even if, *per impossibile*, the rational psychologist could prove the simplicity of the soul, this proof would have no bearing on the question of whether we are, at the noumenal level, of the same kind as the noumenal basis of matter. As Kant says, announcing the result of his thought experiment:

> Even if the simplicity of the soul's nature is granted, such simplicity does not at all sufficiently distinguish the human soul from matter with regard to matter's substratum—if matter is regarded (as it ought to be) merely as appearance.
> (A 359)

If Transcendental Idealism is accepted, the question of the soul's simplicity becomes *irrelevant* to that of its immateriality. For, according to Transcendental Idealism, the soul might for all we know, be fundamentally of the same kind as something—the noumenal correlate of appearances—that appears to us as spatial while also being capable of thinking. Kant is right. But a question remains. Although he has established that—on the assumption of Transcendental Idealism—the question of whether the soul is simple is irrelevant to the question whether it is fundamentally of the same kind as matter, one might still wonder whether the soul's simplicity is also irrelevant to the question of its natural

---

[24] In the *Metaphysics Mrongovius* Kant attributes this version of (what we'd call) monism to Leibniz, while at the same time tailoring it to fit Leibniz's own—from Kant's point of view relatively superficial—version of the distinction between appearances and things in themselves (namely, composites of monads versus individual monads) (29: 905). In the same place, Kant treats a thing's being 'material' as consisting in its substratum's being the same in kind as the substratum of matter and he claims that while it is correct to deny that the soul is *matter*, it is unknown whether or not it is *material*.

immortality. After all, if we had shown that the thinking subject is a single substance₁, then one might suppose that, since it is in this sense non-composite, its divisibility, hence its annihilation through decomposition, would also be ruled out. In short, if we could establish the subject's simplicity (understood as its property of being one substance₁), then it seems we could also establish its natural immortality. We must ask, therefore: Is Kant's insouciance over the hypothetical prospect of the soul's being shown to be simple ultimately misplaced?

The answer is no. For, in Kant's view, the soul's simplicity—that is, its property of not being actually divided—would not entail its indivisibility. An entity that, not being actually divided, is simple, may, in his view, still be divisible since *potentially* divided. As Kant says in a reflection of 1785–88: 'That a being can exist as the unity of the substance and yet be resolved into a plurality of substances involves no contradiction' (R 5650, 18: 299). For all we know, then, a simple soul might still be potentially divisible.[25] And so, even if the second paralogism had accomplished its goal of proving the soul's simplicity, this would not accomplish, or even advance, the rational psychologist's project of proving the soul's imperishability. (We will see a second consideration pointing to this same conclusion when we discuss Kant's criticism of Mendelssohn's attempted proof of the immortality of the soul in the next chapter.)

---

[25] This answer was suggested to me by Ralf Bader, who also alerted me to the supporting text.

7
The Third Paralogism

7.1 Introduction

Kant calls the third paralogism the paralogism of 'personality'. In the A edition it runs as follows:

> What is conscious of the numerical identity of its self [*seiner selbst*] in different times is so far [*ist so fern*] a **person**.
> Now the soul is conscious of the numerical identity of its self in different times. Therefore, the soul is a person. (A 361)

Here, although I have departed from Kemp Smith's translation in certain respects, I have followed him in offering a rather literal rendering of the tricky qualifier, '*ist so fern*'. (I will have more to say about this qualifier later in this chapter.)

This is the first of the A-edition paralogisms whose criticism takes its advertised form, namely, the charge that the argument, though possessing known premises, is a *sophisma figurae dictionis* (A 402). In our jargon, Kant is treating the paralogism as a 'paralogism$_k$'. He is not, however, explicit about the nature of the equivocation he posits. One expects it to lie in the phrase 'I am conscious of my identity at different times'. But in the event Kant emphasizes the availability not of alternative *readings* of this phrase but rather of alternative *perspectives* on the argument. Kant observes that while, from the first-person perspective, the minor premise is a 'completely identical proposition' nonetheless, considered from the third-person perspective—the perspective of an 'outside observer'—no inference can be drawn from the analyticity of the claim that I am the same subject in all my experiences to the persistence over time of an underlying noumenal self (A 362–3).

One task for an interpreter wishing to do justice to Kant's diagnosis of the paralogism as a *sophisma figurae dictionis*, therefore, is to recast these claims about 'perspectives' as claims about the senses of an equivocal middle term. Another is to provide a satisfactory interpretation of the paralogism's major premise, one that explains both the meaning of the term 'person' and the function of the qualifier 'is so far'.

I will argue that Kant uses the term 'person' for a being that is equipped with the capacity for, or power of, 'personality'—understood (to put it anachronistically) as the ability to discern which past *substance₁*-stages are 'temporal stages' of one's own substance₁ at (sufficiently many) different times. Crucially, on my reading, this notion is, for Kant, to be distinguished from that of knowing which *subject of consciousness* one is at different times. (This point should become clearer when we consider Kant's famous 'elastic ball' analogy.)

Kant's use of the term 'person' is, I think, consistent across the editions, as is his equation of the property of *being a person* with that of *having personality*—a status he refers to indifferently as '*Personalität*' and '*Persönlichkeit*'. The supposition that *being a person* is for Kant equivalent to *having personality* would explain why he should title the paralogism that seeks to establish that the soul is a person the paralogism 'of personality'. The supposition that Kant is treating personality as a power or ability is supported by the emphasized part of the following, somewhat cryptic passage, whose purpose and meaning will be scrutinized in due course:

> It is remarkable, however, that the personality of the soul, and its presupposition, permanence, and hence the soul's substantiality must be proved now for the first time. For if we could presuppose the latter [that is, substantiality], then there would follow from it, not yet indeed the continuance of consciousness, but still the possibility of a continuing consciousness in an enduring subject; *and this is already sufficient for personality, which does not itself immediately cease just because its [ihre]* [that is, the soul's] *action is, perhaps, interrupted for a time.*
> (A 365, emphasis added)

The words I have emphasized here suggest that in the *A* edition at least Kant is conceiving of personality [*Persönlichkeit*] as a power of the soul. Powers, after all, are precisely the kinds of things that do not cease to exist just because their possessor's action is temporarily interrupted. The same conclusion is suggested by a passage from the *Metaphysics of Morals* where, in the course of contrasting moral personality—characterized as 'the freedom of a rational being under laws'— with psychological personality, Kant tells us that 'psychological personality [*Persönlichkeit*] is merely the ability [*Vermögen*] to be conscious of one's identity in different conditions of one's existence' (6: 233). Psychological personality, then, is plausibly—at first pass—the ability to keep track of the identity of one's self through its various changes of state and so, trivially, at different times.

In the passage just quoted from A 365 Kant is expressing puzzlement about the rational psychologist's procedure. He is wondering why the rational psychologist should bother to construct a separate argument for the soul's personality such as the third paralogism purports to be. His concern is that if the soul's substantiality really had been proved, then, by the rational psychologist's lights, its personality ought to follow immediately. We will shortly examine the thinking behind this claim, but for now let's just note that all that Kant thinks ought to follow immediately is the possession of a *capacity for* consciousness of one's identity at different times, not *actual* consciousness. Since that is so, and since Kant sees this as sufficient to establish personality, he must also be attributing to the rational psychologist a conception of personality as a capacity or ability. If that is right, then Baumgarten's position would seem to be a better representative of the rational psychologist's position than Wolff's. For while Baumgarten sees personhood as an ability (*Metaphysics*, §783), Wolff seems to see it as an *exercise* of an ability—an actual act of recalling which being one was at an earlier time. For instance, in *GM* Wolff says:

> One calls a *person* a thing [*Ding*] that is conscious that it is the very same [thing] that was previously in this or that state. (*GM*, §924)

And later, in his *Rational Psychology*, he says:

> A **person** is a being which preserves a memory of itself, that is, which remembers that it is that same being that was previously in this or that state.
> (*Rational Psychology*, §741)

On the face of it, then, Wolff conceives of consciousness as an actual state—the product of an exercise of an ability rather than the ability itself. On the other hand, it is possible that he merely means that a person is the kind of being that *habitually* remembers that... etc. *and who therefore has the power to engage in this habitual activity*. If that is what he means, then Wolff would, after all—insofar as this detail goes, at least—be a good representative of the rationalist psychologist's position along with Baumgarten, though, as we saw in Chapter 2 there are other reasons to think that Wolff is a poor candidate for Kant's pure rational psychologist.

Why does Kant think that if personality is a mere power or ability, the rational psychologist ought to regard the soul's possession of it as provably following from its presumed substantiality?[1] This is far from clear; but the following explanation seems possible. The rational psychologist, in Kant's view, would take the soul's personality *in this world* to be revealed by experience. We just do find ourselves able to recognize past stages of our self as our own.[2] It follows that if the self is a substantial soul and therefore, by the rational psychologist's lights, permanent, it will, by those same lights, be guaranteed—barring a miracle—to survive bodily

---

[1] In the *Metaphysics L1* Kant regards the soul's unending existence as following from its substantiality, but not its *necessary* unending existence or immortality (28: 285).

[2] This would follow from the assumption that we just do have the ability to recognize past representations when they are reproduced in memory. And, significantly, Baumgarten makes just this assumption (*Metaphysics*, §579).

death with such abilities as inhere in it intact. This is so because the soul's powers flow from its nature (for Wolff), and are identical with the soul (for Baumgarten).³ Moreover, in the opinion of the rational psychologist these powers and abilities will survive bodily death even if their exercise should happen to be blocked for a while in the afterlife—as this exercise might be if it depended on the possession of a body while the soul existed disembodied for a while after death.⁴ Of course, if this story is correct, then for the rational psychologist personality ought to follow from substantiality not *simpliciter*, but only given the further empirical premise that the soul has the power in question in this life. Accordingly, Kant would have to be interpreted as speaking loosely in the passage quoted from A 365, where he seems to imply that the rational psychologist ought to view personality as following from substantiality alone.

7.2 The major premise

Consider again the major premise:

> What is conscious of the numerical identity of its self in different times is so far [*ist so fern*] a **person**.

The qualifier '*ist so fern*' is apt to call to mind Locke's doctrine that personal identity reaches *as far as* consciousness can be extended into the past.⁵ This is certainly a natural connection to make, but there is reason to think that making it may be a mistake. For when we examine Kant's use of the phrase '*ist so fern*' (along with its variant '*ist sofern*'), we find that it often indicates not relativization (in this case, to a temporal period), but rather the status of one thing as a *ground* of another. The phrase, in short, often simply means 'on that account' or 'in virtue of that fact'. I think this is precisely what it means in the present context. If I'm right about this, then its function in the major premise is merely to indicate that the feature *in virtue of possessing which* a thing should be considered a person is its possession of a capacity for consciousness of its identity over certain (unspecified) times.

But am I right? What is the evidence for this reading? One relevant text is a remark from the Transcendental Aesthetic. There, explaining that a thing's being

---

³ Although he treats the soul as a power, Baumgarten also calls it a substance that subsists per se (*Metaphysics* §§741–3).
⁴ Baumgarten claims that in the afterlife there will be another body with which the soul is in the closest interaction (*Metaphysics*, §786). If one supposes that the soul will receive a *wholly* new body but that it will not do so until the Day of Judgment, the idea of a temporarily disembodied post-existence arises quite naturally.
⁵ *Essay*, bk. II, ch. 27, §§9–10, 14, 17, and 21.

represented through a sense is sufficient to constitute it a part of appearance, Kant says: '*Alles, was durch einen Sinn vorgestellt wird, ist sofern jederzeit Erscheinung*' (B 68). Commentators have differed on how to translate this occurrence of '*ist sofern*'. Kemp Smith chooses the somewhat literal 'is so far', while both Guyer and Wood, on the one hand, and Pluhar, on the other, favour 'to that extent'. Kemp Smith is, I think, on the firmer ground, for there is no suggestion here that being an appearance is supposed to be a matter of degree. The translation that makes more sense, clearly, is 'on that account', for Kant's point seems to be that a thing's possession of the capacity to be represented through the senses grounds its status as an appearance. A second example of this same usage occurs in Kant's *Religion within the Bounds of Reason Alone*. There, in a discussion of the doctrine that Christ is begotten, but not created, Kant says: '*Dieser allein Gott wohlgefällige Mensch "ist in ihm von Ewigkeit her"; die Idee desselben geht von seinem Wesen aus; er ist sofern kein erschaffenes Ding, sondern sein eingeborner Sohn*' (6: 60). Wood and Giovanni render this remark as: 'This human being, alone pleasing to God, "is in him from all eternity"; the idea of him proceeds from God's being, he is not, *therefore*, a created thing but God's only-begotten Son' (emphasis added).[6] Their use of the word 'therefore' expresses the thought that the circumstance of the idea of Christ's proceeding from God's being—or perhaps better essence— would explain why he is not a created being. This circumstance is, as we might say, that *on account of which* he is not a created being.

These points suggest that the qualification '*ist so fern*' in the major premise indicates neither that the notion of personhood occurring there is a matter of degree nor that something counts as a person only for the duration of the interval during which it is aware of remaining the same subject of thoughts. Instead, the phrase serves to indicate that if something is conscious of the numerical identity of itself at different times, then it is, *on that account*, or *in virtue of that fact*, a person. And since Kant endorses the major premise this shows—somewhat interestingly, I think—that he is willing to make use of a notion akin to the contemporary notion of grounding.

A second issue about the major premise concerns the interpretation of the quantifier-deficient phrase 'at different times'. Does this mean 'at *all* different times', 'at *some* different times', 'at *sufficiently many* different times', or something else again? It cannot, I think, mean 'at all different times' both because of the obviousness of the possibility of memory gaps, and because it would have been standard for followers of Leibniz and Wolff to believe in a pre-existence of which we are not, and cannot be, conscious in this life.[7] The 'some' option, for its part,

---

[6] Immanuel Kant, *The Cambridge Edition of the Works of Immanuel Kant: Religion and Rational Theology*, trans. Allen W. Wood and George Di Giovanni (Cambridge: Cambridge University Press, 1996) at 103–4.

[7] For Kant's awareness of Leibniz's views on the pre-existence of the human soul, see *Metaphysics K2* (28: 762).

looks too weak, for one wouldn't be justified in crediting someone with a *general ability* or capacity to φ simply because they managed to φ on a solitary occasion; after all, that one instance of φ-ing might have been a fluke.[8] The most plausible option, to my mind, is 'sufficiently many'. If I should happen to remember a good many incidents in this life then I will be aptly credited with the *general ability* to remember past events as events in my biography, and from this there would follow my possession of the ability to know who I was at those earlier times.

Taken together, these considerations suggest that Kant sees the third paralogism in *A* as running as follows:

> Whatever is conscious of the identity of its current self with its earlier self at sufficiently many times for it to be credited with the general ability of which these acts of consciousness are exercises is, in virtue of that fact, a **person**.
>
> Now, the soul (that is, the thinking I) is conscious of the identity of its current self with its earlier self at sufficiently many times, etc.
>
> Therefore, the soul is a person.   (A 361)

In what follows I will proceed on the assumption that this is how the *A*-edition third paralogism is supposed to run.

7.3 The minor premise

In the *A* edition the crux of Kant's diagnosis of the fallacy vitiating the third paralogism is his (implied) charge of equivocation on the apparent middle term. In a version of the paralogism formulated with 'scholastic precision', that term would be the indefinite noun-phrase, 'a being conscious of the numerical identity of its self in sufficiently many earlier times, etc.'. Kant is treating this phrase as expressing a metaphysically innocent concept in the minor premise and a metaphysically loaded one in the major. The metaphysically loaded concept, I take it, is that of *a being that has the capacity to be aware of which substance₁ it was at (sufficiently many) earlier times*. The metaphysically innocent concept, I take it, is that of *a being all of whose experiences are its own*. This is, of course, a tautological concept—one in the same class as the concept of *a body that occupies precisely the space it occupies*.

It is not entirely obvious that Kant understands the metaphysically innocent concept in the way I am suggesting. In order to see that he does so we need to recall that the minor premise is supposed to be a proposition that we are inclined

---

[8] See John Maier, 'Abilities', *The Stanford Encyclopedia of Philosophy* (Fall 2014 Edition), Edward N. Zalta (ed.), http://plato.stanford.edu/archives/fall2014/entries/abilities/.

to endorse when we attempt to make identity judgments from a point of view in which the usual resources for making such judgments are lacking, the point of view, namely, of inner sense (A 362). Kant does not say what he takes these usual resources to be, but it seems reasonable to suppose that they are intended to include whatever observed facts underwrite the ability to fix one's attention on an object in such a way as to continuously observe it as it traces a path through space and time.[9] Kant maintains that because there is no permanent element in inner sense, this ability cannot be exercised in that domain. He takes it to follow that a rational psychologist who wishes to affirm that the self is a person will be inclined to ground their claim on a proposition that is, unbeknownst to them, merely analytic, a proposition that bears the illusory appearance of being a substantive truth about the identity of the self (or soul) over time. The proposition in question is the minor premise. At one point, Kant glosses this premise as the claim that 'I relate each and every one of my successive determinations to the numerically identical self in all time, i.e., in the form of the inner intuition of my self' (A 362). He explains this gloss as saying: 'in the whole time in which I am conscious of myself, I am conscious of this time as belonging to the unity of my self' (A 362). The first of these glosses is the clearer of the two; it is also the better of the two for Kant's purposes; for it is better fitted for the job of revealing the minor premise to be analytic. We can plausibly take it to mean:

> Every experience or representation I have ever had (or will ever have) is one that has been (or will have been) had by one and the same thinking subject, namely, me.

Such a claim would be true even if my existence should happen to be maximally ephemeral. It means simply that all my experiences, whenever they are experienced, are, when I experience them, experienced by me. But since, obviously, something counts as 'my experience' just in case it is 'experienced by me', this claim is equivalent to the overt tautology: 'All my experiences, whenever I have them, are my experiences.' The minor premise is, of course, unimpeachable when it is understood as making this tautologous claim.

We are now in a position to appreciate why Kant should regard the third paralogism as a *sophisma figurae dictionis* when its premises are treated as correct.

---

[9] Kant's account of what is involved in making trans-temporal identity judgments about external objects runs as follows: 'If I want to know through experience the numerical identity of an external object, I shall pay heed to that permanent element in the appearance to which as subject everything else is related as determination, and note its identity through the time in which the determinations change' (A 362). Kant is plainly implying that we possess such an ability. But as Ralf Bader has observed (in conversation), it is not at all clear that he ought to do so. For although the first analogy tells us that there is some permanent element in space (namely, matter), Kant supposes that we lack the ability to say which apparently outer appearances are caused by matter as opposed to being mere products of the imagination.

For, according to the interpretation we have been developing, the apparent middle term occurs in the major premise with the meaning: 'a being that has the ability to know which substance$_1$ it is at (sufficiently many) earlier times' and in the minor premise with the meaning: 'a being all of whose experiences are its own'. Since the minor premise$_k$ is analytic, the subject knows it to be true at every moment of their existence. This is what Kant means when he says: 'The identity of the person is... inevitably [*unausbleiblich*] to be encountered in my own consciousness' (A 362). Obviously, however, inevitability of encounter is not to be confused with an encounter with the inevitable (that is, the permanent). For even if my existence were to be of infinitesimal duration, I would still 'inevitably' encounter 'the identity of my person' simply because it would remain true that at every moment of my existence I would (in principle) enjoy knowledge of the proposition expressed by the minor premise. In short, my knowledge of the minor premise$_k$ 'does not at all prove the numerical identity of my subject' (A 363)—and by 'my subject' in this context, I take it, Kant means my presumed *ultimate* or absolute subject or, in our terms, the substance$_1$ in which my thoughts are presumed by the rational psychologist to inhere. This is so for more than one reason. In addition to the considerations just mentioned, there is the point that 'despite the logical identity of the I... a change [*Wechsel*] can go on [in the referent of its representation, "I"] that does not allow it [that is, the referent] to keep its identity; and this [is so] even though all the while the identical-sounding ["I"] is assigned to it [as its representative]' (A 363).[10] Kant means that the term 'I', when viewed from an external, third-personal standpoint, might exchange one noumenal referent for another while, from the first-person standpoint, seeming to continue to refer to one and the same subject of consciousness. He illustrates this point with a vivid analogy:

> An elastic ball that strikes another one in a straight line communicates to the latter its whole motion, hence its whole state (if one looks only at their positions in space).[11] Now assuming substances, on the analogy with such bodies, in which representations, together with consciousness of them, flow from one to another, a whole series of these substances may be thought, of which the first would communicate its state, together with its consciousness [of that state], to the second, which would communicate its own state, together with that of the previous substance, to a third substance, and this, in turn, would share the states

---

[10] Although they are clearly required, Kant does not himself supply the quotation marks around this last 'I'.

[11] Kant's parenthetical qualification is needed because for him an otherwise stationary spinning ball would be in motion even though it would not be changing its position in space (that is, the position of its center of mass) (compare 4: 482). Since in the illustration only the rectilinear motion is assumed to be communicated, the *whole* motion (hence the ball's whole state), which includes any rotational motion it may have, may not be communicated.

of all the previous ones, together with their consciousness [of those states] along with [its own consciousness of] its own [states]. The last substance would thus be conscious of all the states of all the previously altered substances as its own states, because these states would have been carried over to it, together with the consciousness of them; and in spite of this it would not have been the very same person in all of these states. (A 363–4, note*)

Kant is pointing to the possibility that a consciousness that is seemingly unified from the first-person perspective might, in spite of this apparent unification, nonetheless be underlain by a series of distinct subtances$_1$. I might, for example, seem to recall seeing the Thames freeze over ten years ago, when I—that is, the substance$_1$ in which all of my present thoughts inhere—had never seen the Thames. I might be in this situation because I had inherited the actual memories of some earlier substance$_1$ that had witnessed the river's freezing.

Here, in short, Kant is agreeing with Locke that consciousness floats free of substantial identity. More precisely, he is agreeing that 'A's thoughts and B's thoughts belong to the same consciousness' does not entail 'A's thoughts inhere in the same substance—that is, in our terms the same substance$_1$—as B's thoughts'.[12] But he is also disagreeing with Locke on the question of whether A's participating in the same consciousness as B is sufficient for A's being the same person as B. Locke takes this to be so, while Kant demurs.[13]

Since Kant himself denies that the self as it is in itself is located in time, the view expressed in the 'elastic ball' passage about what is required for personal identity over time would seem to be stated from a temporarily adopted Transcendentally Realist perspective. Kant, I take it, is bracketing the question of Transcendental Idealism in order to consider what personal identity ought to require from the Transcendental Realist's perspective. Within that perspective, he is clearly siding with the Wolffians—or with a charitably reconstructed version of their view— against Locke on the issue of whether or not remaining the same person over time requires the persistence of the soul—conceived of as a substance$_1$—between those times.[14]

Kant says that when we consider ourselves from the first-person point of view 'the personality of the soul must be regarded not as inferred but rather as a

---

[12] The thoughts in question here must be types rather than tokens. For recall that in the argument of the second Paralogism it had to be assumed that no two things could share the same token thought. In the case of memories, at least, what is carried from one substance to the next in the series would seem to be a type-identified information state which becomes a part of a new state.

[13] This last point has been noted by Béatrice Longuenesse, 'Kant on the Identity of Persons', *Proceedings of the Aristotelian Society*, 107 (2) (2007), 149–67 at 158–9.

[14] The charitably reconstructed Wolffian position differs from (what appears to be) Wolff's own in requiring for personal identity over time the possession of a certain power or ability rather than to an actual state of knowledge. It also differs from Baumgarten's view in seeing personal identity over time as requiring that one remain the same substance$_1$ rather than the same power over time.

completely identical proposition of self-consciousness in time' (A 362). He means, I take it, that from the first-person point of view each of us must hold a belief of the kind I express when I say that all the experiences or thoughts I have had, or will have had, have been had, or will have been had, by myself. To self-ascribe 'personality' in this extremely weak sense of the term is indeed to affirm an identical proposition.

In line with our earlier conventions, let's call the property of being a person in this paper-thin sense of the term, the property of being a 'person$_0$'. And let's call the more interesting property of being an entity that has the ability to be aware of which substance$_1$ it was identical with at (sufficiently many) earlier times the property of being a 'person$_1$'. We can then say that Kant's diagnosis of the third paralogism in *A* involves viewing the middle term as expressing the notion of being a person$_1$ when it occurs in the major premise and as expressing the notion of being a person$_0$ when it occurs in the minor premise$_k$. The paralogism is therefore a *sophisma figurae dictionis* when its premises are taken to be true.

7.4 The practical use of the concept of a person

Kant is committed to denying that in this life we possess the kind of theoretically based a priori knowledge that would ground our status as persons$_1$.[15] He does, however, grant that we know ourselves to be 'persons$_0$':

> [Although it does not extend our self knowledge through pure reason] the concept of personality, just like the concepts of substance and of the simple, can remain (insofar as it is merely transcendental, i.e., a unity of the subject which is otherwise unknown to us, but in whose determinations there is a thoroughgoing connection of apperception)... (A 365–6)

Here Kant is suggesting—or so I take it—that the concept of personality 'can remain' in exactly the sense in which the concepts of substance and simplicity can remain—when, namely, it is construed as an extremely weak concept, one on a par with substance$_0$ and simple$_0$. We have already seen that predicating either of these concepts of the self involves asserting something about the self's *representation*. And something similar would seem to hold of the concept of being a person$_0$. That concept, I would suggest, is just the tautological concept of *being an x such that the 'I' in each of x's 'I'-thoughts has one and the same referent, namely, x*. To ascribe this concept to some entity is, of course, merely to assert an analytic truth.

---

[15] We will shortly address the question whether this means that for Kant we know ourselves not to be persons$_1$.

Kant goes on to claim that this same concept—that is, the concept *person₀*—is both necessary and sufficient for 'practical use' (A 365–6). Faced with such a claim, the reader naturally wonders how such a thin concept could have any use at all, let alone a distinctively moral use.[16] One way of making progress here might be to proceed from the following observation. Kant has persuaded himself that, owing to the combination of transcendental illusion with the specious reasoning of the third paralogism, we are apt to confuse the claim that we are persons₀ with the claim that we are persons₁. Since the former claim is both trivial and analytic it is something that we are inclined to believe. And, therefore, this same confusion inclines us to believe that we are persons₁. It may therefore be that when Kant says that the concept *person* is necessary and sufficient for practical use he is trying, rather clumsily, to express the somewhat more complicated thought that the *belief* that we are persons₀ is, if transcendental illusion is left undiscovered and unchecked, *sufficient* for producing the belief that we are persons₁, which belief is in turn *necessary* for practical use. (We'll consider why it might be necessary in due course.) Admittedly, if this is what Kant means, he is not expressing himself well; for he seems to be saying of one and the same belief that it is *both* necessary and sufficient for practical use. But we should expect some expressive misfires in this part of the first *Critique*; for we know that Kant subjected the A-Paralogisms to a thorough overhaul. And, notably, the claim that the belief that we are persons is necessary and sufficient for practical use is absent from the second edition.

Which practical use might Kant be envisaging for the belief that we are persons₁? What he has in mind, I think, is the role he sees this belief as playing in moral motivation. The idea is that in order to be motivated by the moral law we must believe ourselves to be persons₁. This arises as follows.

At the time of writing the *A* edition Kant had yet to posit respect for the moral law as the sole incentive for distinctively moral action.[17] Instead, he supposed that we can be motivated to act morally only by our concern for our own future happiness.[18] He further supposed that, since we routinely see evil deeds going naturally and socially unpunished, and virtuous deeds similarly unrewarded, we will believe in this prospect only if we believe in a post-mortem state in which

---

[16] Longuenesse rightly presses the question of what exactly this practical use could be. (See Longuenesse, 'Kant on the Identity of Persons', at 159.) I agree with Dyck that her own answer to this question saddles Kant with undue dogmatism; for it involves portraying him as guilty of committing a paralogism of his own. See Corey Dyck, 'The Aeneas Argument: Personality and Immortality in Kant's Third Paralogism', *Kant Yearbook*, 2 (1) (2010), 95–122 at 97. Dyck himself suggests that the practical use to which Kant is referring is the concept's 'use in a proof of the immortality of the soul' (ibid., at 119). But he explains neither how such a proof would go nor how in embracing it Kant could nonetheless steer clear of dogmatism—immortality, after all, is a strong notion.

[17] Thanks to Ralf Bader for reminding me of this point.

[18] This point is spelled out clearly in the *Metaphysics Mrongovius*: 'Morality teaches what I should do. But it gives no ready incentives to do that which reason prescribes as a duty. The sum total of the incentives to actions is happiness' (29: 777).

happiness is proportioned to virtue by a wise and just supernatural being. But in order for a wrong-doer to be justly *punished* rather than merely cruelly harmed by this being it is necessary, Kant thinks, that they should be aware of having performed their former misdeeds (*Metaphysics K2*, 28: 769). Kant seems to assume that we know this, and in consequence he holds—at the time of writing the first *Critique*—that in order to be motivated by the moral law we must believe that we will survive death equipped with the ability to recognize our former misdeeds as our own. But possession of this ability presupposes the ability to recognize which person we were in this world, and since for Kant which person we are is a matter of which substance$_1$ we are, this ability presupposes personhood—in the sense of being a person$_1$.[19] It follows that in Kant's view the belief that we will survive as persons$_1$ is 'practically necessary' in the sense that it is a necessary condition of our being motivated to follow the moral law—or so, at least, runs my reconstruction of his views.

In the first *Critique* Kant makes two brief remarks that seem to correspond to the first part of this line of thought:

> Thus without God and without a world invisible to us now but hoped for, the glorious ideas of morality are indeed objects of approval and admiration, but not springs of purpose and action. (A 813/B 841)
>
> Reason finds itself constrained to assume [a wise Author and Ruler together with our future life in a future world], otherwise it would have to regard the moral laws as empty figments [*leeren Hirngespinste*]. (A 811/B 839)

In these two passages Kant is arguing that we must hope for—or, alternatively, assume [*anzunehmen*]—the existence of God (conceived of as a wise author and ruler) and an afterlife if morality is to motivate us. God and a future life, he says, are thus two 'presuppositions' [*Voraussetzungen*] that are 'inseparable from the obligation imposed on us by [pure reason]' (A 811/B 839).[20] The obverse of this position, however, is that the moral argument will have probative force *only* for

---

[19] To be clear, I am suggesting only that Kant *believes* us to be substances$_1$, but not that he *knows* this to be the case.

[20] The interplay between the roles of hope and assumption (or belief) in this argument is in fact rather complex. For an ingenious account of these matters, see Andrew Chignell, 'Rational Hope, Moral Order, and the Revolution of the Will', in Eric Watkins (ed.), *Divine Order, Human Order, and the Order of Nature* (Oxford: Oxford University Press, 2013), 197–218 at 207–9. And for a suggestion that, late in his career at least, Kant is prepared to characterize the relevant state of assent (*Fürwahrhalten*) indifferently as a 'faith' (*Glaube*), 'assumption' (*Annehmung*), 'presupposition' (*Voraussetzung*), or 'hypothesis' (*Hypothesis*), see *Real Progress*, 20: 297. For illuminating discussions of Kant's moral arguments for God and immortality, see Allen Wood 'Rational Theology, Moral Faith, and Religion', in Paul Guyer (ed.), *The Cambridge Companion to Kant* (Cambridge: Cambridge University Press, 1992), 394–416, and Frederick C. Beiser, 'Moral Faith and the Highest Good', in Paul Guyer (ed.), *The Cambridge Companion to Kant and Modern Philosophy* (Cambridge: Cambridge University Press, 2006), 588–629 at 591.

people who are antecedently convinced that they are subject to the demands of morality—a limitation of which Kant is well aware (28: 289).

7.5 The *B*-edition third Paralogism

In the *B* edition Kant devotes only a single paragraph to the third paralogism:

> The proposition of the identity of myself in everything manifold of which I am conscious [like the claim that I am a simple thing in the second paralogism] is one lying in the concepts themselves, and hence an analytic proposition; but this identity of the subject, of which I can become conscious in every representation, does not concern the intuition of it, through which it is given as object, and thus [this proposition] cannot signify the identity of the person, by which would be understood the consciousness of the identity of its own substance as a thinking being in all changes of state; in order to prove that what would be demanded is not a mere analysis of the proposition: I think, but rather various synthetic judgments grounded on the given intuition. (B 408–9)

In the *B* edition, as in *A*, Kant treats the third paralogism as a *sophisma figurae dictionis* when its premises are taken to be correct. And again, as in *A*, he takes a thing to possess personality (the property of being a person) just in case it possesses an ability to know which thing it was at earlier times. In *B*, however, Kant is considerably clearer about the point that personality presupposes substantiality$_1$ than he had been in *A*, where this point did not become clear until the note about the 'elastic ball'. He also tightens up his requirement on what is required for personality from the ability to tell which substance$_1$ I am at sufficiently many times (that is, sufficiently many times to allow one to treat such determinations as reflective of an ability) to the ability to tell the same thing through *all* changes of state.

According to Kant's diagnosis of the third paralogism in *B*, we imagine that we know ourselves to possess the ability constitutive of personality because we know that we are able to attach the 'I think' to each of our representations whenever they occur, and so are able to become conscious of the identity of the *subject* in each of our representations. The claim that I have such an ability is plausibly analytic, for the ability to attach the 'I think' to one of my representations is plausibly just what constitutes that representation 'mine'.[21] Importantly, this analytic claim does not

---

[21] Being 'mine' for Kant cannot mean 'inhering in that substance$_1$ which constitutes my self', for in his view I don't know if I am a substance$_1$, though I do know my representations are mine. Accordingly, for Kant a representation that inhered in me but which I could not recognize as mine would not *be* mine.

report any fact about the self that appears to me in inner sense (the intuitable self). We nonetheless misconstrue our knowledge of this analytic truth as the knowledge that we possess the ability to discern (on theoretical grounds) whether or not we are identical with any candidate past stage of our supposed soul substance$_1$.

So far, so good. But we have still to consider a loose thread in the B edition's treatment of the third paralogism, namely, the phrase 'the identity of the person'. Today, it would be natural to treat this phrase as referring to a person's property of being numerically the same person at different times. But for Kant it has an altogether different meaning. In the B-edition Paralogism it purports to refer to an *epistemic state*, namely, the subject's supposed *consciousness* of being the same soul-substance through all changes in its state. In Kant's view, if one were to enjoy such consciousness, one would, on that account, be a person$_1$; for such knowledge could result only from several exercises of an ability to discern which past soul-substance one was identical with. For Kant then—at least in the passage quoted from B 408–9—'the identity of the person' refers—perhaps unexpectedly—to the *knowledge* one would have if one were to possess the ability constitutive of personhood and exercise it to the full.

Why is Kant using this phrase in such a misleading way? This is not clear, but one possible answer is suggested by his once having treated the phrase 'the identity of the person in its consciousness' as co-referential with 'intellectual memory [*memoria intellectualis*]' (R 373, 15: 148). This may be significant because Baumgarten treats the latter phrase as co-referential with 'personality [*personalitas*]'—both of these last expressions, for Baumgarten, referring to the faculty of recognizing reproduced intellectual perceptions *as* reproduced, hence as one's own.[22] This suggests that in employing the phrase 'the identity of the person' in the present context Kant may be acquiescing in Baumgarten's practice of treating the phrase 'intellectual memory' as equivalent with 'personality', and so may be implicitly treating 'intellectual memory' as identical with both 'personality' and 'the identity of the person', while also allowing himself the latitude to use the phrase 'the identity of the person' to refer both the faculty in question and to the states of knowledge produced by its exercise.

Kant denies that we know the third paralogism's minor premise$_v$ to be true. It may seem that he is committed, in addition, to maintaining that we know it to be false. After all, if we know nothing of things as they are in themselves, then neither do we know whether the noumenal self that underlies my current thoughts is identical with the noumenal self that underlay the thoughts I had yesterday. This would seem to have the consequence that Kant is dogmatically committed to denying that I am a person$_1$. The only way I can see to avoid this conclusion is to suppose that Kant is understanding the idea of personality slightly differently than

---

[22] See Baumgarten, *Metaphysics*, §579 and § 641. See *Metaphysics K2*, 28: 764; compare *Metaphysics Vigilantius (K3)*, 29: 1038.

we have so far supposed. We can make him consistent if we suppose his considered view to be the following. What it is for something, x, to be a person$_1$ is for *x at some stage in x's existence* to exercise the ability constitutive of personality sufficiently many times for x to be appropriately credited with that ability *at that stage*. This idea comes closer to how Kant explains personhood in the first edition than in the second, and it clearly departs from the text. I therefore offer it only tentatively. Nonetheless, its adoption has the satisfactory consequence that for Kant it is epistemically possible that we should be persons$_1$, since it is epistemically possible that in the afterlife we should come to have a spiritual form of intuition which will enable us to exercise the power of personality sufficiently many times to count as persons$_1$. If we confine ourselves to what we know on theoretical grounds, it is, of course, equally epistemically possible that we will not survive bodily death as persons$_1$—after all, we do not know on theoretical grounds if we will come to have a spiritual form of intuition nor, indeed, whether we even possess souls that will survive our bodily death. It turns out, then, that by appealing to the possibility that our cognitive capacities might be radically different in the afterlife from how they are in this life Kant can secure for himself a non-dogmatic position.[23]

7.6 Immortality

Often in his metaphysics lectures Kant discusses the Wolffian account of what would be required to demonstrate the soul's immortality. We will examine this account before considering Kant's criticisms of various attempts to provide such a demonstration.

In the *Metaphysics Mrongovius* Kant states the Wolffian account succinctly:

> For [proving] immortality it is necessary to prove (1) the natural impossibility of dying (2) the continued existence [*Fortdauer*] of the soul with all its powers and the same [ones], for otherwise life would be nothing (3) the continued existence of its personality, [understood as the fact] that it remains conscious of its previous life.   (29: 911)

A fuller statement occurs in the *Metaphysics Volkmann*:

> [In order to prove the impossibility of the soul's passing away like a body it is necessary to prove] (1) its perdurability, that is, the continued existence of the

---

[23] Kant, I am maintaining, regards our post-mortem acquisition of radically different cognitive capacities as an epistemic possibility. But he often seems to be attracted to the view as more than a mere possibility (see *Metaphysics L1*, 28: 297–8; *Metaphysics Mrongovius*, 29: 920; *Metaphysics Volckmann*, 28: 445–6; compare 29: 857 and 29: 927).

substance, (2) its continued existence as intelligence, that is, of a being whose rational faculty [*Vernunft Vermögen*] and acts <*actus*> also survive, (3) the actual continued existence of the personality [*Persönlichkeit*] of the human soul, [that is] that after death it would be aware that it is the same soul [as it was before death], for otherwise I could not say that **it itself** exists in the future world, but rather [only] that there would be another rational being there. (28: 440–1)

Each of these accounts enumerates the Wolffian 'requisites' [*requisita*] for immortality. And each would seem to be modelled on the account one finds in Kant's early-career textbook for his metaphysics lectures, namely, Baumeister's *Institutiones Metaphysicae*.[24] Speaking on his own account, Kant amends Baumeister's first requirement to say that the soul should persist beyond bodily death *from its nature*, hence with natural necessity (28: 763; 29: 910). In proposing this amendment Kant seems to have been influenced by Baumgarten, who defines immortality as the *impossibility* of dying (*Metaphysics*, §781). Kant sees the strengthening as needed because he regards it as desirable that a proof of immortality should establish a result valid for *all* human souls (28: 764; 29: 911).

Kant's take on the second Wolffian requisite may be stated as follows:

After the death of its associated body, the soul must retain its consciousness and its rational faculty, and continue to exercise (sufficiently many of) its intellectual capacities.

Endorsing this condition, Kant takes its rationale to be that if the soul were either to lose its rational faculties or to cease (permanently) to exercise them, it would have the status of an eternally 'slumbering soul'. But that would be no immortality worth having, for it would permit the soul neither to enjoy the benefits of the afterlife nor to receive divine punishment.[25]

Kant's take on the third Wolffian requisite runs as follows:

In the afterlife the soul must continue to have [Wolffian] personality, continue, that is to say, to be conscious that it is the same soul as it was prior to the bodily death of the human being whose soul it is.

This last condition is not the requirement of Wolffian personality itself but rather the stronger requirement that Wolffian personality should continue to be enjoyed in the afterlife. The condition is not one that Kant could himself endorse, for it

---

[24] Friedrich Christian Baumeister, *Institutiones metaphysicae: ontologiam, cosmologiam, psychologiam, theologiam denique naturalem complexae methodo Wolffii adornate* (Wittenberg: S. G. Zimmerman, 1774) (orig. pub. 1738) at §750.

[25] *Metaphysics K2*, 28: 770, compare *Metaphysics K3*, 1037–8.

contains Wolffian commitments he rejects. For example, personality here seems to be understood as an *actual* state of consciousness rather than an ability to be conscious of something. Kant would presumably endorse a weakened form of this condition—one according to which the soul must retain the ability to recognize sufficiently many of its earlier soul-substance stages as its own.

Both the Wolffian account itself and Kant's modification of it set a high bar for a proof of the soul's immortality. Accordingly, it should come as no surprise that Kant takes theoretically based dogmatic metaphysics to have failed in its attempts to establish this result. In the B edition Kant discusses two of these attempts, one made by Moses Mendelssohn in his 1767 work, *Phädo*, the other by David Fordyce in his *Elements of Moral Philosophy* of 1748.[26] Kant finds the second of these arguments the more congenial of the two because he believes that a version of it succeeds in justifying—or, more precisely, stabilizing—our belief in an afterlife (if not immortality proper).

7.7 Mendelssohn's argument

Kant presents Mendelssohn's argument as an attempt to repair a certain traditional argument for the soul's 'necessary continuation' (B 413). Tacitly assuming the soul to be incapable of perishing except through disintegration, the traditional argument concludes that since the soul is simple, it cannot perish at all. As Mendelssohn notes, the argument is flawed because it overlooks the possibility that the soul might perish, not through disintegration, but simply by 'vanishing' [*Verschwinden*]—that is to say, by instantaneously ceasing to exist, its parts being simultaneously annihilated along with the whole (B 413). Mendelssohn seeks to exclude this apparent possibility by contending that such a vanishing would infringe the principle of continuity. Mendelssohn's argument—or, more precisely, Kant's presentation of it—may be reconstructed as follows:

Assume, as a premise, the principle of continuity. Then time must be a dense ordering (else processes in time would not be continuous). Suppose, for *reductio*, that a simple soul were instantaneously to pop out of existence without leaving a trace. Then there would be no time between two distinct times, namely, the last

---

[26] Moses Mendelssohn, *Phädon oder über die Unsterblichkeit der Seele in drei Gesprächen (Phaedo, or on the Immortality of the Soul, in Three Dialogues)* in Fritz Baumberger and Leo Straus (eds), *Gesammelte Schriften Jubiläumsausgabe*; volume 3/1, *Schriften zur Philosophie und Ästhetik*, 1972, Stuttgart: Frommann-Holzboog, 1767). Fordyce, *The Elements of Moral Philosophy*. French translation 1756, German translation 1757 (in Kant's library). Lewis White Beck identifies an argument in the style of Fordyce's as a distinctive line of reasoning in Kant for a 'doctrinal belief', and notes that he treats it as an argument with a theoretical rather than practical (main) premise. However, he fails to note that Kant expressly credits Fordyce with its invention (29: 916). See Lewis White Beck, *A Commentary on Kant's Critique of Practical Reason* (Chicago: University of Chicago Press, 1960) at 266, n18.

moment at which the soul existed and the first moment at which it did not exist (compare B 414). But then time would not be dense. Contradiction. QED.

Kant endorses the principle of continuity for events and he also agrees that time is dense—and, indeed, necessarily so. Accordingly, he concedes that the soul cannot pop out of existence instantaneously.[27] But he observes that Mendelssohn fails to consider a way in which it might pass out of existence gradually which does not involve disintegration. He contends that the soul could cease to exist through a gradual diminution of its *intensive* magnitude—its degree of being—in virtue of a gradual diminution of its powers (B 414).

The clearest statement of Kant's criticism occurs in some metaphysics lectures from 1794–5.

> [It is true that time is dense] but from that [fact] one cannot declare it to be impossible that the soul can pass away after death.[28] Since it is simple, the parts of the soul cannot indeed pass away, but [the soul can nonetheless pass away] through an **evanescence [*evanescenz*], that is, a gradual remission of its powers.** Just as the clarity of a representation can gradually become obscure so that finally the soul slumbers in it and thus its consciousness is lost little by little, so can all degrees of the powers of the human soul give way little by little, and when they have been diminished through all degrees, finally pass over into a nothing. Here is no leap <*saltus*>, but rather [the soul] observes the laws of continuity by descending through ever smaller degrees, between which there is always again a time.   (*Metaphysics K3*, 29: 1037–8)

The argument assumes that a wholly impotent soul would be no soul at all: it would cease to exist upon its powers' dwindling to zero. Whether this assumption can be justified is a good question; but in the present context it needs no defence; for it is an assumption Kant shares with his Wolffian opponents. At any rate, if we accept it, Kant's argument will be sound.

7.8 Fordyce's argument

Towards the end the B-edition Paralogisms Kant touches on a certain non-dogmatic argument for the afterlife, which he elsewhere attributes to the Scottish philosopher David Fordyce (29: 916).[29] In the first *Critique*, Kant invokes this argument—without mentioning Fordyce by name—in the course of illustrating

---

[27] Since Kant believes that there is only one time (A 31-2/B 47), he supposes that the soul's transition from this life into the next will be governed by the principle of continuity.
[28] Reading 'can' for Kant's 'cannot'.
[29] Compare *Metaphysics Volkmann*, 28: 441–2 and *Metaphysics L2*, 28: 591–2.

the point that even when the flawed dogmatic proofs of 'the schools' have been rejected, certain other proofs retain their 'undiminished worth' (B 424–5). He says:

> [For consider the argument] in accordance with the **analogy** [*Analogie*] **with the nature** of living beings in this world, regarding which reason must assume as a necessary principle that there is to be met with in these beings no organ, no faculty, no impulse [*kein Antrieb*] nothing superfluous [*Entbehrliches*], or disproportionate to its use, hence nothing purposeless [*Unzweckmäßiges*], but rather that everything is to be judged as precisely measured for its function in life. [On the assumption that there is no afterlife] the human being, who after all can alone contain the ultimate final purpose of all this [purposive order], would have to be the only creature excepted from it. For his natural predispositions—not merely concerning his talents and the impulses to make use of them, but above all the moral law in him, go so far beyond all the utility and advantage that he could draw from them in this life that the latter teaches him to esteem above all else the mere consciousness of a disposition to rectitude, even in the absence of any advantage, including even the shadowplay of posthumous fame, and so he feels himself called inwardly to make himself, through his conduct in this world and the sacrifice of many advantages, a fit citizen of a better one, which he has in the idea. (B 425–6)

Kant cannot be said to have gone out of his way to make the structure of Fordyce's argument clear. Nonetheless, we can discern what he takes to be its main contours from certain clearer formulations he offers in his metaphysics lectures. Consider, first, a pithy statement from the *Metaphysics L2*:

> Now we find in human beings powers, faculties, and talents which, if they were made merely for this world, are really purposeless and superfluous. (28: 592)

And, now, a more expansive statement from the *Metaphysics K2*:

> The proof of the immortality of the soul is grounded on the principle of the analogy of nature. Nature has placed in all living organic beings no more predispositions than they can make use of. The faculties, their organs, are not given any larger than it can make use of. It would be absurd to assume predispositions in nature of which no use can be made. In the [non-human] animal everything is purposive.[30] With a human being it is otherwise, for he can extend his faculties, raise himself up to the nebulae, feel himself called to ponder over them, but he can make no use of this [set of capacities] in [this] life, other than that he knows this. With respect to the faculty of desire there is in human beings a predisposition even worthier of admiration. Namely a human being condemns

---

[30] The passage makes clear that here by 'purposive' Kant means 'having a use in this life'.

[*verdammt*] himself and declares duty holy, [even though] without advantage, indeed even if harm rather arises for him from it. We find in us a summons to sacrifice in us the greatest advantages without receiving in life the slightest advantage for it. Here is a predisposition [*Anlage*] in human nature, and it is just as purposive, according to the analogy of nature, as all predispositions of nature. We thus infer a future life, where the use of these predispositions and their end can first be attained. (*Metaphysics K2*, 28: 765–6)

In spite of initially describing the argument as a proof of the immortality of the soul, Kant, with some charity, ends up construing it as an empirically based argument merely for a doctrinal belief in an afterlife. He agrees with Fordyce that in the absence of an afterlife human beings would be unique within organic nature in being equipped with under-utilized, useless, or even harmful faculties. Since we are part of animal nature, the argument goes, we, like the non-human animals, can expect to fully utilize our faculties at some point, and accordingly—it continues—there must be an afterlife in which we can do so.

Kant sees two pairs of human faculties or dispositions as pre-eminently underutilized in this life: *reason* and *cognition*, on the one hand, and *will* and *morality*, on the other. To illustrate the under-utilization of the first pair he cites the fact Newton reached the age of sixty having developed his understanding and cognition to a point at which these faculties could be of great use, only for their further use to be precluded by his death.[31] Both pairs, Kant thinks, positively work against our worldly happiness. The principles of will and morality, he says, 'intend that [the human being] should not attend even to the advantages of life and even life itself'.[32] And even 'the striving after cognition', when carried to a certain degree, appears to be against our 'vocation on earth'. In consequence of this striving, he explains, 'one weakens one's mind... is less able to care for one's physical happiness, cannot fulfil one's animal vocation' (29: 916). He adds—somewhat poignantly in view of his bachelorhood—'Many are thereby prevented from ever marrying' (ibid.). In the *Blomberg* logic he is even more definite: 'If we did not have another life to expect, then learnedness would certainly be more harmful to us than useful' (24: 65).

Of the two pairs of faculties or predispositions Kant takes the moral pair to matter more to the argument.

The moral predispositions, according to which a human being views even life [itself] as nothing if he cannot maintain it without crime, are the best proof of a future existence, for the human being sees by this that he is also determined to develop and to enlarge these predispositions further. (*Metaphysics K2*, 28: 766)

---

[31] 29: 916; compare 28: 294.   [32] 28: 442 and note *.

In other words, the moral dispositions reveal to us that we will develop and enlarge them in the afterlife. They thus convey to us something about the character of that life: it will be a life of moral improvement—or so, at least, the argument would have us believe.

When in the *Metaphysics Mrongovius* Kant attributes the discovery of the argument by analogy to Fordyce, he reproduces a vivid detail of Fordyce's discussion: 'This proof', he says,

> was discovered by Fordyce, who made use of an analogy [*des Gleichnisses*]: if a higher being should perceive in the uterus of a mother a creature that had eyes, ears, and other members, it would infer thus: this creature is determined to a life where these members could be used.   (29: 916)

(In other lecture transcripts Kant is represented as attributing the same thought experiment to 'a French philosopher' (*Metaphysics K2*, 28: 766). We should not allow this to put us off the scent, however, for this remark, in all likelihood, merely reflects a misunderstanding. We know that certain other of Kant's auditors had trouble hearing or deciphering Kant's mention of 'Fordyce'; for one of them took him to be crediting the argument to 'the Englishman Fordon' (*Metaphysics Dohna*, marginal note (28: 688)). The idea that the Scot, Fordyce, was 'English' is explained by the custom in Kant's time of applying the term 'England' to the British Isles—a point reflected in the title page of Fordyce's *Elements of Moral Philosophy*, which describes him as a 'famous professor at Aberdeen in England'.[33] Kant had available to him a French translation of this work, which appeared in 1756; so it is possible that when he was delivering the lectures recorded in the *K2* transcript Kant, who did not read English, had been using this edition and had quoted some of the original formulations in French before offering his own German translations. If this had been his procedure, the transcriber of the *K2* notes might well have formed the mistaken impression that the author under discussion was French—End of digression.)

In the passage just quoted, Kant is accurately describing a thought experiment from the *Elements of Moral Philosophy*. In the course of offering what he calls a 'moral proof of [human] immortality from analogy', Fordyce says:

> [The human being] lives a sort of vegetative life in the womb. He is furnished even there with a beautiful apparatus of organs, eyes, ears, and other delicate senses, which receive nourishment indeed, but are in a manner folded up, and have no proper exercise or use in their present confinement. Let us suppose some intelligent spectator, who had never any connection with man... to see this odd

---

[33] For this point about the broad Eighteenth-century use of 'England' and 'English', see Porter, *Enlightenment*, at *xix*.

phenomenon, a creature formed after such a manner, and placed in a situation apparently unsuitable to such various machinery, must he [that is, the intelligent spectator] not be strangely puzzled about the use of his [that is, the creature's] complicated structure, and reckon such a profusion of art and admirable workmanship lost on the subject; or [alternatively] reason by way of anticipation that a creature endued with such various, yet unexerted capacities, was destined for a more enlarged sphere of action, in which those capacities shall have full play?[34]

Fordyce concludes that we ought to choose the second option and reason 'by analogy' or 'in the way of anticipation' to the conclusion that our present state is only 'the womb of Man's Being', so that the human being is destined for an 'afterpart, and is to be produced upon a more august and solemn stage, where his sublime powers shall have proportioned action' and where the nature of his character shall 'attain its completion'.[35]

Elsewhere, Fordyce underscores the last idea mentioned here, namely, that in the absence of an afterlife certain human capacities would remain, not so much under-exercised, as *unfinished*:

Does nature give the finishing touches to the lesser and ignobler instances of her skill, and raise every other creature to the maturity and perfection of his being, and shall she leave her principal workmanship unfinished?[36]

Kant seems to have regarded this argument as a paradigm of an argument by analogy; for he uses it to illustrate this particular mode of reasoning in the *Jäsche Logic*: '[T]he ground of proof for immortality', he says, 'from the complete development of the natural dispositions of each creature is, for example, an inference according to analogy' (§84, 9: 133). I take Fordyce's argument to have the following form:

Argument by analogy:
P1. Every non-human organism has only such talents, capacities, and predispositions as are fully developed, perfected, and exercised during its existence.
P2. Human beings resemble non-human organisms in being part of organic nature.
Therefore, lest we be anomalous among organic nature:
C. We human beings are such that all of our talents, capacities, and predispositions are fully developed, perfected, and exercised during our existence.

---

[34] Fordyce, *The Elements of Moral Philosophy* (Indianapolis: Liberty Fund, 2003) at 153–4.
[35] Ibid., at 155 and 157.   [36] Ibid., at 156–7.

Coda

P3. Some of our capacities etc. are not fully developed etc. in our mundane life.

So,

Corollary. We enjoy an afterlife in which these capacities etc. are developed etc.

Strictly speaking, only the part of this argument that terminates in the conclusion, C, is an argument by analogy. If formulated in a way that comports with Kant's account of such arguments in §84 of the *Jäsche Logic*, it would take the following form:[37]

P1. *Non-rational organisms* and *rational organisms* agree on all their hitherto observed properties (aside from rationality).

P2. *Non-rational organisms* are observed to perfect, and exercise to the full, all of their capacities and predispositions.

P3. For any kinds, A and B, if As and Bs agree on all their hitherto observed properties (aside from that which distinguishes them into kinds) and As are further found to be F, then Bs are also F. (The principle of analogy)

C. So *rational organisms* also perfect, and exercise to the full, all of their capacities and predispositions.

As Kant makes clear in the *Jäsche Logic*, this argument's conclusion possesses only empirical certainty. We will evaluate the argument later, but the point to note for now is just that Kant is plausibly correct in presenting Fordyce's argument as a paradigm case of an argument by analogy on his understanding of that notion.

When we move back to the first *Critique*, the argument seems to be treated as having a slightly different starting point. At B 425–6 Kant represents the argument by analogy as assuming that among (non-human) living things 'no organ, no faculty, [and] no impulse' is 'superfluous, or disproportionate to its use'. This presupposes that everything living in non-human nature has a 'use', hence a 'purpose' furthered by the feature that is put to this use. Such an assumption is not made explicitly in the version of the argument in the *Jäsche Logic*, though it is perhaps hinted at in the talk of 'predispositions'. Nonetheless, the 'no-superfluity' point would seem to be a clear nod to Fordyce, who says:

> If, besides the immediate Set of Powers which fit [the human being] for Action in his present State, we observe another Set which appears superfluous, if he was to be confined to it, and which point to another or higher [State then], we naturally conclude, that he is not designed to remain in his present State, but to advance to that [one] for which those supernumerary Powers are adapted. Thus we argue

---

[37] 9: 133, note 1.

that the Insect, which has all the Apparatus proper for Flight, is not destined always to creep on the Ground, or to continue in the torpid State of adhering to a Wall, but is designed in its Season to take its Flight in Air. Without this farther Destination, the admirable Mechanism of Wings and the other Apparatus, would be useless and absurd.[38]

Fordyce is thinking of the various 'states' of a human being—that is, in utero existence, post-partum mundane existence, post-mortem existence—on the model of the metamorphic growth stages of an insect. He invites us to draw an inference by *modus tollens*: If humans did not enjoy an afterlife, they would be the only kind of living thing with superfluous faculties. But they are *not* unique in this respect (by the argument by analogy). Therefore, they *do* enjoy an afterlife. In spite of its billing, then, Fordyce's argument is not an argument for *immortality*, proper, but merely an argument for an afterlife—as Kant recognizes. Nor could it have that greater ambition; for as Kant says in the *Mrongovius Metaphysics*: 'I still do not know from this proof whether the human soul will live eternally. Who knows if I do not die once all these predispositions have developed?' (29: 917).[39]

Although, as one might expect, Kant does not endorse Fordyce's argument as a *demonstration* within speculative metaphysics, he does regard it as providing a 'powerful ground of proof' (B 426), which, while not yielding 'insight into the necessary continuation of our existence' (B 426), nonetheless provides a non-conclusive reason to believe in a future life. As we have noted, the kind of belief in question is what Kant in 'the Canon of Pure Reason' terms 'doctrinal belief' [*doktrinalen Glauben*].[40] Such an epistemic state is not mere opinion but a 'strong belief, on the correctness of which I should be prepared to wager many of life's advantages' (A 825/B 853). Plainly referring to the argument by analogy, Kant supposes that we must doctrinally believe in the 'future life' of the human soul 'in view of the surpassing endowment of our human nature, and the shortness of life so ill-suited to this endowment' (A 826-7/B 854-5).

---

[38] Fordyce, *The Elements of Moral Philosophy* at 153. The word 'Destination' is rendered as '*Bestimmung*' in the German translation of Fordyce, 'useless' as '*ohne Nutzen*', and 'absurd' as '*ungereimt*'.
[39] The alert reader will have noted that the commitment expressed in this last remark creates a tension in Kant's position. On the one hand, for the sake of running Fordyce's argument he needs to suppose that human beings will eventually show themselves to be fully analogous to other parts of animal nature by fully realizing their capacities at some point in the afterlife (as is suggested here). On the other hand, however, in his moral philosophy he insists that such a point will never be reached. In the second *Critique*, for example, he says, 'For a rational but finite being only endless progress from lower to higher stages of moral perfection is possible' (5: 123). And again, holiness, which Kant characterizes as 'the complete conformity of the will with the moral law' (5: 122), is 'never fully attained by a creature' (5: 123, note *).
[40] Compare A 826-7/B 854-5. As Chignell notes, Kant's notion of doctrinal belief does not correspond exactly to belief in the ordinary sense ('Belief in Kant' at 359). Having noted the importance of this point, however, I will suppress it in my exposition.

The key premise in the first *Critique*'s version of the argument is that nothing in organic nature is without a purpose. This assumption—or 'principle' (B 425)—is an assent [*Fürwahrhaltung*] that is not 'objectively sufficient' because it doesn't rest on objective grounds.[41] It is rather 'subjectively sufficient' because it is necessary, or so Kant thinks, for inquiry into nature. The assent to the judgment of the existence of an afterlife would seem to inherit the status of doctrinal belief from this more basic assent simply because the proof of the former depends on the latter as a premise. In the case of my belief in the afterlife, the objective grounds are, first, the empirically certain fact that human beings die without fully realizing their potential and, second, the principle of analogy. The subjective ground is the doctrinal belief in the purposiveness of nature, a ground which depends on our possessing the contingent goal of inquiring into nature.

Given the objective grounds that obtain, I have freedom either to doctrinally believe or not to doctrinally believe in the afterlife. Accordingly, my doctrinal belief is a voluntary assent that depends on my goals. It is an indispensable means for securing these goals, but the goals themselves I can take or leave. It is the non-mandatory (or, as Kant says, 'contingent') nature of these goals that distinguishes doctrinal belief (and also prudentially-grounded belief) from moral belief.[42] The contingent goal relevant to the case of doctrinal belief in the afterlife, is inquiry into nature. In Kant's view, if I am to inquire successfully into nature, I must doctrinally believe that empirical inquiry will be advanced by approaching nature with the goal of finding purposes in it. More simply, I must doctrinally believe that nothing in nature is without a purpose. Once formed, this doctrinal belief serves as a subjective ground for another: it functions as a premise in the argument supporting my doctrinal belief in the afterlife—or so, at least, I would argue.

Our doctrinal belief in the afterlife, then, is, by Kant's lights (in a certain special way) justified—or, as Kant prefers to say, 'subjectively sufficient'. However, there remains something 'unstable' [*Wankendes*] about it, namely, that 'one is often put off from it by difficulties that come up in speculation, although, to be sure, one inexorably returns to it again' (A 828/B 855–6). The doctrinal belief in the future life, then, is, in *one* sense, unstable: it can be wrested from us by speculative difficulties. In another sense, though, it is stable: it is a state to which our minds inevitably return after perturbations. By contrast, our *morally* grounded belief in God and an afterlife cannot be even temporarily shaken by speculative difficulties (A 828/B 856). This reveals that for Kant two token beliefs with the same

---

[41] For explanations of Kant's notions of *opinion* and of *objective* and *subjective sufficiency*, see Chignell, 'Belief in Kant'.

[42] By 'prudentially grounded belief' I have in mind, for example, the doctor's non-evidence-based belief that the patient has a certain malady (I'm assuming, for the sake of making this point, that the doctor is *not* morally required to cure the patient). Kant does not adequately disambiguate the word 'practical' in its application to belief: sometimes he means 'morally grounded' and sometimes 'prudentially grounded'.

content—*A*'s morally grounded and *B*'s doctrinal belief in an afterlife, say—can differ in their stability depending on the nature of their grounds.

Kant's attitude to Fordyce's argument is complex. He is critical of the argument's billing as a proof of the soul's *immortality* as opposed to an afterlife. But he still regards it as 'the best of all [arguments] that [have] ever been introduced for the soul' (28: 592). In particular, he admires its ambition to prove a result that is valid of *all* human beings (29: 916; 28: 443–4). He believes that the argument fails to show what it purports to show; but he also describes it as a 'powerful' ground of proof that 'can never be refuted' (B 426). Why should he say such a thing?

The answer has two parts. First and most obviously, even after the argument has been discredited as a demonstration of immortality (B 426), it retains—or so Kant thinks—its probative force as a non-demonstrative, partly theoretically-grounded argument for an afterlife—or, more precisely, as a consideration that produces and sustains a relatively firm belief in an afterlife, a doctrinal belief upon which one would be prepared to wager a great deal.[43] Second, and less obviously, when Kant says that the argument 'cannot be refuted' he does not mean that we will never discover any flaw in it, but rather that we cannot *establish* the falsity of its conclusion. One argument that purports to do precisely that is the argument 'from the contingency of our origins'. One argues that since the effect cannot be greater than the cause, our humble and contingent human origins cannot be the cause of so mighty an effect as our necessary and eternal existence. Kant blocks this argument by observing that its proponent has not excluded the hypothesis that—to the contrary—I lack a contingent origin simply because I have not originated at all. More fully, the argument's proponent has not eliminated the hypothesis that my life, and the life of every other human being, may be without beginning or end in virtue of the fact that we enjoy an eternal spiritual existence of which the series of events we call our 'life' is just an appearance (A 780/B 808). Kant, of course, does not take himself to possess evidence for the truth of this hypothesis, but he believes that its remaining an unexcluded possibility suffices to defeat this particular dogmatic argument against immortality.

One last observation concerns a worry that is not inherited from Fordyce's argument but rather concerns the distinctive twist that Kant gives to it. I have claimed that for Kant the doctrinal belief that serves as a premise in the argument—the belief that nothing in nature is without a purpose—receives its justification from the fact that it subserves the goal of natural inquiry. This is a contingent goal, not mandated by the moral law, and so one that some human beings may have and others lack. But this would seem to suggest that the

---

[43] The argument is partly theoretically grounded because the claims that non-human living things fulfil their purposes, while human beings die before doing so clearly have empirical, hence theoretical, components. Arguably, it might also be taken to be theoretically grounded because Kant describes doctrinal beliefs as theoretical; but whether he holds this of all doctrinal beliefs or only such of them that are means to ends not actually pursued is unclear.

argument is a privilege of the empirical scientist, one quite unavailable to ordinary folk. Kant could, of course, simply accept this consequence of his view: for the rest of us can fall back on the moral argument. But there remains something unsatisfactory about Kant's offering the proof as one that is suitable 'for the world' (that is, for the world of *all* human beings), if its suitability is restricted to practising scientists.

There is reason to think that Kant may have been aware of this problem. For his notion of a doctrinal belief seems to be framed with an eye to addressing it. He holds that I can be credited with a doctrinal belief that p even when proceeding on the assumption that p would subserve only a merely imagined or conceived purpose. This point is already clear from the example he uses to illustrate the notion of a doctrinal belief, namely, his belief that at least one of the planets we see is inhabited. For I am not in a position to undertake any project with respect to those inhabitants. I cannot, in Kant's day, have any dealings with them. Kant makes just this point in a passage in which he is explaining why the judgments we assent to in connection with doctrinal beliefs are merely the *analogues* of practical judgments:

> Even if we cannot undertake anything at all concerning an object, and the assent regarding it is therefore merely theoretical, we can still in many cases conceive and imagine an undertaking for which we suppose ourselves to have sufficient grounds if there were a means of establishing the certainty of the matter. And thus there is in merely theoretical judgments an **analogue** of **practical** judgments, and for an assent to such judgements the word belief [*Glaube*] is appropriate.
> (A 825/B 853)

Here Kant is contrasting doctrinal beliefs with pragmatic beliefs. The latter are assents one must hold, in the absence of objective grounds, in order to bring about some *actually pursued* end. The working doctor, for example, is actually treating the patient and so, in order to act decisively in administering a cure, must, in spite of not knowing the diagnosis, assent to the judgment that the patient has some particular ailment—consumption in Kant's example (A 824/B 852). The alternative is to do nothing and so allow the patient to die. Doctrinal beliefs, on the other hand, bear this same means–end relation to merely imagined (or merely conceivable) projects. And, consequently, Kant is able to hold that each of us may be credited with a doctrinal belief in the purposiveness of nature merely by dint of the fact that we *would* have to assent to the judgment that nature is suffused with purposes if we were to be pursuing natural scientific inquiries. Such a position still seems somewhat unsatisfactory, for it seems to drive a rather deep wedge between doctrinal belief and belief as it is ordinarily understood. But we can at least understand why Kant should have felt compelled to adopt it. Moreover, it explains why he sees the belief that nature is saturated with purposes as (for most of us) a merely theoretical (as opposed to pragmatic) belief: it is a belief we would have to hold if we were to pursue what is for most of us in fact a merely imagined or conceivable project. The belief in the afterlife counts as a theoretical belief partly because it rests in part on this theoretical belief and partly because it rests on the empirically-justified theoretical belief that human beings die before they realize their potential, while animals do not.

7.9 Fordyce's argument evaluated

Kant's version of Fordyce's argument is less ambitious than the original. But one still wonders why he should have been quite so firmly attached to it. The objections it faces, after all, are not few. First, not all human beings have talents that fail to be realized in this life. Some severely cognitively disabled people, for example, *will* be able to fully realize their limited potential precisely because it is so limited. Second, some non-human animals have skills that are in fact far from being realized or perfected during their lifetimes. Indeed, many non-human animals will die in infancy. Worse still, even those that manage to live out full lives may have developmental potentialities that are not actualized. For example, the Peter Pan Salamander (also known as the 'axolotl') often lives and reproduces in an immature larval state, only metamorphosing if its aquatic environment changes its chemical composition.[44] Third, the argument makes the unsupported assumption that human capacities and powers are indeed *analogous* to those of other organisms in nature. But what if the analogy is imperfect? Perhaps some of our powers—the powers we have as part of our animal nature—are analogous to those possessed by non-human animals, but why think that our moral and intellectual—let alone spiritual—powers must be similarly analogous? Why should we think that these powers must be fully exercised and perfected just because of the (alleged) fact that the powers of non-human animals are?

Perhaps, though, some of these objections might be answered. To the first, Kant might perhaps reply that a severely cognitively disabled child arguably does not in fact realize its potential because, given enough time and care, the child could develop its limited powers a little farther while also coming to exercise those it already possesses to a greater degree. To the second, he might reply by reformulating the argument. The proper observation to appeal to, he might argue, is that *some* members of each species of non-human animal live to fully realize their potential; whereas *no* human being does. However, this reply could only succeed if the inhabitants of other planets, in which Kant plainly believes (A 825/B 853), do not have animal natures; for, as Kant himself notes in another connection, we have

---

[44] I am indebted for this example to Roy Sorensen.

no information about whether any of *them* fully realize their potential (8: 23, note *). To the third objection, finally, he might argue that the objection merely goes to shows that the argument has been incorrectly formulated. The crucial point is that there would be something left *unexplained* if humans were unique among the animals in having faculties that far exceeded what they could do with them. If humans survived bodily death, on the other hand, there would be no anomaly to explain.

8
The Fourth Paralogism

8.1 Introduction

Kant titles the fourth paralogism 'the paralogism of ideality (in regard to outer relation)'. It counts as a paralogism of *ideality* because its conclusion is a statement of what Kant calls 'problematic' or 'sceptical' *idealism*: the view that the existence of objects outside of us (that is, in space) is 'merely doubtful'.[1] Kant attributes such a view to Descartes, whom he interprets as holding that only a single empirical assertion is indubitably certain, namely, the assertion 'I am' (B 274).[2] The 'ideality' of the objects of the outer senses alleged by Kant's paralogist, therefore, is a matter of their supposedly enjoying, in contrast with one's own existence, a merely 'doubtful'—or perhaps better, *uncertain and unprovable*—existence (ibid.).

The fourth paralogism is anomalous in appearing to introduce an abrupt change of topic: whereas the other paralogisms speak about 'the soul' or 'the thinking I' it speaks about 'all outer appearances'—a phrase Kant takes to refer to the objects of outer sense (and paradigmatically, to bodies).[3] The appearance of an anomaly can, however, be diminished by an observation made in the previous chapter. We noted that the third paralogism purports to establish something about the *epistemic situation* of the soul. It argues that the soul is a person, which, as we have seen, means that it is capable of having a certain kind of knowledge about its existence over time. The fourth paralogism might also be viewed as attempting to establish something about the soul's epistemic situation, for although it explicitly argues only that the objects of outer sense have an uncertain existence, the implied contrast is with the soul's certainty about its own existence. In keeping with this thought, the table of transcendental predications of

---

[1] B 274; compare 4: 375.
[2] In the *B* edition Kant attributes 'problematic' idealism to Descartes and 'dogmatic' idealism to Berkeley (B 274). He sees these positions as two species of 'material' (B 274) or 'empirical' idealism (A 491/B 519), which he contrasts with his own 'formal' or 'transcendental' idealism. What Kant calls 'dogmatic idealism', however, is not in fact Berkeley's idealism. For Berkeley would agree with the empirical realist that the bodies we perceive are something real in space, and the qualities in them real qualities. He would merely deny that these bodies and qualities are capable of existing unperceived. His target is the reality not of bodies, but of *matter*.
[3] Kant glosses 'outer objects' as 'bodies' at A 370. That said, it is not altogether clear that, strictly speaking, outer objects or appearances should be equated with bodies. For, while all bodies would seem to count as outer appearances, there is a question about whether certain outer appearances that do not display impenetrability—puffs of smoke or rainbows, say—would count as bodies properly speaking. I'm grateful to Brian Cutter for this point.

the soul at A 404 represents the target thesis of the fourth paralogism as the claim that the soul is conscious '*only of the existence of itself* and of other things merely as its representations' (emphasis added). The same idea is suggested when, after formally stating the fourth paralogism, Kant comments on the peculiar nature of the perceptual access we have to the self. 'We may', he says, 'rightly assert that only what is in ourselves can be immediately perceived' (A 367), continuing: 'Descartes therefore also rightly limited all perception in the narrowest sense to the proposition "I (as a thinking being) am"' (A 368). Since Descartes famously took this proposition to be known with certainty, it seems likely that Kant is taking 'perception in the narrowest sense' to entail (apodictic) certainty. Arguably, then, the topic of the fourth paralogism is as much our certain knowledge of our own existence as our uncertainty about the existence of external objects.

8.2 The paralogism

The fourth paralogism runs as follows:

> That whose existence can be inferred only as a cause of given perceptions, has a merely doubtful existence.
>
> Now all outer appearances are of this kind: their existence is not immediately perceived, but can be inferred only as the cause of given perceptions.
>
> Thus, the existence of all objects of the outer senses is doubtful. (A 366–7)

One striking feature of Kant's criticism of this argument is that he alleges an equivocation in a phrase neither identical with nor occurring within the paralogism's apparent middle term. Kant explains this equivocation as follows:

> The expression **outside us** carries with it an unavoidable equivocation [*zweideutigkeit*], since it sometimes signifies something that, **as a thing in itself**, exists distinct from us and sometimes merely something that belongs to outer **appearance**. (A 373)

The nature of the alleged equivocation is clear. Taken in a metaphysically loaded sense, the phrase 'a thing outside us' means 'a thing conceived of as having the features it does independently of its relation to sensibility', or, equivalently, 'a thing conceived of as a thing in itself'. Taken in the metaphysically innocent sense, by contrast, the same phrase means merely 'a thing in space'—hence a spatially located physical object.

If we were to reformulate the paralogism so that it contained the expression 'outside us' as its allegedly equivocal middle term, we would have to understand 'existence' in Kant's original formulation as short for 'existence outside us'. The reformulated paralogism, with its middle term disambiguated as *per* A 373, would then run:

> Whatever is such that its existence outside us (*that is, its existence in space*) can only be inferred as a cause of given perceptions has a doubtful existence.
>
> All objects of outer sense (that is, outer appearances) are such that their existence outside us (*that is, their existence as things in themselves*) can only be inferred as causes of given perceptions. (The minor premise$_k$)
>
> All objects of outer sense (that is, outer appearances) have a doubtful existence.

In addition to incorporating the expression 'outside us', this reformulation involves relocating the word 'only' ('*nur*'), which in the German occurs after the word translated as 'inferred'.[4] The relocation is required to bring out the contrast Kant surely intends to be drawing between two ways in which it might be claimed that we are capable of knowing of the existence of things outside us—the alternatives being 'by causal inference alone' and 'immediately'. The intended contrast is *not* one between two *ways of inferring* the existence of things outside us—'as causes', on the one hand, and in some other (unspecified) way, on the other. This point is confirmed by the following remark:

> If one regards outer appearances... as things in themselves found outside of us, then it is hard to see how their existence could be cognized in any way other than by an inference from effect to cause, in which case it must always remain doubtful whether the cause is in us or outside us.   (A 372)

In other words, if one were to subscribe to Transcendental Realism and so regard objects in space as enjoying a constitution that is wholly independent of our capacity to be sensibly affected by them, then one could not be certain of their existence; for one would have to infer it by means of an untrustworthy inference from effects to causes.

Kant, then, is endorsing the major premise when it is read as saying that if something could be known to exist in space in no other way than on the basis of an inference from effect to cause, then it would enjoy only an uncertain existence. And he is also endorsing the minor premise when it is read as saying that we can know of the existence of *things in themselves* in no other way than on the basis of such an inference. But he is denying the minor premise when it is read as saying what it would have to say in order to mesh with the major premise into a valid

---

[4] In this detail I follow Kemp Smith's translation.

argument, namely, that the objects of outer sense (appearances) are such that their existence can be known by us in no other way than on the basis of an inference from effect to cause. He denies the minor premise so interpreted because he supposes that the objects of outer sense can be immediately known.

8.3 External-world scepticism rejected

Perhaps the most intriguing aspect of the *A*-edition fourth Paralogism is Kant's discussion of his reasons for rejecting the minor premise$_v$. This premise states that the existence of objects outside of us in space can be known only by means of an inference from given perceptions. Kant demurs because he believes that the existence of such objects is known non-inferentially and with certainty. He explains his reasons for rejecting the minor premise$_v$ as follows:

> For the refutation of empirical idealism as a false dubiety [*Bedenklichkeit*] concerning the objective reality of our outer perceptions, it is already sufficient that outer perception immediately proves an actuality in space, which space, though in itself it is only a mere form of representations, nevertheless has objective reality in regard to all outer appearances (which are also nothing but mere representations); and it is likewise sufficient to refute empirical idealism that without perception even fictions and dreams are not possible, so our outer senses, as regards the data [*datis*] from which experience can arise, have actual corresponding objects in space. (A 376–7)

By 'empirical idealism' Kant usually understands a position that comprehends both the problematic idealism he attributes to Descartes and the dogmatic idealism he attributes to Berkeley. But in the present context he is discussing only problematic idealism. Kant clearly takes each of the considerations he mentions to be individually sufficient to refute this kind of idealism. First, there is the claim that we are immediately and non-inferentially aware of external objects in outer perception, so that our perception itself proves their actuality in space. Second, there is the claim that, unless we were to perceive objectively real outer appearances, fictions and dreams would not be possible. Expanding on the first of these points, he says:

> I am no more necessitated to draw inferences in respect of the actuality of external objects than I am in regard to the reality of the objects of my inner sense (my thoughts), for in both cases they are nothing but representations, the immediate perception (consciousness) of which is at the same time a sufficient proof of their actuality. (A 371)

As this passage makes clear, what is supposed to make plausible an account of outer perception as immediate awareness is Transcendental Idealism. Being appearances, objects in space, are, for the Transcendental Idealist, 'nothing but representations'. And, accordingly, our access to them is supposed to enjoy all the intimacy of the relation between a mind and its representations. If I can get so far as to perceptually represent a spatial object as existing then—the thought runs—it must exist, else the binary relation of perceiving, which holds between a mind and a spatial object construed as a representation, would lack one of its relata. In Kant's view at this stage, then, Transcendental Idealism excludes problematic idealism.

The key move in this argument, clearly, is the suggestion that external objects are nothing but representations and so are directly perceived because we directly perceive our perceptual representations. There are two problems with such a move. First, it seems more natural to say that we *have* our representations—that is, we are in representational states—than that we perceive them. Second, if this move is to succeed, Kant will need to say more about the sense in which these objects are, though mere representations, nonetheless occupants of space. In particular, it seems that he would need to replace his simple *identification* of external objects with representations with some kind of 'construction' of them out of representations. Berkeley took a step in this direction when he identified bodies not with individual ideas but with collections of them (and Russell took a further step); but Kant neglects to build on Berkeley's thought.[5]

In the light of these objections, it is worth examining in detail Kant's second argument against problematic idealism. This argument differs from the first in making no appeal to Transcendental Idealism. Instead, Kant claims that the real in space, which he describes as 'the material of all objects of outer intuition' is 'given actually and independently of all invention' (A 375). This is because 'one is not at all able to think up the real [*das Reale*] in intuition *a priori*' (ibid.). Kant's thought, I take it, is that we can't simply dream up the real element in spatial intuition because it is the basic material out of which complex images—which we *can* dream up—are built.

If this is Kant's implicit reasoning, then his argument is vaguely suggestive of the so-called 'painting argument' in Descartes's First Meditation. Descartes's interlocutor—a figure internal to the *Meditations*, whose job it is to create trouble for the meditator's Cartesian line of thought—offers the following argument against the possibility of a fully corrosive dream doubt:

Suppose then that I am dreaming, and that these particulars—that my eyes are open, that I am moving my head and stretching out my hands—are not true.

---

[5] George Berkeley, *Three Dialogues between Hylas and Philonous* (Indianapolis: Hackett, 1979) at Third Dialogue, 81.

Perhaps, indeed, I do not even have such hands or such a body at all. Nonetheless, it must surely be admitted that the visions which come in sleep are like paintings, which must have been fashioned in the likeness of things that are real, and hence that at least these general kinds of things—eyes, head, hands and the body as a whole—are things which are not imaginary but are real and exist. For even when painters try to create sirens and satyrs with the most extraordinary bodies, they cannot give them natures which are new in all respects; they simply jumble up the limbs of different animals. Or if perhaps they manage to think up something so new that nothing remotely similar has ever been seen before—something which is therefore completely fictitious and unreal—[then] at least the colours used in the composition must be real. By similar reasoning, although these general kinds of things—eyes, head, hands and so on—could be imaginary, it must at least be admitted that certain other even simpler and more universal things are real. These are, as it were, the real colours from which we form all the images of things, whether true or false, that occur in thought. (Descartes, *Meditations*, *AT* VII, 19–20; *CSM* II, 13–14)

The painter can invent many things, but not the colours on her canvas; for they constitute the material out of which even her false representations are made. Their presence on the canvas, we might say, already witnesses their reality. Similarly, we cannot—or so the interlocutor suggests—be mistaken about the real existence of the simplest general kinds of things; for these are instantiated by the very medium of representation. And, crucially for our purposes, the interlocutor includes among these simplest general kinds of things 'corporeal nature and its extension' (*AT* VII, 20; *CSM* II, 14).

Given Descartes's conception of corporeal nature as mere *res extensa*, this argument arguably has some merit; and it causes Descartes to switch to the more corrosive deceiving-God hypothesis.[6] In Kant's hands, however, it will not do. For he has a richer conception of corporeal nature: bodies, for him, are, by their very nature, not merely extended but also (to some non-zero degree) resistant to penetration and (to some non-zero degree) prone to attract other bodies. It is therefore hard to see how Kant could argue that our ideas witness the reality of Kantian bodies. And the point generalizes to external objects that are not bodies. For although ideas may perhaps be said to have numbers and temporal durations, and (some of them) arguably to have shapes and extension in *visual* space (think of the shape of the visual field), it seems to be simply false to say that they instantiate the concept of the real in space. After all, shape in visual space is

---

[6] One might, however, question the argument on the grounds that it involves a naïve conception of painting. The realistic painter, after all, does not in fact use quite the same shade of colour she is attempting to depict, for she has to allow for the desaturation of colours seen at a distance through a partly opaque medium. Rather, it seems that the colours on the palette *go proxy for* the colours represented as existing in reality.

not shape in physical space, and extension in the visual field is not physical extension.

For these reasons Descartes's interlocutor's argument cannot be successfully adapted to Kant's purposes. The resemblance that argument bears to the one Kant offers in the fourth Paralogism does, however, suggest that he might have been using it—just how self-consciously is unclear—as his model in that discussion. One supposes that, if that were indeed the case, then he must have initially overlooked the problems we have noted, and that he must have come to see them in time for the *B* edition, where he introduces a new, improved argument for the existence of outer things in which he argues that inner sense presupposes outer sense—the so-called 'Refutation of Idealism' (B 274–9).[7]

8.4 Anti-materialism

At one point, Kant asks after the purpose of *pure* rational psychology. 'For what', he asks rhetorically, 'is a doctrine of the soul founded exclusively on pure principles of reason required?' (A 383). His answer is clear-cut: 'Without doubt, primarily in order to secure our thinking self against the danger of materialism' (ibid.). Why does materialism constitute a 'danger' to our thinking self? The answer, I think, is that, owing to the perishability of matter, this doctrine threatens our hope for an afterlife, and so undermines the incentives towards morality.

Kant is clear that the pure doctrine of the soul is unable to secure us against this danger, but he claims, somewhat surprisingly, that Transcendental Idealism *can* secure us against it. The securing he says, is 'accomplished by means of the rational concept of our thinking self which we have already given' (A 383). The concept in question is the concept of a thinking self that stands outside, and serves as the source of, space and time. This is the thinking self conceived of as the 'transcendental subject'. On this conception, the self has no spatial or temporal parts and so cannot perish through decomposition (29: 1036). Transcendental Idealism, then, is an intrinsically an anti-materialist philosophy of the self—or rather it is such given Kant's understanding of matter as 'the **moveable** in space' (4: 480).

One wonders, however, why any of this should be germane to the question of an afterlife. After all, to the extent that Kant believes in the afterlife such an existence would seem to belong to a temporally embedded subject. But Kant's atemporal noumenal self is no such thing. Perhaps, though, Kant can reply that his timeless noumenal self is nonetheless able to experience the atemporal analogue of an afterlife. The idea would be that, in addition to having its usual experiences, it

---

[7] This topic lies beyond the scope of the present work. For a highly illuminating discussion, see Bader, 'The Refutation of Idealism'.

can, in principle, also be the subject of 'experiences' afforded not by the sensibility associated with the sense organs of its body, but by a certain spiritual form of intuition. That, at least, is the material out of which Kant might try to craft an adequate response to the present worry—though, for the reasons we have already mentioned, its prospects remain unclear.

8.5 Monism

Having made these claims about the anti-materialistic consequences of Transcendental Idealism, Kant registers a caveat. Speaking of Transcendental Idealism's concept of the thinking self, he says:

> Through this concept, to be sure, I do not cognize this thinking self better as regards its properties, nor can I thus gain insight into its permanence, or even into the independence of this self's existence from what may be the transcendental substratum of outer appearances; for I am just as unacquainted with this substratum [of outer appearances] as I am with the thinking self. (A 383)

Insofar as he is open to these possibilities, Kant is conceding that for all we know there might be a single kind of thing that serves as the 'transcendental substratum' of both thinking beings and outer objects—the position we earlier classified as a version of monism.

Kant, however, does not merely note this epistemic possibility: he goes on to enlist it in the service of dissolving the problem of mind–body interaction. To my knowledge, his idea is completely novel. He suggests that the problem will exist only if we take ourselves to *know* that body (or matter) and mind have different natures (extension and thought, respectively). But if we do not know this, and if they might, for all we know, be of the very same nature (in themselves), then for all we know there may be no problem to be solved. He says:

> But if we assume that the two kinds of objects [mind and body] thus differ from each other, not inwardly but only in so far as one **appears** outwardly to the other, and that what, as a thing in itself, underlies the appearance of matter, perhaps after all may not be so heterogenous in character, this difficulty vanishes.
> (B 427–8)

As Kant sees it, then, the problem of mind–body interaction is not to be solved by developing arcane systems of occasionalism or of pre-established harmony. Rather, it is to be dissolved by recognizing how little we in fact know about the nature of mind and body as they are in themselves. In Kant's view, we simply know too little about these matters for the problem to get going.

8.6 The *B*-edition fourth Paralogism

In the *B* edition Kant presents the fourth paralogism as attempting to establish that I, as a thinking being, can exist in the absence of external objects, and so, in particular, in the absence of my own body. In the language of the Wolffian tradition, it attempts to establish my status as a 'spirit'.[8] In the *B* edition the critical discussion of this paralogism is confined to the observation that the minor premise$_k$ of the paralogism$_k$ is merely an analytic proposition, with the consequence that nothing of metaphysical interest can be concluded from it. Kant says:

> I distinguish my own existence, as [that of] a thinking being, from [that of] other things outside me (which include my body)—this is likewise an analytic proposition. For **other** things are things that I think as **distinct** from me. But from this I by no means know whether this consciousness of myself is at all possible without things outside me whereby representations are given to me, and hence whether I can exist as merely [a] thinking being (i.e., without being a human being).
>
> Hence analysing the consciousness of myself in thought as such does not yield the slightest gain as regards the cognition of myself as object. (B 409)

Kant's point is just that the minor premise$_k$ boils down to the mere tautology that I am distinct from everything distinct from me. And, obviously, nothing can be inferred about the possibility of my enjoying a disembodied existence from such a claim.

Kant seems to associate the conclusion of the fourth paralogism with the categories of 'modality' (A 344/B 402). This makes a certain amount of sense in connection with the *A*-edition Paralogism because what had been in question in that Paralogism was the epistemic *possibility* of the non-existence of external objects. In the *B* edition the decision makes still more sense because what is now in question is the *metaphysical* (or real) possibility of the soul's retaining its capacity to think—hence its existence—in the absence of external objects, including its own body.

In his diagnosis of the *B*-edition paralogism Kant is in effect suggesting that the minor premise involves an equivocation between the following two claims.

[A]   I am distinct from all things distinct from me.

[B]   I can exist and think in a world whose inhabitants include no external objects.

---

[8] 'An immaterial being', Kant says, 'is a spirit insofar as it can think without body' (*Metaphysics Dohna*, 1792–93, 28: 683). In the *Real Progress* he defines a spirit as 'a being which, even without a body, can be conscious of itself and its representations' (20: 309).

Kant takes [A] to be analytic and [B] to be substantive but not known to be true. These verdicts are plausible, though one might reasonably doubt whether [A] is really an admissible disambiguation of the minor premise.

8.7 Transcendental illusion again

One consideration speaking in favour of Kant's reformulation of the fourth paralogism in B is that it enables the argument to conform to the pattern required by his account of transcendental illusion—something that the A edition version clearly failed to do. Recall that transcendental illusion is supposed to tempt us to mistake a certain subjective unity for an objective unity, where one way of understanding this objective unity is as the unity that the self might be thought to possess in virtue of being, in some respect or other, an unconditioned condition. Now if the existence of the soul does not depend on the existence of outer objects, it can be thought to enjoy a certain kind of unconditioned status. One worries, of course, that the soul might still depend for its existence on the existence of other non-spatial and non-temporal substances, in which case the lack of conditioning would be only partial. Nonetheless, to think of the soul as enjoying 'the unconditioned unity of existence' even in this limited sense is to predicate something substantive of it. And so the soul's alleged spirituality should, by the lights of Kant's account of transcendental illusion, deserve to be treated as part of that illusion.

It is harder to know how Kant is conceiving of the *subjective* unity that we are supposed to be inclined to mistake for this objective unity.[9] This, he suggests, is the unity of apperception, a unity which, in Kant's view, has various aspects which are expressed by the minor premises$_k$ of the four paralogisms. But in the revised, B-edition version of the fourth paralogism the minor premise$_k$ is a triviality that seems wholly unconnected with the unity that one's consciousness is supposed to enjoy in virtue of the attachment (or attachability) of the 'I think' to each of one's representations. That premise, after all, says merely that I am distinct from all the things distinct from me. It is one thing to suppose that we may, through some confusion, fail to distinguish this trivial thought from the substantive claim that I can exist in the absence of outer things, but it is quite another to see this triviality as an aspect of apperception. In this respect, then, if not in others, the fourth Paralogism must, I think, be adjudged an unconvincing part of Kant's diagnosis of the failings of rational psychology.

---

[9] The diagnosis is repeated in slightly different terms at B 421–2.

8.8 Architectonic and method

In Chapter 2 we noted the distinction Kant draws between the analytic and synthetic procedures in rational psychology. In the former one assumes the existence of the soul and attempts to derive certain results about it; in the latter, leaving the question of the soul's existence to one side, one analyses its concept, turning to a proof of its existence only when that analysis is complete. Which procedure does Kant's paralogist follow? The first *Critique*, unfortunately, offers no clear answer; for while the ordering of the topics of rational psychology in the tables presented at A 344/B 402 and A 404 suggests the synthetic method, that of the table at B 419 suggests the analytic.

The point of each table is to display the content of rational psychology systematically, with the ultimate goal of ensuring the completeness of Kant's critique of this purported science (A 403). The most detailed table, given at A 404, encodes the rational psychologist's claim that the soul cognizes itself as enjoying four kinds of 'unconditioned unity', namely, the unconditioned unity

1. of *relation* i.e., [it cognizes] itself, not as inhering but rather [as] ***subsisting***
2. of *quality* i.e., [it cognizes itself] not as a real whole but rather [as] ***simple***
3. in the *plurality* in time, i.e., [it cognizes itself] not [as] numerically distinct in different times, but rather as ***one*** and the very ***same subject***
4. of *existence* in space i.e., [it cognizes itself] not as the consciousness of several things outside it, but rather [as the consciousness of] ***the existence of itself only***, and of other things merely as its ***representations***. (A 404)

The fourth entry in this table is the hardest to decipher. The idea would seem to be that in being conscious of its representations the soul is thereby conscious only of things inhering in itself, hence of itself (as it appears) alone. And, if it is said to be conscious of other things, then that is only, so to speak, by courtesy because these so-called 'other things' are really only (the objects of) its representations.

The table at A 404 is also organized under the titles of relation, quality, quantity, and modality—though less obviously so. The relevant category of relation in (1) is *inherence-and-subsistence*. And we can infer that the relevant category of quality in (2) must be *reality*, for, as the footnote to A 404 makes clear, the simple is supposed to correspond (somehow) to the category of reality. The category of quantity in question in (3) is unity (as opposed to plurality)—the soul is *one* thing in *many* times, while the category of modality in question in (4), finally, is existence.

Relation, quality, quantity, and modality also occur as the four 'titles' of the table of categories at A 80/B 106.[10] But there they are depicted as having the

---

[10] For this use of 'title' compare R 5663 (18: 323).

following order: (I) quantity, (II) quality, (III) relation, and (IV) modality. Using these roman numerals to abbreviate the titles in this ordering, we can see that in the table presented at A 404 the four kinds of unconditioned unity are presented in the initially curious-seeming order: III, II, I, IV. This curiosity turns out to matter; for it turns out that whether one is operating in accordance with the analytic or synthetic procedure hinges on the order in which these titles are worked through.

A somewhat shorter table, presented earlier at A 344/B 402, is billed as a table of 'the topic of the rational doctrine of the soul'. A doctrine's 'topic' is something from which 'whatever else [this doctrine] may contain must be derived' (ibid.). We should therefore think of this table as presenting the broad contours of rational psychology rather than its fine details. The table runs:

1. The soul is **substance**.
2. In its quality, **simple**.
3. In the different times in which it exists, it is numerically identical, i.e. **unity** (not plurality).
4. It stands in relation to **possible** objects in space. (A 344/B 402)

This table differs from the less pithy one at A 404 with respect to the category that figures under the heading of modality. In the longer-winded table, this category is existence, in this shorter one, possibility. Because of this difference the shorter table is, I think, the better of the two. For Kant claims that the two tables include only those concepts of the understanding that somehow 'ground the unity' of the others contained under the same title (A 403). And these special unity-grounding concepts are the first-mentioned categories in each triad in the table of categories at A 80/B 106 (compare 18: 323). But the first category mentioned under the heading of modality is possibility rather than existence.

If we consider the order in which the headings from the table of categories are presented in the table of topics at A 344/B 402, we again obtain the somewhat curious pattern: III, II, I, IV. And, Kant tells us, somewhat bafflingly, that tackling the headings in this order amounts to going 'backwards' through their series (A 344/B 402). Fortunately, the fog begins to clear when we realize that Kant is conceiving of the headings in the table as forming not just a list but also a 'circle' (B 417). Using arrows to represent the direction in which one proceeds as one treats of the topics mentioned in those headings, we may depict Kant's conception as in Figure 8.1.

In the tables at A 404 and A 344/B 402 Kant is envisaging the rational psychologist as beginning with III: subsistence-and-inherence/substance and working anti-clockwise around this circle until finally arriving at IV: existence/ possibility. In the table at A 404—where IV corresponds to the soul's existence rather than its possibility—this amounts to portraying the rational psychologist as

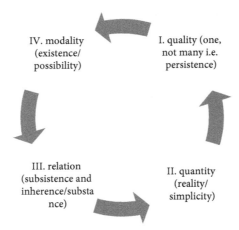

Figure 8.1 Circle of topics

proceeding according to the synthetic method, where the soul's existence is (purportedly) proved only after certain things have been established about its character. As we saw in Chapter 2, if, alternatively, one follows the analytic procedure, although one still works around the circle in an anti-clockwise direction, now, instead of ending with existence one begins with it.[11] Unfortunately, however, Kant's presentation of this idea is complicated by the fact that he illustrates the analytic procedure with reference to a somewhat different table—one occurring only in the B edition—which features no entry corresponding to the fourth paralogism. This third table runs:

1. **I think**
2. **as subject**
3. **as simple subject**
4. **as identical subject** in every state of my thinking (B 419)

Since as we saw in Chapter 6, Kant holds that 'I think' is equivalent to 'I exist thinking', we know that (1) involves a modal category, namely, existence (B 418, compare A 354–5). We also know from Kant's explanations in the *A* edition that (3) involves a category of quality, namely, reality, and that (4) involves a category of quantity, namely, unity. It follows by elimination that (2) involves the category of relation, namely, subsistence-and-inherence. According to this table, therefore, in rational psychology the headings are worked through in the order: IV. modality

---

[11] See Chapter 2, §2.9. As Allison notes, this way of proceeding is plausibly the method that Descartes follows in the *Meditations* (Allison, *Kant's Transcendental Idealism* at 352).

(existence), III. relation (subsistence-and-inherence), II. quality (simplicity (reality)), and finally, I. quantity (unity).[12] We are now straightforwardly 'going backward through the series' of headings (A 344/B 402). And since we begin with existence we are following the analytic method.

Why should Kant retain this picture of rational psychology in the B edition alongside the alternative picture, present in both editions, of rational psychology as starting from a merely problematic concept of the soul—and so proceeding according to the synthetic method? It is hard to be certain, but I would venture the following thought as part of the explanation. As we saw in Chapter 2, the table at B 419 approximates Kant's actual conception of rational psychology in the *L1 Metaphysics* lectures, where he presents the claim 'I am' as included within the basis of rational psychology. In depicting rational psychology as proceeding in accordance with the analytic method, then, the table at B 419 reflects Kant's own pre-critical conception of this putative science—the conception he had of this discipline when he was one of its practitioners. This seems entirely proper because, as we have also seen, the paralogisms often resemble arguments Kant gives in the *Metaphysics L1*.

8.9 Descartes

Which of the two methods or procedures does Kant see Descartes as having followed in his early version of rational psychology? The answer is not straightforward, for while in the *A* edition Kant seems to read Descartes as employing the analytic method, in the *B* edition, although he is plainly not thinking of him as employing the analytic method, neither is there any clear indication that he thinks of him as employing the synthetic method.

The reason why in the *A* edition Kant interprets Descartes as employing the analytic method is that he takes him to begin from an experience of the soul. Descartes, he says, 'rightly limited all perception in the narrowest sense to the proposition "I (as a thinking being [*Wesen*]) am"' (A 367–8). In saying this Kant seems to be attributing to Descartes something close to the view of the *Metaphysics L1* according to which the claim 'I am' is the sole empirically known proposition of rational psychology (*Metaphysics L1*, 28: 263). By the *B* edition, however, he has plainly changed his mind; for he now presents Descartes as attempting to *demonstrate* the soul's existence. The putative demonstration is clearly inspired by Descartes's presentation of the *cogito* in the *Discourse on Method* and the *Principles*:

---

[12] That Kant adopted this new ordering after the first edition is confirmed by his marginal note at E CLVI, 23: 38–9.

Everything that thinks, exists
I think
Therefore, I exist (compare B 422 note)

But although this indicates that in the *B* edition Kant no longer interprets Descartes as employing the analytic method, it is not at all clear that he now thinks of him as following the synthetic method. For Kant nowhere portrays Descartes as prefacing his attempted existence proof with a priori derivations of properties that the soul would have to have if it were to exist.

In the *B* edition Kant offers a novel criticism of the *cogito* (construed as an inference). 'The "I think"', he says,

> [is] an empirical proposition, and contains within itself the proposition 'I exist'. But I cannot say "Everything that thinks, exists"; for then the property of thinking would make all beings possessing it into necessary beings. Hence my existence cannot be regarded as inferred from the proposition "I think" as **Descartes** held (for in order to do that the major premise, "Everything that thinks, exists" would have to be presupposed), but rather it is identical with it.
> (B 422 note)[13]

Here Kant is criticizing the *cogito* as it is presented in the *Discourse* and *Principles* and treating it as an enthymeme.[14] His criticism is not that the enthymematic major premise is *uncertain*, but rather that it is recognizably *false* because it entails the obviously false claim that every thinking being is a necessary being. Kant offers not the slightest hint of the thinking behind his charge. Nonetheless, we can make an educated guess at what he has in mind. He seems to be assuming that any rational psychologist who ran the inferential version of the *cogito* as part of the project of pure rational psychology would have to view the premise 'Everything that thinks, exists' as an analytic truth. But this would require supposing that the concept *exists* is contained in the concept *thinks*. And if that were so, then anything whose essence, according to the rational psychologist, is to think—anything, in Kant's terms, whose concept includes thinking as a mark—would be such that its concept contained existence. But then such a thing would, by the rationalist's lights, be an entity whose existence followed from its very concept. And that is just Kant's conception of an absolutely necessary being (A 606–7/B 634–5). If this reading is to be plausible, the claim 'Everything that thinks, exists'

---

[13] Kant makes the same point at B 420, when he says: '[to] say that every thinking being exists... would at the same time predicate absolute necessity of them, and hence say too much about them'.

[14] Kant shows no interest in the second *Meditation* formulation of the *cogito*, and he seems to be ignorant of Descartes's insistence in the *Second Replies* that the utterance 'I think, therefore I am, or exist' is not to be construed as a syllogism. As Longuenesse notes, his criticism is to that extent unfair. Longuenesse, 'Kant on the Identity of Persons', at 84–8.

must be taken to mean 'Everything whose essence or nature is to think, exists'. And since this gloss may be disputed, there is room to resist this line of reconstruction. Nonetheless, it seems plausible that Kant would read the major premise in this way; for Descartes clearly thinks of the 'I think' as expressing an essence or nature: the essence of the Cartesian soul, after all, is to think.

PART II
RATIONAL COSMOLOGY

9
The Mathematical Antinomies Presented

9.1 Introduction

When Kant uses the term 'antinomy' as a count noun he uses it for a seemingly intractable, two-sided dispute concerning some weighty and enduring metaphysical question. The two sides of the dispute correspond to the two ways in which one might seek to satisfy reason's quest for the unconditioned in a regressive or 'ascending' series of conditions. In the mathematical antinomies, the thesis attempts to halt the regress by positing an unconditioned condition within the regressing series as its highest or ultimate member—for example, an earliest state of the world—while the antithesis attempts to halt it by positing the infinitely regressing series itself (minus its lowest member) as the unconditioned condition of that lowest member—for example, the series of world-states temporally prior to the present world-state (compare A 417–18/B 445–6). In the dynamical antinomies, things are more complicated because the thesis may posit something outside the regress as a condition of the whole (this happens in the fourth antinomy but not the third).

The conditions in these various series bear the *real* conditioning relation to what they condition. Kant offers no very precise characterization of this relation, but his illustrative examples suggest that, *in the Antinomies, at least*, he conceives of it as a binary relation that is irreflexive, asymmetric, and transitive—a relation holding between 'things' broadly construed (including world-states) rather than facts in particular. Since it holds between things rather than facts, the real conditioning relation involved in the Antinomies differs from the grounding relation currently in vogue in metaphysical circles, but it is systematically related to that relation. The kinship consists in the following fact: When in the Antinomies Kant maintains or implies that x is a real condition of y, it is usually safe to assume that the existence of x either grounds—in (one of) today's sense(s)—or partially grounds the existence of y.[1]

In the first *Critique* Kant officially recognizes four antinomies, corresponding, when taken in the order in which they are presented, to the categories of: quantity,

---

[1] However, as Marcus Willaschek has observed, Kant in fact envisages three kinds of real conditioning relation, corresponding to the categories of inherence, dependence, and community. Plausibly, the first of these is relevant to the Paralogisms, the second to the Antinomies, and the third to the Ideal. See Willaschek, *Kant on the Sources of Metaphysics* at 82–3. My exposition has focused on the first two of these relations.

quality, relation, and modality. In practice, however, the first antinomy consists of a pair of sub-antinomies. The four main antinomies concern the age and size of the world; its mereological structure; the existence or otherwise of human free will, and the existence or otherwise of an absolutely necessary being—understood as a being that depends on absolutely nothing for its existence, not even itself.[2] The thesis of each antinomy is congenial to devotees of what is sometimes called 'the enchanted world': thus to theism or free will or a belief in the immortality of the soul; the antithesis to 'Godless materialism': thus to atheism or hard determinism or materialism. Kant believes that there is not a single antinomial proposition among his main eight that has not at some point been accepted by some philosopher or other (4: 379).

Kant takes the arguments supporting each side of each antinomy to be valid (and indeed sound) if, but only if Transcendental Realism is true. But he thinks that in the case of each antinomy the appearance of a contradiction between thesis and antithesis is merely a semblance produced by transcendental illusion.[3] In working out the details of this last idea Kant is guided by a certain Aristotelian taxonomy of 'oppositions' according to which the genus—pairs of 'opposed' propositions—divides into three species, namely: contradictories, contraries, and sub-contraries.[4] Contradictories are pairs of propositions that can neither be true together nor false together; contraries pairs that cannot be true together but *can* be false together; and sub-contraries, finally, pairs that can be true together but cannot be false together. Three points about this trichotomous division are worth noting. First, as Kant indicates in his logic lectures, it applies only to 'oppositions' broadly understood; in the narrow sense of 'opposition' only contradictories count as opposed.[5] Second, the trichotomous form of the division, though emerging naturally from the Aristotelian square of opposition, is, for Kant, most immediately dictated by the fact that sub-contraries are said to contain *less* than is required for *proper* opposition, contraries *more*, and contradictories *exactly as much*.[6] Third, contradictories are *not* treated as a species of contraries.

In the *Real Progress* of 1793 Kant expressly portrays his diagnosis of the antinomies as guided by this trichotomous classification.[7] Each antinomy, he

---

[2] The second antinomy corresponds to the category of quality because the disputed question concerns the existence of simples—entities that the tradition often treated as possessing greater reality than complexes of other things (and, for Kant, reality is a category of quality). Kant accordingly assigns the question of the soul's simplicity to the category of quality (A 344/B 402). Later I will substantiate my claim that specifically *human* free will is in question in the third antinomy.

[3] Kant supposes that there are genuinely contradictory positions in pure psychology and pure theology, but in the case of these putative disciplines he does not think that both sides of the dispute are supported by arguments that are valid if Transcendental Realism is true (A 743/B 771).

[4] This taxonomy occurs in Reusch's *Systema Logicum*, §§476–81. See also definitions 158–60 of Baumeister's *Philosophia Definitiva* at 32–3.

[5] See 24: 281, 24: 770, and 24: 670–1.

[6] See *Real Progress*, 20: 291–2 and 20: 328; compare *Blomberg Logic*, 24: 281.

[7] See 20: 291, 20: 328, R 5962 (18: 404), and 4: 343.

maintains, contains two propositions that, while seeming to be contradictories, are actually either contraries—as in the mathematical antinomies—or sub-contraries—as in the dynamical ones (20: 291). Accordingly, each antinomy is resolved by treating the appearance of a contradiction as deceptive. In the first *Critique*, as we'll see, Kant takes roughly the same approach. However, he does so without explicitly invoking the trichotomous taxonomy—though a hint of it appears in his claim that in the case of contraries one judgment 'not only contradicts the other but says something more than is required for contradiction' (A 504/B 532).[8] As we'll see, however, this neat picture is in fact complicated by Kant's operating in the dynamical antinomies with a non-standard understanding of what it is for two propositions to be 'compatible'.

Kant enlists one of his famous legal metaphors in trying to render vivid the contrasting styles of his envisaged resolutions of the mathematical and dynamical antinomies. Whereas in the mathematical antinomies the claims of the disputants are to be 'dismissed' (as false), in the dynamical antinomies they are rather to be 'settled' by being shown to be non-conflicting, through a 'correction' of their significance—or, more accurately, through an exhibition of their true significance.[9] The mathematical and dynamical antinomies also differ in two respects pertaining to the structure of the series with which they deal. First, whereas the mathematical antinomies are associated with various series generated by the part–whole relation (A 560/B 588), their dynamical counterparts are associated with various series generated by the relation of ground-and-consequence—though Kant tends to express this second relation as a relation of *dependence* rather than ground-and-consequence: causal dependence in the third antinomy, ontic in the fourth.[10] Second, whereas the mathematical antinomies concern series whose members are all of the same kind, the dynamical antinomies concern ones whose members need not all be of the same kind (A 560/B 588). Kant enlarges on this second difference in the *Real Progress*, where he says that the mathematical antinomies deal with various series containing 'parts of a similar quantity' (20: 327; compare 20: 288), while the dynamical antinomies proceed 'from the consequences to the supreme synthetic ground', which is 'something really different' from the other members of the series (20: 327, compare 4: 343).

---

[8] Obviously, in this context what it is for one judgment to 'contradict' another is not to be its contradictory opposite. Rather, Kant is here using 'contradict' with the sense of 'be incompatible with'.

[9] A 529–30/B 557–8; A 532/B 560. The notion of dismissal here is distinct from the one involved in Kant's claim near the beginning of the *A* edition that human reason faces the perplexity of being presented with questions it can neither answer nor dismiss (see A *vii*). In this latter context 'dismiss' means something closer to 'justifiably belittle and ignore'.

[10] A 560/B 588. The first antinomy is concerned with the part–whole relation because the antithesis affirms, and the thesis denies, that each part of the world is enclosed within—hence a part of—a bigger part.

9.2 The phenomenon of antinomy

In the first *Critique* Kant often employs the term 'antinomy' as a mass noun (or 'non-count' noun). This practice reflects his conception of antinomy as a peculiar 'phenomenon of human reason' (4: 339)—one comprising the four (or five) individual antinomies that severally enact reason's apparent dispute with itself.[11] The phenomenon of antinomy is the *appearance* that reason is inherently contradictory.[12] Reason generates this appearance—or so Kant supposes—autonomously and inevitably.[13] It is, he says, not one of the sophist's 'artificial snares' but rather a perfectly natural illusion (A 407/B 434), one to which human beings have, in his view, been immemorially subject. Since it is deeply rooted, the illusion cannot be avoided by disputational skill alone (4: 338). Instead, its resolution calls for *criticism*: a practice that 'requires the philosopher to return to the first sources of pure reason itself' (4: 338). By making this return, Kant thinks, one can discover a deeper illusion lying behind and explaining the illusion that reason is in contradictory conflict with itself. This deeper illusion, he argues, is transcendental illusion, something which, in the context of the antinomies at least, he identifies with the illusion that Transcendental Realism is true (20: 311). In Kant's view, this illusion is for human beings universal and abiding; but, criticism, by drawing it to our attention, enables us to avoid being taken in. Thus, while the illusion abides, the error to which it customarily leads can, if we are careful, be avoided. The antinomies are, we might say, *resoluble* because we can be led to recognize as deceptive the appearance that the thesis and antithesis are contradictory. But since this appearance cannot be removed—but only recognized for what it is—the *phenomenon* of antinomy remains unavoidable (A 407/B 434).

Not only do the thesis and antithesis appear to be contradictorily opposed, their supporting arguments appear to be sound. Indeed, Kant maintains that the opposed proofs in each antinomy would be sound if Transcendental Realism were, *per impossibile*, true. Kant makes this point especially clearly in the *Prolegomena* where, speaking of the phenomenon of antinomy, he says:

> Here is now the strangest phenomenon of human reason... If, as is commonly done, we consider the appearances of the sensible world as things in themselves, if we accept the principles of their connection as principles that are universally valid for things in themselves and not merely for experience (as is just as

---

[11] A 407/B 433; A 497/B 525.

[12] Kant also uses the term 'antithetic [*Antithetik*]' for this phenomenon (A 407/B 433; R 4757 (17: 703–4)). In addition to using this term for the existent phenomenon of *apparent* contradiction, he also occasionally uses it for a merely alleged but actually non-existent contradiction (see, for example, A 743/B 771). The term 'antinomy [*Antinomie*]' has a parallel dual use (see A 564/B 592 for mention of a 'seeming antinomy').

[13] Compare A 407/B 434.

common, nay, is unavoidable without our *Critique*): then there arises an unsuspected conflict, which can never be resolved in the usual dogmatic manner, since both thesis and antithesis can [on the assumptions just adumbrated] be established through equally evident, clear, and incontestable proofs—for I will vouch for the correctness of all these proofs—and therefore reason is seen [on these same assumptions] to be divided against itself, a situation that makes the sceptic rejoice, but must make the critical philosopher pensive and uneasy. (4: 339–40)

Kant sees this state of uneasiness as in a certain respect salutary: it has the power to rouse the critical philosopher from their dogmatic slumber and to set them on the path of critique. It is precisely this ability of antinomy to function as a kind of epistemological smelling salts that makes it reason's 'most remarkable phenomenon'—a phenomenon whose peculiar excellence lies in its working 'the most strongly of all to awaken philosophy from its dogmatic slumber, and to prompt it toward the difficult business of the critique of reason itself' (4: 338). The implied contrast with other, less powerful, agents of awakening would seem to reflect Kant's desire to give Hume due credit for the complementary role Kant sees him as having played in snapping him out of his pre-critical stupor.[14] At any rate, it's clear that this remark has autobiographical significance for Kant. In a well-known letter to Christian Garve of 1798 he explains that it was not the investigation of

> the existence of God, immortality, and so on, but rather the antinomy of pure reason ... [that] first roused me from my dogmatic slumber and drove me to the critique of reason itself, in order to resolve the scandal of the ostensible [*scheinbaren*] contradiction of reason with itself.[15]

The antinomial smelling salts were necessary, Kant seems to imply, because dogmatism, like slumber, is characterized by a certain pleasurable inertia. The business of critique, by contrast, is bothersome and exacting—a rigmarole one would sooner avoid. In a reflection from 1776–78 Kant reflects helpfully on the character of his momentous awakening:

> In the beginning I saw this outlook [*Lehrbegriff*] as if in a twilight. I attempted in all earnestness to prove a proposition and its opposite, not in order to erect a sceptical doctrine, but because I suspected an illusion of the understanding, [and I wished] to discover in what it consisted. The year '69 gave me great light.[16]

---

[14] A role not to be minimized given the *Prolegomena*'s depiction of Hume as setting the agenda for the first *Critique* (see 4: 260–1).
[15] Letter to Garve, 21 September 1798 (12: 257–8). [16] R 5037, 1776–78, 18: 69.

Kant's purpose in constructing antinomies, then, hadn't been to retrace the steps of the *dogmatic* sceptic—a philosopher who defends the doctrine that nothing can be known—but rather to unearth a suspected illusion in order to discover in what it consisted.

It's hard to know which conclusion, if any, he reached at this early stage about the identity of the illusion in question, though, for several reasons, Transcendental Realism is a likely suspect. First, the *timing* of the discovery is right: the doctrine of the ideality of space and time appears for the first time in the *Inaugural Dissertation* of 1770 (2: 400; 2: 403). Second, the *magnitude* of the discovery is right: the illumination afforded by the discovery of Transcendental Idealism would indeed be a 'great light' from Kant's point of view. Third, the *image* is right: Transcendental Idealism is precisely the kind of thing that could have been glimpsed in a twilight if one suspected that the appearance of a contradiction in the antinomies rested on some false assumption common to thesis and antithesis, but couldn't quite say what it was.

That having been said, as Guyer has noted, it is not until the mid-1770s that Kant offers his first tentative formulation of the antinomies.[17] At this stage, he suggests that the principles corresponding to a selection of the theses are 'principles of the spontaneity of pure reason', while those corresponding to a selection of the antitheses are 'principles of the exposition of appearances', and he labels the former principles 'transcendent', the latter 'immanent'.[18] To the extent that there is any recommendation at this stage for how the antinomies ought to be resolved, it seems to be that the antitheses, being 'immanent' principles, should be construed as stating how things stand within the empirical world, while the theses, being 'transcendent' principles, should be construed as stating how things stand outside the empirical world. At a high level of abstraction, such a strategy anticipates the approach Kant eventually adopts in the *dynamical* antinomies, for it involves treating the opposed claims as capable of being true together.

One thing that was clearly already firmly in place in 1769 is the idea that the construction of antinomies can be used as a technique for confirming the existence of an otherwise merely suspected illusion. Antinomy for Kant, then, is not merely a *phenomenon* of reason; it is also an *instrument* of critique—or rather this goes for the *practice* of constructing antinomies.[19]

Both in the 'Great Light' reflection and in others from the same period, Kant indicates that in constructing antinomies he had not merely been reflecting on the proofs, or attempted proofs, of others. Instead, he had been earnestly endeavouring

---

[17] See Paul Guyer, *Kant and the Claims of Knowledge* (Cambridge: Cambridge University Press, 1987) at 393–5.
[18] See R 4757, 17: 703–4, 1775–77.
[19] To construct an antinomy is to construct a pair of apparently sound arguments for apparently contradictory conclusions.

to construct valid proofs of apparently contradictory propositions *for himself*. In doing so, he had been proleptically heeding his own later implied recommendation that the philosopher should be able to develop the 'hidden dialectic' that lies within 'his own breast' (A 754–5/B 782–3). Kant assumes, with some plausibility, that insofar as each of us instantiates 'common human reason' we are thereby in possession of reason's incipient dialectic and so able to develop it for ourselves (compare 8: 226 note *). The development of this dialectic takes the form of a kind of experiment, where we see if we can devise convincing arguments for two apparently contradictory propositions. Nonetheless, the 'do-it-yourself' character of antinomial construction—the fact that in framing antinomies we are not merely rehearsing previously formulated arguments but often devising novel arguments of our own—does not, he thinks, make it inappropriate to borrow a line of proof from another philosopher. Indeed, quite the reverse: 'One must', Kant says, 'weigh the propositions in all sorts of applications and even borrow a particular proof from these [applications], one must try out the opposite, and postpone decision until the truth is illuminated from all sides' (R 5036, 1776–78, 18: 69).

Plainly, the critical method recommended here draws on both historical reconstruction and imaginative innovation. And both techniques are alluded to in the first *Critique*. Kant describes his favoured critical method, which he calls 'the sceptical method', as one of:

> watching or rather oneself occasioning a contest between assertions not in order to decide it to the advantage of one party or the other, but to investigate whether the object of the dispute is not perhaps a mere semblance at which each would snatch in vain without being able to gain anything even if he met with no resistance. (A 423/B 451)

The activity of *watching* a contest corresponds, I think, to rehearsing an extant dispute, *occasioning* one to devising new 'proofs' for apparently inconsistent propositions. Kant plainly regards the sceptical method as *ideally* involving the latter procedure, but whichever procedure one chooses, the goal is to determine whether some kind of illusion lies at the bottom of the dispute and, if so, to gain insight into its nature. As we noted in the introduction, moreover, Kant regards the construction of antinomies as the *best* critical method. 'In the critique of metaphysics', he says,

> one can make use of two kinds of method. The first is to examine and to search for [the disputants'] paralogisms <paralogismos> or instances of begging the question <petitiones principii>. The second is to oppose one proof to another, indeed a proof equally convincing as the opposite. This latter method is the best.
> (R 4454, early-to-mid 1770s, 17: 557)

Why is the construction of antinomies superior to the piecemeal criticism of proofs? Because of the two critical methods only the former forces dogmatic metaphysics to divulge its hidden dialectic:

> The single possible case in which reason would reveal (against its will) its secret dialectic, which it falsely passes off as dogmatics, would be that in which it based one assertion on a universally acknowledged principle, and, with the greatest propriety in the mode of inference, derived the direct opposite from another equally accredited principle. (*Prolegomena*, 4: 340 and compare 5: 107)

Kant means that among the three branches of Wolffian special metaphysics only rational *cosmology*—by his lights, the sole antinomy-engendering putative metaphysical science—has the capacity to reveal reason's secret dialectic. This dialectic, he suggests, arises because 'the concept of a sensible world existing for itself is self-contradictory' (4: 342). And by rehearsing the antinomies on the assumption that the sensible world exists as a thing in itself we reveal this Idea as contradictory. The method of criticism associated with the construction of antinomies, then, serves to reveal both the depth of reason's predicament and its means of escape.

The proofs involved in the antinomies involve 'the greatest propriety in the mode of inference' (4: 340) because, on the assumption of Transcendental Realism, they employ logically *valid* reasoning.[20] This point is vital. If the reasoning of any antinomy were to be flawed in virtue of ordinary logical improficiency—as opposed to the influence of transcendental illusion—then Kant would have failed to isolate the false presuppositions on which the proofs rely. And in consequence, that antinomy would be incapable of serving as the basis for a convincing 'confirmatory' argument for Transcendental Idealism from the need for, and possibility of, its resolution. Kant, then, takes the reasoning of the antinomies to be logically watertight *so long as Transcendental Realism is presupposed*.[21] But he also recognizes that certain earlier attempts to demonstrate the thesis or the antithesis of some antinomy amounted to merely spurious 'lawyers' proofs' (A 430/B 458). Seeking to distance himself from these discredited proofs, Kant insists that the proofs *he* lays out in the first *Critique* are 'drawn from the nature of the case' (ibid.). And, as if to hammer this point home, he occasionally exhibits criticisms of certain specious proofs alongside the argumentation he endorses.[22]

---

[20] As we'll see shortly, the *reductio* inferences in the proofs are valid on—but only on—the assumption that Transcendental Realism is true.

[21] In the *Prolegomena* Kant describes the proofs in the antinomies as proceeding 'in accordance with principles that every dogmatic metaphysician must of necessity acknowledge' (4: 379). Given that each proof presupposes Transcendental Realism, this suggests that he sees dogmatic metaphysics as committed to Transcendental Realism and its consequences.

[22] See, for example, A 430/B 458 and A 453/B 482.

Although Kant is impressed by the special critical and diagnostic power of the antinomies, he is also attuned to their historical dangers. The antinomies, he warns, have traditionally 'led reason into the temptation either to surrender itself to a sceptical hopelessness or to assume an attitude of dogmatic defiance' (A 407/B 434). In other words, the pre-critical speculative metaphysicians have traditionally felt themselves compelled to choose between, on the one hand, declining to adjudicate the dispute—thus joining Kant's inauthentic Pyrrhonian sceptic in permanently suspending belief—and, on the other, hardening their intellects into a rigid dogmatism by denying one side of the dispute a fair hearing (ibid.). As Kant recognizes, antinomy, left unresolved, thus forces us to choose between scepticism and dogmatism—two positions that he sees as, each in its own way, entailing the death of sound philosophy (A 407/B 434).

Scepticism and dogmatism are, of course, precisely the poles in terms of an oscillation between which Kant characterizes the history of philosophy in the A-edition introduction (A ix). The phenomenon of antinomy, he thinks, explains both how the oscillation arises and why it endures. Or rather, this is the first part of his story. His deeper explanation appeals to the role played in sustaining the appearance of intractable conflict by the unrecognized assumption of Transcendental Realism.

9.3 The form of an antinomy

Kant supposes that, if the background assumption of Transcendental Realism is unconsciously made, each antinomy will appear to have the form depicted in Figure 9.1.

Here the two sets of auxiliary premises are assumed to be the minimal sets of mutually-consistent propositions necessary for the derivation of a contradiction from the respective *reductio* assumptions. The auxiliary premises are assumed to be acceptable to both parties to the dispute, though they are not assumed to be either identical or disjoint. Since the antinomy is constructed against the background assumption of Transcendental Realism, each party to the dispute is entitled to include within its set of auxiliary premises not merely logical principles, definitional truths, and conceptual truths but also any premises they can recognize (and expect their opponent also to recognize) as entailed by Transcendental Realism.[23] As we will see, Kant also seems to treat certain antinomial proofs, including the proof of the thesis of the first antinomy, as drawing on certain obvious facts of experience—facts that neither party to the dispute would deny.

---

[23] The Transcendental Realist doesn't, of course, consciously register his reliance on this background assumption.

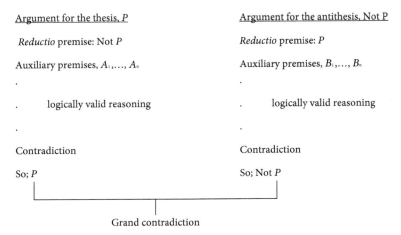

Figure 9.1 The form of an antinomy

Kant associates the opposition between the thesis and antithesis positions with the opposition between Platonism, on the one hand, and Epicurean empiricism, on the other (A 471/B 499; 29: 759). His choice of historical representatives of the two positions reflects his view of Plato and Epicurus as the foremost philosophers of, respectively, the intellect and sensibility (A 853/B 881). He thinks of Plato as regarding genuine insight and certainty as provided by reason alone, Epicurus by the senses alone (compare 24: 207). Kant sees the opposition in question as having originated shortly before the time of Alexander (356–323 BCE) (A 472/B 500)—and so, presumably, during the first half of the fourth century BCE. Such a dating suggests that he may have regarded Epicureanism as an ongoing intellectual tendency even before the adulthood of Epicurus (341–270 BCE), though, obviously, muddled or vague chronology is also a possibility.[24]

Although Kant seems genuinely to regard Plato and Epicurus as historical defenders of at least some of the positions he associates with their names, the correspondence is far from exact. For example, insofar as Epicurus posits the 'swerve' of atoms to make room for free will, he would be more naturally aligned with the indeterministic thesis position of the third antinomy than with its deterministic antithesis.[25] Kant's take on Epicurus is in fact somewhat opaque. In some moods, he allows that Epicurus, whom he occasionally portrays as an anti-metaphysician, might have viewed the antithesis of each antinomy as merely

---

[24] The hedging in Kant's claim that the two camps arose 'Shortly before or during the time of Alexander' suggests vague chronology (29: 749, emphasis added).

[25] Kant was aware of the Epicurean 'swerve' in connection with the Epicurean theory of cosmos formation (see 2: 148 and 28: 664–5); it's less clear that he knew of its role in connection with Epicurus's conception of human free will.

a regulative principle.²⁶ In others, however, he portrays him as treating each antithesis as a constitutive principle straightforwardly opposed to one of the four 'cornerstones' of religion and morality that are constituted by the equally constitutive thesis positions (A 466/B 494). In the latter moods, accordingly, he regards the Epicurean philosophy as having a tendency 'to drive morality and religion into the ground' (R 6317 (18: 626)). And, consistently with this assessment, he regards Epicurus as having merely feigned worship of the gods (29: 763; 29: 951). What does seem clear is that Kant treats the labels 'Platonic' and 'Epicurean' as umbrella terms, suggestive of broad tendencies of mind rather than of worked-out, historically realized positions.

Omri Boehm would disagree with this last claim. In his book, *Kant's Critique of Spinoza*, he argues that, on the contrary, the antitheses of the first and third antinomies are best understood as specifically Spinozistic positions—albeit not identified by Kant as such.²⁷ For four reasons, I remain unpersuaded. First, and most obviously, Kant is conceiving of the antithesis positions sufficiently broadly and abstractly that they may be associated with Epicurus: specific figures are de-emphasized. Moreover, he is encouraging us to share this lofty perspective. Second, insofar as Kant—outside of the first *Critique*—explicitly associates the antithesis of the third antinomy with any particular individual besides Epicurus that person is not Spinoza but Joseph Priestley, who adopts this position in his dispute with Richard Price.²⁸ Accordingly, if Boehm is right that Spinoza exemplifies the antithesis position of the third antinomy, this would merely amount to further evidence that Kant sees the antinomially opposed positions as representing broad and multiply exemplified tendencies of mind. Third, in the second *Critique*, Kant says that Spinozism is 'all that remains' if Transcendental Realism is endorsed (5: 101-2)—a thought echoed by his remark in the L2 metaphysics lectures that if space is a thing in itself then Spinozism is 'irrefutable' (*Metaphysics L2*, 28: 567). Clearly, at the time of making these remarks he can hardly see Spinoza's position as one that is balanced by equally powerful countervailing arguments from a Transcendentally Realist point of view. It follows that, at these stages at least, Spinoza's views are not for Kant good candidates for exemplification by either wing of an antinomy. Fourth, as we will see when we discuss the antithesis of the first antinomy in §9.6, there is in fact good reason to think that Kant takes that antinomy to be a dispute between two Transcendental Realists each of whom subscribes to his own view that space is, in principle, capable of existing while being wholly empty of objects. As Kant would have known, Spinoza is not such a thinker.²⁹

---

²⁶ A 471/B 499; 28: 376; 29: 763-4.   ²⁷ See Boehm, *Kant's Critique of Spinoza* at 7-8.
²⁸ See *Dohna-Wundlacken logic*, 24: 749, and note the talk there of each disputant as being able to conduct a *reductio* of his opponent's position—a feature Kant associates with the antinomies.
²⁹ This, incidentally, may help to explain why Kant views Spinoza's position as the most *nearly* consistent form of Transcendental Realism. As Kant reads Spinoza, he can at least claim that for him the *mathematical* antinomies don't arise.

Kant maintains that if one were to evaluate the thesis and antithesis of each antinomy solely according to their 'grounds', one's allegiance would vacillate unceasingly (A 475/B 503). In practice, however, the oscillation is stabilized by certain 'interests of reason', which cause dogmatic metaphysicians to cluster into stable camps (A 462/B 490). These interests are four in number.

First, there is a certain 'practical' interest of reason, which consists in the need to employ the four thesis positions as the 'cornerstones' of religion and morality (A 466/B 494). Second, there is the 'speculative' interest, which, although it has something to say in favour of each side of each antinomy, nonetheless supports the antithesis more strongly than the thesis (A 468/B 496).[30] This interest might be characterized as the inquiring mind's desire to understand: a desire more fully satisfied by the antithesis because, unlike the thesis, it maintains that *every* condition *within* a given regressive series, has its immediate explanation or ground. Third, there is the interest of 'popularity', which favours the thesis because—Kant supposes—the common understanding feels no qualms about positing the unconditioned (A 467/B 495). And, finally, there is a certain 'architectonic interest'—a penchant for system building—which favours the thesis of each antinomy (A 474–5/B 503). Since all four of these interests support the thesis and only the second, which Kant says is (on both sides) 'only very slight' (A 798/B 826), supports the antithesis, one would expect the camps that form in general to favour the thesis position of each antinomy (and, though Kant doesn't say so himself, this might help to explain the popularity of religion). This fact, however, is *merely* psycho-sociological: the rational grounds for the two positions are, in Kant's view, perfectly balanced.

Echoing both Bayle and Rousseau, Kant claims that each of the parties to an antinomial dispute is in the strongest position when they are on the offensive.[31] And, in keeping with this thought, he presents the argument for each position as a *reductio* of its opposite.[32] As we will see in more detail when we consider the resolution of the mathematical antinomies, Kant distrusted *reductio* arguments in metaphysics—or, as we'll see in Chapter 10, §10.4, in certain parts of it—precisely

---

[30] In the Canon of Pure Reason Kant tells us that the speculative interest of reason in freedom, immortality, and God is only 'very slight' (A 798/B 826).

[31] In a passage from his *Dictionary*, which, because it is quoted by Leibniz in his *Theodicy* Kant would have known, Bayle writes: 'All the hypotheses that Christians have established parry but poorly the blows aimed at them: they all triumph when they act on the offensive; but they lose their whole advantage when they have to absorb the attack' (*Theodicy* §144). In his *Émile* Rousseau places the same thought on the lips of the Savoyard priest, who says of certain philosophers he had read with disappointment before embarking upon his own search after truth: 'Braggarts in attack they are weaklings in defence' (Jean Jacques Rousseau, *Émile, or on Education* (London: Dent, 1974) at 230). Kant would have been familiar with this remark too, for he read *Émile* in the early 1760s and was, initially at least, deeply impressed with it (see Manfred Kuehn, *Kant: A Biography* (Cambridge: Cambridge University Press, 2001) at 227).

[32] In his essay *Real Progress*, Kant goes so far as to suggest that in the case of the first antinomy the proofs of the thesis and antithesis can be obtained *only* by *reductio* (20: 288).

because they figure in antinomies, though he had no objection to their use in logic and mathematics (A 792–3/B 820–1). Such a stance might at first seem puzzling. For if the arguments for the thesis and antithesis are, as Kant supposes, logically watertight, then the *reductio*-style reasoning they employ must also be impeccable. The solution to this puzzle is just that Kant takes the *reductio* reasoning involved in each argument to be valid only *on the assumption that Transcendental Realism is true*. Since the parties to the dispute presuppose Transcendental Realism as a background assumption, each will accept their opponent's *reductio*-style reasoning so long as it is otherwise cogent—and Kant supposes that, on that same assumption, they will be right to do so.

9.4 The thesis of the first antinomy: time

We turn now to the reasoning of the mathematical antinomies. I begin with the argument for the first antinomy's thesis insofar as it relates to time. This half of the thesis states that the world has a beginning in time. Its supporting argument runs as follows:

> If one assumes that the world has no beginning in time, then up to every given point in time an eternity has elapsed, and hence an infinite series of states of things in the world, each following another, has passed away. But now the infinity of a series consists precisely in the fact that it can never be completed through a successive synthesis. Therefore, an infinitely elapsed world-series is impossible, so a beginning of the world is a necessary condition of its existence.
>
> (A 427/B 455)

The argument may be semi-formalized in a natural deduction system as follows ('P' indicates a premise, 'L' a lemma, and 'D' a definition, and the numbers in square brackets indicate the assumptions on which a line depends):[33]

P1. The world has no beginning in time (*reductio* assumption, [1]).

L1. Up to every given point in time, an infinite series of states of things in the world has passed away (from P1—we will save discussion of this step for later [1]). So, in particular,

---

[33] I frame my formalizations in an approximation to the natural deduction system of Warren Goldfarb's *Deductive Logic*, supplemented with such invalid rules of inference as Kant regarded as valid (for example, *per accidens* conversion) and with certain elementary modal inferences (Goldfarb, *Deductive Logic*). Goldfarb's existential introduction and elimination rules may be unfamiliar to some readers. For an explanation, see ibid., at 188–98 and note that existential instantiation steps function as premises in Goldfarb's system.

L2. Up to the present moment, an infinite series of states of things in the world has passed away (from L1, by universal instantiation, [1]).

P2. Let the infinite series affirmed to exist in L2, be S (from L2, by existential instantiation introduction, [1, 2]).

Then,

L3. S is an infinite series of world-states that has passed away (from L2 and P2, [1, 2]).

P3. If an infinite series of world-states has passed away, that series has been completed through a successive synthesis, [3].

So, in particular,

L4. S has been completed through a successive synthesis (from L3 and P3 by universal instantiation followed by *modus ponens*, [1, 2, 3]).

But, D1. The infinity of a series consists in the fact that the series cannot be completed through successive synthesis, [D1].

So, in particular,

L5. S cannot have been completed through successive synthesis (from L3, and D1, [1, 2, D1]).

But then,

L6. S has been completed through successive synthesis and yet S has not been so completed (from L4 and L5, together with truth functional logic and a modal inference from impossibility to non-actuality, [1, 2, 3, D1]).

So,

C. The world has a beginning in time (from L6, discharging the *reductio* premise, P1, and applying existential instantiation elimination, [3, D1]).[34]

Aside from certain assumptions lying behind the transition from P1 to L1 (to be discussed later), the argument rests only on the premise, P3, and the definition, D1. The latter enshrines a conception of infinity that was to be superseded in the nineteenth century by the work of Dedekind and Cantor. The former raises a number of questions: Why should we suppose that P3 is true? Why is the advocate of the thesis permitted to appeal to the Kantian-sounding notion of *synthesis*? Wouldn't such an appeal import an element of Transcendental Idealism into the Transcendental Realist's position, thereby robbing Kant of the part of his argument for Transcendental Idealism that appeals to its alleged power to resolve this

---

[34] Kant warns against a spurious proof of the thesis, which relies on the following defective concept of infinity: 'A magnitude [*Größe*] is **infinite** if[f] none greater than it (i.e., greater than the multitude of a given unit contained in it) is possible' (A 430/B 458). This means 'A magnitude is infinite just in case the cardinality of the set of units contained in it is the greatest natural number'. The definition is defective because, since there is no greatest natural number, nothing will be infinite in this sense.

particular antinomy? Couldn't an infinite series pass away without *any* acts of mind (or syntheses) taking place, let alone infinitely many? Each of these questions is, I think, best approached by way of an examination of Kant's conception of infinity.

9.5 Infinity

Kant distinguishes between the 'real' and the 'mathematical' infinite (28: 568–9). The former is that which is wholly unlimited, the latter, roughly speaking, something immeasurable. A really infinite entity is unlimited in the sense that it is wholly without negations or privations. An example is—or would be if it existed—the *ens realissimum*, or most perfect being. Kant explains the mathematically infinite, by contrast, as follows:

> The true (transcendental) concept of infinity is: that the successive synthesis of the unit in the measurement [*Durchmessung*] of a *quantum* [*Quantum*] can never be completed. (A 432/B 460)

Since it is stated in the form of a 'that'-clause, this characterization needs reformulating. A clue to how we might proceed is provided by three observations of Daniel Sutherland.[35] First, what Kant means by a *quantum* is a concrete thing: a homogeneous multitude or plurality (B 162). Second, Kant understands a *quantitas*, by contrast, as an abstract measure—something that is mentioned in providing an exact numerical answer to the question: 'How large is this?' (compare, A 163/B 204). Third, one assigns a *quantitas* to a *quantum* when one measures it.

For Kant, the correct 'mathematical'—or, equivalently, 'transcendental'—concept of infinity is a concept that holds of precisely those *quanta* whose measurement can never be completed.[36] And here measurement is understood as the successive laying off of an arbitrarily chosen unit—a unit whose magnitude may be gauged without itself being measured—what Kant calls a 'given' unit. Accordingly, our reformulation of Kant's characterization of the true concept of infinity runs as follows:

---

[35] Daniel Sutherland, 'The Role of Magnitude in Kant's Critical Philosophy', *Canadian Journal of Philosophy*, 32 (3) (2004), 411–42 at 427–35.

[36] In identifying the transcendental and mathematical concepts of the infinite I depart from Henry Allison, who views the latter as the schematized form of the former (Allison, *Kant's Transcendental Idealism* at 369). However, as the reference to a unit of measurement in the transcendental concept of the infinite makes clear, the 'transcendental' and 'mathematical' infinite are merely different names for the specifically spatial-or-temporal notion of the infinite—a notion that, as we have seen, contrasts with the concept of a *real* infinity, which is a pure concept of the understanding that makes no reference to space or time, and which amounts to the concept of an *unlimited* being (28: 568–9; 29: 836).

> A *quantum* is infinite in magnitude if and only if the process of measuring it by successively laying off an arbitrarily chosen unit of measure against it can never be completed.

Intuitively, when the *quantum* is infinite, no matter how much of it has been measured off, there is always more of it to come—more, therefore, that *could* be measured off. If there were no lower bound on the time it takes to perform a measurement, this point would not be intuitive. For, arguably, one could complete the process of measuring a line of infinite length by the following Russellian (or Zenoian) method. One would spend one second laying off the first unit, half a second laying of the second, a quarter laying off the third, etc. And after two seconds one would have laid off infinitely many units. Since Kant is clearly presupposing that the feat of measuring off an infinite length is impossible, one suspects that he either failed to entertain the possibility of such a so-called 'supertask' or else assumed that acts of measurement take a minimum time. The latter assumption would be plausible if measurement (or synthesis more generally) were to be a psychological process of a finite being.

Kant fleshes out his definition of mathematical infinity in a footnote:

> This [*quantum*, by dint of being infinite] contains a multiplicity (of [a] given unit) that is greater than any number, and that is the mathematical concept of the infinite. (A 432/ B 460)[37]

Kant seems to be assuming that there are no infinite numbers. If we make this assumption, then his idea amounts to the following:

> A *quantum* is infinite in magnitude just in case for no real number, n, does the result of laying off a unit of arbitrarily chosen measure n times suffice for its measurement.

This formulation is in fact an improvement on the last because it avoids the problem about supertasks.

We can now see why Kant thinks that even the Transcendental Realist is committed to appealing to something like 'synthesis' in the thesis argument. For in Kant's view the notion of synthesis is embedded in the very notion of something's being infinite. An infinite *quantum*, for Kant, is one whose measurement by the successive laying off of an appropriate unit of measure—which process Kant calls 'the successive synthesis of the unit in the measurement'—can never be completed.

---

[37] Compare 2: 154.

'Synthesis' in the present context means the bringing together in thought of certain parts of a thing in the act of measuring it. So, for example, we synthesize—and thus measure—the period of time constituting the previous three years by laying off the unit of a year until the period has been spanned and then counting up the number of layings off thereby performed. All of this suggests that in this context the appeal to synthesis is not a problematic imposition of a Transcendentally Idealist notion on the Transcendental Realist. For synthesis is bound up with the idea of gauging the magnitude of certain kinds of object—objects, roughly, that are not *given as* wholes (we'll come back to this point).

So far, so good. But a crucial question remains: Why should Kant make the assumption that lies behind P3, namely, that to think of the plurality of past states of the world as infinite requires having the idea of the *completion* of a process of successive synthesis? Doesn't it rather just require having the idea that no matter how many previous years we measure off (in imagination), proceeding backwards in time, there will still be more past states of the world to be measured off?

An answer to these questions has been offered by Sadik Al-Azm and elaborated by Henry Allison.[38] Each of these commentators alerts us to a contrast that Kant draws between two kinds of wholes. On the one hand, there is a *totum*, in which the whole is prior to the parts, and, on the other, a *compositum*, in which the parts are prior to the whole. 'Properly speaking', Kant says, 'we should call space not a *compositum*, but a *totum*, because its parts are possible only in the whole, and not the whole through the parts' (A 438/B 466). He goes on to indicate that he regards this terminology as superior to that which he occasionally uses elsewhere, according to which instead of speaking of a *totum* one speaks of an 'ideal composite' (*compositum ideale*), and instead of speaking of a *compositum* one speaks of a 'real composite' (ibid.).[39] He marks the same distinction with yet more suggestive terminology in a reflection, where he refers to a *totum* as a '*totum analyticum*' and a *compositum* as a '*totum syntheticum*' (R 3789 (17: 293))—in the same place explaining that space and time are *tota analytica* while bodies are *tota synthetica*. This last way of marking the distinction has been raised to prominence by Allison, and has gained a foothold in the secondary literature.[40]

The distinction enables one to understand how Kant can conceive of space and time as infinite magnitudes while also denying that the world can be conceived of

---

[38] See Sadik Al-Azm, *The Origins of Kant's Arguments in the Antinomies* (Oxford: Clarendon Press, 1972) at 11–18, and Allison, *Kant's Transcendental Idealism* at 369.

[39] 'A real composite <compositum reale>,' Kant says in the *Metaphysics Mrongovius*, 'is that whose parts can also exist for themselves apart from a connection <nexu> with others—that whose parts can never exist apart from the connection with others is ideal <ideale>' (29: 826). In a reflection apparently from the early 1770s he indicates that space is an ideal composite. 'One can', he says, 'only conceive of spaces insofar as one carves something out of the universal space' (R 4315 (17: 503); and compare the better-known remark at A 25/B 39.

[40] Allison, *Kant's Transcendental Idealism* at 369.

in this way. His idea is that because space and time are *tota analytica* they can be given to the mind as wholes, and so assigned a magnitude as infinite without being synthesized.[41] And, most importantly, what is required for something to be appraised as infinite or finite is that it should be given as whole—something which sometimes requires synthesis, sometimes not. Moreover, being given as a whole requires synthesis neither when the thing given is a *totum analyticum* nor 'when it is given within certain boundaries of any intuition'. The point that being given as a whole is a condition for applying the predicate 'infinite' is not spelled out in the first *Critique*, but it is stated with only a small change of wording— 'taken' for 'given'—in a reflection. 'Infinite', Kant says, 'means...great beyond all measure *when taken as a whole*' (R 5338, around 1771 (18: 155), emphasis added). Because a *totum syntheticum* can be conceived of as a whole only through synthesis, it follows that there is a contradiction in the very idea of assigning an infinite magnitude to a whole of this kind.[42] For, in order to give or adduce this composite for appraisal as infinite—or, indeed, as finite—we must present it to our mind as a whole, and, since it is a *totum syntheticum*, this will require piecing it together in thought—hence, to answer our original question, it will require the completion of a synthesis. But to say that it is infinite is to suppose that—on the contrary—its parts cannot be exhausted by any process that runs through them successively, including this process of piecing them together in thought (synthesis). It thus follows that 'to think of totality [*Totalität*] and infinite composition simultaneously is a contradiction' (29: 855). And, in particular, it is a contradiction to think of the world in space or time as infinite.

These points explain why Kant regards the assumption that the world has no beginning in time as, for the Transcendental Realist, leading to a contradiction. For this figure conceives of the world as a whole of things in space and time, hence as a *totum syntheticum*. They also explain Kant's differential attitude towards the possibility of assessing as infinite the world, on the one hand, and space and time, on the other. For to think of a *totum analyticum* as a whole does not, in Kant's view, require a synthesis. So far, then, so good. But one must register a residual qualm about Kant's assumption that conceiving of the world as a *totum syntheticum* requires a series of mental acts of synthesis. This might make sense from a Transcendentally Idealist point of view, but why, one wonders, couldn't the Transcendental Realist think of the world in past time as an aggregate whose parts exist prior to the whole without conceiving of it through a synthesis? It

---

[41] Though, strictly speaking, to assign a magnitude to space or time is to say not that they *are* themselves infinite but that the regress in them is infinite. As Kant says in the *Metaphysics Mrongovius*: 'One can just as little represent to oneself an infinite space [as an infinite magnitude], but the progression in space can be represented as infinite' (29: 837).

[42] This last claim in fact stands in need of a certain caveat whose explanation it will be convenient to save for later; for it turns out that Kant holds that some wholes can be given as such without synthesis if they are small enough. We discuss this point in §9.7.

seems that, for all Kant has said, they could. And that, I think, is the sticking point of the thesis argument.

We are now nearly ready to examine the antithesis argument, but before we do so, we need to attend to an item of unfinished business, namely, the inference from P1 to L1. Although Kant says nothing about this inference, he owes us an explanation of its validity because at first glance it seems to be an obvious non-sequitur. Why, one wonders, couldn't the world have existed for most of its history without changing? If it could have done so—the worry continues, it might have gone through only a finite number of states. Kant does, I think, have the resources to plug this gap in his proof; for he can reason as follows. Suppose that the world did exist for most of its history in an unchanging state. It is now, unquestionably, changing, for—as both parties to the dispute must agree—change is involved in constructing the arguments for thesis and antithesis. It follows that if it did formerly exist in an unchanging state, there must have been a first moment at which it started changing. Suppose this moment is time t. Since time is a two-way infinite homogeneous manifold there is an arbitrariness in supposing that the world started to change at t rather than at some earlier or later time (why not a second earlier or later?). So, if both parties to the dispute can agree on a rejection of brute or arbitrary facts, this possibility can be ruled out, in which case we would be permitted to conclude that the world has always been changing. As we will see in the next section, there is, in fact, reason to think that—in Kant's view—both parties to the dispute would agree on this envisaged 'no arbitrariness' principle.[43]

9.6 The antithesis of the first antinomy: time

The antithesis of the temporal part of the first antinomy states that the world has no beginning in time but is rather infinite with respect to past time. Its supporting argument runs as follows:

> For suppose that [the world] had a beginning. Since the beginning is an existence preceded by a time in which the thing is not, there must be a preceding time in which the world was not, i.e., an empty time. But now no arising of any sort of thing is possible in an empty time, because no part of such a time has, in itself, prior to another part, any distinguishing condition [*unterscheidende Bedingung*] of its existence rather than its non-existence (whether one assumes that it comes to be of itself or through another cause). Hence although many a series of things

---

[43] Since it is not a truth of logic and not an analytic truth, I take it that Kant would see this 'no arbitrariness' principle as a consequence of Transcendental Realism, though why it should be such a consequence is not altogether clear.

can begin in the world, the world itself cannot have a beginning, and so it is infinite in regard to past time. (A 427/B 455)

In this context, a 'distinguishing condition of the world's existence' is a property of a moment of time the fact of whose possession by that moment would constitute a ground or reason why the world should begin to exist at that moment rather than some other.[44] So when Kant says that 'no part of time has, in itself, prior to another part, any distinguishing condition if its existence rather than non-existence' he means that no part of time is pre-eminently qualified for the role of 'moment at which the world began'. The point is correct so long as we assume, with the proponent of the antithesis argument, that time is a two-way infinite homogeneous manifold. For in such a manifold all moments are qualitatively identical. But then the *PSR*—and also a weaker 'no arbitrariness' principle—entails that the world cannot have begun to exist.

It has been widely noted that in so reasoning on the Transcendental Realist's behalf Kant is borrowing one of the arguments that Leibniz makes against absolute time (and space) in his correspondence with Clarke.[45] It is less often noted that Kant is modifying Leibniz's argument and adapting it to his own, rather different, purposes. Leibniz assumes that the world began to exist, and argues on the basis of this assumption (among others) that time cannot be an empty Newtonian container. It cannot, that is to say, be an 'absolute' temporal manifold that is substantival rather than adherent in nature ('substantival' meaning that it exists as self-subsisting rather than as inhering in some other thing or things). The proponent of the antithesis, by contrast, assumes a component of the Newtonian conception of time, namely, that it is a homogeneous manifold that is capable of being wholly empty, and argues from this assumption (among others), that the world cannot have begun to exist.[46] Since this is how matters stand, the question arises: Couldn't one resolve the temporal part of the first antinomy, not by rejecting Transcendental Realism, but merely by denying that time can be wholly empty? Kant addresses this possible objection, somewhat obscurely, in his

---

[44] Here it's relevant that Kant follows Baumgarten in treating 'ground' and 'condition' as equivalent terms. (See, for example, A 411/B 439 and *Real Progress*, 20: 328. Compare Baumgarten, *Metaphysics* at §14.)

[45] The *locus classicus* for this observation is Al-Azm, *The Origins of Kant's Arguments in the Antinomies*, chapter 1. See H. G. Alexander (ed.), *The Leibniz-Clarke Correspondence* (Manchester: Manchester University Press, 1956) at 3rd letter, §§5–6.

[46] Kant in fact assumes that both parties to the dispute are Newtonians about space and time. But this is not because he takes Newtonianism about space and time to be a consequence of Transcendental Realism. As we will see later in this section, Newtonianism about space and time is rather for him a consequence of Transcendental Realism taken in conjunction with the belief that space and time can be wholly empty. That Newtonian substantivalism is not, for Kant, a consequence of Transcendental Realism taken in isolation is clear from the fact that he takes Spinoza to be a Transcendental Realist who denies the substantiality of space, affirming instead that it is a property of God (5: 101–2; 29: 977; 29: 1008–9).

comment on the antithesis (I have supplied interpolations to make clear how I am reading the passage. I don't mean to imply that this reading is uncontroversial or obviously correct):

> Now it is not unknown to me that attempts are made to evade this consequence [of the assumption that the world is finite and bounded, namely, that it is embedded in a substantival empty Newtonian "absolute" time and similar space which extend beyond it (and so bound it)] by alleging that a boundary of the world in space and time might be possible without having to assume an absolute time before the world's beginning or an absolute space spreading beyond the actual world—which is impossible. I am quite satisfied with the latter part of this opinion of philosophers of the Leibnizian school. Space is merely the form of outer intuition, but not an actual object that can be intuited externally, and not a correlate of appearances but the form of appearances themselves... The same holds also for time. (A 431/B 459)[47]

I take it that what Kant is 'quite satisfied' with is just the Leibnizian view that Newtonian absolute space and time are impossible.[48] He nonetheless departs from the Leibnizians in denying that they can make sense of a boundary to the world on their own conception of space and time. Thus, having concluded his lengthy concession, he continues:

> But all of this being granted, the fact is nonetheless indisputable that these two non-entities [*Undinge*]—empty space outside, and empty time prior to, the world—must assuredly be assumed if one assumes a boundary of the world, whether in regard to space or time. (A 433/B 461)

In other words, though Newtonian ('absolute', substantival) space and time are in fact non-entities, one must nonetheless assume them if one is to assume, in accordance with the thesis position, that the world has spatial and temporal boundaries.

Kant does not explain how he sees the Leibnizians as attempting to make sense of a boundary of the world without absolute Newtonian space and time, but one suspects that he sees them as treating space and time as systems of actual *and possible* relations between actually existing entities. For there are certainly texts in

---

[47] Here I provide a dash where the German has a semi-colon.
[48] Although Kant usually means Newtonian substantival or real space when he speaks of 'absolute' space, he also allows that space can correctly be conceived of as 'absolute' so long as it is conceived of as ideal rather than real. See R 4673 (17: 639). This suggests that what Kant objects to in Newton's conception is not the idea of an ultimate reference frame, but rather the idea that space is a thing in itself.

Leibniz's public writings that suggest such a view.[49] On such a construal of the Leibnizian position, one would conceive of the world as the totality of actual things, and one would conceive of regions of empty space or empty time—in deflationary fashion—as constituted by the merely possible spatial and temporal relations that those actual things might bear to one another. The boundaries of the world in space and time would then be thought of as demarcated by the locations of the maximally separated actual existents—whether bodies or events (though these locations would not themselves be thought to have an independent existence). On this view, there would be no *actual* empty space or time beyond the boundaries of the world. Instead, the world would be 'bounded', not externally by an entity extending beyond it, but internally by its metric geometry.

Kant explains that he rejects this conception because he sees it as involving our 'thinking surreptitiously of an intelligible world, of who knows what kind, in place of a **sensible world**' (A 433/B 461). This suggests that the Leibnizian conception of a finite world would not be a conception of a 'world of sense', for Kant, simply because it would not, in his view, be a spatio-temporal world. Why not? Why should the relations Leibniz envisages be any the less genuinely spatial or temporal for being existentially dependent on the things they relate? In order to answer this question we need to suppose that Kant is at this stage relying on a claim already made in the Transcendental Aesthetic—a claim that, fortunately for him, does not depend on Transcendental Idealism. I have in mind his claim that space can be wholly empty of bodies (A 24/B 38-9) and time of 'appearances'—by which he presumably means 'events' (A31/B 46).[50] I take it that he regards these claims as conceptual truths that are uncovered through the exposition (or analysis) of the concepts of space and time. If so, they will be claims to which neither party can object—indeed, claims enjoying the highest degree of certainty. If one disputes them—as, for example, Leibniz does, one will not, in Kant's view, really be speaking about space or time.

Leibniz is committed to denying that space and time can be wholly empty because he can make sense of empty spaces and times only in terms of the merely possible relations that would hold if certain actually existing bodies or events were arranged in certain counterfactual ways. It follows that even if there were to exist an ordering of actual and possible bodies (or events) of the kind the Leibnizian envisages, it would not, in Kant's view, constitute space (or time) but would rather amount merely to an 'intelligible' ordering—that is, an ordering of things we *can* conceive, but which we cannot conceive of as constituting space or time. And since that is so, Kant finds it natural to suppose on behalf of the Transcendental

---

[49] Consider, for example, a remark from Leibniz's third letter to Clarke: 'For space denotes, *in terms of possibility*, an order of things which exist at the same time, considered as existing together' (Alexander, *The Leibniz-Clarke Correspondence*, emphasis added, 26).

[50] See A 31-2/B 46-8 and A 24-5/B 39-40.

Realist that if the world has a boundary, it must be bounded by a Newtonian absolute space and time.[51]

If I am right that Kant treats both parties to the dispute as sharing his anti-Leibnizian view that space, as a matter of necessity, can be wholly empty of objects (the same, *mutatis mutandis*, going for time), then it follows that Leibniz is not someone whom Kant could have seen as rehearsing the first antinomy. The same, I would claim, goes for Spinoza (or Kant's Spinoza at least), for, believing as he does that God is both necessarily existent and spatially and temporally extended, he cannot regard it as possible that space and time should be wholly empty.

9.7 The thesis of the first antinomy: space

The spatial part of the first antinomy consists in the appearance of a contradiction between the following two claims:

Thesis: The world is enclosed within spatial boundaries

Antithesis: The world is not enclosed within spatial boundaries, but is rather infinite.

The argument for the thesis runs as follows:

> Again, assume the opposite, namely that the world is an infinite given whole of simultaneously existing things. Now we can think of the magnitude [*Größe*] of a **quantum** that is not given within certain boundaries of any intuition in no other way than by the synthesis of its parts, and we can think of the totality of such a quantum only through the completed synthesis, or through the repeated addition of units to one another. Accordingly, in order for the world, which fills all spaces, to be thought as a whole, the successive synthesis of the parts of an infinite world must be regarded as completed, i.e., in the enumeration of all coexisting things, an infinite time would have to be regarded as having elapsed, which is impossible.
> (A 426–8/B 454–6)

We can extract a coherent argument from this passage if we supply certain suppressed premises. The argument runs as follows:

---

[51] In his remark on the antithesis of the first antinomy, Kant uses the term '*Grenzen*' for genuine (sensible) worldly boundaries that would—*per impossibile*—be formed by the existence of a bounding absolute (hence substantival) Newtonian space or time, and '*Schranken*' for the mere limits—bounded by nothing actual—of a merely intelligible ordering masquerading as a genuine spatial or temporal ordering (see A 433/B 461).

232 THE FIERY TEST OF CRITIQUE

P1. The world is infinite in its spatial extent (*reductio* premise, [1]).

P2. We can assign a magnitude to a quantum only if we can conceive of that quantum as a whole or totality (suppressed premise, [2]).

P3. We can conceive of a quantum that is a *totum syntheticum* and not given within certain boundaries of any intuition as a whole or totality only if we can *complete* the synthesis of its parts, [3].

P4. The world is both a quantum and a *totum syntheticum*, and it is not given within certain boundaries of any intuition (suppressed premise, [4]).

P5. No infinite task can (as a matter of metaphysical possibility) be performed in a finite amount of time (suppressed premise, [5]).

P6. Infinitely much time cannot ever have elapsed, [6].

P7. Whatever is infinite in its spatial extent has infinitely many parts of arbitrary finite magnitude (suppressed premise, [7]).

P8. What cannot happen does not happen (suppressed premise, [8]).

From these assumptions we first infer L1: We can assign a magnitude to the world only if we can conceive of it as a totality (from P2 and P4, [2, 4]).

And further, L2. We can conceive of the world as a totality only if we can complete the synthesis of its parts (from P3 and P4, [3, 4]).

So, L3. We can assign a magnitude to the world only if we can complete the synthesis of its parts (from L1 and L2, [2, 3, 4]).

But, L4. Completing the successive synthesis of the world's parts would require infinitely many acts of synthesis (from P1 and P7, [1, 7]).

So, L5. Completing the successive synthesis of the world's parts would take infinitely much time (from L4 and P5, [1, 5, 7]).

But, L6. We have assigned a magnitude to the world (from P1, [1]).

So, L7. Infinitely much time has elapsed (from L3, L5, and L6, [1, 2, 3, 4, 5, 7]).[52]

So, L8. Contradiction (from P6, P8, and L7, [1, 2, 3, 4, 5, 6, 7, 8]).

So, C. The world is finite in its spatial extent and so is enclosed within spatial boundaries (from L8, discharging the *reductio* assumption, P1, and tacitly assuming that space is not itself finite, so that any part of space and any finite thing filling that part is embedded within a more inclusive space, [2, 3, 4, 5, 6, 7, 8]).

Four features of our reconstruction call for comment. First, the argument relies on the assumption that the world is a *totum syntheticum* rather than a *totum*

---

[52] Here it is further tacitly assumed that something that we have actually done is something we can do.

analyticum.⁵³ We saw the same assumption at work in the temporal part of the argument, where it was invoked in support of the thesis argument's third premise. Second, the premise, P5, which denies the metaphysical possibility of what are today called 'supertasks' is needed because if, for example, I could perform the first act of synthesis in one second, the second in half a second, the third in a quarter, and so on, then I would be able to complete the entire task of piecing together an infinite quantum in two seconds, hence in a finite time.⁵⁴ Since in the wake of Paul Benacerraf's work, the weight of philosophical opinion seems to have fallen behind the view that supertasks are at least logically possible, and since some authors have argued that they may even be physically possible, the claim that they are not metaphysically possible would need further argument.⁵⁵ In the face of this problem, Kant might perhaps fall back on the weaker premise that no infinite *synthesis* is possible in a finite time, on the ground that there is some upper bound on the speed with which an operation of synthesis can be performed—perhaps because synthesis is a psychological process. But, such a claim, obviously, would be controversial. The third point to note is that the assumption that infinitely much time cannot ever have elapsed—our P6—is equivalent to a modal strengthening of the thesis of the temporal part of the first antinomy. So, the argument for the thesis of the spatial part of the first antinomy depends on the conclusion of the argument for its temporal part (along with the implicit assumption that this conclusion is knowable a priori, and so necessary). Fourth and finally, in presenting the conclusion as the claim: 'The world is finite (i.e., non-infinite)' rather than as the expected claim: 'The world is not infinite' I am attempting to be faithful to Kant's presentation of the argument (the significance of this all-important distinction will become clearer in the next chapter).

The qualifications occurring in P2 and P3—'not given, etc.'—suggest that in Kant's view there are some kinds of *quanta* which we *can* conceive of as totalities *without* synthesizing their parts, namely those that are 'not given within certain boundaries of any intuition'. Kant vaguely indicates which quanta these are when he says:

> We can intuit an indeterminate *quantum* as a whole, if it is enclosed within boundaries, without needing to construct its totality by measurement, i.e., by the

---

⁵³ For evidence that Kant himself takes the world to be a real composite (hence a *totum syntheticum*) see *Metaphysics L2*, 28: 265.

⁵⁴ A *supertask* is the performance of a *denumerable* infinity of actions in a finite time. A *hypertask* is the performance of a non-denumerable infinity of actions in a finite time. In the present context only the former notion is in question because the synthesis is envisaged as taking place through *successive* steps. See Jon Pérez Laraudogoitia, 'Supertasks', *The Stanford Encyclopedia of Philosophy* (ed. Edward N. Zalta, 2013).

⁵⁵ Paul Benacerraf, 'Tasks, Super-Tasks, and Modern Eleatics', *Journal of Philosophy*, 59 (24) (1962), 765–84.

successive synthesis of its parts. For the boundaries already determine its completeness by cutting off anything further. (A 428/B 456)

He means, I take it, that we can intuit some finite *quanta* as wholes without synthesizing their parts because we can do so simply by inspecting their boundaries in space (or time). The *quanta* in question are those which Kant elsewhere terms 'assignable' or 'givable' *quanta*. Such *quanta*, he says, 'can be exhibited entirely (in [their] totality)'.[56] Kant would seem to be committed to making an exception for these *quanta* because any unit of measure would have to be a *quantum* of this kind. After all, if every quantum had to be measured before its magnitude could be gauged, then a vicious regress would ensue. For any mooted unit would itself have to be measured before it could be thought of as a whole and that would require that some other, smaller unit would have to be taken and laid off against it, but then that unit would need to be thought of as a whole, and so itself measured, etc. There is, moreover, reason to think that Kant was aware of this point. For in the *Metaphysics Vigilantius K3*, having characterized an 'assignable' or 'givable' *quantum* as 'that magnitude which can be presented entirely (in its totality) in intuition', he adds 'every measure must be so constituted'. (By a 'measure' I take it he means a basic privileged unit of measure, for example, the equivalent of today's metre or second.) (ibid.)

Obviously, the world in space and time is not an assignable *quantum*. For even if it were to have boundaries, those boundaries could not be given to us in sensible intuition because in order to intuit them we would have to be able to intuit empty space and time, and that, for Kant, is impossible.[57]

Having got clearer about the meaning of P3, we can see that, for reasons by now familiar, this premise is controversial. It is simply not clear why a Transcendental Realist must agree that in order to conceive of a *totum syntheticum* (that is not given within certain boundaries of any intuition) as a totality we must perform acts of synthesis. Accordingly, there is a real worry that in assuming P3 Kant has illicitly relied on a Transcendentally Idealist assumption.

9.8 The antithesis of the first antinomy: space

The second conjunct of the first antinomy's antithesis states that the world has no boundaries in space but is infinite as regards its spatial extent. The argument for this claim runs as follows:

---

[56] *Metaphysics Vigilantius K3*, 29: 994.
[57] See, for example, B 255 and compare: 'Empty space can neither be perceived nor carry with it a (detectable) existence' (*Real Progress*, 20: 288).

Assume, first of all, the opposite, namely, that the world is, as regards space, finite and bounded. Then it is located in an empty space that is not bounded. We would thus encounter here not only a relation of things **in space** but also a relation of things **to space**. Now since the world is an absolute whole, outside of which there is encountered no object of intuition, and hence no correlate of the world to which the world might stand in relation, the relation of the world to empty space would be the relation of the world to **no object**. But such a relation, and hence also the bounding of the world by empty space, is nothing; therefore the world, as regards space, is not bounded at all, i.e., it is infinite with regard to extension. (A 428–9 / B 457–8)

Omitting its redundant steps, and supplying suppressed premises, we can reconstruct this argument as follows:

P1. The world is finite in its spatial extent and bounded by an infinite empty space (*reductio* premise, [1]).

P2. If the world is finite in its spatial extent and bounded by an infinite empty space, then it is bounded by a self-subsistent (that is, substantial) space to which it bears a relation of occupancy, [2].

Comment: That the envisaged bounding space is self-subsistent is not obvious from the quoted passage, but it comes out in the comment on the antithesis at A 431/B 460.

So, L1. The world is bounded by an infinite otherwise empty self-subsistent space and bears a relation of occupancy to this same space (from P1 and P2, [1, 2]).

P3. The world is an *absolute*—that is, maximally inclusive—whole, [3].

So, L2. There is nothing outside the world (immediate from P3, [3]).

L3. There is something outside the world (namely, a part of a self-subsistent space) (immediate from L1, [1, 2]).

So, L4. Contradiction (from L2 and L3, [1, 2, 3]).

So, C. The world is infinite in its spatial extent and unbounded (from L4, discharging the *reductio* assumption, P1, [2, 3]).

Kant's grounds for holding P2 to be true—namely, his rejection of the Leibnizian alternative—were examined in §9.6. The main problem with the argument lies with premise P3. This premise seems to employ the wrong conception of the world. If P3 is to play its intended role in the argument, it would have to mean that the world is the totality of all things whatsoever. But, thus construed, P3 does not speak of the world in the sense that the Transcendental Realist intends. For the latter thinks of the world as the totality of objects of sense. And when 'the world' is understood in that way the question of whether space, which is not an object of sense, exists outside the world remains open.

Given the weakness of this argument, one wonders why Kant doesn't rather argue for the antithesis of the spatial part of the first antinomy by a means of a strategy paralleling the one he uses in arguing for the antithesis of the temporal part. Why, in other words, doesn't he appeal to the arbitrariness that would be involved in the idea of a spatially finite world's existing with its centre of gravity—or even its geometrical centre—located at one particular point in an otherwise homogeneous empty space? One presumes that Kant must have had his reasons for electing not to pursue this strategy, but it is hard to see what they could have been. The puzzle is especially sharp because Kant appears retrospectively to suggest that he *had* after all given a uniform proof of the antitheses of the temporal *and spatial* parts of the first antinomy, a proof that relied on the idea that if the world does not occupy all of time and all of space then it cannot have a *determinate* position in either one (see A521/B 549, note).

9.9 The second antinomy: preliminaries

The second antinomy concerns the world's mereological structure. Its thesis and antithesis run as follows:

Thesis: Every composite substance in the world consists of simple parts, and nothing exists anywhere except the simple or what is composed of simples (A 434/B 462).
Antithesis: No composite thing in the world consists of simple parts, and nowhere in it does there exist anything simple (A 435/B 463).

The second antinomy is immediately puzzling; for it is hard to see how its thesis and antithesis could even *appear* to be contradictories. Each claim, after all, would be false in a world that contained a gunky composite together with a single isolated simple. (A 'gunky composite' is a composite each of whose parts contains further parts.)

Nor could this difficulty be overcome by treating the second antinomy, like the first, as a two-antinomies-in-one affair; for if we take this tack, the opposed propositions in the two envisaged sub-antinomies will still look like contraries rather than contradictories. Thus:

First sub-antinomy of the second antinomy:
Every composite substance consists of simple parts.
No composite substance consists of simple parts.

Second sub-antinomy of the second antinomy:
Everything in the world is either simple or composed of simples.
Nothing in the world is simple.

In the first sub-antinomy the two propositions have the form of contraries according to the square of opposition. In the second, the two propositions cannot both be true but can both be false: each would be false in a world containing nothing but one gunky object and one simple object. In view of this difficulty, I suggest that we persevere with the original antinomy and seek to attribute to Kant a background assumption that would make the thesis and antithesis at least appear to be contradictories. My candidate for this background assumption is what I will call the assumption of 'uniform mereological structure'. This says that either everything is gunk or nothing is. With this assumption in place, the thesis and antithesis do at least appear to be contradictories. Let's examine their supporting arguments.

9.10 The thesis of the second antinomy

Kant presents the champion of the thesis as arguing for its first conjunct by *reductio* and then inferring its second as a corollary. Since the second conjunct does indeed follow from the first given the assumption of uniform mereological structure, we may confine our attention to the argument for the first conjunct. This runs as follows:

> Assume that composite substances do not consist of simple parts: then, if all composition were to be removed in thought, no composite part, and (since there are no simple parts) also no simple part, thus nothing at all, would remain; consequently, no substance would have been given. Thus either it is impossible to remove all composition in thought or else after its removal something must be left over that exists without any composition, i.e., the simple. But in the first case, the composite would once again not consist of substances (because with substances [that is, substantial composites] composition is only a contingent relation of substances, without [whose obtaining], the latter [that is, these contingently related substances], since they are beings persisting for themselves, must still subsist). Now since this case contradicts the presupposition [*Voraussetzung*], only the second case is left: namely, that what is a substantial composite in the world consists of simple parts.   (A 434 & 436/B 462 & 464)

The argument is hardly transparent. Its method is reasoning by cases, but beyond that little is clear—and not least because the identity of the 'presupposition' is left obscure. Nonetheless, we can make interpretive progress if we keep two points in mind. The first, emphasized by Kant himself, is that the argument concerns only 'composite substances' or 'substantial composites', which Kant also calls 'proper composite(s)' (A 438/B 466).[58] He warns that the proof of the thesis would be spoiled if one sought to establish the result in question for composites in general (A 440/B 468).

What, then, is a 'composite substance' or 'substantial composite'? I take it that it is a composite with two special features. First, it is a composite of 'substances' understood not as substances$_1$ or substances$_2$ but rather as extended things in space.[59] Things in time but not in space, such as thoughts (or, strictly speaking, their appearances), are parts only of *non-substantial* composites, but these composites are not things, but rather *states* of things—for example, the total mental state I am now in, a state that has as parts: thinking about composition, feeling hungry, hearing birdsong, and so forth (*Metaphysics L1*, 28: 195). Second, a composite substance (or substantial composite) is something whose parts stand related by the contingent relation of composition. It is, accordingly, a *totum syntheticum*. The contrast is with a 'formal composite', for example, space, which is something whose parts 'cannot be represented otherwise than in the composition' (28: 566). (A formal composite is a *totum analyticum*.) Kant appeals to the first of these two features of a substantial composite in the argument for the antithesis, the second in the argument for the thesis.

The second point that needs to be borne in mind concerns what it is, in Kant's view, for something to 'consist' of simple parts. One would naturally take this to involve being composed exclusively of simple parts. But, judging by the way Kant develops the thesis argument, this is not what he means. Instead, he takes a composite to 'consist of simple parts' just in case it possesses *some* simple parts. This is clear from the first sentence of the passage in which Kant sets out the thesis argument. For there he indicates that he takes the circumstance that a composite substance should not consist of simple parts to entail that it has *no* simple parts.

With these points registered, we can informally reconstruct the argument for the first conjunct of the thesis.

Suppose a composite substance, *c*, were to contain no simple parts. Since it is a composite substance, *c* is something all of whose parts stand related by the contingent relation of composition (this is the relevant 'presupposition' of calling something a 'composite substance'). Now, either all of a composite's composition can be thought away or it cannot. Suppose it can, then we can conceive of *c* as

---

[58] Kant acknowledges Baumgarten's point that, in all strictness, composite substances do not deserve the name 'substances', for they are composites of other things and composition is merely an accident. But he also downplays the point as a 'mere subtlety' (29: 827). His lack of concern suggests that he recognizes a sense of 'substance' that is looser than his official senses of 'substance$_1$' and 'substance$_2$'.

[59] If substances in this context were understood as substances$_1$, the argument would become question-begging. Substances$_1$, after all, cannot be composite because composites are accidents.

having been completely decomposed. But then what remains after c's complete decomposition will include nothing composite (*ex hypothesi*) and nothing simple (by the *reductio* assumption). In consequence, c will be a plurality containing no members. But a memberless plurality is nothing at all. In conceiving of c's complete decomposition, then, we will be conceiving of an operation of complete dismantling whose product is nothing at all. However, it is of the nature of the dismantling operation that nothing can be completely annihilated through its iteration—some residue will always remain. And so we have arrived at a contradiction. So, suppose instead that c's composition *cannot* be entirely thought away. Then some of its parts must, as a matter of conceptual necessity, be combined. But that contradicts the 'presupposition' of calling c a 'composite substance'. Either way, then, we arrive at a contradiction, and so can infer, by *reductio*, that any composite substance must contain some simples. QED.

The second horn of this argument by dilemma immediately prompts the following question. Why should we suppose that a composite whose composition cannot be completely thought away must contain parts that stand non-contingently combined? Why couldn't it rather be that while every instance of the composition relation holding between parts of the substantial composite is contingent, the composition present in the whole cannot be completely thought away simply because the composite contains parts within parts to infinity—in contemporary terms, it's gunk? Why, in other words, can't it be that the composition cannot be entirely thought away simply because no matter how much decomposing we conceive of as having been done, there is more that could still be done?[60] If this possibility is not excluded, it looks as though the reasoning of the second horn will contain a mis-step; for, with the possibility granted, it won't follow from the fact that not all composition can be thought away that some *particular* composition cannot be thought away. And yet it is not clear how this possibility could be excluded.

Is this conclusion too harsh? I'm inclined to think it may be; for it fails to take full account of the fact that a substantial composite is supposed to be something whose parts exist prior to the whole. (Recall the contrast noted above with a 'formal composite' such as space.) Since this assumption is in place, we may, I think, after all exclude the case in which the reason why not all composition can be thought away is merely that the composite is gunk. For the parts of a piece of gunk plausibly do not exist prior to the whole: we can't think of a gunky whole as built up out of its infinitely many parts.

That's the good news. But the bad news is that the argument now works only because its premises are remarkably strong. Packed into the very notion of a substantial composite, it turns out, is an assumption tantamount to the claim that

---

[60] For this objection, see James Van Cleve, 'Reflections on Kant's Second Antinomy', *Synthese*, 47 (3) (1981), 481–94 at 492.

such a composite is not gunk. But, that being so, it follows trivially that any substantial composite contains some simple parts.

Our reconstruction of the argument for the first conjunct of the thesis brings out that the argument purports to establish its conclusion without invoking any substantive metaphysical principle such as the *PSR*. Is this a problem? Perhaps not, for it was never required of the dogmatic speculative metaphysician that they should exploit resources stronger than logic and conceptual analysis in their antinomial reasoning. Moreover, during his own period as a dogmatic speculative metaphysician Kant prided himself on the fact that his own argument for simples did not rely on the *PSR* but rather proceeded merely by 'ordinary combination of concepts' (1: 477).[61] That argument, which occurs in the *Physical Monadology*, runs as follows:

> Bodies consist of parts, each of which separately has an enduring existence. Since, however, the composition of such parts is nothing but a relation, and hence a determination which is in itself contingent, and which can be denied without abrogating the existence of the things having this relation, it is plain that all composition of a body can be abolished, though all the parts which were formerly combined together nonetheless continue to exist. When all composition is abolished, moreover, the parts which are left are not composed at all; and thus they are completely free from plurality of substances, and, consequently, they are simple. All bodies, whatsoever, therefore, consist of absolutely fundamental parts, that is to say, monads.   (1: 477)

The argument for the thesis of the second antinomy would seem to be the result of attempting to completely reformulate this direct argument while also turning it into an indirect one—a *reductio* argument. If this is correct, it would not be all that surprising that the thesis argument makes no appeal to the *PSR*.

9.11 The antithesis of the second antinomy

The antithesis states that 'no composite thing in the world consists of simple parts, and nowhere in it does there exist anything simple'. The argument for this claim's first conjunct runs as follows.

> Suppose a composite thing (as substance) consists of simple parts. Now all external relation, and hence all composition [of things] out of substances, is

---

[61] Wolff, by contrast, had relied on the *PSR* in offering his own argument for simples (see, for example, *GM*, §76).

possible only in space therefore there must exist as many parts of space as there are parts of the composite thing occupying it. Now space consists not of simple parts, but of spaces. Hence every part of the composite must occupy a space. But the absolutely first parts of every composite are simple. Therefore, the simple occupies a space. Now everything real that occupies a space contains within itself a manifold [of elements] external to one another, and hence is composite, and indeed, as a real composite, is composed not of accidents (for they cannot be external to one another in the absence of substance), but, hence, of substances; therefore, the simple would be a substantial composite, which is self-contradictory. (A 435/B 463)

Proceeding semi-formally, we may reconstruct the heart of this argument as follows:

P1. Some part of a substantial composite is simple (*reductio* premise, [1]).

P2. All the parts of a substantial composite are located in space, [2].

L1. The simple part affirmed to exist by P1 is located in space (from P1 and P2, [1, 2]).

P3. Whatever is located in space occupies (in the sense of 'fills') a part of space, [3].

P4. Whatever fills a part of space has as exactly as many parts as the space it fills, [4].

P5. Parts of space are not simple, but have proper parts, [5].

Therefore,

L2. Nothing simple is located in space (from P3–P5, by a line of reasoning to be discussed shortly, [3, 4, 5]).

L3. Contradiction (from L1 and L2), [1, 2, 3, 4, 5].

Therefore,

C. No part of a substantial composite is simple (from L3, discharging the *reductio* premise, P1, [2, 3, 4, 5]).

Informally presented, the line of reasoning leading to L2 from P3–P5 runs as follows:

Suppose, for *reductio*, that something simple is located in space. Call it m. By P3 m fills a part of space. Call this part of space s. By P5, s has proper parts. By P4, m, since it fills a part of space that has proper parts also has proper parts, and so is not simple. Contradiction. Therefore, nothing simple is located in space.

In P3 the notion of 'filling a space' is so understood that it does not require the space filled to have proper parts. A point-sized particle, if such there be, will, in this sense, 'fill' the space it occupies.[62] Premise P3 is controversial. Crusius, for example, supposes that God is located in space. But he also holds that the way in which God occupies space differs from, and is more perfect than, the way in which bodies do so.[63] It is not clear whether Crusius believes that God fills a point-sized region of space—as his use of the verb *'erfüllen'* would seem to suggest—or whether he rather believes that, although located in space, God does not fill any part of it. In the latter case, Crusius would reject P3. His view, however, is somewhat idiosyncratic. More plainly troubling for P3 is a view according to which monads have locations but do not fill point-sized parts of space because spatial points are not parts of space but rather boundaries of spaces. Kant acknowledges this worry in his remark on the antithesis, but he dismisses it on the ground that the Leibnizian picture could not explain how extensionless monads could compose extended bodies—the point being that they could not do so through mere aggregation (A 440/B 468).[64] With the luxury of hindsight, we can see that Kant is wrong to dismiss this idea so breezily, for current ideas about the continuum suggest that this is indeed arguably possible.[65]

Premise P5 is also controversial. For although, as Kant knows, there is a Euclidean construction by which one can bisect any finite line, the truth of P5 requires, not merely that every extended part of space should be divisible but that no part of space should be a point.[66] But although Kant shares this view with Leibniz, it is open to dispute.[67] And, indeed, Cantorian thinking about the infinite would invalidate its most compelling supporting argument. Let me explain.

One of the main reasons why Leibniz treat points as boundaries of lines rather than as parts of them has to do with the so-called 'paradoxes of the infinite'. In the

---

[62] In this premise, the argument's proponent is temporarily remaining neutral on the question whether space contains any simple parts. That neutrality lapses at P5. In the sense of 'fill' involved in these premises something, x, will be said to fill a space, y, iff x is partly or wholly present in every part of y. If y has no *proper* parts, a point-sized piece of matter will be wholly present in the only part of y, namely, y itself.

[63] Christian Augustus Crusius, *Die Philosophischen Hauptwerke*, 4 vols (Hildesheim: Georg Olms) at vol. 2, 464.

[64] In the *Physical Monadology* Kant had already rejected the idea that bodies could fill space through the mere 'co-presence' of their primitive parts (1: 475, 1: 481). What is required, Kant thinks at this early stage, is rather that the monads should fill space by 'the sphere of [their] activity' (1: 481). However, as Van Cleve notes, this is not so much to fill space as to appear to do so. Van Cleve, 'Reflections on Kant's Second Antinomy' at 490.

[65] See Van Cleve, *Problems* at 66.

[66] Whether the construction amounts to a valid proof, of course, is another question. See Michael Friedman, *Kant and the Exact Sciences* (Cambridge, MA: Harvard University Press, 1992) at 58–61.

[67] For Kant, spatial points, lines, and planes are *boundaries* of spaces; for Leibniz's they are 'extremities of the extended'. See Leroy E. Loemker (ed.), *Gottfried Wilhelm Leibniz: Philosophical Papers and Letters* (2nd edn., Synthese Historical Library, Dordrecht: Reidel, 1969) at 598. 'Solid space', says Kant, 'has the surface as a boundary, planar space the line, and the line the point' (*Metaphysics L2*, 28: 570). A boundary of a spatial object of dimension n, is a mathematical object of dimension $n-1$. For example, a boundary of a plane is a line. Being of a different dimension from a spatial object of type T, a boundary of a T-type object is not to be conceived of as an infinitesimal part of that object. See Richard T. W. Arthur, *Leibniz* (Classic Thinkers; Cambridge: Polity, 2014) at 84.

seventeenth and eighteenth centuries these paradoxes were in effect exploited—without the acknowledgement that they were paradoxes—to generate an argument for the conclusion that points are not parts of lines. The argument runs as follows. Assume that the whole is greater than the part. Assume for *reductio*, that lines have points as parts. On these assumptions, there will be exactly as many points on the base of a square as on its bottom-left to top-right diagonal; for the members of these two sets of points can be put into a one-to-one correspondence. Now there is also a one-one correspondence between the points on the base of the square and the points on a certain proper part of the aforementioned diagonal, namely, the one running from the lower left-hand corner of the square to the point on the diagonal where it would be intersected by the arc generated by rotating the base of the square anti-clockwise until it lay on the diagonal. But then, by the transitivity of the bijection relation, it follows that the whole diagonal has exactly as many point-parts as one of its own proper parts. But such a conclusion infringes the principle that the whole is greater than the part.[68] Contradiction. Therefore, lines do not have points as parts.

Since Kant treats the claim that the whole is greater than its part as analytic (B 17), there is reason to think that, had he known of it, he would have found this argument compelling. Cantor, by contrast, argues that since the points on the diagonal can be put into one-to-one correspondence with the points on the diagonal's own proper part, the two sets of points have the same cardinality. He would thus reject the axiom that says that the whole is greater than the part when 'greater than' is understood as expressing the relation 'has a greater cardinality than'. The sense in which he would take it to be analytic that the whole is greater than the part is another: the set of parts of 'the whole' is a proper superset of the set of parts of 'the part'. The upshot is that modern Cantorians would reject this particular argument for the thesis that points are not parts of lines.

The second conjunct of the antithesis states that 'nowhere in the world does there exist anything simple'. The argument for this conjunct seems to depend on Kant's own metaphysics of experience. He claims—entirely plausibly—that we can never be justified in inferring the simplicity of a thing from a lack of observed composition, adding that 'nothing can ever be given as an absolutely simple object in any possible experience' (A 437/B 465). Combining this claim with the assumption that the world is to be equated with the realm of possible experience, he concludes that the absolutely simple cannot be a part of that world (ibid.).

It is not immediately clear why a Transcendental Realist should be moved by this reasoning. But, on reflection, there may be a line of defence against the worry

---

[68] In Leibniz the argument is highly compressed. He says 'a minimum cannot be supposed without it following that the whole has as many minima as the part, which implies a contradiction'. (See A VI. ii. 264 and, for a discussion: Arthur, *Leibniz* at 83, to which my own presentation of the Leibnizian argument is indebted.)

that Kant's argument imports a Transcendentally Idealist assumption. The defence would run as follows. Since by 'the world' here Kant means 'the world of *sense*', and because it is plausibly analytic that the world of sense is identical with the world of (actual and possible experience), the reasoning may not after all appeal to Transcendental Idealism. The assumption that the world is the world of sense (that is, the world of perceptible things) might *sound* Transcendentally Idealist in character, but since it does not involve the claim that the objects of sense—or features of them—are constituted by the contribution of sensibility, the issue is by no means clear. That having been said, this line of defence does imply that Kant is taking the Transcendental Realist to have a somewhat anti-realist conception of the world of sense: it is the world as we could in principle find it. So, this part of his argument is not uncontroversial. Nonetheless, it is not as flatly question-begging as it might at first appear.

This concludes our exposition of the mathematical antinomies. We have seen that Kant's arguments rest on number of controversial premises that cannot plausibly be taken to be mere consequences of Transcendental Realism. The thesis argument of the first antinomy's temporal part depends on a now-superseded definition of mathematical infinity, as well as on the controversial assumption that we cannot conceive of *tota synthetica* (or such of them as are not given within certain boundaries of any intuition) except through acts of synthesis. And the first antinomy's spatial part is even less promising than its temporal part.

In the second antinomy one does plausibly obtain a contradiction between the first conjuncts of the thesis and antithesis, but only if one makes the assumption of uniform mereological structure, and assumes, further, that spatial points are not parts of lines. And because the second conjunct of the second antinomy's thesis is inferred as a corollary of the first the argument for a contradiction between the second conjuncts depends on these same controversial assumptions.

Unfortunately for Kant, as far as the mathematical antinomies go, there does not seem to be even a single sub-antinomy whose only controversial assumptions are recognizably consequences of Transcendental Realism. In consequence, these antinomies fail to afford even a single successful indirect argument for Transcendental Idealism. It remains possible, of course, that *we* might discover a mathematical antinomy that Kant himself had overlooked; so his project of furnishing an indirect proof of Transcendental Idealism by constructing one or more mathematical antinomies cannot be said definitively to have failed. Nonetheless, Kant's repeated failure to construct even a single convincing mathematical antinomy does leave the prospects for providing such a proof looking rather dim.

10
The Mathematical Antinomies Resolved

10.1 Introduction

Kant seeks to resolve the mathematical antinomies by arguing that the thesis and antithesis, although they appear to be contradictories, are in truth merely contraries—and, further, that each claim is actually false. In the mathematical antinomies the opposed claims are, Kant says, not to be settled 'to the satisfaction of both parties', as they are in the dynamical antinomies, but rather 'dismissed' (as false). They are to be so dealt with because they rest on a false shared presupposition, namely, the unvoiced assumption that the sensible world exists as an absolute whole—a totality of things in themselves.[1]

In a reflection from the late 1780s Kant distinguishes between two kinds of resolution—or 'solution'—of the mathematical antinomies. The less ambitious, 'logical' solution contends that the thesis and antithesis are mere contraries: (R 5962, 18: 404); the more ambitious, 'transcendental' solution, on the other hand, contends, more strongly, that both claims are actually false. Since the first *Critique* contains two distinct lines of resolution of the mathematical antinomies, one might be tempted by this reflection to think of those lines as corresponding to the logical and transcendental solutions. But this temptation is better resisted. In truth, in the first *Critique* both lines of resolution aim at a 'transcendental' solution, for each of them endeavours to show that the opposed claims in a mathematical antinomy are—on the assumption of Transcendental Idealism—false.[2]

Where the two lines of resolution do differ is in how they attempt to show this, and, in particular, in their treatment of the term 'the world'. The first line treats this term as possessing a referent and argues that if we accept the Transcendental Idealist's conception of what kind of thing this referent is, the thesis and antithesis of each mathematical antinomy can be recognized as false because their predicates—'finite' and 'infinite'—contain a common application condition that, owing to the nature of the world, is in both cases unsatisfied. The second line, by contrast, supposes that the term 'the world' fails to refer and, applying a traditional rule for

---

[1] A 529–30/B 557–8. Kant nonetheless treats this dismissal as amounting to *some* kind of 'settling' of the dispute (see A 530/B 558). Varying the image, he also suggests that in the case of the mathematical antinomies the knot—presumably Gordian in nature—is severed (A 529/B 557). One supposes that in the case of the dynamical antinomies it is, by contrast, merely untied.

[2] See A 505/B 533 and A 792–3/B 820–1.

The Fiery Test of Critique: A Reading of Kant's Dialectic. Ian Proops, Oxford University Press (2021). © Ian Proops.
DOI: 10.1093/oso/9780199656042.003.0011

determining the truth values of affirmative judgments with non-referring subject terms, argues that the thesis and antithesis of each mathematical antinomy are both false precisely because of this failure of reference. The first line thus treats the term 'the world' as having the significance accorded to it by the Transcendental Idealist, the second the significance accorded to it by the Transcendental Realist. The two lines of resolution, moreover, turn out to correspond to two traditional ways of attempting to generate counter-examples to the law of excluded middle. The first line exploits the idea of categorial inappropriateness or 'category clash', the second that of failure of reference.

10.2 The first line of resolution

Kant sketches the first line of resolution in the seventh section of the Antinomies chapter. For illustrative purposes he focuses on the spatial part of the first antinomy, but it's clear that he intends his resolution to apply equally to the temporal part, as well as to the second antinomy. In order to illustrate the notion of a common application condition Kant invites us to consider a commonplace example:

> If someone were to say that any body either smells good or smells not good, then there is a third alternative, viz., that the body does not smell (emit an odour) at all; and thus both of the conflicting propositions can be false. (A 503/B 531)

Here, obviously, the common application condition is the possession of an odour. Because this condition can fail to be satisfied, the predicates 'smells good' and 'smells not good'—that is, 'smells bad'—can simultaneously fail to apply to a given object, and so count as contraries or 'disparata'.

Kant wishes to claim that, for parallel reasons, the predicates '(spatially) finite' and '(spatially) infinite' can simultaneously fail to hold of a certain object—the world—and are, accordingly, mere contraries. He regards their common application condition as the property of *being an absolute whole of things in space*. And, maintaining that the sensible world is not such a whole, he concludes that in the mathematical antinomies the thesis and antithesis are both false. He does not, however, give this explanation explicitly. Instead, he just *asserts* that the judgments 'the world is (spatially) infinite' and 'the world is (spatially) finite' are contraries, apparently hoping that the reader will be able to see, without being told, why this is so. He makes this assertion immediately after discussing the example of an odourless body, and he does so, apparently, in the course of drawing a conclusion that he sees as following from the implied comparison between the cosmological and olfactory cases. He says:

If I say that as regards [the world's extent in] space either the world is infinite or it is not infinite (*non est infinitus*), then if the first proposition [in this disjunction] is false, its contradictory opposite, "the world is not infinite" [*nicht unendlich*], must be true.... But if it is said that the world is either infinite or finite (non-infinite [*nichtunendlich*]), then both [disjuncts] could be false.

(A 503–4/B 531–2)

In this passage the free-standing occurrence of '*nicht*' signifies that this word modifies the copula and so serves to express what Kant calls 'logical negation', while the compounded occurrence signifies predicate negation ('transcendental negation').[3] Kant also follows the convention found in Wolffian textbooks of using Latin word order to indicate relative scope.[4] In this remark, for example, the parenthetical interpolation, '*non est infinitus*', serves to indicate that in the sentence 'the world is not infinite' the negation has wide scope with respect to the singular term: it affects the copula rather than merely the predicate.[5] The narrow-scope reading would be indicated by the phrase '*est non infinitus*'.

What is the common application condition in the case of the contrary predicates supposedly involved in the thesis and antithesis of the mathematical antinomies? In addressing this question it helps to revisit the reflection from the early 1770s discussed in the previous chapter. 'Infinite', Kant says, 'means...great beyond all measure *when taken as a whole*'.[6] This strongly suggests that the common application condition must be 'being *given* as a whole'—something

---

[3] Kant is not, however, consistent in observing this syntactic convention; for on one occasion he uses the word '*nicht*' in '*nichtsterblich*' to express *logical* negation (A 574/B 602). This, I think, must be either a slip by Kant or a transcription error by an editor. For when the distinction between logical and transcendental negation is invoked to do actual philosophical work—for instance at A 504/B 532— Kant plainly intends the concatenation of '*nicht*' with a predicate to result in the contrary rather than the contradictory of that predicate, and so to indicate transcendental negation.

[4] See Wolfgang Malzkorn, *Kants Kosmologie-Kritik: Eine formale Analyse der Antinomienlehre* (Berlin: de Gruyter, 1999) at 125. Kant alludes to this convention in the *Jäsche Logic* when he observes that the distinction between infinite and negative judgments is best brought out in Latin (9: 104). As Kant was aware, the convention is an established feature of discussions of infinite judgments in Wolffian logic books. J. P. Reusch, for example, illustrates the same distinction in his *Systema Logicum*—a work Kant knew (24: 701)—with the contrast between 'idolum *est* non Deus' and 'idolum non *est* Deus' (§372, emphases in the original) (Johann Peter Reusch, *Systema Logicum*, ed. J. École (*Christian Wolff Gesammelte Werke Materialien und Dokumente*, 26; Hildesheim: Georg Olms)).

[5] I avoid saying that negation operates on the proposition or that it amounts to 'propositional negation', for Kant lacks a conception of negation as an operator on propositions in general. He does not, for example, recognize negation as applying to conditionals or disjunctions (Kant's taxonomy of judgments does not countenance such judgments as 'not-(if *p* then *q*)' or 'not-(*p* or *q*)'). To say that negation operates on the copula—or as Kant actually says that it affects the copula (9: 104) or attaches to the relation between concepts in a judgment (A 574/B 602)—is tantamount to saying that it is an operator on specifically *categorical* judgments, though Kant does not express the idea in quite this way. I am grateful to Jeremy Heis for reminding me of this point.

[6] R 5338, around 1771, 18: 155, emphasis added.

that makes possible 'being *taken* as a whole'.[7] Kant supposes that this condition fails to be satisfied by the sensible world. He does not say why this should be so, but it seems likely that he's thinking of the sensible world as merely a relative whole and treating the application condition as requiring that the world be an absolute whole. The sensible world exists only as a relative whole, for Kant, in the sense that it exists 'only in the regress', where this means that it plays host only to what he calls an 'indeterminately continued regression'.[8] The solution thus presupposes a Transcendentally Idealist conception of the world as something that does exist but only in the manner of (what we might today call) a potential infinity (compare A 418/B 445–46). If the metaphysics behind this notion of an 'indeterminately continued regression' is murky, the logic of the situation is clear. Kant has in effect distinguished the following three predicates (I confine myself, for illustration, to the case of the spatial part of the first antinomy): 'x is spatially infinite', 'x is spatially non-infinite', and 'x is not spatially infinite'. The application conditions for these predicates may be specified as follows:

[i] x is spatially infinite (that is, infinite in spatial extent) just in case x is given as an absolute whole in space and x is (externally) great beyond measure.

[ii] x is spatially non-infinite (finite) just in case x is given as an absolute whole in space and x is not (externally) great beyond measure.

[iii] x is not spatially infinite just in case x either is not given as an absolute whole in space or is so given but not (externally) great beyond measure.

The predicates dealt with in [i] and [iii] are contradictories. But because it is, in Kant's view at least, a real possibility for something to exist while not being given as an absolute whole in space, the predicates [i] and [ii] are for him mere contraries. The reason why Kant thinks it is possible for something to exist without being given as an absolute whole in space is that, being a Transcendental Idealist, he thinks that the world *actually* exists in this way: it exists 'only in the regress'. Since Kant does not mention anything else as establishing the possibility in question, it appears that, as far as the first line of resolution is concerned, the 'logical' solution of the mathematical antinomies, while *in conception* distinct from the 'transcendental' one, nonetheless in practice presupposes it. We know that the thesis and antithesis *can* both be false precisely because we know that they *are* in fact both false, and we know that because we know that the world exists only as a relative, not an absolute, whole—or so, at least, Kant maintains.

---

[7] In the first *Critique* Kant characterizes the condition as the world's being 'given as a thing in itself' (A 504/B 532), which I take to be equivalent to its being given as an *absolute* whole.

[8] A 518/B 546; compare A 505/B 533 and A 521/B 549.

10.3 The second line of resolution

Before getting into the details of the second line of resolution we need to consider two preliminary points. The first concerns Kant's notion of an 'infinite judgment', the second his understanding—already touched upon—of the predicate 'infinite'.

Infinite judgments are so called because they feature what medieval logicians called 'infinitizing negation'. This is the kind of negation that modifies the predicate term rather than the copula.[9] In Kant's hands at least, infinite judgments are categorical claims of the form '*S* is non-*P*' rather than '*S* is not *P*'—the latter being one form of a negative categorical judgment (another form would be 'No *S* is *P*'). Kant is not alone among his (near) contemporaries in acknowledging a category of infinite judgments. Meier, for example, recognizes them in his *Auszug* (§294), as does Reusch in his *Systema Logicum* (§372). But Kant departs from these Wolffian logicians in regarding infinite judgments not as a sub-species of affirmative judgments, but rather as *sui generis* and, accordingly, as meriting a place of their own in the table of 'functions of unity in judgments' (A 69–70/B 94–5). A second, less important, difference is that for Meier and Reusch, but not for Kant, a judgment counts as 'infinite' when either the predicate term *or the subject term* is negated. Reusch, for example, mentions the following as an example of an infinite judgment: '*non-Deus non debet adorari*' ('A non-God ought not to be worshiped') (*Systema Logicum*, §371).[10]

In the *Jäsche Logic* Kant explains that whereas in negative judgments negation affects (*afficirt*) the copula, in infinite judgements it affects the predicate.[11] And, as we have noted, he terms the former species of negation 'logical', the latter 'transcendental' (A 547/B 602). The choice of terminology may explain why he chooses the term 'transcendental logic' for a taxonomy of judgments that is sensitive to the presence or absence of predicate negation.[12] Kant alludes to this sensitivity when he remarks that, general logic, in contrast to transcendental, 'abstracts from all content of the predicate' (A 72/B 97). His point is that in transcendental logic one looks within the predicate of judgments classified as affirmative by general logic and sorts them into fundamental kinds (infinite versus affirmative), depending on whether that predicate consists of another predicate

---

[9] The adjective 'infinitizing' in turn derives from Aristotle's practice of calling terms with a negative prefix 'infinite names'. Terence Parsons, *Articulating Medieval Logic* (Oxford: Oxford University Press, 2014) at 72.

[10] Parsons notes that in the medieval tradition infinite terms cannot be infinitized. This means that terms featuring double negations, such as 'non-non-donkey', are not permitted (see ibid., at 73n24). This stricture does not, however, seem to have been observed by Meier, for he expressly allows that in particular negative judgments one may apply negation to the predicate, thereby obtaining a particular affirmative judgment (see *Auszug* §351).

[11] See 9: 104; compare *Vienna Logic*, 24: 929–30.

[12] It is also possible, of course, that transcendental negation is so called because it is recognized in transcendental but not general logic.

250 THE FIERY TEST OF CRITIQUE

transcendentally negated. In consequence, transcendental logic contains a finer-grained classification of judgment types than the general logic of Aristotle and Wolff.

The fact that Kant distinguishes between infinite and affirmative judgments is well known. It is less well known that in his second line of resolution of the mathematical antinomies he *in practice* treats infinite judgments as affirmative. This second line thus proceeds from the point of view of general rather than transcendental logic. Polemically, this makes sense; for, insofar as he wishes to persuade a Transcendental Realist that the thesis and antithesis of a mathematical antinomy are not genuine contradictories, Kant will not want his resolution to rest on some potentially controversial feature of his own, innovative taxonomy of judgments.

This point has important ramifications for Kant's notion of the 'logical form' of a judgment. For he holds that one enumerates logical forms within *general* rather than transcendental logic. He says, for example, 'If I say...the soul is nonmortal [*nichtsterblich*], then I have indeed, *in respect of logical form* [*der logischen form nach*], actually affirmed [*bejaht*] something' (A 72/B 97, emphasis added).[13] The judgment 'The soul is nonmortal' is an infinite judgment, and yet Kant is telling us here that it has the logical form of an affirmation. It has that form, however, only insofar as it is catalogued by general, not transcendental, logic. Logical form, then, is a notion that belongs to *general* logic—to, that is to say, a perspective from which infinite judgments are not *sui generis*, but rather a species of affirmative judgments and have exactly the same logical form as the affirmative judgments that are free of transcendental negation.[14]

This point suggests the need for caution in characterizing Kant's 'table of judgments'. Commentators often describe this table as a table of the 'logical forms of judgment'. This, however, is wrong and misleading; for the table distinguishes some judgment types—namely, the affirmative and the infinite—that Kant regards as having the same logical form. The table is rather what Kant says it is, namely, a (more fine-grained) *transcendental* table of the 'moments' of the 'function of thought in judgment' (A70/B 95) or, more loosely, of the 'moments of thought in judgments' (A 73/B 98). The table is transcendental in the sense that it presents a classification that is sensitive to differences in content—especially the

---

[13] Here I follow Erdmann's suggestion of '*nichtsterblich*' for '*nicht sterblich*'. The former is indicated by the occurrence of '*nichtsterbenden*' later in the same sentence. It is also required if we are to make sense of what Kant is saying; for in this context he is clearly intending to contrast the claim that the soul is nonmortal with the claim, discussed in the previous sentence, that the soul is not mortal.

[14] It wouldn't do to suppose that Kant is drawing a distinction between transcendental and general logical form—and maintaining merely that infinite and affirmative judgments differ with respect to the former but not the latter. For there is no such thing as 'transcendental logical form'. After all, the term 'transcendental' in 'transcendental logic' indicates that the categorization of judgments belonging to the latter discipline are sensitive to the *matter* of a judgment. '*Transcendental* logical *form*', accordingly, is an oxymoron.

content of the predicate. The 'moments' it sets out are the various 'functions of unity in judgments' (A 69/B 94): they are not, in Kant's sense, logical forms. Since that is so, we may think of the table as cataloguing (something like) the various kinds of mental acts that are involved in unifying judgmental components into judgments, though the 'judgmental components' unified have to be understood as including, not just concepts (subject and predicate) and judgments (protasis and apodosis), but also predicate negation. The inclusion within the table of the moments of modality, however, suggests that the functions of unity in judgments must include more than this.

Our second preliminary point concerns Kant's understanding of the term 'infinite'. One might have expected him, guided by the presence of affixal negation in the word 'infinite', to treat this term as meaning 'non-finite'. But, like Descartes in the third *Meditation*, he instead takes 'finite' to mean 'non-infinite' (A 504/B 532).[15] He does so because he conceives of finitude as a negation—something understood through its contrast with the reality to which it is opposed. 'No one', he says, 'can think a negation determinatively without using the opposed affirmation as a basis. The person born blind cannot frame the least conception of darkness, because he has none of light' (A 575/B 603). Since Kant regards finitude as a negation, it follows that, for him, we cannot acquire its concept until we have first acquired the concept of infinitude. We cannot, therefore, define the infinite in terms of the finite, but must rather do the reverse.

We are now finally in a position to examine Kant's second line of resolution in the mathematical antinomies. This rests on two claims. First, the phrase 'the world', which in the mathematical antinomies figures as the subject term in (the abbreviated forms of) both the thesis and the antithesis, is a necessarily non-referring term—or more precisely, a term expressing a concept that is necessarily unexemplified (but I'll ignore this complication in what follows). Second, for precisely this reason, a certain logical principle, accepted by all sides, delivers the verdict that both the thesis and the antithesis are false. Kant makes both of these points when he says:

> [In a mathematical antinomy, both parties to the dispute,] being deceived by a transcendental illusion, base their assertions on an impossible concept of the object, and so the rule applies that *non entis nulla sunt praedicata*, that is, both what one asserts affirmatively as well as what one asserts negatively of the object are incorrect and one cannot arrive at cognition of the truth apagogically [that is,] through the refutation of its opposite. So, for example, if it is presupposed that the sensible world is given in its totality **in itself**, then it is false that it must be **either** infinite in space **or** finite and bounded, just because each is false.
> (A 793/B 820-1)

---

[15] Compare third *Meditation* (*AT* VII, 45–6; *CSM* II, 31).

To see what is going on here it's crucial to realize that in this context to 'assert negatively' is to make an *affirmative* judgment: it is to affirm an infinite judgment, where infinite judgments are now construed in Wolffian fashion as a species of affirmative judgment. The rule means: 'No things are predicates of a non-entity', or, more colloquially, 'Nothing is predicated of a non-entity'. And a non-entity in the Wolffian tradition to which this rule (most immediately) belongs is an impossibilium.[16] So the rule means that when the subject term of an *affirmative categorical judgment* is necessarily non-referring, the judgment is false. For convenience, I will refer to this rule as 'the *non entis* rule'.[17]

The rule, which was standard in the medieval tradition, was accepted by the Wolffians. You find a version of it in, for example, J. G. H. Feder's *Logic and Metaphysics* (1769)—a copy of whose fifth edition (of 1778) Kant kept in his library. Kant takes the rule to apply to the thesis and antithesis of each mathematical antinomy—or at least he supposes that the Wolffians are committed to regarding it as so applying. By the Wolffians' lights it ought to apply, Kant thinks, because the subject term of each opposed claim in an antinomy—namely, 'the world'—is, by those lights, internally inconsistent. The upshot is that in any mathematical antinomy both the thesis and the antithesis are false (hence mere contraries). The burning question, of course, is why Kant should take 'the world' to express a concept that is, by the Wolffians' lights, inconsistent.

The answer, I take it, is that he supposes that—by those same Wolffian lights—we will be able to derive contradictory claims from the supposition that it refers—those claims being the thesis and antithesis of each mathematical antinomy (compare 24: 749). On Kant's telling, these claims would indeed be contradictory by the Wolffians' lights, for on their Transcendentally Realist assumptions the arguments for thesis and antithesis will both be sound. There is an interesting wrinkle, however; for, as we will see later in this chapter, the proofs by which these contradictions are derived rely on a kind of *reductio* inference that Kant himself regards as invalid unless Transcendental Realism is true.

The second line of resolution is intended to present the reason why Transcendental Realists run into contradictions in the mathematical antinomies. They do so, Kant thinks, because they wrongly suppose a concept to have reference that is, according to their own commitments, in fact contradictory.

---

[16] Wolff defines an *ens* as 'that which can exist'; a *non ens*, accordingly, is that which *cannot* exist (see Wolff, *Ontologia*, §134).

[17] Kant is in fact appealing to just one half of a longer traditional rule that deals with negative as well as affirmative categoricals, namely:

If the concept expressed by the subject term is necessarily non-exemplified, then the affirmative categorical judgments in which it occurs are false, while the negative categorical judgments in which it occurs are true.

As Terence Parsons observes, this longer rule follows from the principles enshrined in the Aristotelian square of opposition—though Parsons in fact considers a more general rule of which ours is an instance, namely, a rule for assigning truth values to judgments with a (possibly contingently) non-referring subject term. See Parsons, *Articulating Medieval Logic* at 12–13.

A reflection from the mid-to-late 1780s suggests that Kant sees the contradiction in the Transcendental Realists' world-concept as rooted in a clash between two elements of their conception of the world, namely, the idea that it is an *absolute whole*, on the one hand, and that it is something located in *space and time*, on the other. He says: 'The reason why the first two antinomies are both false is that I **had to** ground them both on a contradictory concept, namely, that of a whole in space and time that is also supposed to be an absolute whole, consequently a thing in itself' (R 5962; 18: 402).[18]

The point of the second line of resolution is, I think, to show that, far from being endemic to reason, the contradiction in the antinomies can be traced to the Transcendental Realist's defective concept of the world—taken in conjunction, of course, with the naïve presupposition that this concept refers. The resolution is intended to persuade the Transcendental Realist that this concept needs to be replaced by a coherent one. The first line of resolution can then be used to show that Kant's favoured concept of the world—namely, the concept of a sum of appearances containing an 'indeterminately continued regression' (A 518/B 546)—since it generates no contradiction, can be adopted in its place. The two lines of resolution thus work in tandem to (in effect) recommend a conceptual reform. Or, to put it another way, they combine to persuade each of the Transcendentally Realist parties to the dispute that they share a false presupposition—the assumption, namely, that the sensible world is an absolute whole, a whole of things in themselves. And, indeed, this is precisely the presupposition that Kant mentions in the passage where he discusses the application of the *non entis* rule, where however he treats the presupposition less like a claim than a conception of the world.

One intriguing consequence of Kant's attachment to the *non entis* rule is worth noting before concluding this section. Consider the judgment: 'All round squares are round'. The rule commits Kant to deeming this claim false, but since it is an affirmative judgment in which the predicate is explicitly contained in the subject, he is also committed to deeming it true insofar as he endorses the principle of identity. It seems that he has blundered into inadvertent dialetheism.[19] Nor would

---

[18] The alert reader will have noticed that Kant's second line of resolution anticipates the solution Russell gives to the easy-to-resolve paradox of the Barber who shaves all and only those who don't shave themselves. Russell's solution relies on making three moves: (a) Denying that the barber exists; (b) Assigning Russellian truth conditions to 'The F is G'—truth conditions according to which this claim is false when the F fails to exist; (c) An analysis of 'The barber does not shave himself' which treats the negation particle as not modifying the whole claim (in Russell's terms it is treated as having narrow scope with respect to definite description). Kant's solution features analogues of all three elements, though it differs insofar as Kant does not take the additional Russellian step of suggesting that 'the world' lacks meaning in isolation. He does not suggest, that is to say, that the meaning of this singular term is given only by paraphrasing the whole context in which it occurs; it is not, in Russell's terms, treated as an 'incomplete symbol'. I'm grateful to Roy Sorensen for discussion of this point.

[19] Kant's commitment to the falsehood of the judgment 'All round squares are round' is in fact overdetermined since he also treats universal generalization as existentially committing.

he have embraced this unwitting dialetheism had it been pointed out to him. For if he had done so, he would, by his own lights, have also been free to leave the antinomies unresolved. And yet he sees their resolution as imperative if we are to steer a course between the twin perils of 'sceptical hopelessness' and 'dogmatic defiance' (A 407/B 434). That Kant should have overlooked the present problem is perhaps surprising. For Baumgarten's formulation of the principle of identity, which Kant would have known well, seems to show a certain sensitivity to it. Baumgarten formulates the principle of identity as saying 'Every possible A is A' (*Metaphysics*, §11). This allows the judgment 'All round squares are round squares' to be false.

10.4 Proofs by *reductio*

Although Kant endorses the use of indirect—or 'apagogic'—reasoning in mathematics (A 792/B 820), he deems this style of reasoning illegitimate when employed in 'transcendental proofs' (A 789/B 817). What he means by 'transcendental proofs', however, is not immediately clear. One might be tempted to suppose that he has in mind proofs in philosophy quite generally. But it is also possible that he is referring only to such putative proofs in philosophy as purport to establish results concerning things or states that are not possible objects of experience, for example: God, the self as it is in itself, freedom, and the world treated as an absolute totality.

One consideration favouring the latter interpretation is that Kant's own argument for Transcendental Idealism in the antinomies takes the form of—and is billed as taking the form of—an indirect proof (A 506/B 534). This is plainly an argument belonging to philosophy, but it purports to establish something only about the world conceived neutrally as the world of objects of sense. What it purports to establish is that this world is precisely *not* an absolute totality. Another consideration favouring the same interpretation is that Kant implies that indirect proofs are, on occasion, legitimate even in philosophy. He warns, for example, that *in philosophy* apagogic (that is, indirect) proof, which he equates with proofs by *reductio*, must be used 'very sparingly [*sparsam*]' (*Vienna Logic*, 24: 893). He does not say that it must not be used at all.

To understand Kant's position it helps to distinguish between two patterns of *reductio*-style reasoning. On the one hand, there is what we might call the 'trustworthy' pattern, namely:

[1] For *reductio*, suppose S is not P. Derive a recognizable falsehood (a contradiction or a conjunction of contraries). Conclude that S is P.[20]

---

[20] For Kant's acknowledgement of the validity of the first form of *reductio*, see: *Jäsche Logic* 9: 71. I have presented the *reductio* as a derivation of a recognizable falsehood rather than of a contradiction

On the other hand, there is the untrustworthy pattern:

[2] For *reductio*, suppose S is non-P. Derive a recognizable falsehood (a contradiction or a conjunction of contraries). Conclude that S is P.

The second pattern of inference is untrustworthy because it is possible that the subject term should have an impossible intentional object or that an application condition of the predicate should fail to be satisfied. In either case, the judgment 'S is non-P' will be merely the contrary of 'S is P', and one won't be able to infer from the falsehood of the former to the truth of the latter.

Kant is impressed by the fact that instances of the untrustworthy form of *reductio* can be hard to spot. The danger of missing them, he thinks, is especially acute when we are reasoning about the supersensible; for here illusions lurk that can lead us to imagine that a non-referring subject term refers. Accordingly, Kant deems apagogic proofs impermissible in those sciences in which subreptions are possible (A 791/B 819). On the other hand, he assumes that this kind of mistake cannot occur in mathematics, where one begins by establishing the actuality of the referent of the subject term by means of a construction. And, in line with this thought, he supposes that *reductio* proofs of both kinds—that is, our [1] and [2]—are reliable in mathematics (A 792/B 820).[21]

Kant's advice to use apagogic proof 'sparingly' in philosophy amounts to a tacit acknowledgement of human limitations. Regrettably, we are just not as skilled as we might wish to be either at analysing concepts (for example, the concept 'finite') or at detecting ambiguities of scope. Had we been perfectly versed in these skills, and so able to tell that a negation occurred with narrow scope whenever it did so, the problem that some in fact unexemplified concepts *seem* to be exemplified would not have mattered because, possessing these skills, we would have been able to confine our *reductio* arguments to the safe kind—[1]—where the negation in question has wide scope.

10.5 Regresses *ad infinitum* and *ad indefinitum*

As we have seen, Kant's first line of resolution hinges on a conception of the sensible world as something that is not an absolute totality but rather exists only 'in the regress'. It's time to scrutinize this latter notion. The first point to note is

---

because Kant suggests this flexibility himself. He says: '[In apagogic proof] we need only look at the consequences issuing from the cognition's opposite and find a single one of them to be false; for then this opposite is also false, and hence the cognition that we had to prove is true' (A 791/B 819).

[21] This, of course, cannot be the whole story, for one would want to know why Kant thinks that presupposition failure owing to a clash of categories—as apparently occurs in, for example, the claim 'the number 2 is equilateral'—cannot occur in mathematics. After all, one might fear that this too might be overlooked.

that to think of the world as existing in this way is not, in Kant's phraseology, to think of the regress in it as proceeding *to infinity*—that is, *in* or *ad infinitum*. To think of a regressing series as proceeding to infinity is to 'anticipate the members not yet reached by the regression' and 'to represent their multitude as so great that it could not be reached by any empirical synthesis' (A 519/B 547). To so conceive of the regress in the series that constitutes the sensible world would, Kant suggests, be to determine the world's magnitude (at least negatively) prior to the regression (ibid.). But in Kant's view no such feat is possible because, first, the world is not given, and cannot be given, prior to the regression in it (ibid.), and second, only what is so given can have even a negatively determined magnitude (compare 504/B 532).

In Kant's view, the regress contained in the sensible world proceeds not '*in infinitum*' (to infinity), but rather 'indeterminably far [*unbestimmbar weit*]' or '*in indefinitum*'.[22] The idea—to put it in our own terms—is that the world-series is such that we may extend it as far as we wish by (somehow) actualizing progressively more of its thus-far merely possible members.[23] There is no limit to how far we can extend the series in this way and no time at which all of its members will have been actualized. But to say this is *not* to determine the absolute magnitude of the series (A 520/B 548). On the contrary, to say that the regress in the world-series proceeds *in indefinitum* is equivalent to saying that the world simply has no absolute magnitude (A 521/B 549).[24]

Although in Kant's view *the world* is not given to me prior to the regress in it by means of what he terms a 'collective intuition', he allows that certain parts of it—certain bodies—can be so given, namely, bodies that are—roughly speaking—small enough to be taken in at a glance (hence without a synthesis of their parts).[25] Such bodies can, in his terms, be 'given as a whole in empirical intuition'. In Kant's view, the internal regress in the series of the parts of such bodies *does* qualify as a regress to infinity (A 523-4/B 551-2). And, in such cases, one says that the body is 'divisible to infinity'.[26] Kant insists, however, that a body or a space divisible to infinity must not be regarded as *consisting* of infinitely many parts.[27] It is not to be regarded as an aggregate of the parts into which it is divisible, for an aggregate for Kant is a multitude [*Menge*] of previously given parts (A 163/B 204). It is rather, by definition, only an aggregate of the parts into which it is thought of as already having been divided. As Kant says:

---

[22] A 512/B 540; A 521/B 549.   [23] Compare A 511/B 540 and R 6424; 18: 712.

[24] This is, I think, compatible with later stages in the regress of spatial or temporal conditions being greater in magnitude than earlier ones, hence with one's being able to assign *relative* magnitudes to different, so to speak, constructional phases of what Kant calls 'the regression in the series of the world's appearances' (A 521/B 549). I'm grateful to Jeremy Heis for discussion of this point.

[25] A 522-3/B 550-1; compare A 519/B 547.

[26] See A 512/B 540, A 514/B 542, and A 523-4/B 551-2.   [27] A 524/B 552; R 6425; 18: 712.

> We are by no means permitted to say of [a whole that is given in intuition and] which is divisible to infinity that it **consists of infinitely many parts**. For although the intuition of the whole contains all the parts, it yet does **not** contain the **whole division**; this division consists only in the progressing decomposition, or in the regression itself that first makes the series actual. Now since this regression is infinite, all the members (parts) that it reaches are indeed contained in the given whole taken as an **aggregate**, but not contained therein is the whole **series of the division**, which is infinite successively and never **whole** and hence can exhibit no infinite multitude of parts and no gathering together of such a multitude into a whole. (A 524/B 552)

The claim that the series is first made actual only through the 'regression itself'—or, equivalently, only through 'the progressing decomposition'—means, I take it, that the successive members of the series exist only potentially prior to being 'reached'—and so actualized—by the mind as it performs the mental act of dividing. What exactly this comes to is far from clear: the successive members, after all, are not, in Kant's view, *actually* there to be 'reached'. Nonetheless, we can draw one definite inference from these remarks, namely, that Kant rejects the idea that a body comprises infinitely many *actual* parts.

We may further conclude that the feature of the members of a regress that proceeds 'to infinity' that Kant terms their being 'anticipated' (A 519/B 547) cannot *in this context* be a matter of those members' existing as an actual infinity. It seems rather to amount to our *knowing* certain of their properties prior to the regress—we know, for example, that when actualized they will all exist within certain spatial boundaries—those, namely, of the body that is being divided.

10.6 The cosmological syllogism

As we saw in our discussion of the first paralogism, Kant associates each transcendental Idea with its own distinctive kind of synthesis.[28] In addition, he supposes that the transcendental Ideas correspond one-to-one to the three kinds of syllogism recognized by Aristotelian logic. Thus, the Idea of the soul corresponds to the categorical syllogism, that of the world to the hypothetical syllogism, and that of God to the disjunctive syllogism.[29] Kant takes this correspondence to show that the Ideas are 'grounded in the nature of reason' (A 323/B 380)—reason

---

[28] Or nearly so: the transcendental Idea of freedom remains an awkwardly lodged cousin of the three main transcendental Ideas: self, world, and God. In Chapter 17 I discuss this point further, and also justify my speaking of self, world, and God as (the intentional objects of) transcendental Ideas, rather than as merely corresponding to 'titles' of 'classes' of Ideas.

[29] A 321/B 378 and A 323/B 379.

being the faculty of drawing syllogistic inferences. He plainly intends to model this argument on the so-called 'metaphysical deduction' of the categories, part of whose function is to establish the pure origin of the categories by appealing to their correspondence with the functions of unity in judgments (A 70/B 95).

Kant terms the syllogism associated with the transcendental Idea of the world the 'cosmological syllogism'. He regards this syllogism as grounding each of the antinomial conflicts. It is a dialectical argument, he says, on which rests 'the entire antinomy of pure reason' (A 497/B 525). He means that the syllogism is both unsound and yet sufficiently alluring that it is able to occasion the antinomial conflicts. The syllogism runs as follows: 'If the conditioned is given, then the whole series of all conditions for it is also given; now objects of the senses are given as conditioned; consequently, etc.' (ibid.). Kant regards this argument as a *sophisma figurae dictionis*—a fallacy of an ambiguous middle term. 'It is clear', he says,

> that the major premise of the cosmological syllogism takes the conditioned in the transcendental signification of a pure category, while the minor premise takes it in the empirical signification of a concept of the understanding applied to mere appearances; consequently, there is present in it that dialectical deception [*Betrug*] that is called a *sophisma figurae dictionis*. (A 499/B 527–8)

Kant would seem to be saying that we are inclined to view the inference as a valid hypothetical syllogism—a *modus ponens*—when it is in fact an invalid inference of the following form:

If P then Q (major premise)
R (minor premise)
So, Q

In the fallacious argument P, Q, and R receive the following interpretations:

P: The intelligible conditioned is given.
Q: The whole series of conditions for the intelligible conditioned is given.
R: The empirical conditioned is given.

Kant supposes that, when we commit this fallacy, we treat the minor premise as if it spoke of things as they are in themselves—that's to say, we treat R as if it were identical with P—and so imagine the argument to be valid. He seems to think that we know the major premise to be true; for he is prepared to assert it in his own voice. He says, for example, 'If the conditioned as well as its condition are things in themselves, then when the first is given not only is the regress to the second given as a problem, but the latter is thereby actually [*wirklich*] already given along with it' (A 498/B 526; compare 20: 290).[30] But he thinks that our treatment of the minor premise is mistaken. He supposes that under the influence of transcendental illusion we wrongly regard the objects of sense as things in themselves and so mistake the known truth, R, for the false claim P.[31] The upshot is that we unwittingly arrive at the conclusion, Q, by means of a fallacious inference. And, having made one mistake, we proceed to make another. We presume that we will be able to find 'the whole series of conditions' for any *object of sense*. Finally, since there are two ways in which this series might exist—the finitary and infinitary options—this expectation in turn generates an antinomy.

The cosmological syllogism thus explains how transcendental illusion—construed now as the illusion that the objects of sense are things in themselves—generates antinomies. It thus serves to display the transcendental illusion operative in the antinomies as bound up with pure reason (in the narrow sense), the characteristic mode of inference associated with syllogisms (arguments essentially having two premises). This task needs performing because the central mode of inference that each of the parties imagines him- or herself to be relying on in conducting the arguments of the antinomies—namely, the respectable form of *reductio ad absurdum*—is, on Kant's conception, an inference not of reason, but of the *understanding*, namely, a *single premise* inference of the form 'p is false; so not-p is true' (9: 116–17). The connection of the antinomies with pure reason (in the narrow sense) thus remains uncemented until the cosmological syllogism is introduced.[32]

---

[30] It's an excellent question how Kant could be in a position to know that this claim is true, but there can be little doubt that he does take us to know it—a point that, in my view, deserves a higher profile in the Kant literature.

[31] That Kant takes us to thus misconstrue the minor premise, R, is clear from the following remark: 'It is likewise natural (in the minor premise) to regard appearances as things in themselves and likewise as objects given to the mere understanding' (A 500/B 528).

[32] It is a good question exactly which faculties Kant saw as involved in inference at which stage of his career. For he later apparently came to believe that understanding and reason do not in fact suffice for inference, and that the faculty of judgment is also needed. This point emerges from the rather abstract discussion in his article 'Theory and Practice' of 1793. There, apparently to some degree anticipating, at a high level of abstraction, some of the considerations involved in Lewis Carroll's famous regress argument, he says: 'It is obvious that between theory and practice there is required, in addition [to these two], a middle term connecting them and providing a transition from one to the other, no matter how complete a theory may be; for, to a concept of the understanding, which contains a rule, must be added an act of judgment by which a practitioner distinguishes whether or not something is a case of the rule; and since judgment cannot always be provided with yet another rule by which to direct its subsumption (for this would go on to infinity), there can be theoreticians who can never in their lives become practical because they are lacking in judgment...' (8: 275). To see the parallel with Carroll, think of the rule in question in the Carrollian case (which involves Achilles attempting to logically coerce the Tortoise into accepting the conclusion of a given argument) as: 'You must infer immediate logical consequences of small sets of premises if you see that they are such consequences while also seeing that the premises hold' and think of the application of the rule (the 'subsumption') as a matter of judging that the conclusion is indeed a logical consequence of the premises and the premises true. You may then think of the further premise that the Tortoise urges Achilles to add, as expressing the applicability in a particular case of the rule. The issues here are complex, however, and the question of just how closely Kant is in fact approximating Carroll—or anticipating a generalization of his considerations—

The diagnosis we have presented is not, however, Kant's only diagnosis of the fallacy involved in the cosmological syllogism. For he hints at an alternative which coheres rather better with that part of his account of transcendental illusion that posits a tendency in human beings to mistake an imperative governing inquiry for a description of how things actually stand. According to this alternative diagnosis, the cosmological syllogism is not a *sophisma figurae dictionis* but rather a valid argument with a *major* premise that is not known to be true. When construed in this way, the argument runs:

If the empirical conditioned is given, the whole series of conditions for the empirical conditioned is also given. (major premise—not known to be true)

The empirical conditioned is given. (minor premise—known to be true)

So,

The whole series of conditions for the empirical conditioned is given.

Kant's second diagnosis, if fully spelled out, would take the form of an explanation of why we are inclined to regard the major premise in this argument as known to be true. That explanation is not stated explicitly, but it can be assembled from certain of Kant's remarks. It runs as follows: It is 'indubitably certain' and, indeed, an analytic truth 'beyond any fear of transcendental criticism' that 'if the conditioned [in appearance] is given, then precisely thereby a regress in the series of all conditions for this conditioned is **given** to us **as a problem**' (A 497–8/B 526). Kant supposes that we are prone to confuse this certain truth, whose consequent expresses a norm governing inquiry, with the (in intention) factual claim that 'if the conditioned (in appearance) is given, then the synthesis constituting its empirical condition is also thereby given' (A 499/B 527). Such a confusion is, of course, merely a version of the confusion—already discussed in Chapter 1— between a prescription, on the one hand, and a descriptive claim, on the other. But now the prescription is formulated in the indicative mood. It says: 'The discovery of such-and-such is given to us as a problem', rather than 'Seek, such-and-such'.

Although these two diagnoses of the cosmological syllogism are distinct, Kant cannot be said to have registered their distinctness all that vividly. This, however, is merely a defect of exposition: he is plainly aware that these are complementary diagnoses of the shortcomings of the cosmological syllogism. The two diagnoses arise because, depending on how we resolve the equivocation in question, the cosmological syllogism—like each of the individual paralogisms—can be treated

---

would deserve an article-length discussion. See Lewis Carroll, 'What the Tortoise Said to Achilles', *Mind*, 104 (416) (1895), 691–3.

either as an invalid argument with known premises, or as a valid argument with one or more unknown premise.

Having stated his reasons for regarding the cosmological syllogism as a *sophisma figurae dictionis*, Kant seems to be drawing his discussion of the mathematical antinomies to a close. The two parties to the dispute, he says, once they have been alerted to their common mis-step, 'may justly be dismissed' as disputants whose claims are 'based on no well-grounded title' (A 501/B 529). One might have expected the matter to rest there, but instead the discussion takes an unexpected turn. Kant tells us that even though the parties to the dispute in a mathematical antinomy 'have been instructed by the court of reason to keep their peace', the dispute 'drags on as before' simply because 'nothing seems clearer than that between the two [disputants] one of them has to be right' (ibid.). In Kant's view, then, neither a keen awareness of the fallacy involved in the cosmological syllogism nor the associated awareness that there is, after all, no reason to suppose that the world of sense contains the unconditioned in fact suffices to draw the dispute in a mathematical antinomy to a close. Instead, each party, labouring under the misapprehension that the opposed claims are contradictories, persists in the obdurate conviction that precisely one of them must be in the right. In consequence, in order to lay the matter finally to rest—or, as Kant puts it, to settle the dispute in a 'well-grounded' manner (A 501/B 529)—the disputants must be brought to the realization that the thesis and antithesis are not contradictories. And this requires offering one of the two solutions we have been considering. In Kant's words, it requires that the disputants, who take their dispute to be about the world of sense construed as an absolute totality, recognize that they are in fact 'disputing about nothing and that a certain transcendental illusion has portrayed a reality to them where none is present' (A 501-2/B 530).

10.7 The sceptical representation

The fourth section of the Antinomies chapter takes for its theme the idea that the antinomial questions—all of them—*must*, by virtue of their very nature, admit of a satisfactory resolution. That resolution consists not in *adjudicating* the disputes— that is, in ruling in favour of one side and against the other—but rather in providing a 'critical resolution' [*kritischen Auflösung*] of them (A 481/B 510). Such a resolution proceeds by exposing the 'groundless presupposition' common to the thesis and the antithesis (A 485/B 513). As we have seen, this presupposition amounts to a false conception of the sensible world—a conception of this world as a thing in itself (A 490/B 518). The resolution thus allows us to learn something about the character or constitution [*Beschaffenheit*] of the world of sense, namely, that it is not a thing in itself but rather a sum total of *appearances*—where by 'appearances' here Kant means things that are partly constituted by one or more of the two forms of human sensible intuition—space and time; and by a 'sum total' he means a relative rather than absolute whole.³³ Because, by contrast, we learn nothing about the character or constitution of God or of the soul through transcendental philosophy, Kant supposes that the cosmological questions are unique in their ability to *teach* us something—even if what they teach us is not quite the kind of thing we were expecting to learn at the beginning of our inquiry (A 478/B 506).

Instead of plunging directly into the critical resolution, however, Kant prefaces it with a 'sceptical representation' of the questions involved in the mathematical antinomies (A 485/B 513). This exercise is designed to prepare the reader for the diagnosis and indirect proof of Transcendental Idealism that is to come. It generates what he calls in the *Jäsche Logic* a 'provisional judgment' in the truth of Transcendental Idealism (9: 75), and so allows us to 'get the scent of the cognition' that will arise from the ensuing investigation (ibid.). In this same place he suggests that provisional judgments are an 'indispensable' part of the use of the understanding in all mediation and investigation (ibid.). The 'sceptical representation' is so called, presumably, because insofar as it serves to lengthen inquiry it enacts the Kant-approved 'sceptical' method.

The sceptical representation involves rehearsing the antinomies at a somewhat lofty level of abstraction. One argues that the world—by which in this context Kant means the world of sense as it is conceived of by the Transcendental Realist—is either 'too big' or 'too small' for the empirical regress.³⁴ In the mathematical antinomies, the attitude of regarding the world as 'too small' for the regress corresponds to the thesis position, where one attempts to conceive of the world of sense as finite. Regarding the world as 'too big' for the regress, on the other hand, corresponds to the position of the antithesis, where one attempts to conceive of the world of sense as infinite by thinking of it as incapable of being measured off by successively running through the stages of the empirical regress of conditions.

The 'sceptical representation' cannot be deemed one of the more pellucid parts of the Dialectic. And yet Kant plainly regards it as important. As we noted in the introduction, he believes that one should take care not to arrive too hastily at the

---

[33] Kant tends to use the word '*Inbegriff*' (which is usually rendered 'sum total') when speaking of the sensible world as a whole of appearances. This may seem to be a poor choice of vocabulary for someone who wishes to emphasize the point that the sensible world is not, in the strictest sense, a *totality*. As Courtney D. Fugate, has observed, however, the term '*Inbegriff*' can mean *what* is enclosed within certain boundaries—a point confirmed by the relevant entry in Adelung (1811). This observation may help with the present worry because *what* is in space and time need not have definite or fixed boundaries. See Courtney D. Fugate, 'Baumgarten and Kant on Existence', in Courtney D. Fugate and John Hymers (eds), *Baumgarten and Kant on Metaphysics* (Oxford: Oxford University Press, 2018), 131–53 at 136.

[34] Kant also speaks, rather less clearly, of *the Idea* of the world as being too big or too small for the empirical regress (A 489/B 517). When he does so, what he intends to be speaking of is, I think, the intentional object of the Idea.

critical resolution of any question. Instead, one should work patiently through the problem, approaching it from many sides, and only reaching a definitive conclusion in the light of a meticulous and unhurried investigation. Applying this idea to his resolution of the antinomies, he suggests that before embarking on that resolution we should first to be brought to a 'well-grounded suspicion that the cosmological Ideas, and all the sophistical assertions that have been placed in conflict with one another, are perhaps grounded on an empty and merely imaginary concept of the way the object of these Ideas is given to us' (A 490/B 518). Kant hopes that this suspicion will put us on 'the right track for exposing the semblance that has so long misled us' (ibid.). Since in the section immediately following the sceptical representation Kant portrays Transcendental Idealism as 'the key to solving the cosmological conflict' (ibid.), one can have little doubt that the 'semblance' in question is the appearance that the objects of sense are things in themselves.

10.8 The Lambert analogy

In an attempt to render vivid what he is driving at when he insists that the antinomial questions *must* admit of an answer, Kant draws an analogy between 'transcendental philosophy', on the one hand, and pure mathematics, on the other. The analogy focuses on Johann Heinrich Lambert's proof of the irrationality of π (A 480/B 504). Kant's discussion contains some unnecessary complexity, but we may, I think, distil its main point into the following, somewhat idealized, example. Imagine an otherwise competent mathematician who, after numerous attempts to find an expression for π of the form 'n/m', where n and m are nonzero positive integers, concludes, with misplaced humility, that π eludes us because the limits of our reason are too narrow to permit us ever to attain certainty about which rational number it is.

In Kant's view, to adopt this professedly modest stance is in truth merely to pass the buck. We blame our faculty of reason as too weak, and the object as too elusive, to be known, when the fault actually lies with our mistaken unnoticed presuppositions. As Kant puts it, 'If we are unable to assert and determine anything certain about this object from our own concepts, we must not throw the blame upon the object as concealing itself from us.' Rather, we must 'seek the cause [of this inability] in our very idea [of the object]'.[35] The implication is that we should place the blame where it belongs: namely, in this illustrative example, on the presupposition that π is a rational number—a presupposition that Kant regards as built into the faulty concept (or conception) of π that the confused mathematician

---

[35] A 481–2/B 509–10.

adopts prior to inquiry. The correct way to expose the confusion behind the imagined mathematician's misplaced humility is therefore to draw attention to the presupposition that π has a rational value, and to demonstrate its falsity.

Kant invokes Lambert because he wishes to present himself as having performed for the pre-critical metaphysician a service exactly parallel to the one he takes Lambert to have performed for our imaginary confused mathematician. The confused mathematician presupposes that there is such a thing as the *rational* number, π, and, after a series of unsuccessful attempts to determine its identity, at last concludes that our mathematical faculties are not up to the task (or, equivalently, that the object succeeds in concealing itself from us). Analogously, the confused, pre-critical metaphysician presupposes that there is such a thing as the world conceived of as an absolute totality of objects of sense and, after reaching an impasse in attempting to determine its magnitude, at last concludes that our capacity for determining its magnitude is not up to the task. This, of course, is the attitude of the sceptic (whether tranquillity-seeking or despairing): the dogmatist, by contrast, adheres blindly yet tenaciously to a single side in the dispute.

Developing his analogy further, Kant maintains that, just as the resources for Lambert's proof of the irrationality of π were already contained in the defective concept of π, so the resources for his own proposed 'critical resolution' of the mathematical antinomies are already contained in the Transcendental Realist's defective concept of the world, namely, the concept of the world as an absolute totality of objects of sense. If we use the phrase 'the world$_{TR}$' to express this concept, then Kant's point may be put as follows. Each of the following concepts admits of an a priori proof of their non-exemplification: 'the world$_{TR}$' and 'that ratio, n/m, such that n and m are nonzero integers, and for some circle a, $n = a$'s circumference and $m = a$'s diameter'. It takes some ingenuity, of course, to conceive of the mathematical antinomies as exhibiting the non-exemplification of the concept of 'the world$_{TR}$', but those resources are available and contained a priori in this very concept—or so Kant supposes.

These last remarks make sense of Kant's invocation of Lambert. But two questions about this part of his discussion remain. First, why should one follow Kant in supposing that there *must* be an answer to the antinomial questions, even if it consists only in a 'critical resolution' of them? Second, against whom exactly is he arguing when he insists on this point?

A partial answer to the first of these questions can be gleaned from Kant's maintaining that each question disputed in an antinomy concerns 'an object that can be given nowhere but in our thoughts, namely, the absolutely unconditioned totality of the synthesis of appearances' (A 481/B 509). His thought is that because the Idea of an absolutely unconditioned totality of appearances—'appearances' now being understood as things in space and time—has its origin in reason, the question whether it is exemplified, and if so how, must also be answerable by reason. Kant's grounds for this further claim are unclear, but if this answer is accepted, the rest of his story follows somewhat plausibly. Reason tells us that we cannot tolerate a contradiction, and since the concept of an absolutely unconditioned totality of appearances generates two *contradictory* answers to the question of how it is exemplified, we conclude, by reason alone, that it is not—and cannot be—exemplified at all. In the mathematical antinomies, we further conclude that it follows from the '*non entis*' rule that both the thesis and the antithesis are false.

Our second question admits of a more complete answer. Kant is, I think, seeking to oppose two groups of philosophers who would—officially at least—either hew to the line of irremediable ignorance on the cosmological questions or suppose that these questions can be harmlessly evaded.[36] The first group—the pleaders of ignorance—is made up of those philosophers whom Kant views as non-Academic sceptics, including pre-eminently Pyrrho's (by Kant's lights) inauthentic followers, who see the permanent suspension of belief as the uniquely rational response to the balancing of reasons for and against an antinomial thesis. The second group comprises the so-called 'indifferentists'. These are certain writers who, privately supposing (some of) the questions of dogmatic metaphysics to be answerable, nonetheless publicly affect contempt for these questions and do not even begin to investigate them.

This second group is of particular interest to Kant because he takes indifferentism to be the dominant intellectual outlook of his time (A *viii*, A *x*). He supposes that, while the inauthentic Pyrrhonians fail to adequately prolong their investigation, the indifferentists don't even get started. Rather, affecting disdain for metaphysical questions, they simply deny them a hearing, preferring to indulge in a 'loquacious shallowness' that goes by the name of 'popularity' (B *xxxv–vi*). Kant sees such a stance as contributing to what he calls the 'superficiality' of his age (ibid.). He insists that, on the contrary, his age is—and properly ought to be—'the age of criticism' (A *xi*, note *).

10.9 The indifferentists

But who exactly are the indifferentists? And what is their credo? Kant is frustratingly short on specifics, but his comments on indifferentism do contain some clues:

> Now after all paths [for achieving certainty in metaphysics] (as we [wrongly] persuade ourselves) have been tried in vain, what rules is tedium and complete **indifferentism**, the mother of chaos and night in the sciences, but at the same time also the origin of, or at least the prelude to, their incipient transformation

---

[36] Kant, notably, does not engage with an intermediate position that would hold that the questions are—or might be—answerable but only as a matter of contingent fact.

and enlightenment, when through ill-applied effort they have become obscure, confused, and useless.[37]

For it is idle to affect **indifference** with respect to such inquiries, to whose object human nature **cannot** be **indifferent.**. Moreover, however much they may think to make themselves unrecognizable by exchanging the language of the schools for a popular style, these so-called **indifferentists**, to the extent that they think anything at all, always unavoidably fall back into metaphysical assertions, which they yet professed so much to despise. (A x)

Kant's metaphysics and logic lectures contain further clues:

As for metaphysics: it appears as though we have become perplexed in the investigation of truth; and one finds a kind of indifferentism, where one makes it into an honour to speak deprecatingly of metaphysical ponderings, although [on the contrary] metaphysics is **philosophy proper**. (*Metaphysics L2*, 28: 540)

A kind of **indifferentism** toward this science [that is, metaphysics] now appears, since it seems to be taken as an honour to speak of metaphysical investigations contemptuously as mere **cavilling**. (*Jäsche Logic*, 9: 32)

We can assemble from these remarks a six-point profile of Kant's indifferentist. First, he is one of Kant's immediate predecessors, a figure whose writings, though in Kant's view wholly empty, nonetheless constitute the 'prelude' to the transformation and enlightenment of the sciences (A x). Second, he is disingenuous: he *affects* indifference to questions he in fact takes seriously. Third, and relatedly, he is not a figure for whom Kant has much respect. In addition to the implied charge of hypocrisy, witness: 'tedium' and 'to the extent that they think anything at all'. Fourth, he writes in a popular style. Fifth, he regards the belittling of metaphysics as something honourable.[38] Sixth, he nonetheless ends up embracing the very dogmatism he so volubly disdains (ibid.). However, the indifferentists are not, on the surface at least, indifferent to the *activity* of metaphysics: they despise it (or affect to do so). What they are indifferent to—or affect to be—is the question of where the *truth* in metaphysics lies.

But who exactly are these disreputable characters? Commentators have yet to reach a consensus on this question. Guyer and Wood suggest that Kant has in mind such figures as: J. A. Eberhard, J. G. H. Feder, Christian Garve, Christoph Friedrich Nicolai, and Moses Mendelssohn. Chignell and Pereboom, for their part,

---

[37] Kant had introduced the theme of seeking a 'path to certainty' in the preamble entitled 'Antithetic of Pure Reason' (A 421/B 449).

[38] One suspects that Kant has indifferentism in mind when he distances his *Critique* from 'the stale mockery [that is directed] at attempts [in metaphysics] that have often failed' (A 395).

suggest that the indifferentists are a group of thinkers in the orbit of the Göttingen philosophers, J. G. H. Feder and Christoph Meiners.[39] But while Kant may well have been referring to some of these figures—the well-connected, yet philosophically unsophisticated, Berlin publisher, Nicolai seems to be an especially likely suspect—other thinkers on each list make for a poor fit with our six-point profile. Mendelssohn, for example, could hardly be said to have affected indifference to, or contempt for, metaphysical questions in general, for he argues perfectly seriously for the immortality of the soul in his *Phaedo* of 1762. And in his essay *On Evidence in Metaphysical Sciences* of 1764 he deems the ontological argument sound.[40] Kant, moreover, having read Mendelssohn's *Morning Hours*, judged his philosophy to be not a work of indifferentism but rather the 'final accomplishment' of 'a dogmatizing metaphysics'.[41] It is clear, moreover, that Kant had far too much respect for Mendelssohn to have lumped him in with indifferentists for whom he clearly felt considerable disdain. In the first *Critique* he describes Mendelssohn as 'this acute philosopher [*Dieser Scharfsinnige Philosoph*]' (B 413); and elsewhere he refers to him as 'the excellent Moses' (10: 442), praising his manner of writing as '*gründlich*' (profound, searching, thorough) (4: 262). In his correspondence, he lists Mendelssohn, along with Garve and Tetens, as one of the three philosophers he considers up to the task of properly examining and assessing the first *Critique* (10: 346)—and in one letter—to Marcus Herz—he describes Mendelssohn as the 'most important of all the people who could explain [his] theory to the world' (10: 270). Mendelssohn was one of the four people to whom Kant sent the first edition of the first *Critique* (10: 267), and he even goes so far as to credit him with prompting an author to re-examine his own theories (10: 134). The same broad point applies to Garve. For Kant seems to have had too much respect for his intellect and honesty to have regarded him as an indifferentist. Kant lists him along with Baumgarten and Mendelssohn as one of 'our greatest analysts' (10: 198), and he expressly praises his honesty and talent.[42]

Feder, on the other hand, *was* a figure for whom Kant had little respect—at least in the wake of the former's hostile review of the first *Critique*. But he can hardly be said to have 'exchanged the language of the schools for a popular style' given that in his *Logic and Metaphysics*—a work with which, as we have seen, Kant was familiar—he speaks of God as both as an '*ens a se*', and as an '*ens independens*',

---

[39] *The Cambridge Edition of the Works of Immanuel Kant: Critique of Pure Reason*, trans. Allen W. Wood and George di Giovanni (New York: Cambridge University Press, 1998) at 714, note 5. Chignell, Andrew and Pereboom, Derk (2010), 'Kant's Theory of Causation and its Eighteenth-Century German Background: Eric Watkins (ed. and trans.), *Kant's "Critique of Pure Reason": Background Source Materials* and Eric Watkins, *Kant and the Metaphysics of Causality*', *Philosophical Review*, 119 (4), 565–91 at 573, note 12.

[40] See Moses Mendelssohn, *Philosophical Writings* (Cambridge: Cambridge University Press, 1997) at 281.

[41] Letter to Christian Gottfried Schütz, November 1785 (10: 428–9). The letter makes clear that Kant regards this work of Mendelssohn's as a paradigm of dogmatic speculative rational metaphysics.

[42] See Kant's letter to Garve of 7 August 1783.

while also enunciating the Wolffian principle that 'everything that is actual is entirely determined (*omnitudo determinatem*)'.[43] The same point about a failure to dispense with scholastic vocabulary applies to Meiners, who in his *Grundriss der Seelen-Lehrer* (1786), a copy of which Kant owned, strews scholastic terms liberally throughout his prose. It would be tedious to list them all, but they include: '*operationes mentis*', '*essentia nominalis*', '*essentia realis*', '*ingenia praecocia*', '*definitiones nominales*', and '*definitiones reales sive geneticas*'.

These, then, are unpromising candidates. By contrast, one philosopher whose name appears on neither list, but who does, I think, fit our profile rather well is no less a figure than Voltaire.

Voltaire is a good candidate for several reasons. First, the timing is right. He was one of the critical Kant's immediate predecessors, dying a celebrated figure in 1778. Second, he is plainly not someone for whose philosophical writings Kant has any discernible respect. Indeed, Kant is reported to have said that Voltaire 'does not in the least deserve the title of philosopher'.[44] Third, his work is obviously written in a 'popular' style—indeed, it is self-consciously so written, for in his *Philosophical Dictionary* of 1764 Voltaire overtly scorns the jargon of the schools.[45] Fourth, Voltaire unquestionably expresses contempt for metaphysics, as the article 'Sect' from the *Philosophical Dictionary* makes clear. 'Every sect', says Voltaire, 'of whatever kind is the rallying point for doubt and error. Scotists, Thomists, realists, nominalists, papists, Calvinists, Molinists, Jansenists, are only pseudonyms.'[46] He means, I take it, that these sects would have done better to have uniformly labelled themselves 'purveyors of error'. Nor is Descartes spared Voltaire's withering assessment, for he goes on to condemn the Cartesian system as 'a tissue of erroneous and ridiculous imaginings'.[47]

There is, then, contempt aplenty for metaphysics in Voltaire's writings, but there is also a certain (apparent) indifference to its questions. For example, in the dialogic entry on 'God' in the *Philosophical Dictionary*, the character, Dondindac, with whom Voltaire obviously sympathizes, asks: 'What does it matter to me whether [matter] exists from all eternity? I do not exist from all eternity.'[48] The implication is clear: human beings have no interest in knowing the answer to this—as it happens antinomial—question. Voltaire's (pose of) indifference is sometimes combined, in a way likely, I think, to have made Kant wince, with a certain facetious evasiveness. Imagine the Sage of Königsberg's chagrin on coming

---

[43] Feder, *Logik und Metaphysik* at 257, 387.   [44] *Blomberg Logic*, 24: 210.
[45] See *Philosophical Dictionary*, trans. H. I. Woolf (New York: Dover, 2010) at 142–5. Although the *Dictionary* was published anonymously, its authorship seems to have been an open secret. See Theodore Besterman's editorial introduction to *Philosophical Dictionary* (St. Ives: Penguin, 1972) at 6. Kant, moreover, seems to have been familiar with certain parts of the *Philosophical Dictionary*, for in the *Mrongovius* metaphysics lectures he quotes—closely, though not exactly—from Voltaire's parody of the great chain of being in the entry 'Chain of Created Beings' (29: 922).
[46] Voltaire, *Philosophical Dictionary* at 374.   [47] Ibid.   [48] Ibid. at 153.

across the following not-exactly-Wildean quip from the *Philosophical Dictionary*'s entry on 'Limits of the Human Mind':

> Ruthlessly trenchant fellow, wordy pedagogue, meddlesome theorist, you seek the limits of your mind. They are at the end of your nose.
>
> (Voltaire, Dictionary at 194)

Boom, boom!

The fifth fact making Voltaire a likely indifferentist is that, in spite of expressing contempt for metaphysical doctrines, he occasionally embraces them. In the *Dictionary* entry on 'free will', for example, having denounced all reliance upon 'antecedent principles', he proceeds to invoke the PSR in defending Locke's conception of liberty.[49] Sixth and finally, insofar as he exhibits contempt for the obscurantism of the Schools, Voltaire can at least claim to be preparing the ground for the transformation and enlightenment of the sciences. The preparation, however, consists merely in clearing the ground of scholastic clutter.

Voltaire, then, possesses all six of the characteristics that Kant associates with the indifferentists. And Kant even explicitly attributes two of them to him in a remark from his metaphysics lectures: 'All the despisers of metaphysics', he says, 'who wanted thereby [that, is by professing to despise metaphysics] to give themselves the appearance of having clearer heads, also had their own metaphysics, even Voltaire.'[50]

If the indifferentists do include Voltaire, it seems possible that Kant might have intended to include under that heading not merely (some selection of) the German popular philosophers, but also a number of the French *philosophes*.[51] And Kant's generalizations about the French, as sweeping as they are unflattering, certainly chime with such a thought. In his lectures, he describes the French as having advanced farthest in the popular style of exposition (24: 796), and he accuses them of disclaiming too much against systems, with the result that they develop a prejudice in favour of lazy trust and easiness (24: 741). He says that '[In seeking popularity] one ends up with shallowness, as is the case among the French' (24: 816).[52] And when he claims that the French 'all have popular

---

[49] Ibid. at 142–5.   [50] *Metaphysics Mrongovius*, 29: 765.

[51] A third possible group is the Scottish philosophers of common sense, especially James Beattie. Speaking of certain members of this group in the *Prolegomena*, Kant treats their premature appeal to common sense as a recent phenomenon; so, the timing is right (4: 258–9). He implies that Beattie is a 'popular wag'; so, the idea of a popular style of exposition is plausibly present (ibid.). And Kant seems not to have much respect for Beattie because he seems to be referring to him when he complains that by appealing to common sense 'the dullest windbag can confidently take on the most profound thinker and hold his own with him' (ibid.). In the context, this would appear to be a nod to Beattie's attack on Hume in the former's *Essay on Truth*.

[52] Kant must be speaking loosely here, for there is nothing in his writings to suggest that he would see these unflattering descriptions of the French as applying to the likes of, for example, Descartes, Du Châtelet, or De Mairan.

exposition' he mentions as examples Voltaire and Bernard Le Bovier de Fontenelle.[53]

For evidence that Kant would have included certain German popular philosophers among the indifferentists we need look no farther than his correspondence with Lambert:

> You complain with reason, dear sir, of the eternal trifling of punsters and the wearying chatter of today's reputed writers, with whom the only evidence of taste is that they talk about taste. However, I think [by way of consolation] that this is the *euthanasia* of erroneous philosophy, that it is perishing amid these foolish pranks, and it would be far worse to have it carried to the grave ceremoniously, with serious but dishonest hairsplitting. Before the true philosophy can come to life, the old one must destroy itself; and just as putrefaction signifies the total dissolution that always precedes the start of a new creation, so the current crisis in learning magnifies my hopes that the great, long-awaited revolution in the sciences is not too far off. For there is no shortage of good minds.
>
> (10: 56–7, Kant to Lambert, 31 December 1765)

Lambert had been discussing a Berlin-based coterie of belletrists and critics.[54] But Kant seems to regard the intellectual torpor of this particular literary circle as emblematic of a wider 'crisis in learning'—a crisis that, as Kant's remarks about the French suggest, he associates as much with the French *philosophes* as with the German *Popularphilosophen*.[55]

10.10 The indirect argument for Transcendental Idealism

Kant takes the mathematical antinomies to yield an indirect argument for Transcendental Idealism. 'If the world is a whole existing in itself', he says,

> then it is either finite or infinite. Now the first as well as the second alternative is false (according to the proof offered above for the antithesis on the one side and the thesis on the other). Thus it is also false that the world (the sum total [*Inbegriff*] of all appearances) is a whole existing in itself. From which it follows that appearances in general are nothing outside of our representations, which is just what we mean by their transcendental ideality.   (A 506–7/B 534–5)

---

[53] See *Hechsel Logic* in *The Cambridge Edition of the Works of Kant: Lectures on Logic*, ed. and trans. J. Michael Young (Cambridge: Cambridge University Press, 1992) at 417.

[54] Letter to Kant of 13 November 1765, 10: 52.

[55] It is worth noting the depths to which Kant takes intellectual life to have sunk in his time. 'We live', he says, in a reflection from the late 1780s, 'in an age that has not had its equal in the history of human understanding. The human mind has indeed probably exhausted every possibility for foolishness and madness that belongs to errant reason' (R 6215; 18: 504).

The argument may be set out as follows:

P1. If the world is a whole existing in itself (that is, an absolute whole), then it is either finite or infinite.

But P2. The world is neither finite nor infinite (by the proofs involved in the mathematical antinomies).

So,

C. The world is not a whole existing in itself (by *modus tollens*).

Premise P1 is plausibly analytic (in Frege's sense), hence knowably true. After all, 'finite' and 'infinite' are contradictory predicates on the assumption that the world is a whole existing in itself, and so P1's consequent follows from its antecedent by the law of excluded middle (which deals with contradictory predicates).[56]

One puzzling feature of this argument concerns the meaning of the phrase 'the world'. In premise P1 this phrase cannot mean 'a whole (of objects of sense) existing in itself'. For if it did, the antecedent of P1 would be an analytic truth and the argument's conclusion, accordingly, an analytic falsehood. Yet the truth of P2 requires 'the world' to have precisely this meaning because this premise rests on the arguments of the antinomies, where, if those arguments are to be valid, the world must be conceived of as a whole existing in itself—witness, for example, the fact that these arguments, insofar as they rely on reasoning by *reductio ad absurdum*, treat the predicates 'finite' and 'infinite' as if they were genuine contradictories. As it is stated, then, the argument is invalidated by an equivocation on the term 'the world'. To overcome this difficulty the argument would need to be reformulated in such a way that it appealed to a conception of the world that was neutral between Transcendental Realism and Transcendental Idealism—a conception of the world merely as the totality of objects of sense (where it is left unspecified whether this 'totality' is absolute or merely relative). For convenience, I'll use the term 'the world$_N$' for the world conceived of in this neutral way. One final point that needs to be mentioned before we offer our reconstruction concerns the law of excluded middle. For Kant, as for Baumgarten, this law incorporates a restriction on its quantifier: it concerns only possibilia, running: 'For all possibilia, S, S is P or S is non P' (where 'non P' now expresses the *contradictory* opposite of P).[57] It follows that universal instantiation applied to this law will not be a trustworthy

---

[56] 'The principle of the excluded middle <*principium exclusi medii*>', Kant says, 'does not say that a thing takes one of two disparate predicates <*disparaten praedicaten*>, but rather [one of two] contradictory opposites <*contradictorie opposita*>' (29: 810). Disparates, in the tradition, are contraries. Baumgarten treats the law similarly (*Metaphysics* §10).

[57] In the *Jäsche Logic* Kant formulates the law thus: 'Everything possible is A or non A' (9: 104, note 1); compare Baumgarten, *Metaphysics* §10.

inference if there is any doubt about whether S is a possibilium. Our reconstruction takes this point into consideration.

It runs as follows:[58]

P1. The world$_N$ exists (uncontroversial—or at least not a point of contention in the present context, [1]).

So,

L1. The world$_N$ exists either as the Transcendental Realist conceives of it or as the Transcendental Idealist conceives of it (from P1 and *LEM*).

Suppose for *reductio*,

P2. The world$_N$ exists as the Transcendental Realist conceives of it (that is, suppose that the world$_N$ = the world$_{TR}$, [1, 2])

Then, L2. The world$_N$ is either infinite or not infinite (an instance of *LEM*, [1, 2]).

So, L3. The world$_{TR}$ is either infinite or not infinite (from P2 and L2, [1, 2]).

So, L4. The world$_{TR}$ is either infinite or finite (from L3 because the world$_{TR}$ is an absolute whole, [1, 2]).

P3. The world$_{TR}$ is neither infinite nor finite (by the arguments of the antinomies, [3].)

L5. Contradiction (from L4 and P3, [1, 2, 3]).

So, by the *trustworthy* form of *reductio* (our [1] in §10.4 above):

L6. The world$_N$ does not exist as the Transcendental Realist conceives of it (from L5, discharging P2), [1, 3]).

So,

C. The world$_N$ exists as the Transcendental Idealist conceives of it (from L1 and L6, by disjunctive syllogism), [1, 3]).

The argument is valid. It rests on the uncontroversial assumption that the world$_N$ exists—P1—but also on the controversial assumption, P3. Since Kant sees the arguments of the antinomies as sound on the assumption that Transcendental Realism is true, he will also see our argument as sound on the same assumption. Accordingly, he will regard the argument as proving the conditional that if Transcendental Realism is true, it is false, which of course entails that it is false.

The final claim in the passage from A 506–7/B 534–5—the one that begins 'From which it follows'—registers a corollary of the main conclusion. Kant is

---

[58] Here I set the argument up as a *reductio* proper, rather than as a *modus tollens*. I take this to be justified by the fact that Kant does not seem to distinguish between *modus tollens* and *reductio*, treating both forms of inference as alike in being instances of indirect proof and as belonging to the 'apagogic mode' of reasoning. See, for example, 9: 52.

arguing from the assumption that the *world*—that is, the world$_N$—is nothing outside of our representations to the conclusion that *its parts*—the individual objects of sense—are nothing outside of our representations. This is a reasonable inference to draw because if some part of the world$_N$ were to be something outside of our representations (that is, not an appearance), then some object of sense would be a thing in itself. But then the world$_N$ would not be as the Transcendental Idealist conceives of it, since it is central to that conception that space and time are not features of things as they are in themselves.

If Kant's indirect argument is successful, it will establish the truth of Transcendental Idealism only as that position is understood in the first *Critique*, namely, as the combination of the view that things intuited in space and time are things whose nature is partly constituted by the contribution of human sensibility—'appearances' in Kant's proprietary sense (A 491/B 519)—with the claim that space and time are *nothing but* forms of our faculty of sensible intuition, hence not also features of things as they are in themselves (A 369). It will not, however, establish Transcendental Idealism understood as the more ambitious thesis of the *Prolegomena*, which adds to these two claims a third, namely, that the principles governing the connection of things in space and time hold merely of appearances and are not valid for things in themselves.[59]

A final point to note about the indirect argument (as we have formulated it) is that its form is suited only to the mathematical and not to the dynamical antinomies. However, as we will see in the next chapter, this does not mean that the dynamical antinomies play no role in motivating Transcendental Idealism.

10.11 The road not taken: nonsense

At the beginning of the 'Sceptical Representation' Kant claims that if the consequences of the thesis and antithesis of a mathematical antinomy were to turn out to be nonsense (*'lauter Sinnleeres (Nonsens)'*), then we would have reason to wonder whether the question under dispute might not rest on a baseless presupposition (A 485/B 513). Obviously, to say this is not to suggest that the question itself might be nonsense; and it is not clear what it would be for the *consequence* of a hypothesis to be nonsense while the hypothesis itself, being false, made sense. Nonetheless, this intriguing passage does suggest that nonsense is a live topic for the critical Kant, and so one wonders why he did not seek to resolve the antinomies by arguing that the antinomial questions are nonsense. The mystery deepens when we learn that Kant considered an approximation to this strategy in a reflection from the mid-to-late 1770s. 'Our cosmological concepts', he says,

---

[59] *Prolegomena* 4: 340 and 4: 343.

'have significance only in the world, thus none with regard to the boundary or the totality of the world'.[60] Asking questions with regard to the boundary or the totality of the world, he implies, would be like asking 'where to look for East when I am under the pole star'.[61]

Kant's comparison anticipates Wittgenstein's famous example of a string of words, not immediately nonsensical seeming, to which no truth conditions have nonetheless been attached, namely, 'It's five o'clock on the sun'.[62] Wittgenstein's (immediate) point is that, although this sentence might initially seem to make sense, on reflection it is found not to do so simply because our practices have failed to give any meaning to 'five o'clock' relative to the immediate vicinity of the sun. Consequently, there is no fact of the matter about which time it is on the sun.

Kant's point, similarly, is that, despite initial appearances to the contrary, our practices have failed to give any meaning to 'looking for East'—or, more naturally, 'facing East'—in application to a person located precisely at the North Pole. Since our full system of terrestrial directions does not extend to that location there is no fact of the matter about how to orient one's body so as to face East while standing there. Presumably, we are apt to overlook this fact simply because we—or most of us—have always been located at places on the globe at which all four terrestrial directions exist. In consequence, there is a strong illusion that 'S is facing East' uttered at either of the poles makes sense. Now, we could, of course, *give* the question a sense. We could stipulate, for example, that facing eastwards at the North Pole is a matter of facing southwards along a line of longitude running through Siberia—or through some other stereotypically 'eastern' place.[63] But to make such a move would be to tamper with the original question. If we ask whether the question can be made sense of while giving the words the meanings they have in other contexts (and without ad hoc stipulations), the answer is simply no.

Kant's claim that our cosmological concepts have no significance with regard to the boundary or the whole of the world suggests a possible way out of the antinomies. The idea would be to declare that all questions about the world as a whole—questions about its magnitude included—suffer from a defect analogous to the one of asking in which direction one must face in order to face East at one of the poles. In both cases, a crucial presupposition of the question's making sense fails to be fulfilled. In the case of the question about facing East, this presupposition is that one should be situated on (or near) the earth at some non-polar location. In the case of the questions about the size, age, and mereological structure of the world, the presupposition would be that one should be asking

---

[60] 18: 37, R 4945, 1776–8. [61] Ibid.
[62] Ludwig Wittgenstein, *Philosophical Investigations* (Oxford: Blackwell, 2001) at §350.
[63] We might similarly give the question about the time on the sun a sense by stipulating that it shall be Greenwich Mean Time (the time at the Greenwich Meridian). GMT is in fact the convention used for time-keeping aboard the International Space Station.

about a part of the world rather than the whole. In the event, however, this is not the strategy Kant pursues. Why not?

There are, I think, three main reasons. First, the envisaged way of motivating the strategy—the business about part and whole—limits its effectiveness. After all, questions about part of the world are as apt to generate antinomies as questions about the whole. We can, for example, generate antinomies by inquiring after the magnitude of that part of the temporal world-series that ended a year ago today.[64] Second, even if some other rationale could be found for the nonsense strategy, by adopting it Kant would forfeit his indirect argument for Transcendental Idealism.[65] That argument, after all, requires that, on the assumption of Transcendental Realism, the conjunction of thesis and antithesis should be contradictory rather than nonsensical. Third, the nonsense strategy could not have afforded Kant a *unitary* resolution of the antinomies; for he is committed to treating the antithesis of, for example, the third antinomy as both meaningful and true. He is so committed because this claim amounts to a statement of the causal principle, which principle he takes to express a known truth. I conclude that Kant merely toyed with the nonsense strategy—presumably rejecting it when he fully registered one or more of these points.

10.12 Zeno

The reflection discussed in the previous section suggests that the pre-critical Kant once flirted with the idea that the questions of dogmatic speculative metaphysics might be nonsense specifically because they ask concerning the whole (or, alternatively, concerning a boundary of the whole) a question that may be raised significantly only about the part. Although this idea doesn't survive into the first *Critique*, its less radical cousin does—although only in an illustrative role. This is the idea that sometimes in dogmatic speculative metaphysics we assert something about the whole that can be asserted *truly* only about the part. This idea crops up in §6 of the Antinomies chapter in a passage intended to illustrate how 'a dispute that defies a verdict can nonetheless be settled' (A 502/B 530). 'The Eleatic Zeno', Kant says,

> asserted that God (presumably this was for him nothing but the world) is neither finite nor infinite, neither in motion nor at rest, neither similar nor dissimilar to any other thing.... [I]f by the word **God** Zeno meant the universe, then he did

---

[64] I am indebted to Adrian Moore for this point.
[65] In his religion lectures Kant does appeal to the nonsense strategy without invoking the business about part and whole: 'The question of when, or how long ago, God created the world is the same as how long the year is in fathoms' (28: 1307).

indeed have to say that this universe neither is permanently present in its location (at rest) nor changes its location (moves), because all locations are only in the universe and hence **the universe** itself is in no location.... If two judgments that are opposed to each other presuppose an inadmissible condition, then despite the conflict between them (which, however, is not a contradiction proper) both of them drop out, because the condition drops out under which alone each of these propositions was to hold.   (A 502–3/B 530–1)

Having made this remark, Kant embarks on his (already examined) discussion of common application conditions and their failure to be satisfied, a discussion whose historical illustration this remark about Zeno is intended to provide. The remark thus serves as a bridge between the pre-critical line of thought alleging the nonsensicality of asking questions about the whole that can be significantly asked only about the part and the critical line of thought concerning a common application condition's failure to be satisfied—that condition being 'existing as an absolute whole'. As Kant reads him, Zeno's point is that the universe is neither (permanently) at rest nor (at some time) in motion because each claim presupposes a conception of the universe as something possessing a location. We can bring this out by glossing the relevant predicates in the obvious way:

(permanently) at rest = has a location and never changes it
(at some time) in motion = has a location and at some time changes it

Kant reads Zeno as claiming that neither of these predicates holds of the universe simply because locations are possessed only by the universe's parts. Accordingly, both the claim that the universe is moving and the claim that it is at rest are false. Like the horns of a mathematical antinomy, the two claims look like contradictories but turn out, when we attain the right conception of the universe (or world), merely to be contraries. In Kant's view, then, Zeno both constructs an antinomy of motion and resolves it by means of a strategy formally parallel to the first line of resolution of the mathematical antinomies.

11
The Third Antinomy Presented

11.1 Introduction

Of the two dynamical antinomies, the antinomy of freedom has attracted the bulk of scholarly attention—and deservedly so; for here Kant develops a novel account of how human freedom might be possible, an account whose interest extends beyond its role in resolving the third antinomy. This antinomy is also notable for the fact that Kant seems to have regarded it as the hardest of all to resolve. As late as 1776–78, for example, he is to be found declaring the problem of reconciling freedom with nature 'the only unsolvable metaphysical difficulty'.[1] For these reasons, I will focus my discussion of the dynamical antinomies on the third, though my treatment of the fourth will not be cursory.

11.2 The thesis and antithesis

The third antinomy runs as follows:

Thesis:

Causality in accordance with the laws of nature is not the only one from which the appearances of the world can be one and all derived. It is also necessary to assume another causality through freedom in order to explain them.

(A 445/B 473)

Antithesis:

There is no freedom, but everything in the world happens solely in accordance with the laws of nature. (A 445/B 473)

The thesis affirms the existence of a species of causality that is not in accordance with natural laws. The antithesis seems superficially to deny the existence of this same species of causality. Whether it in fact does so, however, depends on whether

---

[1] R 5121 (18: 98). This remark suggests that the resolution of the third antinomy may have been one of the last parts of the first *Critique* to fall into place—a point consistent with its first appearing in reflections from 1778–80 (see R 5608 and R 5611 (18: 250–2)).

or not a causality's not being in accordance with the laws of nature really entails its producing an event that is not in accordance with those laws. Kant will seek to resolve the antinomy by arguing that, surprising as it may seem, this is not in fact so.

What Kant means by 'the causality of freedom', as we will see, is an agent's power of initiating causal chains entirely off her own bat. This power is the ability either to have omitted actually performed actions or to have performed actually omitted actions (or both). If it existed, such a power would be 'absolutely spontaneous' in the sense that its exercise would not be even partially caused by something other than the agent. The spontaneity of such a power would not, however, require it to be wholly without *grounds*. Indeed, Kant, who believes (on practical grounds) that such a power does in fact exist, states that its exercise rests on 'grounds of the understanding', by which he seems to mean *reasons*—such as those provided by the moral law (A 545/B 573).

The key idea in Kant's resolution of the third antinomy is that, superficial appearances notwithstanding, the thesis and antithesis are not in fact in conflict with one another. On Kant's telling, this is because from the point of view of Transcendental Idealism 'the causality of freedom' affirmed by the thesis is distinct from the 'freedom' denied by the antithesis. I will argue that while the freedom affirmed by the thesis does not, in Kant's view, infringe the laws of nature, that denied by the antithesis would do so if, *per impossibile*, it existed. Since positing the latter kind of freedom involves denying that everything in the world occurs in accordance with the laws of nature, I will refer to it as 'libertarian' freedom. I thus use the term 'libertarian freedom' in the sense favoured by many present-day theorists of free will, namely, as entailing event-causal *in*determinism. Kant scholars, by contrast, sometimes use this term for a notion that does not have this consequence. I say more about this terminological matter in Chapter 12.

In this chapter I argue that, on Kant's view, the reason why the thesis appears to conflict with the antithesis is that, from a Transcendentally Realist point of view, to possess the power that constitutes the 'causality through freedom' requires one to possess the ability to bring about event-causally undetermined events. Incompatibilism, in other words, is, in Kant's view, the default assumption of pre-critical reason.[2] As Kant sees it, one makes such an assumption only because, when in the grip of Transcendental Realism, one overlooks the possibility that an undetermined action should be a timeless exercise of a faculty for bringing into existence an entire 'world-series'—a series of alterations or states of the world each of whose members is event-causally determined. If, however, one acknowledges this circumstance as at least an epistemic possibility, one will recognize that the thesis and antithesis do not in fact conflict.

---

[2] As we will see, Kant views the alleged compatibilisms of Leibniz and Hume as not genuine compatibilisms because not in fact making room for genuine freedom.

It is crucial to note that *insofar as he seeks to resolve the third antinomy* Kant's goal is only to show that the thesis and antithesis do not conflict in the following sense: if they cannot both be true, that is only because one or more of them is necessarily false.[3] In other words, his goal is only to show that neither claim *excludes* or *rules out* the other—something that leaves open the possibility that one of the claims should rule out *itself* through an internal inconsistency. This nuance of formulation matters because Kant denies that in resolving the third antinomy he has shown that freedom is possible. 'It must be noted carefully', he says,

> that by this discussion [of the antinomy] we have not sought to establish the actuality of freedom as one of the powers containing the cause of the appearances of our world of sense... Furthermore, we have not even sought to prove the possibility of freedom... [Rather, our aim has been] to show that that this antinomy rests on a mere illusion and that nature at least does not conflict with the causality through freedom—this was the only goal that we were able to accomplish, and it was, moreover, our sole concern.   (A 557–8/B 585–6)

Kant is right that, *as far as his resolution of the antinomy goes*, he has not established the possibility—whether real or even *logical*—of freedom (by contrast, he does take himself to have established both kinds of possibility through his moral argument for freedom). The moves he makes in resolving the antinomy do not establish the logical possibility of freedom because—as he realizes—they do not show the concept of transcendental freedom to be even logically consistent. That is to say, for all this part of his argument shows, that concept might rather contain a hidden internal contradiction, as is the case, in Kant's view, with—for example—the concept of a 'force of inertia'.[4]

This last claim is controversial. Commentators sometimes suppose that in the passage just quoted Kant is denying only that his resolution of the antinomy has established the real possibility of freedom; and some have claimed that he thinks his resolution does establish the logical possibility of freedom or at least that he aims to establish this result.[5] On reflection, however, such a line of interpretation seems unlikely to be right. For one thing, it is not at all clear how Kant could take

---

[3] My italicized qualification is important: Kant does believe that the thesis and antithesis of the third antinomy are internally consistent. However, he is prepared to affirm the consistency of the thesis only because he takes himself to have a proof of the actuality of freedom on *practical* grounds (A 534/B 562; 20: 309–10). Such a proof, however, is extrinsic to the resolution of the third antinomy. The antinomy is resolved in a way that makes use only of theoretical resources, namely, by arguing that, owing to an equivocation, the thesis and antithesis are merely contraries.

[4] For a discussion of this example, see Michael Friedman, *Kant's Construction of Nature: A Reading of the Metaphysical Foundations of Natural Science* (Oxford: Oxford University Press, 2013) at 364.

[5] Lucy Allais, for example, claims that Kant wants to show that it is at least logically possible for the causality of freedom to exist, Lucy Allais, *Manifest Reality: Kant's Idealism and His Realism* (Oxford: Oxford University Press, 2015) at 96. Though, elsewhere she attributes to Kant only the ambition to

himself to have established the logical consistency of the concept of transcendental freedom *using only the resources he employs in resolving the third antinomy*.[6] For another, the parallel Kant plainly envisages between his resolutions of the third and fourth antinomies strongly suggests that he does not take the former to establish the internal consistency of the concept of transcendental freedom. To see this we need only note that he is explicit in the fourth antinomy that his resolution of that antinomy does *not* establish the logical possibility of an absolutely necessary being; for—as far as his resolution of this antinomy goes—it remains possible that such a being should be 'in itself impossible' (A 562–3/B 590–1). If, as seems likely, Kant has uniform goals in the two dynamical antinomies, this suggests that he would similarly decline to view his resolution of the third antinomy as establishing even the logical possibility of transcendental freedom. And even if one is sceptical about this 'uniform goals' claim this last point at least establishes that his ambitions in resolving a dynamical antinomy need not extend to establishing the logical possibility of the entity for whose existence the thesis contends. A textual reason to suppose that his goals are indeed uniform across the dynamical antinomies occurs in the *Prolegomena* where Kant presents his solution of the third antinomy as entitling him to only a conditional claim, namely: '*If this sort of influence of intelligible beings on appearances can be thought without contradiction*, then natural necessity will indeed attach to every connection of cause and effect in the sensible world and yet that cause, which is itself not an appearance, ... will still be entitled to freedom, and therefore nature and freedom will be attributable without contradiction to the very same thing, but in different respects ...' (4: 344).

What Kant's resolution of the third antinomy does purport to establish, I would argue, is merely that the falsehood of neither of its horns follows from the truth of the other. In other words, it is epistemically possible that both can be true.[7] However, to establish such a claim is emphatically *not* to show that both can be true as a matter of metaphysical or even logical possibility. As an illustration of this point, consider the claims 'Grass is green' and 'Water is not H_2O'. There is no detectable incompatibility between these claims because neither one *logically* entails the negation of the other. Indeed, each might, for all one would have known prior to 1750, be true. Nonetheless, our current metaphysics and chemistry

---

show that freedom is not ruled out by determinism in the spatio-temporal world (ibid., 95, 305). I take this second claim to express the better thought.

[6] In the second *Critique* Kant claims that the internal consistency of the concept of a *causa noumenon* is assured 'by the deduction' (5: 55). He does not say whether he means the transcendental deduction or the metaphysical deduction, but either proof is plainly distinct from the moves Kant makes in resolving the third antinomy—as, of course, is the moral proof of the actuality of transcendental freedom from the principle that *ought* implies *can*.

[7] If successful, the resolution would establish that thesis and antithesis can both be true, *if* transcendental freedom is a real possibility. But Kant doesn't tend to put the point this way himself.

tell us that these claims cannot be true together—simply because the second of them cannot be true *simpliciter*.

For these reasons, it is slightly misleading of Kant to portray his resolution of the dynamical antinomies as establishing that the thesis and antithesis are capable of both being true (A 531–2/B 559–60; A 560/B 588). When he says this kind of thing he must, I think, be taken to mean merely that the falsehood of the one claim cannot be inferred from the truth of the other (compare A 562–3/B 590–1). And, on the assumption of Transcendental Idealism, this is indeed true of the claims involved in the third antinomy, so long as we understand the non-inferentiability claim as (implicitly) one about the logical consequence relation.

11.3 Terminology

The main business of this chapter is to examine Kant's arguments for the thesis and antithesis of the third antinomy. But before tackling that task we must first reach a better understanding of the claims themselves. Complicating this task is a proliferation of Kantian expressions for freedom, as well as a rather hair-raising multiple equivocation on the term 'causality'. I want to begin by scrutinizing these terms, starting with the term 'freedom'.

Kant speaks not only of 'causality through freedom' but also of 'transcendental freedom', and, on one occasion, of 'freedom in the cosmological sense'. It is not immediately clear whether he intends these three phrases to co-refer. On looking into the matter, however, one does get this impression.[8] We know that the phrases 'the causality of freedom' and 'transcendental freedom' are intended to co-refer because, while the thesis of the third antinomy affirms a 'causality through freedom', its supporting argument seeks to establish the existence of 'transcendental freedom' (A 444/B 472). And since these two phrases co-refer, the fact that Kant characterizes transcendental freedom as 'an absolute spontaneity of causes whereby they can begin on their own a series of appearances that runs according to natural laws' (A 447/B 475) suggests that he thinks of the causality through freedom as this same wholly spontaneous faculty.[9] He seems also to use the phrase 'freedom in the cosmological sense' for a wholly spontaneous causal faculty. For he says:

> By freedom in the cosmological sense, I understand the faculty of beginning a state at one's own instigation [*von selbst*], [a faculty] whose causality therefore

---

[8] We'll shortly see that this impression is *slightly* misleading.
[9] Kant speaks not just of spontaneous faculties but also of spontaneously occurring *events* (29: 861). By the latter he means events that arise from causes that are not themselves events.

does not in turn stand, in accordance with the law of nature, under another cause determining it in time. (A 533/B 561)

A faculty that begins a state '*von selbst*' does so unassisted by any other cause, and so is characterized by absolute spontaneity—the very property that Kant takes to belong to transcendental freedom.

A second terminological complication lies in Kant's inconsistent use of the unqualified term, 'freedom'. In the antithesis this term purports to refer to a faculty of bringing about events that are not event-causally determined (A 447/ B 475), and a similar use occurs at A 550/B 578. These uses thus express a 'libertarian' notion of freedom in the sense of that term common among contemporary theorists of free will (a sense according to which 'libertarian' freedom is, by definition, indeterministic). The same use of 'freedom' *sans phrase* for something whose existence entails indeterminism occurs in Kant's metaphysics lectures when he explains that the hypothesis of thoroughgoing natural necessity has the consequence that 'There is...no freedom, because in the previous state the action is already determined, and the previous time is not in my control' (*Metaphysics K2*, 28: 773). Kant makes this remark in the course of arguing that if we assume thoroughgoing natural necessity, it will follow that there is no freedom. Unfortunately, however, in these same lectures he also uses the same unqualified term for a compatibilist conception of freedom, and he does so without signalling the change of usage. Indeed, this happens in the very next sentence of the *Metaphysics K2* lecture transcript, which runs: 'That a human being has freedom cannot be proven psychologically, but rather morally' (28: 773). Since, as I will shortly argue, Kant is a determinist, and since in these lectures he clearly believes that there is a moral proof of the actuality of freedom, it follows that he must be using 'freedom' in this second remark to express a compatibilist notion. The same usage occurs again in Kant's discussion of the resolution of the fourth Antinomy at A 561/B 589.

A third terminological complication arises because Kant sometimes uses the terms 'transcendental freedom' and 'the causality of freedom' for a certain *schematic* conception of freedom that the Transcendental Realist and Transcendental Idealist flesh out in different ways. According to the Transcendental Realist, an exercise of the faculty of transcendental freedom—or, equivalently, of the causality of freedom—would be an event that is not governed by causal laws. According to the Transcendental Idealist, by contrast, an exercise of this same faculty would be a timeless 'action', hence not an event at all.[10] There turn out, then, to be no fewer than three conceptions of theoretical (as opposed to practical) freedom in play in Kant's discussion of the third antinomy. First, there is this just-mentioned

---

[10] A reminder: I will use the term 'event' as though it is analytic that events occur in time. Accordingly, I will assume that a timeless exercise of a faculty is not an event.

theoretically neutral conception of an absolutely spontaneous faculty of bringing about states or events—a faculty whose absolute spontaneity consists in the fact that its exercise—which is not necessarily an event—is caused by nothing but the agent whose faculty it is. This is a conception of freedom for which Kant is prepared to use the terms 'transcendental freedom' and 'causality through freedom'.[11] We know that there must be theory-neutral uses of these terms because they are employed both by the proponent of the thesis position—a Transcendental Realist, who uses the term 'causality through freedom' in stating the thesis of the antinomy (and the term 'transcendental freedom' in arguing for it)—and also by Kant himself (in his own voice) insofar as his resolution of the antinomy involves, *inter alia*, arguing that the thesis does not conflict with the antithesis when the notion of transcendental freedom is properly understood.

The second conception of theoretical freedom occurring in the third antinomy is the Transcendental Realist's conception of what transcendental freedom would have to be if there were to be such a thing. According to this conception, transcendental freedom is a faculty for bringing about event-causally undetermined events, a faculty whose exercise is a non-event-caused event, hence an event not grounded by the laws of nature. As we have seen, Kant sometimes uses the term 'freedom' *sans phrase* for such an envisaged indeterminism-entailing faculty of freedom. For clarity, I will refer to it as a faculty of 'libertarian freedom'.

Third, there is the Transcendental Idealist's conception of what transcendental freedom would have to consist in if there were to be such a thing. According to this conception—Kant's own, of course—transcendental freedom consists in a faculty for bringing about events that *are* event-caused and are governed by the laws of nature. But it is a faculty whose exercise is nonetheless timeless and so not an event, and which, for that reason, is not itself governed by natural laws. This faculty is 'absolutely spontaneous' in the sense that its exercise is caused by nothing except the agent whose exercise it is. Kant does not settle on a term for the faculty of transcendental freedom understood specifically as a faculty of timeless agency. On one occasion he refers to it as 'the causality of reason' (A 555/B 583), on another, as we have seen, as 'freedom in the cosmological sense'.[12] This last point suggests that our initial claim that the three terms of art co-refer must be corrected. Strictly speaking, 'freedom in the cosmological sense' refers to Kant's own specific understanding of transcendental freedom.

A final terminological complication relates to Kant's characterization of freedom in the cosmological sense as the faculty that a thing may possess of 'beginning a state from itself' (A 533/B 561). This phrasing may raise doubts about my

---

[11] In addition, he alludes once in the *Religion* to the causality *of* freedom, but only in the context 'the causality of the same' (6: 145).

[12] In his religion lectures, Kant explains reason's causality as 'the faculty to determine our will not according to matter, but rather such that it sets forth ends for the will' (28: 1309); in his correspondence, he refers to it as a 'supersensible power of causality within us' (11: 76).

understanding of cosmological freedom as a timelessly exercised faculty; for one naturally thinks of 'beginnings' as taking place in time. Kant, however, is prepared to speak of the atemporal first member of a dynamical series—the noumenal subject—as 'beginning' its effect 'from itself' (*von selbst*) (A 541/B 569).

Let's turn now to Kant's notion of 'causality'. Somewhat disconcertingly, in his discussion of the third antinomy alone Kant uses the term 'causality' with at least *five* different meanings. In some places, it purports to refer to a power possessed by an agent (see, for example, A 445/B 473), but in others, it is used, sometimes in the context of the phrase 'the causality of the cause', to refer to an exercise (or manifestation) of this same power—and this exercise is itself sometimes treated as an event in time and sometimes not.[13] Two further uses of the term occur in the proof of the thesis at A 444/B 472. In the fourth sentence of this proof the term 'causality' is used once for a certain token state whose obtaining has causal consequences, and once for a certain token state's property of having the causal consequences that it has. At A 532/B 560, finally, 'causality' is used for a *connection* of temporally ordered states. Mercifully, we will, for the most part, be concerned only with the first two of these usages, though the others should not be forgotten.

One final matter we need to consider before turning to Kant's presentation of the third antinomy is his position on the question: Which kinds of things can be causes?

11.4 Causes in Kant

In the first *Critique*, two of the four traditional Aristotelian causes—the efficient and the final—claim the bulk of Kant's attention.[14] Aristotle characterizes the efficient cause as 'the primary originator of the change and of its succession'.[15] It is 'the cause whence the motion comes'.[16] For him, as for the medieval Aristotelians, the paradigm of an efficient cause is an 'individual substance' in the sense of his *Categories*, and, in particular, a human agent—though Aristotle does not regard agents as the only kind of efficient cause.[17] Paradigm examples of Aristotle's efficient causes include: builders, sculptors, healers, and fathers.[18] Both Aristotle

---

[13] See, for example, A 445/B 473, A 533/B 561, and A 542/B 570—and compare A 203/B 248 and R 5978 (18: 413).

[14] He does, however, recognize certain causes that are neither efficient nor final, namely, so-called 'auxiliary' causes. The canon's powder is the auxiliary cause of its firing, the soldier, the efficient cause (*Metaphysics L2*, 28: 572). Compare Baumgarten, *Metaphysics* at §321.

[15] Aristotle, *The Complete Works of Aristotle*, ed. Jonathan Barnes, 2 vols. (1; Princeton, NJ: Princeton University Press, 1984). *Physics* II. 3, 194b–30–2.

[16] Ibid., 195a5–10.

[17] See R. J. Hankinson, 'Causes', in Georgios Anagnostopoulos (ed.), *A Companion to Aristotle* (Chichester: Wiley-Blackwell, 2009), 213–29 at 220–1.

[18] Aristotle, *Physics* II.3, 194b30–32, 195a30–35, 195b12–30.

and Aquinas describe these agents as causes *potentially* when they are not actually building, sculpting, etc., and *actually* when they are engaged in their characteristic activities—or, as both authors put it, when 'operating'.[19] These agent-causes are said to possess the active *powers* of building, sculpting, and so forth—powers in whose manifestation the cause's operation consists.

Kant follows Aristotle in including human agents among the efficient causes (A 546/B 574).[20] But he recognizes a wider range of entities than does Aristotle as belonging to this category. He takes efficient causes to include: (human) reason (A 317; A 550/B 578), modes of thought [*Denkungsarten*] (A 551/B 579), substances in appearance (A 213/B 260), ideas (A 317), and artefacts—for example, a ball, a glass, or a heated stove (A 202-3/B 248; A 204/B 249).[21] In addition, Kant more than once indicates that he includes *events* among the efficient causes. Since this last point is controversial, I will spend a moment on its substantiation.

In his book, *Kant and the Metaphysics of Causality*, Eric Watkins argues that Kant's 'general model of causality' is substance-causation.[22] Accordingly, he supposes that those passages in which Kant seems to be recognizing event causation as a distinct variety of efficient causation are to be explained away. Because Kant denies that we know any particular thing to be a substance$_1$, charity demands that we interpret Watkins as maintaining that Kant's general model of causality is a model of causation by 'substances' not in Kant's own technical sense—the count-noun sense of 'substances$_1$'—but in (something like) the sense of Aristotle's *Categories*. But if that is what Watkins means, I cannot follow him; for there is just too much evidence that Kant includes events, which he tends to classify as states rather than substances (A 635/B 663), among the causes. For one thing, in his discussion of the antithesis of the third antinomy he treats the series of causes as a series of occurrences: 'any occurrence [*Begebenheit*]', he says, 'always has above it still another occurrence [*Begebenheit*] as its cause'.[23] For another, he says: 'every action, as appearance, insofar as it produces [*hervorbringt*] an occurrence [*Begebenheit*], is itself an

---

[19] Aristotle, however, employs the adjective rather than the adverb, speaking of the 'potential' or 'actual' cause. See Aristotle *Physics*, II.3, 195b4-6. Commenting on this passage, Aquinas says: '[Aristotle] says that besides the causes properly so called, i.e., the causes per se and the causes *per accidens*, some things are said to be causes in potency, as being able to operate [*operari*], while other things are actually operating [*operantes*] causes. Thus, either the builder in habit or the builder in act can be called the cause of the building of a house' (Aquinas, *Commentary on Aristotle's Physics* at bk 2, lecture 6, §191).

[20] Although Kant does not speak expressly of 'efficient' causes in this context, it's clear that they are what he has in mind.

[21] See also A 211/B 256, A 212/B 258, and A 213/B 260.

[22] Eric Watkins, *Kant and the Metaphysics of Causality* (Cambridge: Cambridge University Press, 2005) at chapters 3 and 4, and especially 347-9.

[23] A 467/B 495, compare R 5978, 18: 413.

occurrence [*Begebenheit*], or event [*Ereignis*]' (A 543/B 571).[24] Since the language of 'production' is causal, this remark points to the same conclusion.

The grain of truth in Watkins's position is that Kant does include agents among the efficient causes. This matters for two reasons. First, it suggests that Kant's talk of 'the causality of the cause' is sometimes merely a terminological updating of the medieval Aristotelian notion of the 'operation' of an agent cause, something that consists in an exercise of one of the agent's faculties—which exercise is for Aristotle paradigmatically an event in time. Second, it sheds light on Kant's notion of an intelligible cause; for if one removes temporality from the notion of a faculty's 'exercise', one ends up with Kant's notion of the timeless causality of an intelligible cause—something naturally construed as an atemporal species of agent causation.[25] That notion is, therefore, arguably domesticated, for, as Derk Pereboom notes, it merely involves divesting a notion familiar from the Aristotelian tradition, namely agent causation, of one of its marks, namely, temporality.[26] How convincing one is likely to find that domestication, obviously, will depend on how central one takes temporality to be to the concept of agent causation. But here it might help to recall that one traditional example of atemporal agent causation, namely, the timeless creative act of an extra-mundane God, enjoys an unquestioned centrality in the Christian tradition after Boethius. Kant would seem to be participating in this tradition in his own theology, for in the context of a discussion of God's creative causality in the *Mrongovius* metaphysics lectures he observes that the causality of a noumenal entity is not an event (29: 924). It seems that he might, therefore, claim the precedent of this tradition in countenancing the possibility of an atemporal agent cause of a series of states in the world. Whether he would in fact be willing to claim such a precedent, however, is doubtful; for, as we will see when we discuss the fourth antinomy, he rejects the possibility of a necessary being's engaging in atemporal extra-mundane creative causality when Transcendental Realism is presupposed. If he does claim the precedent, then, it can only be in the spirit of de-fanging his opponent's objections by drawing attention to the fact that he and they have the same or similar commitments. He cannot positively argue that his appeal to atemporal causation is legitimate on the ground that his opponent's appeal is itself legitimate.[27]

In the course of discussing his solution to the third antinomy Kant describes pure reason as a 'merely intelligible faculty' (A 551/B 579), adding that 'the

---

[24] Here I agree with Chignell and Pereboom, who cite this same remark to the same effect in their critical notice of Watkins's book. See Chignell and Pereboom 'Kant's Theory of Causation' at 585.

[25] Kant sometimes refers to exercises of the faculty of intelligible causation as 'actions of reason [*Handlungen der Vernunft*]', which 'actions' he clearly regards as atemporal—hence not events—because not appearances (see, for example, R 5611; 18: 252).

[26] See Derk Pereboom, 'Kant on Transcendental Freedom', *Philosophy and Phenomenological Research*, 73 (3) (2006), 537–67 at 542 note 9.

[27] As we will see in Chapter 14, there is reason to think that Kant does in fact approve of this envisaged kind of defensive use of his opponents' commitments.

causality of reason in the intelligible character does not arise or start working at a certain time in producing an effect' (A 551/B 580). He means that the intelligible cause, which operates in the particular way it does in virtue of its intelligible character, does not operate in time. Rather, 'the intelligible cause, with its causality [that is, with its operation] is outside the series [of empirical conditions]' (A 537/B 565). In the section preceding this one, however, Kant instead locates the cause within time while still placing its causality outside of time (see A 538/B 566). From the point of view of architectonic this would seem to be the better thought; for it supplies the following principled ground for distinguishing between the third and fourth antinomies: while in the fourth antinomy both the cause and its causality are outside of time, in the third, only the causality—the operation of the cause's causal faculty—is extra-temporal.

11.5 Kant's determinism

In our brief sketch of the resolution of the third antinomy (§11.2), we portrayed Kant as committed to a version of determinism according to which every event is event-causally determined. Today, we might say that what it is for an event, *e*, to be event-causally determined is for a statement reporting its occurrence to be entailed by the statement formed by conjoining a complete statement of the laws of nature with a complete specification of the universe at a time earlier (or later) than the time at which *e* occurs. But Kant offers no such characterization in the critical period.[28] Instead, he tends to frame the deterministic antithesis either in terms of the claim that every event has a (preceding) cause (A 467/B 495) or, alternatively, as an epistemic claim of a certain kind (see two paragraphs below).[29] When he says that every event has a cause we can, I think, take Kant to mean that every event has a mundane *total* cause: a set of events jointly necessitating its occurrence.

The question arises: is determinism merely a position held by a champion of the antithesis or is Kant himself committed to this view? The question is worth asking because some philosophers either read Kant as a libertarian or view him as inconsistent in his espousal of determinism.[30] We will consider what has led

---

[28] In the pre-critical period, when he had been happy to speak of an 'initial order of the universe', he came much closer to this conception, characterizing what the context makes clear is the deterministic side of the debate as holding that 'the alterations that occur in the world are... necessary, and necessary in virtue of the initial order of the universe and the laws of nature' (*OPB*, 2: 110).

[29] By assuming that every *event* has a preceding cause Kant is, quite properly, not taking sides in the antinomial dispute over the age of the world. For this assumption is compatible with the events' having a structure isomorphic with some finite segment of the real numbers (a half-closed interval)—or even with some finite segment of the rational numbers, so long as its members form a convergent geometric series. I owe this observation to Brian Cutter.

[30] Allison, for example, speaks of Kant's 'incompatibilist or indeterminist conception of freedom' (Henry Allison, *Idealism and Freedom: Essays on Kant's Theoretical and Practical Philosophy*

some commentators to label Kant a 'libertarian' shortly, but first, in the current section, I want to argue simply that he does indeed embrace determinism in the first *Critique*.

In this work, he expresses his view that human actions are determined by appealing to the concept of in-principle prediction (this is the epistemic formulation mentioned above). 'If we could', he says,

> investigate all the appearances of [the human being's] power of choice down to the bottom, then there would be not a single human action that we could not predict with certainty, and cognize as necessary given its preceding conditions.
> (A 549–50/B 578)

Notice that in the idealized epistemic situation described here we would not, according to Kant, merely possess a precognition of future actions—something that would not entail those actions being determined as opposed to being merely groundlessly *fated* to happen. Rather, we would be able to recognize the existence of every future human action *as necessitated* by preceding conditions. (Such an ability would, of course, require not merely knowledge of the appearances of the human being's power of choice, but also exhaustive knowledge of the laws and of an earlier state of the world. I take it that Kant's omission of these details is accounted for merely by his speaking loosely here.) To claim that in the idealized conditions we would be able to cognize the necessitation of future actions (from a knowledge of the laws, our empirical character, and the past) is to imply that such events are indeed necessitated. Kant is therefore saying—or at least implying—that the relevant facts of necessitation obtain and that we would, under certain idealized conditions, be able to recognize then as obtaining. So, there is reason to think that he believes that all human actions are indeed determined in the sense of being necessitated given the past and the laws (that is to say, 'metaphysically determined').

Evidence for the stronger conclusion that he takes all *events* to be metaphysically determined is provided by the following remark:

> That all events in the sensible world stand in thoroughgoing connection in accordance with unchangeable laws of nature is an established principle of the Transcendental Analytic, and allows of no exception. (A 536/B 564)[31]

(Cambridge: Cambridge University Press, 1996) at 124). And Robert Kane, for his part, numbers Kant among 'the greatest modern defenders of libertarianism' (see John Martin Fischer, Robert Kane, Derk Pereboom, and Manuel Vargas, *Four Views on Free Will* (Oxford: Blackwell, 2007) at 4).

[31] Compare: '[I]n the sensible world everything goes according to the mechanism of nature, according to natural necessity' (29: 924).

Kant means that event-causal determinism is a consequence of the principle of the second analogy—a principle he takes himself to have established in the Transcendental Analytic.

11.6 The antinomies: lessons learned

Before considering the arguments for the thesis and antithesis positions, let us pause to remind ourselves of what we know about the antinomies in general and about the dynamical antinomies in particular. First, if the antinomies are to precipitate the kind of intellectual crisis that Kant envisages, their reasoning must be valid on the assumption that Transcendental Realism is true. Second, if they are to provide indirect arguments for Transcendental Idealism, their reasoning must, in addition, proceed from premises each of which is either a known truth or, alternatively, a falsehood known to be entailed by Transcendental Realism. Third, Kant is committed by his negative verdict on speculative dogmatic metaphysics to maintaining that the arguments for both the thesis and the antithesis are not known to be sound. Fourth, since he regards each antinomy as providing an indirect argument for Transcendental Idealism, he must suppose that the thesis and the antithesis of each antinomy *would* be genuine incompatible, if, *per impossibile*, Transcendental Realism were to be true. This last condition is met in the case of the third antinomy because if Transcendental Realism were to be true, the transcendental freedom contended for in the thesis argument could take no other form than the indeterminism-entailing libertarian freedom denied by the antithesis. With these points in mind, we may now turn to the arguments for the thesis and the antithesis of the third antinomy.

11.7 The thesis argument

The thesis argument runs as follows:

> Assume that there is no other causality than that in accordance with laws of nature. That being so, everything that happens presupposes a previous state, upon which it follows without exception according to a rule. But now the previous state itself must be something that has happened (come to be in a time in which it previously was not), since if it had existed at every time, then its consequence would not have only just arisen, but would have always existed. Thus the causality of the cause through which something happens is itself something that has happened, which according to the law of nature presupposes once again a previous state and its causality, and this in the same way a still earlier state, and so on. If therefore everything happens according to mere laws of

> nature, then at every time there is only a relative [beginning of the series] but never a first beginning, and thus no completeness of the series on the side of causes originating from one from another.[32] But now the law of nature consists just in this: that nothing happens without a cause sufficiently determined a priori. Thus the proposition that all causality is possible only in accordance with laws of nature, when taken in its unlimited universality, contradicts itself, and therefore this causality cannot be assumed to be the only one. (A 447/B 472)

Since the formal presentation of the argument is complicated, it will help to begin with a simplified, informal statement of the reasoning.

Suppose, for *reductio*, that all causality is in accordance with laws of nature (the first premise). Then suppose that an event, e, takes place (the second premise). By the first premise, e must have a cause whose operation is in accordance with laws of nature. But this means that there must be a previous state, S, from which e's occurrence (a finite time later) unfailingly follows according to a rule. But S can't always have existed; for it must precede e by a finite time. Therefore, there exists an event occurring prior to e that consists of S's coming into existence. Let's call this prior event d. By the first premise, d must have a cause whose operation is in accordance with the laws of nature. And we are embarked on a regress. By iterating this reasoning we come to posit an infinite chain of event-causes leading up to e. But now we reason that e cannot, after all, have been caused. We argue that because the chain is infinite, none of the events in e's causal history can have been *sufficiently* determined from before: the acquisition of causal efficacy by each member of the chain, since it depends on the causal efficacy of an earlier event, similarly situated, is, so to speak, regressively indefinitely deferred. And from a Transcendentally Realist point of view, this is not compatible with e's occurring (we will examine this crucial step later). We thus reach a contradiction, and so can infer the falsehood of the *reductio* premise. QED.

This is only a rough sketch of the argument. I take it that the argument Kant's actually states depends on a certain definition of what it is for a causality to be 'in accordance with the laws of nature'. If we understand a 'causality' in this context as the power of a cause to produce its effects, and think of those effects as alterations, the definition may be framed as follows:

Definition D1: A causality c is in accordance with the laws of nature just in case:

---

[32] Here I have followed Kemp Smith's rendering of '*subalternen*' as 'relative' and treated this adjective as qualifying the unvoiced but understood phrase 'beginning of the series'. Guyer and Wood's suggestion of 'subordinate cause' has no warrant in the German, for '*subalternen*' clearly qualifies '*Anfang*' rather than '*Ursachen*'. The word '*subalternen*' literally means 'subordinate' or 'non-original'. I take it that a subordinate or non-original beginning of a causal chain would be a beginning of only a proper part of that chain.

for every alteration, *e*, produced by the cause of which *c* is the power—where *e* consists in the taking on of some new state, *N*, by some object, *O*—there exists some state, *P*, of the altering object, *O*, that exists before *e* occurs and some exceptionless rule of the form "Whenever a state of kind *J* occurs in any object, a state of kind *K* follows in that object a fixed finite time *t* afterwards", where *P* is of kind *J*, and *N* is of kind *K*.

Using this definition, and departing from Kant's presentation in certain minor ways, we may provide the following semi-formal reconstruction of the argument (since the proof is lengthy, I will treat the numerous existential instantiation steps less formally than usual):

P1. There is no causality other than that in accordance with the laws of nature (*reductio* premise, [1]).

P2. Every alteration has a cause that is sufficiently determined a priori (that is, 'from before'), [2].

P3. Every event is an alteration, [3].

P4. Every cause operates through its causality, [4].

P5. No member or set of members of an infinitely regressing series of alterations can sufficiently determine any alteration, [5].

P6. Some alteration, *e*, has just occurred, [6].

L1. Alteration *e* has a cause that operates through the causality *c* (from P2, P4, and P6, [2, 4, 6]).

But then,

L2. Causality *c* is in accordance with the laws of nature (from L1, and P1, [1, 2, 4, 6]).

So, L3. There is some state, *P*, existing before *e* from which *e* unfailingly follows (within a fixed finite period of time *t*) according to a rule (from L1, L2, and D1, [1, 2, 4, 6, D1]).

Comment: L3 follows because *e* just consists in the taking on of some new state, *N*, by some object, *O*, in state *P*, where *O*'s states are governed by a rule of the kind mentioned in D1.

Sub-proof

We wish to show that *P* has not always existed.

Suppose, for *reductio*,

P7. *P* has always existed, [7].

Then, L4. *e* has always existed (from L3 and P7, [1, 2, 4, 6, D1, 7]).

Reasoning: Suppose, for *reductio*, that e has not always existed. Then e began to exist at a given moment m. But since, by P7, P has always existed, there is some time at which P exists that preceeds m by more than the fixed period t mentioned in L3. But this contradicts L3.

But then, L5. e has not just occurred (immediate from L4, [1, 2, 4, 6, D1, 7]).

Contradiction (from L5 and P6, [1, 2, 4, 6, D1, 7]).

So L6. P has not always existed (discharging P7, [1, 2, 4, 6, D1]).

Sub-proof. QED.

So, L7. P has come into existence (from L3 and L6, [1, 2, 4, 6, D1]).

L8. There is some event, d, constituted by P's coming into existence and d hasn't always existed (immediate from L7, [1, 2, 4, 6, D1]).

L9. Event d is an alteration (from L8 and P3, [1, 2, 3, 4, 6, D1]).

And so,

L10. We are embarked on an unending regress and the causal series prior to e is infinitely regressing, [1, 2, 3, 4, 6, D1].

L11. No member or set of members of the infinitely regressing series of causes prior to e can sufficiently determine the cause of e (from L10 and P5, [1, 2, 3, 4, 5, 6, D1]).

But then,

L12. Alteration e does not occur (from L11 and P2, [1, 2, 3, 4, 5, 6, D1]).

So, L13. Contradiction (from L12 and P6, [1, 2, 3, 4, 5, 6, D1]).

So, L14. There is some causality other than that in accordance with the laws of nature (from L13, discharging the *reductio* premise, P1, [2, 3, 4, 5, 6, D1]). QED.

The conclusion of this argument rests on five premises and a definition. Let's now examine these assumptions, taking them in decreasing order of obviousness. Premise P6 is, for the philosopher running the argument, simply an evident fact of experience. Premise P4 seems to be an assumption common to Kant and his Transcendentally Realist opponents. Premise P3 is more puzzling. One wonders, in particular, why Kant should take a Transcendental Realist to be committed to it. The answer, I take it, is that he sees the Transcendental Realist as no less wedded to the principle that (within the world) 'nothing comes from nothing and nothing reverts to nothing' than he is himself. Kant takes this traditional principle to be known a priori because it is a consequence of the principle of persistence of substance (A 185/B 228). He knows, of course, that his Transcendentally Realist opponent won't share his view of *why* this principle is known a priori, but Kant will not begrudge his opponent this knowledge. In premise P2, as Heimsoeth notes, the adverb 'a priori', which modifies 'sufficiently determined', has the pre-Kantian meaning of 'from before' rather than the Kantian meaning of 'independently of any particular experience'.[33] It therefore means that every alteration has a cause that is sufficiently determined by earlier causes, though this observation does not settle whether what is intended by 'earlier' is 'temporally earlier' or only 'causally/dynamically earlier'. The reason why the Transcendental Realist would accept P2 is, I think, because it follows from the causal law when it that law is construed as the Transcendental Realist construes it. I will, however, save discussion of how and why this is so—and of the related premise, P5—for later.

11.8 The antithesis argument

The much simpler argument for the antithesis runs as follows:

> Suppose there were a freedom in the transcendental sense, as a special kind of causality in accordance with which the occurrences of the world could have come about, namely a faculty of absolutely beginning a state, and hence also of absolutely beginning a series of consequences of that state; it then follows that not only will a series begin absolutely, but the very determination of this spontaneity to produce the series, i.e., its causality, will begin absolutely, so that nothing precedes through which this occurring action is determined in accordance with constant laws. But every beginning of action presupposes a state of the not yet acting cause, and a dynamically first beginning of action presupposes a state that has no causal connection at all with the cause of the previous one, i.e., in no way follows from it. Thus, transcendental freedom is contrary to the causal law, and is a connection of such a kind between the successive states of acting causes in accordance with which no unity of experience is possible, which thus cannot be encountered in any experience, and hence is an empty thought-entity.
> (A 445/B 473)

The argument features a terminological oddity: Kant begins by using the term 'causality' to refer to a special kind of faculty, but then immediately switches to using it for 'the determination of this spontaneity [that is, of this spontaneous faculty] to produce a series'. The 'determination' in question would seem to be an *exercise* of the faculty in question; for Kant describes it as an 'occurring action'. This quirk of idiom is, I think, innocuous once registered. Paying it due heed, we may reconstruct the reasoning in the argument for the antithesis as follows:

---

[33] Heimsoeth, *Transzendentale Dialektik* at 239, note 72.

Suppose, for *reductio*, that there exists a faculty of transcendental freedom. Suppose, further, that the causal law holds true. On Transcendentally Realist assumptions, a faculty of transcendental freedom can consist only in a faculty of libertarian freedom (in the sense of that term dominant among contemporary theorists of free will). For, assuming Transcendental Realism, the exercise of such a faculty must be an action that is not determined in accordance with constant laws—an action, as we might say, that is not event-caused. Therefore, either this faculty cannot be exercised at all or there would exist, after its exercise, an event that was caused by no event. But a faculty that cannot be exercised at all would be a faculty in name only. So, by the *reductio* premise, there must be some non-event-caused event. But that infringes the causal law, which requires every event to be event-caused. Contradiction. QED.[34]

Our reconstruction captures the spirit rather than the letter of the argument's reasoning. But it does have the merit of being valid. The main puzzle concerns the Transcendental Realist's appeal to the causal law. How, in Kant's view, do they know this law to be true? The answer, I will argue, is that Kant takes them to regard the causal law as a basic principle known a priori. One might be tempted to suppose instead that he sees the Transcendental Realist as attempting derive the causal law from the *PSR*.[35] The latter principle, after all, is one to whose unrestricted application the Transcendental Realist is, in Kant's view, committed (4: 339–40). But further reflection suggests that this cannot be Kant's view. For while he regards the proof of the antithesis as valid, he also regards the inference from the *PSR* to the causal law as invalid. He takes this view because he denies that one can validity infer absolute contingency from alteration. To see why he sees this inference as invalid we must briefly examine Kant's notions of empirical and intelligible (or absolute) contingency. (We'll return to these notions in Chapter 15.)

Kant calls something empirically contingent just in case it depends for its existence on another thing (or, if you prefer, derives its being from that other thing).[36] He calls something intelligibly (or absolutely) contingent at a time t just in case its non-existence at t is a real possibility. Crucially for our purposes, the version of the *PSR* that Kant attributes to the rationalists is framed only in terms of absolute or intelligible contingency (compare, A 609/B 637). As we will see in more detail in Chapter 15, it may be formulated as follows: 'Necessarily, every absolutely (or intelligibly) contingent fact (or existent object) has some cause (or

---

[34] Here I have formulated the causal law in terms of events rather than alterations. Kant would, I think, acquiesce in such a formulation—and indeed plausibly in fact does so (compare his characterization of 'the natural law' at A 542/B 570).

[35] For such a view, see Boehm, *Kant's Critique of Spinoza* at 120–1.

[36] The idea that the being of a conditioned thing is derived from that of its condition is suggested by a reflection from the mid-1770s, namely, R 4760 (17: 711).

ground) of why it obtains (or exists) rather than fails to obtain (or exist) and, if it is an existent object rather than a fact, a cause (or ground) of why it exists as it does rather than otherwise.' The causal law, on the other hand, runs: 'Necessarily, every alteration has a cause' (B3, B5). Given these understandings, the hoped-for derivation of the causal law from the *PSR* would contain the following reasoning:[37]

> We wish to prove that every alteration has a cause. Proof: Consider an arbitrary alteration e taking place at a time t. Suppose that e consists in some object O's taking on some property F at t. Then O takes on F at t. But, on the assumption that alteration entails intelligible (or absolute) contingency, the state of affairs constituted by O's being F at t is intelligibly contingent. So, by the *PSR*, that state of affairs has a cause. But the cause of that state of affairs' coming to be is just the cause of the alteration e. So e has a cause. But e was arbitrary; so every alteration has a cause. QED.

Kant would not accept this proof because he (rightly) judges the inference from alteration to intelligible contingency to be invalid (A 459–60/B 487–8).[38] And since it is unclear from what other starting point the Transcendental Realist might hope to derive the causal law, the only plausible assumption is that they suppose that the principles invoked in constructing an antinomy can legitimately include certain substantive principles that they take to be known a priori.

What is going on, I think, is this. There are two principles in the vicinity of the causal law that Kant takes to be known a priori. The first holds, roughly, that every event has a cause that is determined by natural laws, the second that whatever is given has an unconditioned condition. In Kant's view, the first principle holds of appearances, the second of things in themselves.[39] Kant further holds that the Transcendental Realist, because he takes appearances to be things in themselves, takes both principles to hold of the objects of sense. And since, according to Kant, the Transcendental Realist takes the idea of having an unconditioned ultimate condition to be a matter of being 'comprehensible' (*Begreiflich*), the second principle can be stated as requiring that every event has a comprehensible cause.

The Transcendental Realist's causal principle thus says:

Necessarily, every event has a *comprehensible* cause that is *natural*.

---

[37] The whole argument would, of course, involve reasoning about how things are at an arbitrary possible world and subsequently generalizing to all worlds. I omit those steps in order to focus on the problematic step.

[38] We examine Kant's criticism of this inference in Chapter 15.

[39] Recall our discussion of the 'cosmological syllogism' in §10.6 and see 29: 860; and R 4117; 17: 423.

A cause's being 'comprehensible' consists in its having a causality—that is, an operation or exercise of its power—that is not conditional on anything else. This feature is aptly described using the epistemic term 'comprehensible' because when a cause is comprehensible one can in principle *understand* how the effect comes about—how, in other words, it is possible. A cause's being 'natural' is a matter of the exercise of its power entailing the existence of its effect, where that entailment is grounded in exceptionless laws of nature. In the thesis and antithesis arguments, instead of speaking of a cause as being 'natural' Kant speaks of its *causality* as being 'in accordance with laws of nature', and instead of speaking of a cause as being 'comprehensible' he speaks of its being 'sufficiently determined a priori'— though the concept of comprehensibility does feature in his 'comment' on the third antinomy.

With this background in place, we can make a key observation, namely, that each horn of the third antinomy relies on a separate part of the Transcendental Realist's causal principle. The thesis argument appeals to the *comprehensibility* of the cause, which assumption it expresses in P2 and P5 taken together, while the antithesis argument appeals to the cause's *naturalness*. The proponent of the thesis in effect alleges that their opponent's position fails to respect the requirement of comprehensibility, while the proponent of the antithesis alleges that their opponent's position fails to respect the requirement of naturalness.[40]

---

[40] Comprehensibility is understood here only in the minimal and technical sense captured by premises P2 and P5. Allais complains that seeing transcendental freedom as consisting in the possession by the agent of a timelessly exercised noumenal faculty of causation makes it seem 'utterly mysterious' (Allais, *Manifest Reality* at 305). She is right that the notion of noumenal agency is, on the face of it, not fully comprehensible in the ordinary sense. And the mystery stems both from the notion of agent causation and from the notion of the timeless exercise of a faculty. However, these concerns are hardly decisive; for, first, the intelligibility of agent causation is in fact an open question. (For a defence see Randolph Clarke, 'Toward a Credible Agent-Causal Account of Free Will', *Noûs*, 27 (2) (1993), 191–203.) Second, Kant's goal insofar as he resolves the third antinomy is not to make the notion of transcendental freedom fully comprehensible *in the ordinary sense*. As I've been at pains to stress, in his resolution of the antinomy he's not even trying to establish that the concept of transcendental freedom is logically consistent. Rather, Kant is trying to show that Transcendental Idealism at least creates the epistemic possibility that freedom and nature might be compatible. He is arguing that, contrary to initial appearances, event-causal determinism does not rule out freedom. The mysteriousness of the notion of noumenal causation will only seem to constitute a problem for what Kant has to say about his resolution of the Third Antinomy if one uncharitably inflates his goals. Allais also suggests that noumenal causation will not be sufficient for explaining moral responsibility. This conception of freedom, she says 'seems to divorce it from the empirical actions for which we want to be able to hold people responsible' (Allais, *Manifest Reality* at 305). I confess I don't follow Allais's thinking here. If freedom is a timelessly exercised absolutely spontaneous faculty for bringing actions into existence, it's hard to know what the 'divorce' could consist in. On this account, after all, the agent remains the 'source' of their actions, and those actions seem to be fully under their control. Moreover, while, as Kant admits, the abstract notion of transcendental freedom does not amount to the entire content of the psychological concept of freedom, it does, on his own telling, make room for the absolute spontaneity of the action, and he is explicit that this is sufficient to provide a 'proper basis for the action's imputability' (A 448/B 476). So, for Kant at least, any account of freedom that makes room for absolute spontaneity keeps freedom and moral responsibility happily married—and the idea of timeless noumenal agency, whatever its other shortcomings, does at least make room for absolute spontaneity.

Kant supposes that you cannot consistently satisfy both components unless you are a Transcendental Idealist—and then you can only have one element for the phenomenal realm (naturalness) and another for the noumenal realm (comprehensibility).[41] Since the Transcendental Realist collapses the distinction between appearances and things in themselves, his causal principle, Kant thinks, amounts to a contradictory attempt to combine these elements. It is, in short, a contradictory consequence of Transcendental Realism.

In the 'comment' on the antithesis of third antinomy Kant portrays the defender of the antithesis position as offering what we might call a 'good-company defence' of their rejection of the comprehensibility requirement. The defender argues that the price of insisting on the comprehensibility requirement is that one will have to reject the idea of basic forces and even of change itself (A 450–1/B 478–9). The implication is that this price is too high to be worth paying. The discussion thus brings out the centrality to the thesis position of an insistence on the comprehensibility requirement. That requirement also looms large in a presentation of (what is in effect) the thesis position that occurs in the *Metaphysics L1* lectures. There Kant says:

> Without a first cause <causa prima>, the series of subaltern causes <causarum subalternen> is not adequately enough determined for reason to derive the effect <causatum>. It is thus not comprehensible [*begreiflich*] to reason; that is: [reason] cannot completely comprehend it, [it cannot completely comprehend] how the existence of a thing, insofar as it is grounded only in subaltern causes <causis subalternis>, is possible – But, although we cannot comprehend the infinite regression <regressum in infinitum>..., we still also cannot say that such [a thing] is apodictically impossible; [rather we can] only [say] that we cannot comprehend such [a thing] without assuming a first cause <causatum primum>.
> (28: 197)

At this pre-critical stage, then, Kant holds that an infinite causal regress—a regress to infinity—would be incomprehensible—or at least not fully comprehensible. But he does not conclude that it would therefore be impossible. In the first *Critique*, by contrast, he comes to hold that in the empirical realm there is no such thing as a regress to infinity but only a regress *ad indefinitum*—or at least he comes to hold that this is so if we begin with an object that is not given within determinate, surveyable boundaries. And he further holds that in the noumenal realm, by contrast, any given thing must have an ultimate unconditioned condition.

---

[41] Kant, I take it, is committed to maintaining that in the empirical realm the demand for comprehensibility is misplaced: the world isn't an actual infinity, and so there's only the permanent possibility of finding further grounds, not an ultimate ground.

Since Kant regards the premises relied on in the proofs of the thesis and antithesis of the third antinomy as including no falsehoods except such as are entailed by Transcendental Realism, he might have resolved the antinomy simply by arguing that comprehensibility and naturalness should be rejected along with the Transcendental Realism from which they follow. In practice, however, he grants these assumptions for the sake of argument and seeks to resolve the antinomy by discerning in its thesis and antithesis an equivocation—one made possible only by Transcendental Idealism—that reveals these claims to be not in conflict after all. Kant is particularly forthright about this point in the *Real Progress*, where he remarks that the opponents in the dynamical antinomies might well have both been right 'if only they had first reached agreement about the meaning of the question' (20: 327). They are, in other words, talking past one another.

12
The Third Antinomy Resolved

12.1 Introduction

Kant seeks to resolve the third antinomy by rejecting a certain assumption that seems inevitable in a Transcendentally Realist setting: the assumption, namely, that an exercise of a genuinely spontaneous faculty of freedom would be an event in time. It is this assumption that makes the thesis and antithesis appear to be contradictories. Calling the spontaneous faculty in question 'reason', Kant says:

> Since reason itself is not an appearance and is not subject at all to any conditions of sensibility, *no temporal sequence takes place in it* even with regard to its causality, and thus the dynamical law of nature, which determines the temporal sequence according to rules, cannot be applied to it.
> (A 553/B 581, emphasis added)

Kant makes the same point more explicitly in a reflection from 1783–84. In the mechanism of nature, he says, the causality of the cause of an occurrence 'is itself an occurrence'; but when the cause is a thing in itself 'the causality is not itself an occurrence, for it does not arise in time' (R 5978 (18: 413)). By raising the possibility that reason's causal power might be exercised atemporally Kant hopes to persuade us that, for all we know to the contrary, a spontaneous causal faculty might co-exist with a fully deterministic temporal realm. Were things to turn out this way, he says, 'freedom and nature, each in its full significance, would both be found in the same actions, simultaneously and without any contradiction, according to whether one compares them with their intelligible or their sensible cause' (A 541/B 569).

Kant regards the thesis and antithesis of the third antinomy as non-conflicting (in the sense explained in the previous chapter) because he thinks that the 'causality through freedom' affirmed by the thesis is distinct from the 'freedom' denied by the antithesis. The former, he supposes, is a timelessly exercised spontaneous causal power, while the latter—if it existed—would be a temporally exercised spontaneous causal power—a power whose exercise would therefore be an event that lacked an event-cause. Since the latter power could be exercised only if something were to take place that was *not* in accordance with the laws of nature, it would count in today's terms as a faculty of 'libertarian freedom'.

In the previous chapter I argued that Kant is a determinist. In the present one I will argue that he is also a compatibilist—albeit one of an unfamiliar kind.[1] In today's terms, he is, I would further argue, a 'soft determinist'—though, again, one of a rather unfamiliar kind. Since I am understanding *determinism* to entail that all *events* are event-caused, and since I am understanding events as essentially temporal, I speak at this stage simply of 'Kant's commitment to determinism' rather than (redundantly) of his 'commitment to determinism *within the phenomenal realm*'. Later we will ask whether a notion of determinism could be framed on which it made sense to think of determinism as holding within the realm of things in themselves.

If I am right that Kant is a determinist, he must be conceiving of the agent's timeless causing of a phenomenal action as amounting to the timeless production of the whole series of causally linked events leading up to, and flowing from, that action. Given determinism, we can think of this 'noumenal choice'—as it tends to be called in the literature[2]—as the choice either of a fully specified state of the universe at a given time, or of the natural laws (given some such state), or of both.[3]

Lucy Allais has astutely observed that whether such a conception is in fact compatible with Kant's other commitments is not immediately clear.[4] The problem is that from the Transcendental Idealist's perspective there is simply no such thing as the *totality* of laws and no such thing as a *complete* description of the universe at a given time. In consequence, it would seem that Kant can neither think of a noumenal choice as a choice of one of these things nor avail himself of the standard 'textbook' characterization of determinism, which makes use of these ideas. This is an excellent point and one that deserves to be more widely noted. I'm inclined to think, however, that Kant would have regarded himself as able to get around the problem by appealing to counterpossibles—that is, to counterfactuals in which the antecedent is not just false, but impossible. He could, for example, say that an event is determined just in case it could be predicted by a being who, *per impossibile*, knew the totality of laws and the state of the world at a given time. Indeed, this is precisely the kind of formulation for which he reaches when affirming his deterministic conception of temporal human actions in the second

---

[1] On this last point I agree with Wood. Allen Wood, 'Kant's Compatibilism', in Allen Wood (ed.), *Self and Nature in Kant's Philosophy* (Ithaca, NY: Cornell University Press, 1984), 73–101 at 75.

[2] Like many other commentators, I will permit myself to speak of a 'noumenal choice' even though in the first *Critique* Kant in fact speaks only of noumenal *causation*. This seems permissible because elsewhere Kant does portray the faculty of freedom as a faculty of choice. For example, in the *Metaphysics Mrongovius* he says: 'Freedom is the faculty of choosing [*das Vermögen, das zu wahlen*] that which is good in itself and not merely good as a means' (29: 899).

[3] As Watkins notes, evidence that Kant sometimes thinks of the causality of freedom as a capacity to produce the laws of nature occurs in the *Prolegomena*, where he maintains that if the rational being brings about effects in the sensible world through its faculty of reason, then 'reason is the cause of [the] natural laws and is therefore free' (4: 346). See Watkins, *Kant and the Metaphysics of Causality* at 303.

[4] In conversation. I am grateful to Allais for permission to discuss these details of her unpublished view.

Critique. There, he says: 'If it were possible for us to have such deep insight into a human being's cast of mind... that we would know every incentive to action... as well as all the external occasions affecting them, we could calculate a human being's future conduct with as much certainty as a lunar or solar eclipse' (5: 99). The next sentence confirms the status of this claim as a counterpossible: 'If, *that is to say*, we were capable of another view, namely an intellectual intuition of the same subject' (ibid., emphasis added). On the reasonable view that Kant takes us to possess our forms of sensibility essentially, this must be a counterpossible.[5] And since Kant is prepared to appeal to counterpossibles, he would seem to be able to conceive of a noumenal choice as the choice of a total world history and a total set of laws if, *per impossibile*, such totalities existed. Accordingly, he would seem to be able to characterize determinism in accordance with the textbook definition when supplemented with the needed '*per impossibile*' riders.

12.2 Empirical and intelligible character

Treating the empirical subject (that is, human being) as an efficient cause (A 539/B 567), Kant distinguishes between this subject's 'empirical' and 'intelligible' character. Whereas the former, existing within time, is entirely shaped by the human being's biography (and its causal antecedents), the latter, being outside of time, is not so shaped.[6] Kant treats empirical characters as capable of being discerned through powers and capacities (A 546/B 574). And an agent's empirical character is, in turn, held to be the 'sensible sign [*sinnliche Zeichen*]' of their 'intelligible character', which is the empirical character's 'transcendental cause [*Ursache*]'.[7] Somewhat surprisingly, Kant seems to maintain that insofar as the intelligible character is indicated by the empirical character we can *know* or *cognize* something about it. For he says that this intelligible character is 'wholly unknown [*unbekannt*] *except* insofar as it is merely indicated [*angegeben*] through the empirical character as its sensible sign' (A 546/B 574, emphasis added). It is possible that he means that we know merely the *existence* of the intelligible character. But it is also possible that his phrasing here is infelicitous and that he is merely intending to convey that we have *justified beliefs* about the nature of the human being's intelligible character—beliefs that are justified by a non-deductive

---

[5] I noted in Chapter 4, §4.3, that in the *Mrongovius* metaphysics lectures Kant flirts with the idea that these forms are not essential, but I also argued that this is *just* a flirtation—one that is broken off as soon as the mistake motivating it is corrected.

[6] Somewhat misleadingly, Kant describes the *empirical* character as 'the ultimate basis' of the appearances constituting the human being's behavior (A 546/B 574). Presumably he does not mean that the empirical character cannot itself be explained by appealing to its event-causal history. What he must mean, I think, is rather that the human being's actions can be fully explained by appealing to this history and without appealing to their intelligible character.

[7] A 546/B 574; cf. A 551/B 579.

inference from effect to cause. These beliefs—or so this line of interpretation would have it—enjoy what Kant elsewhere terms 'empirical certainty' while not amounting to knowledge proper. One reason to think that this may indeed be what is going on is that we know on independent grounds that Kant is prepared to use locutions suggestive of cognition when speaking of the results of non-demonstrative inferences from effects to their causes. He speaks, for example, of our cognizing—the verb is *'erkennen'*—the existence of magnetic matter from our perception of iron filings (A 226/B 273). At any rate, the main emphasis of Kant's remark would seem to fall on the negative point that we can have no *direct* knowledge of the human being's intelligible character (compare A 540/B 568).

Kant maintains that a human being's empirical character determines every one of their voluntary actions (A 553/B 581). This seems to suggest—and has suggested to some commentators—that one's empirical character mediates between one's intelligible character and the empirical causal series in which one's actions are embedded.[8] Such a reading is not unmotivated, for Kant does at one point characterize the empirical character as the 'sensible schema' of the intelligible character, and he treats a schema as a mediating representation (A 138/B 177). Nonetheless, the following remark stands opposed to this otherwise compelling consideration: 'Every action, irrespective of the temporal relation in which it stands to other appearances, is the *immediate* effect [*unmittelbare Wirkung*] of the intelligible character of pure reason' (A 553/B 581, emphasis added). This seems to be about as clear a piece of evidence against the mediation picture as one could ask for. I am therefore going to take it as my guide. But, then, we need to ask: if the empirical character doesn't play a mediating role, why does Kant nonetheless single it out as a seemingly privileged part of the event-causal chain in which one's actions are embedded? This is by no means clear, but one possible answer runs as follows.

A human being's empirical character is something to which *in practice* one would appeal in giving empirical explanations of, and making predictions about, their behaviour. *In principle*, my actions could be explained without reference to my empirical character, but since predictions of human behaviour that invoke a character are—to put it mildly—easier to make than predictions that seek to derive that behaviour from more fundamental natural laws together with a considerably more complete specification of an earlier state of the world, *in practice* it will be necessary to appeal to a human being's empirical character in explaining their actions.[9] Of course, empirical characters would be no less useful

---

[8] For such a reading see Wood, 'Kant's Compatibilism' at 92, and Watkins, *Kant and the Metaphysics of Causality* at 327.

[9] Kant refers to an efficient cause's empirical character as a *law* of its causality (A 539/B 567), and, as we have seen, he treats the human being's powers and capacities as things through which their empirical character can be discerned (A 546/B 574). It might be better, however, to think of an efficient cause's empirical character as, more precisely, a set of dispositions expressible through a law—those

for predicting and explaining the behaviour of inanimate objects; so we should not be surprised that Kant regards these objects as possessing them: 'All natural things', he says, 'have an empirical character' (A 546/B 574).

12.3 What kind of freedom?

I am supposing that the freedom for which Kant wishes to make room in the third antinomy is specifically *human* freedom, which faculty, after all, is one of the three supersensible objects which hold Kant's fascination (29: 947). Ameriks demurs, arguing that nothing so specific has been contended for.[10] I disagree; for there is, I think, ample evidence that in seeking to resolve the third antinomy Kant is trying to make room for specifically human freedom. First, he describes the 'natural antithetic' that constitutes the antinomies as a new phenomenon of 'human reason'.[11] Second, in his summary of the antinomies at A 463/B 491, he presents the question about freedom as being whether 'in my actions *I am free* or, like other beings, led along the course of nature and fate' (emphasis added). It is not implausible to think that here 'I' refers to a representative human being. Third, Kant treats the thesis position of the third antinomy as asserting specifically that 'the human will is free' (A 475/B 503). And fourth, in the first *Critique*'s table of contents—and more specifically in the headings announcing the topics of the appendix to the Transcendental Dialectic—Kant presents the Transcendental Dialectic as a whole as a natural dialectic of specifically *human* reason.

Ameriks does not say which kind of freedom he takes Kant to be endeavouring to make room for in resolving the third antinomy, if not the human kind, but if he is thinking of divine freedom, then his worry can be addressed. For Kant is plainly representing his resolution of the third antinomy as turning on the idea that *reason* is not subject to any conditions of sensibility (A 553/B 581). This suggests that divine freedom is not in fact under consideration simply because Kant is—surprising as it may sound—committed to denying that God has a faculty of reason. He treats reason, after all, as a sub-species of thinking (29: 888–9) and he denies that God can, strictly speaking, think (B 71; 28: 1017).

---

dispositions, namely, that would be invoked by a shallow dormative-virtue style explanation of the patterns in a thing's behaviour. As Stephen Mumford observes, such explanations are not trivial so long as they are construed as answering the kind of question modelled by: 'Why, whenever opium is taken, does sleep follow' rather than by 'Why does opium make one sleep?' (Stephen Mumford, *Dispositions* (Oxford: Oxford University Press, 1998) at 138.

[10] Ameriks, *Interpreting Kant's Critiques*, 167.
[11] A 407/B 433; and compare the heading at A 669/B 697 for a similar take on the Dialectic as a whole.

12.4 Another indirect argument for Transcendental Idealism

I take Kant's resolution of the third antinomy to constitute an independent indirect argument for Transcendental Idealism. In taking this view, I depart from Allison, who maintains that only the resolution of the mathematical antinomies is intended to provide such an argument.[12] On the face of it, however, Allison's claim is at odds with two remarks in the first *Critique*. First, in §7 of the Antinomies chapter Kant says:

> The above proofs of the *fourfold* antinomy... were not deceptions [*Blendwerke*] but well grounded, that is, at least on the presupposition that appearances, or a world of sense comprehending all of them within itself, were things in themselves. (A 507/ B 535, emphasis added)

Second, in a note Kant added to his own copy of the A edition, he says that 'in the case of *each* antinomy' it must be shown that if objects of the senses are assumed to be things in themselves, then 'no resolution of this conflict would be possible'.[13]

The main difference between the mathematical and dynamical antinomies lies not in their differential capacity to provide an indirect argument for Transcendental Idealism, but rather in their different styles of resolution. The opposed propositions in each mathematical antinomy are to be shown to be contraries, those in each dynamical antinomy (loosely speaking) sub-contraries.[14] In his correspondence with Christian Garve, Kant mentions a more subtle point of contrast between the two pairs of antinomies:

> If one takes appearances to be things in themselves and demands of those [appearances] the **absolutely unconditioned** in the series of conditions, one gets nothing but contradictions.... On the other hand, if one takes a **thing in itself... to be an appearance**, one creates contradictions where none are necessary, for example, in the matter of freedom.[15]

---

[12] Allison, *Kant's Theory of Freedom*, 25.

[13] E CLXIX (23: 40), emphasis added, and compare *Prolegomena*, 4: 340–1 and A 505/B 533.

[14] A further difference is that in the mathematical antinomies Kant is committed by his Transcendental Idealism to denying the validity of the *reductio*-style reasoning they employ; in the dynamical, by contrast, he can allow that the *reductio*-style reasoning is valid. For when p and q are sub-contraries—claims that can both be true but cannot both be false—the inference from q's falsehood to p's truth is valid. Kant confirms this last point himself in §50 of the *Jäsche Logic* (9: 117). Note, incidentally, that in (apparently) endorsing this inference, Kant is presupposing the principle that if p is not false then p is true, hence, by contraposition and double-negation elimination, also to the principle that if p is not true then p is false. In consequence, he seems to be committed to the principle that every proposition (or judgment) is either true or false ('no truth value gaps'). This is not yet the principle of bivalence, for that principle additionally holds that no proposition is both true and false ('no truth value gluts'). And we saw at the end of Chapter 10, §10.3, that Kant seems to be unwittingly committed to truth value gluts.

[15] Letter to Garve, 7 August 1783, 10: 341, note **.

Here Kant is registering an aspectual difference between the kinds of mistake that generate the two species of antinomy. If we take appearances (that is, things in space and time) to be things in themselves, we generate the mathematical antinomies. If we take things in themselves—freedom or a necessary being—to be appearances, we generate the dynamical ones.

12.5 Moral responsibility, moral growth, and rational blame

Ralph Walker attributes to Kant the view that in order for my noumenal self to have freely chosen anything it is required that it should have 'freely chosen the entire causal series that makes up the phenomenal world'. He concludes that for Kant

> my responsibility extends far beyond my own character: I can be blamed for the First World War, and for the Lisbon earthquake that so appalled Voltaire. Gandhi is no less guilty than Amin of the atrocities of the Ugandan dictator.[16]

As if this were not dispiriting enough, Walker goes on to claim that taking Kant's view of noumenal freedom seriously leads to 'the complete collapse of our ordinary system of moral evaluations'.[17] Fortunately however, this gloomy assessment is premature. For, as Benjamin Vilhauer notes, even if Kant's position entails that my noumenal self must be causally responsible for the events that must take place if I am to have the empirical character that I noumenally choose to have, it does not follow that it must be morally responsible for those same events.[18] Indeed, it seems reasonable to suppose that in some cases the noumenal agent's information will be sufficiently limited that they would be entirely unaware that some past atrocity constituted an essential part of the causal sequence (or cone) of events leading up to some otherwise morally unproblematic chosen action. In such a case the agent would seem not to be morally responsible for that atrocity—or rather they would be off the hook provided that they could not be reproached for acting recklessly in view of their ignorance of the details of the sequence of events they were realizing. But since the human agent's choice is a forced one between chains of events concerning the content of each of which the agent has only a limited knowledge, the charge of recklessness would be a hard one to make stick.[19]

---

[16] R. C. S. Walker, *Kant*, ed. Ted Honderich (*The Arguments of the Philosophers*; London: Routledge, 1978) at 149.
[17] Ibid.
[18] Benjamin Vilhauer, 'The Scope of Responsibility in Kant's Theory of Free Will', *British Journal for the History of Philosophy*, 18 (1) (2010), 45–71 at 48–9.
[19] I am grateful to David Schroeren for getting me to think about this problem.

In cases in which one does know that one's action causally requires, say, an atrocity to have occurred (e.g., Lincoln's choosing to make the Emancipation Proclamation, which presupposes the atrocity of slavery), the following consideration may be of help. Most of us don't believe we can change the past. I believe that whether I get up this morning or stay in bed, it won't make any difference to the question whether the evil of American slavery happened. So, in making whatever decision I do make I don't take myself to be choosing a history where the institution of American slavery existed *as opposed to one where it did not*. I take myself to be choosing between two actions that will occur in a world whose past contains American slavery. And that is so even if one of the alternatives between which I am choosing—the one left unchosen—would, unbeknownst to me, in fact have occurred only in a world in which the laws and past were such as to preclude slavery. If one supposes that the moral responsibility one shoulders is appraised according to what one takes oneself to be doing then, so long as I don't take myself to be choosing a past, I will seem to be morally off the hook for noumenally producing a world-history in which slavery occurred even if I might, unbeknownst to me, have chosen an alternative where it did not. Indeed, the failure to choose an alternative world-series in which American slavery did not exist (a world-series resembling the actual one in other respects) would seem to be something for which I might be held accountable only if, first, I somehow knew—or had good reason to believe—that my rejected action required a slavery-free past (and an otherwise similar world-history) and, second, I *did* believe (in Kantian fashion) that I had the power to realize a past differing from the one that actually obtains. But given the explosive complexity of the problem of retrodiction, such a situation is hardly likely to arise.

Allen Wood worries that Kant's timeless conception of free, morally responsible choice leaves room for neither moral improvement nor moral progress.[20] Derk Pereboom shares Wood's general concern but focuses on a special case of the problem, namely, on the question how, compatibly with Kant's views, I could be capable of undergoing a genuine *moral conversion*.[21]

These questions deserve a response. They can, I think, be addressed by maintaining that what it is for a noumenal self to grow morally is just for it to produce an empirical series in which, over time, its corresponding empirical self progressively strengthens its disposition to act in accordance with (and for the sake of conformity with) the moral law. Such an answer might be motivated by the formal resemblance it bears to the view that what it is for God to be omnipresent is for Him to 'have locations' everywhere in a way that would involve not His *occupying* space but rather His *acting* everywhere insofar as He sustains every part of the universe—or, at least, His being capable of acting anywhere insofar as he can

---

[20] Wood, 'Kant's Compatibilism' at 97.   [21] Pereboom, 'Transcendental Freedom' at 566.

intervene wherever he wishes to perform a miracle.[22] On such a view, although God is not spatial in Himself, He can nonetheless be attributed the seemingly spatial predicate of 'omnipresence' in virtue of the reach of His causal powers. The present proposal is similar insofar as it combines the concession that the noumenal agent is *not* temporal in itself with the insistence that it can nonetheless be attributed the seemingly temporal predicate of moral growth in virtue of the character of its causal powers. The noumenal self is capable of growing morally, the thought would run, simply because it can realize a series of states of the world in which later stages of its empirical self are more steadily inclined than earlier ones to act in accordance with—and for the sake of—the moral law. This answer may not satisfy everyone, but it ought to satisfy the Christians among Kant's Transcendentally Realist opponents—at least insofar as they are satisfied with the parallel move when it is made in connection with divine omnipresence.

Our second question is whether Kant's view can do justice to our practice of apportioning moral blame. The problem arises in connection with a famous passage in which Kant discusses our practice of blaming a person for a malicious lie in spite of the fact that their actions, including the lie itself, are believed to be empirically determined (A 554–5/B 582–3). In such a case, Kant says, although we believe the action to be determined by prior causes:

> we nevertheless blame the perpetrator.... [W]e presuppose that it can be entirely set aside how that course of life was [constituted], and [also assumed] that the series of conditions that transpired might not have existed, but rather that this deed could be regarded as entirely unconditioned in regard to the previous state, *as if* with that act the perpetrator had started a series of consequences entirely from himself.   (A 555/B 583, emphasis added)

Anticipating the question with what right we could possibly presuppose such a thing if determinism is true, he continues:

> Our blame is based on a law of reason whereby we regard reason as a cause that, irrespective of all the above-mentioned empirical conditions, could have, and ought to have, determined, the agent to act otherwise.   (A 555/B 583)

Kant's picture seems to be the following. Our blame is justified by our knowledge that the noumenal agent could have chosen—or strictly speaking, caused to obtain—an empirical series in which the misdeed did not occur. This knowledge is afforded by fact that we know the agent to be subject to the moral law—a law that we also know requires them to have done otherwise. It is our knowledge of

---

[22] Aquinas's claim that God is 'in all things by His power, inasmuch as all things are subject to his power' (*Summa Theologiae*, 1. 8. 3) is capable of being read in either of the two ways just indicated.

this moral ground that entitles us to assume that the agent is possessed of practical freedom—understood as 'the independence of the power of choice [*Willkür*] from compulsion by impulses of sensibility' (A 534/B 562). As we will see in the next section, this in turn entitles us to assume that the agent is possessed also of transcendental freedom, and so is fully responsible for their actions. As I read him, Kant is saying that, since we know agents to have practical freedom, we have licence, when morally appraising them, to treat them *as if* they had libertarian freedom—a kind of freedom whose exercise entails the falsehood of determinism. More fully, it is legitimate for us to treat someone who could not have done otherwise *given the past and the laws*, but who could have done otherwise *simpliciter*, *as if* they could have done otherwise *given the past and the laws*. Our so treating them is legitimate, Kant supposes, precisely because, possessing practical freedom, they could have done otherwise *simpliciter*—something that would, on Kant's view, have required bringing about a different world-series from the one that actually obtains.

Pereboom regards Kant's position in the 'malicious lie' passage as both philosophically flawed and morally unacceptable. 'But', he objects,

> imagine the offender protesting that he was determined by natural causes to act as he did. Would the following reply count as morally acceptable? "Although we have no evidence of your transcendental freedom, and although we cannot show that such a power of agency is metaphysically possible, yet our belief that you are free in this way involves no inconsistency, and we need to have this belief in order to justify treating people like you as blameworthy and deserving punishing". It would not. Holding an offender blameworthy, expressing one's anger towards him, and depriving him of life or liberty all tend to be harmful to the offender. In general, if one aims to harm another, then one's justification must meet a high epistemic or theoretical standard—much higher than the standard of consistency that Kant advocates...[23]

Pereboom is of course right to reject such an unpromising line of thought. But it is, I think, not the line of thought that is expressed in the 'malicious lie' passage. There, Kant is concerned not so much with justifying our practice of holding agents blameworthy for their morally impermissible actions (and so forth), as with explaining the persistence of that practice in the face of the obvious fact that moral judgers, emoters, and issuers of blame are often well aware of the recent causal history of a wrong-doer, and often regard that causal history as entirely shaping the wrong-doer's character. Kant is suggesting that while knowing how the agent's character was shaped by forces outside of their control we can still muster the

---

[23] Pereboom, 'Transcendental Freedom' at 563–4.

attitude of blame towards them—and regard that attitude as apt—because we employ a regulative principle that bids us to regard the agent *as if* they possessed libertarian (that is, indeterminism-entailing freedom). Kant supposes that we are justified in adopting this 'as if' stance precisely because the agent in fact possesses practical freedom. But he is well aware that that ordinary agents have not reached this conclusion about the justification of their practice of blame for themselves. Instead, they operate with a regulative principle that is, by Kant's lights, in fact justified, without knowing that it is justified.

Pereboom's closing reference to Kant's 'standard of consistency' leads one to suspect that his objection might arise from a failure to tease apart two separate strands in Kant's discussion. On the one hand, for the purposes of resolving the third antinomy, and thereby buttressing his indirect argument for Transcendental Idealism, Kant needs to establish the compatibility of the thesis and antithesis when Transcendental Idealism is assumed. On the other, for the purpose of justifying our practices of praise and blame—including our practice of treating an agent whose actions are event-causally determined *as if* they had libertarian freedom—he needs to show that rational agents possess the capacity to have omitted their actually performed unlawful actions (and to have performed their actually neglected duties). The grain of truth in Pereboom's remark is that we have no *theoretically based* grounds for supposing that an agent possesses such a capacity. But that does not mean we have no *practical* grounds for doing so, and so it does not mean that our practice of treating the agent *as if* they had such a capacity is unjustified. On the contrary, that practice in Kant's view receives its justification from a practical or moral argument for the thesis that the agent possesses a capacity to act in accordance with the moral law. Since that argument is central to Kant's defence of the rationality of our practices of praise and blame, and, by implication, also to his account of the aptness of our moral attitudes and emotions, it seems worth examining closely.

12.6 The moral argument for freedom

The moral argument is most fully articulated in the second *Critique*, where Kant claims that the 'actuality [*wirklichkeit*]' of freedom 'reveals itself through the moral law' (5: 3–4).[24] However, there is reason to think that Kant had already arrived at this view—perhaps somewhat inchoately—in the first *Critique*. For there, in reflecting on the resolution of the third antinomy, he says 'the action must be possible under natural conditions, if the ought is directed to it' (A 548/B

---

[24] Compare 5: 97–8 and also Kant's claim that we 'know' (*kennen*) our freedom insofar as we know that we are not '*necessitated* to act through any sensible determining grounds' (*Metaphysics of Morals*, 6: 226). Presumably, the reason why we know this is that we know we can always act morally.

576).²⁵ The qualifier 'under natural conditions' would seem to be supplied out of deference to the fact that the moral law can obligate us to do only what is physically possible: it cannot mandate a miracle. This limitation, however, is compatible with the moral law's commanding a spontaneous noumenal choice, for such a choice will, given determinism, bring about no event lacking a natural cause.

The point that, already in the first *Critique*, Kant takes us to know that we have transcendental freedom is further confirmed by something he says when spelling out the consequences of his view that an agent's intelligible character is efficacious in the empirical world. He affirms categorically that '[reason] therefore acts freely, without being determined dynamically, whether by external or internal grounds temporally preceding it in the chain of natural causes' (A 553/B 581). If in the first *Critique* Kant had wished to remain agnostic about whether we actually possess transcendental freedom, this would have been a highly misleading thing for him to say.

Later in the first *Critique* Kant tells us that pure reason

> contains—although not in its speculative use but still in a certain practical, viz., the moral, use—principles of the **possibility of** experience, viz., of the experience of such actions as **could** be encountered in accordance with moral prescriptions in the **history** of the human being. For since reason commands that such actions ought to occur, they must also be able to occur. (A 807/B 835)

The epistemological upshot is that our knowledge of standing under the moral law (and of its content), when combined with our knowledge that *ought* implies *can*, allows us to know certain things about what we must be capable of experiencing, namely, the performance of such of our actions as fulfil our moral obligations. These actions, we thus know, must be real possibilities, and so must conform to the conditions of possible experience. This particular passage, notice, suggests that we know that we can *perform* our morally required actions. In this respect it goes beyond certain others that suggest only that we know that we could have *omitted* our actually performed misdeeds.

The moral argument can also be discerned in a famous passage in which Kant argues that practical freedom entails transcendental freedom. 'The abolition of transcendental freedom', he says,

---

²⁵ Compare two partial statements of the moral argument from Kant's *Religion within the Bounds of Reason Alone*: 'Yet duty commands that [the human being] be good, and duty commands nothing but what we can do' (6: 47). And 'if the moral law commands that we *ought* to be better human beings now, it inescapably follows that we must be *capable* of being better human beings' (6: 50). Such statements, as Kant is aware, are closely related to the traditional principle of Roman Law, '*ultra posse nemo obligatur*' ('no one is obligated beyond what they are able to do') (28: 774).

would simultaneously eliminate all practical freedom. For practical freedom presupposes that although something did not occur, it yet **ought** to have occurred, and that therefore the cause of this something in [the realm of] appearance was not completely determinative: not so determinative, that is to say, that there did not lie in our power of choice a causality for producing, independently of those natural causes and even against their force and influence, something that in the time order is determined according to empirical laws—and hence a causality whereby we can begin a series of **events entirely on our own**.
(A 534/B 562)

Contraposing this passage's opening conditional, we obtain the main claim for which Kant wishes to argue, namely, that practical freedom entails transcendental freedom. The second sentence contains the argument for this entailment, but Kant's presentation of that argument is obscured by his failure to tease apart two separate strands of argumentation. One strand argues for the announced entailment, the other for the claim that we do indeed possess practical freedom.

The argument for the entailment proceeds as follows. Kant tacitly invokes the definition of practical freedom he had given in the preceding paragraph, namely, as 'the independence of the power of choice [*Willkür*] from compulsion by impulses of sensibility' (A 534/B 562).[26] He notes that, given determinism, this independence requires the power or ability to bring about an action whose omission is, as things actually stand, causally determined (ibid.). In order to have this ability, Kant claims, the agent must have a causality for producing a counterfactual world-series, hence a causality whereby she can begin a series of events entirely at her own instigation ('*ganz von selbst*').[27] But this is just the causality through freedom (also known as 'transcendental freedom').

---

[26] The *Prolegomena*, by contrast, defines practical freedom as 'that freedom in which reason has causality in accordance with objective determining grounds' (4: 346). Noticing this discrepancy, Ameriks seems to imply that the notion of practical freedom defined in the first *Critique* amounts only to 'comparative freedom' (Karl Ameriks, *Interpreting Kant's Critiques* (Oxford: Oxford University Press, 2003) at 166 n23; compare 163). As we will see later in this chapter, however, when Kant speaks of 'comparative freedom' what he has in mind is not practical freedom in the sense of the first *Critique*, but rather Leibniz's version of a compatibilist conception of freedom. In some metaphysics lectures from the mid-1770s Kant discusses yet a third conception of practical freedom, one that at this earlier stage he equates with 'the freedom of the person', which he contrasts with 'physical freedom or the freedom of one's state' (*Metaphysics L1*, 28: 257). Personal freedom, he says, 'can remain even when physical freedom is missing, as, e.g., with Epictetus' (ibid.). In the *Metaphysics L1*, then, Kant thinks of practical freedom—now under the guise of 'personal freedom'—as the freedom one might possess even on the rack: the freedom of the will. He takes it to 'rest on' transcendental freedom, which at this stage he characterizes in terms similar to those he goes on to employ in the first *Critique* when characterizing practical freedom, namely as 'independence of choice from the necessitation by stimuli' (ibid.).

[27] This claim is controversial because it presupposes the falsity of compatibilism-friendly analyses of the ability to do otherwise. According to one account of this kind, an agent S could have done otherwise (that is to say, has the ability to have done otherwise) just in case if S had chosen to do otherwise, S would have done otherwise. See, for example, G. E. Moore, *Ethics* (London: Home University Library, 1912) at ch. 6. If this analysis is correct, one would be able to possess the ability to do otherwise, while also lacking any power to change either the laws of nature or the state of the universe at earlier times.

Practical freedom is treated in the first *Critique* as a negative property: it is that *independence* of the power of choice from compulsion by sensible impulses that is required by the agent's being subject to the moral law. Kant contends that our power of choice can have this negative property of independence (practical freedom) only if it is also has the positive property of being a power of originating a chain of events with absolute spontaneity (transcendental freedom) (A 553-4/B 581-2).

The second line of argument in the passage just quoted—namely, the argument for the actuality of practical freedom—runs as follows. We know our duties a priori, and know, as a matter of empirical observation, that we sometimes fail to discharge them.[28] Since we also know that *ought* implies *can*, we know that we possess the ability to have acted differently than we actually did.[29] Consequently, we know that our will is to this extent independent of the empirical causal factors impinging on us and so, by definition, practically free.

As Pereboom has astutely observed, transcendental freedom does not consist in, or even require, the ability to have done otherwise. So much is clear, he notes, from Kant's readiness to attribute transcendental freedom to God—a being whom Kant supposes incapable of doing otherwise than He actually does.[30] The entailment rather runs in the opposite direction: our ability to have left our actually performed misdeeds undone entails our practical freedom and therefore also our transcendental freedom.

As an *aide-mémoire* we might summarize the entailments Kant affirms as follows:

For an alternative compatibilism-friendly account of the ability to do otherwise, see David Lewis, 'Are We Free to Break the Laws?', *Theoria*, 47 (3) (1981), 113-21.

[28] Kant shows no hesitation in affirming that we know our obligations. Indeed, he states explicitly that we cannot stand under an obligation of which we are ignorant (A 476/B 504). The fact that the argument contains an empirical premise explains why Kant says that practical freedom is cognized 'through experience' (A 803/B 831).

[29] Here Kant is tacitly assuming that knowledge is closed under known entailment.

[30] Pereboom, 'Transcendental Freedom' at 542. Kant says 'To God pertains transcendental freedom' (28: 1067), and anticipating the objection that 'God cannot decide otherwise than he does', he replies not by claiming that He *can* decide otherwise—indeed, he is explicit that He cannot (28: 1280)—but rather by drawing a contrast between God's being *necessitated by his nature* to decide as he does—which, Kant implies, *would* compromise His freedom, since it would render it a *logical* impossibility for God to do other than he does—and his being *constrained by his understanding* to decide as He does, which he seems to imply would make it only a real impossibility for God to choose otherwise than he does. He concludes that it is 'true freedom in God that he decides only what is in conformity with his highest understanding' (28: 1067-8). He thereby implies that God's property of being constrained in His choices by His understanding, far from limiting His freedom, is actually that in which his freedom consists. This last thought is echoed in a reflection from 1783-84: 'The freedom of the divine will does not consist in having been able to choose something other than the best...but in being necessarily determined by the idea of the best' (R 6078, 18: 443). One suspects that Kant is here trying to formulate the thought that God's freedom consists in his creative act's having its source in His understanding.

Being subject to the Moral Law (in a world in which we do wrong) → Ability to have counterfactually followed the moral law → Practical Freedom → Transcendental Freedom.

It is because Kant takes himself to know that he has practical grounds for affirming the actuality of freedom that he insists in the B edition that my representation of freedom 'contains no contradiction' (*B xxvii*). As he subsequently makes clear, however, his view is merely that I know that transcendental freedom is actual. I know, that is to say, that I have the capacity that constitutes transcendental freedom; I have no insight into how this remarkable capacity is possible (5: 4).

12.7 Is Kant a compatibilist?

I have argued that Kant is a determinist. And since he believes, on practical grounds, that transcendental freedom is actual, there is a natural sense in which he is also a 'compatibilist'. But the label needs to be applied with caution; for, left unqualified, the question 'Is Kant a compatibilist?' in fact admits of no simple 'yes' or 'no' answer. Even if we specify that we are asking about the compatibility of transcendental freedom with event-causal determinism, the question remains underspecified in at least three respects. First, it leaves it unclear whether what is required for compatibilism is the *real* compatibility of free will and determinism (roughly, the metaphysical possibility of their co-existence) or whether it is merely their *logical* compatibility. Second, the question leaves it unclear whether the applicability of the label is supposed to turn on what Kant *believes*, or on what he is *rationally committed to believing*, or, again, on what he takes himself to be able to *prove*. Third, the question leaves it unclear whether the belief (or whatnot) is supposed to be held on *theoretical* grounds or on *practical* ones. Considering every combination of disambiguations of the question thus generates (at least) twelve separate questions. It would be a wearisome chore to consider all twelve, but it's worth considering a couple of them.

To the question whether in the first *Critique* Kant is a compatibilist when that question is construed as asking about what he thinks he can *prove* on *theoretical* grounds, the answer is: no—and that remains so whether we are asking about real or logical possibility. For Kant does not think he can demonstrate the internal consistency of the concept of transcendental freedom on theoretical grounds. To the question whether in the first *Critique* Kant thinks he can prove the (real) compatibility of transcendental freedom with event-causal determinism on practical-cum-theoretical grounds, the answer is yes, and indeed, he further believes he can establish on these same grounds that the actual word is characterized by determinism and contains transcendental freedom. In this sense, then, Kant is a compatibilist and, indeed, a soft determinist.

Kant's compatibilism differs from the compatibilisms of Leibniz and Hume insofar as he requires that a genuinely free will must be wholly spontaneous. He does not, to my knowledge, discuss Hume's compatibilism, but since he has plenty to say about Leibniz's, it is worth pinpointing what he objects to in the Leibnizian position.

12.8 Against Leibnizian compatibilism

Leibniz's compatibilism is best approached via an examination of his conception of freedom. 'Freedom', he says in the *Theodicy*, 'consists in intelligence, which involves a clear knowledge of the object of deliberation, in spontaneity, whereby we determine, and in contingency, that is in the exclusion of logical or metaphysical necessity' (§288). For Leibniz, then, freedom requires intelligence, spontaneity, and contingency. These are supposed to be three individually necessary and jointly sufficient conditions for freedom—in the terminology of Leibniz's day, they are the 'requisites' (*requisita*) for freedom. *Intelligence* involves a 'clear knowledge of the object of deliberation' (*Theodicy*, §288). It thus requires the kind of knowledge traditionally supposed wanting in non-human animals. *Spontaneity* involves 'having within us the source of our actions' (§290).[31] *Contingency* requires that our acting otherwise must be a logical—and it seems also a metaphysical—possibility.

Leibniz thinks that nothing explains spontaneity better than his system of pre-established harmony; for according to that system all simple substances, including intelligent minds, enjoy spontaneity insofar as they are incapable of being influenced (in the strict, philosophical sense of 'influence') by external things (§290). Since Leibniz takes all three requisites for freedom to be satisfied by pre-established harmony, and since that system nonetheless conceives of the states of simple substances as springing naturally from one another in accordance with deterministic laws, Leibniz's is a compatibilist.

Kant memorably dismisses Leibniz's compatibilism as securing for our will a freedom no better than that of the 'turnspit' (5: 97). A turnspit is a kind of rotisserie. In some designs it is powered by a mechanism consisting of a weight suspended from a thread which is wound around the rotisserie's central rod. The suspended weight functions as the turnspit's 'internal principle'. Like the spring of the watch, it is the internal source of the turnspit's motion (compare 28: 267). Since the turnspit operates without being simultaneously moved by an external

---

[31] Compare, 'Aristotle has defined [spontaneity well] saying an action is spontaneous when its source is in him who acts' (*Theodicy*, 301).

cause, it can, Kant concedes, be said to 'move of its own accord' (5: 97). But this means only that 'once it is wound up' it 'accomplishes its movements of itself'. Because its self-movement depends on energy's having been previously put into the mechanism from the outside, the turnspit, for Kant, possesses only a qualified sort of spontaneity (*spontaneitas secundum quid*) (28: 267).

As Kant sees it, Leibniz's free agent similarly possesses only a qualified or 'comparative' kind of freedom (5: 96), a notion Kant illustrates in the second *Critique* with the same example he had used to illustrate the notion of qualified spontaneity (*spontaneitas secundum quid*) in the *Metaphysics L1*, namely, the free motion of a projectile in flight—as it might be, an arrow shot off from a bow. The motion of such a projectile is free insofar as the projectile is not being 'impelled from without' while in flight—that is to say, insofar as it is not being pushed along by something else (compare 5: 96 and 28: 267). In Kant's view, Leibniz's free agent possesses only this kind of freedom because for Leibniz a human soul is endowed at creation with a certain set of temporally ordered states which it runs through as it executes its divinely programmed routine. It is created, as it were, 'already wound up'. Kant would concede that *once wound up by God*, the human soul does, on Leibniz's picture, run through its states without assistance from anything external: the immediate cause of the 'wound up' soul's successive states is always entirely internal. But since the ultimate cause of its running through those states is the creator, Kant believes that it lacks 'absolute' spontaneity (*spontaneitas absoluta* or *spontaneitas simpliciter talis*), which, for him, is really what is in question when we consider the kind of freedom that's bound up with moral responsibility or 'imputation' (5: 96).

Kant's charge is fair. Leibniz does indeed treat God's influence as the ultimate cause of the human soul's running through its states. In the *Theodicy*, he even implies that divine influence is a kind of *physical* influence. The system of pre-established harmony, he says, 'demonstrates beyond a doubt that in the course of nature each substance is the sole cause of all its actions, and that it is free of all physical influence [*influence physique*] from every other substance, *save the customary co-operation of God*' (*Theodicy* §300, emphasis added). One reason why Kant rejects Leibniz's conception of freedom, therefore, is that it fails to satisfy one of Leibniz's own necessary conditions on freedom—a condition that Kant endorses—namely, *genuine* spontaneity, which requires that a free action be caused by nothing except the agent whose action it is.[32]

A second reason why Kant finds Leibniz's conception of freedom unsatisfactory is that it rules out our having the ability to leave our misdeeds undone, and so

---

[32] That Kant endorses this condition, and does so to the extent of prohibiting any role for God as a cooperating or partial cause of free actions, is clear from a reflection conjecturally dated to 1780 or to the late 1770s: 'God cannot concur in the causality of freely acting beings toward his moral ends in the world, for he must not be regarded as a cause <*causa*> of their free actions' (R 6167, 18: 474).

leaves no room for the practical freedom that is, for Kant, bound up with the ability to have done otherwise. This point comes through in a passage that culminates in Kant's famous charge that the Leibnizian view amounts merely to a 'wretched subterfuge'. 'If', Kant says,

> I say of a human being who commits a theft that this deed is, in accordance with the natural law of causality, a necessary result of determining grounds in preceding time, so [that] it was impossible that it could have been left undone; [the question then arises: how] can appraisal in accordance with the moral law [require us to] make any change in it, and [how can we] suppose that it could have been omitted [which is something we have to suppose] because the law says that it ought to have been omitted? That is, how can that man be called quite free at the same point of time and in regard to the same action in which and in regard to which he is nevertheless subject to an unavoidable natural necessity. It is a wretched subterfuge to seek to evade this [issue] by saying that the **kind** of determining grounds of his causality in accordance with the natural law agrees with a **comparative** concept of freedom. (5: 95)

Here Kant is bracketing his 'freedom of the turnspit' objection in order to raise another. He is asking how the kind of freedom that is demanded by our standing under the moral law could be compatible with determinism. His 'wretched subterfuge' zinger is directed at Leibniz's answer to this question—an answer that seeks to treat free actions as a special sub-class of the determined actions, namely, those whose *finite* determining grounds are exclusively internal.[33] The problem with such a conception, Kant is suggesting, is that it fails to do justice to the thought that a freely committed misdeed is one that *could* have been left undone because it *ought* to have been left undone. In Kant's view, Leibniz's determinism, unlike Kant's own, leaves no room for such actions, for a Transcendental Realist cannot situate free human choices outside of time.

So, in summary, while the 'freedom of the turnspit' objection levels the charge that Leibniz's view leaves no room for what is often called 'source freedom', the 'wretched subterfuge' objection levels the charge that it leaves no room for what is often called 'leeway freedom'.

---

[33] A number of philosophers of free will have muddied the waters around Kant's 'wretched subterfuge' remark. Some have taken it to express Kant's wholesale repudiation of compatibilism rather than his rejection of a specifically Leibnizian version of the view. See, for example, Peter Van Inwagen, *Metaphysics* (Boulder, CO: Westview, 1993) at 187; and also Robert Kane, 'Responsibility, Luck, and Chance: Reflection on Free Will and Indeterminism', in Gary Watson (ed.), *Free Will* (Oxford: Oxford University Press, 2003), 299–321 at 300. Others have taken it to signal Kant's rejection of the analysis of abilities in terms of subjunctive conditionals (Gary Watson, *Free Will* (Oxford: Oxford University Press, 2003) at 4). Such a proposal was not in fact made until the twentieth century (see note 27 above in the present chapter).

12.9 Kant's alleged libertarianism

If, as I claim, Kant is a determinist, then why is he so often said to have endorsed libertarianism? There are, I think, two main reasons. First, Kant scholars often employ the labels 'libertarianism' and 'compatibilism' non-standardly, and, in particular use 'libertarianism' as if it did not, as a matter of its very meaning, imply indeterminism. Second, there are certain texts that can seem to suggest that Kant subscribed to libertarianism even when the label is applied in the (more) standard way. In this section, I take up these points, beginning with the matter of nomenclature.

Since I want to claim that a good number of Kant scholars are using their terminology non-standardly, I should first explain what I take the more standard usages to be.[34] To this end, let me briefly survey some leading experts on free will on their use of 'libertarianism', 'compatibilism', and 'incompatibilism'.

Robert Kane says:

> Traditionally, incompatibilists are those who think that free will is incompatible with the world being deterministic.... In the philosophical literature, libertarianism is the view that we have free will and that free will is incompatible with determinism.[35]

Note that Kane is supposing that it follows from libertarianism's very characterization that it is incompatible with determinism. He is also suggesting that 'the philosophical literature' agrees with him on this. Carl Ginet apparently concurs:

> The term *libertarianism* is standardly used in philosophical discussions of free will to refer to a thesis composed of two parts: *incompatibilism* and *indeterminism*-in-the-right-places.[36]

Randolph Clarke is also on board:

> Like any libertarian view, an agent-causal [libertarian] account [of free action] makes room for [the condition that when an agent acts there is a variety of things that she can do] by requiring that determinism be false.[37]

---

[34] Not every contemporary theorist of free will adheres to what I'm calling the 'more standard' usage, but sufficiently many do so to make the usage of a smattering of Kant scholars the outlier.
[35] Kane in Fischer et al., *Four Views on Free Will* at 3.
[36] Carl Ginet, 'Libertarianism', in Michael J. Loux and Dean W. Zimmerman (eds), *The Oxford Handbook of Metaphysics* (Oxford: Oxford University Press, 2003), 587–612 at 587–8.
[37] Watson, *Free Will* at 286.

Turning to 'compatibilism' and 'incompatibilism', we find Peter van Inwagen characterizing these notions as follows:

> Incompatibilists... hold that free will and determinism are incompatible. As I have hinted, however, many philosophers are *compatibilists*: they hold that free will and determinism are compatible. Compatibilism has an illustrious history among English-speaking philosophers... (But compatibilism has not had many adherents on the continent of Europe. Kant for example called it a 'wretched subterfuge'.)[38]

The reason why van Inwagen thinks Kant rejected compatibilism seems to be that he takes the position Kant describes as a 'wretched subterfuge' to be compatibilism in general, rather than Leibniz's specific version of compatibilism. Indeed, he seems to be unaware of the strong current of continental compatibilism in which Leibniz and Wolff, among others, swam.

Ted Warfield says:

> Compatibilists think that metaphysical freedom ('freedom' for short) and causal determinism ('determinism' for short) are consistent. Determinism, according to this view, does not rule out the existence of freedom. Incompatibilists disagree, holding that every situation involving freedom is indeterministic.[39]

Since Kant believes that there is no logical incompatibility between our possessing a faculty of transcendental freedom and the world's being governed by deterministic laws, he is a compatibilist at least in the sense suggested by Warfield (and possibly also in other senses too). When one turns to the scholarly literature, however, one often finds his position described as a version of libertarianism.

Michelle Kosch, for example, claims that Kant 'wanted to maintain something very close to a traditional libertarian conception of free will'.[40] She takes Kant to defend 'freedom construed roughly as libertarians construe it: our actions are causally dependent on us rather than on preceding events, and could at least sometimes be different from what they in fact are'.[41] Kant, she says, 'held what today would be called an agent-causal account of free will. The only aspect of the contemporary form of this position he rejects is its denial of the truth of determinism.'[42] In the context of her other claims, and in the light of our survey, this

---

[38] Van Inwagen, *Metaphysics* at 187. Perhaps for different reasons from van Inwagen, Ameriks speaks both of Kant's rejection of compatibilism and of his anti-compatibilism (Ameriks, *Interpreting Kant's Critiques* at 168–9).

[39] Ted Warfield, 'Compatibilism and Incompatibilism: Some Arguments', in Loux and Zimmerman (eds), *The Oxford Handbook of Metaphysics*, 613–32 at 613.

[40] Michelle Kosch, *Freedom and Reason in Kant, Schelling, and Kierkegaard* (Oxford: Oxford University Press, 2006) at 15. One finds similar claims in Allais, *Manifest Reality* at 95 and 304.

[41] Kosch, *Freedom and* Reason at 16–17.   [42] Ibid., at 15, note 1.

last claim should strike a discordant note. It seems to imply that the denial of determinism is somehow a peripheral aspect of libertarianism—a detail one could take or leave. Kosch—or so one gets the impression—is using the phrase 'a libertarian conception of free will' to mean a view of free will that makes room for an agent both to have the ability to have done otherwise and to be the exclusive ultimate cause of their actions.[43] I've no quarrel with that usage so long as we recognize that it differs dramatically from the usage of many contemporary theorists of free will.

Pereboom, for his part, describes Kant as 'remarkable for his attempt to reconcile an essentially libertarian view of freedom and moral responsibility with a deterministic conception of nature'.[44] To philosophers steeped in the free-will literature this remark is likely to occasion the same puzzlement as Kosch's, and for the same reason: as we have seen, libertarianism is often treated in that literature as *entailing* the falsehood of determinism. The puzzle, however, is resolved by Pereboom's subsequent remarks, which show that he is using the adjective 'libertarian' differently from many contemporary theorists of free will. 'Kant's theory', he says, 'is especially ambitious in that it aims to preserve [widespread intuitions about the capacities for action we have and what is required for moral responsibility] by developing a view of freedom akin to agent-causal libertarianism, while at the same time accepting an uncompromising scientific determinism about the natural world'.[45] It turns out, therefore, that the respect in which Kant's view of freedom is 'essentially libertarian' for Pereboom is not that it entails indeterminism, but just that, first, it makes central use of the notion of agent-causation and, second, that it treats the agent's free choice as not even partially caused by something outside the agent.

Pereboom indicates that in characterizing Kant's position in the way he does he is following Henry Allison.[46] Allison says that Kant's resolution of the third Antinomy 'leaves a conceptual space for an incompatibilist conception of freedom'.[47] But since the freedom for which room is made is compatibilist rather than incompatibilist, Allison would seem to be employing a non-standard understanding of 'incompatibilism'.

A further remark by Allison reveals the likely source of the terminological tangle. He seems to be reserving 'compatibilism' for the kind of position exemplified by the distinctively pre-Kantian compatibilisms of the likes of Leibniz and Hume. He says:

---

[43] The qualification 'ultimate' is needed because on Kant's picture any event brought about by the noumenal agent's timeless act has both an agent cause and an event cause. However, since the event cause is itself brought into existence by the same agent-cause it does not number among the event's ultimate causes.

[44] Pereboom, 'Transcendental Freedom' at 537.   [45] Ibid., 538.

[46] Ibid., at 536. Allison, *Kant's Theory of Freedom*, 1–2, 29–46.

[47] Allison, *Kant's Theory of Freedom*, 11.

The Kantian project requires not merely the reconciliation of free agency with causal determinism (this being the relatively straightforward and non-controversial project of compatibilism, with which Kant was familiar through the writings of Leibniz and Hume, among others) but rather the reconciliation of such determinism with an incompatibilist conception of freedom.[48]

Were we to adhere to standard terminology, we would have to conclude that Allison is portraying Kant as subscribing to an inconsistent triad: determinism, free agency, and incompatibilism. The more charitable conclusion is that non-standard terminology is, once more, in play. Allison's interpretation in fact seems to be a version of a two-aspects view. He says:

> After making the...claim that "if we could exhaustively investigate all the appearances of men's wills, there would not be found a single human action which we could not predict with certainty, and recognize as preceding necessarily from its antecedent conditions", Kant goes on to insist that this does not conflict with the possibility of considering these same actions "in their relation to reason" (A 550/B 578). Moreover, so considered, they are regarded as actions that ought or ought not to have occurred and, therefore, as free in an incompatibilist sense.[49]

If this remark is to give expression to a genuine 'two aspects' view, it seems that by an 'incompatibilist' sense of freedom, Allison must mean a sense of freedom according to which an event's being free requires that it not be determined. The idea would be that when they are viewed as phenomena a human being's actions are determined, but when they are viewed in their relation to reason they are not determined. If that is what he means, I find Allison's position unsatisfactory. Terence Irwin voices the worry crisply: 'if an event is determined, it is true of it under all descriptions that it is determined, even though only some true descriptions, those referring to the relevant laws, show why it is determined'.[50] The upshot is that 'considered in their relation to reason' cannot mean 'considered under such-and-such a description'. But then what does it mean?[51]

Pereboom tries another tack. He offers an inventive analogy to help us make sense of the two-aspects view:

> Suppose I am capable of so-called lucid dreaming, of controlling by my will the contents of my dreams, and imagine that this control is the transcendentally free

---

[48] Ibid., at 28.   [49] Ibid., at 41.
[50] Terence Irwin, 'Morality and Personality: Kant and Green', in Wood (ed.), *Self and Nature in Kant's Philosophy*, 31–56 at 38. For a convincing defence of the thinking behind Irwin's claim, see van Cleve, *Problems from Kant* at 252–3.
[51] For a persuasive case that the two-aspects view cannot be made sense of by any of the obvious strategies, see van Cleve, *Problems from Kant*, 147–50.

sort. One night I freely will myself to dream that I am deterministically manipulated by sophisticated Martian neuroscientists. Furthermore, in this example, by way of reply to Irwin, it turns out that an event—say, the occurrence of the dream-content *my stealing the Mona Lisa*—is causally determined considered or described as a dream occurrence, but is not causally determined (by anything other than the transcendentally free agent) considered or described as an event in the real world.[52]

While the analogy is certainly suggestive, it fails to address Irwin's worry. If the real world—the world in which dream-content producing psychological events occur—is indeed indeterministic and if the production of the dream content is not a determined event, then to say that in the dream my stealing of the Mona Lisa is a determined event can only mean that it is necessitated given the past and laws of *the dream world* as opposed to being necessitated given the past and laws of *the real (waking) world*.[53] But then the sense in which the event in question is 'determined' in the dream world is not the negation of the sense in which it is not determined in the actual world. This seems to spoil the analogy because in order to be apt, it must mirror what the two-aspect theorist wants to say about events. And what that theorist wants to say is that, considered as an appearance, an event is determined, but, considered as a thing in itself, it is *in the very same sense* not determined.[54]

It's time to draw a line under our discussion of matters nomenclatural. We have arrived at two main conclusions. First, some philosophers seem to be prepared to describe Kant's position on free will as 'incompatibilist' simply because he rejects more standard, pre-critical versions of compatibilism, such as those of Leibniz and Hume. Second, several Kant scholars apply the term 'libertarian'—albeit qualified in various ways—to Kant's position on free will without thereby meaning to imply that he rejects determinism. In this respect these scholars depart from the terminological practice of several prominent contemporary theorists of free will.

In order to do justice to what is right in the positions of the Kant scholars I have been discussing, while also avoiding confusion, some new terminology is called for. The idea is to frame a realm-neutral sense of 'determinism' and then to describe Kant's views by qualifying this and related terms with the phrases 'in/with respect to the noumenal realm' and 'in/with respect to the phenomenal realm'. Let us call a position on free will 'determinist' in our new sense just in case it maintains that every action (or omission)—whether that action (omission)

---

[52] Pereboom, 'Transcendental Freedom' at 555.

[53] I am granting for the sake of argument that it is at least metaphysically possible that one's powers of lucid dreaming should be such as to constitute the content of the dream world deterministic.

[54] This is only to scratch the surface of the debate about the viability of two-standpoint readings. For a helpful discussion see Dana K. Nelkin, 'Two Standpoints and the Belief in Freedom', *Journal of Philosophy*, 97 (10) (2000), 564–76.

be a timeless noumenal choice or a phenomenal event—is necessitated to exist by something distinct from the agent performing (omitting) it. And let us call someone a 'libertarian' with regard to a given realm just in case they hold us to be free in that realm while also holding that freedom in that realm requires indeterminism in that realm. Let us call someone an '*intra*-realm' compatibilist with respect to a given realm just in case they affirm the metaphysical possibility of free actions' existing in that realm while determinism also holds with respect to it. And, finally, let us call someone an '*inter*-realm compatibilist' just in case they affirm the metaphysical possibility of free actions' existing in one realm while determinism holds in the other. Then, drawing on our new understandings, we can formulate the following irenic understanding of Kant's position. First, he endorses determinism in the phenomenal realm, while rejecting it in the noumenal realm. Second, insofar as he regards noumenal freedom as requiring the falsity of determinism in the noumenal realm he is a libertarian in that realm. Third, because he endorses determinism in the phenomenal realm while also endorsing noumenal freedom (on practical grounds), he is an inter-realm compatibilist. This new terminology enables us to make sense of Wood's famously paradoxical-sounding—yet ultimately insightful—remark that Kant's project is an attempt to establish the 'compatibility of compatibilism and incompatibilism'.[55] In our terminology, this means that Kant is attempting establish the co-tenability of *inter*-realm compatibilism with *intra*-realm incompatibilism.[56]

The terminological imbroglio would hardly matter were it not for the fact that Kant sometimes speaks in ways suggestive of an adherence to libertarianism as it is (more) standardly understood. Thus, he says, for example:

> Now the actions [of human beings] are in great part occasioned but not entirely determined by sensibility; for reason must provide a complement [*complement*] of sufficiency [*Zulänglichkeit*]. (R 5611; 18: 252)

By 'a complement of sufficiency' Kant means a partial cause that, taken together with certain unspecified others, necessitates an event's occurrence. Kant's view in this reflection therefore seems to be that human actions lack natural *sufficient* causes. It therefore does seem that when he wrote this reflection Kant was at least toying with libertarianism as it is standardly understood. But since the remark can be dated only roughly (and then only conjecturally) to some point in the 1770s, it suggests only that libertarianism may have at one point been a live option for the pre-critical Kant. Does this view survive into the first *Critique*?

The answer would seem to be no. For there Kant at one point expressly rejects this picture of reason as merely providing a complement of sufficiency. He says:

---

[55] Wood, 'Kant's Compatibilism' at 74.
[56] I am grateful Ralf Bader for discussion of the issues in the last two paragraphs.

'One regards the causality of reason not merely as a concurrence [with other causes], but as complete in itself, even if the sensuous incentives were not in the least for this causality but were even entirely against it' (A 555/B 583). The context makes clear that Kant believes that one would be *right* to so regard reason, for here he is appealing to our ordinary practices as support for his own view that reason can be causally efficacious. Here, then, Kant is presenting reason as causally efficacious *on its own*. This fits with his conception of reason as genuinely spontaneous, for a truly spontaneous cause produces its effect without the help of other causes. This passage might itself be read as containing evidence of libertarianism—and we will soon consider other texts that might also seem to suggest this idea—but the present point is just that in the first *Critique* Kant rejects the view expressed in the reflection just quoted.

Does the picture of reason as capable of overpowering sensuous incentives in a kind of metaphysical arm wrestle—a picture arguably sketched at A 555/B 583— point toward libertarianism? Two remarks initially seem to suggest that this is so. The first occurs in the passage we discussed earlier in which Kant maintains that practical freedom entails transcendental freedom:

> The abolition of transcendental freedom would simultaneously eliminate all practical freedom. For practical freedom presupposes that although something did not occur, it yet **ought** to have occurred, and that therefore the cause of this something in [the realm of] appearance was not completely determinative: not so determinative, that is to say, that there did not lie in our power of choice a causality for producing, independently of those natural causes and even against their force and influence, something that in the time order is determined according to empirical laws—and hence a causality whereby we can begin a series of **events entirely on our own**. (A 534/B 562)

This remark makes it sound as though Kant regards our power of choice as capable of *overpowering* the natural causes that would otherwise produce the event so that the event is not naturally caused. Fortunately, however, we can interpret it as consistent with his elsewhere-declared determinism. For we can read him as maintaining merely that our power of choice is capable of instituting a fully determined event-causal order contrary to the one that actually prevails. Such a reading, moreover, is in fact suggested by a closer examination of another passage that might superficially seem to suggest a genuinely libertarian view. 'Reason', Kant says,

> does not yield to the empirically given ground and does not follow the order of things as they exhibit themselves in appearance, but with complete spontaneity makes for itself an order of its own according to ideas. Reason adapts the empirical conditions to accord with these ideas, and in conformity with these

ideas declares to be necessary even such actions as in fact **have not occurred** and perhaps will not occur, but concerning which reason nonetheless presupposes that it can have causality in reference to them, since otherwise reason would not expect from its ideas effects in experience.   (A 548/B 576)

Like the previous passage, this one superficially seems to invoke the image of a struggle of forces in which reason gains the upper hand—an image that in turn conveys the idea of reason's somehow breaking the natural order, as it would do if its exercise entailed indeterminism. But its continuation cancels this suggestion; for it makes clear that what is involved in reason's not yielding to empirically given grounds is its possessing the capacity to completely spontaneously 'make its own order of things according to ideas, to which it fits the empirical conditions'. Not 'yielding' to empirically given grounds, then, consists not so much in pushing back against, or overcoming, them as in suspending the natural order in its entirety and forging a new one. Kant is conveying a picture of reason's first demanding (presumably, on moral grounds) that some action should occur, and then fitting to that occurrence such empirical conditions as make it possible. The suggestion of temporality, however, is merely metaphorical: in truth, for Kant, we timelessly cause to obtain an order into which certain obligatory actions fit—an order in which those actions are bound to occur given the past and the natural laws. Here, then, we have in a compressed and somewhat implicit form an early version of the argument for the actuality of transcendental freedom from four premises: first, that *ought* implies *can*, second, that we sometimes fail to do what the moral law requires of us, third, that we know our obligations and, fourth, that practical freedom implies transcendental freedom. At any rate, the similarity of this second passage to the first gives us some reason to think that our suggested reading of the first is correct.

13
The Fourth Antinomy

13.1 Introduction

At issue in the third antinomy is the existence or otherwise of an unconditioned causality; in the fourth, by contrast, it is the existence of otherwise of an unconditioned being (A 559/B 587). Such a being Kant also calls 'an absolutely necessary being' presumably because, if it existed, it would enjoy an absolutely unconditioned existence. The thesis and antithesis of the fourth Antinomy run as follows:

Thesis
To the world there belongs something that, either as a part of it or as its cause, is an absolutely necessary being (A 453/B 481).

Antithesis
There is no absolutely necessary being existing anywhere, either in the world or outside the world as its cause (ibid.).

On the face of it—and setting aside certain minor differences in wording—the thesis does seem to affirm the proposition denied by the antithesis. Kant nonetheless supposes that both claims can be true (A 562/B 590). We will shortly look into his reasons for thinking so, but first a word about the meaning of the phrase 'an absolutely necessary being'. In the context of the fourth antinomy, Kant uses this phrase for the notion of a being that *depends* on no being for its existence—not even itself—or, equivalently, for a being that *derives* its existence from no being. So much is clear from his referring to the being for whose existence the thesis contends as an 'original being' (A 459/B 487); for Kant contrasts the term 'original' with 'derived' (B 72) and also contrasts the notion of an original being with one that is 'dependent as regards its existence' (ibid.). In the fourth antinomy, then, a necessary being is not characterized as a being that exists at every possible world, and neither is it characterized as a being that exists from its concept.

If the thesis is to appear to contradict the antithesis, the word 'part' occurring in it must have the meaning of 'proper or improper part'. For the antithesis treats as distinct cases the hypotheses that an absolutely necessary being exists as a part of the world and that it exists as identical with the world. This point is not evident from the wording of the antithesis, but it becomes evident when we consider the fact that the antithesis's supporting argument incorporates a *reductio* assumption to the effect that 'either the world itself is a necessary being or that there is such a being in it' (A 453/B 481). The antithesis, accordingly, must be read as denying both of these disjuncts, along with the claim that a necessary being exists outside the world as its cause. It follows that to preserve symmetry the thesis must be read as having three disjuncts, thus: 'Either an absolutely necessary being exists as a proper part of the world, or such a being exists and is identical with the world, or such a being exists outside the world as its cause.' And here 'the world' means 'the whole causally linked series of alterations'. In what follows I will treat the thesis as having this three-disjunct structure.

13.2 The thesis argument

To better understand what is required to establish the thesis, one needs to attend more closely to its logical form. Kant treats it as a claim whose form we might today make perspicuous by means of the following gloss: 'Something is an absolutely necessary being and it is either F or G or H', where the predicates 'F', 'G', and 'H' are such that no two of them can be true together. Such a gloss is not perhaps the first that springs to mind. A modern reader would most likely interpret the disjunction involved as operating upon propositions rather than predicates and as inclusive rather than exclusive. Nonetheless, Kant is perfectly clear that the disjunctive form of judgment effects (what we'd today call) a partition of the domain (compare A 73–4/B 98–9). And in the present case—namely, where the judgment takes the form of a 'particular quantification'—it is the predicates rather than propositions that express an exhaustive and exclusive division of the ways in which an absolutely necessary being might exist. In other words, in the present case the judgment contains a disjunctive predicate of the form 'F or G or H', where 'F', 'G', and 'H' are mutually exclusive and exhaust the ways that a necessary being might exist. It follows that in order to prove the thesis one must do two things. First, one must prove that one of the following three propositions is true: 'Some absolutely necessary being exists as a proper part of the world', 'Some absolutely necessary being exists as identical with the world', and 'Some absolutely necessary being exists outside the world as its cause.' Second, one must establish that the predicates in question are pairwise incompatible (that is, no two of them can ever hold of any one thing). This second task is simple. For nothing can exist both inside the world (whether as the whole or as a part) and merely outside of it, and nothing can be both a proper part of the world and identical with the world. In order to execute the first task, Kant offers a proof of the claim that an absolutely necessary being exists as a proper part of the world. That he proceeds in this way is clear from the details of the reasoning he presents on behalf of the proponent of the thesis, but it is not clear from the conclusion of the thesis argument, which Kant presents as saying that an absolutely necessary being exists inside the world either as its proper or improper part.

The argument for the thesis runs as follows:

> The world of sense, as the whole of all appearances, at the same time contains a series of alterations. For without these, even the temporal series, as a condition of the possibility of the world of sense, would not be given to us. Every alteration, however, stands under its condition, which precedes it in time, and under which it is necessary. Now every conditioned that is given presupposes, in respect of its existence, a complete series of conditions *up to* [*bis zum*] the unconditioned, which alone is absolutely necessary. Thus, there must exist something absolutely necessary, if an alteration exists as its consequence.
> (A 452/B 480, emphasis added)

Here we are invited to assume that a series of alterations exists, and to reason from that starting point to the conclusion that something absolutely necessary exists.[1] Since the absolutely necessary being is described here as something *up to* which the series of conditions leads, Kant would appear to be representing the defender of the thesis position as, at this stage, conceiving of this being as a member of the world-series rather than as identical with it.

The argument's key move is an implicit appeal to the idea that nothing can be a sufficient mediate cause unless it has a sufficient ultimate, unconditioned cause. Application of this principle leads to the positing of a wholly unconditioned cause within the series. But such a cause will have to be an absolutely necessary being because—on the assumption that self-conditioning is impossible—it will depend for its existence on no being within the series, and also upon nothing outside the series because—as the proponent of the thesis goes on to argue—an extramundane atemporal cause is impossible (A 453–4/B 482–3). This last claim is made in the argument against the third disjunct in the antithesis argument and will be discussed when we consider that argument.

13.3 The antithesis argument

On the surface, the antithesis takes the form of a conjunction of two negative claims, but, as we have noted, a stronger claim incorporating a third conjunct is clearly intended. Made fully explicit, the antithesis would say: 'No part of the world is an absolutely necessary being, neither is the world itself such a being, and neither does such a being exist outside the world as its cause.' Kant presents the

---

[1] In spite of Kant's phrasing, the assumption cannot be that an alteration exists *as the consequence of the existence of a necessary being*. For this would plainly beg the question.

advocate of the antithesis as offering one argument for the first two conjuncts taken together, and another argument for the third. The argument for the conjunction of the first two claims begins by assuming the opposite. It runs:

> Suppose that either the world itself is a necessary being or that there is such a being in it; then in the series of its alterations either there would be a beginning that is unconditionally necessary, and hence without a cause, which conflicts with the dynamical law of the determination of all appearances in time; or else the series itself would be without any beginning, and, although contingent and conditioned in all its parts, it would nevertheless be absolutely necessary and unconditioned as a whole, which contradicts itself, because the existence of a multiplicity cannot be necessary if no single part of it possesses an existence necessary in itself. (A 453/B 481)

The assumption to be reduced to absurdity is the following disjunction: 'Either the world-series contains a necessary being as a proper part or the series as a whole is itself such a being.' Kant is treating this disjunction as exclusive, in accordance with his own understanding of such claims (A 74/B 99). The first alternative is ruled out on the ground that an absolutely necessary being within the world would have to be a first member of a temporal dynamical chain and the existence of such a being would infringe the causal law. (The assumption that the absolutely necessary being would have to be a first member of the chain is itself justified on the ground that every other member of the chain would be a *conditioned* being, hence not absolutely necessary.) To assume the second (exclusive) disjunct is to assume that a series of alterations exists all of whose parts are contingent but which is itself absolutely necessary. For, given that only one disjunct can obtain, to suppose that the world is an absolutely necessary being is thereby to assume that no part of it has this status. Kant supposes that this combination of assumptions is contradictory. He doesn't explain why he thinks so, but a plausible answer would run as follows. Since the whole world-series is a *real* composite (a *totum syntheticum*), its parts are prior to the whole. The whole therefore depends for its existence on the existence of each of its proper parts. But if each of those parts is contingent, the whole cannot be absolutely necessary because it would depend for its existence on each of the parts. In short, the whole empirical world-series cannot be a wholly independent being if it existentially depends on dependent beings.

The third conjunct of the antithesis says that no absolutely necessary being exists outside the world as its cause. The argument for this claim runs as follows:

> Suppose, on the other hand, that there were to be an absolutely necessary cause of the world outside the world; then this cause, as the highest member [*oberst Glied*] in the **series of causes** of mundane alterations [*Weltveränderungen*], would first

begin the existence of these alterations and their series. But this cause would itself have to begin to act, and its causality would belong to time, and for this very reason [belong] in the sum total of appearances, i.e., in the world; consequently, it itself, the cause, would not be outside the world, which contradicts what was presupposed. Thus, neither in the world nor outside it (yet in causal connection with it) is there any absolutely necessary being. (A 454–5/B 482–3)

The argument assumes for *reductio* that an absolutely necessary being exists outside the world as its cause. Kant assumes that the operation (or 'causality') of the extra-mundane cause would have to be an event (something in time). But this means—or so he supposes—that the necessary being would itself have to be in time, hence in the world, which contradicts the *reductio* assumption. By discharging the *reductio* premise, therefore, we arrive at the conclusion that there is no absolutely necessary being existing outside the world as its cause.

This last argument is puzzling. One wonders why Kant should now reject the idea of atemporal extra-mundane causation when he had accepted this idea—or something very like it—in proposing his solution to the third antinomy. The answer, I think, is that Kant takes atemporal, extra-mundane causation to be intelligible only on Transcendentally Idealist assumptions, with the consequence that both parties to the antinomy, being Transcendental Realists, are committed to treating all causation as temporal. Unfortunately, however, he does not explain why atemporal, extra-mundane causation should be intelligible only on Transcendentally Idealist assumptions. One possibility is that he believes that if Transcendental Realism is true, then the principle he had dismissed as a subreptive maxim in the *Inaugural Dissertation*, namely, that 'whatever is is somewhere and somewhen', would hold true (2: 413–14). Unfortunately, however, he fails to make such a claim here. Nonetheless, the point does help to explain why Kant takes Spinozism to be 'all that remains' if Transcendental Realism is endorsed (5: 101–2). For, as the reasoning just discussed makes clear, Kant supposes that a consistent Transcendental Realist would have to treat God's causation as temporally exercised and that this would in turn entail that God is not extra-mundane.

13.4 The resolution

Kant resolves the fourth antinomy by arguing that its thesis and antithesis can both be true if each is taken in a different 'respect' [*Beziehung*] (A 560/B 588). The antithesis rules out an empirically unconditioned member of the series and so is true so long as we understand the conditions of which it (implicitly) speaks as empirical conditions. But it is compatible with the antithesis that the unconditioned existence posited by the thesis should be something that exists outside of time performing its causing or grounding function atemporally—hence a merely intelligible condition of what it conditions (A 561-2/B 589-90). When Kant suggests this possibility he is presupposing Transcendental Idealism and one supposes that it is this position that is supposed to create the epistemic possibility that the thesis and antithesis should both be true. Kant's solution thus presents the fourth antinomy's third disjunct as the crux of the matter: from the point of view of Transcendental Idealism, the extra-mundane causality posited by the third disjunct of thesis is understood to be atemporal causation (the cause being an intelligible condition), while the causality denied in the third disjunct of the antithesis is understood to be temporal causation (the cause being an empirical condition). The appearance of a contradiction arises only because, when Transcendental Realism is assumed, the notion of a condition (or cause) can only be understood as an empirical condition (or temporal cause), and so this notion *is* understood in that way by both parties to the dispute, who are, of course, Transcendental Realists. When the assumption of Transcendental Realism is dropped, however, the possibility opens up of understanding the notion of a condition in the thesis as an intelligible condition (or atemporal cause). Transcendental Idealism thus reveals the parties to the dispute to be at cross purposes. Since Kant regards Transcendental Idealism as essential to making this case, he takes the resolution of the Fourth Antinomy to provide yet another independent argument for this position.

As I mentioned in the previous chapter, Kant does not take his resolution of the fourth antinomy to have shown that an intelligible cause of the world-series is possible in itself. '[An] absolutely necessary being of the understanding', he says, 'may, indeed, be in itself impossible' (A 562-3/B 590-1). He means, I take it, that he has not shown that the notion of such a being is free of contradiction; for in Kant's parlance to claim that something is 'possible in itself' is the least one can say of a thing (A 324/B 381), and to affirm the mere consistency of a thing's concept is obviously to affirm something weaker than the thing's real possibility. Since he is not defending even the logical possibility of the truth of the thesis Kant must be speaking loosely when he says of the thesis and antithesis of the fourth antinomy that 'they can **both be true**' (A 562/B 590). What he must mean is what he in fact goes on to say, namely: that the impossibility of an absolutely necessary being 'can by no means be inferred from the universal contingency and dependence of everything belonging to the world of sense' (A 563/B 591). Deploying the terms we used when discussing the resolution of the third antinomy, we may say that the fourth antinomy will be resolved so long as the following condition holds: if the thesis and antithesis cannot both be true, that is only because at least one of them is necessarily false.

13.5 De Mairan and the moon

Kant appends to his presentation of the fourth antinomy a series of remarks on the thesis and antithesis. The remark 'on the antithesis' actually relates to the fourth antinomy as a whole. Or rather, it relates to what remains of that antinomy when it is pruned of the idea that the absolutely necessary being might exist outside the world as its cause. Referring to the absolutely necessary being as an 'original being', Kant says:

> A strange situation is disclosed in this antinomy, namely, that from the same ground of proof, from which in the thesis the existence of an original being was inferred, in the antithesis the non-existence of the same being is inferred, and indeed inferred with the same rigour. (A 459/ B 487)

Kant is supposing that if one is a Transcendental Realist then, depending on which aspect of a certain (alleged) fact one attends to, one will be inclined to draw one or other of two opposite conclusions about the world. The alleged fact in question, which Kant calls a 'ground of proof', is the supposed fact that 'the entire past time comprehends the series of all conditions' (A 459/B 487).[2] If we think of the temporally comprehended series of conditions as a *plurality*, we will treat its members as exhausting the candidates for the role of a wholly unconditioned being, and side with the antithesis. If, on the other hand, we think of the temporally comprehended series as a *totality*, we will include the series as a whole along with each of its members on the list of candidates for occupant of the role of wholly unconditioned being, and consequently side with the thesis. Since nothing rationally constrains the Transcendental Realist to favour one of these aspects over the other, there will arise an antinomial dispute.

Kant compares these observations to an observation previously made by Jean-Jacques d'Ortous de Mairan. According to Kant, de Mairan had observed that when we consider the question whether the moon turns on its axis we are inclined to draw contradictory inferences from one and the same fact: the fact, namely, that the moon always shows the same side to the Earth (A 461/B 489).[3] As Kant points out, in de Mairan's example the opposed views correspond to distinct conceptual 'standpoints'. When one conceives of the situation from an earthbound

---

[2] Here my translation follows Kemp Smith in preference to Guyer and Wood. The German runs: '*Nun heist es: es ist kein notwendiges Wesen, eben darum, weil die ganze verflossene Zeit die Reihe aller Bedingungen (die mithin insgesamt wiederum bedingt sind) in sich faßt.*' The implication of the plural verb in the parenthesis ('*sind*') is that each member of the series of conditions is itself conditioned. It is not—as the Guyer-Wood translation suggests—that the totality is itself conditioned, for this would contradict the claim that the series comprehends *all* conditions.

[3] Jean-Jacques d'Ortous de Mairan (1678–1771), who played a prominent role in the *vis viva* dispute, was secretary of Royal Academy of Sciences in Paris in 1740 and the editor of the *Journal des Sçavans*. A crater on the moon is named in his honour.

perspective—one concludes that the moon does not turn on its axis. But when one conceives of it from a superlunary perspective (from, for example, the standpoint of a position close to the sun), one reaches the opposite conclusion: the moon does indeed turn on its axis precisely because during its monthly orbit it always turns the same face to the Earth.

The comparison is apt: when we view the dynamical series from a perspective within it—from what we might call 'the series-bound perspective'—we will be inclined to think of everything as empirically conditioned and so conclude that there is no original being. If, however, we think of this same series from an external perspective, we will notice that the series itself is a candidate for conditioning and, assuming that every condition exists within the series, we will conclude that it is not itself conditioned and so counts as an absolutely necessary being.

It is hard to be sure which work Kant is alluding to, but one does find the idea he is discussing in de Mairan's 1731 treatise on the *Aurora Borealis*.[4] There de Mairan says:

> Now the moon, properly speaking, does not at all partake of rotation; it turns around a centre which is—more or less—the earth, but not around its own centre, because its lower (in relation to us) hemisphere...always keeps the same position during the course of its [orbital] period in relation to an observer situated at the centre of the earth during its daily revolution—as would the cupola of a dome or the keel of a ship [were they to be rotated about a centrepoint determined by the curvature of the dome or the hull of the ship].[5]

With his use of the phrase 'properly speaking' de Mairan implies that although when, in Berkeley's terms, 'speaking with the vulgar' we might say that the moon turns on its axis, when 'thinking with the learned', we would judge that it does not do so. Since in this passage de Mairan does not attribute the two views in question to 'two famous astronomers', this may not in fact be the passage Kant is referring to at A 461/B 489. But it does plausibly contain the *idea* to which he is alluding.

It is clear that in invoking the lunar example Kant is speaking quite literally of two 'standpoints' on the same object. The availability of two points of view makes possible the drawing of two incompatible conclusions from one and the same set of facts. And each conclusion is perfectly correct relative to the appropriate *spatial* point of view. Kant, we should note, is taking the example to shed light on conflict between the thesis and the antithesis, and so between two Transcendentally Realist theses. The example is therefore not intended to illuminate his distinction between

---

[4] Jean-Jacques d'Ortous de Mairan, *Traité Physique et Historique de L'aurore Boréale (Physical and Historical Treatise on the Aurora Borealis)* (Paris: The Royal Press, 1731).
[5] Ibid., at 264.

phenomena and things in themselves. Whatever truth there may be to a 'two standpoints' interpretation of Transcendental Idealism, it has nothing to do with the present example. Instead, the example is intended to explain a consequence of Transcendental Realism, namely, the tendency—in the absence of non-rational stabilizing factors—for the Transcendental Realist's allegiance to oscillate between the thesis and the antithesis.

This completes our examination of the antinomies. We have seen that Kant takes them to provide four separate indirect arguments for Transcendental Idealism. The cosmological Ideas therefore stand at the heart the Dialectic. The appearance that any one of them has an object is equivalent to the appearance that Transcendental Realism is true. This appearance can be regarded as an aspect of transcendental illusion: it is the illusion that the Transcendental Ideas have an object about whose constitution and magnitude we may legitimately inquire.

PART III
RATIONAL THEOLOGY

14
The Ontological Argument

14.1 Introduction

Kant understands theology as 'the cognition of the original being [*Urwesen*]'. He means, of course, that it is the *purported* cognition of such a being (A 631/B 659). He divides theology into its 'revealed' and 'rational' branches: the former is the purported cognition of God through Scripture, the latter the purported cognition of God independently of Scripture. Rational theology in turn divides into its 'transcendental' and 'natural' sub-branches. The former purports to cognize the original being when it is conceived of by means of highly abstract 'transcendental' concepts such as the concepts of an *ens originarium, ens realissimum*, or *ens entium*; the latter purports to cognize its object as the supreme or highest intelligence—a cause of the world through understanding and freedom (28: 1240–1).[1]

The *object* of transcendental theology is Kant's deist's God: a being regarded as a cause of the world through the necessity of its nature. Kant calls this being a 'blindly acting and eternal nature [that is conceived of] as the root of things' (A 632/B 660). The object of natural theology, on the other hand, is the theist's 'living' God: a being conceived of as the cause of the world through the exercise of its faculties of freedom and understanding, a being conceived of through concepts borrowed 'from nature' and, more specifically, from the nature of one's own soul (A 631/B 659; 28: 1253).

In this third main part of the current work we examine Kant's criticisms of rational theology. We devote two chapters to arguments belonging to transcendental theology, namely, the ontological and cosmological arguments, and one to an argument belonging to natural theology, namely, the so-called 'physico-theological argument'. We begin with the ontological argument.

It was Kant who first introduced the label 'the ontological argument' for the argument in which one attempts to prove God's existence from His essence or concept. This nomenclature may at first seem oddly redundant. Since 'ontology' is the study of being, wouldn't *any* argument for God's existence be aptly described as an 'ontological argument'? This worry, however, arises merely from a lack of familiarity with Kant's technical use of the term 'ontological'. 'Ontology', he says,

---

[1] A third species of rational theology is moral theology, which seeks to establish the existence of God (conceived of as a director of the world) by means of morally grounded arguments (28: 1241).

in the *Dohna-Wundlacken Logic*, 'has to do with nothing but notions' (24: 752). And by 'notions' here he means pure intellectual concepts that are 'given' rather than fabricated (24: 753). Plausibly, then, the ontological argument is so-called simply because it takes for its starting point a pure intellectual concept that is 'given' rather than made up. Such a rationale would certainly make the term appropriate for the Cartesian—as opposed to the Anselmian—version of the argument. For that argument self-consciously begins from a concept that is supposed to be expressive of God's true and immutable essence or nature—a concept that is conceived of as 'given', ready formed, to every human being at birth rather than made up arbitrarily. Once we take into account Kant's understanding of 'ontology', therefore, the label becomes recognizably apt as a term for the Cartesian argument.

Philosophers sometimes speak of 'Kant's objection' to the ontological argument, as if he possessed only one objection, or, at any rate, only one that really mattered.[2] In truth, however, Kant raises a suite of objections against the ontological argument, some intended to be effective against any proponent of the broadly Cartesian (as opposed to Anselmian) version of the argument, others directed against more specific targets. My main thesis in this chapter is that Kant's most celebrated objection, the one that rests on the claim that **being** is not a real predicate (A 598/B 626), is of this second kind. It is intended to have force only against Leibniz's version of the Cartesian argument—whether developed by Leibniz himself or by his followers—and it involves using one of Leibniz's own commitments against him.

This reading is motivated in part by interpretive charity. In my view, Kant's argument that **being** is not a real predicate succeeds if—but only if—a certain Leibnizian commitment, which is rejected by Descartes, is assumed as a background premise. The commitment in question is a certain stance on the Euthyphro contrast (more on which later). This fact does not, however, mean that Kant's broader critical case leaves Descartes unscathed; for, as we will see, that case includes a distinct criticism that succeeds against all proponents of the broadly Cartesian version of the argument—Descartes included. It does mean, however, that if we are to appreciate the power of Kant's most famous objection, we will need to keep in mind that he is treating Leibniz as the caretaker of the Cartesian argument.

Kant's critique of the ontological argument proceeds in two distinct phases. In the opening phase, the relatively soft targets of Wolff and Baumgarten are disposed of (to Kant's satisfaction at least) in a preliminary skirmish. Then, with those opponents driven from the field, Kant concentrates his fire on Leibniz, who becomes his immediate target for the remainder of his discussion. Kant's main

---

[2] See, for example, Alvin Plantinga, 'Kant's Objection to the Ontological Argument', *Journal of Philosophy*, 63 (19) (1966), 537–46.

charge against Leibniz is that the concept of *being* (or, in practice, *actuality* or *existence*) is not a real predicate because its corresponding *property*—being—is not a reality. Kant supports these claims with an argument that makes use of his famous example of 'a hundred thalers' (A 599/B 627). This argument, I will argue, succeeds against Leibniz because (and only because) Kant can appeal to a certain Leibnizian premise to de-fang what would otherwise be a powerful objection.

The bulk of this chapter is devoted to explicating and, to some extent, defending Kant's argument for his thesis that *being*—in its guise as *actuality*—is not a real predicate. But I will also seek to illuminate one of his more obscure—and relatively neglected—criticisms of the ontological argument: the claim, namely, that in attempting to run the ontological argument Kant's opponent is already guilty of a contradiction (A 597/B 625). I will begin, though, by examining the details of Kant's presentation of the ontological argument in the first *Critique*. I do so partly in order to identify the argument's contentious premises, and partly to establish that Kant engages, most immediately, with a characteristically Leibnizian version of the argument.

14.2 Kant's presentation of the ontological argument

Kant introduces the ontological argument under the guise of a putative objection to his own thesis that any concept can be consistently supposed to lack exemplification. He represents his opponent as contending that the concept of the most real being constitutes the sole counter-example to this claim (A 596/B 624). The ontological argument is embedded in a dense thicket of text that I'll call 'the expository passage':

[Against my thesis that every concept can be consistently supposed to lack instances] you challenge me with one case that you set up as a proof [of its falsehood] through the [alleged] fact that there is one and indeed only this **one** concept where the non-being or the cancelling of its object is contradictory within itself, and this is the concept of the most real being [*der Begriff des allerrealsten Wesens*].[3] [This being] has, you say, all reality, and [you say that] you are justified in assuming such a being as possible (which I grant for now, although a non-contradictory concept falls far short of proving the [real] possibility of its object).[4] Now existence is also comprehended under all reality: so

---

[3] Here Kant uses capitalization ('*Einen*') rather than separated type for emphasis.

[4] Kant's own footnote to this passage (not reproduced here) suggests that when he says he concedes the point 'for now' he does *not* mean that he will later take this concession back. Rather, he means that he will for now acquiesce in this (by his lights) loose and potentially misleading way of speaking, even though, strictly speaking, what one is justified in assuming is not that the *being* is possible but merely that its *concept* is (that is to say, that its concept does not contain a contradiction; compare R 5688 (18:

existence lies in the concept of something possible. If this thing is cancelled, then the internal possibility of the thing is cancelled, which is contradictory.

(A 596–7/B 624–5)

There are two points to note before proceeding. First, because Kant portrays the ontological argument as his opponent's attempt to counter-example his own thesis that any concept can fail to be exemplified it will be polemically futile for him to criticize the argument—as he sometimes seems tempted to do (for example, at the beginning of A 598/B 626)—merely on the ground that any concept can fail to be exemplified. For, obviously, to raise such an objection in *this* context would be to beg the question. Second, Kant portrays his opponent as attempting to establish a conditional result, namely, that the most real being exists, on the assumption that this being is logically or 'internally' possible. Since this is how *Leibniz* in fact proceeds, and since, as we'll see, Kant also portrays his opponent as employing a distinctively Leibnizian argument for the most real being's internal possibility (A 602/B 630, compare *Monadology* §45), there is reason to think that Kant is conceiving of his opponent as, in the first instance, either a Leibnizian or a Leibnizian-Wolffian. This impression is confirmed by Kant's subsequent description of the ontological argument as 'Leibniz's completion of Anselm's argument'.[5] This point about Kant's main target is worth pausing to develop further.

In the *New Essays*, Leibniz remarks that the ontological argument 'is not fallacious, but it is an incomplete demonstration which assumes something which should also be proved in order to render the argument mathematically evident'.[6] The demonstration is incomplete, he contends, because 'it is tacitly assumed that this idea of a wholly great or wholly perfect being is possible and does not imply a contradiction'.[7] A proof of the logical consistency of the concept of a wholly great or wholly perfect being is required, Leibniz argues, because if that concept were to prove contradictory, we would be able to demonstrate 'opposite conclusions' from it—including, presumably, both the existence and the non-existence of this very being.[8]

---

327)). But, setting peculiarities of Kantian idiom aside, his main point is that we are not justified in assuming that the being in question is a real possibility—hence my interpolation of 'real'.

[5] 'On a discovery', 20: 349.   [6] *New Essays*, book 4, chapter 10, §7, 437–8.

[7] Ibid. In this same work he nonetheless claims that the argument provides a 'demonstrated moral conclusion'. He does so because he thinks we may assume God to be possible until proven impossible (*New Essays*, book 4, chapter 10, §7, 438).

[8] See 'Meditations on Knowledge, Truth and Ideas' (1684) in Daniel Garber and Roger Ariew, G. W. Leibniz, *Philosophical Essays*, trans. Daniel Garber and Roger Ariew (Indianapolis and Cambridge: Hackett, 1989) at 25. And see G. W. Leibniz, *Discours de Métaphysique et Monadologie* (Paris: Vrin, 1974) at §24. Finally, see 24: 748–9 for Kant's own awareness of this point.

Leibniz's attempted possibility proof occurs in a number of places in his writings, including the *Monadology* (§45)—a work Kant had read. In the *Monadology* Leibniz argues that since we conceive of God as containing 'no limits and no negation', and since negations (as well as positive properties) are required to generate contradictions, the concept of God is guaranteed to be logically consistent. Similar arguments are given by Wolff in the second part of his *Natural Theology* (Wolff 1739–41: §§13, 19, and 21) and by Baumgarten in his *Metaphysics* (§806).

Kant grants that this Leibnizian possibility proof establishes what it sets out to prove: 'The analytic mark of possibility', he says, 'which consists in the fact that mere positings (realities) do not generate a contradiction, of course, cannot be denied of [the concept of a highest being]'.[9] He means that Leibniz's proof does indeed establish the logical or internal consistency of the concept of the most real being. He insists, however, that this does not mean that we know this concept's object to be a real possibility. 'The connection of all real properties in a thing', he says, 'is a synthesis whose possibility we cannot judge a priori' (A 602/B 630).

Against my claim that Kant is targeting a broadly Leibnizian version of the ontological argument it might be objected that he characterizes his target at one point as the famous 'ontological (Cartesian) proof [*ontologischen (Cartesianischen) Beweise*]' (A 602/B 630). Doesn't this indicate that Kant is treating Descartes as his most immediate opponent? The answer is no—and for three reasons. First, Kant sometimes uses the phrase 'the Cartesian proof' as an umbrella term for any version of the modern, post-Anselmian ontological argument, in contrast to the cosmological or physico-theological 'proofs'.[10] Second, he speaks of philosophers other than Descartes as running 'the Cartesian proof'.[11] Third, the very context in which the label 'the ontological (Cartesian) proof' occurs suggests that Kant's immediate target in that part of the Ideal is Leibniz. The relevant context runs: '**Leibniz** was far from having achieved what he flattered himself he had done, namely, gain insight a priori into the possibility of such a sublime ideal being. [New paragraph] Thus the famous ontological (Cartesian) proof of the existence of a highest being from concepts is only so much trouble and labour lost' (A 602/B 630). I take it that 'possibility' here means 'real possibility' and that this—the highest being's real possibility—is something that

---

[9] See A 602/B 630 and R 5269 (18: 138); compare 28: 1016. Kant regards the phrase 'a highest being' as a variant on the phrase 'a most real being' (see 8: 138 and 29: 1001).
[10] See, for example, 2: 162.
[11] See, for example, *Metaphysics L1*, 28: 313, where Kant speaks of 'the **Cartesian** proof, which Wolff and others have assumed' (compare 28: 314). Wolff's version of the argument is Leibnizian in character insofar as it is supplemented by Leibniz's attempted possibility proof (*Natural Theology*, pt. 2, §§13, 19, and 21); so this shows that Kant is prepared to refer to a distinctively Leibnizian version of the ontological argument as 'the Cartesian proof'.

Kant regards Leibniz as having tried and failed to prove by running the ontological argument.[12]

Leibniz and Wolff, Kant supposes, each resort to the ontological argument in attempting to complete the cosmological argument (28: 315; 28: 599). Both authors should therefore be included, along with Descartes, among Kant's likely targets. Another likely target, as we'll see, is Baumgarten.[13] And, indeed, each of Leibniz, Wolff, and Baumgarten develops a version of the ontological argument in a work available to Kant.[14]

Since Wolff and Baumgarten run the ontological argument on the concept of the *ens perfectissimum* rather than that of the *ens realissimum* one might wonder why Kant focuses almost exclusively on the latter concept.[15] The answer, I think, is that he wishes to avoid portraying the argument as begging questions about the most real being's attributes. Since Kant regards the word 'perfection' as 'always presuppos[ing] a relation to a being endowed with cognition and desire' (2: 90), and since he sees these attributes as characteristic of the theist's but not the deist's God (28: 1001–2), it suits him to present the argument using the more neutral term, '*ens realissimum*'—or so, at least, I'd suggest. At other, apparently less cautious, moments, however, he is happy to use the terms '*perfectissimum*' and '*realissimum*' interchangeably (28: 782).[16]

Spelled out, the argument Kant presents in the expository passage runs as follows:

P1. The most real being has all reality, [1] ('[The most real being] has, you say, all reality').[17]

---

[12] For the distinction between the possibility of a concept, which consists in its internal consistency, and that of a thing, which consists in its objective reality, see R 5688 (18: 327). Kant plainly takes Leibniz to have failed to establish the most real being's real possibility (A 602/B 630; 28: 1024).

[13] In his polemical work, 'On a Discovery', Kant at one point describes the first *Critique* as 'the true apology for Leibniz' (8: 250–1). This is not, I think, a reason to doubt that Leibniz is one of Kant's opponents in his critique of the ontological argument. For the context of this remark, and in particular the words that proceed it—'in this way, then' (which are naturally read as meaning 'in the particular way just discussed')—make clear that Kant is referring here specifically to the harmony or union brought about between freedom and nature in his resolution of the third antinomy—a harmony that bears a resemblance to the harmony Kant finds in Leibniz between the kingdoms of Nature and Grace. Crucially, at this point the topic of transcendental theology is not under discussion. For an interesting discussion of other commonalities—or near commonalities—between Kant and Leibniz, see: Anja Jauernig 'Kant's Critique of the Leibnizian Philosophy: *Contra* the Leibnizians, but *Pro* Leibniz', in Daniel Garber and Béatrice Longuenesse, *Kant and the Early Moderns* (Princeton, NJ and Oxford: Princeton University Press, 2008), 41–63.

[14] See, in addition to Leibniz's *New Essays*, Wolff, *Natural Theology* (pt 2, §§1–21), and Baumgarten, *Metaphysics* (§803–23).

[15] 'Almost exclusively', because there are exceptions, for example at R 4659 (17: 628).

[16] Kant identifies a thing's perfections with its realities when the former term is used 'materially' (R 5663 (18: 322)). By contrast, the 'perfection' of a thing 'taken formally' is 'the correspondence of its realities with one ideal' (ibid). One supposes that the perfection (in the formal sense) of an F is the degree to which it corresponds to the concept of an ideal F.

[17] That Kant runs the argument on the concept of 'the most real being' is not evident from Guyer and Wood's translation, but it is clear from the German.

P2. Existence is a reality, [2] ('Existence is comprehended under all reality').

P3. P1 and P2 are conceptual truths, [3] (Suppressed premise).

P4. The concept *the most real being* is logically consistent, [4] ('[You say that] you are justified in assuming such a being as possible').[18]

L1. The concept *the most real being* contains existence and is logically consistent ('Existence lies in the concept of something possible') (By P1–P4, [1, 2, 3, 4]).

L2. So, the concept *the existent most real being* is logically consistent (Immediate from L1, [1, 2, 3, 4]).

P5. The existent most real being does not exist, [5] ('If this thing'—that is, the object of the concept of *the existent most real being*—'is cancelled'; *reductio* assumption).[19]

P6. For any F, if the F does not exist, then the concept of the F contains non-existence as a mark, [6] (Suppressed premise).

But then,

L3. The concept of *the existent most real being* contains non-existence as a mark (from the relevant instance of P6, by *modus ponens*, [5, 6]).

L4. The existent most real being is not possible internally ('then the internal possibility of the thing is cancelled'; from L3 by the meaning of 'internal possibility', [5, 6]).

P7. A thing is not possible internally just in case its concept is not logically consistent, [7] (Suppressed premise).

But then:

L5. The concept of the existent most real being is not logically consistent (from L4 and P7, [5, 6, 7]).

L6. Contradiction (from L2 and L5, [1, 2, 3, 4, 5, 6, 7]) ('which is contradictory').

L7. The existent most real being exists (From L6, discharging the *reductio* assumption, P5, [1, 2, 3, 4, 6, 7]).

Therefore:

C. The most real being exists (From L7 and the first conjunct of L1, for that conjunct entails that 'the existent most real being' and 'the most real being' express the same concept, [1, 2, 3, 4, 6, 7]).

---

[18] I defend my gloss of 'possible' here as 'logically possible' later in the present section.

[19] Although, for expository convenience, I have presented the argument as a *reductio ad absurdum*—that is to say, I have isolated a to-be-discharged counterfactual supposition as a *reductio* premise—as stated, it takes the form of a *modus tollens*. Kant, however, would have seen the argument he states as 'apagogic' or indirect; for he drew no sharp distinction between the apagogic mode of proof and *modus tollens* (see *Jäsche Logic*, 9: 52). What matters for him is that apagogic or indirect mode of proof involves proving a claim by showing that its opposite is false (ibid., 9: 71), and this is clearly how the argument Kant states is supposed to proceed.

A reader familiar with Descartes's discussion of the ontological argument might reasonably regard this formulation as needlessly baroque. But its intricacy is accounted for, first, by the need to register the argument's possibility assumption as an explicit premise and, second, by Kant's desire to present the heart of the argument as an attempt to derive a contradiction from the assumption that the most real being does not exist. Kant presents the argument in this way partly because—as we will see in §14.10—he is bound to do so by the rules of disputation, and partly because he regards the most real being as his opponent's proposed candidate for a being that exists with *absolute necessity* (A 585/B 613)—a notion which in this context he understands as a matter of something's being 'necessary by its very concept' (A 612–13/B 640–1).[20] Since, for Kant, one shows that something's existence follows necessarily from its concept by showing that the assumption of its non-existence entails a contradiction, it follows that the ontological argument must employ a similar proof strategy in arguing for the most real being's necessary existence.[21]

This point helps to explain why Kant's most famous objection involves the concept of *being* rather than that of *necessary being*. For in order to undermine versions of the ontological argument that argue that the *ens realissimum* exists necessarily it suffices—given Kant's conception of a necessary being as a being whose existence follows from its concept—to show that the *ens realissimum*'s existence (or actuality or being) does not follow from its concept. A separate argument that, in addition, its *necessary* existence does not follow from its concept is not required.

It further complicates our reconstruction that we have made tacit premises explicit. I have presented the argument as tacitly relying on premises P3, P6, and P7.[22] Premise P3 is needed to underwrite Kant's transitions from claims about things to claims about the corresponding concepts. If, for example, P1 and P2 were true, but not conceptually true, they would not entail that existence is contained in the concept of the most real being (the first conjunct of L1). The suppressed premise, P6, is required to facilitate the transition from the assumption that the existing most real being lacks existence to the conclusion that the existing most real being is not possible internally.

---

[20] In the first *Critique* itself Kant at one point simply equates absolute necessity of existence with 'existence from mere concepts' (A 607/B 635). This suggests that the rather different notion of an absolutely necessary being that is in play in the fourth antinomy—the notion of a wholly unconditioned being, a being that depends on nothing (not even itself)—is one Kant attributes to the Transcendental Realist without endorsing it himself.

[21] It is possible that Baumgarten's presentation of the argument is at the forefront of Kant's mind at certain points in his exposition; for Baumgarten infers the necessary existence of God from the alleged internal (or '*in se*') impossibility of His non-existence (*Metaphysics*, §823).

[22] It's not surprising that Kant's presentation of the argument leaves certain premises implicit: he was not, after all, operating with anything approaching Fregean standards of rigour.

Let us examine the grounds for premises P6 and P7 more closely, beginning with P7. This says: 'A thing is not possible internally just in case its concept is not logically consistent'. I take this premise to express a corollary of a definitional truth. In the first *Critique*, Kant treats the phrases 'possible internally [*interne möglich*]' and 'possible in itself [*an sich selbst möglich*]' as synonymous (A 324/B 381). The latter phrase is a term of art, one apparently borrowed (most immediately) from Baumgarten's *Metaphysics* (§§15–18, especially §18), where, in line with established Wolffian tradition, something's being '*in se possibile*' ('possible in itself') contrasts with its being '*hypothetice possibile*' ('hypothetically possible'). Kant himself contrasts 'internal [*innere*]' with 'hypothetical' possibility (28: 562; 28: 734); so there is good reason to think he is taking over Baumgarten's distinction—along with his terminology—and using the term 'possible internally' to mean precisely what Baumgarten means by 'possible in itself'. What it is for something to be 'possible internally' (or 'possible in itself') is, I think, just for its concept to be logically consistent. So much, at any rate, is suggested by Kant's remark that: '[to say that something is] possible in itself ([or] internally)... [is] the **least** one can say of an object (A 324/B 381)'. For the least one can say of an object is, plausibly, that its concept is logically consistent. The same interpretation is suggested by Kant's claim in his metaphysics lectures that inner possibility can be cognized 'only in accordance with the principle of contradiction' (28: 562). The tendency of these reflections, then, is that P7 should be viewed as an immediate consequence of (what Kant would have regarded as) the conceptual or definitional truth that a thing is possible internally just in case its concept is logically consistent.

Consider now the relevant instance of P6: 'If the most real being does not exist, then the concept of the most real being contains non-existence.' What would justify Kant in attributing this premise to the rational theologian? One possible answer is: charity alone; for without this assumption the argument of the expository passage would be patently unsound. But one can perhaps say something more. For there exist broadly rationalist principles, known to Kant, that would license P6. One such principle occurs in Descartes's 'geometrical' presentation of the Cartesian system in the *Meditations*' 'Second Replies'.[23] The ninth definition of that presentation runs: 'When we say that something is contained in the nature or concept of a thing, this is the same as saying that it is true of that thing, or that it can be asserted of that thing.'[24] It follows from this 'same-saying' claim that to say that non-existence is true of a thing is the same as saying that non-existence is contained in the nature or concept of that thing. A Leibnizian principle that could do the same work is arguably contained in the following gloss on the Principle of Sufficient Reason from the *Theodicy*: 'There is no true enunciation whose reason

---

[23] Kant owned a copy of the third edition of 1650. See Warda, *Immanuel Kants Bücher* at 47.
[24] *AT* VII, 162; *CSM* II, 114.

could not be seen by one possessing all the knowledge necessary for its complete understanding.'[25]

Since he recognizes the existence of synthetic truths, Kant would himself regard P6 as false. But for two reasons it would be out of place for him to challenge this premise in the present context. First, his case against the ontological argument will be the stronger the less it depends on his own positive—and in his day controversial—views. Second, he would have been well aware that most formulations of the Cartesian ontological argument lack the complexity of the one he offers. Accordingly, he would also have known that to pounce on P6 would be to invite the charge of attacking a straw man.

One final point to note about Kant's presentation of the argument is that it employs two different notions of 'cancellation'. At one stage—P5—it speaks of *the object* of a certain concept as being cancelled; but at another—L3—it speaks of *the internal possibility* of this same object as being cancelled.[26] What it is for the object of a concept to be 'cancelled' is, I think, for the non-existence of such an object to be asserted. On the other hand, what it is for the internal possibility of a thing to be cancelled is for the concept of that object to be shown to be internally inconsistent. No difficulty is caused by supposing that Kant uses the notion of 'cancellation' in these two different ways, though that he does so is worth keeping in mind.

14.3 What is a 'real predicate'?

Kant's most famous objection to the ontological argument involves questioning the truth of P2. In the first *Critique* the objection is framed somewhat obliquely. '**Being**', Kant says, 'is obviously not a real predicate, that is, a concept of something that could be added to the concept of a thing' (A 598/B 626). The meaning of 'real predicate' in this context is controversial. For the reasons given by Ralf Bader in his recent article, 'Real Predicates and Existential Judgments', I will suppose that Kant takes a real predicate to be a synthetic predicate.[27] I also follow Bader in

---

[25] Leibniz, *Theodicy* at 419. I am grateful to Des Hogan for drawing this remark to my attention.
[26] I am indebted to Katherine Dunlop for alerting me to this feature of the argument.
[27] See Ralf Bader, 'Real Predicates and Existential Judgments', *European Journal of Philosophy*, 26 (3) (2018), 1153–8. In following Bader on this point, I depart from my own earlier account in my 'Kant on the Ontological Argument' (*Noûs*, 49 (1) (2015), 1–27). There, I had been guided by Kant's characterization of a real predicate in his religion lectures, where he equates a real predicate with a concept that represents a reality-enhancing or perfecting feature of a thing (*Religionslehre Pölitz*, 1783–84, 28: 1027; compare R 5296 (18: 146), 28: 783, and 24: 510). I now think that the characterization in the religion lectures represents a distinct usage from the one that occurs in the first *Critique*. On the first *Critique*'s conception, real predicates and determinations are synthetic predicates that may represent negations as well as realities. I take this view because in the first *Critique* Kant foregrounds the distinction between a real and a merely logical predicate, and because he characterizes the former in terms of adding something to a concept rather than in terms of perfecting the (intentional object) of that concept. Fortunately, as we will see, accommodating this change requires only a minor

supposing that Kant uses 'determination' and 'synthetic predicate' to mean the same thing. Or rather, I take this to hold of some uses of 'determination'. In truth, Kant uses this word sometimes for a concept and sometimes for the property it represents. When he uses 'determination' in the latter way he indicates that determinations include both realities and negations (A 186/B 229; 28: 14; 28: 652). Realities are determinations that inhere in things; they are what Kant calls 'accidents' (29: 770).

Bader is not entirely explicit about what he takes a synthetic predicate to be. I will suppose that a synthetic predicate is a concept that represents a reality or a negation and which serves as the predicate of at least one synthetic judgment. This characterization allows Kant to avoid classifying *existence* as a synthetic predicate even while classifying claims of the form '*X* exists' as synthetic. The reason why Kant takes the concept of *being* not to be a real predicate, I will argue, is that if it were one, then the *property* this concept represents, namely, being or actuality, would be a reality—a point that Kant denies.[28] As we will see, Kant's argument that being or actuality is a not a reality is just his famous 'hundred thalers' argument.

Kant does not deny that *existence* is a predicate. Rather, he takes both it and the other modal concepts to be logical rather than real predicates. The concept of *existence* is merely a logical predicate because it represents merely the positing of things rather than the things themselves (that is, properties). It represents an *absolute* positing when it occurs in predicate position—as, for example, in the judgment 'God is' (A 599/B 627, 2: 73–4) and a *relative* positing when it occurs as copula—as, for example, in the judgment 'God is omnipotent', where omnipotence is posited relative to God (A 598/B 626, 2: 73–4).[29] 'Were existence to be a determination of a thing', Kant says, 'it would be a relative positing, but it is not such a positing' (28: 630). He means that if, *per impossibile*, existence were to be a real predicate, it would represent a property that was relatively posited of things in the judgments in which it occured. But since it is a modal predicate it plays an altogether different role, namely, that of signifying the positing of things.

If being (or existence) were a property, it would very plausibly be a reality rather than a negation. That being so, we might expect Kant's criticism of the ontological argument to have as one of its central planks the claim that the concept of *existence* or *being* does not represent a reality. Or, to frame the point at the level

---

modification of my interpretation of Kant's argument that *being* is not a real predicate (in 'Kant on the Ontological Argument').

[28] The property of being is not a negation either, of course. But Kant is assuming, with considerable plausibility, that if the concept *being* were a real predicate, then the property of being would be a reality rather than a negation.

[29] Kant's equation of the concept of *being* with the general notion of positing goes back to the early 1760s (*OPB* 2: 73).

of objects rather than concepts, we might expect Kant's criticism of the ontological argument to have as one of its central planks the claim that existence is not a reality. And such, I believe, is indeed the case.

Kant certainly maintains that the ontological argument would be refuted if one could establish that existence is not a reality. For in his religion lectures he says that in the ontological argument 'everything unquestionably depends on whether the existence of a thing is in fact one of its realities'.[30] A reality in the Platonic tradition is a reality-enhancing feature of a thing. Colloquially speaking, it is a feature that beefs up the degree of reality of its possessor, thus making it 'more perfect'.[31] Accordingly, if Kant is following the tradition, then in denying that existence is a reality he should be denying, *inter alia*, that it plays this reality-enhancing or perfecting role. And this is in fact what we find: 'But the fact that a thing exists', he says in these same lectures, 'does not make the thing more perfect in and for itself' (28: 1027). It is, I think, significant that in insisting on this point, Kant is gainsaying a claim that Leibniz attributes to Descartes in reconstructing the Cartesian ontological argument in the *New Essays*—a work with which Kant was familiar.[32]

14.4 Wolff and Baumgarten on existence

In *OPB* Kant attributes to Baumgarten the view that existence is a reality-enhancing feature of a thing. He does so in the course of expressing his dissatisfaction with Wolff's account of existence. 'Wolff's explanation of existence', he says,

> [namely] that it is a completion of possibility [*Ergänzung der Möglichkeit*], is obviously very indeterminate. If one does not already know in advance what can be thought about possibility in a thing, one is not going to learn it from this explanation. **Baumgarten** introduces the concept of thoroughgoing internal determination, and maintains that it is this which is more in existence [*Dasein*] than in mere possibility, for it completes that which is left indeterminate by the predicates lying in or flowing from the essence.[33]

---

[30] 28: 1027. Compare R 3706 (17: 240).

[31] Descartes can be found explicitly equating the notion of being more perfect with that of containing more reality in the second Meditation (*AT* VII, 40–1, *CSM* II, 33).

[32] Leibniz presents the relevant premise of the ontological argument as the claim that 'Existing is something more than not existing, i.e., existence adds a degree to the greatness or to the perfection—as M. Descartes puts it, existence is itself a perfection' (*New Essays*, 437).

[33] See *OPB*, 2: 76 and R 6255; 18: 532; compare Wolff, *GM* §14, Ontology, §174; Baumgarten, *Metaphysics*, §55. Kant attributes the view that existence is the completion of possibility to Baumgarten in the Volckmann metaphysics lectures of 1784–85 (28: 413).

Kant's criticism of Wolff's explanation of existence is simply that it is too sketchy to be useful. His criticism of Baumgarten, by contrast, is substantive and illuminating. Recognizing that Baumgarten follows Wolff in treating existence as the completion of (internal) possibility (see *Metaphysics*, §55), Kant interprets Baumgarten as attempting to explain the actualization of a possibilium in terms of this completion. Moreover, he interprets Baumgarten as treating this completion as a kind of reality enhancement. This is why in the passage just quoted Kant portrays Baumgarten as maintaining that this completion—this rendering of something fully determinate—is that which is '*more* in existence than in mere possibility'. Since a feature whose possession renders something 'more' than it would otherwise be is, in Kant's parlance, a reality, he is, in effect, portraying Baumgarten as treating existence as a reality. And this portrayal is in fact accurate (see *Metaphysics*, §66 and §810). Baumgarten, Kant thinks, is attempting to locate the difference between an actual thing and a mere possibilium in the possession by the former but not the latter of a full set of 'internal'—that is, intrinsic—properties, including those that are not part of the thing's essence and which therefore, for Kant, hold only contingently of the thing in question.[34]

More fully, on the view Kant is attributing to Baumgarten, a mere possibilium—a particular possible human being, say—possesses the intrinsic properties contained in the thing's 'internal possibility' (that is, in its essence) in the present example: rationality and animality—together with those that flow necessarily from that internal possibility (risibility would be a traditional example). On the other hand, it lacks any contingent intrinsic properties such as a position in time or space, or having a particular stature. (At the time of composing *OPB* Kant seems to be treating position in space and time as intrinsic properties.)[35] Most importantly of all, on this picture, it is only upon actualization that a possibilium comes to acquire any intrinsic contingent properties. In doing so, it comes to have more reality than it had possessed prior to actualization.[36]

Kant's Baumgarten thus treats the concept of *existence* as a real predicate—a concept representing, in this case, a reality rather than a negation. But he also attempts to *reduce* the property of existence to thoroughgoing internal

---

[34] For Kant, a thing's *extraessentialia* are contingent properties that may be either intrinsic/internal properties ('modes') or relational properties ('relations'). Compare: 'Those things that belong contingently to the concept of the thing are called extraessentialia' (28: 411). In consequence, Kant—in a departure from the tradition—conceives of a thing's essence as including those properties that would ordinarily be classified merely as its necessary accidents or 'propria'.

[35] Baumgarten treats essence and internal possibility as equivalent notions (§40).

[36] Here, I treat Kant's use of the word 'more' as meaning 'more real'. In suppressing the word 'reality' in this passage—and in others where his point is to claim that one thing contains (or would contain) more reality than another—Kant is following Descartes, who says, for example, that 'there must be at least as much in the cause as in the effect' (*AT* VII, 49; *CSM*, 34). A comparison with the French version of the *Mediations* makes clear that Descartes means 'as least as much *reality*'.

determination. Kant, in effect, attributes to Baumgarten the following definition of existence—or, equivalently, of actuality:[37]

For any possibilium, x,
x is existent (or, equivalently, actual) iff for any intrinsic property, F, such that the proposition $<Fx>$ is contingent, either Fx or not Fx.

Outside of the first *Critique* Kant raises two objections to the specifics of Baumgarten's definition of existence (on his understanding of it). The first charges that the definition infringes the law of excluded middle because it involves treating any *mere* possibilium as a not fully determinate entity (2: 76). As a criticism of the position Kant attributes to Baumgarten, the point seems incisive. Baumgarten *does* treat the law of excluded middle as quantifying over possibilia (*Metaphysics*, §10); so, according to that law, every possibilium—*mere* possibilia included—should be fully determinate.

What if (Kant's) Baumgarten were to bite the bullet and reject the law of excluded middle? Then the second of Kant's objections would gain traction, namely, that (Kant's) Baumgarten's definition of existence is incompatible with the possession by non-omniscient beings of the knowledge that any particular thing exists. We human, non-omniscient knowers can know that the sun exists. But if (Kant's take on) Baumgarten's definition of existence is accepted while the law of excluded middle is rejected, then such an accomplishment will be utterly mysterious. For in order to know that the sun exists we would need to know concerning every intrinsic property significantly ascribable to the sun that either it or its negation holds of the sun. In the absence of knowledge of the law of excluded middle such a cognitive feat would—as Kant himself recognizes—require something approaching omniscience.[38]

---

[37] I take it that Kant reads Baumgarten as treating *existence* and *actuality* as co-extensive concepts. Whether or not this is correct, it is certainly a natural interpretation of what Baumgarten says when laying out the ontological argument in §§810 and 811 of his *Metaphysics*. For there Baumgarten indicates that the inference from 'God has existence' to 'God is actual' is licensed by something contained in §55. The only plausible candidate for what this might be is the apparent parenthetical gloss of 'existence' as meaning 'actuality'. Courtney D. Fugate claims that this is not in fact a gloss. He insists that for Baumgarten existence and actuality are distinct (and, apparently, not even co-extensive) (Fugate, 'Baumgarten and Kant on Existence', at 132). This interpretation, however, leaves the just-mentioned inference looking invalid. And, significantly, Fugate's own reconstruction of the inference represents the relevant step as licensed not by §55 (as is actually indicated in Baumgarten's text), but by §54—a suggestion that has no warrant in the text and which is, on its face, implausible simply because existence is not mentioned in that section. See Fugate, 'Baumgarten and Kant on Existence', 144 (line 14 of the reconstruction).

[38] See 28: 554; and compare 28: 410. Strictly speaking, I would not need to know every detail of the farthest corner of the universe in order to know which intrinsic properties hold of the sun, but Kant is certainly correct that, on the assumptions we've mentioned, knowledge of the existence of the sun would far outrun our actual cognitive capacities.

14.5 The 'inconsistency' objection

In the first *Critique* itself Kant raises a third objection, distinct from each of these, which, although not expressly directed against the views of Baumgarten and Wolff, nonetheless makes sense if we suppose them to be its targets. It runs:

> I answer: you have already committed a contradiction when you have brought the concept of its existence, under whatever concealed [*versteckten*] name, into the concept of a thing which you would think merely in terms of its possibility.
> (A 597/B 625)

Even though it contains Kant's official answer to his (implied) interlocutor's objection, this remark is often ignored in discussions of the ontological argument; and, when it is discussed, it is sometimes not treated as expressing a criticism in its own right.[39] This is understandable; for without a good deal of context the remark can seem utterly baffling. In particular, one wonders how the assumption that existence is contained in the concept of a most real being could amount to a contradiction. Surely, one supposes, that would require the concept of the most real being to contain *non-ex*istence as a constituent concept. And surely that is the *last* thing a champion of the ontological argument would wish to maintain. On the hypothesis that Kant's interlocutor is a Wolffian, however, his point snaps crisply into focus. The contradiction Kant is alleging to exist holds not between the concept of existence and marks of the concept of the most real being, but rather between the Wolffian *explanation* of existence as the 'complement of (internal) possibility' and the claim that existence is part of God's essence.

The inconsistency arises—or so I would argue Kant supposes—because if one follows Baumgarten in understanding the general (putative) property of existence—that is, existence as it applies to both finite and infinite beings—as the *complement* of (internal) possibility (*Metaphysics*, §55), then because Baumgarten equates essence with (internal) possibility (§40), one cannot also understand God's existence as a part of His essence. A 'complement' of something, after all, is not a part of that thing—as Kant's own use of this term in unrelated contexts attests.[40]

To feel the force of Kant's objection one must appreciate that Baumgarten and Wolff are defining not the existence of finite things in particular but rather

---

[39] Michelle Grier, for example, conflates the charge of contradictoriness with the charge of tautologousness by which it is immediately followed (see Michelle Grier, 'The Ideal of Pure Reason', in Paul Guyer (ed.), *The Cambridge Companion to Kant's Critique of Pure Reason* (Cambridge: Cambridge University Press, 2010), 266–89 at 278). By contrast, I take it that Kant's words at A 597/B 625, 'If one allows you to do that', in fact serve to waive his first objection for the sake of raising a further (and very different) worry about tautologousness.

[40] Compare, for example, *Jäsche Logic*, §§27–8 and 9: 602–3.

existence in general. Their explanation of existence must accordingly apply to God's existence as much as to the existence of anything else.[41] The contradiction Kant alleges is not, of course, an explicit one. But it could be made explicit if we were to provide an appropriate definition of the notion of a 'complement of (internal) possibility'.

Baumgarten has two lines of possible reply to this objection. First, he might resist Kant's implication that he takes existence to be part of the essence of God. For he might insist that though existence pertains to that essence (flows from it in the way that a proprium flows from an essence) it is not *part of* that essence. And such a line would certainly be compatible with what Baumgarten says at crucial stages of his presentation of the ontological argument (see, for example, *Metaphysics*, §810). If Baumgarten were to insist on this line of reply, then Kant would also be on correspondingly thin ice in his reconstruction of the argument, since Baumgarten would deny the first conjunct of L1.

Alternatively, he might say that to claim that existence is part of the concept of God does not mean that God's essence (absurdly) contains as members a full, and fully determinate, set of intrinsic extra-essentialia. It rather means that the concept of God contains the concept of *a being that is completely determinate with respect to its intrinsic extra-essentialia*. And *that* concept *can* consistently be part of God's concept (hence part of his essence). As stated, then, Kant's first objection seems unpromising. However, owing to the unclarity of the notion of the 'complement of internal possibility' one can hardly blame Kant for getting the wrong end of the stick. Moreover, once Baumgarten's position is clarified, Kant's second criticism actually gains in force.

Kant continues: 'If one allows you to do that, then you have won the illusion of a victory, but in fact you have said nothing; for you have committed a mere tautology' (A 597/B 625). This point is surely correct. Even if the concept of God is the concept of something that, *inter alia*, exists, it does not follow that there is anything that falls under that concept. Caterus had famously made a similar criticism of Descartes, arguing that in deriving God's existence from his concept one has not demonstrated God's existence outside of thought; one has not, as Caterus puts it, shown the existence in question to be anything 'actual in the real world'.[42] In reply, Descartes had claimed that, although the objection does apply

---

[41] I offer a more succinct, but less carefully qualified, version of this same reading in 'Kant on the Ontological Argument' at 14. Nicholas Stang takes my view there to be the obviously mistaken one that since existence for Baumgarten is not contained in the concept of any *finite* thing, neither is it contained in the concept of the *ens realissimum* (see Nicholas Stang, *Kant's Modal Metaphysics* (Oxford: Oxford University Press, 2016) at 61, note 57). This is not how I meant to be arguing, and it is certainly not the argument I meant to be attributing to Kant, but I accept full responsibility for not having made that clear. Stang might have possessed a good objection to my actual line of reconstruction if Baumgarten and Wolff were seeking to define specifically *finite* existence rather than existence in general. But there is, so far as I can tell, no indication of any such qualification or restriction in the relevant texts (see Wolff *Ontologia* §174 and Baumgarten *Metaphysics*, §§54–5).

[42] *AT* VII, 99; *CSM* II, 72.

THE ONTOLOGICAL ARGUMENT   353

to Anselm's version of the argument, it does not apply to his own, for, unlike his famous precursor, he had begun not from a mere name or signification of God ('that than which nothing greater can be thought') but from a concept that is genuinely expressive of God's 'true and immutable nature or essence'.[43] This concept, Descartes supposed, provides the proper starting point for a demonstration that God exists in reality and not merely in thought. Descartes does not explain *why* this difference in starting concept should matter, but given that he makes this move, Kant would need to have something to say back to this Cartesian defence. In the event, however, he attempts no such reply. Indeed, in a reflection he even seems to endorse the Cartesian defence and so reject Caterus's criticism.[44] I therefore take this second criticism to be, by Kant's own lights (but not our own), somewhat inconclusive. It is therefore no great surprise that Kant rests the weight of his case on other points, and, in particular, on the claims that P1 is not known to be true, on the one hand, and that P2 is false, on the other.

14.6 *Existence*, *being*, and *actuality*

On examining Kant's argument for the claim that *being* is not a real predicate, the first thing one notices is that the thesis for which he in fact argues is the claim that *actuality* ('*Wirklichkeit*') rather than *being* ('*Sein*') is not a real predicate. How are these claims related?

The answer, I think, is that Kant simply draws no distinction between actuality and existence understood as what is expressed by the concept of *being* when it is used to express absolute positing. So much is clear from the fact that, while in both the first *Critique* and *Prolegomena* (4: 303) Kant lists the modal categories as 'possibility-impossibility', 'existence-non-existence' (*Dasein-Nichtsein*),[45] and 'necessity' (A 80/B 106), he also, on the one hand, lists the unschematized categories as 'possibility', 'actuality' (*Wirklichkeit*), and 'necessity' (A 144–5/B

---

[43] *AT* VII, 115–16; *CSM* II, 82–3.

[44] Kant says:
Against [the Cartesian ontological argument] one objects in vain that such a possible thing includes existence within itself only in the understanding...but not outside of thought.... The latter indeed occurs when one arbitrarily combines something with a concept that is not necessarily posited thereby; e.g., in this way wings are posited of a horse in thought in order to form a Pegasus, hence wings belong to some horse or other only in thought.... On the contrary, where the connection of a predicate with a thing is not arbitrary, but is combined through the essence of the things themselves, the predicate does not belong to it [merely] because we think it in the thing, but rather it is necessary to think such a predicate in it because it belongs to the thing itself. For this reason I cannot say that the equality of the angles with two right angles belongs to a triangle only in thought, but rather it belongs to it in itself... *This is how matters [would] also stand with existence, if it could be regarded as a predicate of things.* (R 3706, 17: 240–1, emphasis added).
The clear implication is that if existence could be regarded as a predicate of things, the second objection would be answerable.

[45] In the *Prolegomena* Kant lists '*Dasein*' rather than '*Dasein-Nichtsein*'.

184) and, on the other, treats the principles of modality as definitions of possibility, actuality (*Wirklichkeit*), and necessity (A 219/B 266). In addition, although in some places in his writings he offers 'absolute positing' as the definition of existence (2: 73; 2: 82; R 5710, 18: 332), in others he offers this same phrase as the definition of actuality (28: 556; 29: 822). Nor should this equivalence surprise us; for in treating existence and actuality as the same notion, differently expressed, Kant is simply following in the footsteps of Wolff (*Ontology*, §174). All of this suggests that when Kant denies that *being* is a real predicate what he means is that *being*—construed as *existence* or, equivalently, as *actuality*—is not a real predicate.

14.7 *Actuality* is not a real predicate

In the first *Critique* Kant formulates his argument that actuality is not a real predicate somewhat inexplicitly at A 599/B 627. When fully spelled out, this argument takes the form of a simple (and obviously valid) *modus tollens*:

AP1. If *actuality* were a real predicate, then the actual would contain more (reality) than the merely possible (Suppressed premise).

AP2. The actual contains nothing more than the merely possible (Quotation from A 599/B 627).

Therefore:

AC. Actuality is not a real predicate.

On the entirely natural assumption that the concept *actuality*'s being a real predicate would involve the property of actuality's being, specifically, a *reality*, premise *AP1* follows from the following principle:

R: For any property *F*, if *F* is a reality, then an arbitrary object, *x*, that has *F* will have more reality than an object, *y*, that lacks *F* while differing from *x* only as far as it needs to in order to lack *F*.

Principle *R* gives precise expression to the informal thought that a thing's possessing a reality serves to increase its degree of reality.

Kant's reason for endorsing *AP2* is provided by an argument involving his famous example of a hundred thalers. In order to understand this argument we need, I think, to appreciate that Kant is thinking of the concept of *a hundred thalers* in a quite specific way: not as the concept of a concrete pile of coins, but rather as the concept of a particular abstract debt—as it might be, the balance of thalers residing in a certain Prussian's bank account at the close of business on a particular day. This bank balance, of course, is both a debt the bank owes the depositor and an asset to the depositor.

Kant's choice of example enables him to argue for AP2 roughly as follows. Suppose for *reductio* that AP2 is false. That is, suppose that actualization does beef up the degree of reality of a possibilium. Then for any concept F, an actual F will have more reality than a merely possible but otherwise identical F. But then, in particular, an actual deposit of (exactly) a hundred thalers will have more reality than a merely possible deposit of a hundred thalers. But from this it follows—and this is the most controversial step—that the former would be a larger deposit than the latter. But then, absurdly, what actualizes the possibilium in question would not fall under the concept of (exactly) a hundred thalers. I will scrutinize the most controversial step in this argument in the next section.

Such an argument would not have been available to Kant if he had been thinking of the concept of *a hundred thalers* as the concept of a concrete pile of coins. For had that been so, he would not have been able to conclude that a hundred actual thalers was a larger sum of money than a hundred merely possible thalers from the assumption that the former had more reality than the latter. If warmth, for example, is a reality, then a concrete pile of coins might take on an additional reality just by warming up, while, of course, remaining the same sum of money. For this reason, it is crucial to think of a hundred thalers as an abstract debt.

Though Kant is not explicit that he is thinking of a hundred thalers as an abstract debt in the first *Critique*, the point is made less startling by the observation that when he first uses the example of a hundred thalers in his published writings—in his 1763 work, *Negative Magnitudes*—Kant treats the sum in question as a debt. He introduces the example in the course of explaining the concept of a 'real repugnancy'. 'Real repugnancy', he says, is:

> based upon the relation of two predicates of the same thing to each other; but this relation is quite different from that which is present in logical repugnancy. [In real repugnancy] that which is affirmed by the one is not negated by the other. [Rather, in this case] both predicates, A and B, are affirmative. However, since the consequences of the two, each construed as existing on its own, would be a and b, it follows that, if the two are construed as existing together, neither consequence a nor consequence b is to be found in the subject; the consequence of the two predicates A and B, construed as existing together, is therefore zero. (2: 172)

Since in the preamble to this passage Kant glosses the notion of a 'truly affirmative' predicate as a '*realitas*', it is clear that here the species of opposition that he is contrasting with logical repugnancy is real opposition. In the continuation of the passage Kant illustrates this idea of a real opposition with a monetary example:

356   THE FIERY TEST OF CRITIQUE

> Suppose that someone has the active debt $A = 100$ thalers with regard to another person; that active debt is the ground of a correspondingly large [interest] income. But suppose that this same person also has a passive debt $B = 100$ thalers; then that passive debt is the ground of a correspondingly large expenditure [on interest payments]. The two debts together are the ground of zero, that is to say, the ground for neither giving nor receiving money.   (2: 172)

The specifics of the point Kant is making here need not concern us. All that matters for our purposes is, first, that the example of a hundred thalers enters Kant's published writings in a context in which it is clearly intended to be understood as a debt; second, that the debt in question—whether active (an asset) or passive (a liability)—would have been considered by Kant to be a positive ground (2: 175) of its consequence (that 'consequence' being a stream of interest income in the active case, and a series of interest payments in the passive case); and third, that Kant would have thought of the property of having (or, in the active case, being owed) the debt in question as a reality as opposed to a negation. I take these points to indicate that it is not at all far-fetched to suppose that in the hundred thalers argument Kant is conceiving of his example of a hundred thalers as the example of a debt, while also supposing that a debt is something that has a positive degree of reality.

14.8   The 'hundred thalers' argument

We are now in a position to examine the argument for *AP2* more closely. Kant says:

> A hundred actual thalers contain not an iota more [*das mindeste mehr*] than a hundred possible ones. For since the latter signifies the concept and the former the object and its positing in itself, then, in case the former contained more than the latter, my concept would not express the entire object and thus would not be a commensurate [*angemessene*] concept of it.   (A 599/B 627)

The reasoning stated here constitutes the core of a longer argument, which might be spelled out as follows:

HTP1.   If the actual contained more than the merely possible, then, in particular, an actual deposit of a hundred thalers would contain more than a merely possible deposit of a hundred thalers.

HTP2.   If an actual deposit of a hundred thalers contained more than a merely possible deposit of a hundred thalers, then my concept of a deposit of a hundred thalers would not express the entire object and would not be a commensurate concept of it.

HTP3. But my concept of a deposit of a hundred thalers *does* express the entire object and *is* a commensurate concept of it.

Therefore, by a two-step *modus tollens*:

HTC (= *AP2*). The actual does not contain more than the merely possible.

This argument, too, is valid. Premise *HTP1* is unobjectionable: it simply amounts to the claim that if actuality were a reality-enhancing property of a thing, so that an actualized possibilium contained more reality than the possibilium it actualized, then, in particular, an actual deposit of a hundred thalers would contain more reality than a merely possible deposit of a hundred thalers. Our scrutiny should therefore fall on *HTP2* and *HTP3*. Each of these premises calls for interpretation, for we need to know what it would be for a concept to 'express the entire object' and be a 'commensurate' concept of it.

I suggest that what it is for a concept to be a 'commensurate' concept of its object is for it to represent its object as having exactly as much reality as it does in fact have and that what it is for a concept to 'express its entire object' is just for it to represent its object as having at least as much reality as it does in fact have. These glosses accord with our emphasis on the framework of degrees of reality, but the main reason to accept them is just that they make possible a plausible interpretation of Kant's argument for *AP2*.

Kant's appeal to the notion of a 'commensurate' concept is in fact an unnecessary complication. The argument will remain valid if we, first, simplify *HTP2* to:

HTP2 (simplified): If an actual deposit of a hundred thalers contained more reality than a merely possible deposit of a hundred thalers, then what actualizes a merely possible deposit of a hundred thalers would not fall under the concept of a deposit of (exactly) a hundred thalers.

(It should not yet be apparent why this premise is plausible. Its justification will be discussed shortly.)
And, second, simplify *HTP3* to:

HTP3 (simplified): What actualizes a merely possible deposit of a hundred thalers falls under the concept of a deposit of (exactly) a hundred thalers.

I take the reasoning supporting the crucial premise *HTP2* (simplified) to rest on the following principle.

M: The only way that one bank deposit, *A*, could have more reality than another, *B*, is if the monetary magnitude of *A* were to exceed that of *B* (where the bank deposits are conceived of as abstract debts).

The argument for *HTP2* (simplified) then runs: Assume the antecedent of *HTP2* (simplified). Assume, that is to say, that an actual deposit of a hundred thalers were to have more reality than a merely possible deposit of a hundred thalers. Then, by principle *M*, the monetary magnitude of the former would exceed that of the latter. Assume, further, that a merely possible deposit of a hundred thalers has a monetary magnitude of exactly a hundred thalers.[46] Then an actual deposit of a hundred thalers, since it has a greater monetary magnitude than a merely possible deposit of a hundred thalers, will not fall under the concept of *a hundred thalers*. QED.

The argument appears to be valid, but one might question its soundness on the ground that its crucial premise, *M*, seems dubious. Principle *M* in effect treats monetary magnitude as a proxy for degree of reality. But one might wonder whether bank deposits differing in their degree of reality really need differ in their monetary magnitude. The problem arises because in the case of deposits a better proxy for degree of reality than monetary magnitude would seem to be the *value* of the deposit to the depositor. This is not merely a function of the deposit's monetary magnitude because two deposits of a hundred thalers might differ in their value to the depositor merely because they earn different rates of interest, or reside in banks differing in their degree of security, or with different chances of becoming insolvent, and so forth. But, although genuine, this problem may be addressed simply by modifying Kant's example in a minor respect (and modifying principle *M* accordingly).[47]

First, we need to replace the example of the concept of a deposit of a hundred thalers with a concept that builds in a determinate value rather than just a determinate monetary magnitude. One such concept might be that of a deposit of a hundred thalers residing in the Königsberg branch of the Royal Prussian Bank (in a fund earning five per cent interest annually) at the close of business on 22 April 1781. If this specification is not sufficiently detailed to fix the value of the deposit, one may further complicate the example as needed. This repair is available simply because Kant needs to find just one concept to serve as a counter-example to the relevant instance of the consequent of principle *R*. In this respect the argument enjoys a certain robustness.

Second, principle *M* needs to be reformulated so that it speaks not of all deposits but of all deposits of a highly specific kind. Let us call something 'a

---

[46] I am supposing that '*x* is a merely possible deposit of a hundred thalers' should be understood to mean: '*x* is a deposit of a hundred thalers and *x* exists merely possibly'.

[47] I am indebted to Jon Litland for this suggestion.

deposit of kind k' just in case it is a deposit in the Königsberg branch of the Royal Prussian Bank (in a fund earning five per cent interest annually) at the close of business on 22 April 1781. Then we may reformulate M as follows:

M (revised):

The only way one deposit of kind k, A, could have more reality than another of kind k, B, is if the monetary magnitude of A were to exceed that of B.

With these small modifications in place, the argument for $HTP2$ (simplified) would now run as follows: Suppose, first, that the antecedent of $HTP2$ (simplified) is true. That is, suppose that a hundred actual thalers (construed as a deposit of kind k) had more reality than a hundred merely possible thalers (construed as a deposit of kind k). Suppose, second, that the monetary magnitude of anything falling under the concept of a deposit of kind k of a hundred possible thalers is: a hundred thalers. Then, by principle M (revised) and our first assumption, the monetary magnitude of a deposit of kind k of a hundred actual thalers will exceed a hundred thalers. But, then, by our second assumption, a deposit of kind k of a hundred actual thalers will not fall under the concept of a deposit of kind k of a hundred thalers. But that is absurd. QED.

14.9 Evaluation of the argument

Principle M (revised) is in fact ambiguous between two different principles:[48]

M (weak):   Necessarily, for any deposits of kind k, x and y, if x is more real than y, then x has a larger monetary magnitude than y.

M (strong):   For any *possible* deposits of kind k, x and y, if x is more real than y, then x has a larger monetary magnitude than y.

In M (weak) the values of the variables 'x' and 'y' are possibilia in the same possible world; in M (strong), by contrast, the values may or may not be worldmates.

A difficulty now arises because neither disambiguation seems to be suitable for the job assigned to principle M. Although M (weak) is plausibly true, it is not the principle relied on in the argument. For in $HTP2$ a comparison is made between the degrees of reality of a merely possible deposit and its actualization. M (strong), on the other hand, *is* relied on, but it seems to render the argument question-begging because it would be true only if *actuality* were not to be a real predicate. After all, if *actuality* were a real predicate, then one possible deposit might, for all

---

[48] This section has benefited from discussions with Brian Cutter, Jon Litland, and Martin Lin.

we have argued, be more real than another simply by dint of being actual. Should we conclude that Kant has stumbled by conflating these two interpretations of M, and so unwittingly rendered his argument question-begging?

Possibly, but there's a more charitable interpretation. If I am correct in thinking that the hundred thalers argument is directed exclusively against Leibniz (and his close followers), Kant will be able to use Leibnizian commitments as premises in his critical argument. And with the help of these additional resources Kant is, I would argue, in a position to defend principle M (strong) against the charge of begging the question.

But first let me spell out the objection. Kant's envisaged opponent takes issue with principle M (strong) on the ground that it is in fact possible to conceive of two possible deposits of kind k, x and y, such that x is more real than y even though x and y have precisely the same monetary magnitude. The difference in degree of reality, Kant's opponent claims, derives merely from the fact that x is actual and y merely possible. In other words, it derives from nothing over and above the fact that x has a reality that y lacks, namely, actuality. And to deny that one possibilium could be more real than another merely by dint of being actual (when the other is merely possible) is—his opponent continues—simply to beg the question in favour of the view that actuality is not a reality.

Kant, however, can reply that this objection is not available to Leibniz, with the consequence that the hundred thalers argument is effective against him at least. This is so because Leibniz, as Kant would have been aware, takes a stand on the Euthyphro contrast that is incompatible with pressing the present objection to M (strong). In the *Theodicy*—a text familiar to Kant—Leibniz takes the position that the actual world is actualized by God because it is the best; it is not the best because it is actualized. 'Those who believe that God established good and evil by an arbitrary decree', Leibniz says, 'deprive God of the designation good: for what cause could one have to praise him for what he does, if in doing something quite different he would have done equally well?'[49] For Leibniz, then, God is praiseworthy and good because he chooses to actualize the best possible world—a world that is best quite independently of his choice. Substituting 'most real' for 'best'—as the tradition would plausibly warrant (compare *Theodicy* §201)—we obtain the conclusion that, for Leibniz, the actual world is not the most real world because it is actualized by God, rather it is actualized by God because its corresponding unactualized possibilium is the most real. To put the point slightly differently: for Leibniz, differences in the degree of reality between worlds must exist prior to God's creative choice and must serve to ground that choice; they cannot be

---

[49] Leibniz, *Theodicy* at 236. Similar reasoning occurs in Leibniz's *Discourse on Metaphysics*, which, however, was not available to Kant. Leibniz says: '[If we say] that things are not good by virtue of any rule of goodness but solely by virtue of the will of God, it seems to me that we unknowingly destroy all of God's love and all his glory. For why praise him for what he has done if he would be equally praiseworthy in doing the exact contrary?' (Leibniz, *Discours de Métaphysique* at §2).

consequent upon it. But since there seems to be no reason why this reasoning should not apply, *mutatis mutandis*, to world-parts as much as to world-wholes, it seems that Leibniz cannot counter-example M (strong) in the way we have envisaged. He cannot suppose that one possible deposit of kind k is more real than another merely by dint of being actual (that is, merely by dint of having been actualized) when the other is merely possible. For that would involve portraying God's actualizing activity as bestowing extra reality on the deposit in question. Instead, for Leibniz the actual deposit has to be supposed to have been actualized on account of having occupied—independently of God's free choice—the most real possible world.

Since Kant would likely have read the relevant passage from the *Theodicy*, there is good reason to think he would also have known of Leibniz's position on the Euthyphro contrast. I conclude that the hundred thalers argument is effective against Leibniz at least—or at least against the time-slice of him with whom Kant would have been familiar. It should also appeal to anyone attracted to Leibniz's stated argument for his stance on the Euthyphro contrast.

Whether Kant's most famous criticism tells also against Wolff (and his followers) is less clear. For it is hard to know where they stand on the Euthyphro contrast.[50] But since Wolff treats existence as the completion of a possibility (*Ontologia*, §174), it seems likely that Kant—who, as we have seen, would have taken this idea to entail that a thing's existence is extrinsic to its essence—would in any case have treated him as vulnerable, like Baumgarten, to the 'inconsistency' objection. As we noted at the outset, however, the crucial interpretive point is that, having (at least to his own satisfaction) whittled down his German rationalist opponents to Leibniz through preliminary arguments, Kant can appeal to a particular Leibnizian commitment to construct an argument—*viz.*, the hundred thalers argument—that is effective specifically against him.

Since Descartes famously espouses a voluntarist conception of God's powers, Kant's hundred thalers argument will not work against him.[51] This doesn't mean, however, that Kant lacks an effective criticism of Descartes. For the Cartesian argument also relies on premise P1 of the argument we set out in §14.2, namely, 'The most real being has all reality'. In the first *Critique* Kant argues convincingly that this premise cannot be known to be true because we cannot know a priori that the realities are compossible (A 601–2/A 629–30). He makes the same point even more clearly in his religion lectures: 'When I know that a being is the highest in its reality', he says, 'I still do not on that account know whether it has all realities nor [do I know] how many of them it has' (*Danzig Rational Theology*, 28: 1251). What might provide us with that knowledge, of course—if we could come by it—would

---

[50] There is, however, some reason to think that one of Wolff's followers, Baumgarten, does side with Leibniz on the question. See *Metaphysics*, §934.
[51] See *Sixth Replies*, AT VII, 431–2; CSM II, 291–2.

362 THE FIERY TEST OF CRITIQUE

be a proof that a being having every reality is a *real* possibility. For then we might interpret 'a being that is highest in its reality' as meaning one that has the most reality that any being *could* have, and such a being would, given the assumption just stated, have every reality. But, as Kant recognizes, Descartes offers no such proof, and Leibniz also fails to provide one because he demonstrates only the logical possibility of some being's having every reality. We may note, finally, that since Kant regards P1 as not known to be true, he would also seem to be committed to questioning P3: 'P1 and P2 are conceptual truths.'

These last points underscore a main theme of this chapter, namely, the need to recognize Kant's critical case as multiply layered and variously targeted. I hope to have made it plausible that when it is taken as a whole, it succeeds against both Descartes and Leibniz.

14.10 The disputational form of Kant's criticism

Before saying goodbye to the ontological argument, it is worth pausing to note that my interpretation is able to explain an otherwise puzzling feature of Kant's discussion. It explains why Kant should have presented his criticism of the ontological argument in the form, not of an attack on that argument, but rather as a *defence* of the thesis that any concept can fail to be exemplified. For it turns out that according to his own strictures on disputational conduct, Kant *must* present the argument in this form if he is to use one of Leibniz's own commitments against him.

In the tradition of disputations, the technique of using one's opponents' commitments as premises in one's own argument was known as arguing '*ad hominem*'. This did *not* mean that one was committing the fallacy of attacking the person rather than the argument. Rather, an *argumentum ad hominem* was a species of *legitimate* move in a fully rational disputation (see, for example, Meier, §504).[52] It was an argument *ex concessis*: the drawing out of a consequence or commitment of one's opponent's position in order to use that consequence or commitment as a premise in an argument for the falsehood of one's opponent's claim.[53] But, crucially, Kant insists that one is justified in using this anodyne species of *ad hominem* argument *only* as a 'defensive weapon' (8: 134): one can use it to repel an attacker, but not when it is oneself on the attack. It follows that Kant can argue against Leibniz in the way I am suggesting only if he adopts the disputational role of 'defendant' or 'respondent'—as indeed he does according

---

[52] For discussions of this form of argument, see Henry W. Johnstone, *Philosophy and Argument* (University Park, PA: Pennsylvania State University Press, 1959), chapters 5 and 6, and Maurice A. Finocchiaro, 'The Concept of Ad Hominem Argument in Galileo and Locke', *The Philosophical Forum*, 5 (1974), 394–404. I am grateful to Roy Sorensen for these references.

[53] Kant himself speaks of refuting an opponent '*ex concessis*' in his correspondence (11: 50).

to my reading.[54] This otherwise puzzling feature of Kant's presentation is thus fully explained. Also explained is the fact that Kant portrays the party attacking him as couching the ontological argument in the form of an apagogic argument. For Meier lays it down that the attacking party '[seeks to refute] the contested proposition by an apagogical proof' (Meier, *Auszug*, §504).

---

[54] According to Meier, whom Kant seems to be following insofar as he casts his arguments in the form of a disputation, the party tasked with defending the thesis in a disputation is the '*adversarius defendens*' (defender), while his adversary is the '*adversarius opponens*' (attacker) or opponent. Kant presents the ontological argument as being adduced by his opponent in order to attack the contested thesis ('*thesis controversa*') (Meier, *Auszug*, §500) that he is himself defending—the thesis, namely, that any concept can fail to be exemplified. His opponent attacks this claim by adducing the most real being as an alleged counter-example to it, thus applying Meier's seventh rule for the conduct of the attacking party (ibid., §508), namely, the rule that licenses adducing an 'instance [*instantia*]' as an exception to a general claim. Kant, as defending adversary or respondent, first 'takes up the argument' ('*assumere argumentum*') by stating this objection (ibid., §516), with the words 'You argue that...' (A 596/B 624), and then responds using the words: 'I respond: you have already committed a contradiction...' (A 597/B 625). All of this, I would argue, displays Kant's remarkably close adherence at this point of his discussion to the rules of scholastic disputation.

15
The Cosmological Argument

15.1 Introduction

As we saw in the previous chapter, Kant's criticism of the ontological argument is complex and multiply layered. In the Ideal of Pure Reason he constructs a no less richly layered critique of the so-called 'cosmological proof'.[1] He portrays the cosmological argument—as I shall more neutrally term it—as having (or at least purporting to have) three main phases. In the first phase, one observes that there is at least one existent being—the self—and proceeds to argue that it is contingent (28: 1006). In the second, appealing to the *PSR*, one argues from the existence of this contingent being to the existence of an absolutely necessary being as its ultimate cause (A 605/B 633 n*) or ground (28: 1006). In the third, one argues that this absolutely necessary being is a most real being—or *ens realissimum* (A 605–6/B 633–4). In the first *Critique* Kant presents this last step as drawing the argument to a close (A 605–6/B 633–4). But elsewhere he presents the argument as being rounded off by a sort of coda in which one argues that the absolutely necessary being for which one has argued, since it is an *ens realissimum*, must possess every one of the traditional 'divine attributes'—uniqueness included.[2]

These are the main steps of the argument that Kant finds in Leibniz and Wolff, among others—an argument he takes to have enjoyed particular 'prestige' as a result of the efforts of Wolff's followers (2: 157). Nonetheless, he regards the argument set out in these steps as incomplete because it requires the insertion of a further step between the third step and the coda. In this step one argues that the *ens realissimum* is a being that could not fail to exist. As we will see, this further step is needed because in the traditional Leibniz-Wolffian argument the 'absolutely necessary being' argued for by the second step turns out—as surprising as it may seem—to be conceived of *not* as a being that cannot fail to exist (which in the present context is the correct understanding, according to Kant), but rather as an existent being that can exist only in a single way.

---

[1] A 603/B 631–A 614/B 642.
[2] See 28: 1037 and 28: 1047–9 for some of the relevant arguments. Kant alludes to this step in the first *Critique* (A 580/B 608), but ignores it in his official critical discussion of the argument at A 603–6/B 631–4. In what follows I will, for convenience, sometimes speak of the arbitrary *ens realissimum* whose existence the argument strives to establish as 'the *ens realissimum*' even though, strictly speaking, all that has been argued for is *an* entity of this kind. The argument for uniqueness traditionally appeals to the identity of indiscernibles, and involves reasoning that any 'two' most real beings would have all of their non-haecceitistic properties in common, and so, by the principle would be identical.

Kant raises three main objections to this augmented form of the cosmological argument. First, it 'presupposes' the correctness of the ontological argument in the sense, apparently, of tacitly incorporating that argument as a part.[3] Second, and relatedly, it commits an *ignoratio elenchi*—a fallacy of arguing for a conclusion weaker than the one advertised as the argument's goal (A 609/B 637). It commits this fallacy, in Kant's view, because the proponent of the cosmological argument, having promised to establish the existence of an *absolutely necessary*, 'highest' being—that is, a necessarily existent *ens realissimum*—in practice, first contends for a weaker conclusion and then, in order to arrive at the stronger, desired conclusion, reverts to the well-trodden (a priori) path of the ontological argument (ibid.). Third, the cosmological argument presupposes the ontological argument, but not merely because it tacitly assumes its soundness as a premise (A 608/B 637). Since he takes himself to have established the unsoundness of the ontological argument earlier in the Ideal, Kant concludes that the cosmological argument must, for this reason, itself be unsound. He also raises certain other objections to the cosmological argument, including the charge that it attempts to employ the *PSR* beyond its legitimate domain of application (A 609–10/B 638). But it is clear that he wishes to rest the weight of his criticism on the three points just mentioned.

Although commentators tend to agree that Kant announces these three criticisms, not every commentator has been persuaded that he really *develops* all three of them. Most notably, in his path-breaking study of Kant's philosophy of religion, Allen Wood contends that, in spite of presenting himself as developing all three criticisms in the Ideal, Kant in practice makes a case only for the third of them.[4] Wood is certainly right that this is how things seem, but I will argue that, on closer inspection of the relevant texts, his assessment can be seen to be mistaken. Kant does, indeed, develop all three criticisms in the Ideal. Moreover, I will argue that it matters greatly that he should have done so. For it is the two criticisms that Wood takes Kant to have failed to develop that turn out to have the most going for them.

The key to recognizing all three of Kant's announced objections as working parts of his criticism is to consider the following question: To what kind of contingent fact does Kant see the cosmological argument as appealing? The answer is somewhat unexpected: Kant takes his opponent to be appealing not to the assumption that something observably existent *might not have existed at all*, but rather to the assumption that such a thing might have existed in some other way. Accordingly, he supposes that the most that the combination of the first two phases of the argument could hope to establish is that there is some being that cannot exist in a way other than the way in which it actually exists, a being that, as Kant puts it himself, is capable of existing 'only in one single way [*nur auf eine*

---

[3] A 607/B 635; A 608–9/B 636–7.
[4] Allen Wood, *Kant's Rational Theology* (Ithaca, NY: Cornell University Press, 1978) at 124–5.

einziger Art]'.[5] Such a being would be one for which the question: 'Why does this being exist thus and not otherwise?' fails to arise simply because it is conceptually impossible for this being to exist otherwise than it actually does. Henceforth, I will refer to a being so conceived as an 'essentially unimodal being'.

Because, in Kant's view, the first two phases of the cosmological argument could at best—and waiving other objections—establish the existence of an essentially unimodal being, those phases must, he thinks, be supplemented by an a priori train of reasoning in which it is argued first, that this essentially unimodal being is an *ens realissimum* (a most real being), and, second, that this *ens realissimum* exists necessarily or, to put it another way, that it is a necessary being. Kant takes the cosmological argument to depend on the ontological argument because he sees the ontological argument as being enlisted—whether consciously or not—to provide this step in the overall argument. It should not be immediately obvious that Kant conceives of the first two phases of the argument as constituting an argument for the existence of an essentially unimodal being, and much of this chapter will be concerned with substantiating this point. I will argue that four considerations support this conclusion.

First, such a view is the natural one to hold if we make the assumption of interpretive charity on Kant's part. For, it is only if one conceives of a *contingent* being in the way that this view would demand—that is, as a being that *is* capable of having existed in some other way—that the crucial contingency assumption even appears to be capable of being supported by argument (as Kant supposes that it would have to be).[6] To be clear, Kant does not think that his opponent *succeeds* in establishing the contingency assumption, but he does think that they possess an argument for this assumption that is at least *prima facie* cogent. Second, I think it is only by taking this view of what (in Kant's opinion) the first phase of the argument purports to establish that we can make sense of an otherwise obscure passage in the heart of Kant's discussion (A 605–6/B 633–4)—see §15.3 for discussion. Third, one of Kant's actual historical opponents—Christian Wolff— since he conceives of a contingent being as a being that is capable of having existed in some way other than that in which it actually exists, turns out to be committed to thinking of an absolutely necessary being as an essentially unimodal being—see §15.2. Finally, on the assumption that the combination of the first two phases of the argument purport to establish only the existence of an essentially unimodal being we can explain why the notion of a being that is capable

---

[5] A 605/B 633; 28: 1029. Kant speaks on some occasions of an 'absolutely necessary being' and, on others, merely of a 'necessary being'. In the present context, it is clear that the latter phrase is intended to abbreviate the former.

[6] Here it is worth noting that Kant denies the validity of an inference from the possibility of annulling a thing 'in my thought' without contradiction to that thing's having 'objective' contingency 'in itself' (A 244/B 302). He means that we cannot infer from the fact that there is no inconsistency in supposing a thing's concept non-exemplified to the real possibility of its non-existence.

of existing 'only in one single way' should figure in Kant's discussion at A 605/B 633 (compare: 28: 1029).

15.2 Kant's presentation of the cosmological argument

When Kant criticizes the cosmological argument, he telescopes its first two phases into a *modus ponens*:

> If something exists, then an absolutely necessary being also has to exist. Now I myself at least, exist; therefore, an absolutely necessary being exists.
>
> (A 604/B 633; compare A 584/B 612)

This formulation suggests that Kant views the proponent of the cosmological argument as starting not from the assumption that something exists contingently—the starting point usually suggested in the literature—but rather from the assumption that something—namely, the self—*exists*.[7] That Kant views the argument as proceeding in this way is confirmed in the religion lectures by his describing the argument's starting assumption as 'the simplest experience that I can take for granted [*voraussetzen*]: the experience **that I am**' (28: 1006). From this starting point, he explains, 'I infer with **Leibniz** and **Wolff**: I am either necessary or contingent. But the alterations [*Veränderungen*] which go on in me show that I am not necessary; therefore I am contingent' (ibid.). We will examine Kant's criticisms of this argument later in this chapter. But, for now, it will suffice to note that for Kant's cosmological arguer the self's contingency is supposed to be established by certain observed alterations. Although this way of proceeding may not square with Leibniz's actual practice, it does arguably square with Wolff's. For in his *Ontologia* Wolff enunciates the principle that 'Whatever is alterable [*mutabile*] is contingent' (§296).[8] By including Wolff among his chief

---

[7] For accounts that portray the cosmological argument as proceeding from an unsubstantiated contingency assumption, see C. D. Broad, *Kant: An Introduction* (Cambridge: Cambridge University Press, 1978) at 297 and Wood, *Kant's Rational Theology* at 130. Kant himself helps to create the misleading impression that the contingency assumption is not argued for by neglecting to sound the needed note of caution when reporting the label that Leibniz and Wolff use for the argument, namely, 'the proof *a contingentia mundi*' ('the proof from the contingency of the world') (28: 1029; A 604/B 632).

[8] Baumgarten, incidentally, also subscribes to this Wolffian principle (*Metaphysics*, §131). Some evidence that Kant would have agreed with my rendering of '*mutabile*' as 'alterable' is provided by his once having glossed '*Veränderung*' (which is standardly translated as 'alteration') as '*Mutation*' in a reflection (R 5225 (18: 124)). And compare the ease with which he toggles between these terms in the Pölitz religion lectures (28: 1039). Also relevant here is the fact that Baumgarten, whose translations Kant often follows, suggests rendering '*Veränderung*' as '*mutatio*', and '*veränderlich*' as the translation of '*mutabile*'. (See *Metaphysics*, §§125-7.)

opponents, then, Kant is charitably targeting a version of the argument that at least has the merit of attempting to *argue* for its crucial contingency assumption.[9]

In his religion lectures, Kant portrays the cosmological arguer as appealing to the *PSR* in attempting to infer the existence of an absolutely necessary being from the existence of a contingent self. He presents the argument as running as follows:

> If I am contingent, then there must be somewhere **outside me** a ground for my existence, which makes it the case that I am as I am and not otherwise. This ground of my existence must be absolutely necessary. For if it too were contingent then it could not be the ground of my existence, since it would once again have need of something else containing the ground of its existence. This absolutely necessary being, however, must contain in itself the ground of its own existence, and consequently the ground of the existence of the whole world.[10]

Here Kant does not mention the *PSR* by name, but it is clear, both from this passage and from its counterpart in the first *Critique* (A 584/B 612), that he sees the cosmological argument as making use of it.[11] And, notably, the passage makes clear that Kant takes the contingent fact whose explanation initiates the explanatory regress to be the fact that the self exists *as it does and not otherwise*.[12] As we will see, this choice of contingent fact has a crucial bearing on the way in which Kant's criticisms of the argument unfold.

Drawing these points together, we may offer the following reconstruction of the first two phases of the version of the cosmological argument that Kant selects as his first-pass—and not yet charitably emended—target:

P1. I exist and undergo alteration.

P2. Whatever alters is contingent (in the sense of being capable of having existed in some other way).

---

[9] Of course, if the self were *not* to be contingent, the argument would *immediately* reach the conclusion that *a* necessary being existed. However, since that being, in the Wolffian version of the argument, would be the person conducting the argument—a being who is, therefore, in many obvious respects limited—this limb of the dilemma would not establish the existence of God. The argument, accordingly, is *not* most happily construed as an argument by dilemma.

[10] 28: 1006; compare A 584/B 612 and A 605/B 633 n*.

[11] Though he is prepared to call the principle 'the principle of sufficient reason', Kant shares Crusius's dissatisfaction with the label. He complains that the term 'sufficient' is 'ambiguous [*ambigua*]' because 'it is not immediately clear how much is sufficient' (1: 393). Presumably, he means not 'ambiguous' but rather 'vague'. For this reason, he prefers to call the *PSR* either 'the principle of the determining ground' (1: 391) or, as in the first *Critique*, 'the allegedly transcendental natural law of causality' (A 605/B 633 n*).

[12] A remark from Kant's pre-critical writings reveals this conception of contingency to be one he had settled on early in his career (2: 124). The conception shows up again in Kant's religion lectures, where he portrays the proponent of the cosmological argument as positing an 'absolutely necessary cause' as the terminus of an explanatory series generated by asking of each contingent thing in the series why it exists 'so and not otherwise' (28: 1029).

So,

L1. I am contingent (in this sense).

P3. If a being exists that is contingent (in this sense), then, by the *PSR*, an absolutely necessary being (conceived of as a being that contains within itself the ground of its own existence) must also exist.

So,

C. An absolutely necessary being (so conceived) exists.

The argument is valid and its first premise relatively uncontroversial. However, for reasons Kant states in the Fourth Antinomy—and which we examine in §15.5— the warrant for premise P2 is unclear. The warrant for P3 is also unclear given, among other things, its reliance on the *PSR*—a point that we also examine in §15.5.

Although in his religion lectures Kant (correctly) portrays the traditional cosmological argument as seeking to establish the existence of a being that is absolutely necessary in the sense of containing the cause or ground of its existence within itself, he believes that what it properly *ought* to seek to establish is the rather different conclusion that there exists a being 'whose nonbeing is impossible' (A 592/B 620).[13] By this he means a being whose non-being is *logically* impossible in the sense that the supposition of its non-being is contradictory (compare A 607/ B 635). Because it incorporates this feature, Kant's understanding of the kind of being for which, in his view, the argument ought to be arguing represents a clear departure from the stated positions of Leibniz and Wolff. But what this departure amounts to, I think, is less a distortion of their views than a charitable emendation of them. The departure is motivated by Kant's view that Leibniz and Wolff are operating with an incoherent conception of what an absolutely necessary being would have to be.

This view is one at which Kant arrived early in his career. In the *New Elucidation* of 1755 he deems 'absurd' [*absonum*] the idea that something should be capable of containing within itself the ground of, or reason for, its own existence (1: 394).[14] In this same place, he draws the moral that if anything is said to exist with absolute necessity, 'that thing does not exist because of some ground [*propter rationem*]; [rather] it exists because the opposite cannot be thought at all' (ibid.). He puts the point this way because—in some moods at least—he maintains that to think a self-contradictory concept is, strictly speaking, to think nothing at all (compare A 291/B 348). Kant rejects the very idea of a

---

[13] For versions of the argument that have this traditional feature see Wolff, *Natural Theology*, 1, §29 and Leibniz, *Theodicy* §7, 127.

[14] In classical Latin '*absonum*' means 'discordant', or 'inharmonious'; but for Kant it has the stronger meaning of 'absurd'. In the *Inaugural Dissertation*, for example, he applies it to the notion of an infinite number—a notion he plainly considers absurd (2: 389 n*).

self-grounding being as incoherent because he supposes that such a being would have to be its own cause, while also supposing that 'the concept of a cause is by its nature prior to the concept of that which is caused' (1: 394).[15] The *New Elucidation* is, of course, an early work, but in the critical period Kant continues to reject the coherence of the notion of self-causing or self-grounding—along with the attempt to construe absolute necessity in terms of it. In the *Prolegomena*, for example, he characterizes the concept of causality as that concept 'whereby through one thing, something *completely different from it* is posited' (4: 343, emphasis added). In the *Real Progress* he describes the idea that a thing exists as a consequence of itself as an absurdity (20: 278).

And, in same vein, in *On a Discovery*, he claims that to say of the supreme being that it has a ground of its existence that 'lies within it' leads to 'a contradiction' (8: 198). In the first *Critique*, he says: 'Reason cognizes [*erkennt*] as absolutely necessary *only* what is necessary from its concept' (A 612–13/B 640–1; compare 28: 1032, emphasis added).[16] Since he does not think that reason *knows* anything to be absolutely necessary (28: 1033), he must mean that reason cannot *conceive* of absolute necessity except in this way.[17] And, in line with this thought, Kant at one point simply equates absolute necessity with 'an existence from mere concepts' (A 607/B 635). It follows that he cannot, officially at least, think of an absolutely necessary being as a self-grounding being.

In Kant's view, then, the *proper* goal of the cosmological argument is (and can only be), to prove the existence—and status as an *ens realissimum*—of an absolutely necessary being, construed as a being whose non-existence is a conceptual impossibility (A 607/B 635). In the first *Critique* he treats his opponents as though they are attempting to offer such a proof *in lieu* of pursuing their actually professed goal of demonstrating the existence of a being that contains within itself its reason for existing. Lest it might seem unfair of him to proceed in this way, we should stress that his motive for doing so seems to be simply the charitable one of

---

[15] Kant presumably does not mean 'temporally prior' for he allows the coherence of simultaneous causation; he means, rather, 'prior in the causal series'. As Laurie Paul has observed (in conversation), Kant's bald assumption that the notion of a self-caused being is incoherent might be challenged by adducing time-travel cases in which I figure as a partial cause of my own existence. It is worth nothing, therefore, that Kant in fact needs only a weaker assumption to motivate his rejection of a self-grounding or self-caused being, namely, that no *atemporal* being can be its own *total* cause. Since the necessary being to be demonstrated in the cosmological argument is to be shown to have (what Kant takes to be) the traditional divine attributes—atemporality among them (A 641–2/B 669–70; 28: 1067)—this would suffice to address the problem.

[16] A related remark occurs in metaphysics lectures from 1782–83: 'The concept of a self-sufficient being is not the concept of a necessary being' (29: 843).

[17] It follows that when in his reconstruction of the cosmological argument he treats absolute necessity as a matter of being capable of existing in only one way, Kant must be granting this understanding to his opponent solely for the sake of argument. It also follows, as we noted in the previous chapter, that Kant is not being entirely consistent since the fourth antinomy, whose terms Kant does not question, conceives of the absolutely necessary being as an original, hence wholly independent, being.

securing as his target a version of the argument whose conclusion he views as at least *coherent*.

A second point to keep in mind is that the term 'absolutely necessary being' changes its meaning in the course of Kant's discussion of the cosmological argument. According to his reconstruction of the argument, its first two phases purport to demonstrate only the existence of 'an absolutely necessary being' conceived of as what I have termed 'an essentially unimodal being'. But he treats the argument's proper ultimate goal as being to demonstrate the existence and attributes of 'an absolutely necessary being' in the rather different sense of a being whose non-existence is (logically or conceptually) impossible. It is precisely Kant's failure to alert the reader to this shift in meaning that accounts for much of the obscurity in his discussion.[18] The hypothesis of such a shift, I will argue, enables us to understand why Kant should suppose that the cosmological argument derives all of its force from the ontological argument (A 607/B 635). As we will see, it also illuminates certain central passages in Kant's discussion that are otherwise rather obscure.

15.3 The role of contingency

As we have seen, Kant's formulation of the cosmological argument departs from his opponents' with regard to its understanding of the notion of *an absolutely necessary being*. It also *seems* to depart from those formulations in its understanding of contingency. For, at first glance, neither Leibniz nor Wolff seems to be conceiving of the self's contingency as consisting in the fact that it is capable of having existed in some way other than the way in which it actually exists. On closer inspection, however, it becomes apparent, first, that Kant is not in fact misrepresenting Wolff's position—or, at least, his position in *GM*—and, second, that, although he is to some extent misrepresenting Leibniz's position, that is only because he is—once again—offering a charitable emendation of the Leibnizian argument. Wolff's version of the cosmological argument in *GM* is worth examining in detail, for, as we will see, it seems likely to be the version of the argument with which Kant is most directly engaging.

Wolff's presentation of the cosmological argument in *GM* agrees with Kant's insofar as it portrays the argument as beginning with the observation that the self exists, and as proceeding to argue that it exists contingently. Since at the start of

---

[18] Both conceptions of a necessary being come from the tradition. The idea of a necessary being as one that cannot exist otherwise than it actually exists is found in Aristotle and comes down to the modern period by way of the Averroes-influenced St Thomas. The idea of a necessary being as one whose non-existence is contradictory is found in Anselm and Avicenna, and also in St Thomas before he reads Averroes. See Anthony Kenny, *The Five Ways: Saint Thomas Aquinas' Proofs of God's Existence* (London: Routledge, 1969) at 47–8.

his discussion Wolff is conceiving of an absolutely necessary being as an (exclusively) self-grounding (hence self-subsistent) being, his strategy at this point is to argue that the self is contingent because it depends on something distinct from itself (§938). That dependence, he argues, follows from the self's having its 'being and nature' in a faculty of representation whose component representations depend on the states of things in the mind-external world (§941; compare §§755–6). Nonetheless, immediately after making this argument for the self's contingency (in this special sense of 'contingency'), Wolff goes on to consider a way in which his opponent might seek to resist it. The idea would be to raise the sceptical possibility that the world might be nothing beyond (the content of) the self's representations. If this were so, the aforementioned grounds for contingency would be lacking—or so the imagined objector reasons. And therefore, the objector continues, if the cosmological argument is not to depend on an antecedent proof of the existence of the external world, it had better argue for the contingency of the self by some other means.

Wolff's response to this envisaged objection is, in effect, to concede its force, and to fall back on a revised conception of contingency that renders the objection moot.[19] He argues that, even if the 'egoist' were right that the external world does not exist (§944), there would still have to be a reason why the self represents the world as existing thus and not otherwise.[20] The clear implication is that, since the self might have represented things differently—something presumably attested to (in Wolff's view, but not, as we will see, in Kant's) by the fact that it represents the world differently at different times—it qualifies as contingent in the sense of being capable of having existed in some other way. Wolff concludes that, for this reason, even the egoist's self can be known to be a contingent being (§943)—now, of course, in this revised sense of contingency.

Since he depicts the cosmological argument as appealing to the contingent fact that 'I am as I am and not otherwise' (28: 1006). Kant is not, as it turns out, misrepresenting Wolff's *considered* position in GM. But just how faithfully is he representing Leibniz's position? One might have doubts on this score because in a passage from the *Theodicy* (with which Kant would likely have been familiar) Leibniz suggests that the contingent fact to be explained in the cosmological

---

[19] As we saw in Chapter 2, Wolff himself regards the existence of external objects as indubitable (*GM* §1 and §6). He might therefore have stuck to his guns at this point. Instead, he chooses the conciliatory path of granting the objection for the sake of argument.

[20] Wolff says: 'If the world is not actually there but is only constituted by the soul's thoughts, even then it is still true that *the reason why it represents this and not another world* is to be sought in its nature' (*GM*, §943, emphasis added and reading the initial '*Welt*' as '*Wenn*'). I take it that Wolff is not implying that the chain of explanations terminates in the soul's nature. His view rather seems to be that once the soul's nature has been appealed to, the question will then arise why the soul has this particular nature and not some other; for, as he goes on to observe, other kinds of souls are possible (ibid.). In consequence, the chain of explanations generated by asking why the soul exists as it does and not otherwise will, on Wolff's way of thinking, not end until one posits the existence of a being that is itself the sole (hence sufficient) cause of its being the way it is and not otherwise.

argument is the fact that the world exists *at all*. We must, he says, 'seek the reason for the existence of the world' (*Theodicy*, §7, 127). But, although this discrepancy cannot be denied, two points serve to lessen the appearance of a misrepresentation. First, in this same section of the *Theodicy*, Leibniz appeals *also* to the fact that the world exists as it does and not otherwise. 'Time, space and matter', he says, 'might have received entirely other motions and shapes, and [existed] in another order' (ibid.). And the same starting point for the argument is suggested—as an option, at least—by a formulation of the *PSR* that occurs later in the *Theodicy*. 'Nothing', Leibniz says, 'ever comes to pass without there being a cause or at least a reason determining it, that is, something to give an *a priori* reason why it is existent rather than non-existent, *and in this wise rather than in any other*' (emphasis added).[21] The second point that lessens the appearance of unfairness is the fact that by assimilating Leibniz's version of the argument to Wolff's Kant is in fact treating the former charitably. For—as we will shortly see—the version of the argument that proceeds from the assumption that the self is contingent in the sense that it might have existed in some other way turns out, by Kant's lights, to have a better chance of establishing the existence of an *ens realissimum* than the version that begins by assuming merely that the self (or the world) exists.

15.4 The remaining phases of the argument

In the first *Critique* Kant depicts the cosmological argument as containing two further phases. In the third phase, it is argued that the essentially unimodal being, whose existence was purportedly established in the first two phases, is an *ens realissimum*. In the fourth phase, it is argued that this *ens realissimum* is a conceptually necessary being. Kant equates this fourth phase with the ontological argument.

He describes the reasoning of the third phase as follows:

Now the proof further infers: The necessary being can be determined only in one single way, that is, in regard to all possible opposed [*entgegengesetzten*] predicates, it can be determined by only one of them,[22] so consequently it must be *thoroughly* determined through its concept. Now only one single concept of a thing is possible that thoroughly determines the thing *a priori*, namely that of an *ens realissimum*. Thus the concept of the most real being is the only one through

---

[21] Leibniz, *Theodicy* at §44, 147. The clause I have highlighted runs: 'et pourquoi cela est ainsi plutôt que de toute autre façon'. Insofar as it incorporates the clause about ways of existing, Leibniz's formulation of the *PSR* here resembles Clarke's in his third reply. See Alexander (ed.), *The Leibniz-Clarke Correspondence* at 30.

[22] Kant means 'by only one member of each pair'.

which a necessary being can be thought, that is, there necessarily exists a highest being. (A 605–6/B 633–4)[23]

The claim that the necessary being 'can be determined only in one single way' is not, I think, intended to report the conclusion of the 'further' inference mentioned in this passage. Instead, it is intended to remind the reader that the 'necessary being' under discussion at this point is something that is conceived of merely as an essentially unimodal being. That reminder having been issued, the further inference—indicated by the word 'consequently'—then proceeds from the alleged existence of an absolutely necessary being (conceived as an essentially unimodal being), via the idea of thoroughgoing determination, to the existence of an *ens realissimum*.[24]

This reading draws support from the somewhat clearer presentation of this same phase of the argument that occurs in the religion lectures. 'The cosmological proof', says Kant,

> infers further from the purported existence of an absolutely necessary being to the conclusion that this being must also be an *ens realissimum*. The inference runs as follows: This necessary being can be determined in only one way: this is, with respect to all possible *praedicatorum contradictorie oppositorum* [contradictorily opposed predicates] it must be determined by one of these opposed predicates, consequently it must be thoroughly determined by its concept. But there is only one possible concept of a thing which determines it thoroughly *a priori*, and this is the concept of the *ens realissimum*, since in every possible pair of *praedicatis contradictorie oppositis* only the reality belongs to it. Hence the concept of a most real being is the only concept by means of which a necessary being can be thought. (28: 1029–30)

Both this passage and its counterpart in the first *Critique* seem to have caused Kant's commentators a good deal of trouble. Wood declines to engage with the details of either passage, deeming the second of them 'obscure'.[25] Van Cleve quotes the passage from the first *Critique*, but makes no attempt to explain its reasoning.[26] And Bennett, commenting on this same passage, complains that we

---

[23] I take it that this last remark means that the concept of the most real being is the only one that fits the role of the absolutely necessary being *as that notion is understood at this stage*, namely, as the notion of the essentially unimodal being. And, as we will see, Kant thinks that if one wanted to establish the stronger conclusion that the most real being cannot fail to exist, the ontological argument would need to be sound.

[24] Kant attributes this inference to Wolff: 'Now from the absolute necessity of such a being Wolff inferred its highest perfection' (28: 1006). Kant, recall, uses 'highest being' as synonymous with both 'most real being' and '*ens realissimum*' (8: 138; 28: 1013–14; 29: 1001).

[25] Wood, *Kant's Rational Theology* at 125.   [26] Van Cleve, *Problems* at 200.

are not told why a necessarily existing being must be completely determined through its concept.[27]

Nonetheless, the fog begins to clear—or so I would argue—if we suppose that when explicating the first phase of the cosmological argument Kant is using the term 'absolutely necessary being' to mean 'essentially unimodal being'. If that is so, then, contrary to Bennett, we *have* been told why a necessary being must be thoroughly determined through its concept: it must be so determined precisely because it is an essentially unimodal being (we will examine the reasoning behind this explanation shortly).

According to the present reading, each of the two passages just quoted contains the following argument:

AP1. Any essentially unimodal being is an object that is thoroughly determined through its concept.

AP2. Any object that is thoroughly determined through its concept is a most real being.

So,

AC. Any essentially unimodal being is a most real being.

Although the validity of this argument is obvious, the truth of its premises is not. To convince ourselves that Kant would have regarded the premises as true—or, at least, as sufficiently plausible that he might have charitably attributed them to the rational theologian—we need to arrive at a clearer understanding of what it is for an object to be 'thoroughly determined through its concept'.

I want to suggest that—to a first approximation, at least—an object is 'thoroughly determined through its concept' just in case the content of its concept— that is, the content of the concept that expresses its traditional Aristotelian essence—fixes the object's intrinsic properties determinately. So, to illustrate, no human being is thoroughly determined through their concept—namely, the concept *human being (rational animal)*—because the content of this concept fails to settle whether or not the individual in question has, for instance, the property of being tanned. By contrast, on the assumption that all realities are necessarily compossible, the concept of *the most real being*—that is, the concept of *the most real being there could possibly be*—*does* plausibly fix its object's intrinsic properties. The argument for this last conclusion runs as follows. We make two assumptions: first, that all realities are necessarily compossible,[28] second, that for

---

[27] Bennett, *Kant's Dialetic* at 249.

[28] In his discussion of the ontological argument Kant objects that this assumption has not been proven (A 602/B 631). I take it, however, that in the present context he is granting it for the sake of argument.

each intrinsic property, F, exactly one of F and its negation is a reality.[29] Then, it follows by the first assumption that the most real being—that is, the most real being there could possibly be—must have every reality. And, by the second, it follows that the most real being will be determined by its concept to have exactly one property from each pair of contradictorily opposed intrinsic properties, for it will possess the reality (and only the reality) in the pair. It will therefore be thoroughly determined through its concept.

We can make the idea of 'thorough determination' more precise by enlisting the concept of entailment. We will say:

> An object, x, is thoroughly determined through a concept, F, just in case, for any intrinsic property, G, the proposition that x is F either entails that x is G or entails that x is not G.

So, for example, Madonna is not thoroughly determined through the concept *human being* because—among other things—the proposition that Madonna is a human being entails neither that she is tanned nor that she is not tanned. On the other hand, given our two assumptions, the most real being *is* thoroughly determined through the concept, *the most real being*. To see this, consider an arbitrary intrinsic property, G. By our second assumption, exactly one of G and its negation is a reality. Call the reality in this pair, R. And call the proposition that the most real being is a most real being, p. Then, by our first assumption, p entails the proposition that the most real being is R. If R is identical with G, this means that p entails that the most real being is G. If, on the other hand, R is identical with G's negation, then p entails that the most real being is not G. But, since R is, by construction, identical with exactly one of G and G's negation, this means that one or other of these entailments must hold. Finally, since G is arbitrary, that means that the most real being is thoroughly determined through its concept.

With this understanding of 'thoroughgoing determination' in place, we may return to the argument for the claim that any essentially unimodal being is a most real being (our *AC*). I take it that the first premise of this argument—*AP1*—would be established by the following reasoning. Suppose, for *reductio*, that some essentially unimodal being, x, were not thoroughly determined through its concept. And suppose that the concept of any essentially unimodal being is *an essentially unimodal being*. Then there would be some intrinsic property, G, such that the proposition that x is an essentially unimodal being entailed neither that x was G nor that x was not G. But then it would be metaphysically possible—or, as Kant says, a 'real' possibility—for x to be G, and it would also be

---

[29] That Kant is operating on this assumption is clear from his saying that in every pair of contradictorily opposed predicates only '*the* reality [*das Reale*]' belongs to the most real being (28: 1029, emphasis added).

metaphysically possible for x not to be G. But then x would be capable of existing in more than one way, and so would not be an essentially unimodal being. Contradiction. QED.

This argument is arguably sound.[30] Premise *AP2*, on the other hand, is distinctly dubious. There is no obvious argument in its favour and—worse—it faces plausible counter-examples. One wonders, for example, why a Leibnizian complete individual concept should not qualify as a concept that thoroughly determines its object.[31] Take, for example, the complete individual concept—or 'notion'—of Caesar. If, as Leibniz supposes, this concept contains a constituent concept for every property that has ever held or will ever hold of Caesar, then, surely, it will thoroughly determine its object. Another concept that might seem to thoroughly determine its object—if the concept of a most real being does—is the concept of *a thing possessing every reality save benevolence*.

Why these concepts should not be thought of as thoroughly determining their objects is a good question. But I think Kant would not wish to challenge *AP2* on these grounds. For, in the first place, even if he had known of it—and that seems unlikely—he could not have regarded the Leibnizian conception of a complete individual concept as coherent.[32] For a concept of this sort would have to contain *infinitely* many component concepts—something that is, by Kant's lights, impossible (B 40) (The concept of the most real being, by contrast, contains only a handful of constituents, namely, the concepts *most*, *real*, etc.). Our second putative counter-example requires more delicate handling because the concept in question contains only finitely many component concepts. The reason why Kant would not, I think, see this example as providing grounds for rejecting *AP2* is that he is acquiescing in the traditional idea, found in Descartes among others, that the divine attributes are somehow inseparable or reciprocally grounding.[33] As Kant's contemporary, Moses Mendelssohn, puts the point:

> A single chain of inferences combines all perfections of [the supreme being]. His independence, infinity, immensity, his supremely perfect will, unbounded intellect, and unlimited power, his wisdom, providence, justice, holiness, and so forth are reciprocally grounded in one another in such a way that, without the others, each of these properties would be contradictory.[34]

---

[30] There is perhaps room for doubt about its second premise, though such a doubt might be quelled if we supposed that in the argument 'an essentially unimodal being' means 'an essentially unimodal being *considered merely as such*'.

[31] Bennett seems to be raising this worry, or something like it, when he claims that the concept of the *ens realissimum* is not the only 'saturated concept' (Bennett, *Kant's Dialetic* at 249).

[32] As is well known, Kant did not have access to the works in which the theory of complete individual concepts is developed.

[33] Descartes presents God's attributes as enjoying 'inseparability' [*inseparabilitas*] in the third Meditation (*AT* VII, 50; *CSM* II, 34).

[34] 'On Evidence in Metaphysical Sciences', in Mendelssohn, *Philosophical Writings* at 279.

Kant shows himself to have a similar conception of how the divine attributes are mutually related in his religion lectures. There, speaking of God's divine attributes, which he characterizes as 'single realities without limitation', he says: 'I think of each such unlimited reality equally as a ground from which I understand every other unlimited reality' (28: 1015). Mendelssohn's talk of a single chain of *inferences* suggests that mutual or reciprocal grounding is supposed to imply mutual or reciprocal *entailment*. But if so, the present objection may be resisted. For, given such a view, the argument for AC may be trivially reformulated in a way that gets around the problem, namely, thus:

A*P1: Any essentially unimodal being is thoroughly determined through its concept, where this concept is capable (as a matter of real possibility) of exemplification.

A*P2: Anything that is thoroughly determined through its concept, where this concept is capable (as a matter of real possibility) of exemplification, is a most real being.

So,

A*C: Any essentially unimodal being is a most real being.

The new argument circumvents the present objection because, on the assumption that the perfections (or realities) of the most real being are mutually entailing, the concept of *a being with every reality save benevolence* is not capable of exemplification and so will not constitute a counter-example to A*P2. To be sure, a positive argument for A*P2 has not been provided, but, so long as counter-examples to this premise are not in the offing, we can plausibly suppose that Kant would have been prepared to grant it for the sake of argument—and the same would go for premise A*P1.

One moral we may draw from all of this, independently of the finer details of our discussion, is that Kant sees the argument for the thesis that the absolutely necessary being is an *ens realissimum* as proceeding along strikingly different lines from the argument for the similar-sounding thesis that Leibniz offers in the *Theodicy*.[35] There, Leibniz had argued that the absolutely necessary being allegedly proved to exist in the first phases of the cosmological argument would—in virtue of its assumed role in choosing and actualizing the best of all possible worlds—have to be absolutely perfect in respect of its power, wisdom, and goodness (*Theodicy* 1, §7). Since Leibniz's argument relies on substantive assumptions about how the necessary being goes about creating the world, it is not all that surprising that Kant should proceed differently when trying to offer a sympathetic

---

[35] Only 'similar-sounding' because, for Leibniz, the absolutely necessary being is not merely an essentially unimodal being.

reconstruction of the cosmological argument. Instead, he first conceives of an absolutely necessary being as an essentially unimodal being, and then proceeds to argue (on his opponent's behalf) that such a being must be an *ens realissimum*. And he does so by introducing a consideration—the concept of thoroughgoing determination—to which Leibniz's argument for the corresponding conclusion makes no appeal.

This observation helps to explain why Kant should be more concerned with Wolff's version of the argument than Leibniz's. We have already seen that he would in any case likely prefer Wolff's version because it troubles to argue for its crucial contingency assumption. We now see that Wolff's version additionally suggests a natural route by means of which one might attempt to argue that the 'absolutely necessary being' contended for in the combination of the first two phases of the cosmological argument—that is an essentially unimodal being—is an *ens realissimum*. For, as we have just seen, there is a passably coherent—if not in the end demonstrably sound—argument that any essentially unimodal being must be an *ens realissimum*. And Wolff's version of (the first phase of) the argument, since it starts by assuming a being that is conceived of as contingent in the sense of being capable of having existed in some other way, is naturally viewed as properly culminating in the positing of an essentially unimodal being— even if Wolff does not draw this conclusion himself.[36]

Let us now turn our attention to what I have described as a supplementary step that Kant sees as intervening between the third step of the traditional argument and the coda. Here one attempts to deduce the existence of a being that cannot fail to exist from the supposed existence of an *ens realissimum*. Kant sees such an inference as relying on the ontological argument. He says that the proponent of the cosmological argument, having established (to his own satisfaction) the existence of a 'being of the highest reality' (that is, an *ens realissimum*) then presupposes [*voraussetzt*] that from the concept of such a being the concept of an absolutely necessary being may be inferred (A 607/B 635). This inference, Kant says, is something that the ontological proof 'asserted' and which 'one thus assumes in the cosmological proof and takes as one's ground [*zum Grunde legt*], although one had wanted to avoid it' (ibid.). The reason he offers for equating this last step with the ontological argument is that he now construes absolute necessity as 'an existence from mere concepts' (ibid.). Clearly then, at the close of his reconstruction of the cosmological argument Kant is understanding the phrase 'an absolutely necessary being' as meaning a being whose existence follows from

---

[36] Wolff attempts to establish that the necessary being has the traditional divine attributes by appealing to its status as an *ens a se*—that is, a being that contains within itself the sufficient reason for its existence (*Natural Theology*, 1.2, §31. For some of the relevant arguments see §§24–74 of this work). Kant, however, since he rejects the very idea of an *ens a se* thus understood, would also reject Wolff's argumentative path to the divine attributes.

its very concept, rather than, as he had done earlier, a being that is capable of existing in only one way.

In his religion lectures, Kant remarks that the ontological argument gives the cosmological argument 'all its probative force [*Beweiskraft*]'.[37] We will shortly consider why he should say such a thing. But the point to note for now is just that, even if the argument for the existence of a most real being were to be sound, it would not establish the existence of an absolutely necessary being—understood now as a being that cannot fail to exist. This point, I take it, is what Kant is driving at when he says: 'The greatest perfection, no less than the smallest, hovers without support before speculative reason' (A 613/B 641).[38] He means that, unless we assume the ontological argument as an inferential subroutine—and unless that argument is sound—even the most real (or most 'perfect') being will lack a proof of its *necessary* existence. Accordingly, Kant supposes that the ontological argument is required to license the inference from the most real being's (supposed) existence to its necessary existence. Since this extra step is required, the cosmological argument, as it stands, could establish—at best, and waiving certain other objections that Kant will make—only the existence but not the necessary existence of an *ens realissimum*. And since the argument establishes less than it purports to establish, its proponent (who fails to recognize this fact) commits an *ignoratio elenchi* (A 609/B 637). The second of Kant's three main charges against the cosmological argument is thus substantiated.

In connection with this last point, it is important to note that the conclusion of an *ignoratio elenchi* need not be unrelated to the conclusion for which one is supposed to be arguing: indeed, it might even be a step on the way. Committing the fallacy of *ignoratio elenchi* consists merely in overestimating the strength of an actually attained conclusion—and, in particular, in wrongly supposing that it is the conclusion one was supposed to be proving. This point is illustrated by an example of an *ignoratio elenchi* that Kant gives in his logic lectures, namely, the fallacy of arguing merely for a 'future life' when one was supposed to be arguing for the soul's immortality.[39] A weaker—if still interesting, and to some extent pertinent—conclusion is thus unwittingly passed off as the desired, stronger conclusion.

---

[37] 28: 1006–7; compare A 607/B 635. I owe this felicitous translation to W. F. Vallicella. See W. F. Vallicella, 'Does the Cosmological Argument Depend on the Ontological?', *Faith and Philosophy*, 17 (4) (2000), 441–58.

[38] Here, I favour Kemp Smith's rendering of '*wie*' as 'no less than' over Guyer and Wood's 'as well as'. Kant is surely trying to convey that, for all the argument has so far shown, the most real being—for all its perfection or reality—is no more firmly supported in existence than a being with the lowest (non-zero) degree of reality.

[39] Immortality involves the natural impossibility of the soul's ever ceasing to exist, an afterlife merely the soul's existing—perhaps contingently—for some, possibly finite, period after bodily death. See 28: 778 and compare: 28: 284; 29: 911.

In Kant's view, the cosmological arguer embarks upon an a priori 'digression' when he reasons from the conclusion that the essentially unimodal being exists to the conclusion that an *ens realissimum* exists. But if that is so, one wonders why Kant should claim that this digression brings us back to the 'old path' of the ontological argument (A 609/B 637). The opening assumption of the ontological argument, after all, is quite obviously *not* the assumption that an *ens realissimum* exists.[40] To resolve this difficulty it helps to recall that Kant's quarry is a version of the ontological argument that begins with an attempt to demonstrate the logical consistency of the concept of the *ens realissimum*.[41] Accordingly, we can think of the reasoning of the 'digression' as bringing us back to the beginning of the ontological argument because, if sound, it will establish a conclusion from which we can trivially infer the *consistency* of the concept of the *ens realissimum*—the conclusion, namely, that the *ens realissimum* exists.

It may seem odd for Kant to write as though the proponent of the cosmological argument succeeds in establishing a result as strong as the existence of an *ens realissimum*. But we may, I think, view this as merely yet another symptom of his thoroughgoing concessiveness. Officially, he thinks that his opponent cannot establish this result—indeed, he sees the relevant reasoning as riddled with error (A 609–10/B 637–8). But Kant's purpose is not merely to raise objections to the cosmological argument: he wishes to raise the deepest and most telling objections he can. And he believes that none of his objections to the argument for the existence of an *ens realissimum* can rival in power his charge that the inference from the existence of an *ens realissimum* to its necessary existence depends on the ontological argument. From Kant's point of view, this is an especially damning criticism because he supposes himself already to have *proved* the unsoundness of the ontological argument in its Leibnizian setting and, outside of that setting, to have revealed its status as not-known-to-be-sound (recall that his criticism of P1 in that argument is that it is not known to be true and that *this* criticism is not *ad hominem*). Consequently, if he can prove the dependence of the cosmological argument on the Leibnizian ontological argument, his objection to the former will (he thinks) have something approaching demonstrative force. (Only 'approaching' because Kant officially reserves the word 'demonstration' [*Demonstration*] for such arguments as have that kind of dependence on intuition that enables them to generate conclusions enjoying the highest degree of theoretical certainty. When being careful he reserves the word 'proof' [*probatio*] for arguments which, not being thus anchored in intuition, produce not 'evidence' in his technical sense (that is, apodictic *intuitive* certainty), but only conviction (that is, apodictic

---

[40] I am grateful to Randolph Clarke for posing this question.

[41] Recall that Kant attributes the relevant logical possibility assumption to the proponent of the ontological argument when he says: 'and [you say that] you are justified in assuming [the most real being] as possible' (A 596–7/B 625).

discursive certainty). Arguments in the former category—that is, demonstrations—turn out to belong exclusively to mathematics; those in the latter category include certain sound arguments in philosophy.)[42]

It therefore suits Kant's purposes to consider how far the argument would carry us if we were to allow his other objections to lapse. And the answer turns out to be: not far enough to attain the goals of the dogmatic speculative theologian. We would, at best, establish the existence of a most real being; but we would lack the warrant to clothe this being in its traditional theological garb. For, if one is to earn the right to treat the *ens realissimum* as (something like) the God of the Abrahamic tradition, one will need to argue that it exists necessarily (A 641-2/B 669-70).

Given this diagnosis, one can easily see why Kant should not have bothered to develop his other criticisms of premise P3 in the argument presented in §15.2. Since he regards the argument from a contingent self to the essentially unimodal being as a red herring, the issue of that argument's cogency becomes moot. The important point for Kant is just that if the ontological argument is sound, there is no need for the elaborate train of reasoning that leads from the existence of the self, by way of the essentially unimodal being, to existence of a most real being.[43] If, on the other hand, the ontological argument is not cogent, then the cosmological argument will also lack cogency. For, even if it were otherwise impeccable, the elaborate chain of reasoning in question would bring us only as far as the existence, but not the necessary existence, of an *ens realissimum*, and so would need to be supplemented by an appeal to the ontological argument. This, I think, is why Kant says that the cosmological argument draws '*all* its probative force' from the ontological argument (emphasis added).[44]

But in what way exactly does Kant see the cosmological argument as tacitly relying on the ontological argument? In tackling this question it pays to keep in mind that, in the present context at least, Kant is conceiving of an absolutely necessary being as a being whose existence follows from its concept (A 607/B 635). That being so, in order to show that the *ens realissimum* exists necessarily the cosmological arguer will need to exhibit, through a derivation, the alleged fact that its existence follows from its very concept. Kant agrees with Leibniz that such a feat would require establishing *two* things. First, one would need to establish the consistency of the concept of the *ens realissimum*; second, one would need to derive the *ens realissimum*'s existence from its very concept. As we have seen, Kant

---

[42] See A 734/B 762, R 5645 (18: 290-1), and 24: 892. In the *Dohna Wundlacken Logic* Kant makes clear that the difference between discursive and intuitive certainty—which he now calls 'mathematical certainty'—is a difference of degree (24: 748).

[43] Recall that Kant does not object to Leibniz's demonstration of the *logical* consistency of the concept of the *ens realissimum*. In consequence, the reasoning of the cosmological argument is not, from his point of view, required in order to establish this result.

[44] See 28: 1006-7, compare A 607/B 635.

takes the first of these tasks to be assigned by the cosmological arguer to the line of reasoning that leads from the existence of the self to the alleged existence of the *ens realissimum*. And this seems entirely appropriate, for, if sound, this stretch of reasoning would indeed trivially prove the consistency of the concept of the *ens realissimum*. He takes the second to involve arguing that, since the *ens realissimum* has every reality, and since existence is a reality, the *ens realissimum* exists. If Kant is correct in holding that this reasoning—the heart of the ontological argument—is unsound, the derivability in question will remain undemonstrated, and so one will fail to show that the *ens realissimum* is a necessary being.[45] This, I think, suffices to establish the correctness of Kant's first main criticism of the cosmological argument—or rather, it does so if we grant him his favoured conception of what it is to be an absolutely necessary being (that is, to be a being whose existence follows from its concept). For, given that conception, the cosmological argument does indeed assume (the soundness of) the ontological argument as a tacit premise.

15.5 Contingency and the *PSR*

Although Kant regards as moot the question of the soundness of what in §15.1 I identified as the first phase of the cosmological argument, he does raise certain objections to this reasoning.[46] One of the more important among them alleges that the cosmological arguer in fact has no occasion to employ the *PSR*—styled as 'the transcendental principle of inferring from the contingent to a cause' (A 610/B 638)—in the course of the cosmological argument because the relevant contingency is not proven. Although in the Ideal Kant touches on this point only briefly (A 609/B 637), it amounts to a trenchant criticism of Wolff's manner of proceeding.[47] The problem is that in order to apply the *PSR* in the Wolffian cosmological argument one needs to know that the self is contingent in the sense that it can exist in more than one way. Naïvely, one imagines that this may be established by appealing to the fact that the self actually exists in more than one way (at different times) when it alters. As Kant explains in the comment on the thesis of the fourth antinomy, however, alteration does not in fact serve to establish the requisite kind of contingency.[48]

---

[45] We should not worry that the *ens realissimum*'s existence has (allegedly) already been established earlier in the cosmological argument for at this stage the question is whether that existence follows merely from the *ens realissimum*'s concept.

[46] *Contra* Wood (Allen Wood, 'Rational Theology, Moral Faith, and Religion', in Guyer (ed.), *The Cambridge Companion to Kant*, 394–416 at 399).

[47] In his religion lectures Kant portrays Leibniz and Wolff as attempting to infer the contingency of the self from the fact that it alters (28: 1006). This seems to be a fair representation of how Wolff might reason, since in his *Ontologia* Wolff claims that 'Whatever is alterable [*mutabile*] is contingent' (§296).

[48] A 459–60/B 487–8; compare B 290n and R 4306 (17: 501).

To put the point in contemporary terms, what Wolff needs to show is that there is one possible world in which the self is *F* at a given time and another world at which it is not *F* at that same time. To show this it will not suffice to show that there is a world in which the self is *F* at one time and not *F* at another. The self's (intelligible) contingency is therefore not established.

15.6 Kant's third main criticism: the *nervus probandi* and its converse

In his third main criticism Kant imagines that his opponent had after all succeeded in establishing the existence of an 'absolutely necessary being' (words whose meaning at this point he leaves unclear). He now contends that if the inference from the absolutely necessary being to the most real being were to be sound, the ontological argument would also be sound. And, supposing himself to have established the unsoundness of the latter, he infers by *modus tollens*, to the unsoundness of the former. Kant presents this objection as follows:

> If the [following] proposition is correct: "Every absolutely necessary being is at the same time the most real being" [*das allerrealste Wesen*] (which is the *nervus probandi* of the cosmological proof), then, like any affirmative judgment, it must at least be convertible *per accidens*, thus: "Some most real beings are at the same time absolutely necessary beings". But now one *ens realissimum* does not differ the least bit from another, and thus what holds of **some** beings contained under this concept holds also of **all**. Consequently, I will also be able (in this case) to convert the proposition **absolutely**, i.e., [infer from it] "Every most real being is a necessary being". Now, because this proposition is determined merely from its concepts *a priori*, the mere concept of the most real being must carry with it also the absolute necessity of this being—which is just what the ontological proof asserted, and the cosmological proof did not want to recognize, despite the fact that it underlay its inferences, though in a covert way. (A 608–9/B 636–7)

Informally spelled out, Kant's objection takes the form of the following (somewhat dubious) argument:

[1] Suppose, it is a conceptual truth, and so known a priori, that every absolutely necessary being is a most real being. (Premise)

[2] Then, by the rule of *per accidens* conversion, some most real being is an absolutely necessary being.[49]

---

[49] The rule licences the inference from 'All *F* are *G*' to 'Some *G* is *F*'.

[3]   But what holds of some most real being holds of all. (Because all most real beings have exactly the same properties).

[4]   By [2] and [3], all most real beings are absolutely necessary beings.

[5]   But our derivation of [4] begins from a conceptual truth and employs only logically or conceptually valid reasoning. So [4] itself is a conceptual truth—it is, as Kant puts it, 'determined merely from its concepts a priori' (A 608/B 637).

But then, the mere concept of a most real being carries with it the absolute necessity of this being.

[6]   But *that*—the conclusion of [5]—is just what the ontological argument purports to establish.

So,

[7]   If it is a conceptual truth that every absolutely necessary being is a most real being, then the ontological argument must be sound. (Discharging our premise [1]).

[8]   But the ontological argument is not sound.

So, by *modus tollens*,

[9]   The absolutely necessary being cannot be shown to be a most real being. QED.

If we suppose that Kant is granting for the sake of argument that the cosmological argument has established on empirical grounds the existence of an absolutely necessary being (a phrase whose meaning for now we leave unsettled), then the first part of this argument—that is, steps [1]–[4]—is, by *our* lights at least, valid. (We'll shortly ask whether Kant himself is really entitled to view it as valid given his other commitments.) For, as Wood has observed, given this assumption it does not matter that the argument relies on the nowadays discredited rule of *per accidens* conversion. For the existential commitment of that inference, while not warranted generally, is nonetheless warranted in this particular instance by the assumption that the first phases of the cosmological argument have already proved the existence of an absolutely necessary being.[50]

To put the point slightly differently, the following argument is (by our contemporary lights) logically valid:

---

[50] See Wood, *Kant's Rational Theology* at 127. Wood generously credits this observation to Peter Remnant, 'Kant and the Cosmological Argument', *Australasian Journal of Philosophy*, 32 (7) (1959), 152–5. But his own formulation of the point is considerably clearer. Lest, influenced by reflection on the apparent truth of 'Some things don't exist', one wonder whether it may not be anachronistically Quinean to suppose that Kant is treating the particular quantifier as existentially committing, we may note that non-ampliated particular affirmatives—that is, claims of the form 'Some S is P' that are free of words indicating tense or modality—are, in the tradition stemming from Buridan, treated as existentially committing, see Gyula Klima, 'The Nominalist Semantics of Ockham and Buridan', in Dov M. Gabbay and John Woods (eds), *Handbook of the History of Logic*, volume 2: *Mediaeval and Renaissance Logic* (Amsterdam: Elsevier, 2008), 417–21.

BP1: Every absolutely necessary being is a most real being.

BP2: There exists some absolutely necessary being.

BP3: Every most real being has exactly the same properties as every other.

So

BC: Every most real being is an absolutely necessary being.

The validity of this argument can be established by the following reasoning. Consider an arbitrary most real being, *a*. We want to show that *a* is an absolutely necessary being. Now consider the absolutely necessary being—or beings—asserted to exist by BP2. Call it—or one of them—*b*. We know that *b* is an absolutely necessary being; so by BP1, *b* is a most real being. But because both *a* and *b* are most real beings, we know, by BP3, that they have exactly the same properties. So, in particular, since *b* has the property of being an absolutely necessary being, *a* has that property, too. QED.[51]

This shows that the initial part of the argument—steps [1]–[4]—is valid in the context (of what we have supposed to be) Kant's concessive assumption that an absolutely necessary being exists. Nonetheless his argument as a whole—steps [1]–[6]—remains problematic in virtue of—among other things—the dubiousness of his claim that if the absolutely necessary being is the most real being, then it follows that the converse of this assumption—our proposition *BC*—is knowable a priori. Kant needs to make such a claim because it is the alleged status of *BC* as a conceptual truth that is supposed, as Kant sees it, to show that the most real being exists from its very concept. And the conclusion that the most real being exists from its concept was required because one wanted to show that the most real being was a necessary being (which, for Kant, just means that its existence follows from its very concept).

The problem for Kant is that he has *not* demonstrated that his opponent's assumption of premise [1] entails the a priori status of *BC*. For, as we have already seen, a valid argument for *BC* would depend on the empirical premise, *BP2*. In the end, then, the fact that *per accidens* conversion—understood as an inference with an existentially committing conclusion—is not today recognized as logically valid *does* turn out to matter. For, although in the present context it does not undermine the reasoning of parts [1]–[4] of the argument, it does undermine the claim (our step [5]) that that reasoning is logically or conceptually valid. Kant's third criticism accordingly fails.

But does the fault lie with Kant's criticism or merely with his formulation of it? The question is worth asking because it turns out that his third criticism can be reformulated in a way that gets around the present difficulty, namely, by

---

[51] I agree with van Cleve that this argument does not rely on the identity of indiscernibles. See van Cleve, *Problems* at 305 n51.

disambiguating the phrase 'absolutely necessary being' by interpreting it as meaning 'conceptually necessary being'. Kant's third criticism would then run as follows: Suppose for the sake of argument that the cosmological argument had somehow succeeded in showing that a conceptually necessary being exists, and suppose, further, that it had also shown that any conceptually necessary being is a most real being. Let's call these imagined results P1 and P2 respectively. Kant's contention would then be, first, that on the basis of these assumptions, we would also be able to establish the converse of P2—which I will call 'L1'—namely, that any most real being is a conceptually necessary being, and second, that L1 would itself suffice (in the context of P1 and P2) to prove the soundness of the Leibnizian ontological argument. Since that argument is, in Kant's view, unsound, this suffices to refute the cosmological argument.

The argument for the second of these claims would run as follows. Call the (or one of the) conceptually necessary being(s) whose existence, according to P1, has been established, a. By P2, a is a most real being. So, we know that a is both a conceptually necessary being and a most real being. Let us further assume that a's concept is the concept *most real being*. Then since a is a conceptually necessary being, a's existence can be derived from a's concept, and so from the concept *most real being*. And since a is an existent most real being, it follows trivially that the concept *most real being* is consistent. We thus arrive at the two propositions that the Leibnizian ontological argument aims to establish.

The task of reconstructing a viable version of the third objection therefore reduces to that of showing that it follows from P1 and P2 that any most real being is a conceptually necessary being (our L1). The argument for this claim runs along by now familiar lines. Suppose P1. Call the (or a) conceptually necessary being thus assumed to exist, a. Then by P2, we know that a is a most real being. Let b be any most real being. Then since all most real beings have all their properties in common, and since a is a conceptually necessary being, b must be one too. But b was an arbitrarily chosen most real being; so, any most real being is a conceptually necessary being. QED.

Thus reformulated, the argument is an improvement on the version Kant offers. But certain difficulties remain. First, it is not clear why one should grant the assumption that 'the' concept of the most real being is: *most real being* (after all, for any object there are many concepts that it exemplifies). This assumption might follow if a thing's concept could be equated with its unique essence and if the essence of a most real being were *to be a most real being*, but the warrant for such claims is unclear. Second, and more decisively, the argument seems to rest on a deeply un-Kantian assumption. As we have seen, it is central to Kant's critique of the ontological argument to deny that the property of being (construed as the property of existence or actuality) is a reality. It would seem to be no less central to that critique to deny that the property of being a conceptually necessary being is a reality; for if it were, the ontological argument could be run directly on this property.⁵² This matters in the present context because the assumption that all most real beings have the same properties seems to rely on the background assumption that any most real being has all and only the realities. (Kant, let us suppose, is conceding this background assumption to his opponent for the sake of argument.) The idea would be that if every most real being has the same properties that is only because those properties are supposed to include all and only the realities. But with that understanding of the ground for this assumption (our BP3) in place, it seems that 'properties' in BP3 must be understood in a restricted sense; for, with the exception of certain identity-involving properties, the properties all most real beings can be assumed to have in common are just the realities. But if that is so, it follows that Kant could not endorse the inference to the conclusion that *b* is a conceptually necessary being. For such an inference would be valid only on the un-Kantian assumption that the property of *being a conceptually necessary being* is a reality.⁵³ It seems, then, that Kant could not regard even our reformulated version of his third criticism as sound.⁵⁴

This concludes our discussion of Kant's case against the cosmological argument. I hope to have shown that it does—in spite of Wood's doubts—contain all three of his announced criticisms. These criticisms are, I think, most illuminatingly presented in the following order. First, the Wolffian cosmological argument, since it starts from the assumption that the self is contingent in respect of its character—the way in which it exists—rather than in respect of its very existence, locks itself into building a case only for the existence of an essentially unimodal being. This is unsatisfactory because what is actually required is an argument for the existence of a being that could not fail to exist.⁵⁵ And—this first objection continues—even when the first two phases of the argument are supplemented by the step leading from the essentially unimodal being to the *ens realissimum* we still reach—waiving certain other objections—only the conclusion that an *ens*

---

⁵² The point that the property of being a conceptually necessary being is not a reality is suggested by Kant's claim in the *Metaphysics Mrongovius* that possibility, existence, *and necessity* are not determinations (29: 821).

⁵³ I owe these points about the problems for the reformulated version of the argument to Brian Cutter.

⁵⁴ Could one read Kant as treating the phrase 'a most real being' at this stage of the argument as meaning 'a being that has more reality than any other being'? If one could, then the conclusion that all most real beings have the same properties would follow immediately from the uniqueness of such a being. One would not need to assume that the property of being a conceptually necessary being is a reality (and, arguably, Kant would be prepared to grant that it is at least a property). Such a line is attractive, but unfortunately it does not seem to be how Kant is arguing, for if he were, he would not need to bother with the assumption that all most real beings have all their properties in common. Instead, he would argue as follows: 'All conceptually necessary beings are most real beings; so by *per accidens* conversion, some most real being is a conceptually necessary being; but since there is only one most real being it follows that all most real beings are conceptually necessary beings.' (I owe this point to Brian Cutter.)

⁵⁵ Kant would, I think, have been aware that if the argument had instead begun with the assumption that the self is contingent in respect of its very existence, the problem of establishing the contingency assumption would have been even more obvious.

realissimum exists, and not the desired conclusion that such a being exists *necessarily*. The proponent of the cosmological argument thus—at best—establishes something weaker than the desired conclusion, and so commits an *ignoratio elenchi*.

Second, if a defender of the argument should seek to remedy this problem by arguing that we can use this same argument for the existence of an *ens realissimum* as a proof of the consistency of its concept, and they should argue by means of the (rest of) the Leibnizian ontological argument to the conclusion that the *ens realissimum* is a necessary being, then, obviously, the argument would rely on the ontological argument and so inherit its vulnerabilities.

Third, waiving these objections, if the empirical stage of the argument *had* managed to show that there is an absolutely necessary being (construed as a conceptually necessary being), and if it had also shown that this being is a most real being, then—by the reasoning we have just considered—the ontological argument would also have to be sound. But the ontological argument has been shown earlier in the Ideal not to be sound. So, by a simple *modus tollens*, the cosmological argument is not sound either.

In addition to doing justice to all three of Kant's advertised criticisms, our interpretation has three further advantages—or so I would claim. First, it explains why Kant should represent the cosmological arguer as maintaining that the 'absolutely necessary being' can be determined 'only in one single way' (A 605/B 633). Second, it explains why Kant should think that this being is 'thoroughly determined through its concept', and, indeed, why he should see this claim as playing a central role in the third phase of the argument. Third, it brings out Kant's exact grounds for denying that the *PSR* can have application in the argument (to wit: alteration does not imply intelligible contingency).

There are, finally, two broader morals to be drawn from our discussion. First, we have seen that for Kant the only way in which there could be 'an absolutely necessary being' worthy of its name would be if there were to exist a being that existed from its own concept. Since Kant affirms that there is no such thing (A 594–5/B 622–3), it follows that the God in which he believes is not *in this sense* an 'absolutely necessary being'. Second, we can explain why Kant sees his criticism of the empirically-grounded cosmological argument as forming part of a critique of distinctively *pure* reason. For it turns out that he regards the cosmological *argument*—to the extent that it aims at its proper (immediate) goal, namely, demonstrating the existence of a conceptually necessary being—as deriving whatever force it has entirely from the a priori ontological argument. Indeed, at bottom it is merely that old argument in new dress (A 606/B 634). It is, as Kant puts it, a merely 'covert' ontological proof (A 629/B 657). The deepest criticism of the cosmological argument, therefore, is a criticism of the ontological argument, and so, because the ontological argument is wholly a priori, it is a criticism—or critique—of pure reason.

16
The First *Critique* on the Physico-Theological Argument

16.1 Introduction

The final 'proof' scrutinized in the Ideal of Pure Reason is a version of the argument from design. Since its defenders conceive of this argument as belonging to the discipline of 'physico-theology' Kant dubs it 'the physico-theological proof'. Although he denies that it amounts to a demonstration of God's existence, he defends the argument as capable of generating and sustaining a stable doctrinal belief in "a god" [*einen Gott*] (A 826–7/B 854–5). As we will see, this god may, for all we know, be something less than the God of the Abrahamic tradition (which point, I take it, explains Kant's use of the indefinite article). In its Kant-approved role, the argument claims for its conclusion only empirical certainty—the kind of certainty that Kant regards as characteristic of the conclusions of arguments by analogy (9: 132–3), as well as those of the (presumably abductive) arguments of natural science (24: 857). It is because Kant regards rational theology as containing a justification of—or at least stabilizing grounds for—a doctrinal belief in a god, understood as a 'wise and great originator of the world' (ibid.), that I have claimed that he regards this traditional discipline as yielding a nugget of silver when it is subjected to the fiery test of critique. The mention of silver, however, is merely my own.

In getting to grips with Kant's attitude to physico-theology, it will be convenient to begin with an examination of his pre-critical discussion of this enterprise in his 1762 work, *The Only Possible Basis for a Demonstration of the Existence of God*. In this work, Kant takes physico-theology to be the project of attempting to prove God's existence from observations of apparently end-directed natural structures and apparently harmonious natural arrangements.[1] His early attitude towards this

---

[1] At this stage Kant refers to the physico-theological argument, somewhat confusingly, as 'the cosmological proof'. This terminology foreshadows his critical view that the physico-theological argument is merely a concealed form of the cosmological argument. The relevant terminological correspondences are as follows:

Critique of Pure Reason	Only Possible Basis
Ontological proof	Cartesian proof
Cosmological proof	Cosmological proof 'from the accidental arrangement of universe as a whole'

The Fiery Test of Critique: A Reading of Kant's Dialectic. Ian Proops, Oxford University Press (2021). © Ian Proops.
DOI: 10.1093/oso/9780199656042.003.0017

enterprise is one of ambivalence: like weight lifting, there's a good way to do it and a bad way—and the bad way can be dangerous. The bad project he calls the 'ordinary' physico-theology, the good one the 'revised' or 'restricted' physico-theology (2: 117).

16.2 The ordinary physico-theology

Although he recognizes that ordinary physico-theology goes back at least as far as Anaxagoras and Socrates (28: 1004), Kant singles out two more recent thinkers as having 'conferred honour' on human reason by pursuing it (2: 160). The first is the Dutch theologian, Bernard Nieuwentyt (1654–1718), the author of a mammoth work entitled *The Religious Philosopher, or the right use of contemplating the works of the Creator*, published in Dutch in 1718. The second is the English 'parson-naturalist', William Derham (1657–1735), the author of another doorstopper, *Physico-Theology, or a demonstration of the being and attributes of God* (1713), translated into German in 1730. Since Kant read Dutch, both works were available to him.

These works contain numerous detailed descriptions—often fanciful and sometimes soporific—of the supposed 'uses' of certain natural structures or arrangements, which are treated as the immediate ends towards which the natural structures and arrangements in question seem—to the physico-theologist at least—to be directed as so many means. Thus, for example, on Derham's telling, mountains, although at first sight 'inconvenient', are actually of great utility. They serve for: '[taming] the violence of [the] greater rivers, [strengthening] certain joints within the veins and bowels of the earth, [breaking] the force of the sea's inundation, and [protecting] the earth's inhabitants, whether beasts or men'.[2] Nieuwentyt, for his part, affirms that mountains serve, among other things, 'to collect the watery vapours from the air'.[3]

Having enumerated these supposed 'advantages', these writers then proceed to portray the structures affording them as the immediate provisions of a wise and benevolent Author of Nature. Derham, for example, claims that the fact that the parts of the land lying farthest from the ocean are 'commonly the highest' is a 'sign' of an

---

Physico-theological proof Cosmological proof 'from properties of things'
The proof from the existence of possibilities Ontological proof
(not labelled in the first *Critique*)

---

[2] William Derham, *Physico-Theology, or a Demonstration of the Being and Attributes of God from His Works of Creation* (6 edn.; London, 1723) at 76, note (a); compare 73. Here Derham is quoting approvingly from John Wilkins, who is himself quoting from Pliny.
[3] Bernard Nieuwentyt, *The Religious Philosopher*, volume 2 (1718) at Contemplation 19, §31.

'especial providence'. It is an 'admirable provision' of 'the wise creator' for 'carrying off the superfluous waters from the whole earth'.[4] The rival hypothesis that these elevations, and the rivers flowing from them, have natural efficient causes—whether 'natural gravity' or 'earthquakes'—is, he thinks, to be rejected as manifestly less plausible.[5] And, not surprisingly, he takes the same view of the hypothesis that they come about through 'blind chance'.[6]

The significance of calling mountains and rivers *direct* or 'special' provisions is that, on this conception, they are not merely concomitants of processes governed by natural laws. Instead, they are the products of a direct divine intervention—one that takes place in the teeth of the (otherwise) prevailing physical laws. 'If one listened to what the physico-theological authors have to say', Kant observes, 'one would be persuaded to imagine that the river-beds had all been hollowed out by God' (*OPB*, 2: 120). With these words, he seems to be implying that the direct-provision model portrays the Creator as doing work that is beneath the dignity of the divine office.

In Kant's view, the direct model of divine provision is the hallmark of ordinary physico-theology. And it is for him a feature that, for numerous reasons, renders it problematic. First, the direct model leaves divine providence looking unduly *patchy*. Referring to direct provision as 'provision made by wisdom', Kant says:

> Precisely because [in the ordinary physico-theology] no other method of assessing nature's perfection is admitted other than that which involves appealing to the provision made by wisdom, it follows that any widely extended unity, insofar as it is obviously recognized as necessary, constitutes a dangerous objection [*Einwurf*]. (2: 119)

This remark needs some unpacking. To appeal to 'the provision made by wisdom' is, I think, to treat certain natural features as wisely chosen—in a direct and piecemeal fashion—by a benevolent originator rather than as necessary concomitants of natural processes. To gauge the perfection of the world solely by appealing to this provision is to treat these natural features as conducing to the world's perfection only to the extent that they are direct divine provisions. By a 'unity recognized as necessary', Kant means any cluster of features or powers in a thing whose co-occurrence is attributable to necessary physical laws. He gives the example of the air's property of co-instantiating its several capacities to draw up vapours, to become rarer at higher altitudes, and to produce the winds (2: 119). Kant regards these features as necessarily interrelated in the sense that the air must have each of them, if it is to have any. By a 'widely extended unity recognized as

---

[4] Ibid., at 78.   [5] Derham, *Physico-Theology*, at 79.   [6] Ibid.

necessary', finally, he means the circumstance that this kind of necessary interrelation is found in a good many samples of the kind in question. Such a unity constitutes a 'dangerous objection' because, given the ordinary physico-theologian's assumptions about what conduces to the world's perfection, its existence makes the world seem sub-optimal. For example, in Kant's view, since God chooses to impart to the air the properties by virtue of which it absorbs moisture, it follows by the laws of physics that He couldn't but have created it as having the other interrelated capacities that he ascribes to it. And so, given that choice, those other capacities cannot be regarded as individually chosen direct divine provisions. In consequence, the entailed features will seem to the ordinary physico-theologian to be properties of the air that fail to be imbued with divine purposes. Since they have no artificial purposes either, they will seem, for this same point of view, to be telicly barren corners of an imperfect world—a point that in turn will seem to derogate from the perfection of the Author of Nature. This is the first shortcoming of the ordinary physico-theology and it relates to theology.

The second, by contrast, relates to natural science. The problem is that insofar as it explains useful features as immediate divine provisions the ordinary physico-theology works to bring empirical inquiry to a premature close. When, for example, we seek to explain the 'beautiful' and 'well-ordered' arrangement of rivers on earth as the direct or immediate provision of a benign and wise originator, we 'put an end to all scientific research into the causal factors which bring rivers into existence' (2: 128). This is a cost because these (efficient) causal explanations tend to be more illuminating than their teleological counterparts.

The charge is clear, but is it fair? Why can't the ordinary physico-theology suppose piecemeal teleological explanations to happily co-exist with explanations in terms of efficient causes and physical laws? Part of the answer, Kant tells us, is to be found in the 'pious' style of reasoning employed in ordinary physico-theology. Wishing not to seem ungrateful recipients of God's benefaction, and viewing that benefaction as *directly* bestowed, we decline to look into the mechanisms of its provision lest we become guilty of a 'prying curiosity' (2: 119). Another part of the answer is that the ordinary physico-theology treats explanations in terms of universal laws of nature as either impossible, or, if possible, then tantamount to appeals to pure chance, and so as robbing the divine Author of a role (ibid.). In consequence, teleological explanations crowd out (efficient) causal ones, so that the ordinary physico-theologian ends up imposing a 'reverential silence' on reason in its inquiries (2: 127). Such a story, obviously, amounts to no more than a psycho-sociological explanation of why ordinary physico-theology impedes the progress of science. Kant is plainly open to the possibility that physico-theology might be practised in some better way.

The third shortcoming of ordinary physico-theology is that its explanations invite ridicule; for they often involve positing comically ad hoc solutions to specifically human problems. One hypothesizes, for example, that the Aurora Borealis has been directly instituted to provide illumination for the Lapps (2: 136). Kant is certainly right that the works of the traditional physico-theologians abound in this kind of delicious silliness. Nieuwentyt, for example, suggests that without the winds the air would become 'infected by our breath'.[7] Kant's personal favourite in this genre is the idea that God has equipped Jupiter with its moons specifically to assist humans in calculating longitude (2: 131). Apropos this and similar examples, he warns that one should take care 'not to incur the legitimate mockery of a Voltaire who, in a similar tone, asks: "Why do we have noses?" and then replies: "No doubt so that we can wear spectacles"'(ibid.).

A fourth worry is a sharpened version of the 'patchy provision' objection. The concern is that the direct-provision model seems to generate the wrong empirical predictions. If we hypothesize that some physical feature exists because it has been directly furnished by a wise originator to meet some specifically human need, we would expect to encounter the feature wherever the need existed. But, as Kant observes, this is manifestly not the case:

> Take, for example, the supposition that the forests and fields are for the most part green in hue because green is the one colour which has an intermediate intensity and which thus does not strain the eye. The objection may be raised that the inhabitants of the Davis Straits get almost blinded by the snow and have to resort to snow-goggles. (*OPB*, 2: 136)[8]

Is this quite fair? Did any historical proponent of the direct-provision model really offer such a ludicrously anthropocentric explanation of the greenness of vegetation? The answer is yes. In his work, *The Wisdom of God*, the English parson-naturalist, John Ray (1627–1705), declares that 'the whole dry Land is, for the most part, covered over with a lovely Carpet of Green Grass, and other Herbs, of a colour...most useful and salutary to the Eye.'[9] The context makes clear that Ray does indeed see this useful feature as a direct divine provision; so Kant is in fact being scrupulously fair.

Yet a fifth objection is a variation on this theme of empirical inadequacy. The worry is that the direct-provision model is unable to accommodate the imperfections we observe in seemingly purposive arrangements. Kant says:

---

[7] *The Religious Philosopher*, volume 2, at 23.

[8] Voltaire had already made the same point using a different example. 'Those who taught', he says, that the tides were made to bring our ships into port ([for instance,] the Abbé Pluche in "The Spectacle of Nature"), were somewhat ashamed when the reply was made to them that the Mediterranean has ports and no ebb. (Voltaire, *Dictionary* at 194)

[9] John Ray, *The Wisdom of God Manifested in the Works of Creation* (6th edn; London: William Innys, 1714) at 207.

If God had immediately imparted motion to the planets and established their orbits, one would not expect to find the character of imperfection and deviation which is to be met with in all the products of nature. If it had been a good thing for [the planets] to relate to a single plane, then one would expect that God would have fixed their orbits in that precise plane. If it had been a good thing for their orbits to approximate to circular motion, one would expect that their orbits would have been exactly circular. It is not clear why there should have been any exceptions to the strictest precision, particularly in the case of things which are supposed to be the immediate product of God's own activity as an artist. (2: 142)

More generally,

In an immediate divine arrangement, one can never encounter purposes which are only imperfectly realized: rather, the greatest precision and accuracy will be manifest everywhere. (2: 144)

The objection, obviously, is a good one.

A final objection focuses on another aspect of perfection: not precision, but *unity*. The appeal to the divine power of choice, Kant says, 'does not adequately explain why a given means, necessary to the achievement of a single end, is advantageous in so many other respects as well' (2: 131). The point is illustrated by the example of gravity. For Kant, this force is the single cause of a range of effects: it gives the earth its spherical form, it prevents bodies from flying off the earth as a result of the centrifugal force of its rotation, and it keeps the moon in orbit (2: 106). Since, from the point of view of the ordinary physico-theology, there is no particular reason to expect God to directly institute forces and structures that are in this way multiply advantageous, the unity described here is left looking like an unexplained coincidence. Nor can the ordinary physico-theologian reply that, on the contrary, God should be expected, as an aspect of His concern for perfection, to choose a unitary means to secure multiple ends. For Kant can reasonably reply that this is not typically a consideration that carries *any* weight for the ordinary physico-theologian. If it became one, Kant might add, the physico-theologian would no longer be practising the *ordinary* physico-theology.

Kant, then, has some good objections to physico-theology as it is ordinarily practised. But how important are they in the grand scheme of things? One might have doubts on this score, simply because Derham, Ray, and Nieuwentyt are not exactly household names. Might Kant just be shooting fish—long-forgotten minnows—in a barrel? The answer, I think, is no. For one thing, in spite of their obscurity to us, these thinkers were major figures in their day. John Ray's work, for example, ran to some fourteen editions. For another, it wasn't only a handful of now-obscure naturalists and theologians who favoured this approach. Distinguished scientists did so too. Indeed, no less a figure than Newton occasionally appealed to the direct-provision model of divine providence. In the General Scholium to book 3 of the *Principia*, for example, he claims that God has placed the systems of fixed stars at great distances from one another 'lest they should, by their gravity, fall on each other'.[10] Although Kant doesn't approve of Newton's appeal to direct provision, he seems to regard it merely as a forgivably desperate expedient, one resorted to only when a mechanical explanation could not be found (2: 121). For Kant, this sets Newton apart from many other practitioners of ordinary physico-theology, figures who, out of a pious incuriosity, are actively committed to eschewing explanations of useful features in terms of physical causes.

Kant's own 'revised' physico-theology is characterized by its insistence on the points, first, that the teleological mode of explanation should never impede or exclude the mechanical, and, second, that it should never be permitted to cut short the telic chains we might otherwise seek to trace. Both points, as we will see in §16.5, are sufficiently important that they survive into the first *Critique*.

I close this section with a caveat. Although in *OPB* Kant warns against assuming all divine provision to be direct, and although he often gives examples of non-directly bestowed inorganic features, he does allow that some inorganic features may indeed (for all we know) be specially or directly instituted. 'The cohesiveness of the parts of matter', he says, 'may, in the case of water, for example, be a necessary consequence of the possibility of matter in general, *or it may be an arrangement which has been specially instituted*' (emphasis added, 2: 102).

16.3 Kant's revised physico-theology

In *OPB*, Kant plainly regards his objections to ordinary physico-theology as identifying deep flaws in this traditional project. But, because he regards physico-theology as possessing a special persuasiveness for the ordinary human understanding, he recommends reform over abandonment. Properly construed, physico-theology can, he thinks, generate a 'firm and unshakeable' belief in a being who is 'worthy of our worship' (2: 118).[11]

---

[10] Newton, *Principia* at vol. 2, 544. As Martin Schönfeld notes, Newton also appeals to a direct divine choice as the cause of the planets' moving 'one and the same way in orbs concentric' (*Opticks*, book 3, part 1, 402). See Martin Schönfeld, *The Philosophy of the Young Kant* (Oxford: Oxford University Press, 2000) at 105.

[11] Kant regards the better aspects of this project as praiseworthy. He describes the physico-theological argument as 'powerful' (2: 162), 'very beautiful' (2: 162), and—in its best form—possessed of 'great probative force' [*Beweiskraft*]. What he finds attractive about the argument is its appeal to the common understanding or common imagination. Since it is 'natural' and 'persuasive' the argument will, he thinks, 'endure as long as rational beings wish to engage in [the project of seeking] to know God from his works' (2: 160).

One of Kant's aims in *OPB*, then, is to reform physico-theology by reining in its ambitions and changing its methodology. The appeal to apparent design in nature can, he thinks, provide a polemically forceful, yet non-demonstrative, argument for the existence of an immensely wise and powerful Author of Nature—something less than a supreme being.[12] As far as method is concerned, Kant's idea is that the originator does not produce the seemingly end-directed features we observe in inorganic nature through a series of intelligent individual choices. He is not, as Kant puts it, their 'special ground' (2: 103). Instead, he grounds the harmony and unity we find in the world in a wholesale manner by instituting a system of laws that eventuates in the best inorganic structures overall. 'Each particular effect', he says, 'shows signs of an intermingling of laws, which were not aimed exclusively at producing the individual effect alone. This is why deviations from the greatest possible exactitude in respect of a particular purpose also occur' (2: 143). This solves the problem that ordinary physico-theology faced of wrongly predicting perfection in inorganic structures.

As Kant freely admits, in making this move he is following in the footsteps of the French mathematician and philosopher, Pierre Louis Maupertuis, who, in his *Essay on Cosmology* of 1750, himself advocates the wholesale approach (*OPB*, 2: 99). 'It is not', says Maupertuis,

> in petty details, but in those phenomena whose universality allows of no exception, and whose simplicity is such that they are wholly within our comprehension, that we are to search for the proofs of a Supreme Being.... Let us search for Him in the fundamental laws of the cosmos, in those universal principles of order which underlie the whole,... rather than in the complicated results of those laws.[13]

Kant, then, is echoing Maupertuis. But he is also departing from him in holding that when the complicated details in question happen to be *organic* we may after all search in them for evidence of a wise originator. He takes this view because he regards the structures of plants and animals to be direct divine provisions (*OPB*, 2: 118). Moreover, he fully embraces the obvious implication that organisms are perfect: 'In an arrangement which is the product of an immediate divine intervention', he says:

---

[12] Kant sometimes speaks loosely of 'God' or of 'a supreme being' when he has this lesser being in mind. I will do the same.
[13] Pierre Louis Maupertuis, *Essai de Cosmologie* (1751) (orig. pub. 1750) at 54–62.

one can never encounter purposes which are only imperfectly realized: the greatest precision and accuracy will everywhere be present. Such is the case, for example, in the structure of animals. (*OPB*, 2: 144)[14]

More generally, Kant claims that the structure of organisms 'cannot be explained by appeal to the universal and necessary rules of nature' (2: 114; compare 2: 118). He takes this point to be obvious. 'In the case of the spider', he says,

> the uniting together into a system of the different eyes by means of which it watches out for its prey, the warts from which the spider's thread is drawn out, as through hawseholes, the delicate claws and even the balls of its feet by means of which it sticks the thread together or holds on to it. In this case, the unity of all the combined advantages (in which perfection consists) *is obviously contingent and ascribable to a wise choice.* (2: 119, emphasis added)

As Kant goes on to make clear, what it is for the spider's perfection to be 'contingent' is for the possibility to exist that this animal should have possessed some of its advantageous features without possessing the others.[15] The intended contrast is with certain useful inorganic structures or stuffs—air, for example—whose advantageous features, Kant supposes, come in a necessarily indivisible bundle (2: 106, compare 2: 119).

Kant's picture at this stage, then, is a bifurcated one: the harmonies and unities found in inorganic nature are often merely concomitants of universal and necessary laws, while those belonging to organic nature are, for the most part, direct divine provisions.[16] This is relatively clear, but Kant's revised physico-theology also contains a more fundamental idea, namely, that God operates in two quite distinct ways. Some natural features He intelligently chooses, but others He simply *grounds*, and this grounding does not involve His faculty of intelligent choice or wisdom.

---

[14] This remark makes one wonder just how closely Kant could have examined the structure of the animals with which he would have interacted. Domestic cats, for example, fail to show the greatest precision and accuracy in their structural features because they vary in the number of toes they have. If five toes on each front paw is the most perfect or appropriate number for some cats, why do others (polydactyl cats) have six?

[15] In virtue of this possibility the 'unity of the combined advantages' itself counts as contingent.

[16] I say 'for the most part' because Kant appears to think that organic structure may sometimes be merely the necessary consequence of certain developmental dispositions. This point comes out when he is outlining the rules by means of which the revised physico-theology ought to proceed. 'One will presume', he says, 'that the necessary unity to be found in nature is greater than meets the eye. *And that presumption will be made not only in the case of inorganic nature, but also in the case of organic nature.* For even in the case of the structure of the animal, it can be assumed that there is a single disposition, which has the fruitful adaptedness to produce many different advantageous consequences' (*OPB*, 2: 126, emphasis added). We have already noted that he also supposes that some inorganic structures may be direct divine provisions.

The features He directly grounds include, on the one hand, the essences of things and, on the other, the harmonious relationships between those essences—harmonies that manifest themselves in certain law-governed relationships between the things that have those essences.[17] As a result, the harmonies we observe in the inorganic world can be taken to be signs of God's perfection, signs of His nature or essence. They are effects that carry information about their cause, as footprints carry information about their causes.

Importantly, the originator grounds not only the harmonies we find in nature but even their very possibilities. As Kant says, 'That being which is by nature completely independent can only be wise insofar as it contains the grounds of even such **possible** harmony and perfections as offer themselves for realization by that being' (*OPB*, 2: 126, note). This leads him to an intriguingly subtle picture of the relation between God's wisdom and the unity and harmony we find in inorganic nature. The widely extended necessary unity we find there is not, Kant says,

> inferred from the wise choice as its cause; it is rather derived from a ground in a supreme being which [ground] is such that it must also be a ground of great wisdom in him. [The unity in question] is thus derived from a wise being, *but not though his wisdom.*[18]

The harmony obtaining between the possibilities of things is not an object of God's choice because which possibilities there are is not something that God chooses. Accordingly, this harmony is not something that He brings about *through His wisdom*. Rather, the harmony found in the possibilities of things, which is identical with the harmony found in the things that actualize those possibilities, is grounded in something that exists in a supreme being—presumably its essence or nature (compare 28: 1035). And this ground is also the ground of the originator's great wisdom.

That, at least, is Kant's position in *OPB*. Unfortunately, however, his elaboration of this picture contains a tension. Two remarks in particular seem especially hard to reconcile. The first runs:

> Without doubt the reasons why Jupiter should have moons are complete, and they would have been complete even if the moons of Jupiter had never, as a result of the invention of the telescope, been employed for calculating longitude.
>
> (2: 131–2)

Kant's point is that God doesn't equip Jupiter with moons in order to give human beings the means for calculating longitude. Rather, He has sufficient reason to

---

[17] 2: 91; 2: 96–7.   [18] See 2: 119, emphasis added. Compare 2: 103.

400 THE FIERY TEST OF CRITIQUE

equip Jupiter with moons independently of any consideration of human needs or purposes. Nonetheless, Kant also holds that the fact that the moons of Jupiter can be used for calculating longitude figures as part of a proof of the infinite greatness of the originator. Referring to this 'use' (that is, this useful natural feature) among others, he says:

> Although these uses are to be construed as ancillary consequences, they are, notwithstanding, relevant to establishing the infinite greatness of the originator of all things. For they, along with millions of other things of like kind, are proofs of the great chain which links together, in the very possibilities of things, parts of the creation which seem to have no connection with one other. (2: 132)

How can Kant have it both ways? If the originator doesn't equip Jupiter with moons *in order to* help humans with the longitude problem, how can the fact that its moons do in fact help us in this way constitute evidence of His infinite greatness? Kant doesn't answer this question himself, but it might, I think, be answered in the following way.

We need to think of the originator's motives for creating the moons of Jupiter as indeed unconnected with human needs, but also think of His motives for designing human beings in the way He does as including the wise and benevolent desire to equip them with certain faculties by means of which they might use those moons to calculate longitude. With the matter viewed in this way, the harmony between the organic and inorganic parts of the world will after all redound to the originator's credit: it is—in a weak sense—a 'proof' of His greatness. However, the object of God's wise choice, on this conception, will be a whole world that plays host to a chain of purposive links—one of these links being manifested in the ability of human beings to use the moons of Jupiter to calculate longitude.

On this picture, God does not choose the inorganic structures we find in the world with an eye to human convenience. Instead, we have a two-step model of creation: First, God emanatively grounds the possibilities and the necessary laws inherent in those possibilities. This presents Him with a plurality of possible worlds among which to make His wise and benevolent creative choice. Next, God chooses the best among these worlds, using a procedure that's 'lexically ordered' in the following sense: He has two criteria of choice, but the second one kicks in only when the first has been fully satisfied. His first criterion requires that any choice-worthy world should contain inorganic structures that may be deemed maximally harmonious if we confine our attention only to the world's inorganic parts. This narrows the candidates for God's choice down to a set of worlds sharing their inorganic laws but differing in their initial conditions, where each world is second to none with respect to its inorganic harmony. A second criterion then comes into play. Among these optimal inorganic worlds, God chooses the one into which the flora and fauna can be so designed as to fit most harmoniously. The result is a world in which human beings are equipped with features that enable them to use Jupiter's moons for calculating longitude. God's motive or reason for equipping Jupiter with moons is complete because that decision was made at the first stage, before human needs were considered.

These reflections show that Kant has an interestingly mixed picture of the way in which the reformed physico-theologian ought to *cognize* (in a broad sense of that term) the Author of Nature. On the one hand, the fact that the possible worlds containing matter are one and all governed in their inorganic aspects by harmony-producing laws is evidence of the author's greatness. This is an inference from effect to cause that rests on the assumption that the effect resembles the cause—or otherwise carries information about it. It is *not* an inference by analogy. On the other, we do reason by an analogy when we argue for the originator's great wisdom and benevolence from the fact that the actual world contains organisms displaying intrinsic unity (while also harmonizing with the inorganic realm). We reason as follows: Both human artefacts and the natural world manifest the appearance of wise design, so because artefacts have wise designers, the world has one too.

Several remarks suggest that Kant recognizes that the traditional physico-theological argument proceeds by analogy. Consider, for example, the following remark from a reflection: 'Physicotheological proof: Primordial originator by analogy' (R 5505; 18: 202). Or again: 'In theology ... the relation of a supersensible object lying behind the world to the things of the world can only be cognized in accordance with the analogy with an intelligence in nature' (R 5552; 18: 221). Or, yet again, consider Kant's implication in the first *Critique* that the ground of proof of the physico-theological argument is 'the analogy with human art' (A 627/ B 655).

Kant's new physico-theology improves on the old one by expanding the range of ways that God is considered to be a cause of the apparently end-directed features we find in the world. Whereas the old physico-theology had conceived of divine causality as uniformly operating though a faculty of wise choice, the new one sees God—or, strictly a wise and great Author of Nature—as generating some structures through an exercise of this faculty, others merely by emanative grounding. This development enables Kant to free physico-theology from a fundamental limitation, namely, its treatment of all harmonious structures as directly divinely chosen—a limitation that, as we've seen, exposes physico-theology to a range of trenchant criticisms.

Kant maintains that it is only the *combinations* of things that presuppose an intelligent plan (2: 124). Since the ordinary physico-theology finds evidence of divine origin only in the products of a wise chose, this means that, for him, it is constrained to argue only for an architect—a combiner or arranger of matter, not a creator of matter *ex nihilo*. The revised physico-theology, by contrast, since it expands our conception of how God can be a cause, can argue for a creator. One does so by arguing that matter itself bears tell-tale traces of its divine cause—perhaps because its essence makes possible certain harmonious arrangements that betoken a divine origin. And, crucially, these traces are thought of not as wisely *chosen* but rather as somehow emanatively grounded in the creator—but grounded in such a way that laws expressive of intelligence nonetheless govern the matter that is created. None of this, of course, means that Kant regards the revised physico-theology as entirely free of shortcomings. Indeed, he holds that even the revised argument fails to establish the existence of God with either precision or certainty. It lacks precision because it argues only for a perfectly wise being, not an 'incomprehensibly great Author' (2: 160). And it—or more precisely its conclusion—lacks certainty because it possesses not demonstrative, but only moral certainty—by which, at this stage, Kant means a conviction strong enough to produce virtuous conduct (*OPB*, 2: 117).

For Kant these limitations are acceptable, while those of the original physico-theology are not. If the originator were indeed merely an arranger, then it would be limited by the possibilities of combination of the matter it arranges. Not even the most skilled architect, after all, can create a sky-scraper out of custard pudding. On the assumption—apparently tacitly made by Kant—that all matter will come with *some* limits on its possibilities of combination, it follows that any mere arranger of matter will be limited in its combinatory powers and so not identical with God. For this reason, Kant calls the belief implicit in the ordinary physico-theology merely a 'refined atheism' (2: 122). The revised physico-theology, by contrast, although its mode of argument is relatively obscure, can at least claim to avoid this difficulty.

Kant sums up his view of physico-theology in *OPB* as follows:

> From the *contingent* connections of the world one will infer the existence of a Being who has originated the manner in which the universe is assembled. From the *necessary* unity of the world, however, one will infer the existence of that self-same Being, construed as the Author even of the matter and fundamental stuff of which all natural things are constituted. (2: 128)

By the 'necessary unity of the world' Kant means the unity that is grounded in the world's necessary and universal laws. The most fundamental among these laws—an inverse square law of attraction and inverse cube law of repulsion—are, for Kant, constitutive of the very essence of matter because without a balancing of the forces they describe matter simply would not exist. Kant had already sown the seeds of this idea in his *Physical Monadology* of 1756, but it comes to fruition in the *Metaphysical Foundations of Natural Science* (hereafter '*MFNS*'). 'It is now manifest', he says there, 'that, whether one takes neither [of the two basic forces] as a ground, or assumes merely one of them, space would always remain empty, and no matter would be found therein.'[19]

The obtaining of the laws constitutive of the essence of matter, in other words, is a condition of the very possibility of matter. And Kant's picture, accordingly, is one according to which we can infer a creator of matter as the cause of the very laws that make matter possible. These laws are not contingent and so not chosen, but rather, for Kant, flow necessarily from the very geometry of the diffusion of the basic attractive and repulsive forces through space. Nonetheless, through their unity and harmony, they serve as signs of the unity and harmony of the emanative cause of the matter they govern. The traditional idea that the effect resembles the cause thus retains a foothold in Kant's philosophy.

16.4 The pre-critical revised physico-theology: concluding remarks

We can now state the three main lessons of Kant's revised physico-theology. The first is that we ought to favour one side of a certain Euthyphro contrast. According to the ordinary physico-theologian, the natures of divinely created things mutually harmonize because the things themselves (have been wisely chosen to) exist. For Kant, by contrast, divinely created things exist because their natures harmonize. For the ordinary physico-theologian, it is as if God first decides to create a set of things and then so shapes their natures that they dovetail with one another and with human interests. For Kant, it's rather that the most harmonious world is actualized partly in virtue of the harmony that already exists between the inorganic things it contains when those things are considered as merely possible. On this point, then, Kant is on the Leibnizian, the ordinary physico-theologian on the Cartesian, side of the Euthyphro contrast.

The second main lesson is that we must not allow our scientific inquiries to be curtailed by our observation of apparently end-directed natural features. In particular, we must not regard it as an act of prying presumption to inquire into the mechanism of divine provision in inorganic nature (compare 28: 1282). As Kant sees it, there's no impiety here because in looking into the natural causes of worldly phenomena we are not seeking to uncover the trick behind the magic; we are rather examining a structure of possibilities, or essences, that exists quite independently of any exercise of God's matter-creating faculty.

The third main lesson is that we ought to expand the range of ways in which God may be thought of as the source of the features and structures we find in the world. God is to be thought of as bringing about these structures and features not

---

[19] *MFNS*, 1786, 4: 511.

exclusively through His faculty of wise choice, but rather—with regard to the inorganic parts of the world—also through a kind of direct emanative grounding. Only by expanding our conception of God's causal activity in this way will we obtain a proper physico-*theology* as opposed to a kind of refined atheism—or so Kant supposes.

Having examined these pre-critical views, we are now equipped to consider Kant's treatment of physico-theology in the first *Critique*.

16.5 The revised physico-theology in the first *Critique*

As we saw at the end of §16.2, Kant's view that the teleological and nomological/efficient-causal modes of explanation can peacefully co-exist persists into the first *Critique*. 'The advantage provided by the earth's spherical shape', he says in a footnote,

> is familiar enough;[20] but few people know that the flattening of the earth as a spheroid is what alone prevents the prominences of the mainland—or even those consisting of smaller mountains, thrown up perhaps by earthquakes—from shifting the earth's axis continuously and appreciably in a fairly short time. Such shifts would indeed occur if the earth's equatorial bulge were not a mountain so enormous that [the earth] can never be noticeably displaced with regard to that axis by the momentum of any other mountain. *And yet we do not hesitate to explain this wise provision from nothing more than the equilibrium of the earth's formerly fluid mass.* (footnote to A 687/B 715; compare 28: 1035, emphasis added)

The immediate advantage of the earth's flattening into an oblate spheroid is that its axial tilt—the angle between its orbital and rotational axes, technically known as its 'obliquity'—is not continuously altered as new mountain ranges and volcanoes spring up around the globe. This stability is in turn salutary—or so one presumes—because it reduces the severity of summers and winters, thereby making possible stable patterns of human farming and settlement, while also, of course, stabilizing the environment for wildlife.[21] Nieuwentyt had already noted the advantages of the stability of the earth's obliquity in the second volume of *The Religious Philosopher*. There he suggests that in the absence of the needed

---

[20] In *OPB* Kant mentions as one advantage of the earth's sphericity that a spherical surface is capable 'of the most uniform dispersion of light' (2: 102).

[21] In *OPB* Kant speaks of certain 'deleterious effects' that would accompany the displacement of the earth's axis of rotation (2: 121), but he doesn't say what they are.

stabilization creatures accustomed to hot climates would be plunged into colder ones (and vice versa), with fatal consequences.[22]

Nieuwentyt had also known about the earth's flattening, but he didn't anticipate Kant in seeing it as the means by which the earth's obliquity is stabilized. Instead, he supposed that the stabilization was provided directly by a providential miracle. He says:

> Now [the circumstance] that... the Globe has unchangeably kept its state and condition can result from nothing else than the miraculous operation of a mighty providence. (*The Religious Philosopher*, book 2, contemplation 20, §29)

For the critical Kant, Nieuwentyt's appeal to a miraculous operation of a mighty providence is flawed in two ways: first, it preempts and precludes the positing of a zetetically promising telic chain; second, it precludes explanation in terms of universal laws of nature. Kant does think that the earth's stabilization can be *usefully viewed as* a wise and benevolent provision. But he supposes that this is only because such a stance prompts us to look for the means by which it is brought about. By inquiring into the means by which this useful stability is provided—that is by treating the stability 'as if' it were a divine provision—we come to conjecture the earth's equatorial bulge as providing the necessary gyroscopic stabilization.

As an account of the actual historical discovery of the earth's flattening this story is, I think, somewhat dubious. For the flattening was in any case predicted by Newton's theory (on the assumption that the earth had once been in a fluid state), and one supposes that this fact alone might have prompted us to try to verify its existence. Nonetheless, it does illustrate the operation of Kant's 'as if' stance. It also brings out a point that Kant clearly considers of the utmost importance, namely, that there need be no *harm* in taking up this stance. For, as Kant knew, one thinker who did not 'hesitate to explain this wise provision from nothing more than the equilibrium of the earth's formerly fluid mass' was Newton, who provides just this explanation in propositions 18, 19, and 20 of book 3 of *Principia* (2: 121).[23] Actual scientific practice—of the highest calibre—therefore makes clear that, in contrast to the ordinary physico-theology, Kant's critical *as if* teleology does not in the least prevent us from giving explanations in terms of powers, laws, and effective causes.

---

[22] *The Religious Philosopher*, volume 2, Contemplation 20, §27.
[23] For an illuminating discussion of this case, see Friedman, *Kant's Construction of Nature*, at chapter 4, §§33–4.

16.6 The first *Critique* on the physico-theological argument

Kant presents the dogmatic physico-theological argument as an argument for a supreme intelligence as the 'principle' of natural order and perfection (A 632/B 660). He divides the argument into four 'chief moments' (see A 625–6/B 653–4):

1. Everywhere in the world we find signs of wisely instituted, purposive arrangement.
2. This purposive arrangement is *contingent*: it has not come about as a necessary consequence of the natures of the things so arranged. Rather, it has been specially selected and designed by a rational cause that chooses between genuine options.
3. Therefore, there exists a sublime and wise cause (or several such causes) of this arrangement—an intelligent cause (or several such) whose causality operates through *freedom* rather than mere *fecundity*.
4. The observed unity of this arrangement—the reciprocal purposive relations that the parts of the world exhibit as parts of an artistic structure—allows us to infer with certainty the unity (that is, singleness) of the cause of such purposive arrangements as we observe, and with probability (by analogy) the unity of the cause of the whole (unobserved as well as observed) universe.

Although Kant tells us only that the fourth moment features an inference by analogy, he seems to also take the argumentation spanning the first three moments to have this form. The heart of this latter argument is the following argument by analogy:

We observe contingent, apparently end-directed natural structures in the world. Insofar as they are contingent and apparently end-directed, these natural structures resemble the end-directed products of human artifice (houses, ships, clocks, and so forth). By the principle of analogy, they therefore further resemble these human artefacts in possessing a cause (or causes) relevantly similar in nature to the causes of these human artefacts (9: 132–3). The cause of end-directed human artefacts is a being (or a plurality of beings) that operates through a freely acting intellect. Therefore, the cause of natural structures is also a being (or a plurality of beings) that operates through a freely acting intellect (or a plurality of them).

Although Kant doesn't see the argument as perfect, his treatment of it is conciliatory. He declines to challenge the tacit assumption that there is an analogy (that is to say, a similarity) between the products of nature and the end-directed products of human art (or artifice) (A 626/B 654). And he concedes that, although the argument lacks demonstrative force, once we grant that the purposive order we take ourselves to observe has a cause (that is, that it didn't come about by mere chance), there is no better conclusion than that this cause possesses a will and an understanding. This last concession is related to a remark whose significance is not immediately apparent. 'Reason', he says, 'would not be able to answer for itself if it wanted to pass over from a causality with which it is acquainted to obscure and unprovable grounds of explanation, with which it is not acquainted' (A 626/B 654). With these words, he is charitably defending the argument against an envisaged objection, which advances a rival hypothesis about the causality of the cause of the apparently end-directed products of nature. These products, the rival hypothesis maintains, are caused to exist by a being whose causality operates not through intelligence and freedom, but in some other manner. *Which* other manner Kant doesn't say, but the third 'moment' suggests that the envisaged alternative is 'through *fecundity* [*Fruchtbarkeit*]'. A cause that operated in this manner would be one whose causality was of the kind exercised in the generation of an organism from its parent (or parents), hence wholly without intelligence or understanding: in short a blindly working fecundity.

Unless Kant can eliminate this rival hypothesis, he will have to reject the physico-theological argument even when it is construed as he himself wants to construe it, namely, as a piece of reasoning capable of producing and stabilizing a doctrinal belief in a wise and benevolent originator of nature, a being that designs some parts of the universe. The stakes, then, are high, and especially so because the rival hypothesis is no idle possibility, but rather a concrete suggestion made by Philo in the seventh part of Hume's *Dialogues Concerning Natural Religion*.[24]

It may seem surprising that in the A edition Kant should be seeking to rebut a suggestion that appears for the first time in Hume's *Dialogues*. For the German translation of the *Dialogues* appeared only after the A edition of the first *Critique* had gone to press. However, we should not forget that Kant read French, and the French translation of the *Dialogues* appeared in the same year as the *Dialogues* itself, namely, 1779.[25] Moreover, as Gary Hatfield reports, Kant had seen J. G. Hamann's translation of Hume's work by September 1780.[26] The text was therefore in all likelihood available to Kant during the final stages of the composition of the A edition. There are also some 'internal' reasons to think that he would likely have read the *Dialogues* before completing the A edition.

First, he seems to be borrowing Hume's terminology in the second 'moment' when he describes the type of cause contended for in the physico-theological argument as 'an arranging *rational principle*' [*vernünftiges Princip*] (A 625/B 653,

---

[24] David Hume, *Dialogues Concerning Natural Religion* (Indianapolis, IN: Bobbs-Merrill, 1970) at 238–43.
[25] David Hume, *Dialogues sur la religion naturelle* (Edinburgh, 1779).
[26] Gary Hatfield, 'Kant und die Berliner Aufklärung', in Rolf-Peter Horstmann, Gerhardt Volker, and Ralph Schumacher (eds), *Akten des IX. Internationalen Kant-Kongresses Band 1* (Berlin and New York: De Gruyter, 2001), 185–208 at 188.

emphasis added). This italicized expression, rare in Kant, seems likely to be of immediate Humean provenance because Philo lists reason among the four 'principles' that he sees as equally good candidates for explaining the order and organization we find in the world. These principles are: reason, instinct, generation, and vegetation.[27] Whereas Philo asks why the last two principles on this list should not be the causes of worldly order, Kant lobbies for the first. This consideration is not dispositive, of course, but to suppose that Kant had been reading the *Dialogues* while he was crafting his argument against the hypothesis of a fecund cause would certainly explain the alignment of terminology. A second, more decisive, consideration is that Kant frames the crux of his argument against the fecund-cause hypothesis in language that is the mirror image of Philo's when Philo claims that the character and manner of operation of each of the four explanatory 'principles' is equally *unknown*. Thus, whereas Philo says that in the case of each of the four principles 'the principles themselves and their manner of operation are totally unknown',[28] Kant says that the rational species of cause—the kind of cause that is operative in the production of human artefacts—is, on the contrary, 'fully known' [*völlig bekannt*], adding that the same goes for its 'manner of operation' [*Wirkungsart*] (A 626/B 654). When combined with the fact that the objection to which Kant is responding in the first *Critique* is in fact precisely the one raised by Philo in the *Dialogues*, these points suggest that Kant had indeed read this work before completing the A edition.[29] Incidentally, it is also worth noting in this connection that Kant echoes Hume's Cleanthes when he likens sceptics to *nomads* (A ix, compare *Dialogues*, 249). This is the first time Kant draws this particular comparison, and its presence in the A-edition preface is consistent with his having read the *Dialogues* around the time he was composing this preface—presumably as he was finishing up the A edition in the second half of 1780.

In the light of these textual points, it is striking just how closely Philo's criticism of the physico-theological argument resembles the objection Kant is describing—and attempting to answer—when he rejects the hypothesis of a fecund cause. Philo argues for that hypothesis as follows:

> If the universe bears a greater likeness to animal bodies and to vegetables, than to the works of human art, it is more probable that its cause resembles the cause of

---

[27] Hume, *Dialogues Concerning Natural Religion* at 240.
[28] Ibid. In the French: '*L'experience nous fait connaître tous les effects de ces principes: mais les principes eux-même & le maniere dont ils operent nous sont absolument inconus*' (Hume, *Dialogues sur la religion naturelle* at 147).
[29] Kant indicates that he knows that the objection he had addressed in the first *Critique* is Hume's when he presents Hume as the advocate of the fecundity hypothesis in the *Pölitz* religion lectures from 1783–84. In these lectures he uses the same word for 'fecundity'—'*Fruchtbarkeit*'—as he uses in both editions of the first *Critique* (28: 1064).

the former than that of the latter, and its origin ought rather to be ascribed to generation or to vegetation than to reason or design.[30]

Affirming the antecedent of this conditional, Philo continues:

> The world plainly resembles more an animal or a vegetable, than it does a watch or a knitting loom. Its cause, therefore, it is more probable, resembles the cause of the former. The cause of the former is generation or vegetation. The cause of the world, therefore, we may infer to be something analogous to generation or vegetation.[31]

In other words, since what is in question is the causal origin of the universe as a whole rather than that of this or that natural structure within it, a closer analogy would be the one that holds between the universe and a living thing; for the universe resembles a living thing more closely than it does an artefact. It follows that, insofar as an argument for analogy makes it plausible—or probable—that the universe has a cause, that cause would have to be conceived of as operating through generation or vegetation, rather than through wisdom and free choice.

Hume concludes that it simply begs the question to assume that the signs of order we observe in the world are signs of *design* rather than of a blindly working fecundity. As Philo says:

> A tree bestows order and organisation on that tree which springs from it, without knowing the order: an animal, in the same manner, on its offspring; a bird, on its nest: and instances of this kind are even more frequent in the world, than those of order, which arise from reason and contrivance. To say, that all this order in animals and vegetables proceeds ultimately from design, is begging the question.[32]

These objections are powerful and deserve a convincing reply. Kant, rather gamely, makes a stab at meeting them. His (tacit) rejoinder involves suggesting that the hypothesis of a fecund cause would be lacking in explanatory power relative to that of an artificer. For only in the case of the products of human artifice are we 'fully acquainted with the causes *and the manner of their action*' (A 626/B 654, emphasis added).[33] When, for example, I observe a house being built, I am in a position to *understand* how the house comes to be. I can observe the operation of the builder's causality and see how the organization of the house flows from the

---

[30] Hume, *Dialogues Concerning Natural Religion* at 238.   [31] Ibid.   [32] Ibid., at 241.
[33] We might offer on Kant's behalf the additional consideration that we don't in fact observe the world *as a whole*. It is a little puzzling that Kant doesn't buttress his response with this further observation.

410 THE FIERY TEST OF CRITIQUE

builder's plans and intentions. I can appreciate how the builder's free choices cause the building materials to come be organized into a house. More generally, I can outwardly observe the operation of free will and understanding in the causality of other persons and know it inwardly in my own case. In the case of the generation of an animal, by contrast, I have not the least understanding of how the causality operates. I don't know how the animal produces its seed or how the seed grows into a new animal. Nor would observing my own generative activity afford me any insight into these things. These last claims—true ones given the limited biology of Kant's time—mean that citing one animal as a cause of another, while no doubt amounting to saying something *true*, nonetheless constitutes a relatively shallow explanation of the existence and character of the animal.

At this point in his discussion Kant is on the verge of treating the physico-theological argument as an inference to the best explanation of the appearance of design. Moreover, recognizing that Philo's rival explanation lacks explanatory power relative to the hypothesis of a designer, and wishing to critique the argument from analogy in its most plausible form, he favours a starting point according to which certain *parts* of the world—and one supposes pre-eminently the organs of animals—are analogized to the products of human contrivance.

It is, however, unclear whether this amounts to a fully satisfactory reply to Hume. For arguably the world does resemble an organism more closely than an artefact. After all, it's not at all clear what the world's function or purpose would be.[34] If that is right, then each way of framing the argument has an advantage over its rival: Hume's involves a closer analogy, Kant's a deeper explanation. Since it is not immediately clear how to weight these apparently incommensurable virtues, we reach a standoff.

16.7 Kant's criticisms of the dogmatic physico-theological argument

The first *Critique*'s opening salvo against the dogmatic physico-theological argument is a charge recycled from *OPB*, namely, that the argument 'could at most establish a highest **architect of the world** [*Weltbaumeister*], who would always be greatly limited by the suitability of the material on which he works, but not a **creator of the world**, to whose idea everything is subject' (A 627/B 655). The key point is that no mere architect—that is to say, no mere arranger of previously existing matter—could be a highest (that is, unlimited) being; for the suitability of

---

[34] As we will see in the next chapter, Kant holds that the purpose of natural structures in the world is to promote the interests of rational beings. But such a view is hardly obvious, and it would not provide a compelling premise in a defence of the thesis that the world resembles an artefact in having a purpose.

the material would impose constraints on the architect's creative activity. The point is well taken; but Kant does not leave it at that. Instead, he goes on to consider how the argument might be charitably reformulated as an argument for an originator of the world's *matter* along with its form. This would require establishing the contingency of the world's matter—establishing that is to say, that the matter of the world might not have existed. And establishing that, he says, would require proving that 'unless the things of the world were the product of a supreme wisdom even **as regards their substance**, they would in themselves be unsuitable for acquiring such order and harmony [as they are taken to have] according to universal laws' (A 626–7/B 654–5).

The envisaged proof would try to show that the law-grounded order and harmony manifested in nature could exist only as the order and harmony of a particular kind of stuff, a stuff that could be created only by a wise and great being. Kant does not argue that these things could not be proved at all. Instead, he contents himself with observing that they could not be proved *by means of the analogy with human art*. It is possible, therefore, that while critiquing the ordinary physico-theology Kant is at the same time remaining open to a modified version of the physico-theological argument that proceeds along the lines of the proof envisaged by the revised physico-theology.[35] Equally clearly, however, he is not actually *supplying* such an argument, and he is certainly not endorsing the argument he leaves room for as a dogmatic proof. That argument is rather, I think, envisaged as merely supporting a doctrinal belief.[36]

Kant's second criticism questions whether, even if the argument could establish the existence of a wise and powerful architect, it could also show that this being possessed omnipotence, *supreme* wisdom, *absolute* unity, and so forth. 'I trust', he says,

> that no one will presume to have insight into the relation of the magnitude of the world as he has observed it (in its scope as well as its content) to omnipotence, or

---

[35] The theme of the inadequacy of the ordinary physico-theology is not abandoned in the first *Critique*. On the contrary, Kant now elaborates that criticism, offering a diagnosis of the emergence of the direct-provision model of divine providence. He says: 'Because the concept of such a supreme intelligence [as is assumed in the ordinary physico-theology] is in itself quite inscrutable, one determines it anthropomorphically; and then one thrusts purposes upon nature forcibly and dictatorially, instead of seeking them—as is proper—along the path of physical investigation. Thus the result is not only that teleology, which was to serve merely to supplement the natural unity in terms of universal laws, now works rather toward annulling this unity' (B 720). Kant now understands the direct-provision model as involving an unduly 'anthropomorphic' understanding of the supreme intelligence and he does so—presumably—because he sees that being's causality as operating through freedom and understanding.

[36] In his lectures on religion Kant sketches what seems to be a distinct line of argument for the thesis that the designer must also be a creator. The idea seems to be that the very interaction of substances requires a creator of them (28: 1299). Kant's line of thought here isn't altogether clear, though it is plain that he is not despairing of reaching this stronger conclusion. One presumes, however, that he would have conceived of the argument as producing only a doctrinal belief.

> the world-order to supreme wisdom, or the unity of the world to the absolute unity of its originator, etc. Thus physico-theology cannot give any determinate concept of the supreme cause of the world. (A 628/B 656)

A 'determinate' concept of the supreme cause of the world would be the concept of something that had all perfection—that is to say, all power, wisdom, and so forth; it would, in Kant's terminology, be an 'all-sufficient being' (A 628/B 656). Kant's point is that, since we are ignorant of the *absolute* degree of perfection of the observed world, we cannot gauge whether it is sufficiently perfect that its cause would have to be an all-sufficient being. He proceeds to claim that the conclusions we *are* entitled to draw about the nature of the world-originator—if we waive other criticisms—are of the following kind: that it is 'very great', 'astonishing', and has 'immeasurable' power and excellence. But these are only 'relative representations' through which the observer of the world 'compares the magnitude of the object with himself and his power to grasp it' (A 628–9/B 656).[37]

Kant's idea is straightforward: what is 'very great' *for a flea* is hardly great *tout court*, and what is 'astonishing' *to a dullard* need not be astonishing *sans phrase*. More generally, owing to the phrase's implicit relativization to a judger, one can make an object fit the description 'very great' either by increasing its magnitude or by decreasing the magnitude of the observer (A 628/B 565). The upshot is clear: since we cannot in general infer '*x* is very great *tout court*' from '*x* is very great as compared with us' we have no reason to conclude that the former predicate applies to the originator.

Kant's third line of criticism charges that the dogmatic physico-theological argument rests on the cosmological argument, hence, ultimately, on the ontological argument. In consequence, the whole of dogmatic rational theology, insofar as it rests on theoretical rather than practical grounds, turns out to have the status of *pure* rational theology—a putative science that Kant sees as already having been discredited by his critique of the ontological argument. 'The physico-theological proof', he says,

> stymied in its undertaking, in its embarrassment suddenly jumped over to the cosmological proof, and since this is only a concealed ontological proof, it actually carried through its aim merely through pure reason, even though at the beginning it had denied all kinship with it and had proposed to base everything on evident proofs from experience.[38]

In Kant's view, the physico-theological argument reveals itself to rest on the ontological argument through the following process. When the physico-

---

[37] Compare 'Nothing is absolutely large' (R 6338a; 18: 660).
[38] A 629/B 657; compare the final paragraph of A 630/B 658.

theologian realizes that the most he can prove is the existence of a being possessing great power and wisdom relative to the power and wisdom of human beings he immediately changes tack and treats the world's alleged order and purposiveness as establishing nothing more than the premise of the cosmological proof, namely, that the state of the world is *contingent* (A 629/B 657). Arguably, this *is* a reasonable inference to draw; for things that might have been arranged less wisely are things that might have been arranged differently. Insofar as things appear to have been wisely arranged or chosen, therefore, they also appear to be contingent in the sense (relevant to the cosmological argument) that they could have been arranged differently. Having reached this conclusion, the physico-theological argument thereafter follows the path of the cosmological argument and so, in Kant's view, inherits that argument's dependence on the ontological argument.

Kant draws the grand conclusion that all of the merely speculative proofs boil down to the ontological proof. And he further concludes that the physico-theologians are, in consequence, guilty of a kind of, perhaps unwitting, hypocrisy. They have, he says 'absolutely no cause to be so prim [*spröde*] when it comes to the transcendental kind of proof [that is, the ontological argument] and to look on it with the self-conceit of clear-sighted students of nature looking down on the webs spun by gloomy brooders' (A 629/B 657). The physico-theologians have no right to primly condescend to the gloomy, apriorist, web-spinners Kant thinks, because they merely affect to approach rational theology in a fashionably modern and empirical spirit. In truth, they are, at the end of the day, just re-hashing the old a priori argument—the ontological argument—while passing it off as something new.

Although Kant sees speculative reason as failing to accomplish its traditional goal of demonstrating the existence of God (A 638/B 666), he does regard it as having 'one great benefit' (A 640/B 668), namely, that of '**correct[ing]** the cognition of [the highest being]' (A 639–40/B 668). He means that speculative metaphysics enables us to arrive at a clear and fitting conception of God—one purged of extraneous empirical elements. In Kant's view, it is worth possessing such a conception because we can—and do—arrive at a stable (and, by implication, justified) belief in the existence of God 'from somewhere else', namely, from certain arguments having practical (in the sense of 'moral') grounds (A 640/B 668).

Kant supposes that the correct way to 'precisely determine' the concept of the highest being is to conceive of it as the God of *theism*—namely, a 'living God' or 'highest intelligence' (A 633/B 661), a supremely perfect originator of nature. Such a being exists outside of space and time (A 641/B 669), and its causality operates through understanding and free will (A 633/B 661; 28: 1063). It is conceived of as cause of the world 'through its ideas of the greatest harmony and unity' (A 678/B 706). Kant reserves the terms '*Urheber*' and '*Welturheber*' for a being so conceived.

In thus 'determining' the concept of the highest being Kant is rejecting three rival conceptions of the divinity. The first is that of an 'original being' or 'highest cause', something that Kant describes as a 'blindly acting and eternal nature as the root of things' (A 632/B 660). Such a being is 'blindly acting' insofar as its causality operates through its nature—through emanation or fecundity—rather than through freedom and understanding.[39] The second is that of a mere architect of nature—a being that creates the world's form but not its matter. The third is that of a being possessing spatial or temporal properties.

Kant equates the first of these three rival conceptions with that of the deist—a figure who, because he does not conceive of the cause of the world as possessing freedom and understanding, might be alleged not really to believe in God.[40] With characteristic diplomacy, however, Kant stops short of making such an allegation; for he sees the deist as at least open to the idea that the original being might, *for all they know*, operate through understanding and freedom (A 633/B 661). Properly speaking, then, Kant's considered position is that the deist is neutral on the question of God's mode of causality.

Somewhat disconcertingly, Kant labels the second of his three disfavoured conceptions of the divinity the 'atheistic' conception (A 640/B 668), and the third that of 'anthropomorphism' (ibid.).[41] He means, I take it, that while the second conception purports to be a conception of God, it is really no such thing. It is rather a conception belonging to what Kant in *OPB* had called merely a 'refined atheism' (2: 122).[42] The idea would seem to be that if one believed merely in an architect of the world who is *limited* by the materials with which he works, one's position would amount to a kind of atheism. The label 'anthropomorphism' is not ideal either, but it is clear that Kant sees placing God in time and, more generally,

---

[39] See 28: 1064, and compare: 28: 1054, 28: 1265, and 28: 1270. Kant ascribes to the Tibetans the idea that human souls emanate from, and are eventually reabsorbed into, the Godhead (28: 1050, 1054). And, though he does not conceive of Spinoza as a deist, he supposes that Spinoza's system involves a similar idea (8: 335). He also speaks of 'the principle of emanation', which states that 'all things are actual **by the necessity of God's nature**'—a notion that contrasts with their being actual through God's freedom—the latter being the so-called, 'system of creation' (28: 1054-5).

[40] A 632/B 660; 28: 1063.

[41] The label 'anthropomorphism' for such a conception derives from Baumgarten (see *Metaphysics*, §848).

[42] This is not the only context in which Kant's use of the terms 'atheism' and 'atheist' departs from ordinary use. In his religion lectures he defines 'sceptical atheism' in terms that would perfectly describe his own view, namely: the belief in God coupled with the denial of the soundness of the dogmatic speculative (that is, theoretically grounded and apodictic-certainty seeking) proofs of God's existence (28: 1010, compare 28: 1241). Kant thus seems to be committed to self-identifying in his own idiom as a (sceptical) 'atheist'—though in our terms, he is clearly a theist. On the other hand, in a reflection from 1783-84, he claims that in order to counter sceptical atheism it would suffice to show that there are practical grounds for moral conviction, even if not speculative grounds (R 6287 (18: 556)). This, I think, is the better thought, and it would mean that Kant is not, after all, a sceptical atheist—understood now as a figure who would deny that there are *any* grounds for belief in God (whether practical or speculative).

attributing to Him properties that belong to mere appearance, as involving what he calls 'anthropomorphism, broadly understood' (A 640/B 668).

16.8 Do we observe end-directedness?

It is time to address a question that has been hovering in the background this whole chapter. Does the Kant of the first *Critique* think that we observe actual end-directness in nature or only the appearance thereof?[43] The texts are equivocal. They do make clear that at this stage Kant conceives of human beings as capable of observing *purposiveness* [*Zweckmäßigkeit*]. Kant describes the inference involved in the physico-theological argument as running 'from the thoroughgoing order and purposiveness that is observed [*beobachtenden*] in the world, as a thoroughly contingent arrangement, to the existence of a cause **proportioned to it**' (A 627/B 655). And later, in the 'Doctrine of Method', when speaking of purposive unity [*Zweckmäßige Einheit*], he remarks that 'experience liberally supplies examples of it' (A 826/B 854).

But it is not immediately clear whether he uses the technical term, 'purposiveness', to refer to end-directedness itself or merely to the appearance thereof. Customary usage suggests the former: this German word ordinarily means 'suitability', 'adaptedness', or 'convenience'. But we can't rely on this point; for Kant does not always employ telic vocabulary factively. At one point, for example, he speaks of ends as 'manifesting themselves in nature' [*in der Natur zeigende*] while at the same time saying that these same 'manifested' ends are often merely 'made up by us' [*von uns selbst dazu gemachte*] (A 691/B 719). Here, obviously, he is using 'manifesting' non-factively while also taking 'ends' to mean 'apparent ends'.

One reason to doubt that Kant really believes that we are capable of observing end-directedness in nature is that this assumption would render him vulnerable to one of his own criticisms of physico-theology. The criticism occurs in the Appendix to the Transcendental Dialectic, where Kant warns against what he calls the fallacy of 'perverted reason (*perversa ratio*)', which he also calls the fallacy of 'later first of reason': '*ὕστερον πρότερον rationis*'—the fallacy of making prior what is in fact posterior (A 692/B 720). At the close of his discussion of this fallacy he warns against 'a vicious circle in one's proof, where one presupposes what really ought to have been proved' (A 693/B 721). Since the 'proof' in question is the physico-theological argument (A 692–3/B 720–1), there is reason to think that Kant regards the physico-theologian as somehow begging the question. Such a

---

[43] The alert reader will have noticed that I addressed this question in my discussion of Fordyce's argument in Chapter 7. There I suggested that on Kant's first-*Critique* view, we do not observe purposes, but merely have a doctrinal belief in their existence. Owing to certain textual complexities, however, the question is worth re-opening here.

verdict would not have been idiosyncratic, for when explaining this same fallacy, Wolff treats the physico-theological argument as paradigm of a circular demonstration.[44]

In what way is the physico-theologian begging the question? Most plausibly, I think, by assuming, controversially, that we observe the actual end-directedness of things. The question is begged because, first, the verb 'to observe' is factive and, second, it is analytic that nothing could be end-directed unless there were at least one being whose end or ends it subserved as a means. In consequence, to assume that we observe end-directedness is tantamount to, and no more certain than, assuming the existence of a being with ends to which the end-directed features in question serve as so many means. A properly formulated physico-theological argument ought, therefore, to begin by assuming the existence of *apparent* rather than *observed* end-directedness.

A second reason to think that in the first *Critique* Kant does not take us to observe end-directedness in nature is the following. He tells us that although we may regard purpose-like [*Zweckähnliche*] arrangements as (indicative of) intentions, we may do so only on the condition that it remain a matter of indifference to us whether the arrangement has been brought about by a divine wisdom or whether it is merely the product of natural processes (A 699/B 727). This suggests that we are not at liberty to understand our act of 'regarding the purpose-like arrangements as intentions' as a matter of *perceiving* intentionally formed structures as intentionally formed. Instead, we are merely to act *as if* the arrangements in question are intentionally formed as we conduct our empirical inquiries. His choosing to use the term 'purpose-like' in the context of making this point suggests that, when he is being careful, he recognizes that we are entitled to say only that we observe purpose-like arrangements, not arrangements that have purposes.

Other evidence, however, points to the opposite conclusion. In the Pölitz religion lectures of 1783–84, for example, Kant is reported to have said:

> In a few cases the wise will of God and his aim [*Absicht*] are obvious, e.g., the whole structure of the human eye shows itself to be a wise means to the end of seeing.... [But] the presupposition that everything in the world has its utility and good aim, if it is supposed to be constitutive, would go much farther than our observations up to now can justify. (28: 1069)

This remark seems to imply that we do observe *some* instances of end-directness in nature. Kant seems to be cautioning merely against over-generalizing from the

---

[44] Wolff, *Philosophia Rationalis* at §884. Baumeister, in a similar vein, remarks that every end 'presupposes an intelligent being, therefore the existence of an end cannot be proved unless the existence of an intelligent being was antecedently proved' (*Institutiones Metaphysicae*, §377).

data. And later in the same lectures, speaking now of a maxim to the effect that nothing in the whole of organized nature is without an 'aim' [*Absicht*], he says: 'This is an established principle in the study of nature, and it has been confirmed by every experiment made in this case' (28: 1098). This seems to suggest that in Kant's view we do have empirical evidence for the existence of some aims or purposes in nature.

How are we to reconcile these remarks with the eminently sensible, and apparently also textually well grounded, thought that the proper starting point for the physico-theological argument is the assumption merely that nature contains the *appearance* of end-directness? One strategy would be to distinguish two things one may mean by calling a certain natural product—or feature of a natural product (but let's set that complication aside)—'purposive' or 'end-directed'. On the one hand, we may mean that the natural product has a certain *function*—as the eye has the function of seeing and the heart of pumping blood. On the other hand, we may mean that the structure has a certain *design*. The former would be (loosely speaking) an observable, the latter an unobservable feature of the thing in question. There is, after all, nothing question-begging in commencing the physico-theological argument with the assumption that the function of the eye is to see, for even a modern Darwinian evolutionary biologist—a person who might well be an atheist—could agree with such a claim. Though, to be fair, this would be something we take ourselves to 'observe' only in a somewhat expansive sense of the term—one that counts as 'observed' certain facts obtained by low-level inferences from the data proper.[45] Such a biologist would simply argue that the functional properties of certain structures or traits were not *designed* but rather *selected for* in virtue of their property of promoting the reproductive fitness of the organism in question. In taking such a line, they would exhibit their implicit belief that there is no analytical connection between '*x* has a function' and '*x* is designed by an intelligent being'.

The distinction between function and design having been drawn, it becomes apparent that the non-question-begging basis for the physico-theological argument would be our observation of functional features and traits in organisms. On the basis of these observations, the methodologically correct physico-theologian would infer—relying on an analogy with the products of human art (which also have functions)—that these features and traits have a wise designer. This would be an inference to the best explanation of the *appearance* of design.

To make sense of the second remark from the Pölitz religion lectures one would merely need to suppose that in that remark 'purpose' means 'function'. And, similarly, to make sense of the first remark, one would merely need to suppose that

---

[45] I'm assuming that, strictly speaking, functions are not among what are usually called 'the admissible contents of perceptual experience'. If I'm not right about this, the problem motivating this qualification disappears.

in speaking of certain parts of the world as having 'utility' and 'good aim' Kant means that they have functions. Now, because Kant certainly *believes* in a theistic God—or at least an exceedingly wise and great being—who creates the world through its free will and understanding, *he* will regard these functional parts of the world as designed, and so it will be natural for him to refer to them in ways suggestive of his own conception of them as realizing this being's intentions. However, when he speaks in this way, he will be speaking loosely. He will mean not that we observe some features *to be designed* but merely that we observe (in the permissive sense mentioned earlier), concerning certain structures that he himself happens to believe to be designed, that they have functions. I think this characterization of Kant's position manages to do justice both to his belief that certain natural features are designed, and to what I am claiming to be his belief that we nonetheless only infer, rather than observe, that they are designed. At any rate, by reading Kant this way we can make his position in the religion lectures consistent with his position in the first *Critique*.

16.9 The doctrinal belief in an Author of Nature

In the first *Critique*, Kant sees the revised physico-theological argument as justifying—or at least stabilizing—a doctrinal belief in the existence of a god (understood, now, merely as a 'wise and great originator of the world [*Welturheber*]' (B *xxxiii*)).[46] He says:

> Even in this theoretical relation we can say that I firmly believe in a god; but in this case this belief must not strictly be called practical, but must be called a doctrinal belief, to which the **theology** of nature (physico-theology) must *necessarily* everywhere give rise. (A 826–7/B 854–5, emphasis added)

If he is right, therefore, speculative rational theology is neither wholly dogmatic nor wholly fruitless. It can rightly boast of its role in producing and justifying a firmly held, theoretically grounded belief in an exceedingly great and wise Author of Nature. However, as Kant is acutely aware, to deploy the physico-theological argument in the justification of this belief is not to establish anything with apodictic certainty (A 624/B 652). Since the argument is an inference by analogy, it rather produces only empirical certainty. Nonetheless, although arguments of this kind are not, in Kant's view, capable of producing knowledge or apodictic certainty, they are, he thinks, to be respected because they enable the common

---

[46] In a reflection Kant indicates that the belief in question is a 'taking something to be true in a way that is sufficient for acting' (R 2793 (16: 514)).

understanding to arrive at 'a belief that is sufficient to comfort us though not to command unconditional submission' (A 625–6/B 653).

Kant supposes that the argument by analogy for our doctrinal belief in 'a supreme and unconditioned originator [of nature]' (A 624/B 652), like that for our doctrinal belief in an afterlife, relies on the more basic doctrinal belief that nature is suffused with purposes. This more basic doctrinal belief is justified—or, as Kant prefers to say, rendered 'sufficient'—by the fact that it is an indispensable presupposition of the contingent aim of acquiring guidance in the investigation of nature (ibid.).[47] Having formed this belief, we are in a position to argue by analogy from (what we believe to be) the pervasive possession of purposes by the things in nature to the existence of a designer possessing (at least relative to ourselves) immense wisdom and power. And, beyond this, the apparent unity of worldly ends—their seeming to subserve a single plan—gives us reason to think that there is only *one* being with such ends. The doctrinal belief, however, is not formed on the basis of observation or other evidence: its justification consists in the fact that it is an indispensable means to a contingent end.

The particular argument by analogy that Kant would seem to be envisaging *is* nonetheless *partly* empirically grounded; for it relies on the empirical premise that the world contains actually designed things—namely, human artefacts—to which the things of nature bear a resemblance insofar as they share the appearance of being designed.[48] This empirical assumption combines with the doctrinal belief in the purposiveness of nature, on the one hand, and the principle of analogy, on the other, to generate the doctrinal belief in a wise and powerful Author of Nature. The usefulness of this doctrinal belief is *confirmed* by the progress we actually make in investigating nature when we form it (A 829/B 857). For, by possessing it, we become more able to detect previously unnoticed apparent natural harmonies—or so, at least, Kant supposes.

Since Kant subjects the dogmatic physico-theological argument to powerful criticisms, it will be worth asking why he supposes that the non-dogmatic (non-demonstrative) argument fares better.

16.10 The non-dogmatic argument: criticisms and prospects

The non-dogmatic argument remains vulnerable to two criticisms. First, it seems powerless to rationalize our belief in a being that is perfect—hence, all-powerful,

---

[47] The belief, it should be noted, was widespread in Kant's day. Hume, for example, has Philo remark: '*That Nature does nothing in vain*, is a maxim established in all the schools...and, from a firm conviction of its truth, an anatomist, who had observed a new organ or canal, would never be satisfied, till he had also discovered its use and intention' (*Dialogues Concerning Natural Religion*, 12.9 at 277).

[48] In the *Pölitz* religion lectures Kant describes the source of the proof as 'wholly empirical' (28: 1007), adding that 'Here I use my actual perception of the world as [the proof's] ground' (28: 1008).

all-wise, etc.—a *supreme* intelligence. For the criticism still holds that the apparently intention-directed features that we observe in the world indicate nothing about the absolute magnitude, or absolute perfection, of their posited cause. Second, the reconceptualization of the argument leaves intact the problem that the available evidence points, at best, only to an intelligent originator of world's *form*—an architect rather than a creator of matter *ex nihilo*. In response to the first criticism Kant would seem to have to thin out his conception of the target of the physico-theological argument—as he seems to have done by the second edition at least—and conceive this being only as immensely great and wise (relative to us). This means that the doctrinal belief in the existence of a 'supreme' Author of Nature, in all strictness, parallels the belief in an afterlife in being—in truth—a belief only in a weakened counterpart of one of the cardinal propositions of dogmatic speculative theology.

The second criticism is addressed in the Pölitz religion lectures of 1783–84. Speaking there of the stabilization afforded to the earth's axial tilt by its equatorial bulge, Kant says:

> But wise as this arrangement is, I may not derive it immediately from the divine will, as something contingent, but I must rather consider it as a necessity of the earth's nature, just as has actually been demonstrated in this case. Yet this takes nothing away from God's majesty as creator of the world; for since he is the original being from whose essence the nature of all things is derived, this natural feature, in accordance with which an arrangement is necessary, is also to be derived from his essence, not from his will, for otherwise he would be only the world's architect, not its creator. (28: 1035)

Kant is now suggesting that we *may* argue from certain worldly features to the existence of God as a creator, so long as we think of Him as grounding the necessary arrangements of nature through His essence rather than His will. By regarding God as the *ens originarium* 'containing in itself the ground of all possible things', he suggests, we derive the *matter* of those things from the divine essence (ibid.). It is unclear exactly how this is supposed to work. If the argument is to appeal to the common human understanding, it is not supposed to rely, surely, on Kant's arguments in the *MFNS* about the diffusion of forces through spaces of various dimensions and their balancing. But it does seem that Kant takes the non-dogmatic physico-theological argument to be capable of generating a 'firmly and unshakeably' held belief in God, construed now as an independent, hence 'original' being—an *ens entium*, from whose essence the essence or possibility of all things derives.[49] And since it is characteristic of doctrinal beliefs that

---

[49] Compare: 28: 1035–6; 28: 1248; 28: 1252; and R 6251 (18: 531).

they are firmly held, there is reason to think that Kant is now regarding the *OPB* argument as gaining a second life when reconceived as an argument for a doctrinal belief in an originator of matter.[50] If this is right, then Kant's most famous criticism of the physico-theological argument—namely, that it argues only for an arranger of matter, not a creator of it *ex nihilo*—is directed only against an argument that treats the apparently end-directed arrangements in nature as contingent arrangements that are supposed to proceed directly from God's will (or wise choice). It is directed, in other words, against the kind of proof afforded by the ordinary physico-theology. And, notably, the style of explanation in which ordinary physico-theology trades is rejected during the critical period more comprehensively than it had been in *OPB*: 'We must', Kant says in the *Prolegomena*, 'refrain from *all* explanations of the organization of nature drawn from the will of a supreme being' (4: 331).

This concludes our examination of Kant's views on physico-theology. We have seen that although he subjects the dogmatic version of the physico-theological argument to trenchant criticism, he nonetheless harbours a genuine respect for the non-dogmatic argument—and he endorses that argument when it is interpreted as arguing only for a very great and wise Author of Nature. Moreover, of the three arguments criticized in the Ideal, the physico-theological argument is, he thinks, the only one capable of appealing to the common human understanding.[51] The argument has the further merit, in Kant's view, of being the source of genuine scientific discoveries; for by conducting our inquiries into nature on the assumption that the world is designed by a wise and benevolent being we will, he thinks, be able to discover natural features we would otherwise have overlooked. This last theme—that of the role of an 'as if' stance in empirical inquiry—is one whose importance it would be hard to overstate. Indeed, it is a theme for the sake of whose further development Kant adds to the Dialectic an appendix entitled 'On the Regulative Use of the Ideas of Pure Reason'. We devote the next chapter to this appendix.

---

[50] It is clear that Kant regards the *OPB* proof as surviving as a 'foundation for a hypothesis', though what this amounts to exactly is not altogether clear (28: 1258, compare 28: 1261).

[51] In *OPB* Kant cites Herman Samuel Reimarus's book on natural religion as a paradigm of what he means by arguments that, while lacking scholastic rigour, nonetheless appeal to the common human understanding or sound common sense (2: 161).

17
The Regulative Use of the Ideas

17.1 Introduction

Kant borrows the word 'Idea' from Plato and—implying that, on this point at least, he understands Plato better than Plato understood himself—he attaches to this word a meaning that, he claims, ought to have been its original Platonic sense (A 312/B 368–A 314/B 370).[1] According to Kant's usage, an 'Idea' is a concept whose intentional—or, in Kant's terms, 'imagined'—object is idealized or maximal along some dimension of variation. Kant mentions a broad range of Ideas in the first *Critique*. In addition to the Ideas of the soul, the world, and God, they include the Ideas of: an (absolutely) basic power (A 649/B 677); absolute simplicity (A 784/B 812); immortality (B 395 note *); freedom (A 533/B 561); maximal systematic unity (A 647/B 675); pure earth, pure water, and so forth (A 646/B 674); a continuum of forms (A 661/B 689); the most perfect creature of its kind (A 318/B 374); perfect wisdom (A 328/B 385); a state that maximizes the freedom of its citizens (A 316–17/B 372–4); the highest good (A 816/B 844); and the moral world (A 808/B 836).

The Ideas of the soul, the world, and God enjoy a special status: they are 'transcendental Ideas' or 'pure concepts of reason' (A 321/B 378). They are special both in being Ideas of the three putative objects of Wolffian 'special' metaphysics and in being associated with the three kinds of Kantian synthesis (categorical, hypothetical, and disjunctive), which are themselves patterned on the three kinds of Aristotelian syllogism (A 323/B 379).[2] Kant claims that these three Ideas exhaust the transcendental Ideas.[3] His argument for this claim, which is modelled

---

[1] Kant's tortured apologetics here seem intended to avoid running afoul of Locke's strictures on the abuse of words, especially the rule against using an old word with a new signification. See Locke, *Essay*, book 3, chapter 10, §6.

[2] Each Transcendental Idea is the unconditioned in (or, more accurately, corresponding to) *some* series of conditions, and Kant indicates that this unconditioned might even be the *totality* of the conditions in the series (See A 322/B 379 and A 336/B 394).

[3] Willaschek claims that Kant identifies 'precisely nine' transcendental Ideas (*Kant on the Sources of Metaphysics* at 168–9) and—rather strikingly—his list includes neither the Idea of the soul nor that of the world (as opposed to what I'd call their various, more determinate, 'sub-Ideas'). He is certainly right that Kant speaks of three *classes* of Ideas (see A 334/B 391) and that there are in fact a plethora of transcendental Ideas, not just the familiar three. However, I can't follow him in (apparently) downplaying two out of those original three. For Kant simply does speak of 'the three different transcendental Ideas' (see A 671/B 699). And, he clearly identifies the Ideas of the world and of God as Ideas in their own right and not merely as titles of classes of Ideas (see A 684/B 712 and A 685/B 713). I will therefore speak in the traditional way of the three (main) transcendental Ideas of the soul, the world,

The Fiery Test of Critique: A Reading of Kant's Dialectic. Ian Proops, Oxford University Press (2021). © Ian Proops.
DOI: 10.1093/oso/9780199656042.003.0018

on his metaphysical deduction of the categories, shares much of the implausibility of its more famous archetype. Whereas the categories—or so the metaphysical deduction alleges—earn their right to be recognized as pure concepts of the understanding in virtue of their correspondence with the twelve functions of the understanding in judgments, the Ideas are supposed to earn their right to be recognized as pure concepts of reason through their correspondence with the three forms of Aristotelian syllogism (also known as 'inferences of reason').

Kant takes the intentional object of each transcendental Idea to be that thing which would be reached if a certain kind of 'synthesis'—understood now in the broad sense of a series-generating iterative *process*—were, *per impossibile*, to be completed. So, the Idea of the soul, for example, is the Idea of something that constitutes the terminus of the series generated by attempting to construe every apparent subject as merely a property of a more fundamental subject. To think of the soul as the terminus of this series is to think of it as resisting such a construal. The Idea of the world, for its part, is the Idea of a presupposition that presupposes nothing further, hence the terminus of a series of presuppositions. And the Idea of God, finally, is the Idea of an unconditioned condition in the series of originations (compare A 624/B 652).

Kant holds neither that all Ideas lack objective reality nor that all have it: rather, the picture is mixed. The Idea of the world is clearly supposed to lack objective reality, while the Idea of God, he supposes, might for all we know on *theoretical* grounds have it. The Idea of a moral world, Kant thinks, does have objective reality, presumably as a state that would prevail at the limit of human moral improvement—a state that must be possible because it is a state that we are obligated to strive to realize (A 808/B 836).

He further holds that the *transcendental* Ideas (non-contingently) lack *sensible* exemplification. But he does not view them as intrinsically defective. Instead, they become problematic—or, in his terms, 'dialectical'—only when we misconstrue them as concepts known to be exemplified on theoretical grounds. This mistake arises merely because of 'misunderstanding and carelessness' (A 680/B 708). To avoid it we must attend to their true nature, namely, as the conceptual correlates— or expressions—of certain 'regulative' principles. These are certain 'logical'—by which in this context Kant means 'methodological' (A 648/B 676)—principles that tell us 'not what the character of the object is', but rather 'how we ought, under this concept's guidance, to **search** for the character and connection of experiential objects as such' (A 671/B 699).[4] Construed in this way, the Ideas advance empirical

---

and God, while also speaking, less traditionally, of their sub-Ideas. One caveat: the transcendental Idea of freedom (A 448/B 476; A 533/ B 561), which Willaschek does not include on his list of nine, must also be acknowledged. It is discussed in the third Antinomy, so it is perhaps best treated as (somehow) a sub-Idea of the transcendental Idea of the world.

[4] Kant applies the adjective 'heuristic' to both the principles and their associated Ideas (A 663/B 692; A 671/B 699).

inquiry partly by suggesting to us novel hypotheses and partly—as we'll see—by getting us to notice certain natural features we would otherwise have overlooked. In doing so, they 'open up new paths unknown to the understanding' (A 680/B 708). Handled properly, then, the Ideas serve as indispensable tools in natural-scientific inquiry. It is this fact that constitutes their justification, and the exercise of exhibiting this justifying fact constitutes their transcendental deduction (A 671/B 699).[5]

Regulative principles can be formulated either as commands or as 'ought'-claims. Construed as commands, they have the following form: 'We ought to regard/investigate/study X as if it were Y'. The Dialectic contains the following instances of this schema, among others (the table includes abbreviated paraphrases).

The Idea of	*What* is to be investigated	*How* it is to be investigated
The Soul	all appearances, acts, and the receptivity of our mind (A 672/B 700)	as if the soul were a simple substance that (at least in [this] life) exists permanently and with personal identity (A 672/B 700)
The World (considered as a mathematical series)	the conditions of inner and outer natural appearance (A 673/B 700) the regressing or ascending series of conditions (A 685/B 713)	as if nature were in itself infinite without a highest member (A 672/B 700) as if it were in itself infinite (A 685/B 713)
The World (considered as a dynamical series)	the series of states (A 685/B 713)	as if it had begun absolutely (through an intelligible cause) (A 685/B 713)
God (as the highest intelligence or supreme reason)	whatever may belong to the nexus of possible experience (A 672/B 700)	as if the sensible world (that is, the sum of all appearances) had outside its own range (that is, outside of space and time) a single highest and all-sufficient ground, namely, an independent, original, and creative reason (A 672/B 700)
	all arrangements (A 678/B 706)	as if they were made by a supreme reason of which our reason is only a faint copy (A 678/B 706; compare A 826/B 854)
	all arrangement in the world (A 686/B 714) everything (A 688/B 716)	as if it had sprung from the intention of a most supreme reason (A 686/B 714) as if it were caused by a purposive causality, which, as supreme intelligence, brought it about according to the wisest intention (A 688/B 716)

[5] At A 664/B 692 Kant seems to contradict this claim when he denies that the Ideas are capable of a transcendental deduction. But elsewhere he seems to maintain merely that they cannot be given a deduction of the same kind as the deduction of the categories (A 336/B 393; A 669–70/B 697–9).

As this table makes clear, the Idea of the world is anomalous and, on first appearances at least, puzzling. This is so for three reasons.

First, whereas in the case of the other transcendental Ideas what it is to proceed in the way enjoined is, *inter alia*, to proceed as if the Idea in question were exemplified, in the case of the world this is not so. On Kant's conception, after all, the Idea of the world is a *contradictory* concept (in our terms, it is the concept of the $world_{TR}$).[6] But to think of a contradictory concept as exemplified is to think of a contradictory state of affairs as obtaining. And that, in Kant's view, is, strictly speaking, to think nothing at all (29: 792). Accordingly, if one were to attempt to formulate the relevant principle on the model of the others, it would be as if one were to make a nonsensical recommendation—as it might be: 'One ought to act as if the intentional object of the concept *abracadabra* existed.' And such a recommendation, obviously, could afford us no guidance whatsoever. In consequence, there is no good explanation of the connection between the Idea of the world and its associated principle.

The second way in which the Idea of the world is anomalous is that it generates two different principles of inquiry, depending on whether we consider the world as a mathematical or as a dynamical series. This seems problematic because these principles themselves seem to stand in contradiction. One principle, in effect, bids us to accept nothing at all as an unconditioned member of the series, the other to treat the series as though it contains an unconditioned first member, and so, presumably, to search for this member.[7] One wonders how there could be a coherent state of mind that consisted in a resolution to follow both principles simultaneously. This problem may, I think, be addressed by appealing to the considerations raised in Chapter 3 in connection with the application of principle *P* to the series generated by the inherence relation. There, we suggested that part of what is involved in striving to find a non-inhering entity might be the attempt to construe every entity in the relevant series as inhering in something else. Repeated failure in this endeavour, we suggested, might constitute empirical evidence for the existence of a non-inhering entity. The current thought is that we might similarly hope to use compliance with one of these seemingly opposed principles as a means of complying with the other.

The third respect in which the Idea of the world is anomalous is that there seems to be something arbitrary about the way Kant associates the two regulative principles just mentioned with their corresponding sub-Ideas. The mathematical Idea of the world is associated with a recommendation to regard the world as infinite, the dynamical with a recommendation to regard it as finite. But Kant fails

---

[6] That the Idea in question is the concept of the $world_{TR}$ is suggested by the fact that the relevant way of proceeding is 'as if nature is *in itself* infinite' (A 672/B 700, A 685/B 713).

[7] The alternative reading, according to which the principle enjoins us to regard the world as if it had an intelligible cause outside of itself, is to be rejected because such a principle corresponds to the Idea of God rather than to that of the world.

to say why the associations should not rather have been made the other way around.

For these reasons, it will be best to focus on the less problematic among Kant's regulative principles: those, namely, associated with the Ideas of the soul and of God.

17.2 The Idea of the soul as a regulative principle

The various regulative principles associated with the Idea of the soul bid us to regard the appearances of the thinking I—the properties it manifests in inner sense—as if they inhered in a soul of the kind envisaged by the dogmatic rational psychologist. In particular, we are enjoined

> to regard all determinations as [united] in a single subject; to regard all powers as—to the greatest extent possible—derived from a single basic power; to regard all existence change [*Wechsel*] as belonging to the states of one and the same permanent being; and to represent all **appearances** in space as entirely different from actions of **thought**. (A 682–3/B 710–11)

The second of these injunctions is the clearest of the four. It amounts to an application of the principle of genera, which is associated also with the Idea of systematic unity (A 647/B 675) (we discuss this principle later in this chapter). It is not altogether clear why this injunction should be associated with the Idea of the soul. One's first thought is that Kant must be focusing on the soul's traditional attribute of simplicity while also supposing that its simplicity would dictate that it should possess, at the most fundamental level, merely a solitary power— something amounting to a 'complete and necessary unity of all mental powers' (A 771/B 799). This makes a certain amount of sense; for a composite soul, being a composite of simple substances, would have to possess at least as many fundamental powers as it had members—though, of course, it would have none of them *qua* composite.[8] On reflection, however, one worries that if this were indeed Kant's view, he would seem to be committed to the dogmatic position that the soul is *not* simple. For in the A edition of the first *Critique* (A 94), and also in certain later works, he claims that the soul has a plurality of distinct fundamental powers.[9]

---

[8] Recall that a composite may be credited with a power provided that one of its members has that power. But in such a case the composite would not be thought to have the power *qua* composite. See Chapter 6 for details.

[9] See, for example, the essay 'On the use of teleological principles in philosophy' of 1788 (8: 181), and also *Critique of the Power of Judgment* (5: 177–8).

In order to accommodate this point, one would need to assume that Kant does not himself hold that a simple thing must possess only a single power. His view would rather have to be taken to be that *the rational psychologist's* concept of the soul incorporates a traditional Wolffian conception of what it is for a substance to be unitary, namely, that it should possess a solitary basic power. In the case of the soul-substance the Wolffian would take this power to be the soul's power of representing the world. If this is right, then, in acting as if the Idea of the soul were exemplified, we would—temporarily occupying the perspective of the rational psychologist—be acting as if the soul had a single basic power from which all its other powers derived. In so acting, however, we would just be following the second injunction on the just-quoted list.

Kant seems to think that the third injunction advances inquiry because by following it we avoid getting distracted by inquiries that are, in his view, guaranteed to be inconclusive. In particular, by acting as if the soul is permanent, we exclude from consideration certain 'windy hypotheses' about 'the generation, destruction, and palingenesis of the soul' (A 683/B 711). Quite why the hypothesis of the soul's permanence is not itself 'windy', however, Kant does not explain.

The two remaining injunctions on Kant's list are 'to regard all determinations as [united] in a single subject' and 'to present all **appearances** in space as entirely different from actions of **thought**'. Neither one is all that well explained. The former provides no clear direction for inquiry; the latter makes only a dubious claim to be a genuine heuristic for investigating one's own mind. It is quite unclear, after all, why a philosopher or empirical scientist who thought of spatial appearances (outer objects) as inhering in the divine mind should, on that account, be in any way hamstrung when investigating their own mind. Perhaps, though, Kant is using 'thought' here in the strict sense according to which God's ideation does not, in all correctness, amount to thought (28: 1017).[10] If so, then the fourth injunction might be construed as bidding us to investigate bodies on the presupposition that they are more than the products of *human* thought. That suggestion, however, faces the difficulty that it seems that we would be able to do natural science perfectly well even while regarding our experience as merely a coherent dream.

17.3 The Idea of God as a regulative principle

Kant characterizes the Idea (or 'rational concept') of God as the Idea of a being considered as 'the single and all-sufficient cause of all cosmological series' (A 685-6/B 713). He regards the regulative principle associated with this Idea—the

---

[10] See also Chapter 2, §2.7.

428   THE FIERY TEST OF CRITIQUE

so-called principle 'of the unity of purposes'—as the 'foremost' among the regulative principles of reason (A 702/B 730). It bids us to view all arrangement in the world as if it had sprung from a 'single and all sufficient cause' (A 685–6/B 713–14). Kant thinks that by so regarding the world—as we do in practising physico-theology—we open up 'entirely new prospects for connecting the things of the world according to teleological laws and of arriving thereby at their greatest systematic unity' (A 687/B 715).[11] The physico-theological argument, he says, 'enlivens the study of nature' since it 'brings in purposes and aims [*Zwecke und Absichten*] where our observation would not have discovered them on its own, and it expands our acquaintance with nature through the guiding thread of a particular unity whose principle is outside nature' (A 623/B 651). In other words, the teleological stance essential to the physico-theological argument enables us to discover purposes—or perhaps more correctly, *purpose-like* features—and arrangements in the physical world that we would otherwise have overlooked. It thus alerts us both to otherwise unnoticed instances of apparent end-directedness and to otherwise unnoticed physical features and arrangements.[12] One instance of this phenomenon, discussed in the previous chapter, is the discovery of the earth's flattening into an oblate spheroid (an apparently end-directed feature of the earth—since apparently aimed at stabilizing the earth's axial tilt)—which leads us to hypothesize its formerly fluid state (an otherwise overlooked physical feature).

The idea that the teleological stance can advance empirical science was already in place in *OPB*, where Kant had alleged a number of intriguing instances of the phenomenon. For, example, by supposing that rivers are designed to bring water to dry regions of the world without flooding the surrounding land we are led to notice certain *ceteris paribus* physical laws: for example, rivers, *ceteris paribus*, build up their banks in their lower reaches until they no longer flood the surrounding land as much as they once did (2: 128–9).[13] By adopting this same stance we also come to notice certain unexpected facts—for example, that

---

[11] Kant supposes that the world would be the more systematically unified the richer the chains of means–end connections it contained. One example of such a chain would be the following. The seasons are uniform in duration so that animals and plants might inhabit stable environments; the earth's axial tilt is stable so that the seasons might be uniform in duration; the earth is somewhat flattened in order that its axial tilt might be stable, and so forth. In his religion lectures Kant suggests that the ultimate ends subserved in these chains are those of rational creatures (28: 1102). If so, we might presumably extend the chain as follows: animals and plants inhabit stable environments in order that they might live, and they live in order that the ends of rational creatures might be served. To be clear, Kant does not claim that such purposive chains actually exist, but he thinks that by acting as if they do we make progress—indeed, more progress than otherwise—in discovering and explaining natural features.

[12] Kant is especially clear about this point in his religion lectures. In adopting the teleological stance, 'We will often err', he says, 'but yet still also pay attention to many things that would otherwise have escaped us' (28: 1314).

[13] Compare Ray: 'if we shall consider the great Concepticula and Congregations of Water, and the Distribution of it all over the dry Land in Springs and Rivers, there will occur abundant Arguments of Wisdom and Understanding' (Ray, *Wisdom of God* at 78).

some *riverbeds* are, in the river's lower reaches, higher than the surrounding land (2: 129).

Another example, not developed by Kant himself but of which he would likely have been aware, is that of the honeycomb. Very plausibly, a standing alertness to the appearance of means and ends would enable us to discover the honeycomb's feature of being so constructed as to maximize the storage of honey in cells of equal volume for a given outlay of wax—a feature that might otherwise have been overlooked. Derham is adopting just such a stance when he remarks: 'And with what prodigious geometrical subtlety do [bees and wasps] work their deep hexagonal cells, [the hexagon being] the only proper figure that the best mathematician could choose for such a combination of houses.'[14] In making this optimality claim, Derham is alluding to the so-called 'honeycomb conjecture' of Marcus Terentius Varro (116 BCE–27 BCE), though he seems to regard it (wrongly) as a proven result rather than a mere conjecture.[15] Derham's elaboration is worth noting:

> Circular cells would have been the most capacious; but this would by no means have been a convenient figure, by reason [that] much of the room would have been taken up by vacancies between the circles; therefore, it was necessary to make use of some of the rectilinear figures.[16]

Kant presents a special case of the honeycomb conjecture as a fact when he says:

> [The hexagon is the figure that] encloses the greatest space with the shortest boundary [among those with the property that when they are] externally juxtaposed with other [congruent] figures no interstices [are] left. (2: 133–4)

So, for example, the isosceles triangle and the square are, like the hexagon, figures that tile the plane; however, they enclose less space than the hexagon for a given boundary. What Kant states here amounts only to a special case of the conjecture because it speaks only of tessellating figures rather than figures of equal area, the circle included. Nonetheless, the fact that he is aware of this special case suggests that he may have known of the more general conjecture. If he had, the connection with the teleological *as if* stance would have been obvious.

---

[14] Derham, *Physico-Theology* at 233.
[15] The result was proved in 1999 by Thomas C. Hales. Precisely formulated, it runs: 'Any partition of the plane into regions of equal area has perimeter at least that of the regular hexagonal grid.' A mathematically more informed Kant might therefore have said: 'By acting as if apparently useful natural features are designed by a maximally wise being in order to advance benevolent ends we are, among other things, led to formulate and try to prove the honeycomb conjecture.'
[16] Derham, *Physico-Theology* at 233, note 'o'.

17.4 Laws expressing the purposes of nature

In *OPB* Kant maintains that there exist certain laws whose character suggests that nature has certain *high-level* ends. He sees these laws as illuminating the relationship between the laws of physics, on the one hand, and the harmony and order found in the natural world, on the other (2: 129). One such law runs: 'nature, when left to universal laws, tends to produce regularity out of chaos' (2: 151). Another runs: 'the forces of motion and resistance continue to operate on each other until they afford each other the least impediment' (2: 129).

This second-mentioned law belongs to a family of high-level principles expressive of nature's apparent drive for economy. Other examples in this genre include: 'nature does the most with the least' and 'nature does nothing in vain'. Kant accords pride of place among these laws to Maupertuis's 'law of least action'. 'Maupertuis', he says:

> proved that even the most universal laws of matter in general—whether [this matter] be in equilibrium or in motion, whether in elastic or in non-elastic bodies, whether in the attraction of light in refraction or in its repulsion in reflection are subject to one dominant rule, according to which the greatest possible economy of action is always observed. (2: 98–9, compare 2: 134)

Kant illustrates the law governing the forces of motion and resistance as they act on matter using two examples. The first is the case of so-called 'epicycloidic' or 'planetary' gearing, the second that of a river's tendency to even out its gradient by erosion.

The gearing example is the more obscure of the two. Kant says: 'The epicycloid, an algebraic curve, is of the following nature: the teeth and gearwheels: when they are curved according to it, friction is reduced to a minimum' (2: 130). The epicycloid is the curve described by a point on one circle as it rolls around the outside of another. Kant is referring to a system of gearing in which several 'planet' gears are arranged around a central 'sun' gear, while the whole assembly is set within an internally toothed ring (an 'annulus'). In such a gearing system a point on the circumference of each planet gear traces out an epicycloid as it rolls around the central circular 'sun' gearwheel (the epicycloid is described relative to the frame of reference of this central wheel). The advantage of such a gearing system is that it reduces friction, wear, and noise relative to simpler systems. Kant says that A. G. Kästner mentions 'somewhere' that an engineer had shown him a mechanical system in which this 'epicycloidic' form was eventually produced by the friction of the system. It's not immediately apparent what Kant has in mind. Not, presumably, that he was told that the gearing arrangement actually reconfigured itself over time. More likely, Kästner had learned from engineers that the pattern of wear on the teeth of gearwheels arranged in certain non-epicycloidic configurations was precisely the one that would be produced if the wheels were striving to move in epicycloidic curves rather than circles, so that it was *as if* the wheels were endeavouring to reconfigure themselves into a lower-friction arrangement.

Kant's second example is more familiar. He observes that the force of the water flowing in a waterfall erodes the rock until the river achieves a 'fairly uniform gradient' (2: 131). In such a case, it is *as if* the river were working to even out its gradient. Insofar as this happens, the river is tending towards an anthropocentrically 'convenient' arrangement, namely, navigability (2: 130).

Since these examples are drawn only from the inexact sciences, it is worth mentioning that Kant is (at least dimly) aware of one case in which certain *exact* laws of nature may be derived by acting as if one is imputing intentions or goals to natural phenomena. I have in mind Leibniz's derivation of the laws of reflection and refraction from his 'Most Determined Path Principle'. In some metaphysics lectures of unknown date, Kant says:

> Many philosophers assumed the principle of the connection of finality <*principium nexus finalis*>, and also thought to discover much from it. Thus, *Leibniz* assumed, e.g., that a ray of light traverses the shortest path from one location to another, from which [assumption] he then derived the laws of dioptrics.
>
> (*Metaphysics L2*, 28: 574)

If his student note-taker is to be believed—and, in this case, that's a big 'if'—Kant is not stating the principle accurately. For if light were to take the *shortest* path between two points located in media with different refractive indices, it would not be refracted. Kant's remark would have made more sense if he had said not 'shortest' but 'quickest'. For, as Jeffrey McDonough observes, a refracted ray will spend more time in the rarer medium, where it travels faster, than in the denser medium, where it travels slower, and so will travel faster than a ray travelling in a straight line between the same two points.[17] But even this is not quite Leibniz's example, for, as McDonough also observes, Leibniz's principle does not in fact appeal to maxima or minima. Rather, it is tantamount to the claim that 'from among all the possible paths between a source and a sink, a ray of light will travel along the path which is [locally] unique with respect to ease; where ease is understood as the quantity obtained by multiplying the distance of the path by the resistance of the medium'.[18]

---

[17] Jeffrey K. McDonough, 'Leibniz on Natural Teleology and the Laws of Optics', *Philosophy and Phenomenological Research*, 78 (3) (2009), 505–44 at 509–10.
[18] Ibid., at 512.

17.5 Lazy reason and perverted reason

Kant sees two kinds of error as flowing from the original sin of construing a regulative principle as constitutive. The first is the fallacy of 'lazy reason' (*ignava ratio*). For Kant, this is the fallacy of prematurely curtailing one's investigation of nature by assuming that it is, at some stage, 'absolutely complete' (A 689/B 717–18). As we saw in the previous chapter, the 'ordinary' brand of physico-theology commits precisely this error when it treats certain natural arrangements as the directly instituted products of a divine choice instead of seeking their causes 'in the universal laws of the mechanism of matter' (A 691/B 719). In doing so, it 'bypass[es] at a stroke' all the relevant natural causes that would otherwise have been discovered through empirical investigation (A 773/B 801). In rational psychology, Kant supposes, one makes a mistake of the same kind when one assumes oneself capable of cognizing the simple, immaterial, and permanent nature of the soul, but he makes no effort to explain why this is so.

We might attempt an explanation on Kant's behalf by reflecting once again on Fordyce's argument. Since Kant's dogmatic spiritualist imagines that he cognizes the permanence of the soul a priori (from its simplicity taken together with the principle of continuity), it follows immediately that he will also take himself to cognize a priori his own post-mundane existence. But if so, he will have no incentive to try to construct the somewhat less compelling empirical argument for the soul's immortality attempted by Fordyce. He will, accordingly, have no incentive (from this quarter) to engage in the kind of close study of nature that might furnish evidence for the empirical premise of that argument—the premise, namely, that each part of every observed non-human organism has a function useful to the organism. The study of organic nature will thus lose one of its motivations.

The second mistake Kant sees as flowing from the more basic mistake of construing a regulative principle as constitutive is the error of 'perverted reason (*perversa ratio*)' (A 692/B 720). This is the mistake of begging the question. The dogmatic metaphysician makes this mistake in the course of conducting the physico-theological argument when they assume without warrant that we observe in nature *design* rather than merely the appearance of design. This mistake was discussed in the previous chapter; so I'll not belabour it here.

17.6 The Idea of systematic unity

The transcendental Ideas are not the only ones whose legitimate regulative use Kant wishes to describe. Of no less importance to him is the regulative use of the

Idea of 'systematic unity' (A 647/B 675).[19] Kant terms the regulative principle associated with this idea 'the logical principle of reason' (A 649/B 677). This principle urges us to strive to bring about a certain systematic unity among our concepts (ibid). Its concrete articulation generates three distinct methodological principles—those, namely, of genera (or homogeneity, or unity), species (or variety, or specificity), and affinity (or kinship).

The principle of genera urges us to search for ever higher genera in nature, that of species to seek ever lower species, while that of affinity urges us to inquire on the assumption that such species as belong to the extension (in Kant's sense—more on which below) of a given genus are linked to one another by continuous gradations (A 660/B 688; compare A 657/B 686).

Kant employs a vivid example to illustrate the operation of the logical principle of genera (which he also calls 'the logical law of homogeneity'). 'The various appearances of one and the same substance', he says:

> show, at first glance, so much heterogeneity that one must at the outset assume almost as many kinds of power of this substance as there are effects putting themselves forth, just as in the human mind there are [for example:] sensation, consciousness, imagination, memory, wit, the power to differentiate, pleasure, desire, etc. Initially, a logical maxim bid us to reduce this apparent variety as far as possible by discovering hidden identity through comparison and seeing whether imagination combined with consciousness may not be memory, [and whether] wit [may not be] the power to distinguish, or perhaps even understanding and reason. (A 648–9/B 676–7)

The logical maxim in question bids us to diminish the apparent variety in the mind's powers 'as far as possible' by means of certain theoretical reductions, which take the form of identity claims (A 649/B 677). In heeding this injunction, we endeavour to represent the mind's powers in a taxonomic tree that has at its root a single fundamental power. This taxonomy, however, is merely an ideal to which we approximate. 'The idea of a **fundamental power**', Kant says, is 'the problem set by a systematic representation of the manifoldness of powers' (ibid.).

Kant takes the logical principle of genera (or 'homogeneity') to entail the principle 'there is no vacuum of forms <Non datur vacuum formarum>', which he interprets as meaning 'there are not original and first genera that are, as it were, isolated and separated from one another (by empty and intermediate space); rather, all the manifold genera are only divisions of a single highest and universal genus' (A 659/B 687). It is not immediately clear whether he takes the entailed 'Non datur' principle to be itself a logical principle or whether he regards it as a

---

[19] Kant also terms this idea the Idea of 'the form of a whole of cognition' (A 645/B 673).

constitutive transcendental principle (more on which later). But if the former is the case, we would have to take the principle to enjoin us to proceed in our inquiries as if nature never contains a plurality of irreducibly basic natural kinds—a plurality, that is, of natural kinds sharing no common genus. We should not, for example, ever settle for the conclusion that there are different kinds of *basic* matter.

Kant takes the logical principle of genera to be tempered by a second, countervailing principle, which 'limits the inclination toward unanimity [*Einhelligkeit*]' (A 660/B 688). 'The logical principle of genera, which postulates identity', he says:

> is opposed by another, namely that of **species**, which requires manifoldness and variety in things regardless of their agreement under the same genus, and prescribes to the understanding that it be no less attentive to variety than to agreement.   (A 654/B 682)

This last remark indicates that the logical principles do their work by directing the understanding's *attention*. Kant's idea is that if we allow ourselves to be guided by them, we will give our natural-scientific inquiries a boost because we will come to attend to things—natural laws as well as natural features, kinds, traits, and structures—that we would otherwise have overlooked.

The logical principle of species urges us never to conclude that a given species lacks sub-species. Kant illustrates the principle, which he also terms the law of specificity, with an example from chemistry:

> That there are absorbent earths of different species (calcareous earths and muriatic earths) required for its discovery an antecedent rule of reason that made it a task for the understanding to seek variety in nature.   (A 657/B 685)

The absorbent earths were found to divide into, the calcareous earths—various crystalline structures of calcium carbonate, such as calcite and aragonite—on the one hand, and, on the other, the muriatic or 'magnesian' earths—including 'magnesia alba' (magnesium carbonate) and 'calcinated magnesia' (magnesium oxide).[20] Kant would seem to be advancing the rather strong thesis that but for the principle of species the hypothesis that the absorbent (that is, hygroscopic) earths

---

[20] Magnesia alba is, more precisely, basic carbonate ($xMgCO_3;yMg(OH)_2;zH_2O$). See J. R. Partington, *A Short History of Chemistry* (3rd edn; New York: Dover, 1989) at 95. In eighteenth-century chemistry books the Latin term 'Terra muriatica' can be found glossed as 'magnesia'. See, for example, *Comparative view of ancient and modern names of chemical substances*, appendix to Antoine-François de Fourcroy, *Elements of Natural History and Chemistry*, Volume 3 (London, 1790), translated from the Paris edition of 1789. And for a classification of the 'simple earths' into the 'the calcareous, the ponderous, the magnesian or muriatic, the argillaceous, and the siliceous' see: Richard J. Sullivan (1794), *A View of Nature in Letters to a Traveller Among the Alps* (6 vols) (London: T. Becket) at vol. 1, 434.

subdivide into these two sub-species could not have been seriously entertained. This point suggests that reason, for Kant, is the faculty that, among other things, extends the horizon of taxonomic inquiry, while the understanding, by contrast, is a faculty that merely keeps in its judgments to the kinds already discovered.[21]

Kant's example is worth dwelling on, for it sheds important light on his knowledge of the chemistry of his day. He is, I think, alluding to certain experiments that had been conducted in the 1750s by the Edinburgh chemist, Joseph Black (1728–1799). These experiments are described in Black's famous paper of 1756, 'Experiments upon magnesia alba, quick-lime and other alcaline substances'. In these experiments, the calcareous earths were distinguished from magnesia alba (magnesium carbonate) through their differential reactivity with various acids.[22] Although Kant unquestionably knew of Black's work, *how* he knew of it is not altogether clear: Black's article was translated into German in 1757 and into French in 1774, but I have been unable to find it mentioned either in Kant's own writings, or in any of the chemistry books found in his library after his death.[23] Given this partial lacuna, it's worth considering a rival suggestion owed to Michael Friedman.

Wishing to stress Kant's Stahlian orientation, Friedman interprets Kant's division of the absorbent earths into the '*Kalk- und muriatische Erden*' as a differentiation between 'calx and muriatic earths'.[24] However, the calx (singular) of phlogiston chemistry is a poor candidate for what Kant means by '*Kalk-Erden*' (plural) in this context. And this holds true for reasons of chemistry as well as grammar. For calces (metal oxides) are not in general absorbent (consider, for example, lead dioxide). Of course, none of this detracts from Friedman's important observation that the Kant of the first *Critique* is, in both editions, operating squarely within the framework phlogiston chemistry. What it does mean—if I am correct—is that Kant knew (so to speak, *de re*) of the first steps taken beyond that chemistry (though he does not seem to have recognized them under that description). For the experiments discussed in Black's article show glimmerings of the first great advance beyond Stahl, namely, pneumatic chemistry. In particular, the article shows recognition of the fact that 'fixed air' (carbon dioxide) is a chemically distinct component of atmospheric air, with its own distinctive properties. This fact has the anti-Stahlian corollary that 'pure' (that is,

---

[21] That horizon, it should be noted, continues to be extended today. As recently as 2020, for example, a genetic study revealed that 'red pandas' are in fact two distinct species.

[22] See Joseph Black (1893), *Experiments upon magnesia alba, quick-lime and other alcaline substances*, orig. pub. 1756 (read 1755), Alembic Club Reprints (Edinburgh: Clay), at 11–12.

[23] Kant shows himself aware of Black's work in his anthropology lectures for 1784–5. He says: "Black in Edinburgh invented the analysis of the air" (*Anthropology Mrongovius*, 25: 1410). He does not mean that Black *completed* that analysis, but rather that he began the project of isolating the distinct chemical components of pure (that is, completely dephlogisticated) air. For details of the translations of Black's article, see J. R. Partington, *A History of Chemistry* (4 vols.), vol. 3 (London: Macmillan, 1961–64) at 136–7, n7.

[24] Friedman, *Kant's Construction of Nature*, at 273, n267.

completely dephlogisticated) atmospheric air is a heterogeneous stuff.[25] Kant was aware of the corollary (see note 23 above), but he does not seem to have been fully aware of its anti-Stahlian import.

Kant claims that the logical principle of variety (or 'species' or 'specificity') has as a consequence another principle (or law), namely, 'There is a continuum of forms' <Datur continuum formarum>' (A 659/B 687).[26] If taken as a logical principle, this principle would have to be read as urging us never to conclude that between two particular species in our division there is no third. Kant expresses this idea by saying that in drawing up our taxonomic systems we are to proceed on the assumption that 'all differences of species border on one another and permit no transition to one another by a leap, but [rather] permit a transition only through all the smaller degrees of difference through which we can get from one species to another' (ibid.). In its condensed form the principle says that there are no species or sub-species that are 'nearest to one another'.

These formalisms fail to settle whether Kant intends to be recommending (a) that the *branches* of each taxonomic tree be regarded as dense orderings of concepts (let's call this the recommendation to seek 'vertical denseness') or (b) that such polytomies as a tree incorporates be regarded as dense orderings of concepts (the recommendation to seek 'horizontal denseness') or (c): both. I'm inclined to favour (c) for three reasons: First, as we will see in the next section, in the first *Critique* Kant illustrates the principle of affinity, which is supposed to incorporate the principle of variety, with an example—namely, the paths of the planets and comets—that takes the form of a polytomy whose members are a horizontal continuum of conic sections. Second, the way Kant formulates the principle of affinity suggests that the gradual transition between species is supposed to unify species located on *different* branches of a taxonomic tree (A 660/B 688). This suggests that the envisaged gradual transition is one between nodes dwelling on different branches—as would be the case in a division that incorporated genuine, irreducible polytomy. Third, as Watkins has noted, (a) is nonetheless plainly *part* of what Kant has in mind.[27] So much is clear from Kant's

---

[25] For an illuminating discussion of the milestones passed in the wake of Stahl's chemistry, see Friedman, *Kant and the Exact Sciences*, at chapter 5, part 3.

[26] Translators have generally taken Kant to be claiming that this principle is a consequence of the principle 'Non datur vacuum formarum'. But this hypothesis seems unlikely simply because the entailment so obviously fails to hold: the fact that there is just one tree—recall Kant's gloss on the principle—entails nothing about the length or structure of its branches. It makes more sense, I think, to read the word *'diesem'* in the phrase *'aus diesem Grundsetze'* not as meaning 'this' and so as referring to the principle 'Non datur vacuum formarum', which he has just mentioned, but rather as meaning 'the latter' and so as referring to the second-mentioned basic logical principle, namely the law of specification. This reading has the additional merit of restoring symmetry to Kant's discussion; for one would have expected both basic methodological principles to have corollaries if either did.

[27] That said, I disagree with Watkins's view that (a) is the whole of what Kant has in mind. See Eric Watkins, 'Kant on Infima Species', in C. La Rocca (ed.), *Kant und die Philosophie in weltbürgerlicher Absicht* (Berlin: de Gruyter, 2013) at 217.

associating the *scala naturae* tradition with the principle of affinity at A 668/B 696, and also—as Watkins himself notes—from the reflection, R 2893, in which Kant explicates the word '*proxima*' ('nearest') as it figures in the claim 'there is no nearest species' with the phrase '*immediate subordinata*' ('immediately subordinate'). That Kant should have been committed to vertical denseness is not all that surprising; for the same commitment occurs in his favourite logic textbook, namely Meier's *Auszug*. In this work Meier claims that 'through an opposition one *gradually* [*nach und nach*] connects the differences [of the lower concepts that figure in the divided concept's extension] with the higher concept' (emphasis added).[28]

Kant is transforming a traditional constitutive claim about the existence of a gradualism in the hierarchies of nature into a regulative principle expressing an injunction always to seek new species lying between any already recognized genus and its apparent immediate sub-species (Meier, since he is discussing the *representation* of species in a logical division stands at an intermediate point between Kant and this older, ontologically orientated tradition). If the word 'always' in Kant's injunction is taken seriously, I think we must judge him to be making a mistake. For it is possible to imagine a branch of science advancing by, on the contrary, actually *eliminating* nodes from a taxonomic tree. Some species, after all, might turn out to be gerrymandered categories that fail to correspond to natural kinds. To take an imaginary example, one might begin with a taxonomy that incorporated the concept *growing thing*, supposing this concept to express a basic natural kind intermediate between *extended thing* and *living thing*.[29] Such a species might, for example, be taken to include within its sphere not only plants and animals but also certain crystals, for example stalactites and stalagmites. But, since the concept *growing thing* is not in fact the concept of a natural kind, natural science would be advanced if one were to eliminate it and instead recognize a direct subordination relation as holding on the newly pruned tree between *extended thing* and *living thing*. The injunction, in short, ought to be to seek genuine *natural* kinds, not mere species. But that, unfortunately, is not what it says.

Kant represents the opposition between the first two logical principles as expressive of a conflict in the very interests of reason (A 654/B 682).[30] On the one hand, reason has an interest in 'comprehensiveness' [*Umfang*] or 'universality' in regard to genera; on the other, it also has an interest in 'content' [*Inhalt*] or 'determinacy' in regard to the manifoldness of species (A 654/B 682). Kant

---

[28] Meier, *Auszug*, §285.
[29] The example is inspired by Kant's including 'growing things' as a concept in one of his divisions in the *Dohna-Wundlacken Logic* (24: 755), though he does not himself treat this concept as the genus of which *plant* is a species.
[30] Kant's retraction of this claim at A 667/B 695 is discussed later in this chapter. The claim should plainly be softened because the demands are obviously co-satisfiable.

maintains that in promoting the first interest the understanding thinks much 'under' its concepts, while in promoting the second it thinks progressively more 'in' them. The understanding thinks more 'under' a given concept to the extent that the tree-like division on which the concept is located contains more concepts beneath it—the set of concepts occurring below a given concept (usually in the left-most branch of the tree) being that concept's 'extension'.[31] By contrast, the understanding thinks more 'in' a given concept to the extent that the division on which the concept is located contains more concepts above it—the set of concepts above a given concept on a given branch of the tree being that concept's 'intension'.[32]

We turn now to the principle of affinity, which is a hybrid principle that combines the principle of genera with the principle of species. Calling this principle 'the third law', Kant says:

> The third law unites [the first two] inasmuch as amidst the utmost manifoldness it yet prescribes that we seek homogeneity through the gradual transition from one species to another—a transition which indicates a kind of kinship of the different branches insofar as all of them are offshoots from one stem.[33]
>
> (A 660/B 688)

Kant is thinking of a principle that requires us to seek *family resemblances* between the individuals falling under a given genus, but he is also envisaging the principle as urging us to treat the properties of the family members as related to one another by a maximally gradual spectrum-like transition. To get a better sense of what the principle means, it will help to consider how it might be applied in an actual case—for example, Kant's early discussion of the discovery of the perisolar celestial bodies in his 1755 work, *Universal Natural History and Theory of the Heavens*. At this early stage, Kant is not explicitly discussing the principle of affinity, but he is identifying a case that we can retrospectively recognize as one to which it might appropriately be applied.

In the third chapter of *Universal Natural History* Kant claims that, for the most part, the eccentricity of the paths of the planets and comets increases with their distance from the sun.[34] Speaking of this loose correlation, he says:

---

[31] A Kantian extension thus differs from a Fregean extension (the set of objects falling under a given concept), the latter corresponding to a Kantian 'sphere'. If the tree features genuine, irreducible polytomy, the extension will include concepts not on the left-most branch.

[32] See Allison, *Kant's Transcendental Idealism* at 111. Note that since Kant denies that there is a lowest species, the set of concepts occurring under a given concept will be infinite, and, accordingly, the notions of 'less' and 'more' in the above explanation of extension will have to be understood in terms of set inclusion rather than cardinality.

[33] Notice that the passage makes clear that a 'law' for Kant need not be a descriptive claim: it can take the form of a *prescription*.

[34] Kant says that there are two exceptions which infringe the law (*Gesetz*) of increasing eccentricity with solar distance, namely Mercury and Mars—planets which he thinks have highly eccentric orbits in

This determination leads, through all possible stages of eccentricity, via a continuous ladder from the planets finally to the comets and although this connection appears to be severed at Saturn by a great chasm, which completely separates the cometic family from the planets... there may well be other planets beyond Saturn, which approach the orbits of the comets more closely by a greater deviation from the circular nature of the orbits, and that it is only as a result of a lack of observation, or of the difficulty of observation, that this relationship is not just as visible to the eye as it has been shown to be for the understanding.

(1: 278)

Here Kant is counselling us never to yield to the appearance that there is a gap in the sequence of increasingly eccentric occupied orbits between Saturn and the comets. Instead, we are to keep inquiring, and, in particular, to seek further planets intermediate in eccentricity between Saturn and the comets. This, I think, is the part of the principle that corresponds to the principle of species; the part corresponding to the principle of genera, on the other hand, bids us to regard the heavenly bodies as sharing a kinship with one another insofar as they are, one and all, made up of matter of fundamentally the same kind—matter, namely, that is constitutively governed by an inverse square law of attraction and an inverse cube law of repulsion.

Here is Kant articulating this very conception:

It is not possible to create a special genus of heavenly bodies out of the comets that is entirely distinct from the family of planets. Nature acts here, as elsewhere, through imperceptible gradations, and, by passing through all stages of change, it connects the remote properties to the closer ones by means of a chain of links.

(1: 277-8)

The claim about nature acting through imperceptible gradations cannot, I think, be an empirical claim. It is rather an assumption that guides inquiry. We assume the gradualism in assuming the principle of affinity—and, to be precise, in assuming the vestige of the principle of species that results from its absorption into the hybrid principle of affinity. We also assume that the heavenly bodies share a uniform constitution and so are all governed by the same fundamental laws—laws constitutive of the stuff of which they heavenly bodies are composed. This is the part of the principle of affinity that corresponds to the principle of genera. Since the planets are observed to have elliptical paths, we know that their paths are conic sections—a point that can, as Kant knew, be explained by their being

---

spite of orbiting close to the sun (1: 280). In the case of Mars, he attributes the exception to the gravitational influence of Jupiter (ibid.). This suggests that he is regarding the *ceteris paribus* law as having the status of a genuine law on certain idealizing assumptions that do not in practice obtain.

governed by an inverse square law of attraction (4: 321; compare 5: 363). We therefore reason that the paths of the comets must be governed by the same law and so themselves be conic sections. Since the comets are observed to appear only at irregular intervals it seems reasonable to assume that they orbit the sun at great distances, if they orbit it at all. Applying the *ceteris paribus* law that tells us that the farther out a heavenly body orbits the sun, the more eccentric its orbit, we conclude that the comets have highly eccentric orbits that take the form of conic sections.[35]

I should emphasize that I am not suggesting that this reasoning occurs explicitly in the *Universal Natural History*. My point is rather that the materials for it are present in chapter 3 of that work. The reasoning I have just sketched does, however, lie behind the first *Critique*'s appeal to the paths of the heavenly bodies in illustrating the operation of the principle of affinity in the first *Critique*. It is now time to consider that discussion.

17.7 The first *Critique* on the courses of the heavenly bodies

In the first *Critique* Kant indicates that the three logical principles that collectively unpack the logical principle of reason are to be applied in the following order: species (or 'manifoldness'), affinity (or 'kinship'), genera (or 'unity') (A 662/B 690). He illustrates their application with reference to the example of theorizing about, and ultimately discovering, the paths of the planets and comets. This same example serves to illustrate a point about the scope of the three principles, namely, that they concern 'not merely things but even more the mere properties and powers of things' (A 662/B 690). The 'properties' in question are the properties possessed by the planets and comets of having paths of certain shapes, while the 'power' is the force of gravity.

Kant offers the following explanation of how the principle of affinity might have guided the construction of a theory of the planetary courses:

> Thus, e.g., if through an experience (that is not yet fully corrected) the course of the planets is given to us as circular and we then find differences, we presume them to lie in what can change a circle in accordance with a constant law, through each of an infinity of intermediate degrees, into one of these divergent orbits; i.e., we presume that the planetary motions that are not circles will more or less approximate the properties of a circle; and thus we hit upon the ellipse. The comets show in their paths an even greater difference from the circle, since (as far as observation extends) they do not even loop back. Yet we guess that they

---

[35] In the first *Critique* Kant supposes that these 'orbits' are parabolas or hyperbolae (A 662–3/B 690–1).

follow a parabolic course, which is still akin to the ellipse, and which in all our observations is indistinguishable from an ellipse if the latter's major axis is extended very far. (A 662/B 690)

Kant supposes that at the start of our inquiry, relying on our rough preliminary observations, we hypothesize that all the planets have circular paths. Later, when we notice that some planets do not seem to move in perfect circles, we hypothesize elliptical paths for them.[36] In framing this more accurate hypothesis we thereby 'correct' our original observation. The hypothesis of an elliptical path is the natural one to test after the circle because of the *affinity* between the two figures—something that consists, I think, partly in the fact that the properties of the ellipse approximate those of the circle as the distance between the former's foci approaches zero, and partly in the related fact that between any given ellipse and the circle constituting its limit there is a further, less eccentric, ellipse.[37] When we come to consider the comets, since observation never, so far as we can tell—and here I speak only from Kant's point of view—shows them to return, we make an informed guess at a parabolic orbit. This new hypothesis is anchored in our previous one because (as we'd say) the parabola is the limiting case of an ellipse as the distance between the latter's foci goes to infinity.[38] Our hypothesizing is thus once again guided by the principle of affinity.

It bears mentioning that the division of non-circular non-degenerate conic sections into ellipse, parabola, and hyperbola is for Kant a genuinely irreducible polytomy. Since its objects, being geometric curves, are intuitable, it is *not* a logical division, which is the kind of division that must be dichotomous (see 9: 146–8). Watkins claims that, on the contrary, Kant treats *all* polytomy as reducible to dichotomy, not just logical polytomy. And by this he seems to mean that when there appears to be three or more (immediate) species of a given genus, all but two of those species are really immediate subspecies of concepts distinct from, and lower in the division than, the genus.[39] But, so far as I can tell, the first *Critique* does not support this claim. It is true that Kant does say something arguably suggestive of it elsewhere. 'Polytomy', he says at R 3019 (16: 662), 'is a subordinate dichotomy'. This might perhaps be taken to mean that every polytomy is the

---

[36] Here Kant's reconstruction of the discovery actually fails to agree with the historical facts. For, immediately after the circle, Kepler in fact tried the hypothesis of an egg-shaped path (or 'ovoid') before hitting on the ellipse. If this fact had been pointed out to him, Kant would no doubt have replied that this merely shows a lack of full rationality on Kepler's part. See A. E. L. Davis, 'Kepler's Unintentional Ellipse: A Celestial Detective Story', *The Mathematical Gazette*, 82 (493) (1998), 37–43. My thanks to Roy Sorensen for alerting me to both article and fact.
[37] Since in the first *Critique* Kant thinks of the affinities in question as holding between *properties* he must see the properties 'having an elliptical path' and 'having a circular path' as enjoying an affinity in virtue of the more basic affinity between the curves.
[38] Kant does not himself treat the parabola or the circle as kinds (limiting cases) of ellipse. Instead, he speaks of one kind of curve as approximating another as its eccentricity increases or decreases.
[39] Watkins, 'Kant on Infima Species' at 216.

misrepresentation of what is in fact a dichotomy that incorporates another dichotomy (see 24: 928)—a violation of Meier's fifth rule for the construction of a logical division: 'the members of the subdivision must not be put among the members of the division' (Meier, *Auszug*, §288). But this is hardly a natural reading of the remark. It treats Kant as saying that what is superficially presented as a polytomy in an inaccurate taxonomic tree is really a set whose members are shared between subordinate and superordinate dichotomies. But that is not the same thing as saying that a polytomy is a single subordinate dichotomy. It seems more likely that Kant had meant to write 'Polytomy is a subordinate *division*' and that 'dichotomy' was either a slip or a loose use of that term. If that had been so, Kant would be saying that polytomy is always a subordinate division, never the first dividing step. I take this to be a likely reading because Kant clearly holds that any division I might draw up, although it must *begin* with a dichotomous classification may incorporate non-dichotomous divisions lower down (a dichotomous 'division' now in the sense of 'an *act* of dividing into two') (taken together, the following passages make this point clear: 24: 928, R 3022, R 3025, R 3027). When insisting on this point, he goes on to say that subsequent acts of dividing—so-called 'subdivisions'—may be polytomous *so long as the subdivision is synthetic rather than logical*, where a subdivision is synthetic if it is a classification of entities (conic sections included) whose cognition involves intuition. These points tell against Watkins's reading. For if Kant did take all (apparent) polytomy to be reducible to dichotomy—so that taxonomic trees apparently incorporating polytomies were always merely superficial and misleading representations of (objective) taxonomies that were in fact dichotomous at every level—his insistence that a division must *begin* with a dichotomy would be redundant. It would raise the question: why the focus on the *first* step if what holds there must hold everywhere?

Incidentally, these reflections suggest that a claim I made in Chapter 9 needs refining. There I represented Kant's division of oppositions (in the broad sense) as a trichotomy (contradictories, contraries, and sub-contraries). However, since this is a logical (that is to say, non-empirical and non-synthetic) division it *would* have to be considered reducible to a dichotomous division.[40] The first dichotomous division in the formal division would presumably be that between pairs of claims that can both be true and those that can't both be true. The next would divide the latter category into contradictories and mere contraries.

Owing to the hybrid nature of the principle of affinity, Kant's illustration involves, in addition to an appeal to a series of conic sections, an appeal to a subsuming genus. He tells us that under the guidance of the principle of unity— recall that 'the principle of unity' is a variant term for the principle of homogeneity or genera—we arrive:

---

[40] See *Jäsche Logic*, §77, n2 (9: 130).

at a unity of the genera in the forms of these paths, but thereby also at unity in the cause of all the laws of this motion (gravitation); from there we extend our conquests, seeking to explain all variations and apparent deviations from those rules on the basis of the same principle; finally we even add on more than experience can ever confirm, namely in accordance with the rules of affinity [*Verwandtschaft*], even conceiving hyperbolical paths for comets in which these bodies leave our solar system entirely and, going from sun to sun, unite in their course the most remote parts of a world system, which for us is unbounded yet connected through one and the same moving force. (A 662–3/B 690–1)[41]

The principle of genera is operative in the hypothesis that the conic section is the genus relative to which the paths of the planets and comets are species.[42] But it is also operative in our positing a unitary cause for the various motions of all of these heavenly bodies, namely, the force of gravity—a force whose existence explains why the paths are all conic sections. Having posited this cause, we then 'extend our conquests' by explaining the deviations of certain planets, including Mercury and Mars (1: 280), from their predicted courses. We do so by factoring in the mutual gravitational attraction of all the perisolar celestial bodies. Finally, recurring to the principle of affinity, we experiment with the hypothesis that certain comets should have hyperbolic rather than parabolic paths. This will—or so Kant thinks—be the natural hypothesis to frame about a comet whose orbit could not be fitted to a parabola; for the hyperbola is akin to the other curves we've mentioned in being a conic section obtainable from the circle by means of a certain continuous transformation, which transformation is, I think, what Kant is referring to when he speaks of 'a constant law' in the first of the two passages just quoted—that is, the one at A 662/B 690.

Before we describe this transformation, we should note that the affinity in question does *not* consist merely in the hyperbola's sharing with the other planetary paths the property of being a conic section. For, first, the hypothesis that the paths of the planets are all conic sections is recommended by the principle of genera rather than affinity, and second, the mere idea of a conic section doesn't yet bring out the thought, reflective of the principle of affinity, that we are to seek a gradualism in the properties of the paths. We should also note that the principle of affinity does not merely recommend that we treat the series of orbits ordered by increasing eccentricity as continuous. For the investigation Kant actually describes

---

[41] A version of this hypothesis turns out to be true of *some* comets from *other* solar systems. In August 2019, the Crimean amateur astronomer, Gennadiy Borisov, discovered the first known interstellar comet, the so-called '2I/Borisov'. Because it has an orbital eccentricity of 3.36, its trajectory is classified as 'extremely hyperbolic'.

[42] In the *Prolegomena* Kant asserts, yet more strongly, that all possible orbits of the celestial bodies are conic sections (4: 321).

involves seeking ever *later* members of the series rather than merely in finding further members lying between those already discovered.

The transformation that brings out the idea of the affinity of the planetary paths involves taking a plane that intersects a cone and rotating it around a certain axis in such a way that it generates further conic sections. We begin by considering a plane *P* which intersects a cone to form a circular conic section *C*. At this initial stage, the plane is parallel to cone's base. We then take one of the tangents to *C*, *T*, as an axis of rotation and rotate *P* around *T* in the direction of the cone's base. By performing this operation we obtain a continuous ordering—'continuous' in our sense as well as Kant's—of non-degenerate conic sections. We first (that is, before the rotation starts) obtain a circle, then a continuous series of ellipses, then a continuous series of parabolas (the first parabola being formed when the rotated plane becomes parallel to one of the 'sides' of the cone), and finally a hyperbola—or, technically half of one—as the plane becomes perpendicular to the cone's base.

In the course of this process we generate infinitely many curves lying between each of the salient curve kinds—for example, infinitely many ellipses lying between a given ellipse and the first parabola obtained. Kant's thought, I take it, is that if it proceeds in the order dictated by this continuous transformation, our hypothesizing about the paths of the perisolar celestial bodies will proceed in a properly systematic—hence non-haphazard—way. The principle of affinity thus affords concrete guidance about the order in which our hypotheses are to be tested.

As we have seen, by approaching the comets with the expectation that their paths will always be some kind of conic section we, in effect, act upon the assumption that their matter, like that of the planets, is constitutively governed by an inverse square law of attraction. We thus, in effect, proceed on the assumption that the matter of the comets is like in kind with the matter of the planets.

In employing the example of the comets Kant would seem to be revealing his knowledge of actual scientific practice; for when Newton considers a number of hypotheses concerning planetary paths in his *System of the World* each hypothesis involves assuming that the comets move in conic sections.[43] Kant, moreover, is clearly aware that Newton's inverse square law of gravitational attraction entails that the only physically possible orbits for the planets are conic sections (4: 321; compare 5: 363).

---

[43] Appearing as it did in 1728, this Latin work (*De Mundi Systemate*) was available to Kant. An English translation is available in volume 2 of Newton, *Principia* (see 614–15, for the relevant discussion). Kant's use of the example of the planetary paths to illustrate the idea of a series of successively corrected hypotheses is anticipated by Émilie du Châtelet in her *Foundations of Physics*. There, du Châtelet defends the use of hypotheses as guiding threads capable of leading us to 'the most sublime discoveries'. See *Foundations of Physics* (1st edition, 1740), chapter 4, §§57–8, in Émilie Du Châtelet, *Selected Philosophical and Scientific Writings*, trans. Isabelle Bour and Judith P. Zinsser (Chicago: University of Chicago Press, 2009) at 148–51.

The methodological principle Kant wishes to defend in the first *Critique* under the heading of 'the law of affinity' in fact incorporates a certain crucial indeterminacy. It does not, he says,

> indicate the least mark of the affinity according to which—nor how far—we are to seek the sequence of degrees of difference, but contains nothing further than a general indication that we are to seek this sequence. (A 661/B 689)

This suggests that we should not regard the logical law of affinity as entailing the following claim: 'For any two sub-species, we should seek a third intermediate between them', for such an injunction contains a perfectly precise indication of how far we are to seek, namely: without end. But how, then, should we build the envisaged indeterminacy into a statement of the injunction? If we opt for vagueness and read the injunction as saying that the search is to be carried 'sufficiently far', the principle will afford us next to no guidance. It will certainly rule out complete incuriousness about whether there may be individuals intermediate between those belonging to species recognized as closely similar, along with complete incuriousness about whether a range of phenomena are of a unitary kind. But guidance this weak is of little value. And yet the point that the principle ought to contain nothing more than a general indication that we are to seek affinity is one on which Kant clearly places considerable weight. He adopts this position because he takes each methodological principle to entail a corresponding transcendental principle and he supposes that the latter must be treated as indeterminate if we are to avoid dogmatism. This point is explored in the next section.

17.8 The transcendental principles

Kant maintains that each of the three logical principles that collectively unpack the logical principle of reason requires us to presuppose a corresponding 'transcendental' principle. 'It is impossible', he says,

> to see how there could be a **logical** principle of the rational unity of rules, if we did not presuppose a **transcendental** principle whereby such systematic unity, construed as attaching to the objects themselves, is assumed *a priori* as necessary. (A 650–1/B 678–9)

If we were not to assume a transcendental principle for each logical principle, Kant claims, reason would set itself a goal that 'would entirely contradict nature's arrangement' and so 'proceed in a manner contrary to its vocation' (A 651/B 679). On the face of it, this means that if reason bids us to proceed as if nature has a certain structure, then it must indeed have that structure. But if so, Kant would seem to have committed the very mistake he attributes to the Transcendental Realist when offering his diagnosis of dogmatic metaphysics in terms of a tendency to slide from a regulative to a constitutive principle. After all, since we *are* commanded by reason to proceed in our inquiries as if the soul has a single fundamental power, it follows that if this kind of link between logical and transcendental principles were to hold—and be known to hold—we would also know that the soul does indeed have a single fundamental power. But to make such a claim would, in Kant's view, be both dogmatic and—as we've already noted—actually false.[44] Again, if our being commanded to seek ever more richly detailed taxonomic trees did entail that nature itself contains for any two individuals belonging to apparently adjacent species a third belonging to an intermediate species, then we would be committed to the existence of infinitely many individuals of different species. Again, this would be both dogmatic and, since Kant denies the existence of actual infinities, by his lights, actually false.[45]

Kant chooses an unexpected way out of these difficulties. Instead of reminding us not to infer the constitutive principle from the regulative one, he insists that each regulative principle *does* presuppose a constitutive one, but he adds that the constitutive principle is not as determinate as one might have expected. The transcendental principles affirm the existence—in nature itself—of only some indeterminate degree of homogeneity, specificity, and affinity. Our knowledge of their truth, he wants to suggest, is in every case a priori knowledge, grounded in the ways previously recognized as legitimate in the first *Critique*. Presumably, by treating the transcendental principles as indeterminate Kant is attempting to make it more plausible that these claims can be shown to be knowable a priori. For, in the present context, a less determinate claim is also a weaker claim.

To illustrate this idea, consider the principle of homogeneity (genera). In this case, the a priori knowledge Kant takes us to possess is, he thinks, grounded in the fact that what is known is a condition of the possibility of experience. 'Homogeneity', he says,

> is necessarily presupposed in the manifold of a possible experience (although we cannot determine a priori the degree of this homogeneity); for without homogeneity no empirical concepts and hence no experience would be possible.
>
> (A 654/B 682)

---

[44] See A 94, 5: 177–8, and 8: 181.
[45] Kant says that 'the species in nature are actually [*wirklich*] separated and therefore in themselves [*an sich*] have to constitute a *quantum discretum*' (A 661/B 689). If, as seems likely, the species 'in themselves' are the *members* of the kinds, then Kant's view must be that the individuals in nature do not in fact sit in a dense linear ordering, for a *quantum discretum* is a finite plurality (A 527/B 555).

In the complete absence of homogeneity, Kant is saying, we would have no occasion to make comparisons, hence no opportunity to form or apply empirical concepts—something that is itself a necessary condition of experience. If we were to apply this idea to the case of the soul's powers, we would take the logical principle to presuppose only the weak conclusion that some of the soul's powers are sub-powers of others, not the strong conclusion that there is a single basic power from which all the others derive. And Kant seems to confirm this interpretation when he says that if the transcendental principle (of homogeneity) were to fail, reason would admit it as possible that '*all* powers are heterogeneous' (A 651/B 679, emphasis added).

Kant, then, does have a strategy for avoiding dogmatism. But a worry remains. If the inference from a prescriptive methodological principle to a descriptive one—one stating that what we are bidden to seek in fact exists—is not, as Kant insists, generally valid, then he owes us an explanation of why it should be valid in the particular case in which what is inferred is one of Kant's favoured weak transcendental principles. This is a story, however, that Kant simply fails to tell.

One last point worth registering about the transcendental principles is the importance Kant attaches to them. Indeed, his primary purpose in discussing the logical principles sometimes seems to be merely to emphasize that they can have force only if the corresponding transcendental principles are presupposed as 'objectively valid and necessary' (A 650-1/B 678-9). Kant's caring so much about the transcendental principles is in turn explained by their relevance to his work in the philosophy of physics. Kant indicates that the demand for some degree of unification of powers applies just as much to the powers of matter as to those of the mind (ibid.). In making this point he would seem to be alluding to his own view that we know a priori that *all* specific kinds of matter—including, for example, the kind of matter that generates a magnetic force (B 273)—are governed by the same two fundamental laws, laws which hold of 'matter in general' (ibid.). This example concerns our a priori knowledge of homogeneity or unity, but Kant is also committed to our having—perhaps tacit—a priori knowledge of the transcendental principle that underlies the logical principle of affinity. The latter principle, as we saw in the previous section, bids us, among other things, to seek planets with ever more eccentric paths. We are, for example, never to rest with the conclusion that Saturn's is the most eccentric path possible for a planet. This logical principle is backed by a transcendental one, for we know a priori from the geometry of conic sections the truth of the transcendental principle affirming that for any possible planetary path there exists another more eccentric.[46]

---

[46] It is a good, but difficult, question whether Kant would have seen the transcendental principles as part of the valuable residuum of speculative metaphysics. I am inclined to think that this is so, but that is only a hunch. I am grateful to Bennett McNulty for asking this question.

17.9 The co-applicability of the logical principles

As his example of the paths of the perisolar celestial bodies shows, Kant believes that his various 'logical' (that is, methodological) principles can be reconciled and applied simultaneously. And although, as we've seen, he sometimes suggests that reason possesses a variety of competing interests (A 666–7/B 694–5), his more considered view is that (theoretical) reason has, at root, only a single interest, namely: the attainment of an unfettered insight into nature (A 666/B 694). Accordingly, he supposes that his various methodological principles are merely so many different yet complementary means to the end of satisfying this single interest (ibid.). This fact, Kant thinks, is in itself unproblematic. But because investigators are prone to misconstrue these merely regulative principles as insight-affording constitutive principles, a perfectly normal, and in itself innocuous, variation in the tastes of investigators—a variation that leads each of them to emphasize certain methodological principles over others—will, Kant supposes, tend to spawn fruitless disputes that actually hinder our inquiries (A 667–8/B 695–6).

Kant illustrates this point by reference to the example of the nature–nurture controversy (A 666–7/B 694–5). Are the biological characteristics that—Kant supposes—sort the members of a single species into different sub-species inherited, or are they merely environmentally determined? In the first *Critique* he maintains that the science of his day is not up to the task of settling, or even meaningfully advancing, this quarrel. He therefore regards the very persistence of the dispute as calling for explanation. What are the disputants doing if not citing empirical evidence for their side of the dispute? His answer is that the opposed parties are, unwittingly, relying on methodological principles that, when interpreted as constitutive, become opposed. One party, feeling greater attachment to the principle of unity, regards nature as having made a single, unitary provision for all members of the species, and so regards the variation in question as wholly explained by environmental factors. The other, feeling greater attachment to the principle of manifoldness or (specification), sees the variation in question as wholly explained by the inheritance of distinct traits. Kant supposes that, because they misconstrue these methodological principles as constitutive principles, both parties labour under the illusion that they possess a kind of a priori insight into the matter in question—and the dispute, irresoluble given the state of eighteenth-century biology, drags on.

17.10 The *focus imaginarius*

Kant borrows a metaphor from optics to clarify the relationship between the transcendental Ideas and the regulative principles. The transcendental Ideas, he says, have an excellent and indispensably necessary regulative use, namely, that of directing the understanding to a certain goal upon which the lines of direction of all its rules converge in one point which, even though only an idea (*focus imaginarius*), that is, a point from which the concepts of the understanding do not actually proceed, because it lies entirely outside the boundaries of possible experience, nevertheless serves to provide for these concepts the greatest unity as well as the greatest extension. (A 644/B 672)

The metaphor relates to the diagram from Newton's *Opticks* shown in Figure 17.1.[47]

What particularly impresses Kant about the example of the mirror and the *focus imaginarius* is an idea expressed by Newton himself:

[The light rays incident on the spectator's eyes] make the same picture in the bottom of the eyes *as if* they had come from the object really placed at [the *focus imaginarius*]. (*Opticks*, book 1, part 1, axiom 8, emphasis added)[48]

The key phrase here, is 'as if'. Just as a spectator with properly functioning visual faculties will be affected when she looks at the mirror exactly *as if* the light rays had come from a point on its far side, so the methodologically correct inquirer will take herself to be affected exactly *as if* her experience had been caused by an object lying outside of experience. (For the reasons discussed earlier,

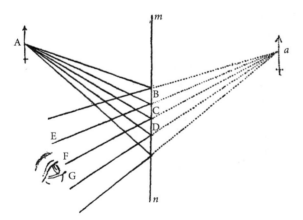

Figure 17.1 Diagram from Newton's *Opticks* (1704)

---

[47] Isaac Newton, *Opticks* (Great Minds; New York: Prometheus, 2003), Book 1, part 1 at 18.
[48] Ibid.

the image works better with the Ideas of the soul and of God than with the Idea of the world.)

Although vivid and illuminating, the analogy is imperfectly expressed.[49] It requires two emendations. First, the *focus imaginarius* should be compared not with the Idea itself but with what it purports to represent: its intentional—or as Kant says, 'imagined'—object.[50] Second, the rays of light should be compared not to rules or 'concepts of the understanding', but to 'the patterns of regularity, order, harmony, and [apparent] purpose we find in the world of experience'—patterns that run through experience and which seem to point back to a unitary cause outside of it (compare, A 623/B 651). These emendations are, I think, sufficiently minor to be considered clarifications and precisifications of Kant's position rather than revisions of it.

With the metaphorical comparison sharpened in these ways, Kant's point emerges as the following. The situation of the inquirer who allows herself to be guided by the transcendental Ideas—or at least by the Idea of God—is analogous to that of a spectator who sees an object viewed in a mirror as existing at a point behind the mirror's plane. Just as the perceiver's experience is exactly as if it had been caused by something located at the *focus imaginarius*, so the character of the inquirer's experience is exactly as if it had been produced by a certain entity located outside of the world of experience. However, just as there may, for all the spectator knows, be no object of the kind apparently perceived behind the mirror, so too, there may, so far as the inquirer's theoretically grounded knowledge goes, be no object outside of experience exemplifying the transcendental Idea of God. (A similar point can be made in connection with inner experience and the Idea of the soul.)

So far, so good. But Kant also has a subsidiary point to make. Developing the metaphor, he continues:

> Now of course from [the workings of this Idea] there arises the illusion [whereby it seems] as if these lines of direction emanated from an object lying outside the field of possible empirical cognition (just as objects are seen behind the mirror's plane); yet this illusion (which can be prevented from deceiving) is nevertheless indispensably necessary if besides the objects before our eyes we want to see those that lie far behind our back, i.e., when, in our case, the understanding wants to go beyond every given experience (beyond this part of the whole of possible experience), and hence wants to direct it to its greatest possible and utmost extension. (A 644–5/B 672–3)

---

[49] This analogy improves on another Kant sometimes uses, namely, that between seeking the unconditioned and seeking the square root of a negative integer (see, for example, his letter to J. S. Beck of 1791, 11: 290, note *). The latter analogy is less successful because it relies on a view of imaginary numbers as impossibilia (compare the letter to A. W. Rehberg of 1790, 11: 209 note *) rather than—as is proper—extensions of the number system.

[50] See A 670/B 698 for Kant's talk of an Idea's 'imagined object'.

In other words, just as the mirror enables the spectator to see objects that, although not falling within her visual field, nonetheless lie on her side of the mirror's plane (that is, behind her), so the kind of illusion that is bound up with the Ideas—transcendental illusion—enables the subject to cognize objects that, while not given in actual experience, nonetheless belong within the realm of possible experience.

Kant does not explain how transcendental illusion is supposed to play this role. Henry Allison suggests that he is thinking of empirical enumerative induction, which does indeed advance from actual observations to cognition of—or justified beliefs about—objects outside our current purview.[51] But the suggestion lacks plausibility. If Allison is right, Kant would be claiming that transcendental illusion is somehow operative in justifying induction. But first, it is wholly unclear how it could play such a role, and second, there are, to my knowledge, no texts in which such a suggestion is made. Nonetheless, Allison is surely on to something when he stresses that transcendental illusion is supposed to play some positive role in empirical inquiry. I would suggest that it plays such a role not because it makes induction possible but rather because—among other things—it, or the part of it connected with the Idea of God, creates the illusion that nature contains *end-directed* features.

In more detail, transcendental illusion disposes us to believe that there exists a wise and benevolent extra-mundane God who produces such natural features as are apparently directed toward the fulfilment of wise and benevolent ends. This in turn inclines us to believe that the world is shot through with purposes. Proceeding on this assumption, we develop a standing alertness or attentiveness to purpose-like natural features and laws, which enables us to notice natural phenomena we would otherwise have overlooked. The laws in question, as we saw in the previous chapter, include the laws of reflection and refraction. The features include: the earth's equatorial bulge, the honeycomb's feature of exemplifying a structure that enables it to maximize storage capacity for a given outlay of wax; the conventional gearing system's feature of manifesting a characteristic pattern of wear; and the silt-heavy river's feature of possessing in its lower reaches a riverbed higher than the surrounding land. In coming to observe these features we benefit from transcendental illusion, rather as the person looking into a mirror benefits from its characteristic illusion: in each case the observer is, or can be, made sensible of something hitherto unnoticed or unseen. This, I would suggest, is Kant's model for understanding how transcendental illusion enables the understanding to reach objects of possible experience that lie beyond every given experience.

It is time to take stock. We have seen that Kant's account of the regulative use of the Ideas is at its most successful in connection with the Ideas of God and of

---

[51] Allison, *Kant's Transcendental Idealism* at 426–7.

systematic unity. The regulative principles associated with the Idea of the soul seem either to be somewhat mysterious or to overlap with the principle of genera—the principle officially associated with the Idea of systematic unity. And the regulative principles associated with the Idea of the world seem to be both anomalous and somewhat arbitrary. Nonetheless, the regulative principles associated with the Ideas of God and of systematic unity do—at least some of them—yield concrete guidance for framing hypotheses and—in Kant's view at least—have facilitated actual discoveries in empirical science.

18
Closing Reflections

We have found that Kant regarded rational metaphysics as yielding two sorts of valuable residue when subjected to the fiery test of critique. The nugget of gold, which is contained within rational cosmology, is an indirect proof of Transcendental Idealism (A 506/B 534). The nuggets of silver include the arguments Kant endorses for the doctrinal beliefs in a god and an afterlife. These are non-a priori arguments that nonetheless belong (on Kant's conception of these disciplines) to rational theology and rational psychology respectively.

Kant sees the indirect proof of Transcendental Idealism as facilitating a philosophical discovery about the nature of the objects of sense. This discovery, he supposes, is illuminating in itself, but also of tremendous instrumental value insofar as it makes room for a practically grounded extension of our cognition beyond the limits of possible experience (B *xxi*). This room is made because the discovery shows that, for all we know on theoretical grounds, there might be genuinely spontaneous human actions—the timeless choices of an agent equipped with a faculty of intelligible causality. The room that speculative reason thus makes for an extension of our knowledge on practical grounds therefore turns out to be the realm of the noumenal. The extension is made when we argue that because we ought to have left some misdeed undone, we were capable of doing so, and therefore can rightly be held accountable for not leaving it undone (compare B *xxi*). Kant, of course, sees such an argument as viable only if Transcendental Idealism is true. For him, then, speculative reason, since it facilitates the discovery of Transcendental Idealism, is not illegitimate per se. Rather, it becomes illegitimate when it develops 'pretensions to transcendent insight' (compare B *xxxx*). Moreover, although it lies within the remit of speculative reason to make room for freedom—and hence also for morality—by resolving the third antinomy, this resolution does not by itself afford any insight into the supersensible. That insight *is* possible, but only through the morally grounded proof of the existence of transcendental freedom.

I have argued that each antinomy is intended to furnish an apagogic confirmatory argument for the Transcendental Idealism already contended for in the Transcendental Aesthetic. But I have not explained why Kant regards this confirmatory project as necessary. If the direct arguments in the Aesthetic for Transcendental Idealism are, as Kant supposes, cogent, why aren't these additional indirect proofs otiose? Kant answer is given in the 'Doctrine of Method'. 'Apagogic proofs', he tells us there, 'are superior to direct proofs in regard to evidence' (A 790/B 818). The advantage of a direct proofs, by contrast, is that they provide 'insight into the sources of [a] truth' (A 789/B 818). The two kinds of proof are thus complementary: whereas the direct proof yields greater insight into the sources of the truth of Transcendental Idealism (24: 234)—that is, greater 'comprehensibility' (A 789/B 817)—the indirect proofs severally produce an epistemic state whose certainty is equal in degree to, though different in kind from, the state that Kant calls 'evidence' or 'intuitive certainty'—a state attainable only by means of mathematical proofs (9: 70–1).[1] The indirect proofs have this status because Transcendental Realism entails contradictions, and, for Kant, reductions to contradictions always carry with them more 'clarity in the presentation' (A 790/B 818) than direct proofs. An indirect proof, therefore, more nearly approximates 'the intuitive character of a demonstration' (ibid.).[2] Accordingly, the direct proof is better for preaching to the choir, the indirect ones for making new converts.

So much, then, for the gold at the bottom of the crucible. What of the silver? I have argued that the silver consists, at minimum, of the arguments Kant endorses for the doctrinal beliefs in an Author of Nature and in an afterlife. Each of these firmly held beliefs is argued for on grounds that are in part empirical. The argument for an afterlife is overtly of the form of an argument by analogy and so—Kant would later come to suppose—involves an exercise not of reason but of the power of judgment (9: 132–3). Rather less obviously, the abductive argument for the existence of an Author of Nature from the order and unity of nature is also of this form; for Kant treats abductive reasoning as a species of argument by analogy (A 790/B 818).

18.1 Further conclusions

These conclusions about the valuable products of Kant's fiery test are far from exhausting the higher-level results of our investigation. A further significant conclusion is that Kant accords the antinomies a special place in the Dialectic:

---

[1] See A 734/B 762, R 5645 (18: 290–1), and 24: 234. In this last-cited passage, from the *Blomberg* logic lectures, Kant observes that one 'makes use of apagogic proof only *ad interim*', which presumably means 'until one can exhibit the grounds for the indirectly proven claim through a direct proof'. This suggests that in the first *Critique* the order of presentation of the direct and indirect proofs of Transcendental Idealism is in fact the reverse of their order in the construction of knowledge. The remark from reflection R 5645 shows that Kant sometimes uses the word 'evidence' [*evidentia*] for his technical notion of 'intuitive certainty'—the kind of certainty produced by demonstrations, which are found exclusively within mathematics, as opposed to acroamatic or discursive proofs, which are found in philosophy (compare 9: 71 and 24: 892). In the *Blomberg Logic*, he indicates that apagogic proof produces an epistemic state that is, in his view, the closest approximation to 'evidence [*Evidenz*]' in this technical sense (24: 233).

[2] Kant holds that only mathematics contains demonstrations proper, because in mathematics intuition guides the proof at every step (A 734/B 762).

they are the smelling salts that serve to rouse human reason from its dogmatic slumber and to prod it towards its long-overdue critical self-examination. Kant thinks of the antinomies—and of the sceptical procedure with which they are connected—as playing a 'preparative' role in arousing reason's 'cautiousness' and setting it on the path of genuine knowledge (A 769/B 797). Were we to experience only the 'one-sided' illusion involved in the Paralogisms and the Ideal, we would not, Kant thinks, be faced with the intellectual crises that prompt us to ferret out the sources of dogmatic metaphysics (B 434). As an agent of critical awakening, then, the phenomenon of antinomy is distinguished by its potency, but no less importantly it is also distinguished by its universal availability: it is an inner dialectic that lies within *every* human breast. It thus affords precisely the kind of equalizing, 'think-for-yourself' critical technique that we might expect to appeal to Kant's enlightened, anti-elitist sensibilities.

Another main conclusion is that Kant's critical philosophy takes a stand against an extraordinarily broad range of figures and approaches. He numbers among his opponents not only the dogmatists, but also the 'dogmatic sceptics'—including the Academic sceptics, on the one hand, and (what Kant considers to be) the inauthentic Pyrrhonians, on the other. A third group of opponents are the indifferentists, who present an obstacle to critique insofar as they affect not to take metaphysical questions seriously. The threat from this quarter is not a body of doctrine so much as a certain *attitude*, namely, that of glib (and ignorant) dismissiveness. Kant finds this attitude not only unhelpful but also disingenuous. The indifferentists, he supposes, having flippantly evaded serious philosophical engagement too often proceed to quietly take a stand on the very issues they purport to disdain. For Kant, this attitude isn't merely annoying: it is also ruinous to philosophy because it precludes our taking the first step towards critical enlightenment, namely, the recognition that the problems in question deserve to be taken seriously. Yet a fourth group of opponents, we have learned, comprises an assortment of lesser-known British moralists, natural theologians, and 'parson naturalists', including, Ray, Derham, and, most notably, Fordyce, whose argument for the immortality of the soul Kant modifies for his own purposes.

More broadly still, we have arrived at a deeper understanding of Kant's relation to the Western philosophical tradition. We have seen that whereas in the case of rational *theology* his targets are for the most part identifiable historical figures, including Descartes, Leibniz, and Wolff, in the case of rational psychology, he engages for the most part with a charitably purified and somewhat abstracted version of this purported science—though he does also engage specifically with Descartes, Mendelssohn, and Fordyce. We have seen that the abstracted pure rational psychology Kant takes as his main target in the Paralogisms chapter seems to be a view distilled from elements of Baumgarten's rational psychology, on the one hand, and Kant's own immediately pre-critical rational psychology in the *Metaphysics L1*, on the other.

As for rational cosmology, we have seen that Kant does not engage explicitly with any of his immediate predecessors, but rather constructs antinomies from arguments largely of his own devising, arguments that he associates, loosely at least, with certain broad tendencies of mind that he claims to find in Plato and Epicurus. From Kant's point of view, this somewhat lofty level of abstraction is entirely fitting; for he regards it as both permissible and salutary for each of us to autonomously develop the 'dialectic' that lies in our own faculty of reason, and which, he thinks, is apt to lead us into genuine contradictions so long as we adhere to the viewpoint of Transcendental Realism. In keeping with this last idea, some of the lines of thought that Kant exploits in constructing the antinomies bear the traces of his own pre-critical ruminations.

At a higher level of abstraction yet, we have learned something about Kant's conception of the best philosophical method. It is the method of developing the inner dialectic that lies within the human breast. Kant's properly rational inquirer, having constructed an antinomy, continues to inquire—both by checking the proofs already constructed and by searching for an illusion underlying the apparent contradiction. Since Kant sees the construction of antinomies as a critical method superior to the mere detection of fallacies, the former might be considered the principal method of philosophy in the Dialectic, whereas the construction of transcendental arguments arguably has a claim to be the principal method of philosophy in the Analytic of Principles.[3]

We have also seen that Kant's procedure in the Antinomies enacts the Kant-approved 'sceptical method' (A 507/B 535). The Antinomies and their resolution thus exhibit Kant himself as belonging to the class of philosophers whom he views as *authentic* followers of Pyrrho. These 'critical sceptics' adhere not to the aporetic, tranquillity-inducing scepticism usually associated with Pyrrho, but rather to a method of unhurried, lengthened, painstaking investigation aimed, ultimately, at knowing some things with apodictic *certainty*—in Kant's case, the truth of Transcendental Idealism.

'Where reason would conduct its business through mere concepts', Kant tells us, 'only a single proof is possible if any proof is possible at all' (A 789/B 817). We have seen that in connection with dogmatic rational theology this claim is best construed as a *counterpossible*. It means: 'If, *per impossibile*, there were to exist a dogmatic speculative demonstration of the existence of God, then there could be only one.' Kant thinks that the single proof in question would be the ontological argument.[4] He takes this view because the other putative theistic proofs are, for

---

[3] Adrian Moore has claimed that in the first *Critique* Kant sees transcendental arguments as constituting philosophy's 'most characteristic methodological tool' (Adrian Moore, 'The Transcendental Doctrine of Method', in Paul Guyer (ed.), *The Cambridge Companion to Kant's Critique of Pure Reason*, 310–26 at 314 and 316). I'm inclined to disagree simply because, as we have seen, the method of constructing antinomies is at least as centrally philosophical for Kant.

[4] A 630/B 658, A 788/B 816.

him, merely disguised versions of the ontological argument since they all rest essentially on that argument. This point bears a special importance for Kant because he is keen to debunk the implicit claim of physico-theology to be the counterpart within rational theology of a modern, and empirically minded, scientific theory.

18.2 Denying knowledge (again)

In the introduction I offered some preliminary explanations of why Kant should have found it necessary to deny knowledge in order to make room for faith. One idea was that, in Kant's view, speculative dogmatic metaphysics leads to Spinozism, which he equates not with faith but with a kind of dogmatic fanaticism. Another was that by aiming at knowledge we land ourselves in antinomies and so end up either seeing reason as entailing absolutely *anything* (because self-contradictory) or with a principled permanent suspension of belief. Either way, faith becomes impossible. A third idea was that the speculative scholastic proofs, on account of their very subtlety, tend to arouse suspicion, with the consequence that in relying on them we do damage to faith. It therefore behoves us to abandon those proofs in favour of the more digestible moral proofs, which possess a kind of robustness and stout-yeoman persuasiveness that suits them for the promotion of faith (compare 28: 1246-7).[5] Our discussions of the third antinomy and of the fourth paralogism suggest yet a fourth explanation of Kant's famous remark: one that perhaps comes closest to the letter of B *xxx*. Let me explain.

In Chapter 12 we saw that Kant takes the resolution of the third antinomy to require the rejection of Transcendental Realism. The argument ran that if Transcendental Realism were true, human freedom would have to be an ability whose exercise required one or more events to lack an event-cause—a kind of freedom, therefore, ruled out by the causal principle. Since Kant himself embraces the causal principle he accordingly supposes that Transcendental Realism entails the non-existence of human freedom. And since he supposes that 'ought' implies 'can'—the kind of 'can' that itself requires human freedom—he takes Transcendental Realism to further imply that there can be no moral requirements on human beings. It follows that by denying Transcendental Realism, which for

---

[5] Like the moral proofs, the arguments supporting the doctrinal beliefs lack the hair-splitting quality of the dogmatic proofs, and so the current point applies equally to them. In his famous remark about denying knowledge in order to make room for faith at B *xxx*, however, Kant is explicit that he is speaking of what we must assume for the sake of 'the *necessary* practical use of reason' (emphasis added). This strongly suggests that the assumptions in question are so many means to a *necessary* practical end. But if that's right, it must be the moral, not doctrinal, beliefs that Kant is thinking of here, for the latter serve only as so many means to contingent, non-moral ends. On this point I depart from Chignell ('Belief in Kant' at 335), who suggests that, on the contrary, both kinds of belief may well be in question at this point.

Kant is equivalent to denying that we have, or could have, knowledge *of things as they are in themselves*, one makes room for morality—and so also for a set of arguments that seek to establish the beliefs in God, freedom, and immortality (or at least an afterlife) as assumptions that we must make in order to be motivated by the moral law (B *xxix–xxx*). We thereby make room for an argument for the (conditional) necessity of faith (understood as specifically *moral* belief). We also make room for faith itself; for if God exists, then His commands, or such of them as are directed at human beings, though not for Kant the *source* of morality, will have the same content as a specification of our duties. Accordingly, if Transcendental Realism is true, so that neither human freedom nor freely chosen moral behaviour are saved, we will be incapable of *obeying* God's commands (as opposed to acting in accordance with them), and consequently those commands, being thus vain and bootless, will seem unworthy of a supremely authoritative being. The upshot is that the belief in Transcendental Realism, since it leads—in Kant's view—to the belief that we lack freedom, will generate doubt about God's existence (or, at least, it will do so in anyone who believes that God is, by His nature, a legislator, and that His commands are co-extensive with the demands of morality). We thus have a plausible line of argument supporting Kant's claim that by denying knowledge (of things in themselves)—which denial I am supposing equivalent to endorsing Transcendental Idealism—we make room for faith.[6]

How well does this reconstruction cohere with Kant's stated rationale for his famous claim about the need to deny (or annul) knowledge? The answer, I think, is: tolerably well. He says:

> I cannot even **assume God, freedom, and immortality** for the sake of the necessary practical use of my reason, if I do not at the same time **deprive** speculative reason of its pretensions to transcendent insight.   (B *xxix–xxx*)

His rationale for this claim runs as follows:

> In order to [try to] reach God, freedom, and immortality, speculative reason must use principles that in fact extend only as far as objects of possible experience; and when these principles are [in spite of this limitation] nonetheless applied to something that cannot be an object of experience, they actually do always transform it into appearance, and thus they declare all **practical expansion** of reason to be impossible. I therefore had to annul [*aufheben*] knowledge in order to make room for faith.   (B *xxx*)

---

[6] To be clear, I am supposing that Transcendental Realism and the possibility of knowledge of things in themselves are mutually entailing. I have not argued for this view on textual grounds, but if it is accepted, the present reading would, I'd contend, be viable.

In this cryptic passage Kant is claiming that the error of enlisting principles that in fact hold only within possible experience in the vain hope of acquiring theoretical knowledge of matters lying beyond experience, and in particular, theoretical knowledge of the existence of God, freedom, and immortality, causes us to transform these supersensible objects into appearances. He further claims that this transformation in turn stymies the practical expansion of reason—understood, it would seem, as the acquisition of specifically *morally* grounded beliefs about the supersensible.[7] In what sense is the supersensible object 'transformed into appearance'? This is far from clear, but we can gain a foothold on the problem by observing that in Kant's day the term '*Erscheinung*' had a range of meanings including: 'appearance', 'apparition', and 'manifestation' (in the sense of 'epiphany').[8] Since that is so, it's possible that when he says 'they actually do always transform it into an appearance' Kant is playing on the multiple meanings of '*Erscheinung*'. It is possible, in particular, that he is claiming that the dogmatic metaphysicians do indeed succeed in their ambition of turning God, human freedom, and immortality into so many '*Erscheinungen*', *but not in the sense they had intended*. While the dogmatists had hoped to render these things *manifestly* existent—that is, *shown* to exist by the light of reason (intellectually manifest), in practice they turn them into '*Erscheinungen*' in the sense of *apparitions* (non-existent entities that merely seem to exist)—or rather this is the conclusion that we must reach if we follow their principles.

18.3 Transcendental Realism as a logical impossibility

In the course of resolving the mathematical antinomies Kant makes clear that he sees Transcendental Realism as entailing a logical contradiction. This presents a deep, if seldom noted, difficulty. Kant holds that to say that something is thinkable is to say that its representation is non-contradictory (compare B *xxviii*).[9] It follows that if something's representation is contradictory, it is, in some sense, unthinkable (compare 8: 195). The antinomies would therefore seem—from Kant's point of view at least—to show that we cannot so much as *think* of the world as a totality of things existing in themselves; for he maintains that they show that the effort to represent the world in this way is the effort to represent something whose concept is in fact contradictory. This point raises two urgent problems. First, recall that

---

[7] The parenthetical remark is needed because Kant uses 'practical' sometimes for prudential, sometimes for moral considerations (see A 824/B 852).

[8] The word has the second of these senses in, for example, the context '*eine Erscheinung haben*' (to imagine oneself to see an object that is in fact invisible). See the entry, '*Erscheinung*', in Adelung, *Grammatisch-kritisches Wörterbuch der hochdeutschen Mundart*, at 1933–4.

[9] Here he makes the point in connection with the concept of freedom, but he clearly takes it to generalize. Relatedly, he sometimes says that a contradictory concept is no concept at all (see, for example 28: 1016).

I have argued that Kant takes a component of transcendental illusion to be the illusion that Transcendental Realism is true.[10] This creates a difficulty: if Transcendental Realism forms part of the content of an illusion, it's hard to see how it could be unthinkable. Second, if there's nothing I think when I assert p, then there's no state of the world I rule out by asserting not-p and the statement 'not-p' thus has no truth-conditions. It would therefore appear that if Transcendental Realism is unthinkable, Transcendental Idealism must be too.

It seems that if his position is to be made consistent, Kant will need to soften his position on the unthinkability of contradictions. There are two reasons to suppose that, in any case, he *ought* to do so. First, his appeal to the '*non entis*' rule, discussed in Chapter 10, suggests that he is committed to holding that judgments with self-contradictory subject terms are truth-evaluable—a view it would be hard to square with their containing non-significant subject terms. Second, as we have seen, Kant accepts the general validity of *reductio* arguments in mathematics. But the *reductio* premises of these arguments would need to make sense if *specific* inferences are to be drawn from them. I conclude that in maintaining—or at least flirting with—the idea that contradictions are unthinkable Kant is, even by his own lights, making a mistake.

18.4 The loss of innocence

The difficulty discussed in the previous section is one that arises only if one accepts Kant's conclusion that Transcendental Realism entails a genuine contradiction. A second difficulty which similarly arises only for someone who has already entered some way into the critical system, relates to Kant's account of transcendental illusion. Suppose that reflection on the antinomies has led some reader to agree with Kant's contention that the attempt to locate an absolutely unconditioned condition within the world of sense must result in failure. What is that reader to make of the injunction—supposedly in itself anodyne—to *seek* the unconditioned within the world of sense? As we saw in Chapter 1, this injunction is a vital part of Kant's diagnosis of the workings of Transcendental Illusion (it corresponds to step [3] in our account—or does so if 'series' is understood to include the minimal, one-member series). Kant sees it as giving expression to a perfectly genuine demand of reason. But with the reader's loss of innocence or naïvety—that is to say, with their newfound insight into the nature of the world of sense—they must recognize this injunction as bidding them (and the rest of us) to seek something that in fact does not, and cannot, exist. The problem is sharp because it is very plausible that one cannot try to do what one believes to be

---

[10] Indeed, we have seen that he sometimes even equates the two (see A 504–5/B 532–3).

impossible. Since for Kant *ought* implies *can*, this would seem to entail that one cannot be obligated to try to find what one knows we cannot find. But since to try to find something is to seek it, it seems that none of the initiated can stand under an imperative of inquiry to seek the unconditioned. If this is right, then once we have bought into the critical system, we can no longer accept Kant's claim that we stand under such an imperative. And, in consequence, we can no longer accept a central component of his diagnosis of metaphysical error, namely, his story about transcendental illusion's giving rise to metaphysical error through its power to prompt a misinterpretation of such an injunction. Sadly, this difficult seems insuperable.

18.5 Exhaustiveness

Kant takes it to be the philosopher's duty to carry out 'an exhaustive examination of the vain elaborations of speculative reason' (A 703/B 731).[11] Does Kant discharge this duty in the first *Critique*? We might reasonably have doubts on this score; for we might wonder: How can the Kant of the first *Critique* be taken to have examined—let alone diagnosed—Spinoza's doctrine that the finite mind, far from being a substance$_1$, is merely a mode of the divine intellect? Wasn't Spinoza led by purely rational considerations to this—by Kant's lights dogmatic— doctrine?[12] Or, again: How can Kant be taken to have subjected to critic-diagnostic scrutiny the materialism of Thomas Hobbes or of Julien Offray de La Mettrie? Doesn't materialism about the mind have just as much right to be regarded as belonging to dogmatic speculative metaphysics as the pneumatism Kant does scrutinize?

Turning to rational theology, we must ask: Where does Kant offer a critique of Descartes's third-Meditation argument for the existence of God? He boldly claims that experience 'never offers us the greatest of all possible effects (such as would bear witness to [the supreme being] as its cause)' (A 637/B 665). But he does not consider Descartes's subtle claim that the presence in our minds of the idea of God

---

[11] Kant clearly places great weight on exhaustiveness: 'In this inquiry', he says, 'I have made completeness my chief aim' (A *xiii*).

[12] In Kant's defence we might observe that he did *eventually* get around to diagnosing this view. For in his religion lectures of 1783–4 (or later) he argues that it has its source in Spinoza's faulty conception of substance (as something whose existence depends on the existence of nothing else). This flawed conception, Kant thinks, led Spinoza to treat the world itself as the only substance and to identify it with God. And this, in turn, had the consequence that human souls can only be dependent entities and so must be treated as accidents (see 28: 1041). Kant diagnoses Spinoza's faulty conception of substance as itself arising from his use of arbitrary definitions in philosophy rather than in mathematics where the requisite safeguards are present (ibid.). The deepest analysis of Spinoza's mistake, therefore, is that he was applying mathematical *method* outside of its legitimate domain. This story did not make it into the B edition. Moreover, it plainly fails to conform to the pattern of Kant's diagnosis of dogmatic metaphysics in terms of the workings of transcendental illusion.

is precisely such an effect—a claim that relies crucially on Descartes's distinction between objective and formal reality. Or again, we may ask: How can Kant be supposed to have diagnosed the impulse behind what he takes to be the Stoic's belief that God is the soul of the world (28: 1042–3)?

Kant's claims for the exhaustiveness of his critique seem to be on shaky ground. Owing, perhaps, to the constraints of his architectonic, he lacks the flexibility to offer diagnoses of the full range of doctrines belonging to dogmatic speculative metaphysics. But another part of the story, surely, is that in practice the target of (the negative part of) Kant's critique is, for the most part, the body of doctrine belonging to the three disciplines that grow out of Wolffian special metaphysics. Since a sizeable chunk of the Wolffian project is devoted to establishing that the soul satisfies the Wolffian requisites on immortality, the topics discussed in the Paralogisms are skewed towards a critique of pneumatism rather than of materialism. Kant knows that he needs to say *something* about materialism; but while one might have expected him to treat this position as antinomially opposed to pneumatism, in practice he merely argues that, for all we know, materialism might be true because (and in the sense that) the soul (as an object of inner sense) might have a noumenal basis of the same kind as the noumenal basis of the objects of outer sense. To assign materialism about the soul or mind to the realm of the unknown, however, is not to offer an account of how transcendental illusion has predisposed us—or some of us—to find this dogma attractive. It is rather merely—from Kant's point of view—to draw attention to a hypothesis that the pneumatist must exclude, while also observing that they have in fact failed to exclude it. Nor can one plead that Kant's duty is merely to critically diagnose such dogmas as have their source in transcendental illusion—adding that these other dogmas do not have such a source. For such a plea would undermine Kant's claim that transcendental illusion is the fundamental cause of our impulse towards dogmatic speculative theorizing. I conclude, with some regret, that Kant fails to substantiate his claim to have engaged in an exhaustive critique of pure reason in the first *Critique*. What he has done is to offer a broad, yet incomplete, critique of the efforts of pure speculative reason to accomplish the 'two great goals' of dogmatic metaphysics, namely, the construction of demonstrative proofs of God's existence, on the one hand, and of human immortality, on the other (A 805/B 833). Beyond this, in recommending Transcendental Idealism as the uniquely correct way of resolving the antinomies, he has—or so he believes—provided the surest possible validation of his own Copernican revolution.

APPENDIX

Abbreviations

A substance$_0$	A thing whose representation cannot be the predicate of a judgment.
A substance$_1$	A necessarily non-inhering subject of inherence. (The unschematized concept of substance).
Substance$_2$	Some stuff that exists at every moment. (The schematized concept of substance).
A simple$_0$	A thing whose representation is (a) singular and (b) contains nothing manifold.
A person$_0$	A thing that has the property of being such that all the experiences or thoughts it has had (or will have had) have been had (or will have been had) by that thing.
A person$_1$	A thing that has the ability to be aware of which substance$_1$ it was identical with at (sufficiently many) earlier times.
A paralogism$_v$	A (rectified) paralogism in which the middle term of a paralogism is so construed that (a) the argument is valid and (b) the minor premise is not known to be true.
A paralogism$_k$	A paralogism in which the middle term is so construed that (a) the minor premise is known to be true but (b) the argument is invalid.
The minor premise$_v$ (or the minor$_v$)	The minor premise of a paralogism$_v$.
The minor premise$_k$ (or the minor$_k$)	The minor premise of a paralogism$_k$.
The world$_{TR}$	the sensible world as it is conceived of by the Transcendental Realist.
The world$_{TI}$	the sensible world as it is conceived of by the Transcendental Idealist.
The world$_N$	the sensible world conceived neutrally as the world we experience.

Abbreviations of Works

AG	Ariew R., and Garber D. (eds), 1989. *G. W. Leibniz: Philosophical Essays*, Indianapolis: Hackett.
AT	*Oeuvres de Descartes*. Edited by Charles Adam and Paul Tannery. 11 vols. Paris: Libraire Philosophique. J. Vrin, 1973-82.
CSM	*The Philosophical Writings of Descartes*. Edited and translated by John Cottingham, Robert Soothoff, Dugald Murdoch, and (vol. 3 only) Anthony Kenny. 3 vols. Cambridge: Cambridge University Press, 1984-91.
G	Leibniz, Gottfried Wilhelm. *Die philosophischen Schriften*. Edited by C. I. Gerhardt. 7 vols. Berlin 1857-90. Reprinted Hildesheim 1965.
GM	Christian Wolff (1751), *Vernünfftige Gedancken von Gott, der Welt und der Seele des Menschen, auch allen Dingen überhaupt, den Leibhabern der Wahrheit mitgetheilet*, in Christian Wolff *Gesammelte Werke* (Hildesheim: Olms, 1983).
L	Leibniz, Gottfried Wilhelm. *Philosophical Papers and Letters*. Translated by L. Loemker, 2nd edn. Dordrecht, 1969.
Latin Logic	Christian Wolff (1740c), *Philosophia rationalis, sive Logica*, 3rd edn. 3 vols. in Christian Wolff (part 1 of this work is known as 'Preliminary Discourse on Philosophy in General' ('*PD*' in our abbreviations)), *Gesammelte Werke*, Pt. 2. Lateinische Schriften, vols. 1.1-1.3 (Hildesheim: Olms, 1983).
MFNS	*The Metaphysical Foundations of Natural Science. Metaphysiche Anfangsgründe der Naturwissenschaft*, in Kant 1900, vol. Academy edition: 4: 467-565.
New Elucidation	*Principiorum primorum cognitionis metaphysicae nova dilucidatio*, in Kant 1900, 1: 385-416. English translation in Walford 1992, 1-45.
On a Discovery	*Über ein Entdeckung nach der alle neue Kritik der reinen Vernunft durch eine ältere entbehrlich gemacht werden soll*, in Kant 1900, 8: 185-251. English translation in Henry Allison et al., *The Cambridge Edition of the Works of Immanuel Kant: Theoretical Philosophy after 1781*, Cambridge: Cambridge University Press, 2002, 271-336.
Ontologia	Christian Wolff (1736), *Philosophia prima seu Ontologia methodo scientifica pertractata, qua omnis cognitionis humanae principia continentur*, in Christian Wolff, *Gesammelte Werke*, Part 2, Lateinische Schriften, vol. 3 (Hildesheim: Georg Olms, 1962).
OPB	*Der einzig mögliche Beweisgrund zu einer Demonstration des Daseins Gottes*, in Kant 1900, 2: 63-163.
PD	*Latin Logic*. Part 1.
PE	Wolff, Christian (1738), *Psychologia empirica* (2nd edn) (first published 1732), in Christian Wolff, *Gesammelte Werke*, Part 2. Lateinische Schriften, vol. 5. (Hildesheim: Olms, 1968).

Rational Psychology	Christian Wolff (1740a), *Psychologia rationalis*, 2nd edn, Christian Wolff, *Gesammelte Werke*, Part 2. Lateinische Schriften, vol. 6 (Hildesheim: Olms 1972).
Theodicy	G. W. Leibniz, *Theodicy*, trans. E. M. Huggard (La Salle, IL: Open Court).

Bibliography

Adelung, J. C. (1811), *Grammatisch-kritisches Wörterbuch der hochdeutschen Mundart* [online text], http://lexika.digitale-sammlungen.de/adelung/online/angebot.

Adickes, Erich (1889), *Immanuel Kants Kritik der reinen Vernunft* (Berlin: Meyer & Müller).

Agricola, Georgius (1556), *De re metallica* (Basel: Froben).

Ahluwalia, A. (1978), 'An Intra-Cultural Investigation of Susceptibility to "Perspective" and "Non-Perspective" Spatial Illusions', *British Journal of Psychology*, 69 (2), 233–41.

Al-Azm, Sadik (1972), *The Origins of Kant's Arguments in the Antinomies* (Oxford: Clarendon Press).

Alexander, H. G. (ed.) (1956), *The Leibniz-Clarke Correspondence* (Manchester: Manchester University Press).

Allais, Lucy (2015), *Manifest Reality: Kant's Idealism and his Realism* (Oxford: Oxford University Press).

Allison, Henry (1990), *Kant's Theory of Freedom* (Cambridge: Cambridge University Press).

Allison, Henry (1996), *Idealism and Freedom: Essays on Kant's Theoretical and Practical Philosophy* (Cambridge: Cambridge University Press).

Allison, Henry (2004), *Kant's Transcendental Idealism: An Interpretation and Defense* (New Haven: Yale University Press).

Ameriks, Karl (1982), *Kant's Theory of Mind: An Analysis of the Paralogisms of Pure Reason* (Oxford: Clarendon Press).

Ameriks, Karl (2000), *Kant's Theory of Mind: An Analysis of the Paralogisms of Pure Reason* (New Edition; Oxford: Clarendon Press).

Ameriks, Karl (2003), *Interpreting Kant's Critiques* (Oxford: Oxford University Press).

Angelelli, Ignacio (1970), 'The Techniques of Disputation in the History of Logic', *Journal of Philosophy*, 67, issue 20 (3), 800–15.

Aquinas, Thomas (1999), *Commentary on Aristotle's Physics*, trans. R. J. Spath, R. J. Blackwell, and W. Edmund Thirkel. Rev. (South Bend, IN: Dumb Ox Books).

Ariew Roger and Garber, Daniel (1989), *G.W. Leibniz, Philosophical Essays*, trans. Robert Ariew and Daniel Garber (Indianapolis and Cambridge: Hackett).

Aristotle (1984), *The Complete Works of Aristotle*, ed. Jonathan Barnes, 2 vols (Princeton, NJ: Princeton University Press).

Arthur, Richard T. W. (2014), *Leibniz* (Classic Thinkers; Cambridge: Polity).

Bader, Ralf (2017), 'The Refutation of Idealism', in James O'Shea (ed.), *Kant's Critique of Pure Reason: A Critical Guide* (Cambridge: Cambridge University Press), 205–22.

Bader, Ralf (2018), 'Real Predicates and Existential Judgments', *European Journal of Philosophy*, 26 (3), 1153–58.

Baumeister, Friedrich Christian (1738), *Philosophia recens controversa complexa definitiones theoremata et quaestiones nostra aetate in controversiam vocatas* (Leipzig and Görlitz: Marcheana).

Baumeister, Friedrich Christian (1767), *Philosophia Definitiva* (Wittenberg) (orig. pub. 1735).

Baumeister, Friedrich Christian (1774), *Institutiones Metaphysicae Ontologiam, Cosmologiam, Psychologiam, Theologiam denique Naturalem Complexae Methodo Wolffii Adornate* (Wittenberg: S. G. Zimmerman).
Baumgarten, Alexander (1773), *Acroasis Logica* (2nd edn; Halle and Magdeburg).
Baumgarten, Alexander (2013), *Metaphysics: A Critical Translation with Kant's Elucidations, Selected Notes, and Related Materials*, trans. Courtney D. Fugate and John Hymers (London: Bloomsbury).
Beck, Lewis White (1960), *A Commentary on Kant's Critique of Practical Reason* (Chicago: University of Chicago Press).
Beck, Lewis White (1969), *Early German Philosophy: Kant and His Predecessors* (Cambridge, MA: Belknap).
Beiser, Frederick C. (2006), 'Moral Faith and the Highest Good', in Paul Guyer (ed.), *The Cambridge Companion to Kant and Modern Philosophy* (Cambridge: Cambridge University Press), 588–629.
Benacerraf, Paul (1962), 'Tasks, Super-Tasks, and Modern Eleatics', *Journal of Philosophy*, 59 (24), 765–84.
Bennett, Jonathan (1966), *Kant's Analytic* (Cambridge: Cambridge University Press).
Bennett, Jonathan (1974), *Kant's Dialectic* (Cambridge: Cambridge University Press).
Berkeley, George (1979), *Three Dialogues between Hylas and Philonous* (Indianapolis: Hackett).
Birken-Bertsch, Hanno (2006), *Subreption und Dialektik bei Kant: Der Begriff des Fehlers der Erschleichung in der Philosophie des 18. Jahrhunderts* (Stuttgart: Frommann-Holzboog).
Black, Joseph (1893), *Experiments upon magnesia alba, quick-lime and other alcaline substances*, orig. pub. 1756, Alembic Club Reprints (Edinburgh: Clay).
Boehm, Omri (2014), *Kant's Critique of Spinoza* (Oxford: Oxford University Press).
Broad, C. D. (1978), *Kant: An Introduction* (Cambridge: Cambridge University Press).
Carroll, Lewis (1895), 'What the Tortoise Said to Achilles', *Mind*, 104 (416), 691–3.
Chignell, Andrew (2007), 'Belief in Kant', *Philosophical Review*, 116 (3), 323–60.
Chignell, Andrew (2013), 'Rational Hope, Moral Order, and the Revolution of the Will', in Eric Watkins (ed.), *Divine Order, Human Order, and the Order of Nature* (Oxford: Oxford University Press), 197–218.
Chignell, Andrew and McLear, Colin (2010), 'Three Skeptics and the *Critique*: Critical Notice of Michael Forster's *Kant and Skepticism*', *Philosophical Books*, 51 (4), 228–44.
Chignell, Andrew and Pereboom, Derk (2010), 'Kant's Theory of Causation and its Eighteenth-Century German Background: Eric Watkins (ed. and trans.), *Kant's "Critique of Pure Reason": Background Source Materials* and Eric Watkins, *Kant and the Metaphysics of Causality*', *Philosophical Review*, 119 (4), 565–91.
Cicovacki, Predrag (2006), 'Kant's Debt to Leibniz', in Bird Graham (ed.), *A Companion to Kant* (Oxford: Blackwell), 79–92.
Clarke, Randolph (1993), 'Toward a Credible Agent-Causal Account of Free Will', *Noûs*, 27 (2), 191–203.
Crusius, Christian August (1745), *Entwurf der Nothwendigen Vernunft-Wahrheiten, wiefern sie den zufälligen entgegengesetzt werden*, ed. Giorgio Tonelli, 4 vols (*Die Philosophischen Hauptwerke*, 2; Hildesheim: Georg Olms 1964).
Cudworth, Ralph (1845), *The True Intellectual System of the Universe*, 3 vols (London).
Davis, A. E. L. (1998), 'Kepler's Unintentional Ellipse: A Celestial Detective Story', *The Mathematical Gazette*, 82 (493), 37–43.
De Mairan, Jean-Jacques d'Ortous (1731), *Traité physique et historique de L'aurore boréale (Physical and historical treatise on the Aurora Borealis)* (Paris: The Royal Press).

Derham, William (1723), *Physico-Theology, or a Demonstration of the Being and Attributes of God from His Works of Creation* (6th edn; London).
Descartes, René (1973–82), *Oeuvres de Descartes*, ed. Charles Adam and Paul Tannery, 11 vols (Paris: Libraire Philosophique, J. Vrin).
Descartes, René (1984–91), *The Philosophical Writings of Descartes*, ed. and trans. John Cottingham, Robert Soothoff, Dugald Murdoch, and (vol. 3 only) Anthony Kenny, 3 vols (Cambridge: Cambridge University Press).
Descartes, René (1990), *Meditations on First Philosophy: Meditationes de prima philosophia: A bilingual edition*, trans. George Hefferman (Notre Dame, IN: University of Notre Dame Press).
Diogenes, L. (1925), *Lives of Eminent Philosophers* (Loeb Classical Library; Cambridge, MA: Harvard University Press).
Du Châtelet, Émilie (2009), *Selected Philosophical and Scientific Writings*, trans. Isabelle Bour and Judith P. Zinsser (Chicago: University of Chicago Press).
Dummett, Michael (1978), *Truth and Other Enigmas* (Cambridge, MA: Harvard University Press).
Dyck, Corey (2009), 'The Divorce of Reason and Experience: Kant's Paralogisms of Pure Reason in Context', *Journal of the History of Philosophy*, 47 (2), 249–75.
Dyck, Corey (2010), 'The Aeneas Argument: Personality and Immortality in Kant's Third Paralogism', *Kant Yearbook*, 2 (1), 95–122.
Dyck, Corey (2014), *Kant and Rational Psychology* (Oxford: Oxford University Press).
Feder, Johann Georg Heinrich (1778), *Logik und Metaphysik* (5th edn; Göttingen: J. C. Dieterich).
Finocchiaro, Maurice A. (1974), 'The Concept of *Ad Hominem* Argument in Galileo and Locke', *The Philosophical Forum*, 5, 394–404.
Fischer, John Martin, Kane, Robert, Pereboom, Derk, and Vargas, Manuel (2007), *Four Views on Free Will* (Oxford: Blackwell).
Fordyce, David (2003), *The Elements of Moral Philosophy* (Indianapolis: Liberty Fund).
Forster, Michael N. (2008), *Kant and Skepticism* (Princeton, NJ: Princeton University Press).
Fourcroy, Antoine-François de (1790), *Comparative view of ancient and modern names of chemical substances*, appendix to *Elements of Natural History and Chemistry*, volume 3 (London, translated from the French (Paris) edition of 1789 (3 vols)).
Friedman, Michael (1992), *Kant and the Exact Sciences* (Cambridge, MA: Harvard University Press).
Friedman, Michael (2013), *Kant's Construction of Nature: A Reading of the Metaphysical Foundations of Natural Science* (Oxford: Oxford University Press).
Fugate, Courtney D. (2018), 'Baumgarten and Kant on Existence', in Courtney D. Fugate and John Hymers (eds), *Baumgarten and Kant on Metaphysics* (Oxford: Oxford University Press), 131–53.
Ginet, Carl (2003), 'Libertarianism', in Michael J. Loux and Dean W. Zimmerman (eds), *The Oxford Handbook of Metaphysics* (Oxford: Oxford University Press), 587–612.
Goldfarb, Warren (2003), *Deductive Logic* (Indianapolis: Hackett).
Gottsched, Johann Christoph (1762), *Erste Gründe der gesamten Weltweisheit* (7th edn; Leipzig: Breitkopf).
Grier, Michelle (1993), 'Illusion and Fallacy in Kant's First Paralogism', *Kant-Studien*, 83, 257–82.
Grier, Michelle (2001), *Kant's Doctrine of Transcendental Illusion* (Cambridge: Cambridge University Press).

Grier, Michelle (2010), 'The Ideal of Pure Reason', in Paul Guyer (ed.), *The Cambridge Companion to Kant's Critique of Pure Reason* (Cambridge: Cambridge University Press), 266-89.
Guyer, Paul (1987), *Kant and the Claims of Knowledge* (Cambridge: Cambridge University Press).
Hankinson, R. J. (2009), 'Causes', in Georgios Anagnostopoulos (ed.), *A Companion to Aristotle* (Chichester: Wiley-Blackwell), 213-29.
Hatfield, Gary (2001), 'Kant und die Berliner Aufklärung', in Rolf-Peter Horstmann, Gerhardt Volker, and Ralph Schumacher (eds), *Akten des IX. Internationalen Kant-Kongresses Band 1* (Berlin and New York: De Gruyter), 185-208.
Hatfield, Gary (2018), 'Baumgarten, Wolff, Descartes, and the Origins of Psychology', in Courtney D. Fugate and John Hymers (eds), *Baumgarten and Kant on Metaphysics* (Oxford: Oxford University Press), 61-77.
Heimsoeth, Heinz (1966-71), *Transzendentale Dialektik: Ein Kommentar zu Kant's Kritik der reinen Vernunft.*, 4 vols (Berlin: De Gruyter).
Henrich, Dieter (1989), 'Kant's Notion of a Deduction and the Methodological Background to the First *Critique*', in Eckart Förster (ed.), *Kant's Transcendental Deductions: The Three 'Critiques' and the 'Opus postumum'* (Stanford, CA: Stanford University Press), 29-46.
Hogan, Desmond (2009), 'How to Know Unknowable Things in Themselves', *Noûs*, 43 (1), 49-63.
Hume, David (1779), *Dialogues sur la religion naturelle* (Edinburgh).
Hume, David (1970), *Dialogues Concerning Natural Religion* (Indianapolis: Bobbs-Merrill).
Hume, David (1975), *Enquiries Concerning Human Understanding and Concerning the Principles of Morals* (Oxford: Clarendon Press).
Irwin, Terence (1984), 'Morality and Personality: Kant and Green', in Allen Wood (ed.), *Self and Nature in Kant's Philosophy* (Ithaca: Cornell University Press), 31-56.
Jauernig, Anja (2008), 'Kant's Critique of the Leibnizian Philosophy: *Contra* the Leibnizians, but *Pro* Leibniz', in Daniel Garber and Béatrice Longuenesse (eds), *Kant and the Early Moderns* (Princeton, NJ and Oxford: Princeton University Press), 41-63.
Johnstone, Henry W. (1959), *Philosophy and Argument* (University Park, PA: Pennsylvania State University Press).
Kalter, Alfons (1975), *Kant's vierter Paralogismus: Eine entwicklungsgeschichtliche Untersuchung zum Paralogismenkapitel der ersten Ausgabe der Kritik der reinen Vernunft* (Meisenheim am Glan: Anton Hain).
Kane, Robert (2003), 'Responsibility, Luck, and Chance: Reflections on Free Will and Indeterminism', in Gary Watson (ed.), *Free Will* (Oxford: Oxford University Press), 299-321.
Kant, Immanuel (1900-), *Gesammelte Schriften* (Berlin: Königlich-Preussischen Akademie der Wissenschaften zu Berlin [now De Gruyter]).
Kant, Immanuel (1992), *The Cambridge Edition of the Works of Kant: Lectures on Logic*, ed. and trans. J. Michael Young (Cambridge: Cambridge University Press).
Kant, Immanuel (1996), *The Cambridge Edition of the Works of Immanuel Kant: Religion and Rational Theology*, trans. Allen W. Wood and George di Giovanni (Cambridge: Cambridge University Press).
Kemp Smith, Norman (1992), *A Commentary to Kant's Critique of Pure Reason* (2nd edn; Atlantic Highlands, NJ: Humanities Press International).
Kemp Smith, Norman (2003), *Immanuel Kant: Critique of Pure Reason* (Basingstoke and New York: Palgrave Macmillan) (orig. pub. 1929).

Kenny, Anthony (1969), *The Five Ways: Saint Thomas Aquinas' Proofs of God's Existence* (London: Routledge).
Kitcher, Patricia (1982), 'Kant's Paralogisms', *Philosophical Review*, 91 (4), 515–47.
Kitcher, Patricia (2011), *Kant's Thinker* (Oxford: Oxford University Press).
Klemme, Heiner F. (1996), *Kants Philosophie des Subjekts: Systematische und entwicklungsgeschichtliche Untersuchungen zum Verhältnis von Selbstbewußtsein und Selbsterkenntnis* (Hamburg: Felix Meiner).
Klima, Gyula (2008), 'The Nominalist Semantics of Ockham and Buridan', in Dov M. Gabbay and John Woods (eds), *Handbook of the History of Logic*, volume 2: *Mediaeval and Renaissance Logic* (Amsterdam: Elsevier), 417–21.
Knutzen, Martin (1744), *Philosophische Abhandlung von der immateriallen Natur der Seele* (Königsberg).
Kosch, Michelle (2006), *Freedom and Reason in Kant, Schelling, and Kierkegaard* (Oxford: Oxford University Press).
Kossler, Matthias (1999), 'Der transzendentale Schein in den Paralogismen der reinen Vernunft nach der ersten Auflage der *Kritik der reinen Vernunft*', *Kant Studien*, 90 (1), 1–22.
Kreines, James (2008), 'Metaphysics Without Pre-Critical Monism', *The Bulletin of the Hegel Society of Great Britain*, 29 (1–2), 48–70.
Kuehn, Manfred (2001), *Kant: A Biography* (Cambridge: Cambridge University Press).
Lange, J. J. (1770), *Einleitung zur Mineralogica Metallica* (Halle: J. J. Curt).
Langton, Rae (1998), *Kantian Humility: Our Ignorance of Things in Themselves* (Oxford: Clarendon Press).
Leeson, Peter T. (2012), 'Ordeals', *Journal of Law and Economics*, 55, 691–714.
Leibniz, G. W. (1974), *Discours de Métaphysique et Monadologie*, ed. André Robinet (Paris: Vrin).
Leibniz, G. W. (1985), *Theodicy*, trans. E. M. Huggard (La Salle, IL: Open Court).
Lewis, David (1981), 'Are We Free to Break the Laws?', *Theoria*, 47 (3), 113–21.
Loemker, Leroy E. (ed.) (1969), *Gottfried Wilhelm Leibniz: Philosophical Papers and Letters* (2nd edn, Synthese Historical Library; Dordrecht: Reidel).
Longuenesse, Béatrice (2007), 'Kant on the Identity of Persons', *Proceedings of the Aristotelian Society*, 107 (2), 149–67.
Longuenesse, Béatrice (2017), *I, Me, Mine: Back to Kant and Back Again* (Oxford: Oxford University Press).
McDonough, Jeffrey K. (2009), 'Leibniz on Natural Teleology and the Laws of Optics', *Philosophy and Phenomenological Research*, 78 (3), 505–44.
McLear, Colin (2011), 'Kant on Animal Consciousness', *Philosophers' Imprint*, 11 (15), 1–16.
Malzkorn, Wolfgang (1999), *Kants Kosmologie-Kritik: Eine formale Analyse der Antinomienlehre* (Berlin: De Gruyter).
Maupertuis, Pierre Louis (1751), *Essai de Cosmologie* (orig. pub. 1750).
Meier, Georg Friedrich (1752), *Auszug aus der Vernunftlehrer* (Halle: Gebauer).
Meier, Georg Friedrich (1765), *Metaphysik*, 4 vols (3; Halle: Gebauer).
Meiklejohn, J. M. D. (1855), *Critique of Pure Reason: translated from the German of Immanuel Kant* (London: Henry G. Bohm).
Meiners, Christoph (1786), *Grundriss der Seelen-Lehrer* (Lemgo).
Mendelssohn, Moses (1767), *Phädon oder über die Unsterblichkeit der Seele in drei Gesprächen (Phaedo, or on the immortality of the soul, in three Dialogues)* (*Gesammelte Schriften Jubiläumsausgabe*; Stuttgart: Frommann-Holzboog).

Mendelssohn, Moses (1997), *Philosophical Writings* (Cambridge: Cambridge University Press).
Moore, Adrian (2010), 'The Transcendental Doctrine of Method', in Paul Guyer (ed.), *The Cambridge Companion to Kant's Critique of Pure Reason* (Cambridge: Cambridge University Press), 310–26.
Moore, G. E. (1912), *Ethics* (London: Home University Library).
Mumford, Stephen (1998), *Dispositions* (Oxford: Oxford University Press).
Nelkin, Dana K. (2000), 'Two Standpoints and the Belief in Freedom', *Journal of Philosophy*, 97 (10), 564–76.
Newton, Isaac (1934), *Philosophiae Naturalis Principia Mathematica (Mathematical Principles of Natural Philosophy)*, trans. Florian Cajori, 2 vols (Los Angeles: University of California Press).
Newton, Isaac (2003), *Opticks* (Great Minds; New York: Prometheus).
Parsons, Terence (2014), *Articulating Medieval Logic* (Oxford: Oxford University Press).
Partington, J. R. (1961-64), *A History of Chemistry*, 4 vols (London: Macmillan).
Partington, J. R. (1989), *A Short History of Chemistry* (3rd edn; New York: Dover).
Pereboom, Derk (2006), 'Kant on Transcendental Freedom', *Philosophy and Phenomenological Research*, 73 (3), 537–67.
Pérez Laraudogoitia, J. (2013), 'Supertasks', *The Stanford Encyclopedia of Philosophy* (ed. Edward N. Zalta).
Pinder, Tillmann (1998), *Immanuel Kant Logik-Vorlesung Unveröffentlichte Nachschriften, Logik Hechsel; Warschauer Logic* (2; Hamburg: Meiner).
Plantinga, Alvin (1966), 'Kant's Objection to the Ontological Argument', *Journal of Philosophy*, 63 (19), 537–46.
Plato (1992), *Republic*, trans. G. M. A. Grube (Indianapolis: Hackett).
Porter, Roy (2000), *Enlightenment: Britain and the Creation of the Modern World* (London: Penguin).
Powell, C. Thomas (1990), *Kant's Theory of Self-Consciousness* (Oxford: Oxford University Press).
Proops, Ian (2003), 'Kant's Legal Metaphor and the Nature of a Deduction', *Journal of the History of Philosophy*, 41 (2), 209–29.
Proops, Ian (2010), 'Kant's First Paralogism', *Philosophical Review*, 119 (4), 449–95.
Proops, Ian (2015), 'Kant on the Ontological Argument', *Noûs*, 49 (1), 1–27.
Ray, John (1714), *The Wisdom of God Manifested in the Works of Creation* (6th edn; London: William Innys).
Reimarus, Hermann Samuel (1756), *Die Vernunftlehre, als eine Unweisung zum richtigen Gebrauche der Vernunft in der Erkenntnis der Wahrheit als zwoen ganz natürlichen Regeln der Einstimmung und des Wiederspruchs hergeleitet* (Hamburg: H.S.R. P.J.H).
Remnant, Peter (1959), 'Kant and the Cosmological Argument', *Australasian Journal of Philosophy*, 32 (7), 152–5.
Reusch, Johann Peter (1734), *Systema Logicum*, ed. J. École (*Christian Wolff Gesammelte Werke: Materialien und Dokumente*, 26; Hildesheim: Georg Olms, 1990).
Rohlf, Michael (2010), 'The Ideas of Pure Reason', in Paul Guyer (ed.), *The Cambridge Companion to Kant's Critique of Pure Reason* (Cambridge: Cambridge University Press), 190–209.
Rosefeldt, Tobias (2017), 'Subjects of Kant's First Paralogism', in A. Stephenson and A. Gomes (eds), *Kant and the Philosophy of Mind: Perception, Reason, and the Self* (Oxford: Oxford University Press), 221–44.
Rousseau, Jean Jacques (1974), *Émile, or On Education* (London: Dent).

Schönfeld, Martin (2000), *The Philosophy of the Young Kant* (Oxford: Oxford University Press).
Sextus Empiricus (1933), *Outlines of Pyrrhonism*, trans. R. G. Bury (Loeb Classical Library; Cambridge, MA: Harvard University Press).
Sorensen, Roy (2003), *A Brief History of the Paradox: Philosophy and the Labyrinths of the Mind* (Oxford: Oxford University Press).
Spinoza, Baruch (2002), *Complete Works*, trans. Samuel Shirley (Indianapolis: Hackett).
Stang, Nicholas (2016), *Kant's Modal Metaphysics* (Oxford: Oxford University Press).
Sullivan, Richard J. (1794), *A View of Nature in Letters to a Traveller among the Alps* (6 vols) (London: T. Becket).
Sutherland, Daniel (2004), 'The Role of Magnitude in Kant's Critical Philosophy', *Canadian Journal of Philosophy*, 32 (3), 411–42.
Thiel, Udo (1997), 'Varieties of Inner Sense: Two Pre-Kantian Theories', *Archiv für Geschichte der Philosophie*, 79 (79), 58–79.
Thümmig, Ludwig Philipp (1725–26), *Institutiones Philosophiae Wolffianae in usus academicos adornate*, 2 vols (1; Frankfurt am Main and Leipzig: Renger).
Tonelli, Giorgio (1962), 'Die historische Ursprung der kantischen Termini "Analytik" und "Dialektik"', *Archiv für Begriffsgeschichte*, 7, 120–39.
Tonelli, Giorgio (1978), '"Critique" and Related Terms Prior to Kant: A Historical Survey', *Kant-Studien*, 69 (2), 119–48.
Tucker, Abraham (1768–78), *The Light of Nature Pursued*, 7 vols (1; London: R. Faulder and T. Payne).
Tye, Michael (2019), 'Homunculi Heads and Silicon Chips: The Importance of History to Phenomenology', in Adam Pautz and Dan Stoljar (eds), *Blockheads! Essays on Ned Block's Philosophy of Mind and Consciousness* (Cambridge, MA: MIT Press), 545–70.
Vallicella, W. F. (2000), 'Does the Cosmological Argument Depend on the Ontological?', *Faith and Philosophy*, 17 (4), 441–58.
Van Cleve, James (1981), 'Reflections on Kant's Second Antinomy', *Synthese*, 47 (3), 481–94.
Van Cleve, James (1999), *Problems from Kant* (Oxford: Oxford University Press).
van Inwagen, Peter (1993), *Metaphysics* (Boulder, CO: Westview).
Vilhauer, Benjamin (2010), 'The Scope of Responsibility in Kant's Theory of Free Will', *British Journal for the History of Philosophy*, 18 (1), 45–71.
Vitruvius (Marcus Vitruvius Pollio) (1960), *The Ten Books on Architecture* (*De Architectura*), trans. Morris Hicky Morgan (New York: Dover).
Voltaire (1972), *Philosophical Dictionary*, trans. T. Besterman (St. Ives: Penguin).
Voltaire (2010), *Philosophical Dictionary*, trans. H. I. Woolf (New York: Dover).
Walker, R. C. S. (1978), *Kant*, ed. Ted Honderich (The Arguments of the Philosophers; London: Routledge).
Warda, Arthur (1922), *Immanuel Kants Bücher* (Bibliographien und Studien; Berlin: Martin Breslauer).
Warfield, Ted (2003), 'Compatibilism and Incompatibilism: Some Arguments', in Michael J. Loux and Dean W. Zimmerman (eds), *The Oxford Handbook of Metaphysics* (Oxford: Oxford University Press), 613–32.
Watkins, Eric (2005), *Kant and the Metaphysics of Causality* (Cambridge: Cambridge University Press).
Watkins, Eric (2013), 'Kant on Infima Species', in *Kant und die Philosophie in weltbürgerlicher Absicht*, ed. C. La Rocca (Berlin: De Gruyter).
Watson, Gary (2003), *Free Will* (Oxford: Oxford University Press).

Willaschek, Marcus (2018), *Kant on the Sources of Metaphysics: The Dialectic of Pure Reason* (Cambridge: Cambridge University Press).
Wittgenstein, Ludwig (2001), *Philosophical Investigations* (Oxford: Blackwell).
Wolff, Christian (1736), *Philosophia prima seu Ontologia methodo scientifica pertractata, qua omnis cognitationis humanae principia continentur* (first published 1730), in Christian Wolff, *Gesammelte Werke*, Part 2, Lateinische Schriften, vol. 3 (Hildesheim: Olms, 1962).
Wolff, Christian (1738), *Psychologia empirica* (2nd edn) (first published 1732), in Christian Wolff, *Gesammelte Werke*, Part 2. Lateinische Schriften, vol. 5. (Hildesheim: Olms, 1968).
Wolff, Christian (1739–41), *Theologia naturalis, methodo scientifica pertracta*, 3 vols (first published 1736-7), in Christian Wolff, *Gesammelte Werke* Part 2, vols 7.1–7.2, 8 (Hildesheim: Olms, 1978).
Wolff, Christian (1740a), *Psychologia rationalis* (2nd edn) (first published 1734), in Christian Wolff, *Gesammelte Werke*, Part 2. Lateinische Schriften, vol. 6 (Hildesheim: Olms 1972).
Wolff, Christian (1740b), *Anmerkungen zur deutschen Metaphysik* (first published 1724), in Christian Wolff, *Gesammelte Werke*, Part 1, vol. 3 (Hildesheim: Olms, 1983).
Wolff, Christian (1740c), *Philosophia rationalis, sive Logica* (3rd edn), 3 vols (first published 1728, vol. 1 known as 'Preliminary Discourse') in Christian Wolff, *Gesammelte Werke*, Part 2. Lateinische Schriften, vols 1.1–1.3 (Hildesheim: Olms, 1983).
Wolff, Christian (1751), *Vernünftige Gedancken von Gott, der Welt und der Seele des Menschen, auch allen Dingen überhaupt* (first published 1719), in Christian Wolff, *Gesammelte Werke* (Hildesheim: Olms, 1983).
Wood, Allen (1978), *Kant's Rational Theology* (Ithaca, NY: Cornell University Press).
Wood, Allen (1984), 'Kant's Compatibilism', in Allen Wood (ed.), *Self and Nature in Kant's Philosophy* (Ithaca, NY: Cornell University Press), 73–101.
Wood, Allen (1992), 'Rational Theology, Moral Faith, and Religion', in Paul Guyer (ed.), *The Cambridge Companion to Kant* (Cambridge: Cambridge University Press), 394–416.
Wood, A. and Guyer, P. (eds) (1998), *The Cambridge Edition of the Works of Immanuel Kant: Critique of Pure Reason* (New York: Cambridge University Press).
Wuerth, Julian (2014), *Kant on Mind, Action, and Ethics* (New York: Oxford University Press).

Index

Note: Figures are indicated by an italic "*f*", following the page number.

For the benefit of digital users, indexed terms that span two pages (e.g., 52–53) may, on occasion, appear on only one of those pages.

Academic scepticism/sceptics 5, 55, 57–8, 265, 455
Achilles argument 140–8, 259n.32
actuality 94, 155, 193, 255, 338–9, 344, 347, 350n.37, 353–7, 359–60
  concept of not a real predicate 339, 353–4
  definition of 349–50, 353–4
  not a reality 360
achromatic doublet 41n.5
ad hominem arguments 362–3
Adickes, Erich 33, 128n.5
affinity 4n.14, 432–3, 440, 443–6, *see also* kinship, principle of affinity
affirmative judgments 245, 249–50, 252–4, 384
afterlife 4, 27, 29, 120, 136, 164, 172–7, 179, 181–2, 186, 196, 380n.39, 457–8
  argument for 29–30, 178–9, 184, 186, 454
  belief/faith in 4–5, 13–14, 26–7, 119–21, 177, 180, 185–8, 196–7, 419–20, 453
  existence of 25–6, 185
agent-causation 286, 296n.40, 317–19
Al-Azm, Sadik 225, 228n.45
Allais, Lucy 279n.5, 296n.40, 300–1, 318n.40
Allison, Henry 84n.38, 143, 155n.20, 202n.11, 223n.36, 225, 287n.30, 304, 319–20, 438n.32, 451
Ameriks, Karl 106n.6, 128n.6, 129, 303, 311n.26, 318n.38
  on the *B*-edition first paralogism 125–6
  on Kant's *A*-edition criticism of the first paralogism 128–9
Angelelli, Ignacio 91n.2
analogy 1n.2, 29, 53, 62–3, 85n.43, 93, 117–19, 144, 167–8, 167n.9, 179, 181–2, 184n.39, 188, 264, 274–5, 289, 320–1, 406–7, 409–10, 450, 454
  of nature 13–14, 179–80, 401
  with human art 401, 411, 417
  see also arguments by/from analogy, elastic ball analogy, Lambert analogy
animals 81n.36, 178n.29, 187–9, 194–5, 397–8, 408–10, 428n.11, 437, *see also* cats
Anselm 337–8, 340–2, 352–3, 371n.18

antinomies 5n.17, 7–8, 14, 18, 22, 24–5, 29, 32–3, 45n.14, 55–6, 130–4, 132n.14, 209–10, 212–14, 216–17, 253–4, 258–9, 271–2, 274–5, 289, 453–5, 460–1
  and Pyrrhonism 19–20
  and the sceptical method 19–20
  and Transcendental Idealism 254, 270, 273
  and transcendental illusion 55–6, 131–4
  construction of 19–20, 23–4, 214–16, 295, 456
  form of 217–21, 218*f*
  pre-eminence of 29–30
  resolution of 14–15, 25–6, 29–30, 55, 214, 262–3, 275, 279, 456, 462
apperception 77n.31, 80–4, 128, 132, 134–5, 137, 155, 157, 170
  unity of 85–6, 132–3, 135, 156, 199
applied logic 40n.2
Aquinas, Thomas 100, 100n.24, 284–5, 307n.22, 371n.18
Arcesilaus 21
architect of the world 410–11, 414–15, 419–20
architectonic and method 200–3
arguments by/from analogy 13, 29, 53–4, 181–4, 390, 401, 406, 409–10, 418–19, 454
Ariew, Roger 340n.8
Aristotelianism 26n.62
Aristotle 100, 249–50, 284–6, 285n.19, 314n.31, 371n.18
  efficient causes in 284–5
  essence in 375–6
  notion of an infinite name 249n.9
  notion of primary substance 128n.3
artefacts 285, 401, 406–10, 419
Arthur, Richard T. W. 243n.68
atheism/atheists 25–6, 116, 209–10, 402–4, 414–15, 414n.42, 417
Averroes 371n.18
Avicenna 371n.18

Bacon, Francis 30–1
Bader, Ralf 59n.2, 65n.12, 93n.9, 117–18, 117n.26, 121, 122n.32, 150n.13, 160n.25, 167n.9, 171n.17, 196, 322n.56, 346–7

Baumeister, Friedrich Christian 62n.6, 176, 210n.4, 416n.44
Baumgarten, Alexander 27–8, 45n.15, 60, 69n.19, 70–1, 73n.25, 79–80, 88n.48, 91, 98, 106n.6, 164n.4, 169n.14, 176, 228n.44, 266–7, 271–2, 271n.56, 284n.14, 338–9, 341, 345, 352n.41, 361, 361n.50, 367n.8, 414n.41
  and the ontological argument 342, 344n.21
  on composites 94n.12, 238n.58
  on existence 348–52
  on identity 174, 253–4
  on immortality 176
  on paralogisms 98
  on psychology 68–71, 75, 162–3, 163n.2, 455
  on sophisms 98, 101
  on the soul 70–1, 73n.25, 106n.6, 164n.4
Bayle, Pierre 17–18, 143n.4, 220–1
Beattie, James 269n.51
Beck, Jakob Sigismund 450n.49
Beck, Lewis White 4–5, 4n.13, 68–9, 69n.18, 71n.22, 177n.26
Beiser, Frederick C. 172n.20
Benacerraf, Paul 232–3
Bennett, Jonathan 32n.82, 92, 122–3, 128–9, 374–5, 377n.31
Berkeley, George 190n.2, 193–4, 194n.5, 332
Black, Joseph 435
Boehm, Omri 48n.21, 219, 294n.35
Borisov, Gennadiy 443n.41

Carroll, Lewis 259n.32
Cartesian
  causal principle 147
  concept of 'I' 72–4
  doubt 111, 125–6
  'I exist thinking, therefore I exist' (sum cogitans, ergo sum) 155
  'I think, therefore I am' (cogito, ergo sum) 87–8, 155
  ontological argument 337–8, 341–2, 344, 346, 348, 353n.44, 390n.1
  side of the Euthyphro contrast 403
  soul 204–5
  system 268, 345–6
  see also Descartes
cats
  as subject to transcendental illusion 53n.29
categories
  as distinct from functions of the understanding 122–3
causal
  activity 403–4
  chain 277, 290n.32, 302
  determinism 289, 296n.40, 313–14, 318, 320
  efficacy 290
  explanations 393
  faculty 27–8, 281, 286–7, 299
  law 282–3, 293–5, 328
  over-determination 142, 152n.15
  power 299, 307
  principle 30, 44, 147, 151–2, 275, 295–7, 457–8
  regress 297
  series 291, 302, 305, 370n.15
causality 142, 277–8, 281–2, 290–1, 293, 296, 299, 311, 315n.32, 323–5, 328–30, 369–70, 401, 406, 409–10, 411n.35, 413–14, 424, 453
  law of 302n.9, 316, 368n.11
  of a noumenal entity 286
  of freedom 278, 279n.5, 281–3, 300n.3
  of reason 283, 322–3
  of the cause 284, 286–7, 289–90, 299, 329, 406–7
  through freedom 277–9, 281–3, 299, 311
causation 151n.14, 370n.15
  agent causation 286, 296n.40, 319
  atemporal causation 286, 299, 329–30
  efficient causation 145, 151–2, 284–6, 301–2, 302n.9, 391–3
  extra-mundane causation 286, 327, 329–30
  noumenal causation 296n.40, 300n.2
  substance causation 285–6
  temporal causation 329–30
certainty 5–7, 15–18, 23, 29, 39, 74–5, 79–80, 187, 190–1, 193, 218, 230, 263, 265–6, 288, 300–1, 320, 402, 406, 414n.42, 418–19, 456, see also evidence, intuitive certainty
charity 24–5, 51n.27, 180, 285–6, 338, 345–6, 366–7
chemistry 14–15, 188, 280–1, 434–5, 434n.20, 435n.23 see also phlogiston chemistry, pneumatic chemistry
Chignell, Andrew 4n.15, 19–20, 45n.15, 50n.26, 172n.20, 184n.40, 185n.41, 266–7, 267n.39, 286n.24, 457n.5
Christianity/Christians 8–9, 164–5, 220n.31, 286, 306–7
Cicero 17n.47
Cicovacki, Predag 48
Clarke, Randolph 296n.40, 317
Clarke, Samuel 26n.64, 228–9, 230n.49, 373n.21
cogito 65, 203
  Kant's criticism of 204–5
  see also Cartesian
cognition 3n.9, 14, 17–18, 27–8, 42, 75, 83–4, 93, 115, 135, 156, 180, 249n.10, 262, 301–2, 342, 441–2, 450, 453
  grounds of 73f, 79, 82
  object of 47–9
  of God 337

of objects 28, 30–1, 57, 198, 451
of the objects of the senses 72–3
of the original being 337, 413
sources of 6–7
see also cognitions
cognitions 46–7, 49
cognitive
　capacities 174–5, 350n.38
　faculties 1, 2n.4
　penetration 5, 66
　power 85
　states 64–5
collective intuition 256
collective unity of a thought 146–7
Collins, Anthony 26n.64
column entasis 41n.5
comets 436–41, 443–4
common sense 269n.51, 421n.51
compatibilism 278n.2, 282, 311n.26, 313–20, 316n.33, 322
　pre-critical versions of 321
composite substance 94n.12, 142–4, 236–9
conic sections 436–7, 439–44, 443n.42, 447
consciousness 8n.24, 78–81, 85, 90, 95, 107, 117, 120, 122, 132–7, 161–9, 173–9, 193, 199–200, 433
　and the soul 59, 62, 68–9, 73–5, 161, 176, 190–1, 200
　of myself 84, 198
　see also intellectual consciousness, self-consciousness, unity of consciousness
contingency 294–5, 371–3, 384
　and the Principle of Sufficient Reason (PSR) 383–4
Copernican revolution 1–2, 462
Copernicus, Nicolaus 1, 30–1
corporeal nature 195–6
cosmological
　concepts 273–5
　conflict 262–3
　dispute 30
　freedom 281–4
　Ideas 55n.34, 94, 130, 262–3, 333
　proof 341–2, 364, 374, 379–80, 384, 390n.1, 412–13
　questions 261–2, 265
　series 427–8
　syllogism 257–61, 295n.39
cosmological argument 24–5, 30–1, 54n.32, 56, 74, 342, 348, 364–73, 370nn.15,17, 378–9, 382–3, 389, 390n.1, 412–13
　Kant's presentation of 367–71, 373, 375, 379–83, 385, 387–9
　Wolff's presentation of 371–2, 383, 388–9

Crusius, Christian August 18–19, 27–8, 67n.15, 96n.14, 241–2, 368n.11
Cudworth, Ralph 143n.5
cupellation test 9–12, *see also Feuerprobe*, fiery test of critique, fire assay
Cutter, Brian 190n.3, 287n.29, 359n.48, 388

Davis, A. E. L. 182n.36
deist's God 337, 342, 414
de Mairan, Jean-Jacques d'Ortous 269n.52, 331–2
　and the moon 331–3
demand of reason 42–3, 46n.16, 52, 94–5, 460–1
denying knowledge 25–7, 457–9, 457n.5
Derham, William 391–2, 392n.5, 395–6, 429, 429nn.14,16, 455
Descartes, René 2, 22–3, 23n.59, 27–8, 43n.10, 45n.15, 51, 60, 81n.36, 146–7, 147n.11, 151–5, 155n.19, 190–1, 194–6, 202n.11, 203–5, 204n.14, 251, 268, 269n.52, 338, 341–2, 345–6, 348, 348n.31, 349n.36, 352–3, 362, 377, 377n.33, 455, 461–2
　and the fourth paralogism 190
　and the ontological argument 344
　on corporeal nature 195–6
　on God's power 361–2
　see also Cartesian
determination 23–4, 94, 118, 121, 125–8, 142, 152n.15, 167n.9, 170, 173, 240, 328, 346–50, 374, 376–9, 439
　as a property 92
determinations 46, 94n.13, 107n.8, 112, 154, 166–7, 170, 346–7, 388n.52, 426–7
determinism 209–10, 279n.5, 287–9, 300, 307, 309–11, 316–18, 320–3
determinist 282, 300, 313–14, 317, 321–2
dialectic 47n.17, 214–16, 303, 454–6, *see also* Transcendental Dialectic
dialetheism 253–4, 304n.14
Diogenes Laertius 21
disputation 91–2, 102, 129n.10, 344
　'argument' method of 91n.2
　'question' method of 91n.2
　role of defendant in 362–3
disputational
　conduct 362
　form of Kant's criticism of the ontological argument 362–3
　skill 212
doctrinal belief 4, 8, 26, 29, 177n.26, 184, 186–7, 411, 415n.43, 457n.5
　contrasted with pragmatic belief 187–8
　in a god 13, 390, 418, 453
　in an afterlife 4–5, 13–14, 27, 180, 185–6, 453
　in an Author of Nature 17n.47, 418–20, 454

doctrinal belief (*cont.*)
  in an originator 13, 407, 419–21
  in the purposiveness of nature 185, 187–8, 419
  Kant's notion of 184n.40
doctrine of spirits (*Geisterlehre*) 8–9, 67–8
dogmatic
  arguments 186
  beliefs 41, 51–2, 57, 95
  doubt 5n.18
  error 17n.47, 57–8
  idealism 190n.2, 193
  metaphysicians 24, 216n.21, 220, 432, 459
  physico-theological argument 406, 410–15, 419–21
  pretensions 27
  proofs 26, 178–9, 411, 414n.42, 457n.5
  rational psychologists 59, 90, 136–7, 426
  rational psychology 6n.19, 8–9, 13n.39, 17, 25, 39, 59–61, 63, 85–9
  rational theology 412, 418–19, 456–7
  reason 2n.5, 28
  scepticism/sceptics 5–6, 5n.18, 15–16, 16n.44, 25–8, 214, 455
  slumber 213, 454–5
  speculative metaphysics 1–3, 5, 14, 19, 23–5, 27–8, 39, 41–2, 44, 47n.18, 48, 51–2, 54, 177, 216n.21, 249, 265, 267n.41, 289, 445–6, 457, 461–2
  spiritualist 136, 432
  systems 18–19
  theology/theologian 382, 419–20
  see also non-dogmatic
dogmatism 2n.4, 3n.11, 6n.21, 13–14, 16, 18, 30, 45–6, 50–1, 51n.27, 77, 99, 105, 111, 117–19, 121–2, 129, 140n.1, 159, 171n.16, 174–5, 212–13, 216, 266, 426, 445, 447
dogmatists 26, 142, 264, 455, 459
Dollond, John 41n.5
doubt 5–6, 19–20, 22–3, 26n.64, 90, 109n.11, 111, 125–6, 130, 133–4, 149–50, 190–2, 194, 196, 199, 268, 271–2, 315, 372–3, 377n.30, 388–9, 393–6, 399, 409–10, 415–16, 457–8, 461
  of decision 5n.18
  of postponement 5n.18
  species of 15–16
dream world 321
Du Châtelet, Émilie 269n.52, 444n.43
Dyck, Corey 32n.82, 60n.3, 61n.5, 67n.15, 68n.16, 70n.20, 74n.27, 75n.29, 79n.34, 85, 85n.43, 87n.45, 105n.2, 110n.12, 143, 143n.4, 146n.9, 171n.16

Earth 331–2, 391, 404–5, 420, 427–8, 451
  axial tilt of 404–5, 427–8, 428n.11
  oblate spheroid 404–5, 427–8

earths (in chemical sense) 434–5
Eberhard, J. A. 266–7
efficient-causal modes of explanation 404
elastic ball analogy 161–2, 168–9, 173
empirical psychology 7, 31–2, 39–58, 41n.4, 60, 61n.5, 64–7, 70–9, 73f, 80n.35, 82, 86, 88–9, 96–7
  Baumgarten on 69
  Gottsched on 67–8
  in Kant's *Metaphysics L1* lectures 68–9
end-directedness 415–18, 427–8, *see also* purposive, purposiveness
ens originarium 337, 420–1
ens realissimum 50–1, 223, 337, 342, 344, 352n.41, 364–6, 370–4, 377n.31, 378–84, 388–9
Epicurus 21n.54, 27–8, 218–19, 218n.25, 219, 456
epicycloids/epicyclic gearing 430–1, 451
Euthyphro contrast 338, 360–2, 403
evidence 13, 19–20, 28n.69, 91–2, 96–7, 111–12, 116n.25, 118–19, 122, 125, 164–5, 186, 219, 233n.53, 270, 285–6, 288, 300n.3, 302–3, 308, 401–2, 416, 419, 432, 448
  for the existence of purposes in nature 416–17
  Kant's technical sense of 13n.38, 381–2, 453–4
  of an intelligent/wise originator 397, 419–20
  of divine origin 401–2
  of God's infinite greatness 400–1
existence of God 2–3, 2n.4, 25–6, 74, 151–2, 172–3, 213, 337–8, 337n.1, 344n.21, 351–3, 368n.9, 390–1, 401–2, 413, 414n.42, 420–1, 456–9, 461–2
existence of the soul 3n.10, 69, 74, 75n.29, 76, 87–8, 199–200
existential
  commitment 253n.19, 385, 385n.50, 386
  dependence 230, 328
experience
  that I am 367–8
  unity of 293
  see also inner experience, objects of experience
experiment 1, 1n.2, 14–15, 84, 214–15, 416–17, 435, 443, *see also* thought experiment
external-world scepticism 193–6

fallacies 97–8, 101–2, 111, 128–9, 139, 150–1, 258–9
  classification of 97
  detection of 456
fallacy
  of equivocation (*sophisma figurae dictionis*) 91–2, 98, 101, 104, 106n.4, 129, 138, 148, 157, 161, 167–8, 170, 173, 258, 260–1
  of lazy reason (*ignava ratio*) 432
  of perverted reason (*perversa ratio*) 415–16

of *heterozeteseos* 100–2, 128
of *ignoratio elenchi* 91–2, 100–1, 128–9, 139, 157, 365, 380, 388–9
of subreption (*vitium subreptionis*) 85, 85n.43
family resemblances 438
fanaticism 6n.20, 25–6, 116, 457
fecundity 406–10, 408n.29, 414
Feder, Johann Georg Heinrich 98, 100n.26, 266–8
Feuerprobe 8–14 *see also* cupellation test, fiery test of critique, fire assay
fiery test of critique 7–8, 390, 453 *see also* cupellation test, *Feuerprobe*, fire assay
Finocchiaro, Maurice A. 362n.52
fire assay 9–14 *see also* cupellation test, *Feuerprobe*, fiery test of critique
focus imaginarius 33, 448–52
Fontenelle, Bernard Le Bovier de 269–70
Fordyce, David 455
　argument of 26n.64, 177–84, 182n.34, 184n.38, 186–9, 415n.43, 432
Forster, Michael N. 19–21
Fourcroy, Antoine-François de 434n.20
freedom 2–3, 6n.21, 24, 27–8, 30, 70, 114, 185, 217, 254, 277, 281, 296n.40, 299, 302–5, 314–16, 318–22, 337, 342n.12, 406–7, 411n.35, 414, 422, 457–9, 459n.9
　in the cosmological sense 281–4
　moral argument for 309–13
　of the turnspit 314–16
　possibility of 279–80
　reconciled with nature 277
　see also free will, incompatibilist conception of freedom, libertarian freedom, practical freedom, transcendental freedom
free will 3n.7, 28n.69, 209–10, 218–19, 269, 278, 282, 294, 311n.26, 313–14, 316n.33, 317–19, 321–2, 393, 409–10, 413, *see also* freedom
French philosophers, Kant on 269–70
French *philosophes* 27–8, 269–70
Friedman, Michael 242n.66, 279n.4, 405n.23, 435
Fugate, Courtney D. 262n.33, 350n.37

Garber, Daniel 340n.8, 342n.13
Garve, Christian 213, 213n.15, 266–7, 304, 304n.15
genealogical metaphor 11–12
Ginet, Carl 317
God 2–3, 3n.11, 6n.21, 29, 94, 106–7, 109n.11, 117, 124, 131, 146, 152, 164–5, 172, 195–6, 220n.30, 228n.46, 231, 241–2, 254, 257–8, 267–9, 275–6, 303, 312, 315, 337, 340n.7, 342, 347, 360–1, 382, 389–90, 392–6, 397n.12, 398–404, 413, 416–18, 420, 422–4, 422n.3, 424, 426–7, 451, 458
　creative causality of 286
　attributes of 67–8, 152–3, 378
　belief in 13, 124–5, 185–6, 414, 457–8, 461–2
　character of 261–2
　cognition of 337
　concept of 74, 119, 124–5, 341–2, 352–3, 413–15
　Descartes's argument for the existence of 147n.11, 201
　essence of 351–2
　in Descartes's third *Meditation* 151–2, 461–2
　in the first paralogism 116, 124
　in the third antinomy 329
　intellect of 106n.5, 113n.16
　judgment of 8–9
　nature of 72, 337–8, 414n.39
　omnipresence of 306–7
　powers of 361–2
　unity of 153
　will of 360n.49, 420–1
　see also existence of God, Idea of God
Goldfarb, Warren 32–3, 210n.3
Gottsched, Johann Christoph 67–70, 71n.22, 72
Grier, Michelle 41–2, 46–7, 47n.17, 55, 57, 110n.13, 351n.39
group minds 90, 142, 148–9, 155
Guyer, Paul 8, 11, 99n. 20, 164–5, 214, 266–7, 290n.32, 331n.2, 342n.17, 380n.38

Hales, Thomas C. 429n.15
Hamann, J. G. 407
happiness 25–6, 171–2, 180
Hankinson, R. J. 284n.17
Hatfield, Gary 45n.15, 407
heavenly bodies 438n.34, 439–35, *see also* Jupiter, Mars, Mercury
Heine, Fredericus 91n.2
Henrich, Dieter 12n.36
Herz, Marcus 266–7
Hobbes, Thomas 461
Hogan, Desmond 67n.14, 346n.25
homogeneity 432–4, 438, 442, 446–7
honeycomb conjecture 429
Hume, David 28, 213, 269n.51, 319–20, 407–10
　Dialogues Concerning Natural Religion 407–8, 409n.30, 419n.47
　Enquiries Concerning Human Understanding 26n.64
　criticism of the design argument 407–10
　on compatibilism 278n.2, 314, 321
　on scepticism 5–6, 27–8, 27n.66, 407–8
hundred thalers argument 347

idealism 190, 190n.2, 193–4, 275, 296n.40,
    see also Transcendental Idealism
ideality
    of the objects of the outer senses 190
    of space and time 3n.7, 214
    paralogism of 190
    transcendental 270
Idea of God 151–3, 422n.3, 423–4, 425n.7, 426,
    449–52, 461–2
    as a regulative principle 427–30
Idea of systematic unity 422, 426–8, 432–40, 445,
    451–2
Idea of the soul 95–6, 130–2, 257–8, 422n.3,
    423–4, 426–7, 450–2
    as a regulative principle 426–7
Idea of the world 258, 262n.34, 422n.3, 423–6,
    449–52
Ideas
    regulative use of 422–52
identity 161, 169, 237–8, 264, 434
    claims 433
    hidden 433
    judgments 109n.11, 167n.9
    of indiscernibles 2n.4, 364n.2, 386
    of the person/personal 164, 167–9,
        173–4, 424
    of the self 161–7
    of the subject 167–8, 173–4
    principle of 253–4
    rule of 147
ideological parsimony 43–6, 93n.10
ideology 42–3
illusion 11, 17n.47, 18, 22, 29–30, 40, 42, 48–9, 53,
    55–8, 85–6, 97, 103, 213–15, 255, 274, 279,
    352–3, 448, 450, 454–6, 459–60, see also
    dialectical illusion, empirical illusion, optical
    illusion, logical illusion, moon illusion,
    Müller-Lyer illusion, transcendental illusion
immortality 2–3, 6n.21, 59, 172n.20, 176, 181–2,
    184, 213, 220n.30, 422, 457–9, 462
immortality of the soul 2–3, 26, 70, 75–6, 90,
    102, 159–60, 163n.1, 171n.16, 175–7,
    179–80, 186, 209–10, 231, 380, 432, 455
imperative 48–9, 54, 253–4, 260, 460–1
    categorical 49–50
    hypothetical 49–51
impure rational psychology 60, 80
incompatibilism 278, 317–22
incompatibilist conception of freedom 287n.30,
    319–20
incompatibilists 317–19
indeterminism 278, 282–3, 289, 309, 317, 319,
    321–2, 324
indifferentism 5–6, 19, 265–7, 266n.38, 269

indifferentists 19, 27–8, 248, 265–70, 455
infinite
    judgments 247n.4, 249–50, 252
    length 224
    magnitude 55, 224–7
    numbers 224, 369n.14
    series 222–3
    series of conditions 45
    series of states 45n.14, 221
    space 226n.41
    see also paradoxes of the infinite
infinity 93–4, 133–4, 221, 223–7, 239, 247–8,
    255–7, 259n.32, 377, 440–1
    concept of 221–3
    regress to 297
    see also mathematical infinity
inner experience 82–3, 450
inner sense 59–60, 72–4, 73f, 77, 77n.31, 84nn.
    40–41, 88, 95–6, 113, 117–19, 121, 121n.29,
    166–7, 173–4, 193, 196, 426, 462, see also
    objects of sense, outer sense
intuition 14–15, 78, 83–4, 95, 106, 112–13, 121, 123,
    159, 173, 225–6, 229, 234–5, 256–7, 261–2, 273,
    300–1, 319, 381–2, 441–2, 454n.2
intuition
    boundaries of 196–7, 231–4, 244
    into another world 120
    of an object 86
    of my self 166–7
    of noumenal stuff 158
    of space 158–9
    of the permanent 93n.9
    of the self 84
    of the soul 96, 120–1
    of the subject 86
    of this world 119–20
    spiritual form of 174–5, 194
intuitive certainty 13n.38, 381–2, 453–4
intuitive plausibility 68
Irwin, Terence 320–1

Jakob, Ludwig Heinrich 98n.19
jargon 32–4, 42, 47, 78–9, 148, 161, 268
Jauernig, Anja 342n.13
Johnstone, Henry W. 362n.53
Jupiter 423n.4
    moons of 393–4, 399–401, see also longitude

Kalter, Alfons 128n.5
Kane, Robert 287n.30, 316n.33, 317
Kästner, Abraham Gotthelf 430–1
Kemp Smith, Norman 9n.25, 99n.20, 103n.31,
    143n.5, 161, 164–5, 192n.4, 290n.32, 331n.2,
    380n.38

INDEX 481

Kenny, Anthony 371n.18
Kepler, Johannes 441n.36
kinship 209, 412, 432–3, 438, 439, 440, *see also* affinity, principle of affinity
Kitcher, Patricia 84n.41, 111–12
Klemme, Heiner F. 96n.14, 143
Klima, Gyula 385n.50
Knutzen, Martin 143n.5, 144n.7
Kosch, Michelle 318–19
Kossler, Matthias 128n.5
Kreines, James 48n.21, 54n.32
Kuehn, Manfred 220n.31

La Mettrie, Julien Offray de 461
Lambert analogy 263–5
Lambert, Johann Heinrich 263–4, 270
Lange, Johann J. 10
Langton, Rae 110n.12
Laraudogoitia, Jon Pérez 233n.54
law of excluded middle 245, 271–2, 271n.56, 350
laws of nature 277–8, 283, 287–91, 296, 299, 300n.3, 311n.27, 393, 405, 431
Leeson, Peter T 9n.26
Leibniz, Gottfried Wilhelm 2, 18n.50, 27–8, 51, 159n.24, 165–6, 242n.67, 316, 319–20, 342, 360–4, 367–9, 371, 377, 382–3, 383n.47, 455
  argument against spatial points as minimal parts of lines 242–3
  Discours de Metaphysique et Monadologie 340n.8, 360n.49
  Euthyphro contrast 361, 403
  free agent 315
  identity of indiscernibles 2n.4
  laws of dioptrics 431
  laws of reflection and refraction 431
  Monadology 340–1
  New Essays 155n.20, 340, 342n.14, 348
  on compatibilism 278n.2, 311n.26, 314–18, 320–1
  on determinism 316
  on *ens realissimum* 382n.43
  on freedom 311n.26, 314–15
  on pneumatology 67n.15
  on space and time 228–31, 242
  on the concept of *being* 338–9
  on the ontological argument 339–42, 348, 381–2, 386–7, 389
  on the soul 165n.7, 315
  Preliminary Dissertation on the Conformity of Faith with Reason 100
  and Principle of Sufficient Reason 377n.31
  and principle of the connection of finality 431
  Theodicy 100, 220n.31, 314–15, 345–6, 360–1, 369n.13, 372–3, 378–9

Leibnizian
  conception of a finite world 230
  cosmological argument 371
Leibnizians 229–31
Lewis, David 311n.27
libertarian freedom 278, 282–3, 289, 294, 299, 307–9, 317–19
libertarianism 287n.30, 317–19, 321–3
  Kant's alleged 317–24
Locke, John
  conception of liberty 269
  on consciousness 169
  on personal identity 164
  on the abuse of words 422n.1
  on the persistence of the soul 169
Loemker, Leroy E. 242n.67
longitude 394, 399–401, *see also* moons of jupiter
Longuenesse, Béatrice 122–4, 169n.13, 171n.16, 204n.14, 342n.13

magnesia alba 434–5
magnesian earths 434–5
magnitude 62, 178, 214, 222n.34, 231–2, 234, 255–6, 256, 264, 274–5, 275, 333, 411–12, *see also* infinite magnitude, monetary magnitude
Maier, John 166n.8
McDonough, Jeffrey 431
McLear, Colin 19–20, 81n.36
McNulty, Bennett 447n.46
Malzkorn, Wolfgang 247n.4
Mars 423n.4, 443
materialism 196, 209–10, 461–2
mathematical infinity 223–4, 244 *see also* infinity
mathematicians 263–4, 397, 429
mathematics 13n.38, 28, 30–1, 220–1, 223, 254–5, 263–4, 340, 381–2, 424–6, 429n.15, 453–4, 454, 460, 461n.12
Maupertuis, Pierre Louis 397, 430
Meier, Georg Friedrich 71–2, 98, 100–1, 104, 249, 437
  Auszug aus der Vernunftlehrer 32n.83, 99n.21, 100, 101n.27, 125n.38, 249, 249n.10, 362–3, 436–7, 441–2
  Grundriss der Seelen-Lehrer 267–8
  Metaphysics 71
Meiklejohn, John M. D. 10n.28
memory 45–6, 64–5, 163, 163n.2, 165–6, 174, 433
Meiners, Christoph 266–8
Mendelssohn, Moses 2, 27–8, 377–8, 455
  Morning Hours 266–7
  On Evidence in Metaphysical Sciences 266–7
  on the immortality of the soul 26, 160, 177–8

Mendelssohn, Moses (*cont.*)
    Phädon 143n.5, 177, 266–7
    Philosophical Writings 267n.40, 377n.34
Mercury 423n.4, 443
metallurgical assay 9–11
metallurgical metaphor 11–12
metallurgy 14–15
metals myth 11–12
metaphysics 1, 5n.16, 6n.20, 7–8, 12–14, 18–19, 21, 25–6, 26n.62, 29–31, 34, 39, 44, 77, 146n.9, 177, 184, 215–16, 220–1, 247–8, 265–9, 280–1, 413, 422–3, 440, 447n.46, 453–5, *see also* rational metaphysics, Wolff on dogmatic speculative metaphysics
mind–body interaction 197
modality 50, 96n.14, 125–6, 198, 202–3, 202*f*, 209–10, 250–1, 385n.50
    and the fourth paralogism 198
    categories of 198, 200–1
    principles of 353–4
monads 70, 143n.5, 159n.24, 240–2
monism 158–60, 197–8
moon 331–3, 395
moon illusion 40–1
moons of Jupiter 393–4, 397n.12, 399–401
Moore, Adrian 275n.64, 456n.3
Moore, G. E. 311n.26
morality 3n.11, 10, 25–6, 30, 31n.78, 57, 172–3, 180, 196, 218–20, 453, 457–8
morally based/grounded
    arguments 26, 30, 337n.1
    beliefs 29, 185–6, 459
    faith 22, 25–6
    proof 453
Müller–Lyer illusion 42, 53–4
Mumford, Stephen 302n.9

natural science 49, 390, 393, 427, 437
natural theology 337
nature–nurture controversy 448
negation (in logical sense) 247, 247nn.3,5, 249–51, 255
    affixal 251
    and transcendental logic 249–51
    infinitizing 249, 249n.10
    in law of excluded middle 271n.56
    logical (as opposed to 'transcendental') 247, 249–50
    operates on categorical judgments 247n.5
    scope of 253n.18, 255
    transcendental/predicate 247, 249–50
negation (in metaphysical sense) 51n.27, 341, 347–8, 347n.28, 350, 356, 376, 376n.29
nervus probandi 91, 140–2, 145–51, 153, 384–9

Nelkin, Dana 321n.54
Newtonian
    absolute space and time 229–31
    conception of time 228–9
    substantivalism 228n.46, 229n.48
Newton, Isaac 180, 229n.48, 395–6, 449
    Opticks 396n.10, 449*f*, 449
    Philosophiae Naturalis Principia Mathematica 144, 396n.10, 405, 444n.43
    System of the World 444
Nicolai, Christoph Friedrich 266–7
Nieuwentyt, Bernard 391, 393–6, 405
    The Religious Philosopher 391, 391n.3, 394n.7, 404–5
non entis rule 251–4, 264–5, 460
non-dogmatic
    arguments 27, 178–9, 419–21
    metaphysics 29–30
    physico-theological argument 420–1
nonsense 273–5
noumenal
    agency 296n.40
    agent 305–8, 319n.43
    basis of matter 159
    basis of objects 462
    causation 296n.40, 300n.2
    choice 300–1, 309–10, 321–2
    correlate of appearances 159–60
    entity 286
    freedom 305, 321–2
    realm 297, 321–2, 453
    self 135, 161, 174–5, 196–7, 305–7
    stuff that thinks 154, 159
    subject 283–4
    substance 134
    substratum of matter 158–9

oath taking 4n.14
objective reality 93, 115, 151–2, 193, 342n.12, 423
objective side of critique 6–7, 12–14
objects of experience 3n.8, 52, 72–3, 119, 254, 458
objects of sense 2–3, 14–15, 45, 52, 72–3, 215, 235–6, 243–4, 254, 258–9, 262–4, 271–3, 295, 304, 453, *see also* inner sense, outer sense
ontological argument 32n.83, 266–7, 337–42, 344, 346, 348, 351, 353n.44, 365–6, 371, 373, 374n.23, 375n.28, 379–84, 389, 412–13, 456–7
    Baumgarten's presentation of 350n.37, 352
    Kant's criticism of 346–8, 362–4, 387–8, 412
    Kant's presentation of 339–46, 354

Leibnizian version of 341n.11, 381–2, 386–7, 389
  Wolff's presentation of 342
ontology 42–3, 337–8
optical illusion 2–3, 41, 41n.4, 53–4
outer sense 59, 72–4, 73f, 117, 121, 158–9, 190–3, 196, 462, *see also* inner sense, objects of sense

painting 194–5, 195n.6
painting argument 194
paradox, characterization of 1n.3
Parsons, Terence 249nn.9,10, 252n.17
Partington, James Riddick 434n.20, 435n.23
Pereboom, Derk 266–7, 267n.39, 286, 286n.24, 287n.30, 306, 308–9, 312, 319–20, 321n.52
Pérez Laraudogoitia 233n.54
person₀ 170–1
person₁ 170, 174–5
personality 70, 161–4, 169–70, 173–7
Peter Pan Salamander 188
Philo of Larissa 17n.47
phlogiston chemistry 15n.41, 435
physico-theological argument/proof 22, 29, 341–2, 390, 390n.1, 401, 406–13, 415–21, 427–8, 432, *see also* dogmatic physico-theological argument
physico-theology 13, 390, 403–4, 411–12, 418, 427–8, 456–7
  Kant's criticisms of 395–6, 415–16
  Kant's revised version of 396–406
  ordinary 390–7, 405–6, 420–1, 432
physics 72–3, 73f, 392–3, 430, 447
physiology 72–3, 73f
Pinder, Tillmann 44n.12
planetary motions/paths 430, 440–1, 443–4, 447
planets 4, 187–9, 395, 396n.10, 423n.4, 430–1, 436–41, 443–4, *see also* heavenly bodies, Earth, Jupiter, Mars, Mercury
Plantinga, Alvin 338n.2
plants 397, 428n.11, 437
Plato 27–8, 218–19, 348, 422, 453, 456
  myth of the metals 11–12
  Republic 11–12
Pliny 391n.2
pneumatic chemistry 435
pneumatism 8–9, 11–14, 90, 461–2
pneumatology 8n.24, 67–8, 72
Pölitz religion lectures by Kant 116, 118, 367n.8, 408n.29, 416–18, 419n.48, 420
polysyllogisms 44–6, 49n.23, 125n.37
polytomy 314, 438n.31, 441–2
Porter, Roy 26n.64, 181n.33

positing 347, 347n.29, 353–4, 356
Powell, C. Thomas 107n.7
practical freedom 282–3, 307–13, 315–16, 323–4
prescription 42–3, 46–8, 46n.16, 93n.10, 260, 310, 438n.33
Price, Richard 219
Priestley, Joseph 219
principle of
  affinity 436–44, 447
  analogy 4, 179–80, 183, 185, 406, 419
  bivalence 304n.14
  continuity 432
  contradiction 68, 345
  emanation 414n.39
  genera 426, 433–4, 438–40, 443–4, 446, 451–2
  homogeneity 442, 446
  identity 253–4
  manifoldness 448
  modal continuity 177–8
  natural order 406
  persistence of substance 118, 292–3
  possible experience 118–19
  pure reason 44, 48, 76
  reason 4, 11, 432–3, 440, 445
  species 434–5, 438–40
  the connection of finality 431
  the determining ground 368n.11
  the first analogy 121–2
  the second analogy 289
  unity 442, 445, 448
  variety 436–7
Principle of Sufficient Reason (PSR) 2, 48, 66–7, 93, 118n.27, 143–4, 228, 240, 269, 294–5, 345–6, 364–5, 368, 368n.11, 369, 372–3, 383–4, 389
privation 223
problematic idealism 190n.2, 193–4
Proops, Ian 12n.36, 48n.21, 97n.15, 114n.19, 123n.34, 133n.16, 346n.27, 352n.41
psychologists, *see* dogmatic rational psychologists, rational psychologists
psychology, *see* dogmatic rational psychology, empirical psychology, impure rational psychology, pure rational psychology, rational psychology
pure rational psychology 60, 63, 68–9, 78–80, 85–9, 143, 196, 204–5, 455
  as the science of self-consciousness 79–85
  two ways of proceeding in 87–9
pure reason 2–3, 6–8, 6n.20, 23n.59, 40, 51–2, 55–6, 72–4, 93–6, 103, 133–4, 170, 172–3, 212, 214, 286–7, 310, 364, 389, 412, 462
  antinomy of 213, 258–9
  paralogism of 85–6

pure reason (cont.)
  principle of 44, 48, 76
  system of 5n.16
purposive
  arrangements 406, 427
  causality 424
  chains 428n.11
  links 400
  natural product 417
  order 179, 406–7
  unity 415
purposiveness 179–80, 412–13, 415
  of nature 185, 187–8, 419
  see also end-directedness
Pyrrho 5–7, 17–21, 23, 30–1, 265, 456
Pyrrhonian
  postponement 22–4
  sceptics 5–6, 19–20, 23, 27n.66, 217, 456
  sect 15–16
Pyrrhonians 15–16, 17n.47, 18–20, 265, 455
Pyrrhonism 5–6, 15–20, 17n.47, 22

Quine, W. V. 42–3

rational animal 375–6
rational beings 49, 54, 162, 175–6, 300n.3, 396n.11, 410n.34
rational cosmology 8, 55–6, 216, 453, 456
rational metaphysics 4–5, 12–14, 267n.41, 453
rational numbers 263–4, 287n.29
rational psychologists 45–6, 79–82, 88, 93n.10, 114, 116, 128–9, 136, 139, 143–4, 147, 153–4, 158–60, 163–4, 166–8, 200–2, 204–5, 426–7, see also dogmatic rational psychologists
rational psychology 4–5, 7–8, 13–14, 17n.47, 32, 57–64n.10, 73f, 89
  and the soul 74–5, 88–9
  as a route to knowledge 66–7
  Baumgarten on 69–71, 75
  in *Metaphysics L1* 72–9, 88–9
  Kant-approved empirically grounded 60
  Kant's conception of 68–9, 72–4, 77
  Kant's constraint on 75
  Meier on 71–2
  Wolff on 65, 67–9, 71, 75, 86–9, 87n.45
  see also dogmatic rational psychology
rational theology 5, 8, 13, 17n.47, 337, 390, 412–13, 418–19, 453, 455–7, 461–2
rationality 26, 39, 54, 183, 309, 349, 441n.36
Ray, John 395–6, 455
  The Wisdom of God 394, 428n.13
real predicates 338–9, 346–50, 353–6, 359–60
realism, see Transcendental Realism

realists, see Transcendental Realists
reductio arguments/apagogic proofs 13, 146n.9, 219n.28, 220–1, 220n.32, 254–5, 460
  in metaphysics must be used 'very sparingly' 254
  trustworthy *versus* untrustworthy patterns of 254, 254n.20
refraction, law of 431
regress 45, 133–4, 209, 226n.41, 234, 247–8, 255–60, 259n.32, 262, 290–1, 297, 368
  ad indefinitum 255–7, 297
  ad infinitum 255–7
regression 247–8, 253, 255–7, 256n.24, 297
  series 94–5, 131–2, 134, 209, 220
  series of appearances 130n.12
  series of conditions 94, 130–1, 132n.14, 133–4
  series of subjects 95
Reimarus, Hermann Samuel 100n.26, 421n.51
religion 25–6, 31n.78, 57, 218–20, 365, 421n.51
  lectures 50–1, 116, 118, 124, 275n.65, 283n.12, 346n.27, 348, 361–2, 367–9, 368n.12, 374, 378, 380, 383n.47, 408n.29, 411n.36, 414n.42, 416–18, 419n.48, 420, 428n.11, 461n.12
Remnant, Peter 385n.50
repugnancy 355
Reusch, Johann Peter 97n.17, 210n.4, 249
Rohlf, Michael 53n.30
Rosefeldt, Tobias 44n.11, 127n.2
Rousseau, Jean Jacques 220–1
Russell, Bertrand 194, 253n.18

scepticism in Hume 5–6, 27–8, 407–8
scepticism/sceptics 5–7, 5n.18, 17–19, 21, 27–9, 41–2, 193–6, 212–13, 217, 264, 279–80, 407–8, 456, see also Academic scepticism/sceptics
Schönfeld, Martin 396n.10
Schütz, Christian Gottfried 267n.41
sciences 1, 8, 30–1, 72–3, 255, 265–6, 269–70, 431
self-consciousness 79–85, 88, 106, 125–6, 136–7, 169–70, 196, 268, 304n.14, 337–8
self-knowledge 7, 30–1, 77
sense, see inner sense, objects of sense, outer sense
Sextus Empiricus 15–16, 16n.46
Socrates 30–1, 391
Socratic method 31n.78
sophisms 97–8, 101–2, 128, 129n.10
Sorensen, Roy 1n.3, 41n.5, 91–2, 188, 253n.18, 362n.52, 441n.36

soul
  concept of 59, 63, 66–7, 69, 71, 73–6, 87, 107n.8, 119, 203, 427
  constitution of 59, 75–6
  doctrine of 8, 59–60, 74, 78–9, 82, 98, 196, 201
  essence of 61–5, 67–8, 71, 80n.35, 82
  existence of 3n.10, 69, 74, 75n.29, 76, 87–8, 199–200
  experience of 61–2, 66–7, 76, 136, 203
  nature of 3n.8, 19, 59, 68, 72n.24, 76, 86–7, 96, 432
  properties of 61–2, 70–1, 77
  science of 59–60, 71, 74, 87n.46
  see also consciousness and the soul, Idea of the soul, immortality of the soul, Transcendental Idea of the soul
speculative reason 27–9, 39n.1, 56–7, 380, 413, 453, 458, 461–2
Spinoza, Baruch 106–7, 116, 116n.24, 118, 140n.1, 219, 228n.46, 231, 414n.39, 461
spontaneity of thought 149–51
Stang, Nicholas 352n.41
Stoics 462
square of opposition 210, 252n.17
substance
  minimal concept of (substance$_0$) 128–30, 128n.3, 139, 170
  schematized concept of (substance$_2$) 33, 92–3, 118, 124–5, 128–9, 238n.58
  unschematized concept of (substance$_1$) 92–7, 103, 109–11, 114–15, 117–18, 122–5, 128–30, 132, 135, 140n.1, 142, 144, 150–1, 155n.19, 156–62, 166, 168–74, 169n.14, 173n.21, 238, 238nn.58,59, 285–6, 461
substantiale, the 130n.12, 134–5, 137
substance-causation 285–6
Sullivan, Richard J. 434n.20
sum total of
  appearances 261–2, 270, 328–9
  incentives 171n.18
  substance$_2$ 93
sun, the 274, 274n.63, 331–2, 350, 430–1, 438–40, 443
supersensible
  the 4, 28, 39, 255, 453
  object/objects 2–3, 303, 401, 459
  power of causality 283n.12
supertasks 224, 232–3
suspension of belief 20, 20n.53, 265, 457
Sutherland, Daniel 223
synthesis 131, 217, 221–7, 231–4, 244, 255–8, 260, 341, 422–3
  categorical 131–2, 453
  empirical 255–6
  hypothetical 131–2, 422–3
  of appearances 264–5
  of thoughts 57, 85, 132n.15
systematic unity, *see* Idea of systematic unity

taxonomy 101, 210–11, 433–7, 441–2, 445–6
  of judgments 247n.5, 249–50
  of oppositions 210
  of the sciences 72–3
teleology 393, 396, 404–5, 411n.35, 427–9
Tetens, Johannes Nikolaus 266–7
Thiel, Udo 84n.41
thinking I 3n.10, 59–60, 78, 88–90, 92, 95, 105, 115, 118, 127–9, 140, 148, 157–8, 166, 190–1, 426
thinking self 59, 79, 106–7, 196–7
thought experiment 158–9, 181
Thümmig, Ludwig Philipp 88n.48
Tonelli, Giorgio 7n.23, 39n.1
totum analyticum/ideal composite 45n.14, 225–7
totum syntheticum/real composite 45n.14, 225–7, 232–4, 238, 328
tranquility 5–6, 15–16, 264, 456
transcendental
  concepts 82, 223, 337
  deduction 280n.6, 454–5
  freedom 3n.9, 75–6, 257n.28, 279–83, 289, 293–4, 296n.40, 307–8, 310–14, 318, 323–4, 453
  ideality 270
  logic 249–50
  negation 247, 249n.12, 250
  paralogisms 99, 102–3
  philosophy 72–3, 73f, 261–3
  principles 47, 383, 434, 445–8
  proofs 254
  subject 59–60, 77, 137, 155, 196
  theology 337, 342n.13
Transcendental Aesthetic 14–15, 164–5, 230, 453–4
Transcendental Analytic 3n.12, 288–9
Transcendental Dialectic 1–2, 39, 41–2, 41n.3, 57–8, 136, 303, 415–16
Transcendental Idea
  of freedom 257n.28, 422n.3
  of God 40, 422n.3, 450
  of the soul 95, 130–2, 422n.3
  of the world 40, 422n.3
Transcendental Idealism 159–60, 169, 190n.2, 194, 196, 222–3, 230, 243–5, 271–3, 278, 281, 296n.40, 298, 332–3, 457–60, 462
  and the cosmological conflict 262–3
  anti-materialist consequences of 196
  confirmatory argument for 216
  direct proof of 13, 454n.1
  discovery of 214

Transcendental Idealism (*cont.*)
  doctrine of 25–6
  indirect argument for 14, 18, 27–30, 244, 270–3, 275, 289, 304–5, 309, 329–30, 333
  indirect proof of 23, 244, 262, 453, 454n.1
  truth of 1, 14–15, 262, 273, 453–4, 456
Transcendental Idealist 59, 194, 225–7, 234, 243–5, 247–8, 272–3, 282–3, 297, 300–1, 329
Transcendental Ideas 2–3, 130–1, 257–8, 333, 422–5, 432–3, 448, 450
transcendental illusion 29, 39–42, 44, 46–57, 85n.43, 88–93, 95–6, 102–3, 111, 130–4, 171, 199, 210, 212, 251, 259–61, 333, 451, 459–62, 461n.12, 462
  affinities with empirical illusion 40–1
  characterization of 47n.17, 53n.29, 133–4
  existence of 39, 41–2
  in the first paralogism 93–7
  influence of 125–6, 216, 258–9
  nature of 7
  necessity of 53–5
  persistence of 42
  recalcitrant texts relating to 55–8
  simplified account of 52–3
  sources of 40, 42–52
Transcendental Realism 14–15, 24–5, 26n.62, 29–30, 32–3, 53, 55–6, 192, 212, 214, 219–21, 228–9, 252, 271–2, 278, 286, 298, 329, 453–4, 456, 460–1
  as a logical impossibility 459–60
  assumption of 14, 216–17, 275, 289, 294, 329–30
  belief in 55, 457–8
  consequences of 227n.43, 228n.46, 244, 297, 332–3
  rejection of 457–8
Transcendental Realist 24–5, 55–6, 169, 217n.23, 219, 222–9, 234–6, 243–5, 250, 252–3, 262, 264, 272, 278, 282–3, 290, 292–7, 299, 306–7, 316, 329–33, 344n.20, 445–6
truth conditions 253n.18, 274, 459–60
Tucker, Abraham 10
Tye, Michael 149–50
typographical conventions used in this book 33, 107n.8
unity of consciousness 85–6, 110n.13, 113, 132, 156

Vallicella, W. F. 412n.37
Van Cleve, James 92n.7, 122–3, 239n.60, 242n.65, 321, 374–5, 386n.51
van Inwagen, Peter 316n.33, 318, 318n.38
Varro, Marcus Terentius 429
Vilhauer, Benjamin 305
vitium subreptionis 85
Vitruvius 41n.5
Voltaire 268–70, 305, 393–4, 394n.8

Walker, Ralph C. S. 305, 305n.16
Warda, Arthur 10n.30, 69n.18, 345n.23
Warfield, Ted 318, 318n.39
Watkins, Eric 172n.20, 267n.39, 285–6, 286n.24, 300n.3, 302n.8, 436–7, 441–2
Watson, Gary 316n.33, 317n.37
Wilkins, John 391n.2
Willaschek, Marcus 139n.25, 209n.1, 422n.3
Wittgenstein, Ludwig 274
Wolff, Christian 2, 7, 18–19, 45n.15, 46, 60–7, 85, 87n.46, 100, 106n.6, 118n.27, 165–6, 249–50, 318, 338–9, 341n.11, 364, 366–7, 369, 371, 374n.24, 379, 383–4, 455
  German Metaphysics/GM 60–8, 82, 100, 106n.6, 162–3, 240n.61, 348n.33, 371–3, 372n.19
  Latin Logic (*Philosophia Rationalis sive Logica*) 64n.10, 85, 85n.43, 87n.46, 97–8, 97n.17, 416n.44
  Natural Theology 341, 341n.11, 342n.14, 369n.13, 379n.36
  and cognitive penetration 66
  account of the soul's immortality 175–6
  on consciousness 163
  on dogmatic speculative metaphysics 27–8
  on empirical psychology 68–9
  on existence 68, 337, 348–52, 361
  on personal identity 169
  on possibilia 124–5
  on psychology 60–8
  on rational psychology 65–9, 72, 75–6, 79–80, 86–9, 426
  on syllogisms 97–8
  on the cosmological argument 364, 371–3, 383, 388–9
  on the ontological argument 342
  on the physico-theological argument 415–16
  on the soul 62–6, 68, 70–1, 73–5, 82, 88–9, 163–4, 427
  special metaphysics of 2–3, 8, 216, 422–3, 462
  Ontologia 252n.16, 348n.33, 352n.41, 353–4, 361, 367–8, 383n.47
  Psychologia Empirica 85
  Psychologia Rationalis 64n.10, 66–7, 163
Wolffians 8, 32n.82, 66–7, 76, 88n.48, 169, 252
Wood, Allen, W. 8, 11, 42n.8, 99n.20, 164–5, 266–7, 290n.32, 300n.1, 306, 321–2, 331n.2, 342n.17, 365, 367–8, 374–5, 380n.38, 383n.46, 385, 388–9
Wuerth, Julian 114–15, 114nn.18,20, 116n.23, 116n.25, 122, 133n.16, 134–7
  interpretation of the *B*-edition first paralogism 115–16

Zeno 224, 275–6